The Journals of the Lewis & Clark Expedition, Volume 13

Comprehensive Index

Sponsored by the Center for

Great Plains Studies,

University of Nebraska–Lincoln,

and the American

Philosophical Society, Philadelphia

A Project of the Center for
Great Plains Studies,
University of Nebraska–Lincoln
Gary E. Moulton, Editor

The Journals of the Lewis & Clark Expedition

Comprehensive Index

University of Nebraska Press

Lincoln and London

Publication of this book has been assisted by a grant
from the National Endowment for the Humanities, an
independent federal agency.

Library of Congress Cataloging-in-Publication Data
(Revised for volume 8)
The Journals of the Lewis and Clark Expedition.
Vol. 2 – Gary E. Moulton, editor; Thomas W. Dunlay,
Assistant editor.
Vol. 2 – has title: The Journals of the Lewis & Clark
Expedition. "Sponsored by the Center for Great Plains
Studies, University of Nebraska–Lincoln, and the
American Philosophical Society, Philadelphia" – vol. 1,
t.p. Includes bibliographies and indexes.
Contents: v.1. Atlas of the Lewis & Clark Expedition –
v.2 August 30, 1803–August 24, 1804 – [etc.] –
v.8. June 10–September 26, 1806. 1. Lewis and Clark
Expedition – (1804–1806). 2. West(U.S.) –
Description and travel – To 1848. 3. United States –
Exploring expeditions. 4. Lewis, Meriwether, 1774–
1809 – Diaries. 5. Clark, William, 1770–1838 –
Diaries. 6. Explorers – West (U.S.) – Diaries. I. Lewis,
Meriwether, 1774–1809. II. Clark, William, 1770–1838.
III. Moulton, Gary E. IV. Dunlay, Thomas W., 1944–.
V. University of Nebraska–Lincoln. Center for Great
Plains Studies. VI. American Philosophical Society.
VII. Journals of the Lewis & Clark Expedition.
F592.4   1983   917.8′042   82–8510
ISBN 0-8032-2942-9 (v.13)

Contents

Preface

I have a number of people to thank for their continuing contributions to *The Journals of the Lewis and Clark Expedition* and to this thirteenth volume in particular. Two dedicated people are responsible for much of the hard and tedious work of preparing this index. Lisa K. Roberts and Stephen Witte not only assisted in the sometimes wearisome chore of rechecking the indexes of all the previous volumes and bringing them to a new standard of excellence and consistency, but they also provided valuable suggestions for ways to make the comprehensive index better in its own right. They challenged me with tough questions and a strong desire to get it right. Thanks to them this index is much better than I had expected or even hoped it could be. There came a time though when we had to close the door on the project and end the work. As I had reluctantly let each of the twelve volumes go to press, knowing that I could have done better with each one, so too did I want to keep at this comprehensive index a bit longer (but not too much longer). Readers will find here a much better index than those in the single volumes and can now trace persons, ideas, and events across the entire series of books. I've already found it useful a number of times.

Readers will also find in this volume an appendix that lists errors discovered in previous volumes. It makes apparent why I wished to press on toward perfection in each volume. Flawless editing is an impossibility, however, and surely was not attained in this volume either. Neither time, circumstance, nor Lisa or Steve are to blame for this; it's just the way things are, and I accept whatever deficiencies remain.

I want to thank the keen-eyed people who noticed errors and inconsistencies in the volumes and were kind enough to inform me gently of the mistakes. While working back and forth between volumes over the years, the editor and staff discovered many of these problems; they became especially apparent while we worked on this index. The authors of new books, monographs, and essays on Lewis and Clark also corrected points in the annotations. I list only the most conspicuous mistakes that have been discovered over the years and skip simple spelling and typographical errors, although I do show correct spellings of proper and scientific names. Otherwise,

the intent of the list is apparent. The following persons shared their discoveries with me, hoping to make the books better in the future.

John Eliot Allen, Portland, Oregon
Irving Anderson, Portland, Oregon
Robert N. Bergantino, Butte, Montana
William K. Brunot, Bisbane, California
Steve Brunsfeld, Moscow, Idaho
Keith Burgess-Jackson, Fort Worth, Texas
Michael F. Carrick, Salem, Oregon
E. G. Chuinard, Tigard, Oregon
James M. Denny, Jefferson City, Missouri
Nancy Eid, Astoria, Oregon
Harry Fritz, Missoula, Montana
Walter J. Gary, Walla Walla, Washington
Robert J. Hoyle, Lewiston, Idaho
Frithiof V. Johnson, Binghamton, New York
Glen E. Kirkpatrick, Portland, Oregon
Robert E. Lange, Portland, Oregon
Jack Mahley, Lewiston, Idaho
Rick Minor, Eugene, Oregon
Steve C. Plucker, Touchet, Washington
Henry M. Reeves, Amity, Oregon
Robert Saindon, Wolf Point, Montana
Robert Lee Sappington, Moscow, Idaho
Jack Schmidt, Council Bluffs, Iowa
Phil Scriver, Great Falls, Montana
Arthur H. Smith, Davis, California
Larry M. Southwick, Cincinnati, Ohio
James Alexander Thom, Bloomington, Indiana
Bruce P. Van Haveren, Evergreen, Colorado
Mike Venso, Lewiston, Idaho
James Wallace, Columbia, Missouri
W. Raymond Wood, Columbia, Missouri

The following people contributed financially to this volume: Samuel H. Douglas, III, Whittier, California; Jay Maxwell, Atlanta, Georgia; William P. Sherman, Portland, Oregon; and Nelson S. Weller, Healdsburg, California. The National Endow-

ment for the Humanities, an independent federal agency, also supported the project. I sincerely appreciate the generosity of all. I also had the support of persons at the Center for Great Plains Studies: James Stubbendieck, Linda Ratcliffe, Gretchen Walker, and Belinda Hall.

In 1979 my mission was to edit and publish the journals of the Lewis and Clark expedition. For me the effort is accomplished. On May 14, 1999, 195 years after Lewis and Clark began their mission, I completed mine and closed the project. On September 23, 2000, 194 years after Lewis and Clark ended their expedition, I turned this final volume over to the University of Nebraska Press.

This has been the most gratifying and intellectually challenging work of my career as well as the most personally rewarding. I count myself the luckiest historian of my time. I am deeply honored to have served as editor of the expedition's journals for this generation. It is my sincere hope that my work will help to keep this incredible story of courage and endurance alive for another two hundred years.

GARY E. MOULTON
Lincoln, Nebraska

Introduction to Volume 13

The journals of the Lewis and Clark expedition present considerable challenges to the indexer. First among these is the fact that the writers made multiple and varied references to single topics and then applied alternate spelling and nomenclature to the very same matter. These factors require editors, indexers, and readers to negotiate conflicts between the perspective of expedition writers and that of contemporary users.

The guiding principles for this comprehensive index were to index from the perspective of the party, to categorize items under the most feasibly specific entry, and to limit multiple citations to a single entry as much as possible. If, for example, Lewis had discussed the guns of the Mandan Indians in a journal entry, the index could conceivably have three citations for the single topic: "Lewis," the "Mandans," and "guns." We tried whenever possible to develop guidelines that would prevent such occurrences but decided to choose inclusiveness when there was doubt. Redundancy was accepted in a number of instances. In seeking specificity in the annotations to the volumes, we were often definitive about vague references in the journals. The index reflects those conclusions in our choosing the specific rather than the generic classification.

The index deviates from the party's perspective with regard to variant spellings, anachronistic names, and misidentifications. Information is indexed according to current orthography, nomenclature, and scholarship. For this reason, the notes are indexed more thoroughly here than they are in most works. Attention to the notes is essential for locating the party by modern place-names, citing Indian nations by their modern denominations, and identifying species by their current popular and scientific names. Correct spellings are used in the index, often without reference to the journalists' variants, since a gloss or textual note at the point of origin usually corrects the misspelling. Usual but understandable variants appear in parentheses after the correct word in the index. Distinctive and repeated misspellings (such as Sharbono for Charbonneau) are given as cross-references to the correct word in

addition to appearing as a gloss in the index. This is particularly the case with names of members of the party and Indian tribes.

In an effort to be as clear and concise as possible, prepositions were not included in subheadings wherever ambiguity did not result. This comprehensive index uses the subheading "abundance" rather than "abundance of," "habitat" rather than "habitat of," and so on, because the concept is clear without the preposition. But prepositions are used whenever a meaning might otherwise be ambiguous. The index includes prepositions to distinguish between "information from" and "information about" a particular person or item and between instances when the "food" of an animal is discussed and when that species is discussed "as food." Certain long entries have not been subcategorized, such as "astronomical observations" and "mosquitoes." Divisions that appeared likely under such terms ultimately seemed of little practical use to readers.

Many index entries contain a reference to a major informative discussion—an overview or a sketch—either in the text or the notes. Such overviews are subdivided and labeled in three ways: for animals and objects under the subcategory "described," for members of the party under "biographical sketch," and for Indian nations under "historical sketch."

MEMBERS OF THE PARTY

The preparation of index entries for Captains Lewis and Clark presented a special challenge. As the commanding officers and primary record-keepers of the expedition, Lewis and Clark naturally appear in the expedition's journals far more frequently than anyone or anything else. Just as naturally, the captains themselves are a principal focus of interest for readers of the journals. The challenge was to prepare index entries for them that convey essential information to readers while limiting those entries to a manageable size.

As a general rule, the captains are not indexed when they interact with other persons who are indexed. This follows the principle of limiting multiple citations. For example, the captains' council with the Oto Indians on August 3, 1804, is referenced under "Oto Indians, councils," not under "Lewis, Meriwether" or "Clark, William." This rule also holds true for Lewis's and Clark's interactions with other members of the expedition. On April 17, 1804, Clark records that he sent four men to find a horse. Clark himself is not indexed for this event. The men who went to look for the animal are indexed under "members of the party, sent out."

A similar rule was followed for geographic features and plant and animal species. When the officers report observances of named geographic features—for example, rivers, creeks, and mountains—the name of the feature is indexed, but Lewis and

Clark are not. The captains generally are not indexed separately when they merely describe plant and animal species, but they are referenced when they themselves collect specimens. For example, Clark records that he collected grass samples on August 17, 1804. This appears in the index as "Clark, William: and species." The "and species" subcategory is also used when the captains have a significant encounter with a species, such as an attacking grizzly bear. The subheading "ecological observations" under the captains' headings covers detailed and lengthy references to ecological zones, such as the Great Plains.

The index notes instances of the captains' absences from the main body of the expedition. During the voyage up the Missouri River, Lewis and Clark often disembarked from the keelboat and proceeded on foot to examine adjacent country. For such cases, the captains are referenced under the subheading "reconnaissance." When one of the captains leads a scouting, hunting, or fishing party, the index reflects the appropriate activity. If while separated Clark recorded Lewis's whereabouts, Lewis is indexed and vice versa. Instances when Lewis and Clark sent messages to each other are also indexed.

The largest subcategory for the captains' index entries is undoubtedly "journal-keeping methods." We decided to index as completely as possible all references that indicate the manner in which the captains composed or made use of their journals.

The principles that guided the indexing of references to the captains are generally applied in the same way to the other members of the party, but they do call for some additional explanation. These guidelines apply to enlisted soldiers, *engagés* (hired boatmen), and other civilian members of the party, such as Sacagawea, the infant Jean Baptiste Charbonneau, Toussaint Charbonneau, York, and George Drouillard.

Our general practice was to index references to expedition members as completely as possible. In many cases, a journal entry refers to one or more members of the party without giving their names. When we could not identify the specific person or persons meant, the reference is indexed under the generic category "members of the party." When we were able to identify at least one person, the person appears in the index under his or her own name, and any remaining unidentified members of the party are indexed as such. For example, Clark records that on August 15, 1804, he took ten men fishing. An editor's note informs the reader that according to his own journal, Sgt. Charles Floyd accompanied this group. The sergeant is therefore indexed as "Floyd, fishing," even though Clark did not specifically mention his name. Floyd's unidentified companions are indexed as "members of the party, fishing."

As the above example indicates, the notes contain numerous references to the

journals of John Ordway, Charles Floyd, Patrick Gass, and Joseph Whitehouse. In these cases, we index the appropriate person under the subcategory "journal." In the fishing example just given the entry is "Floyd, journal."

Several other subcategories for the members of the party require explanation. Understanding the use of "mentioned" is important. We use this term when a person is named in a journal entry or in a note, but the reference does not fit a more specific subcategory. A common situation for which we use "mentioned" in indexing the captains' journals is the appearance of a person's name in a journal entry when little else of substance about that person is conveyed. For example, on July 8, 1804, Clark wrote, "we appoint a Cook to each mess to take Charge of the Provisions. in Serjt. Pryor's = *Collens* in Sjt. Ordway's *Werner* in Sergt. Floyd's *Thompson*." In this case, we indexed Pryor under the subheading "mentioned," while Collins, Werner, and Thompson fall under "duties." An exception to the this last rule occurs when a person appears more than once on the same page. In such cases, we did not index a person as "mentioned" when another reference on the same page fits a more specific subcategory. In the above example, Ordway is not indexed as "mentioned" because earlier in the same journal entry, Clark noted that Ordway had rejoined the party after an absence. Ordway is therefore indexed as "Ordway, John: returns." Another common use of "mentioned" applies to the enlisted men's journals (volumes 9, 10, and 11). In these later volumes, many of the notes simply identify persons without further commentary. In these cases, the person's appearance in the note is indexed under "mentioned."

Other common subcategories in the expedition members' index entries are "sent out," "returns," "duties," and "scouting." "Sent out" is used when members of the party are detached from the main body to perform some task that is not covered under a more specific activity such as "hunting," "fishing," or "scouting." Examples include rounding up stray horses, accompanying one of the captains while walking onshore, and bringing in meat from a hunter's kill. "Returns" is used when a member of the party rejoins the main body. As Lewis and Clark did not record every instance in which a person was sent out and returned to the main body, there is not a one-to-one correspondence between "sent out" and "returns" in most expedition members' index entries. The term "duties" is used when a member of the party is given a task that does not require his or her absence from the main body or from their current camp, such as cooking. "Scouting" is used either when the scouting mission involves traveling a significant distance from the main body or when the actual word "scouting" is used in regard to a person's absence. Shorter excursions are covered under "sent out."

NATIVE AMERICANS

When we indexed Native Americans we applied virtually the same procedures as we used for members of the party. Again, we sought specificity. When a diarist uses a generic term like "Indians," we indexed the mention under the appropriate tribal designation whenever possible. Otherwise, we placed the group in the appropriate subcategory under "Indians." So too we treated Indian individuals much the same way we treated unnamed members of the party in the category "members of the party." Unnamed individual Indians fall under the general category "Indians" and in a subcategory according to the activities in which they are engaged. When an Indian's name has the article "The" as a part of the name, we alphabetized it under the next word. For example, "The Shake Hand" is found under the letter S.

To index the Indian languages, tribal languages were distinguished from language families. For example, references to the language of the Sioux tribe are indexed under the entry "Sioux Indians" and subheading "languages." References to the Siouan language family, however, can be found under "Siouan language." The same is true for the language of the Chinook Indians, as opposed to the Chinookan language. Under the general entry "Indians," readers will find the subcategory "sign language" and, for Indian tongues that are not identified specifically, "languages."

PLACES

The expedition's camps are listed by county and state. Modern archaeological sites are indexed through their references in the notes, but references in the text to such areas are indexed according to the formations, rivers, Indian villages, and the like that the text specifically mentions. Some redundancy has been deemed appropriate because it aids the reader. For instance, descriptions of the Great Plains are indexed twice—under the entry "Great Plains" and under the entries for Lewis and Clark beneath the subheading "ecological observations."

Those place-names that locate campsites or give information on geographic situations associated with the expedition are of primary concern. Incidental place-names in the notes—that is, references to sites, towns, and states that do not relate to the expedition specifically—do not appear in the index.

ANIMALS AND PLANTS

The focus on members of the party in this comprehensive index extends even to the use of subcategories. The term "discovered" is used as a subcategory for plants or animals that the party has first scientifically described or identified for the Euro-American community, although the species may have been long known to Native Americans.

If a textual reference to "grouse" is identified in a note as "probably ruffed grouse," both the note and text are indexed as "grouse, ruffed." But if the note lists a variety of possible species, the note is indexed to each of these specific possibilities while the text is indexed simply to the generic entry "grouse."

Whenever possible, the index avoids redundancy by indexing information under the one entry most relevant to its context in the journals and to the members of the party. Horses of the Indians, for instance, are indexed under "horses: and Indians" rather than "Indians: horses" or both. In such cases, we tried to determine the subject under discussion and create the entry from that perspective.

OBJECTS

The comprehensive index uses a few major collective entries: "arms and ammunition," "clothing," "equipment," "provisions," and "tools." These entries refer to objects associated with the party in particular. Thus the collective entry "clothing" lists references to the clothes of the party; further, it lists references for which neither the type of clothes nor the specific member of the party is known. When the specific party member is identified the person takes priority and the reference to clothes is indexed under the entry for that person's name and the subcategory "clothes." Alternatively, when we do not know the person involved but the specific type of clothing has been identified, the reference is indexed under that specific type, such as "moccasins" or "hats." When references to articles of clothing are not those of the party, they are indexed to the appropriate Indian tribes or persons under the subcategory "clothes," whether or not the items have been specified.

Likewise, when a journal writer identifies a weapon, or it is identified in a note, the item is indexed under its specific name. On October 21, 1804, Clark wrote, "Little gun all my hunting," which the note explains as meaning that Clark evidently did all his hunting with a relatively small-caliber "Kentucky" long rifle. Accordingly, this information is indexed under "rifle, Kentucky," not "guns" or "arms and ammunition." The arms and ammunition that are associated with the party but have not been specifically identified are indexed in a way similar to that used for the party's unspecified clothes: they are listed under the collective entry—"arms and ammunition," in this case—and placed in an appropriate subcategory, if possible. But when the arms and ammunition mentioned are associated with the Indians, they are indexed according to the relevant tribe or individual. Collective entries list cross-references to specific types of arms and ammunition, clothing, equipment, provisions, and tools.

In the case of specific objects like axes, beads, or bedding, this comprehensive

index emphasizes that specificity. Objects such as these have achieved an importance that argues against their being placed in a subcategory. Such specific objects are indexed under their own separate entries without regard to the party member, Indian, or trapper to whom they belong. The alternative, which was to index such references under entries for the relevant people and then under the subcategory "artifacts," was rejected to retain specificity and avoid massive, undifferentiated lists of references. In creating entries for specific objects, we again err on the side of inclusiveness. A good example is the entry for kegs. "Kegs" most often refers to an object, but it may at times indicate a unit of measurement. Since we cannot be sure which is indicated, we group all references to kegs under one entry.

MEDICINE AND MEDICAL PROBLEMS

The collective entries of "medicine" and "medical problems" offer further exceptions to the rule of foregrounding the party and avoiding redundancy. The entry "medicine" includes all references to medicinal substances and medical practices, no matter which person mentions, dispenses, performs, or receives them. The journals note that medicine was exchanged between different members of the party and between the party and the Indians. Given this knowledge, indexing the medicines to only one of the persons involved could produce arbitrary and misleading distinctions and perhaps miss important references. Since "medicine" includes references to both materials and activities, substances such as laudanum and practices such as bleeding are both found under this entry.

The collective entry "medical problems" also adopts a perspective broader than that of the party alone. To make them easily accessible, references to all illnesses, injuries, and accidents mentioned in the journals are collected under "medical problems" without regard to which persons are afflicted. Cross-references under specific illnesses send readers to the "medical problems" entry. The unique issue of medical problems required us to break our rule against redundancy as well. Readers will find that afflictions identified specifically by name under the entry "medical problems" are also indexed under the specific person who is afflicted, if the person is known.

WEATHER AND ASTRONOMICAL OBSERVATIONS

The entry "weather conditions" does not list all references to weather but only those that impede the progress of the party or are noted by the party as significant. Routine conditions of rain and snow and other climatic occurrences are not indexed. References to the astronomical instruments, such as the chronometer, octant, and sextant, are indexed under those three terms but only when some signifi-

cant mention of them is made (for example, when Lewis mentions that the chronometer is slow). Other routine references to these instruments are found under the entry "astronomical observations."

Finally, in navigating subcategories, readers should understand that the subheadings are arranged chronologically rather than alphabetically, for the most part. The arrangement of the journals by volume, however, takes precedence over chronology; that is, an item in the index from a later date in volume 8 precedes a chronologically earlier reference noted in volumes 9, 10, or 11.

The Journals of the Lewis & Clark Expedition, Volume 13

Comprehensive Index

Index

A

Abalone, **5**: 140n
Abdomen. *See* Medical problems
Abel, Annie Heloise, **1**: 6
Abert, James, **3**: 291n
Abies alba, **5**: 195n. *See also* Fir,
European
Abies amabilis, **6**: 284n. *See also*
Fir, Pacific silver
Abies grandis, **5**: 210n, **6**: 28n,
7: 37n, **8**: 12n, **9**: 212n, **10**:
144n, **11**: 286n. *See also* Fir,
grand
Abies lasiocarpa, **5**: 202n. *See also*
Fir, subalpine
Absaroka Range, **8**: 187, 188n,
198, 203n, 217, 221n, 235n
Abscesses. *See* Medical problems
Absentee Shawnee Indians. *See*
Shawnee Indians, Absentee
Academy of Natural Sciences,
Philadelphia, Pa., **2**: 210n,
531, **3**: 450, 473, **8**: 307n,
12: 2, 5–8
Accipiter cooperii, **6**: 378n. *See also*
Hawk, Cooper's
Accouterments. *See* Equipment
Acer circinatum, **6**: 296n, **7**:
114n, **10**: 207n. *See also*
Maple, vine
Acer glabrum, **5**: 85n, **8**: 30n, **10**:
207n. *See also* Maple, Rocky
Mountain
Acer macrophyllum, **6**: 19n, **7**:
14n, **9**: 287n, **10**: 166n. *See
also* Maple, bigleaf
Acer negundo, **4**: 19n, **8**: 418n,

9: 182n, **11**: 182n. *See also*
Boxelder
Acer saccharinum, **2**: 78n, **9**:
377n, **10**: 15n. *See also* Maple,
silver
Acer saccharum, **2**: 78n, **8**: 418n,
9: 377n, **10**: 15n. *See also*
Maple, sugar
Acer sp., **9**: 42n. *See also* Maples
Achillea millefolium, **7**: 338n, **9**:
164n, **11**: 189n. *See also* Yar-
row, western
Acipenser medirostris, **6**: 70n, **9**:
275n, **10**: 195n, **11**: 396n. *See
also* Sturgeon, green
Acipenser transmontanus, **6**: 346n,
7: 14n, **9**: 275n, **10**: 195n,
11: 425n. *See also* Sturgeon,
white
Ackomokki (The Feathers), **1**:
5, **4**: 269n
Acorus calamus, **9**: 28n. *See also*
Flag, sweet
Actitis macularia, **6**: 383n. *See also*
Sandpiper, spotted
Adams, John, **3**: 214n, **10**: 186n
Adel Mountains, **4**: 391n, 397n
Adena culture, **2**: 78n
Adzes, **3**: 309, 309n, **4**: 370
Aechmophorus occidentalis, **6**: 98n,
391n. *See also* Grebe, western
Aedes hendersoni, **8**: 22n. *See also*
Mosquitoes
Aedes spenserii, **8**: 22n. *See also*
Mosquitoes
Aedes vexans, **2**: 305n, **3**: 15n,
4: 19n, **5**: 10n, 58n, **8**: 22n,
9: 15n, **10**: 106n. *See also*
Mosquitoes
Aesculus glabra, **2**: 69n, **8**: 418n,

9: 20n, **10**: 15n. *See also* Buck-
eye, Ohio; Buckeye, western
Aesculus octandra, **2**: 69n, **10**:
15n. *See also* Buckeye, yellow
Agastache urticifolia, **7**: 285n. *See
also* Hyssop, giant-, nettle-
leaved
Agate, **5**: 147n
Agelaius phoeniceus, **3**: 86n. *See
also* Blackbird, red-winged
Agency Creek, **5**: 75, 76n, **9**: 73,
74n
Ageneotetix deorum, **4**: 308n. *See
also* Grasshoppers
Agkistrodon contortrix, **7**: 312n.
See also Copperhead
Agropyron sp., **5**: 60n, **7**: 338n.
See also Wheatgrasses
Agropyron spicatum, **5**: 228n, **6**:
368n, **7**: 204n, **8**: 38n. *See also*
Wheatgrass, bluebunch
Ague. *See* Medical problems,
ague and fever
Ahnahawa, Ahwaharway (and
similar spellings) Indians. *See*
Hidatsa Indians, Awaxawi
Aiaouez, Aieway (and similar
spellings) Indians. *See* Iowa
Indians
Air, dry. *See* Weather conditions
Aird, James, **8**: 346, 347n, 348–
49, 356n, 367, 368n, **9**: 358,
358n, **10**: 275, 275n
Air gun, **2**: 65, 66n, 439, 441,
492–93, **3**: 24, 156–57,
158n, 209–10, 216, 221,
275, **4**: 271, 275, **5**: 55, 112,
6: 233, 235, **7**: 55, 66, 137,
242, 244, **8**: 155, 419, **9**: 50,
67, 79, 92, 121, 165, 198,

1

Air gun (*continued*)
205, **11**: 65–66, 192, 259. *See also* Arms and ammunition

Aiten, **8**: 360, **10**: 279n

Aix sponsa, **2**: 101n, **4**: 310n, **5**: 13n, **7**: 41n, **10**: 208n. *See also* Duck, wood

Akicita, **3**: 25–26n

Alabama Indians, **3**: 447, 449

Alamotin village, **5**: 264n

Albertosaurus, **8**: 229n

Alces alces, **7**: 330n, **8**: 96n. *See also* Moose

Alcohol. *See* Medicine

Alcoholic beverages. *See* Beer; Brandy; Grog; Liquor; Porter; Rum; Tafia; Whiskey; Wine

Alder, black, **8**: 7, 11, 12n. *See also* Alder, red

Alder, red, **5**: 356, 358n, **6**: 9, 26–27, 29n, 65, 81, 96, 98, 98n, 103, 104n, 183, 194, 284n, 290, 293, 293n, 297, **7**: 19, 21, 22n, 32, 45, 113, 114n, 192

Alder, Sitka, **5**: 224n, **9**: 214, 215n, 216

Alder, thinleaf, **8**: 7, 11, 12n, 79

Alder, white, **7**: 22n, 113, 114n, 193

Alder Creek, **6**: 276n, **7**: 169n

Aldrich Point, **6**: 41n, **7**: 11n, **10**: 201n, **11**: 433n

Alectoria jubata, **7**: 233n. *See also* Lichen

Alexander, John Henry, **1**: 12

Algonquian Indians, **10**: 48n. *See also* Chippewa Indians

Algonquian language, **2**: 82n, 127n, 192n, 226n, 281n, 361n, **3**: 109n, 167n, 206n, 236n, **4**: 214n, **5**: 131n, **6**: 432n, **7**: 165n, **8**: 132n, 235n

Alice Creek, **8**: 96n, **10**: 250, 251n

Alitan Indians. *See* Shoshone Indians; Ute Indians

Alkali Creek (Elk River), **8**: 236–38, 240n, 390, 407

Alkali Flat Creek, **5**: 266n

Allegheny Mountains, **10**: 34n, **12**: 4

Allegheny River, **10**: 229n

Allen, John L., **2**: 542

Allen, Paul, **2**: 37

Allfour's Run, **2**: 68, 69n

Allium acuminatum, **5**: 21n. *See also* Onions

Allium brevistylum, **4**: 422n, **9**: 189n, **11**: 238n. *See also* Garlic

Allium cernuum, **4**: 418n, **10**: 116n. *See also* Onion, nodding

Allium douglasii, **7**: 312n. *See also* Onion, Douglas's

Allium geyeri, **4**: 418n, **7**: 266n, **10**: 116n. *See also* Onion, Geyer's

Allium schoenoprasum, **7**: 31n, **9**: 283n. *See also* Chive, wild

Allium sp., **5**: 170n. *See also* Onions

Allium textile, **4**: 28n, **5**: 21n. *See also* Onion, white wild

Allium tolmiei, **7**: 312n. *See also* Onion, Tolmie's

Allogona townsendiana, **6**: 405n, **7**: 46n. *See also* Snails

Allspice, **6**: 174, 197

Allum, **10**: 30

Alluvium, **4**: 135n

Almota Creek, **5**: 264n, **6**: 467, **10**: 153n, **11**: 349n

Alnus glutinosa, **8**: 12n. *See also* Alder, black

Alnus incana, **8**: 12n. *See also* Alder, thinleaf

Alnus rhombifolia, **7**: 22n. *See also* Alder, white

Alnus rubra, **5**: 358n, **6**: 29n, **7**: 22n. *See also* Alder, red

Alnus serrulata, **5**: 224n

Alnus sinuata, **5**: 224n, **9**: 215n. *See also* Alder, Sitka

Alopecurus sp., **5**: 60n. *See also* Foxtail

Alpaweyma village, **7**: 208n

Alpowa Creek, **5**: 261, 263n, 279, **7**: 205–7, 208n, **8**: 384, 402, **9**: 304, 304n, **10**: 221, 222n

Alps, **10**: 93n

Alsea (Neck-e-to, Ul-se-ah) Indi-

ans, **6**: 201, 202n, 237n, 432n, 476, 485, 490–91

Alsean language, **6**: 202n, 237n

Alum, **2**: 500–501, **3**: 372–73, 473, 475–76, 478, 481, **4**: 36, 41, **8**: 379, **9**: 42, 59, **11**: 59

Amahami site, **3**: 205–6n, **9**: 91n, **10**: 78n, **11**: 134n

Amblyomma americanum, **2**: 305n. *See also* Tick, lone star

Amdol, **2**: 191

Amelanchier alnifolia, **3**: 492n, **4**: 57n, **5**: 35n, **7**: 111n, **8**: 13n, **9**: 187n, **10**: 119n, **11**: 242n, **12**: 9n. *See also* Serviceberry

Amelanchier arborea, **2**: 217n, **4**: 396n. *See also* Juneberry; Serviceberry

American Bottom, **2**: 156n, 166n, 197

American (Corvus) Creek, **2**: 18, **3**: 74–76, 76n, 79n, 80, 85–87, 85n, 88n, **8**: 326, 327n, 417, **10**: 40, 40n

American Fur Company, **3**: 91n, **4**: 80n, **8**: 280n, 347n, 362n, 368n

American Island, **3**: 80n, 86–87, 88n

American Philosophical Society, **1**: 4, **2**: 1–2, 4–5, 9, 38, 40, 225n, 530–31, 536–39, 541, 544, **3**: 334–35, 383n, 386, 388, 450, 472, 491n, **6**: 488n 494n, **7**: 89–90n, **8**: 414n, **9**: xvii, **12**: 3–4, 6–8

Amorpha fruiticosa, **3**: 466. *See also* Indigo, false

Amorpha sp., **8**: 193n

Amphicarpa bracteata, **2**: 382n, **3**: 16on, **4**: 18n, **8**: 344n, **9**: 227n, **10**: 54n, **11**: 92n. *See also* Peanut, hog

Amputations. *See* Medicine

Anabrus simplex, **5**: 174n. *See also* Cricket, Mormon

Anas clypeata, **7**: 169n. *See also* Shoveler, northern

Anas discors, **3**: 69n, **4**: 47n, **5**: 272n, **6**: 384n. *See also* Teal, blue-winged

Anas platyrhynchos, **3**: 223n, **4**:

24n, **5**: 13n, **6**: 98n, **7**: 11n, **10**: 160n. *See also* Mallard

Anas sp., **6**: 384n. *See also* Teals

Anchors, **3**: 121, 123–25, 127, 129, 132n, **9**: 25, 71–72, 87, **10**: 43, 47, **11**: 83, 85–86, 88–90

Anchovies, **6**: 344, 346n. *See also* Eulachon

Anckas, week, a chappa. *See* The Half Man

Anderson, Richard Clough, **2**: 142, 142n, 205

Andropogon gerardi, **2**: 349n, **3**: 167n, 468. *See also* Bluestem, big

Ane, a, wish, a Shaddie La, dom. *See* The Half Man

Angelica, small-leafed, **10**: 137, 137n

Angelica pinnata, **10**: 137n. *See also* Angelica, small-leafed

Angelica sp., **8**: 31n, **10**: 137n

Anise, **7**: 264

Ankles. *See* Medical problems

Annahhose Indians, **3**: 217n

Anomiidae, **6**: 409n. *See also* Bivalves

Anser albifrons, **6**: 420n. *See also* Goose, greater white-fronted

Ant, carpenter, **7**: 194n

Ant, harvester, **3**: 7, 10, 12n, **9**: 44, 45n

Ant, western harvester, **5**: 11, 14n

Antelope. *See* Pronghorn

Antelope brush, **8**: 93, 94n

Antelope Butte, **4**: 381n, **10**: 111n

Antelope Creek (Broadwater County, Mont.), **4**: 416, 418n

Antelope Creek (Jefferson County, Mont.), **8**: 178n, **9**: 335n

Antelope Creek (McCone County, Mont.), **11**: 145n

Antelope Creek (Madison County, Mont.), **5**: 21n, **11**: 249n

Antelope Creek (Phillips County, Mont.), **10**, 92, 92n, 120n, **11**: 167–68, 169n

Antelope (High Water) Creek

(S. Dak.), **3**: 107–8, 109n, **9**: 65, 66n, **10**: 43, 43n, 44n, **11**: 82n, 83, 84n

Antelope Flat, **8**: 114n

Antelope Lake, **8**: 114n

Anthus spragueii, **6**: 383n. *See also* Pipit, Sprague's

Antilocapra americana, **3**: 46n, **4**: 21n, **5**: 17n, **6**: 317n, **7**: 53n, **8**: 92n, **9**: 54n, **10**: 36n, **11**: 75n. *See also* Pronghorn

Aowa (Roloje) Creek, **2**: 493n, 500–501, 502n, **9**: 42, 42n, **10**: 30, 30n

Apash Wyakaikt (We-ark-koomt, Big Horn), **7**: 2, 202–8, 204n, 211, 214–18, 220, 222, **9**: 304, 304n, 306, **10**: 221, 221n

Aphelocoma coerulescens, **5**: 214n. *See also* Jay, scrub

Apiaceae, **7**: 266n, 277n. *See also* Parsley

Apios americana, **2**: 224n, 365n, **3**: 120n, **8**: 360n, **9**: 23n, **11**: 89n. *See also* Potato, Indian

Apis mellifera, **4**: 277n, **7**: 312n. *See also* Bee, honey

Aplodinotus grunniens, **2**: 484n, **10**: 29n. *See also* Drum, freshwater

Aplodontia rufa, **6**: 78n, **9**: 260n, **10**: 174n, **11**: 405n. *See also* Mountain beaver

Apocynum androsaemifolium, **5**: 131n. *See also* Dogbane, spreading

Apocynum cannabinum, **5**: 131n, **8**: 120n. *See also* Dogbane, hemp

Apocynum medium, **5**: 131n. *See also* Dogbane

Apocynum sp., **6**: 217n. *See also* Dogbane

Appalachian Mountains, **2**: 3, 6

Appaloosas, **5**: 225n, **6**: 313, 315, 317n, **10**: 224, 224n

Appendicitis. *See* Medical Problems

Apple, crab. *See* Crabapple

Apple, white. *See* Breadroot

Apple Creek (Mo.), **2**: 108, 109n, 111–13, 113n, **3**: 446

Apple (Shepherd's) Creek (N. Dak.), **3**: 186–87, 188n, **9**: 88, 88n, **10**: 57, 57n, **11**: 102, 103n

Apples, **2**: 208, 209n, 433, **9**: xvi, **10**: 67, **11**: 113. *See also* Mayapple

Aquila chrysaetos, **3**: 120n, **4**: 95n, **5**: 141n, **6**: 94n, **7**: 17n, **8**: 146n, **9**: 194n, **11**: 252n. *See also* Eagle, golden

Aquilegia canadensis, **3**: 471. *See also* Columbine

Aquilegia formosa, **8**: 30n. *See also* Columbine, red

Arapaho (Ca-ne-na-vich, Cas-ta-ha-na, Kun-na-nar-wesh, and similar spellings) Indians, **3**: 135, 137n, 167n, 217n, 206n, 403, 423, 426–27, 439, 448–49, 487, **4**: 214n, **5**: 86n, **8**: 90n, 235n

Arborvitae. *See* Redcedar, western

Arbutus menziesii, **6**: 105n. *See also* Madrone, Pacific

Archilochus alexandri, **7**: 47n. *See also* Hummingbird, black-chinned

Arctic Ocean, **10**: 6n, 67n, 226n

Arctostaphylos uva-ursi, **3**: 305n, 471, **5**: 353n, **6**: 237n, **7**: 17n, **12**: 9n. *See also* Bearberry

Ardea herodias, **2**: 178n, **6**: 98n, **9**: 51n. *See also* Heron, great blue

Area Creek, **8**: 183, 186, 188n

Argali, **3**: 119, 120n. *See also* Sheep, bighorn

Argillite, **5**: 141n, **8**: 124n

Arikara (Ree, Ricara, Rickaree, and similar spellings) Indians: villages, **1**: 8, **2**: 352n, **3**: 2, 31, 37n, 126–27, 127n, 132, 134, 143–44, 144n, 146–49, 147n, 150–52, 150n, 155–57, 156n, 157n, 158–59, 158n, 160n, 162, 164, 166, 167n, 181n, 194–97, 198n, 221–22, 227n, 252, 294, 305n, 309, 316n, 361, 372–73, 376, 380–81, **4**: 7, **8**: 307, 307n, 309–12,

Arikara (*continued*)
316n, 318, 322–23, 323n,
358n, 369n, 380, 398–99,
417, **9**: 72, 74, 76, 78–79,
81, 83, 90, 90n, 119n, 352–
53, 352n, 367, **10**: 48, 51–
54, 269, 270n, **11**: 91, 92n,
96–99, 97n, 172; chiefs, **1**: 8,
3: 2, 179, 181, 200n, 201n,
210, 217–19, 221, 224, 230–
31, 292, 300, 327, **4**: 7, 11,
93, **8**: 288–89, 289n, 312,
314, 316n, 317, 357, 358n,
9: 79, 82, 82n, 126, 361,
10: 76n, 77, 269, **11**: 100n;
listed, **2**: 195, **3**: 448; language, **2**: 438, 442n, **3**: 127n,
137–38n, 148–49, 161, 163,
178, 178n, 184n, 190, 196,
205n, 217n, 247n, 490, **4**: 7,
7: 343n, **10**: 274, 274n, **11**:
103n, 126n; trade, **2**: 482n,
3: 76n, 135–36, 137n, 155n,
161, 238, 484, **8**: 360n; distances, **2**: 485; and members
of the party, **2**: 512, 514–15,
521, 525–26, **8**: 4, 312, 314,
9: 83, 85, **10**: 53–56, 56n,
270, **11**: 100; encountered,
3: 2, 221–22, **8**: 312, **9**: 78,
10: 52, **11**: 97, 99–100; and
Pawnee Indians, **3**: 126–27,
127n, 16¹, 163, 232n, 244–
45, 247n, 251, 251n; name,
3: 127n, 251, 251n; lodges,
3: 143, 161, 166n, **9**: 77–78,
82n, **10**: 52–54, **11**: 96, 98,
105; located, **3**: 153n; medical problems, **3**: 153n, 161,
401, **4**: 11; historical sketch,
3: 153–54n, 161–64, 400–
401; councils, **3**: 156–58,
160–66, **8**: 312–16, **9**: 79,
10: 269, **11**: 98; and liquor,
3: 157, 157n, 183; clothes,
3: 161–62, 164, 196, 488, **8**:
318, **9**: 83; customs, **3**: 161,
163–64, 167n, 168–69, 172,
180, 196, 313, 315, 488, **6**:
169, 191, 405–6, **8**: 314–15,
317n; war, **3**: 161, 213n,
243–45, 284, 331, 414–15,
424, 427–28, 430–31, 437,

5: 91, **8**: 159n, 301, 303–4,
308, 313, 315–16, 316n, **11**:
108–9, 110n; relations with
the party, **3**: 161, 284; **8**: 314,
317n; information from, **3**:
169, 308, **4**: 321, 375, **8**: 323,
9: 119, **10**: 74; camps, **3**:
173–76, 175n; speech for,
3: 252; and horses, **3**: 292, **8**:
319; visits, **3**: 304, 307, 332,
10: 76–77, **11**: 132; tobacco,
3: 460–61, 466, 471–72n, **5**:
81, **10**: 53; character, **3**: 482;
hunting, **3**: 484–85, **9**: 84,
86, **10**: 55–56, **11**: 10; appearance, **3**: 487, **8**: 318;
gifts, **3**: 496; and other Indians, **5**: 91, 130, **8**: 306, **9**:
125–26, **11**: 106, 131; mentioned, **2**: 309n, **3**: 128–29,
232n, 244, 249, 251, 297,
305, 315n, 409, 413, 418,
420, 423, **4**: 12n, **6**: 172n, **8**,
198n, **9**: 73n, 77, 94, **10**: 49,
11: 92, 126
Ariolimax columbianus, **6**: 146n.
See also Slug, Pacific woods
Arkansas River, **1**: 12, **2**: 147,
150n, 266, 439, 514, **3**: 339,
343–44, 391–93, 435–38,
445–46, 473, 479, 483, 486,
4: 188, 204, **8**: 355, 355–
56n, 367n
Arketarnarshar, **3**: 156n, 175–
76, 209–10. *See also* Eagles
Feather
Ar-lo-quat, **6**: 148n
Armbands, **6**: 173n, 195, 221, **7**:
271–72, **9**: 205, 369n. *See also*
Clothing
Armells Creek (Rosebud
County, Mont.), **8**: 241, 243–
44, 245n
Armells (South Mountain)
Creek (Fergus County,
Mont.), **4**: 189–91, 192n, **8**:
400, **9**: 154, 154n, **11**: 166–
67, 167n
Arms. *See* Medical problems
Arms and ammunition: distrib-
uted, **2**: 188; inspected, **2**:
248–50, 261, 317, 370, 416,
429, **4**: 136, 139, 306, **5**: 289,

326–27, **6**: 48–49, 265, 272,
7: 146, **8**: 311, 324, 332, **9**:
7–8, 16, 146, 375, 377, 382,
384, 387, **10**: 9, 11, 16, **11**:
12; cleaned, **2**: 293; orders
concerning, **2**: 332, **6**: 158;
and Indians, **3**: 114n, **4**:
221n, **5**: 91, 96, 115, 122,
166, 229, **8**: 131, 280n, **10**:
223, **11**: 280, 282; Indian, **3**:
122, 356, 428, 484, **7**: 247–
48, 251n, **11**: 89–90, 439;
fired, **3**: 261, 261n, **6**: 137,
151, 153, 312, 314, **8**: 346,
369–70, **10**: 184, **11**: 113,
115, 285; repaired, **4**: 271, **8**:
80, **9**: 165–66, **11**: 56, 193–
94; cached, **4**: 275, 334, **7**:
232, **10**: 151, **11**: 339; as
trade items, **7**: 146, 183, 185,
229, 301, **8**: 88, 132n, **9**: 209,
214, 302, 309, 318; secured,
7: 148; accidents, **7**: 206–7;
stolen, **8**: 113, **9**: 87, **10**: 56,
171, 268; problems with, **9**:
226; as gift, **10**: 266; mentioned, **3**: 112, 321n, **4**: 267,
338, 371n, 426, **5**: 113, 333,
6: 267, **8**: 134, 155, **9**: 126,
307. *See also* Air gun; Balls,
bullets, and shot; Bayonets;
Blunderbusses; Bows and
arrows; Canisters; Cannon,
swivel; Cannons; Cartridges;
Cloth, wiping; Cutlasses; Daggers; Dirks; Espontoon; Eyedaggs; Flintlocks; Flints; Frizzen; Fusils; Guard, trigger;
Gunpowder; Guns; Hatch-
ets; Horns, powder; Knives;
Lances; Lead; Musket, North
West; Musket, U. S. Model
1795; Muskets; Pan; Pistols;
Poggamoggan; Portfire;
Pouch, shot; Rifle, Kentucky;
Rifle, Model 1803; Rifles;
Rod, ram; Rod, wiping;
Shields; Shotguns; Spears;
Swords, Tomahawks
Armstrong, Erica, **12**: 8
Arnold, John, **2**: 92n
Arnold's chronometer. *See*
Chronometers

Arrastra Creek, **8**: 94, 95n, 102
Arrowbeach site, **5**: 252n
Arrow Creek (Slaughter River),
  4: 217–18, 220–21n, **6**: 449,
  463, **8**: 140n, 382, 401, **9**:
  158, 158n, 343n, **10**: 96n,
  260n, **11**: 177–78, 179n
Arrowhead, **6**: 17, 20n, **7**: 36n,
  38. *See also* Wapato
Arrow Prairie, **2**: 288–90, 290n,
  3: 370, 377, **8**: 377, 395, **9**:
  368n, **10**: 13, **11**: 21
Arrow Rock (Mills) Island, **2**:
  286–87, 288n, **9**: 11, 11n,
  11: 21n
Arrows. *See* Bows and arrows
Arrowsmith, Aaron, **1**: 5, 16nn.
  25, 29, **4**: 266, 269n, **7**: 219n
Arrowwood, **6**: 44, 45n, **8**: 359n.
  See also Dogwood, red osier;
  Haw, black
Arsenic, **2**: 500–501
Artemisia abrotanum, **4**: 40n. *See
  also* Southernwood
Artemisia cana, **3**: 470, **4**: 41n,
  419n. *See also* Sagebrush,
  silver
Artemisia dracunculus, **3**: 469. *See
  also* Wormwood, silky
Artemisia frigida, **3**: 469–70. *See
  also* Sagewort, prairie
Artemisia longifolia, **3**: 470. *See
  also* Sage, long leaf
Artemisia ludoviciana, **3**: 467. *See
  also* Sage, white
Artemisia nova, **4**: 145n. *See also*
  Sagebrush, black
Artemisia sp., **4**: 40n, 419n,
  10: 81n. *See also* Sagebrush
Artemisia tridentata, **4**: 41n,
  419n, **5**: 67n, **7**: 151n, **8**:
  94n, **9**: 140n, **10**: 133n, **11**:
  154n. *See also* Sagebrush, big
Artemisia vulgaris, **4**: 40n. *See also*
  Wormwood
Artichoke, Jerusalem, **3**: 326,
  327n, 483, **4**: 15–16, 18n,
  5: 143, 147n, **8**: 50–51, 52n,
  11: 196
Artichoke (Shield's) Creek,
  3: 142n
Articles. *See* Equipment
Artificial horizon, **2**: 94, 94n,

411–12, **3**: 257, 275, **4**: 25.
  See also Instruments, scientific
Artiodactyla, **6**: 405n
Arundinaria gigantea, **2**: 104n.
  See also Cane, large
Arwarharmay (and similar spell-
  ings) Indians. *See* Hidatsa
  Indians
Asarum canadense, **3**: 467. *See also*
  Ginger, wild
Asarum caudatum, **8**: 59n. *See also*
  Ginger, long-tailed wild
Ash, **2**: 275, 286, 306, 313, 428,
  430, **3**: 221–22, 229, 361–
  62, **5**: 365, **6**: 9, 17, 449, **8**:
  272–73, 286, 311, 354, 359,
  9: 10, 10n, 12, 44, 61, 137–
  38, 377, 377n, **10**: 11, 15,
  11: 361–62, 435
Ash, blue, **2**: 314, 315n
Ash, broad-leafed. *See* Maple,
  bigleaf
Ash, green, **2**: 314n, **3**: 76, 182,
  184n, **4**: 26, 28n, 39, 54, 69,
  73–74, 216, 220, 221n, 222–
  23, **8**: 150, 151n, 268, 270n,
  345, 345n, 355n, 359n, 417,
  418n, **9**: 130, 130n, **10**: 11n
Ash, Greene mountain, **8**: 12n
Ash, large-leafed. *See* Maple,
  bigleaf
Ash, Oregon, **5**: 356–57, 358n,
  6: 20n, 98n, 294–95, 296n,
  7: 14n, 19, 21, 25, 32, 55, 77,
  112, 114n, **9**: 287, 287n, **10**:
  164, 164n, 202, 202n, 207,
  207n
Ash, Pacific mountain, **5**: 217,
  223n
Ash, prickly, **8**: 359, 359n, 417,
  418n
Ash, volcanic, **6**: 14n, **7**: 204n,
  208n, 225n, 236n
Ash, white, **2**: 314n, **8**: 345n,
  359n, **10**: 11n
Ashley, William, **2**: 515, **8**: 316n
Ashley Island, **3**: 151–52, 153n,
  154n, 380, **8**: 316n, 317n,
  380, 399, **9**: 78, 78n, 353n,
  10: 52, 52n, 270n, **11**: 97,
  97n
Ash Rapids, **8**: 150, 151n
Asimina triloba, **8**: 12n, **9**: 361n,
  10: 280n. *See also* Pawpaw

Asio otus, **4**: 175n. *See also* Owl,
  long-eared
Aspen, quaking, **4**: 2, 94, 96n,
  386, 391n, 394, 396, 399,
  401, 406, **8**: 79, 81n
Ãs-sáy. See Buffaloberry
Asses, **3**: 435, 437–38
Assiniboine House (Mouse
  River Fort), **2**: 225, 226n,
  8: 212n
Assiniboine (Osnaboin, Ossiniboin, Stone) Indians: trade,
  1: 5, **2**: 167n, **3**: 278–79,
  403–5, 466, 484, **4**: 34–35,
  38, **8**: 289, **10**: 69, **11**: 119;
  encountered; **3**: 3; stealing
  horses, **3**: 196–97, 237, 292;
  and Hidatsa Indians, **3**: 230,
  236–37, historical sketch,
  3: 230n, 429–32; chiefs, **3**:
  235n, 278n; and Mandan In-
  dians, **3**: 236, **8**: 289, **9**: 96;
  located, **3**: 236n; war, **3**:
  246–47, 262, 279, 292, 309,
  312, 317, 412–13, 424, 426–
  28, 442–43, **4**: 48–49, **8**:
  289; and liquor, **3**: 430,
  4: 34–35, 38; listed, **3**: 448;
  hunting, **3**: 484–85, **4**: 35,
  39, 42, 44; appearance,
  3: 487; language, **3**: 490;
  camps, **4**: 2, 23, 28, 30, 33–
  34, 42, 44, 48, **10**: 79; feared,
  4: 20, 136; lodges, **4**: 34;
  tipis, **4**: 38–39; customs, **4**:
  55, 100–101, **6**: 169, 191;
  search for, **4**: 136, 139; mentioned, **3**: 198n, 433, 440,
  4: 10–11, 88n, 126–27, 136,
  5: 86n, **8**: 90n, 289n, **9**: 96n,
  11: 120n
Assiniboine (Ossiniboin) River,
  1: 5, 8, **2**: 144n, 219–20,
  225, 225–26n, **3**: 196–97,
  198n, 199, 210n, 218–19,
  220n, 224, 235, 235n, 241,
  251n, 253, 257, 262n, 308,
  309n, 317, 363–64, 402–4,
  429–33, 441–43, 487, 491,
  492n, **4**: 30, 33–34, 42, **8**:
  74, 77, 212, 212n, **10**: 66n,
  67n, 70n, 265n, **11**: 111n

Astacus sp., **5**: 228n, **6**: 398n, **9**: 227n, **11**: 326n. *See also* Crayfish

Astor, John Jacob, **6**: 94n, **8**: 368n

Astoria Formation, **6**: 67n, 179n, 185n

Astorians, **6**: 37n, 61n, 91n, 94n, 148n, 333n, **8**: 316n, 344n, 352n, 358n, 368n

Astoria (Point Meriwether), **6**: 92, 94n, 459, 471, **8**: 387, 406

Astragalus canadensis, **3**: 469. *See also* Milkvetch, Canada

Astragalus crassicarpa, **3**: 467. *See also* Plum, ground

Astragalus missouriensis, **3**: 469. *See also* Milkvetch, Missouri

Astragalus sp., **8**: 193n. *See also* Milkvetch

Astringent. *See* Medicine; Cherry, choke

Astronomical observations, **2**: 11, 20, 59, 85, 87, 87n, 91, 94, 97, 110, 111–12, 117, 118n, 119–21, 122n, 123–24, 128, 134–39, 145, 150, 151n, 152–53, 155, 167, 215, 228, 229n, 232–33, 235, 237–40, 261–63, 269–74, 282–83, 289–92, 296, 298–99, 303, 311, 317–20, 325–32, 334–36, 339, 348, 360, 368, 370–72, 379, 381–82, 385, 387–90, 393, 396–97, 410, 415–20, 422–23, 432, 434–35, 446n, 451–52, 457, 459, 462, 464–65, 467–70, 472, 474, 476–78, 480–82, 484, 487, 489, 497, 499, 532, 534, 542, **3**: 17–18, 25, 28, 34, 44–45, 56–60, 63, 64n, 77, 82–83, 85, 91, 100, 102–3, 106, 140, 153, 159–60, 181, 212, 216, 232n, 233, 260–61, 269–70, 273–75, 275n, 277–80, 288–89, 300–302, 320–21, 324, 329, 333, **4**: 24–25, 37–38, 43, 52, 61–62, 72, 76, 114, 119, 122–23, 133, 138, 143, 149, 157, 172–74, 177, 187–88,

208–9, 243–46, 251, 272–74, 276, 310, 318, 321, 345, 352, 356, 370, 372–73, 377, 387, 393, 400, 408–9, 413–14, 424–25, **5**: 9, 11–13, 54–56, 59, 98–99, 118, 123–24, 129–30, 138, 178, 192–93, 195, 197, 236–37, 240n, 244–48, 253, 255–56, 259n, 264–65, 280, 284–85, 291–92, 327–28, 340–41, 344, 346n, 366–67, **6**: 62n, 71n, 82–83, 179, 255, 257, 259, 277, 347, 410, 417, 495, **7**: 1, 39, 41, 50, 53, 55, 71, 74–76, 74n, 78n, 127, 285n, 286–87, 335–36, 340, 346, 349, **8**: 2, 116–17, 122, 125–26, 156, 293, 322, **9**: 9, 14, 17–18, 24, 26–27, 34, 78, 83, 113, 129, 137, 151, 161–62, 198, 207, 240, 245, 341, 354, 376, 387, 389, **10**: 63–64n, 98, 119, 122, 140, 158, 161, 177, **11**: 4, 17, 31–32, 37–40, 44, 51, 184–85, 245–46, 259, 277–79, 310, 349–50, 358–59, 367–68, 431, **12**: 2

Astronomy Notebook, **2**: 122n, 542, 564–65, **7**: 177n

Athabasca, **10**: 7n

Athapascan Kwalhiokwa (Killaxt-ho-kle) Indians, **6**: 475, 486, 491

Athapascan language, **6**: 432n

Atkins's Riffle, **2**: 70

Atlantic Ocean, **3**: 368, **6**: 259, 340, 342, 396–97

Atsina (Big Bellies, Fall, Gros Ventres, Minetares of Fort de Prairie, Pah-kee) Indians: name, **3**: 206n, **5**: 83, 86n, **8**: 65n, 235n; historical sketch, **3**, 433–35, **4**: 214n; listed, **3**: 448; language, **3**: 490; signs, **4**: 211, 213, 216, 219, **8**: 64, 93–94, 142; camps, **4**: 222, 224, **9**: 159, 159n; war, **5**: 80, 83, 96, 226, **7**: 242–43, 245n, 248, 250–51, 251n, 256, 258, 301, 333–34, **8**: 48, 63, 66, 68, 82, 85, 88,

278; peace, **5**: 91, **8**: 75, 78; trade, **5**: 95n, **9**: 159n; trails; **8**: 88; lodges; **8**: 94, 142; reputation, **8**: 113, 129; supposed encounter, **8**: 130, 132n; mentioned, **4**: 221n, **5**: 142, **7**: 334n, **8**: 48n, 78n, 90n, 125, **9**: 343n, **10**: 259–60n. *See also* Blackfeet Indians; Hidatsa Indians

Attacapa Indians, **3**: 447, 450

Audubon, John James, **2**: 38, **6**: 148n

Augers, **4**: 275, 279, **9**: 166, **11**: 193–94

Augite, **8**: 26n

Au-ho-ne-ga, **2**: 439, 441

Au-ho-ning ga, **2**: 439, 441

Auner-hoo Indians, **3**: 136

Aurelia sp., **6**: 425n. *See also* Jellyfish

Aurora borealis, **2**: 187, 190n, 208, **3**: 230, 231n, 249, **8**: 335, 336n, **9**: 94, 94n

Auxvasse (Big Miry, Big Muddy, Muddy) River, **2**: 265, 266n, 269–70, **3**: 339, 370, 376, **8**: 377, 395, **9**: 9, 9n, 368n, 376, **10**: 11, 11n, **11**: 16–17, 17n

Avocet, American, **4**: 96–100, 100n, **8**: 113, 114n

Awatixa Hidatsa Indians. *See* Hidatsa Indians, Awatixa

Awaxawi Hidatsa Indians. *See* Hidatsa Indians, Awaxawi

Awls, **3**: 428, 484, **5**: 70, 78, 112, **6**: 214, 216, **7**: 148, 161, 253–54, 271–72, 275–76, 284–85, **9**: 369n, **10**: 67, **11**: 113

Awnings. *See* Pirogues; Pirogue, white

Ax, battle, **3**: 281, 286–87, 287n, 293, 296, 308, 313, 484

Axes: cached, **2**: 287, **4**: 275–76, 279, **9**: 166; as trade item, **3**: 226–27, 233, 298, 303, **5**: 158, **8**: 23, **9**: 297, 318, 369n, **10**: 71; Indian, **3**: 264, 268, 356, 401, 403, 413, 428, **5**: 139, 150, **6**: 16–17, 265, 271, **7**: 129, 253–54,

9: 106n; use, 3: 285, 300, 5: 113, 115, 234, 8: 209, 9: 111; stolen, 6: 90, 327, 7: 105, 109, 9: 83, 87, 240, 290, 10: 54, 11: 99; left, 9: xv, 184; repaired, 9: 106–7; broken, 9: 119; mentioned, 2: 137, 3: 232, 4: 334–35, 370, 372, 374, 374n, 375–77, 386–87, 6: 113, 158, 243–44, 8: 208, 9: 174, 11: 212, 228, 334, 403

Axletree. *See* Wagons

Ayauwa (and similar spellings) Indians. *See* Iowa Indians

Ayer, Edward Everett, 2: 543

Ayoway Creek. *See* Aowa Creek

Aythya collaris, 7: 26n. *See also* Duck, ring-necked

Aythya valisineria, 5: 312n, 6: 37n, 7: 25n, 10: 160n. *See also* Canvasback

B

Bachelor (Green Bryor, Quathlahpotle) Island, 6: 21, 23, 24n, 56, 7: 28, 31n, 32, 34, 9: 250, 250n, 283n, 10: 203n, 11: 387, 388n, 436n

Back. *See* Medical problems

Backgammon, 3: 3, 265, 266n, 6: 118–19

Bacon, 2: 333, 4: 362

Badger: hunted, 2: 173, 173n, 429–30, 431n, 3: 148–49, 4: 256, 9: 32, 32n, 110, 164, 340, 10: 24, 24n, 52, 70, 11: 47–48, 48n, 96–97, 301–2; described, 2: 429–30, 431n, 8: 352–53, 357–58, 10: 24, 24n, 11: 47–48; signs, 3: 7, 12n, 8: 200, 203n; abundance, 3: 7, 12n, 482; as specimen, 3: 330–31, 8: 418, 9: 77, 126, 127n; and Indians, 5: 188, 189n, 6: 19, 21n; observed, 6: 313, 315, 317n; habitat, 6: 352, 357, 8: 417;

behavior, 6: 352–53, 357–58; mentioned, 2: 481, 483n, 4: 34n, 6: 355n, 8: 418n, 9: 312n, 11: 121

Badger Creek (Mont.), 8: 127–28, 132n, 133n

Badger (Fish) Creek (S. Dak.), 9: 87, 87n, 10: 57, 57n, 11: 102, 102n

Badger Lake, 9: 37n, 10: 27n

Badgley (Bagley), David, 2: 166, 166n

Bad Place site, 5: 348n

Bad (Askow) River (Canada), 3: 365, 367, 434

Bad (Teton) River (S. Dak.), 3: 2, 107–9, 109n, 110n, 111–12, 114n, 359, 372, 375, 380, 401, 415–16, 419, 8: 323, 324n, 330, 380, 398, 411–12, 9: 65, 66n, 81, 354n, 367n, 10: 43, 44n, 272, 272n, 11: 83, 84n, 172

Bad Route Creek, 8: 258, 260, 262n

Bad Village, 3: 15n

Baggage: dried, 3: 1, 76–77, 132n, 4: 121, 275, 378, 5: 8, 53, 55–56, 252, 271–72, 340, 342–43, 345, 6: 51, 83, 85, 96, 7: 23, 277–80, 8: 140–41, 146, 9: 191, 235, 344, 347, 364, 10: 23, 119, 152, 172, 253, 262, 270, 276, 11: 244–45, 277, 352–54, 394, 398, 400, 411; secured, 3: 1, 76–77, 5: 172–73, 177, 229, 6: 36, 7: 261, 263, 275; portaged, 4: 3, 300, 302, 317–19, 323–27, 330, 334, 336, 338–40, 342, 344–45, 351–52, 5: 92, 111, 113, 117, 129, 153, 159, 165–66, 171, 173, 178–79, 277, 283, 320, 323, 329, 338, 357, 366–67, 6: 7, 7: 104, 108, 111–13, 137, 139, 142–44, 146, 152, 154, 156–57, 8: 74, 77, 110, 9: 168, 170, 172–73, 176–77, 206, 209, 239, 244, 248, 254, 273, 278, 290, 294, 10: 104, 106–7, 110–11, 126–28, 156, 160, 162, 165, 209,

212–14, 247, 254, 258, 11: 199, 201, 203–4, 206–16, 273, 275–77, 282–83, 287, 292, 355, 365–66, 370, 379–81; wet, 4: 63–64, 261, 368, 5: 52–53, 55, 251, 271–72, 276–77, 340, 342–43, 6: 39–40, 48–49, 51, 91–92, 108, 127, 169, 9: 238, 10: 88–89, 151, 155, 11: 211, 352–53, 393; loaded, 4: 64, 309, 330, 332, 371, 378, 5: 115, 119, 133, 158, 7: 7, 116, 181, 183, 249, 255, 257, 8: 40, 42, 52, 54, 83, 107, 111, 169, 174–75, 217, 280, 306, 328, 9: 125, 165, 174, 176, 182, 184, 198, 207, 209, 219, 334, 351, 10: 75, 151, 11: 222–24, 227, 259, 278, 291, 302–3, 313, 340–41; unloaded, 4: 121, 435, 6: 40–43, 7: 102–3, 256, 8: 178–79, 9: 115, 289, 10: 180, 11: 217, 286, 340–41; cached, 4: 269, 5: 125, 133, 8: 32–34, 34n, 53–54, 67, 69, 106, 137, 9: 207–8, 324, 327, 10: 100–101, 103, 241, 244, 253, 11: 202, 217, 278–81, 334; Indian, 5: 121, 6: 119, 190, 216–17, 246, 253, 305, 307, 8: 39–41, 43, 135, 295, 319, 11: 334; lost, 5: 271–72, 10: 145; damaged, 5: 272, 342, as trade item, 6: 135, 147, 7: 343; on horses, 7: 54, 56, 126, 128, 131, 160, 166, 168; guarded, 7: 98–99, 104, 11: 289–90; endangered, 8: 31, 33; stolen, 8: 113; problems, 8: 138; mentioned, 1: 4, 4: 22, 70, 276, 333, 350, 354, 363, 365, 369–70, 376, 379, 382, 5: 142, 182, 187, 6: 50, 172n, 328–29, 8: 209, 284, 371, 413, 9: 170, 174, 182–83, 182n, 213, 230, 272, 290, 300, 310, 339, 10: 108, 194, 217, 227, 241n, 247, 255, 11: 368, 391, 402, 421–22

Bagnell site, 3: 198n, 9: 90n

Bailey (Deer) Creek, **2**: 262–63, 264n, **9**: 8, 8n, 375, **10**: 10, 10n

Baker, H., **2**: 138

Baker, James, **6**: 47–48n

Baker (Haley's) Bay, **6**: 46–47, 47n, 49–50, 51n, 53–54, 61, 66, 67n, 81, 113, 154, 201–2, 282, 284, 284n, 387, **9**: 232, 254–55, 254n, 255n, **10**: 171, 171n, 173, 175n, 186, 186n, 195, 195n, 199, 203, **11**: 393, 394n, 397

Bakers Oven Island. *See* Oven Islands

Balaenoptera musculus, **6**: 185n, **9**: 266n, **10**: 188n, **11**: 412n. *See also* Whale, blue

Balch. *See* Bowles, William

Baldhead (Piaheto, Eagles Feather) Creek, **3**: 172, 173n, **9**: 84, 84n, **10**: 55, 55n, **11**: 100, 100n

Bald (Chauvin) Island, **2**: 383–85, 386n, 389–90, 392

Bald Island, **10**: 21n

Bald Mountain, **5**: 214n, **8**: 55n, **9**: 226, 226n, 327n, **10**: 144n, 245n, **11**: 321, 321n

Bald-pated Prairie, **2**: 383–85, 386n, 388, 392, 406–7, 409, 479, 487, **3**: 94, 346–47, 371, 375, 378, **4**: 145, **8**: 354, 354n, 378, 396, 417, **9**: 26, 27n, 80–81, 360, 360n, 367n, **10**: 21, 21n, 277, 277n, **11**: 35, 36n, 40, 40n, 172, 174

Ball Creek (Lyman County, S. Dak.). *See* Bull Creek (Shannon's River)

Balls, **2**: 174, 193, 236, 239, **8**: 372. *See also* Members of the party, singing and dancing

Balls, bullets, and shot, **2**: 213–14, 214n, 438, 459, 497, 504, **3**: 28–31, 34, 65–66, 125n, 142–43, 144n, 166, 246–47, 290, 310, 356, 401, 484, **4**: 151, 153, 341, 343, 351, 367, 368n, 416, **5**: 23, 151, 168, 178, 232, 235, 248, **6**: 74, 76, 121, 187, 205–6, 208–9, **7**: 137, 139, 177, 179, 198, 236, 247–50, 256, 258, 343–44, **8**: 80, 135, 155–56, 289n, 290, 305, 311, 319–20, 324, 330, 359, **9**: xviii, 48, 58, 68, 177, 300, 369n, 393, **10**: 38, 224, 265, **11**: 72–73, 178n, 215–16. *See also* Arms and ammunition

Balsam, **6**: 89, 281, 283. *See also* Fir, grand

Balsam copaiba. *See* Medicine

Balsamorhiza sagittata, **7**: 122–23n. *See also* Balsamroot

Balsamroot, **7**: 121, 122–23n

Baltimore Bar, **2**: 309n

Banks, Joseph, **12**: 5

Bannock Indians, **5**: 94n, 260n, **8**: 180n

Bannock Trail, **8**: 43n

Baptesia sp., **8**: 193n. *See also* Indigo, wild false

Barbarea orthoceras, **7**: 195n. *See also* Cress, winter

Barbarea verna, **7**: 195n. *See also* Cress, Belle Isle

Barbour, Edwin H., **3**: 472

Barbs. *See* Bows and arrows

Barbs, fishing, **5**: 139, 141n

Barge. *See* Keelboat

Bark, Peruvian. *See* Medicine, barks

Bark, walnut. *See* Medicine, barks

Barkers Island, **4**: 438n, **10**: 119n, **11**: 244

Barkley, T. M., **12**: 7

Barley, **2**: 487

Barley, foxtail, **4**: 333n

Barn Mountain. *See* Square Butte (Barn Mountain)

Barrels, **2**: 156, 191, 201–3, 202n, 217–18, 329, 332, **3**: 52–53, **4**: 14, 338, **6**: 368n, **8**: 349, 363, **9**: 27, 28n, 40, 387, **10**: 30, **11**: 41

Barton, Benjamin Smith, **2**: 6, 8n, 16, 33, 38, 352n, 530–31, 533–35, **3**: 76, **4**: 54, 142, 184, 352, 391, 400, **6**: 98, **7**: 90, **12**: 2–4, 6, 9n

Bartram, William, **2**: 35

Bartramia longicauda, **4**: 419n,

8: 78n. *See also* Sandpiper, upland

Basalt, Columbia River, **5**: 266n, 300n, 313n, 319n, **6**: 9n, 10n, 28n, **7**: 114n, 169n, 204n, 208n, 225n, 236n, **8**: 26n

Basalt, Grande Ronde, **5**: 319n, **7**: 114n

Basalt, Pomona, **6**: 34n

Basalt, Saddle Mountain, **5**: 313n, **7**: 169n

Basalt, Wanapum, **5**: 300n, 313n, 319n, 326n, 336n, 340n, 348n

Basalt, Yakima, **5**: 300n, 313n, **6**: 10n, **7**: 169n

Basalts, **5**: 102n, 265, 311, 331, 363n, **6**: 8, 10n, 27, 179n, **7**: 112, 114n, 166, 168, 169n, 236n

Basilicon. *See* Medicine

Baskets: use, **5**: 300, 311, 320, 347–48, 348n, 361, 371, **6**: 74, 76, 137, 192, 196, **7**: 246, 301, **9**: 289, **10**: 158; described, **5**: 323, 325, **6**: 215–17; materials for, **5**: 348n, **6**: 78n, 218n, 296n, 307n, 435, 439, **8**: 55n; stolen, **6**: 47; types, **6**: 77n, **7**: 59, 82, 246, 301; as gift, **6**: 137; mentioned, **3**: 148–49, **6**: 32, 119, 187, 336–37, **7**: 59, 82, **8**: 419, **9**: 77

Bass, **2**: 71, 483, 485–86, **9**: 40

Bass, largemouth, **2**: 72n, 484n, **9**: 40n

Bass, smallmouth, **2**: 72n, 484n, **9**: 40n

Bass, striped, **4**: 279n

Bass, white, **2**: 486n

Bass Creek, **8**: 162n

Bateaux, **8**: 278, 280n, 346, 360, 367, 412. *See also* Keelboat

Bates Island, **2**: 254, 259n

Batholith, **5**: 157n, 203n, 223n, **8**: 65n

Baths. *See* Medicine

Bats, **3**: 12, 13n, **4**: 94, 96n, 346n, **6**: 405–6, 409, 409n, **7**: 46, 48n

Battle (Char-part, Girl, So-harch, Woman) Creek, **3**: 175–76, 178n, **9**: 85, 86n, **10**: 56, 56n, **11**: 101, 101n

Baxter Creek, **8**: 181, 185, 188n

Bayonets, **8**: 41, 177, 177n, **9**: 325. *See also* Arms and ammunition

Bayou Teche, **3**: 447

Bay View site, **6**: 34n

Ba Za conja, **2**: 439, 441

Bazile (White Paint) Creek, **3**: 46–47, 47–48n, 357, 372, 380, **8**: 379, 398, **9**: 53, 54n, **10**: 35, 35n, **11**: 69, 69n. *See also* Lost Creek

Beacon Rock, **5**: 358, 362, 363n, **6**: 7–9, 9n, 54, **7**: 78–79, 89n, 96, 98, 100, 101n, **8**: 404

Beadow Creek, **2**: 380, 382n, **9**: 25, 26n

Beads: as trade item, **2**: 6, **3**: 174, 484, **5**: 89, 226–27, 235, 243, 246, 294, 296, 367, 371, **6**: 72–74, 81, 83, 85, 88, 113, 118, 120–21, 123, 134, 142, 144, 165, 168, 181, 187, 190, 199, 204–5, 214, 216, 221–22, 314, 316, 360, **7**: 28, 36, 98–99, 129, 145–49, 154, 163–64, 253–55, 326, 328; **8**: 45–46, **9**: 100, 105, 229, 237, 239, 256, 292, 295, 302, **10**: 165, 176, **11**: 329–30, 341–42, 380, 397; as clothing, **3**: 488, **5**: 122, 127, 134–35, 139, 222, 258–59, 289, 318, **6**: 15, 75, 142, 435–36, 439, **7**: 129, 151n, 224, 253, 255, **8**: 318–19, **9**: 205, **11**: 276–77, 344–45, 355–56; as gift, **5**: 69–70, 77–79, 105, 112; gambling with, **6**: 119, **7**: 137–38, 140, 154, 249–50; mentioned, **3**: 135, 173n, **6**: 82n, 172n, **9**: 309, 309n, **10**: 149, **11**: 369–70. *See also* Clothing; Wampum

Bean, potato-, **3**: 120n

Bean, wild, **8**: 359, 360n

Bean Lake (Pond Creek), **10**: 18, 18n

Beans: listed, **2**: 203, 217; cultivated, **3**: 151–52, 161, 163, 399–407, 410, 483, **8**: 350, **9**: 78, 82n, **10**: 53, **11**: 91–92, 106, 132; as gift, **3**: 158–60, 162, **8**: 314, **9**: 79, 82–83, 350, **10**: 53–54, 267,68, **11**: 98; as food, **3**: 261; **4**: 362, **5**: 144, 147n, **8**: 285, 308, 315, **9**: 93, 208, **11**: 122; as trade item, **3**: 261, 484, **9**: 92, 103, 105–106, 111, 120, **10**: 67, 270, **11**: 113, 115; and Indians, **3**: 272; mentioned, **3**: 389

Bear, black: observed, **2**: 142, **4**: 44, 48, **6**: 290–92, 293n, 317n, 318, **7**: 3, 94, **8**: 25, 187, **9**: 132, 363, 383; food, **2**: 222, **8**: 145; hunted, **2**: 284–85, 285n, 293, 296, 298, 304, 306–7, 307n, 315, 317–18, **7**: 267–68, **8**: 13, 17, **9**: 11, 12, 14, 16, 139, 286, 311–12, 314, 321, 326, 344, 379, 381, 383, **10**: 205, 235n, **11**: 19–20, 20n; skins, **2**: 266, **9**: 376; signs, **2**: 319, **7**: 50, 53, 127; scarcity, **2**: 432, **4**: 180, 182n, 287, **7**: 288, 313–15; described, **4**: 82, 84, **7**: 261, 287–88, 332; and Indians, **7**: 264; classification, **7**: 312–15, 315n; name, **7**: 315n, **8**: 39, 41; as food, **8**: 145; as trade item, **9**: 286; mentioned, **2**: 142n, 151, 224, 347, **3**: 492n, **4**: 45n, 113, 115, **6**: 290–91, 293n, 312, 315, 317n, 318, 324, **8**: 21n, 43n, 145n, 416, 418n, **9**: 11n, **10**: 15–16, 15n, 84

Bear, cinnamon, **3**: 482, 492n, **7**: 3, 312–15, 315n, 331–32, 332n, 335–36, **8**: 13, 21n, 39, 41, 43n, 145, 145n, **10**: 235, 235n

Bear, grizzly (brown, white, yellow): habitat, **3**: 133, 135, 482, **6**: 318, 324; described,

3: 148–49, **4**: 84–85, 113–15, 180, 286–87, **7**: 260–61, 269–70, 286–88, **9**: 143, 178, **10**: 84, **11**: 141, 146–47, 156, 214–15; hunted, **3**: 186, 188, 188n, 222, **4**: 39–40, 81–82, 84–87, 113–15, 118, 141, 143, 149–51, 154–56, 159, 161, 166, 168, 181, 184–86, 242, 244, 255, 259, 280, 308, 310, 336, 350–52, 354, 431, 433, **7**: 256–58, 260, 262, 264–65, 267–69, 286, 288, **8**: 99, 141, 144–45, 147–48, 150, 179, 205–6, 259, 271–72, 274, 282, 334, **9**: 88, 140, 143, 146–50, 153, 163, 167, 171, 175, 178, 190, 193, 225, 310–13, 311n, 325–26, 335, 343–46, **10**: xii, 57, 57n, 86–88, 91, 97–99, 102, 107–8, 227, 229, 242, 261, 261n, **11**: 103, 141, 146, 152–53, 155–57, 159–61, 164–66, 180, 183, 188–89, 197, 204–5, 214–16, 239, 243–44; specimen, **3**: 330, **4**: 88n, **8**: 418; attacked by, **4**: 2–3, 84–85, 141, 151, 154–55, 157, 242, 256, 292–93, 308, 331, 350–52, **8**: 2, **9**: 178, **10**: 253–54; signs, **4**: 23, 31, 48, 54, 108, 281, 336, **5**: 17, **9**: 128; and Indians, **4**: 31, **5**: 135, 140, 159, **7**: 241n, 257, 259, 264–65, **9**: 51, **11**: 310–11; observed, **4**: 36, 48, 52, 54, 108, 113, 115, 118, 155, 157, 186, 212–13, 259, 305, 336, 338, 354, 423, 426, 428, **5**: 18, 28–29, **8**: 25, 110–12, 146, 149, 154, 162, 189–90, 208, 253, 281, 283, **9**: 132, 143, 153, 163, 189, 193, 338, 345, **10**: 106, 252n, 253–54, **11**: 145, 148, 177–78, 239–40, 250–51; food, **4**: 74–75, 78, 111, 113, 115, 126, 146, 303–4, 336, 417; grease, **4**: 113, 115, 141, 151–52, 180–81, **7**: 256, 267, **8**: 145, **9**: 153, 178; as food, **4**: 113,

Bear (*continued*)
155, 259, 280, **7**: 257, **11**: 188–89; skins, **4**: 141, 151, 275, 279, 336, **7**: 287, **8**: 141, 272, 282, **9**: 166, 178, 222, **10**: 235, 235n, **11**: 153, 161, 164–65, 216, 310–11; feared, **4**: 145, 338; behavior, **4**: 338, 348, 350, **8**: 259, **10**: 254; claws, **5**: 135, 140, **7**: 257, 259, **10**: 33; classification, **6**: 312, 315, **7**: 3, 259–60n, 262, 312–15, 315n; name, **7**: 315n; mentioned, **3**: 37n, 38, 39n, 492n, **4**: 3, 34n, 56, 155n, 182n, 295, 309, **6**: 317n, **8**: 26n, 109, 145n, 275n, **9**: xii, xv, 5n, 51–52, 51n, 88n, 155, **10**: 33n, 57n, 84n, 238, **11**: xii, 6n, 103n, 141n

Bearberry (saccacommis): as gift, **3**: 304; and Indians, **3**: 305n, **5**: 348, 351, **6**: 235–36; specimen, **3**: 464, 471; as food, **5**: 348, 351 **6**: 118, 373, 375; abundance, **6**: 116; as trade item, **6**: 133–34; scarcity, **6**: 134; described, **6**: 245–46, 251, 253; use, **7**: 15–16, 17n; mentioned, **5**: 353n, **6**: 237n, **7**: 110, 112, 193

Bear Creek (Ravalli County, Mont.), **8**: 161, 162n

Bear (Calf Brook, No Water) Creek (McCone County, Mont.), **4**: 130, 134, 135n

Bear (Plum) Creek (Mo.), **2**: 294–95, 295n, **9**: 12, 13n, 380

Bear Creek Island, **2**: 267, 269n

Bear Den (Charbonneau's, Indian) Creek, **4**: 36–37, 39, 41n, **6**: 447, 462, **8**: 295, 296n, 381, 400, **9**: 131, 131n, **10**: 80n, **11**: 153n

Beargrass: observed, **3**: 42; and Indians, **5**: 363, 371, 373, **6**: 7–8, 74, 76, 144n, 215, 217, 221–22, 246, 249, 335, 337, 435–36, 439–40, **7**: 98–99, 100, 146–47, 149, 254, **9**:

241, 243, **10**: 160n, 175, **11**: 395; abundance, **8**: 53–54; mentioned, **3**: 43n, **5**: 326n, **6**: 9n, 77n, 78n, **7**: 3, 100n, **8**: 55n, **9**: 241n, **11**: 396n

Bear Rapid. *See* Yellow Bear Rapids

Bears: as trade item, **3**: 27, 32, 390–444 passim; food, **3**: 77; as food, **4**: 56, **5**: 91, **7**: 71, 74, 259, 271, **11**: 370–71; behavior, **4**: 195, 198, 397, **8**: 175; signs, **5**: 32, 156, 342–43, 355, **6**: 116, 122, **7**: 262, **8**: 35–36, 38; observed, **5**: 39, **8**: 25, 365, **10**: 80; skins, **5**: 139, **6**: 434, 438, **8**: 107, 138; hunted, **5**: 183, **7**: 90, 92, 95, 257–58, 271–74, **8**: 39, 41, 45–46, 48, **10**: 227, 230n, 236, 238, 243, 252, 254, 260, 262, **11**: 22–29, 37, 295, 319–20; oil, **5**: 211, 342–43, **7**: 267, 336, **8**: 57–58, 63, **11**: 27–28; claws, **6**: 436, 440, **7**: 224, 253, **8**: 318; and Indians, **6**: 206, 208, 210, **11**: 370–71; abundance, **7**: 286, **11**: 33, 45; scarcity, **7**: 269, 271–73, 297, 299; captured, **7**: 76–77; specimen, **8**: 419; mentioned, **10**: 91n

Bears claw. *See* Larkspur, Menzies's

Bears Paw (North) Mountains, **4**: 2, 198, 200, 200n, 207n, 238–39, 241n, 253, 257n, 268, **8**: 115, 116n, **11**: 181–82, 182n

Beartooth Mountains, **8**: 187, 188n, 203n, 217, 221n

Beatles, **2**: 185, **4**: 235. *See also* Box-elder bug

Beauchamp (Grouse) Creek, **4**: 179, 182n, **6**: 448, 463, **8**: 382, 400, **9**: 152, 153n, **11**: 164, 165n

Beausoleil, Eugene Pouree *dit*, **2**: 386n

Beaver: hunted, **1**: 12, **2**: 420, 434–35, 487–88, 503, **3**: 39, 68–71, 96, 101, 192, 208,

226–27, 236, 327, **4**: 20, 23, 25, 27, 30, 32, 45, 48, 51–53, 55–57, 57n, 58, 60, 62, 73, 78, 96, 100, 102, 108, 118, 120–21, 123, 126, 128, 136, 139–40, 144, 147, 165–77, 185, 217, 219, 244, 256, 308, 344, 356, 358, 362, 365, 430, **5**: 71–72, 118–19, 126, 197, **6**: 135, 174, 196, 215–16, 290–91, 293, **7**: 188–89, 196–97, **8**: 94, 96, 114, 141, 145, 157, 178, 266, **9**: 30, 32–33, 37, 40, 42, 55–56, 59, 61, 88, 96, 128–34, 136–37, 139–51, 153, 158, 161–63, 165–66, 171, 179–80, 189, 193, 206–7, 265, 267–70, 286, 301, 311–12n, 335–36, 342, 344, 348, **10**: 22–23, 37, 39–40, 79, 81–82, 87, 133, 192, 199, 218, 220, 260–261, **11**: 45, 71, 74–76, 101, 142–44, 147–48, 150, 152–54, 158, 160–64, 183–84, 186–88, 190–91, 194–95, 204–5, 217–20, 241, 249–50, 276–79, 411, 417; as trade item, **2**: 89, 277, 279, **3**: 27, 32, 159, 165, 390–444 passim, **6**: 187, 358, 360, **8**: 319, 351, **11**: 280–81; observed, **2**: 344, 431–33, **4**: 53–54, 118, 250, 252, 259, 385, 403, 420, 430, 438, **5**: 37, 43, 71, 84, **8**: 119, 146, 179–80, 184, 237, **9**: 87, 106, 208, 376, 378, **10**: 24, **11**: 188–89, 232; habitat, **2**: 350, 445, 464, 483, **3**: 37–39, 482, **6**: 313, 315, **8**: 217, **9**: 20, 52, 195, 198–200, 216; abundance, **2**: 362, 471, 474, **3**: 269, **4**: 25, 45, 53–54, 62, 75, 78–79, 103, 105, 125–26, 128, 428, 431, 433, **5**: 14, 18, 39, 57, 59, **7**: 200–201, **8**: 171, 175, 177, 182, 186, 219, 245, 248, 278, 412, 414, **9**: 22, 52, 138, 186, 189, 192, 196, 198–200, 204, 301, 333, 348, **10**: 125, 266, **11**: 227, 233, 238–39, 246–

47, 261–62; as food, **2**: 433, **4**: 22, 48, 50, 111, **5**: 25–26, 167, 169, **6**: 166–67, 197, 307, 309, **10**: 133, **11**: 411; signs, **2**: 448, 464, 466–67, **3**: 78, 180, 192, **4**: 79, 436, **5**: 37, 46, 55, 337, 340, **8**: 102, 170, 181, 191, 237, **9**: 53, 142, 145, 334–35, **11**: 68, 139, 144, 149, 151–52, 176, 235, 251–52, 254, 280–81; dams, **3**: 8, **5**: 14, 32–33, 37, 68, 97, 124, 184, 203, **8**: 95, 102, 181–82, 185–86, 392, **9**: 54, 136, 192, 194–96, 198–200, 216, 223, 330, 333, **10**: 120, **11**: 69, 246–48, 253–56, 296–97, 313–14; skins, **3**: 27, 32, **4**: 275, 279, 308, **5**: 92, 126, 139, 286, **6**: 25, 27, 31, 33, 74, 76, 161–62, 205, 434, 438–39, **8**: 131, 294, 314, **9**: 87, 106, 166, 208, 283, 359, 369n, 376, 378, **10**: 131, **11**: 16, 102, 193–94, 395; scarcity, **3**: 133, 135, **4**: 189–90; food, **4**: 45–46, 60, 125, 281; behavior, **4**: 45–46, 81–82, 100–101, 118, 132, 281, 422–25, **11**: 152, 255–56, 264–65; dens, **4**: 49, 118, 399, 401, 423, 425, **9**: 21, 136, 194, 200, **11**: 251–53, 264–65; nails, **4**: 54, 56; attacked by, **4**: 166, 168; castoreum, **6**: 174–75, 178n, 197–98; and Indians, **6**: 208, 210; specimen, **8**: 419; mentioned, **2**: 420n, 423n, 429–30, **3**: 148n, 153n, **5**: 2, **6**: 77n, 317n, 337–38, **8**: 95n, 167, 232, 295, 320n, **9**: xi, 20n, 197n, **10**: xi, 22n, 91n, 122n, 123, 149, **11**: xi, 6n, 45n, 49, 49n, 258n

Beaver, mountain. *See* Mountain beaver

Beaver Creek (Lewis and Clark County, Mont.), **4**: 407–8, 410n, 411n, **8**: 94, 95n, 102, **9**: 187, 187n, **10**: 115, 115n, **11**: 234, 234n

Beaver (Hornet) Creek (Williams County, N. Dak.), **4**: 46, 47n, **9**: 132n, **10**: 80n, **11**: 136, 136n

Beaver (Little Willow) Creek (Nebr.), **3**: 351–52, 384n

Beaver (War-re-con-nee, Wardepon) Creek (Emmons County, N. Dak.), **3**: 176–77, 178n, 360–61, 373, 381, 386n, 409, 417, 419, 421, **8**: 310, 311n, 380, 399, **9**: 85, 86n, 367n, **10**: 56n

Beaver (White Paint, White Earth, Pryor's Valley) Creek (Broadwater County, Mont.), **4**: 407, 410n, 411n, 415n, 416–17, 418n, 419n, **6**: 450, 464; **9**: 188n, **10**: 116n, **11**: 237n

Beaverhead (Jefferson) River: arrive at, **1**: 10, **5**: 2, 40–41, 47, **8**: 172–73, 173n, **9**: 196–97, **10**: 121, **11**: 257–58; conditions, **5**: 40–41, 84, 97, 107, **8**: 264, **9**: 198–200, 203–4, 207, **10**: 124, 127n, 128; characteristics, **5**: 44, 58, 60, **10**: 126, **11**: 259–61, 263–64, 270–71; valley described, **5**: 45, 57–58, 62, 63n, 106–7, 108n, **9**: 198–99, **11**: 259–60; described, **5**: 54–55, **8**: 175; navigational problems, **5**: 58, 62, 71, 75, 92–93, 106, **11**: 260–61, 264–65, 270–71; distances, **5**: 115, **8**: 172, **9**: 231, 231n; listed, **6**: 465, **8**: 409; hunting on, **8**: 80, 182; explored, **8**: 414; forks, **9**: 207, **11**: 270–73; mentioned, **5**: 3, 43n, 52n, 67n, 76n, 87, 87n, 92, 114, 116n, 117, 140, 163n, **7**: 334n, **8**: 1, 3, 74, 78n, 174, 176n, **9**: 196–97n, 197n, 206n, 210n, 333n, 334n, **10**: 121, 121n, 122n, 123n, 124n, 125n, 126n254n, **11**: 256n, 258n, 261n, 262n, 266n, 267n, 272n, 275n, 284n

Beaverhead Mountains, **5**: 83,

86n, 140, 141n, **8**: 167, 169n, 170

Beaverhead Rock, **5**: 2, 59, 61, 61n, 66, 67n, 73n, 83–84, 100, **6**: 451, 465, **8**: 77, 173n, 176n, 177, 299n, **9**: 200, 200n, 201n, **10**: 124n, **11**: 264n, 265n

Beaver Island, **8**: 392

Beaver River, **2**: 70, 70n

Bedding, **4**: 343, **5**: 163, 271–72, **6**: 39–40, 42–43, 48–49, 83, 85, 91–92, 108, 119, 120, 122, **7**: 23, 25, 266, 274, **8**: 282, 317–18, 349, **9**: 238, **11**: 352–53. *See also* Indians, bedding

Bedrock Creek, **7**: 220, 222, 224–25n, **9**: 306, 307n, **10**: 223n

Bee, bumble, **7**: 309, 311, 312n

Bee, honey, **4**: 276, 277n, **7**: 309, 311, 312n

Beech, **2**: 79, 80n, **5**: 355–56. *See also* Alder, red

Beech, American, **5**: 356, 358n

Beech, eastern, **6**: 98n

Bee (Parques) Creek, **2**: 340, 342, 343n, **9**: 19, 19n, 384, **10**: 18, 18n

Bee plant, Rocky Mountain, **3**: 464, 468

Beer, **5**: 315, 318. *See also* Porter

Bees, **11**: 426

Beeswax, **4**: 363, **7**: 336, **9**: 181, 181n, 276, **11**: 220–21

Beetles, **7**: 78n, 192, 309, 311, 312n, **12**: 6

Beinecke, Frederick, **2**: 41

Beinecke Collection, Yale University, **2**: 542

Bel-larsara, **3**: 212, 213n, 214n

Bellefontaine, Ill., **2**: 124–25, 125n

Belle Fontaine, Mo., **8**: 4

Belle Fourche River, **3**: 136n

Bellonius, **10**: 93n

Bellows, **3**: 262, 262n, 263, **4**: 271, 275, **9**: 165, **11**: 192–93

Bells, **5**: 294, 296, **6**: 113

Bellsman Creek. *See* Deadman Creek

Belmont Creek, **8**: 90, 92n, 101

Belt (Portage) Creek, **1**: 7, **4**: 299–304, 299n, 302n, 310–13, 316–18, 321, 323, 327, 335, 338–39, 342, **6**: 449, 464, **8**: 111n, 382, 401, **9**: 169, 169n, 174–75, 176n, 340, 340n, 341n, **10**: 102n, 103, 103n, 255n, 257–58, 257n, 258n, **11**: 199–202, 199n, 201n, 202n

Belt Group, **5**: 141n, 148n

Belts, **7**: 134, **11**: 397. *See also* Clothing

Bennie Peer Creek, **8**: 272, 274n

Benoit, François M., **2**: 322n, 377–78, 379n, **9**: 17n, 25, 25n, **10**: 17n, **11**: 30n

Bentonite, **8**: 321, 321n

Berberis aquifolium, **6**: 28n, **7**: 60n. *See also* Grape, Oregon

Berberis nervosa, **6**: 28n, **7**: 60n. *See also* Grape, dull Oregon

Berberis repens, **10**: 135n. *See also* Grape, Oregon creeping

Berdaches. *See* Indians, customs; Mandan Indians

Berries: abundance, **2**: 350–51, 380, **5**: 168–69, **9**: 161–62, **10**: 135, 141, **11**: 404; as food, **5**: 81, 87–88, 90–91, 95, 128, 145–46, 153, 162, 167–68, 187–89, 219, 222, 229, 296, 300, 323, 349, 351, 355, 357, 371, **6**: 118–19, 132, 139, 256, 366, 368, **7**: 119–20, 147, 158, **9**: 70n, 213, **10**: 146; and Indians, **5**: 115, **6**: 32, 118–19, 139, 216–17, 307, **7**: 100, 119–20, **9**: 70n, 213, 219, 246, **10**: 128, 130, 134, 138, 141, 146, 176; as trade item, **5**: 227, 232, 306, 309, 311, 346–47, 349, 351, **6**: 139, 152–53, 161–63, 214, 216, **7**: 100, 147, 158, **10**: 130, 146; mentioned, **5**: 335, **6**: 132, 256, 366, 368, **9**: 185n, **11**: 404

Berry, rabbit. *See* Buffaloberry

Berry, red. *See* Buffaloberry

Berry (Dry) Creek, **8**: 203, 204n, 391, 408

Betsy, **6**: 160n

Betula glandulosa, **5**: 39n, **7**: 195n, **9**: 194n, **11**: 254n. *See also* Birch, scrub

Betula nigra, **8**: 418n. *See also* Birch, river

Betula occidentalis, **4**: 253n, **5**: 58n, **6**: 29n, **7**: 191n, **8**: 162n, **9**: 194n, **10**: 164n. *See also* Birch, water

Betula papyrifera, **3**: 79n. *See also* Birch, paper

Bibionidae, **7**: 47n. *See also* Flies

Bicarbonate, **8**: 120n

Bice Island, **3**: 76n

Biddle, Charles, **2**: 536

Biddle, Edward, **2**: 85n, 536

Biddle, Nicholas: emendations in journals, **1**: 10, 18n. 108, **3**: 13n, 26n, 37n, 115n, 120n, 137n, 142n, 148n, 171n, 194n, 226n, 270n, 273n, 319n, 328n, **4**: 12n, 76n, 129n, 214n, 220n, 277n, **5**: 198n, 199n, 205n, 207n, 263n, 264n, **6**: 14n, 25n, 30n, 34n, 37n, 42n, 68n, 145n, 202n, 239n, 257n, 317n, 409n, **7**: 31n, 122n, 125n, 151n, 330n, **8**: 55n, 58n, 59n, 61n, 65n, 69n, 78n, 80n, 90n, 94n, 98n, 176n, 177n, 228n, 240n, 241n, 250n, 279n, 287n, 288n, 300n, 344n, **9**: 104n, 128n, 131n, 140n; and maps, **1**: 12, 19n. 133; collaboration with Clark, **2**: 9, 11–12, 37, 530, 534, 539–40, **3**: 335, 388, 479, 491n, **5**: 198n, 214n, **6**: 41n, 51n, 120n, 172n, 206n, **7**: 89n, 225n, 241n, **8**: 34n, 124n, 279n; editorial methods, **2**: 37–38, 51, 85n, 234n, 249n, 252n, 253n, 259n, 261n, 265–66n, 269n, 274n, 283n, 288n, 291n, 292n, 293n, 306n, 316n, 323n, 332n, 333n, 343n, 351n, 354n, 356n, 361n, 366n, 368n, 373n, 375n, 386n, 393–94n, 397n, 400n, 404n,

413n, 423n, 431n, 435n, 444n, 456n, 463n, 465n, 474n, 486n, 494n, 506n, 532–33, 544, **3**: 268n, **6**: 471n, **8**: 111n, 158n, 162n, 166n, 168n, 173n, 187n, 221n; writes expedition history, **2**: 37–39, 521, 530, 544, **5**: 141n, 187n, 263n, **6**: 19n, 59n, 440n, **8**: 228n, 303n, 309n, 317n, 332n, 349n, 359n, 411n, **9**: xvi, **10**: xvii, **12**: 3–4; papers, **2**: 40–41, 225n, 531, 535–37, 539–41; notations in journals, **3**: 12n, 25n, 45n, 64n, 73n, 85n, 103n, 106n, 120n, 198n, 206n, 214n, 238n, 280n, 311n, 324n; marks in journals, **3**: 15n, 48n, 79n, 148n, 214n, 220n, 234n, 236n, 270n, 273n, 293n, 297n, 305n, 331n, **4**: 57n, 76n, 121n, 129n, 145n, 148n, 175n, 187n, 233n, 241n, 245n, 253n, 257n, 260n, 269n, 277n, 279n, 282n, 289n, 298n, 308n, 325n, 333n, 346n, 354n, 365n, 368n, 376n, 377n, 381n, 386n, 396n, 402n, 410n, 415n, 418n, 419n, 422n, 429n, 433n, 438n, **5**: 10n, 13n, 21n, 29n, 35n, 39n, 67n, 76n, 85n, 94n, 95n, 124n, 125n, 131n, 132n, 147n, 164n, 174n, 223n, 224n, 225n, 228n, 328n, 364n, 380n, **6**: 29n, 51n, 71n, 78n, 94n, 99n, 148n, 158n, 162n, 164n, 179n, 185n, 198n, 214n, 221n, 225n, 227n, 230n, 232n, 235n, 237n, 242n, 244n, 248n, 249n, 278n, 280n, 284n, 286n, 290n, 293n, 296n, 302n, 307n, 316n, 317n, 321n, 324n, 327n, 330n, 333n, 335n, 342n, 346n, 351n, 355n, 358n, 362n, 368n, 373n, 377n, 383n, 387n, 391n, 394n, 397n, 401n, 405n,

408n, 414n, 416n, 420n,
425n, 428n, 432n, **7**: 14n,
17n, 25n, 31n, 41n, 60n,
78n, 89n, 93n, 96n, 110n,
114n, 129n, 135n, 165n,
169n, 173n, 186n, 190n,
202n, 205n, 209n, 225n,
233n, 237n, 251n, 263n,
264n, 297n, 302n, 307n,
312n, 325n, 330n, 337n,
342n, 346n, **8**: 13n, 21n,
30n, 38n, 151n, 188n, 208n,
229n; mentioned, **2**: 34,
301n, 303n, 311n, 318n,
328n, 360n, 363n, 365n,
535n, **3**: 23n, 36n, 125n,
127n, 227n, 251n, 261n,
269n, 386, **4**: 321n, **5**: 63n,
9: 106n. See also *History of the
Expedition under the Command
of Captains Lewis and Clark*
Biers. *See* Cradleboard; Nets,
mosquito
Big Ax (NeeSworunja), **2**: 491,
493, 493n
Big Bellies. *See* Atsina Indians;
Hidatsa Indians
Big Belt Mountains, **4**: 247,
252n, 260n, 282n, **8**: 116n,
9: 164n, **10**: 99n, 115, 115n,
11: 235n
Big Bend of the Missouri River.
See Missouri River, Big Bend
of the
Big Berger (Shepherd) Creek,
2: 253–54, 259n, **3**: 370,
376, **8**: 377, 395, **9**: 368n
Big Blue Eyes (Stargrahunja),
2: 491, 493, 493n
Big Blue River (Nebr.), **2**: 324n,
369–70, 372–73n
Big Blue (Blue Water) River
(Mo.), **2**: 323–24, 324n,
372n, **3**: 317, 318n, 342–44,
346, 370, 378, 383–84n, **8**:
378, 396, **9**: 17, 17n, 368n,
383, **10**: 17, 17n
Big Bone Lick, **2**: 78n, 85n,
4: 194, 197, 199n
Big Canyon (Mosquito) Creek,
7: 221, 223, 225n, 235, 322,
324–25, 325n, **9**: 307n, **10**:
223, 223n

Big Creek (Mont.), **8**: 161, 162n
Big Creek (Oreg.), **11**: 438n
Big Dry Creek (Big Dry River),
4: 130, 133–34, 135n, 142,
6: 448, 463, **8**: 147, 148n,
381, 400, **9**: 145, 145n, **10**:
87, 87n, **11**: 150–51, 151n
Bigelow Creek, **2**: 249–50, 251n
Big Hidatsa site, **3**: 206n, 319n,
10: 78n, **11**: 134n
Big Hole Pass, **5**: 148n, **8**: 167,
168n, 169n, 171n, 393, 409,
9: 332n, 333, 333n
Big Hole (Sensable, Wisdom)
River: arrive at **1**: 10, **5**: 40–
41, 46–47, **9**: 196–97, **10**:
121; characteristics, **5**: 39n,
47, 51–52, 54, 61, 83–84,
10: 255; conditions, **5**: 41,
44, **8**: 264, **9**: 198, 334; navigational problems, **5**: 44, 46–
47, **11**: 255–57; distances,
6: 451, 465, 494–95, **8**: 170;
described, **8**: 166–67, 175,
176n, **11**: 255–57; explored,
8: 173n, **10**: 121–22; listed,
8: 393, 410, 415; mentioned,
5: 2, 43n, 51–52n, 53, 55n,
56–58, 62, 100, 146, 148n,
8: 168n, 169n, 171n, 177,
177n, 299n, **9**: 196n, 200,
335n, **10**: 121n, 122n, 123n,
255n, **11**: 256n, 258n, 259,
259n, 261, 262n, 263–64
Big Hole Valley, **8**: 167, 168n,
169n, 170–71, 171n, **9**:
332n
Big Horn. *See* Apash Wyakaikt
Bighorn. *See* Sheep, bighorn
Bighorn (Ar-sar-ta) River, **1**: 13,
4: 71, 73, **3**: 234n, 242n, 351,
365, 374, 383, 385n, 427, **8**:
212, 212n, 217, 221n, 228n,
230–32, 234–40, 234n,
235n, 245n, 277–78, 279n,
390, 407, 410n
Bighorn Canyon, **8**: 234n
Bighorn Mountains, **8**: 175,
202, 228n, 235n, 250n
Big Horse (Shingto-tongo),
2: 439, 441, 443n, 491–92,
493n, 494n, **9**: 40, 41n, 395,
11: 57

Big Horsetail Ripple, **2**: 67, 68n
Big Man (Oh-he-nar), **3**: 199,
200n, 211, 213n, 215, 217n,
224, 245, 265, 288, 299
Big Muddy (Avaise, Cow) River,
1: 5, **2**: 112, 113n
Big Muddy Creek (Martha's
River, Yellow River), **4**: 85–
87, 88n, **6**: 447, 462, **8**: 150,
151n, 381, 400, **9**: 140,
140n, **10**: 84n, **11**: 141, 141n
Big Nemaha River, **2**: 366–67,
368n, 369, 372n, 373n, 406,
409, 480, 487, **3**: 94, 346,
371, 375, 378, 393–94, **8**:
355–56, 356n, 357n, 378,
396, 417, **9**: 23–24, 24n, 80–
81, 360n, 367n, 387, 387n,
10: 20, 20n, 277n, **11**: 38,
38n, 172, 174
Big Osage River. *See* Osage River
Big Papillion Creek. *See* Papillion (Butterfly) Creek
Big Pipestone (Panther) Creek,
5: 35n, 37–39, 39n, 50, **8**:
177, 178n, **9**: 194n, **11**:
252n
Big Porcupine (Little Wolf
Mountain) Creek (Little
Wolf River), **3**: 374, 382,
8: 236, 240n, 241, 243–44,
245n, 390, 407
Big Sheep Mountain, **8**: 258,
261n
Big Shoal Creek (Sharriton-Car-
tie), **2**: 319–20, 320–21n, **9**:
16, 16n, 383, 383n, **10**: 16n
Big Sioux River (Rivière des
Sioux), **2**: 286–87, 288n,
497–501, 499n, **3**: 7–8, 11,
23, 27, 94, 171n, 355–56,
372, 379, 384n, 386n, 398,
413, 476, **8**: 4, 349, 349n,
379, 397, 411, 416, **9**: 11,
11n, 42, 42n, 367n, 378,
379n, **10**: 29, 29n, **11**: 20,
20n, 59, 59n, 172
Big Sni a Bar Creek, **9**: 15, 15n,
368n, 382, **10**: 16n
Big Soldier (Heart) Creek, **3**:
344, 383–84n
Big Stealer (Mar-noh-tah),
3: 212, 213n, 241, **9**: 98n

Big Stranger (Stranger's Wife) Creek, **3**: 344, 383n
Big Swamp Creek, **8**: 170, 171n
Big Tarkio Creek, **3**: 346, 371, 378. *See also* Tarkio River
Big Tavern Creek, **2**: 264n, 265, 266n
Big Timber Creek (Rivers Across), **8**: 193, 195–96, 197n, 391, 409
Big Track, **3**: 391
Big Wheeling Creek, **2**: 74
Big White (Sheheke): and maps, **1**: 8, 18n. 82; visits Washington, **3**: 153n, 205n, **8**: 4, 304–5, 316n; visits, **3**: 209, 211, 224, 233, 254, 265, 269, 288, 296, 299, 309, 317, **9**: 103, 350–51, 350n, **10**: 64, 64n, 268, 268n; biographical sketch, **3**: 213–14n; medal for, **3**: 215; information from, **3**: 270n, **8**: 308, **9**: 101, **11**: 110, 111n; village, **8**: 306; brother, **8**: 307; speech, **8**: 314; gifts, **8**: 338, **9**: 95, 95n; death, **8**: 357, 358n; clothes, **8**: 370; mentioned, **2**: 10, 514, 518, 521, **3**: 154n, **8**: 305n, 312–13, 352, **11**: 133
Bijou Hills, **3**: 68n
Bile. *See* Medical problems
Billman Creek, **8**: 184–85, 188n, 392
Biloxi Indians, **3**: 447, 449–50
Bindweed, hedge, **3**: 458, 463, 467
Birch, **5**: 60, **10**: 218
Birch, black. *See* Birch, river
Birch, paper, **3**: 78, 79n
Birch, river, **8**: 416, 418n
Birch, scrub, **5**: 36, 39n, 58n, **7**: 193, 195n, **9**: 194, 194n, 201, 201n, **11**: 253–54, 254n
Birch, water, **4**: 250, 253n, **5**: 57, 58n, **6**: 26–27, 29n, **7**: 188–89, 191n, 197, **8**: 161, 162n, **9**: 194n, **10**: 163, 164n
Birch (Battle) Creek (Pondera County, Mont.), **8**: 136, 137n
Birch Creek (Ravalli County, Mont.), **5**: 191n

Birch (Thompson's) Creek (Chouteau County, Mont.), **4**: 211–14, 214n, **6**: 448, 463, **8**: 382, 401, **9**: 157, 157n, **11**: 176, 176n
Bird, cherry. *See* Waxwing, cedar
Bird Coulee, **4**: 289n, **10**: 102n, **11**: 196n
Bird Creek, **9**: 184, 185n, **10**: 112, 113n, **11**: 228, 229n
Bird (Elk Fawn) Rapids, **4**: 202–3, 205–6, 207n, **6**: 448, 463, **8**: 382, 401, **9**: 155, 156n, **10**: 93, 93n, **11**: 169–70, 170n
Birds: observed, **2**: 173, 344, 383–84, **4**: 265–66, 325, **5**: 37, **6** 364, 457, **8**: 119; as specimen, **3**: 4; behavior, **3**: 7, 10–11, 457, **4**: 329, **6**: 175, 347n; and Indians, **4**: 140, 219, **5**: 134, 140, **6**: 74, 76, 207, 210, **8**: 214; food, **4**: 146, 303; abundance, **4**: 347, 380, 414, 417, **5**: 11, 314–15, **6**: 36, 55, 70, 145, **7**: 200–201; hunted, **5**: 174, **6**: 60–61, 72–73, 93, 96–97, 105, 163–64; mentioned, **2**: 459–60, **3**: 294, 456, **5**: 24n, **6**: 382–83, 409n, **7**: 219, 267. *See also specific species;* Waterfowl
Birds Bill Hill, **3**: 186n
Biscuits, **2**: 84, 203, 217, **3**: 81, **4**: 13, 22, 334–35, **6**: 187, 205, **7**: 106, **8**: 360, 363, 365, **9**: 127, 174, 362, 364, **10**: 279–80, **11**: 212–13
Bison, mountain, **8**: 166, 168n
Bison, plains, **8**: 168n. *See also* Buffalo
Bison bison, **2**: 283n, **8**: 106n, **9**: 18n, **10**: 30n, **11**: 60n. *See also* Buffalo
Bison bison athabascae, **8**: 168n. *See also* Bison, mountain
Bison bison bison, **8**: 168n. *See also* Bison, plains
Bissell, Daniel, **2**: 105, 109n, 510, 519, 524, **11**: xiv
Bissell, Russell, **2**: 510, 513–15, 523–24, 529n, **9**: xiv, **10**: xiv, **11**: xiv

Bits, **2**: 157, 157n, **3**: 428
Bitter Creek, **8**: 216, 221, 222n
Bittern, American, **3**: 13n
Bitterroot, **5**: 143, 147n, **8**: 80–81n
Bitterroot (Clark's, Flathead) River: arrive at, **1**: 10, **5**: 185, 190n, **9**: 220, **10**: 139n, **11**: 304–5; and maps, **1**: 10–11, 18nn. 103, 108, **6**: 308–10; distances, **1**: 11, **5**: 193–94, **6**: 494–95, **8**: 82, 161, 167, **10**: 173, **11**: 338–39; name, **2**: 26, **6**: 325n, **7**: 216–18, **10**: 140n, 157, 246n; conditions, **5**: 192, 195n, **8**: 69, 263, **10**: 140–41; valley, **5**: 196n; listed, **6**: 452, **8**: 393, **9**: 231; Indians, **7**: 148, 151n, 331–32, 341, **8**: 53–54, 62, 85, 87, 290–91; hunting on, **8**: 77, 80; described, **8**: 100, **10**: 246; and plants, **11**: 308–9, **12**: 7; mentioned, **3**: 298n, 382, **5**: 164n, 187, 188n, 191, 191n, 198n, **6**: 311n, 472n, **7**: 219n, 332n, **8**: 2, 26, 27n, 36, 66, 68, 69n, 72, 75, 80n, 83, 86n, 162n, 163, 164n, 166, 388, 413–14, **9**: 220n, 221, 221n, 329n, 330, 330n, 331n, **10**: 135n, 157n, 247, 248n, **11**: 305n, 306, 306n, 308n
Bitterroot Range, **8**: 81n, 161, 162n, 169n
Bitterroot (Snow) Mountains, **1**: 10, **2**: 8, **5**: 3, 148n, 164n, 185, 191, 191n, 199, 199n, 201n, 203, 204n, 207, 207n, 218, 223n, **6**: 493, **7**: 3, **8**: 1, 27n, 164n, **9**: 220, 221n, 222n, 231, 319, 326–27, **10**: 139, 140n, 173, **11**: 304–6, 305n, 306n, 315–16, 316n, 374n
Bitterroot Valley, **8**: 164n
Bivalves, **6**: 407, 409n, 420
Blackberries, **2**: 286, 288n, **7**: 96n
Blackberry, Pacific, **6**: 16, 18, 20n, 26–27, 103, 104n, 297–98, 298n, 302–3, **7**: 12–14, 14n, 22n

Blackbird, **2**: 466–67, 469, 470n, 472, 480, **3**: 13–14, **9**: 37, 37n, 394, **10**: 27, 27n, **11**: 54, 54n, 174

Blackbird, Brewer's, **4**: 237n, **6**: 375, 377, 378n, **7**: 28, 32n, **8**: 78n, **9**: 181n, **10**: 106n, **11**: 222n

Blackbird, red-winged, **3**: 83, 86n

Blackbird, rusty, **4**: 237n, **6**: 378n, **8**: 78n, **9**: 181n, **10**: 106n, **11**: 222n

Blackbird Hill, **2**: 466–69, 467n, 472, 480, **3**: 379, 386n, **9**: 37, 37n, 394, **10**: 27, 27n, **11**: 54n, 174

Blackbirds, **3**: 11, **4**: 36, 236, 265, 298, 331, 348, 364, 368, **8**: 75, 266, 267n, **10**: 106, **11**: 221

Blackbird (Wau-Condi peche, Bad Spirit) Creek, **2**: 467–70, 471n, **3**: 371, 379, 384n, **8**: 379, 397, **9**: 367n, 394, 394n

Black Bluff Island, **4**: 296n

Black Buffalo (Un-tongar-Sar-bar), **3**: 110n, 111–12, 114, 114n, 122–24, 305, **8**: 330, 332n, **9**: 65, 67, 68n, 71, **10**: 45, 45n, 47n, **11**: 85, 86n

Black Cat (Necasawa), **2**: 491, 493, 493–94n

Black Cat (Posecopsahe): information from, **3**: 207–8, 259; biographical sketch, **3**: 208n; appointed chief, **3**: 209, 211; speech, **3**: 218–19; visits, **3**: 223, 235, 237, 239–40, 242, 253, 256, 267, 271, 289–90, 293, 306, 308–9, **4**: 9, 13–14, **8**: 298–99, 301, **9**: 97n, 99–100, 120, 120n; mentioned, **3**: 200n, 205n, 282, 303, 317, **4**: 12n, **8**: 300n, 304, **11**: 107, 107n, 133

Black Cat site, **3**: 205n, **9**: 91n, **10**: 60n, **11**: 107n, 133n

Black Coulee (Lark Creek), **4**: 257–58, 259n, 261, 296n, **9**: 167n, **10**: 102n, **11**: 198n

Black Eagle (Upper) Falls, **4**:

290, 296n, 307, 312, 315, **6**: 449, 464, **9**: 175, **10**: 107, 109, 109n

Blackfeet Indians: chiefs, **1**: 5; and members of the party, **1**: 9, **2**: 8, 29, 515–17, 520, 523, **5**: 10n, **7**: 3, 248, 301, 333–34, **8**: 130–31, 132, 134–35, 136n, 293–95, 414, **9**: xvi, 341–42, **10**: 259; historical sketch, **3**: 444–45; listed, **3**: 449; camps, **4**: 2, 222, 224, **8**: 131, **9**: 159; lodges, **4**: 108–9, 110n, 379n, **10**: 111, 111n, **11**: 177–79; war, **4**: 159–61, 407, **8**: 198n, 278, 280n, 298, 364n; trade, **4**: 214n, 222, 224, **8**: 131, 133n, 280n, 294, **9**: 159n; signs, **4**: 216, 219; located, **4**: 222, 224, **11**: 177–78; and other Indians, **5**: 2, 85n, 86n, 95n, 188n, **7**: 3, 248, 250–51, 251n, 301; encounter, **8**: 2, 128–30; reputation, **8**: 113; and horses, **8**: 129; danger from, **8**: 129, 139n, 303n; customs, **8**: 131; information from, **8**: 131, 294; bands, **8**: 132n; arms and ammunition, **8**: 135, 137n; name, **9**: 343n, **10**: 259n; mentioned, **3**: 109n, 435, **4**: 221n, 269n, **7**: 334n, **8**: 90n, 213. *See also* Atsina Indians

Blackfeet Indians, Blackfeet proper, **8**: 132n

Blackfeet Indians, Blood, **3**: 433, **8**: 132n

Blackfeet Indians, Piegan, **8**: 2, 132–33n, 136n

Blackfoot (East Fork Clark's) River **1**: 11, **8**: 85, 87, 87n, 88–89, 90n, 89n, 92n, 94n, 95, 95n, 96n, 100–2, 104, 291, 383, 401, 415, **9**: 338, 338n, **10**: 249n, 250, 250n, 251n

Black Hills, **1**: 8, **2**: 327, 328n, **3**: 25–26, 26n, 47, 48n, 85, 133–35, 136n, 137n, 153n, 167n, 179–82, 183n, 222, 226, 227n, 234, 234n, 343,

350–51, 353, 357–60, 363, 421–22, 424–26, 482, 486–88, **4**: 16–17, 26–27, 118, 130, 188, 192n, 202, 204, 241, 321, 375, **6**: 337–38, **8**: 159n, 235n, **9**: 74, 75n, 352

Black Horse Lake, **4**: 288n

Blackleaf Formation, **4**: 260n, 296n, 299n, **8**: 114n

Black Man, **3**: 267, 288, 310

Black Moccasin (Omp-se-ha-ra), **3**: 209, 211, 213n, 214n, 249, 303, 311, **8**: 298, 300n, 303, 303n, **10**: 61n

Blacksmithing, **2**: 112, 175, 176n, 179, 182, **3**: 3, 262, 262n, 264, 284, 286, 288, 292, 298, 313, 486, **4**: 271, 275, 279n, **7**: 93n, 95, **9**: 105–6, 110, 111n, 113–14, 120, 166, **10**: 71, 268, 268n. *See also* Shields, John; Willard, Alexander

Blacktail Deer (McNeal's) Creek, **5**: 63, 63n, 67n, 76n, 83–84, 87n, 101, **6**: 451, 465, **8**: 175, 176n, **9**: 201, 202n, **10**: 125, 125n, **11**: 266–67, 266n, 267n

Blackwater River, **2**: 286, 288n

Blalock Island, **5**: 306, 307n, **10**: 158n, **11**: 361n

Blanchard Creek, **8**: 92, 92n

Blanket-coat, **10**: 234. *See also* Clothing

Blankets: wet, **2**: 142, **6**: 69; as gift, **3**: 121–22, 128, 130, **9**: 74, 283; Indian, **3**: 428, 488, **5**: 69–70, 188n, 317, **6**: 17, 74–75, 187, 195, 205, 336, 434, 438, **7**: 29, **8**: 131, 294, 329, **9**: 248, 266, 314, **10**: 188, **11**: 272, 274; Hudson's Bay Company, **5**: 126, 131n; dried, **6**: 40; as trade item, **6**: 49, 72, 88, 423, **7**: 147–48, 253–54, **9**: 318–19, **11**: 22–23, 397; scarcity, **6**: 92, **7**: 308, 310, **8**: 280, **10**: 234, 241; infested, **6**: 123, 138, 142; attempted theft, **6**: 181; mentioned, **3**: 256, **4**: 100n, 418, **5**: 20, 30–31, **6**: 77n,

Blankets (*continued*)
189, 192n, **7**: 141, 283–85,
8: 36, 71, 204, 263, 354,
9: 115, 272, 281, 324, 369n,
10: 104, 120, 170, 192, 229n,
11: 142, 352–53, 420. *See also*
Clothing

Blean (Blear), **2**: 125

Blechnum spicant, **6**: 307n. *See
also* Fern, deer

Bleeding. *See* Medicine

Blodgett Creek, **8**: 162–63,
162n, 164n, **9**: 330n

Blood Indians. *See* Blackfeet Indians, Blood

Bloody Dick Creek, **5**: 73, 76n,
6: 465, **10**: 127, 128n

Blouin, Daniel, or Louis, **2**:
126n

Blowing Cave, **4**: 320, 321n,
361–62

Blubber. *See* Whales

Bluebells, **7**: 193, 195n

Bluebells, tall, **8**: 28, 30, 30n

Bluebird, eastern, **4**: 276, 277n

Bluebird, mountain, **6**: 131n

Blue Blanket (Grouse) Island,
3: 148–50, 150n, 151, **8**:
318, 320n, **9**: 353, 353n,
10: 52, 52n, 271n, **11**: 96–
97, 97n

Bluegrass, **8**: 218

Bluegrass, fowl, **8**: 222n

Bluegrass, Kentucky, **8**: 222n

Bluegrass, Sandberg's, **4**: 41n, **7**:
188–89, 190n, 204n, 335–
37, 337n, **10**: 218, 218n

Bluegrass, western. *See* Bluegrass, Sandberg's

Blue (Horse) Creek, **8**: 218,
221, 222n, 391, 408

Blue Lake (Coupée à Jacques),
2: 465–66, 467n

Blue Lake Park, **7**: 61n

Blue Mountains, **5**: 214n, 274–
75, 276n, 286, 288, 290n,
10: 217, 217n, 220, 220n

Blue River. *See* Big Blue River
(Mo.)

Blue (Southwest, Southeast)
Mountains, **7**: 149, 151n,
182, 184, 186n, 187, 189,

190n, 203–5, 205n, 207,
208n

Blue Springs site, **2**: 373n

Bluestem, big (leek green
grass), **2**: 346, 349n, 373n,
3: 163, 167n, 457, 463, 468

Bluestone Bluff, **8**: 350, 351n

Bluewater River. *See* Big Blue
River (Mo.)

Blunderbusses, **2**: 264n, **3**:
125n, **4**: 215, 218, 334–35,
8: 298, 369, **9**: 68, 105, 107,
349–50, 352, 355, 359, **11**:
177, 178n. *See also* Arms and
ammunition; Cannon, swivel

Boat, iron-frame: assembled, **4**:
149, 323–24, 326–27, 330,
333, 336–37, 343–44, 349,
350–51, 354, 356, 359, 362–
66, **9**: 169, 172, 178–81,
10: 103, 105, 106n, 107, 109,
11: 201, 203, 207–10, 207n,
213–20; examined, **4**: 306,
8: 108; attention to, **4**: 309;
oars, **4**: 368; seats, **4**: 368;
failure, **4**: 368–71, **9**: 181,
11: 221–22; cached, **4**: 371,
9: 183, **10**: 110, **11**: 221–24;
described, **11**: 207; mentioned, **4**: 3, 242, 261, 300,
324n, 339, 346n, 371n, **9**:
182

Boat, leather. *See* Boat, iron-
frame

Boat, Schenectady, **8**: 367, 368n

Boat Island, **3**: 55

Boats, **2**: 123, 179, 187, 193,
211, **8**: 362, 412, **9**: 39. *See
also* Bateaux; Boat, iron-
frame; Boat, Schenectady;
Bullboats; *Cajeux;* Canoes;
Flatboats; Keelboat; Pirogues;
Rafts

Bobcat, **2**: 167, 167n, **3**: 256n,
6: 327, 328n, 333, **8**: 266,
267n

Bobcat, Oregon: discovered, **6**:
3; skins, **6**: 76, 206, 208, 352,
354, 434–35, 438–39, **9**:
260, 260n, **11**: 405, 405n;
as trade item, **6**: 187, 205–
6; habitat, **6**: 313, 315; de-

scribed, **6**: 327, 333–34;
hunted, **7**: 24, 26n, **9**: 282,
282n, **11**: 435, 435n; specimen, **8**: 419; mentioned, **6**:
77n, 114, 124, 124n, 192n,
317n, 328n

Bobwhite, northern, **6**: 375,
377n, **7**: 87–88, 89n, 90–91

Bodmer, Karl, **3**: 229n

Boeuf (Beef) Island, **2**: 253–54,
259n

Boggs Island, **4**: 241n, **9**: 161n,
10: 97, 97n, **11**: 181–82,
182n

Bogs, **6**: 117

Boils. *See* Medical problems, abscesses and boils

Bois des Sioux River, **3**: 171n

Boise River, **8**: 344n

Bois rouge. See Dogwood, red
osier

Bolch. *See* Bowles, William

Boley, John, **2**: 148–49, 179,
188, 195, 198–99, 212,
229n, 256, 415, 417n, 511,
514, **4**: 12n

Boley site, **3**: 192n

Bombus sp., **7**: 312n. *See also* Bee,
bumble

Bombycilla cedrorum, **3**: 250n, **4**:
95n. *See also* Waxwing, cedar

Bonasa umbellus, **2**: 134n, **4**: 45n,
5: 29n, 223n, **6**: 24n, **7**: 46n,
8: 55n. *See also* Grouse, ruffed

Bonasa umbellus sabini, **5**: 223n,
6: 24n, **8**: 30n, **10**: 136n. *See
also* Grouse, Oregon ruffed

Bonhomme (Good Man's)
Creek, **2**: 245–46, 246n,
264n, **3**: 338, 369, 376, **9**: 7,
7n, 368n, 374, **10**: 8, 8n, **11**:
11, 11n

Bon Homme (Good Man's) Island, **3**: 38–39, 39n, 42, **6**:
488n, **8**: 338, 342–43, 344n,
372n, 379, 398, 417, **9**: 52,
52n, 53n, 367n, **10**: 33–34,
33n, 34n, **11**: 67, 67n, 68n

Bonne Femme (Good Woman's)
Creek (Howard County,
Mo.), **2**: 284–85, 285n, **3**:
341, 370, 377, **8**: 377, 395,

9: 11, 11n, 368n, 378, **10**: 12, 12n, **11**: 19, 20n

Bonne Femme (Little Good Woman's) Creek (Boone County, Mo.), **2**: 277, 279, 281n, **3**: 340–41, **9**: 10, 10n, **10**: 12, 12n, **11**: 19, 19n

Books, **4**: 152, 154, 334–35, **8**: 419, **11**: 156–57. *See also specific books*

Boone, Daniel Morgan, **2**: 249n

Boone, Daniel, **2**: 234n, 249n, 253n, 522, **3**: 338, **11**: 12, 12n

Boone's Settlement, **2**: 248, 249n, 253n, **3**: 338, **8**: 153n, 158n, **11**: 12, 12n

Bore-tree. *See* Elderberry

Borromeo, Charles, **2**: 234n

Boston Athenaeum, **1**: 12

Botaurus lentiginosus, **3**: 13n. *See also* Bittern, American

Boudin blanc. See Pudding, white

Bougainville, Charlotte Peman-pieh, **2**: 107–8, 109n

Boulder River (Reubin Field's Valley Creek) (Jefferson County, Mont.), **4**: 431–32, 433n, **5**: 25–27, 29, 29n, 30n, 48, **6**: 450, 465, **8**: 175, 176n, 178, **9**: 193, 194n, 335n, **10**: 120, 120n, **11**: 250–51, 251n

Boulder River (Rivers Across, Stinking Cabin Creek) (Sweet Grass County, Mont.), **3**: 365, 383, 385n, **8**: 192–93, 192–93n, 195–96, 197n

Bourgmont, Etienne Véniard de, **2**: 147, 150n, 288n, 305n, 351, 352n

Bouteloua gracilis, **4**: 308n, **8**: 188n. *See also* Grama, blue

Bow (Little Bow, Petie Arc) Creek, **3**: 13–14, 15n, 41, 43, 44n, 356, 372, 379, **8**: 379, 397, **9**: 45, 45n, **10**: 31, 31n, **11**: 62, 62n

Bow piece. *See* Cannon, swivel

Bow River, **8**: 133n

Bowels. *See* Medical problems

Bowl Creek, **5**: 215, 217n

Bowles, William, **6**: 155, 160n, 427

Bowling Green Bend, **2**: 295–96, 299n

Bowls, **5**: 311, 347–48, 361, **6**: 118–19, 215–16, **7**: 59, 82, **11**: 122, 352

Bowmon, J., **6**: 74–75

Bows and arrows, **2**: 210, 504–5, **3**: 23–24, 112–13, 114n, 121–22, 177, 213n, 244, 254–55, 288–89, 296, 329–30, 484, **4**: 31, 194, 198, 221n, 430, **5**: 68, 80, 87, 118, 122, 143, 149–52, 160, 196, 235, 290, 323, 335, 351, **6**: 16–17, 19, 27, 206–10, 210n, 211n, 248–49, 274, 336, 338, **7**: 105, 109, 140, 253–54, 261, 263–65, **8**: 75, 135, 294–95, 329, 338, **9**: 47, 50, 70–71, 85, 190, 205–6, 209, 314, 341–42, 357, 369n, **10**: 64, 228, **11**: 65–66, 89–90, 241–42, 274, 276, 372, 385–86. *See also* Arms and ammunition

Bowyer's Sulphur Springs, **4**: 300

Box, common, **4**: 27, 29n

Boxelder, **4**: 17, 19n, 26, 54, 69, 108, 216, 222, 250, 324, 326, 330, 358, 372, 374, 388, 392, 417, 435, **8**: 417, 418n, **9**: 182, 182n, **11**: 181–82, 182n, 222–23

Box-elder bug, **2**: 186n

Box Elder Creek (Willow Run), **4**: 302n, 325, 326n, 329, 335, 338–40, 342–43, 345, **9**: 174, 174n, 340–41, 340n, **10**: 105, 105n, 257–58, 257n, **11**: 210–13, 211n

Boxes, **5**: 125, **10**: 75, **11**: 216

Boyer (Bowyer) River (Pott's Creek), **2**: 425–27, 428n, **3**: 353, 371, 379, **8**: 379, 397, **9**: 31, 31n, 367n, 391, **11**: 47, 48n

Boyley. *See* Boley, John

Bozeman Creek, **8**: 181–82, 183n, 185, 392, 409

Bozeman Pass, **8**: 180, 180n, 186, 187n, 191, 392, 409

Brackenridge, H. M., **2**: 494n

Bradbury, John, **3**: 207n, **8**: 347n

Bradbury Slough (Fanny's Bottom), **6**: 458, 470, **8**: 387, 405

Bradford (Brant) Island, **5**: 359, 362, 364n, **6**: 7, 9n, 54, **9**: 288, 289n, **7**: 97–98, 100n, 101–2

Branding iron, **4**: 277n, **5**: 246, 246n, **6**: 82n, **7**: 151n, **9**: 234, 234n, **11**: 18n, 192–93, 193n, 338, 339n

Brandon Butte, **4**: 169n

Brandy, **2**: 166, **10**: 68, **11**: 113–14. *See also* Alcoholic beverages

Brant: migration, **2**: 208, **3**: 98, 131, 141, 232, **4**: 31, 33, 92; abundance, **3**: 96, **4**: 14, 17, 23, 103, **6**: 11–13, 21–23, 75, 88, 96, 457, **9**: 249–50, **11**: 385–86, 411; observed, **3**: 145, 147, 221, **4**: 111, 114, 204–5, **6**: 59–60n, 161–62, 171, 261, **9**: 128, 128n, **11**: 381–84; hunted, **6**: 8, 16, 19, 53–54, 60–62, 71, 73, 81, 83, 85, 92–93, 119–21, 414–15, **9**: 254–55, 264, **10**: 165, 165n, 171–72, 175, 177, **11**: 387, 394–96, 410; described, **6**: 9n, 394; as food, **6**: 65–67; mentioned, **2**: 185, 187n, **3**: 146n, **4**: 112, 18n, 115n, **6**: 383, 385, 391–93, 394n, 417–20, **11**: 382n

Brant, white. *See* Goose, snow

Branta bernicla, **3**: 146n, **4**: 18n, **6**: 9n, **9**: 128n, **10**: 165n, **11**: 382n. *See also* Brant

Branta canadensis, **2**: 186n, **3**: 88n, **4**: 21n, **6**: 10n, **7**: 11n, **9**: 128n, **10**: 79n, **11**: 140n. *See also* Goose, Canada

Branta canadensis hutchinsii, **4**: 115n. *See also* Goose, Hutchins's

Branta canadensis leucopareia, **4**: 115n, **6**: 10n, **7**: 11n. *See also* Goose, lesser Canada

Branta canadensis minima, **4**: 115n. *See also* Goose, cackling

Braro, brarow (and similar spellings). *See* Badger

Brass, **5**: 222, 227, 259, 289, 296, 359, 361, **6**: 15, 139, 142, 187, 195, 205, 221–22, 436, 440, **7**: 147–48, 160–61, 253, 255, **9**: 42, 239, 369n, **11**: 355–56

Brassicaceae, **7**: 338n. *See also* Mustard

Brassica sp., **3**: 466, **7**: 338n. *See also* Mustard

Bratton (Bratten), William E.: listed, **2**: 147, 187, 189, 194, 197, 199, 255, **3**: 170, **4**: 9, 11, **8**: 162n, 179, 277, **11**: 4n, 7n, 62n, 395n, 408n; in permanent party, **2**: 229n; sent out, **2**: 361, 363n, 397, 455, 488, **3**: 7, 9, **4**: 373, 375, 377, **6**: 42–43, 60, **8**: 209, 211, 285, **9**: 22, 35, **10**: 26, 255, **11**: 52, 61, 407; hunting, **2**: 395, **4**: 141, 193, 196, **8**: 266, 326, **9**: 108, **11**: 152–53; biographical sketch, **2**: 515; one of "nine young men from Kentucky," **2**: 529n; medical problems, **4**: 138, 374n, 375, **6**: 293, 295, 297, 307, 309, 311n, 312, 314, 318, 321, 324, 329–30, 332–33, 336–37, 384–85, 388, 390–91, 393–96, 416, 419, 441–43, **7**: 3, 10, 30, 104, 146, 152, 154, 282–86, 285n, 302, 304, 330–31, 346, **9**: 271–72, 314, **10**: 110n, 192n, 193, 203, 203n, 232–33, 232n, **11**: 419–20; creek named for, **4**: 162, 163n, **10**: 89n; and iron-frame boat, **4**: 350–51; returns, **4**: 376, **9**: 27, **10**: 28, **11**: 57; duties, **6**: 65, **8**: 276; votes, **6**: 83; and saltmaking camp, **6**: 138, 140, 166, 172n, **9**: 263, 263n, **10**: 184; visits whale

site, **6**: 177; and Indians, **7**: 334, 336; loses horse, **8**: 41; river named for, **8**: 196, 198n; scouting, **9**: 44, 254, **10**: 175, **11**: 395; mentioned, **2**: 500–501, **9**: 28n, 45n, 271n, 255n, 279, **10**: 26n, 29n, 175n, 184n, 193n, 233n, 256n, **11**: 153n, 419n, 420n

Brave Man (War-sar sha co), **2**: 491, 493, 494n

Brazeau Creek, **2**: 117n

Bread, **2**: 75–77, 223–24, 333, **3**: 19, 32, **5**: 219, 222, 227, 231–32, 315, 318, 341–42, 346–51, 353, **6**: 79, 96–97, 113, 118–19, 121, 166, 238–39, **8**: 44–45, 214, **9**: 92, 106, 316, **10**: 130, 134, 147, 147n, 159, 211, 221, 225, **11**: 330, 336, 362–63. *See also* Camas; Cous; Roots

Breadroot (white apple), **3**: 32, 37n, **4**: 125–26, 128, 129n, 146, 309, **8**: 282, 283n, 288, 288n, **9**: 69, 70n, **10**: 47n

Breaks of the Missouri River. *See* Missouri River, Breaks of the

Breckenridge, William Clark, **2**: 542

Breechcloths, **3**: 462, **6**: 113, **9**: 129, **11**: 276. *See also* Clothing

Breeches, **6**: 163–64, **7**: 266, 268. *See also* Clothing

Bricks, **5**: 8, 10n

Bridger Creek (Bratton's River) (Sweet Grass County, Mont.), **8**: 196, 198n, 391, 408

Bridger Creek (Gallatin County, Mont.), **8**: 181–82, 183n, 185, 392, 409

Bridger Range, **8**: 180, 183, 180n, 186, 187n, 188n, 191, 193n, 409

Bridles, **5**: 68, 92, 149, 161, **7**: 165, 167, **8**: 137, **9**: 107, 309

Brier, green. *See* Blackberry, Pacific

Brinton, Daniel G., **2**: 39

Britain, **3**: 120n, 281, 363–64, 367, **4**: 266, **8**: 348n

British, **1**: 3, 8, **2**: 1–3, 5, 122, 225, **3**: 3, 27, 29–30, 32, 163, 203, 208n, 224, 225n, 231, 242n, 258n, 311n, 365, 403, 439–42, 444, 484, 487, **4**: 30, 33–35, 39, 42, 103, **5**: 95n, **6**: 36n, 62n, 76n, 94n, 148n, 160n, 187, **7**: 61n, **8**: 74, 346, 347n, 356n, 412, **9**: 29, 43, 45, 49, 75, 219n, 250, 280, 306n, 361–62. *See also* Hudson's Bay Company; North West Company; Traders

British Columbia, **8**: 364n, **10**: 226n

Brodiaea douglasii, **7**: 135n. *See also* Hyacinth, wild

Brodiaea grandfolia, **7**: 135n. *See also* Hyacinth, wild

Broken Arm (Tunnachemootoolt): and Twisted Hair, **7**: 229–30, 232; relations with the party, **7**: 230, 232, 237–40, 246, 248–51, 256, 258, 300–301, 333–34, 339–41, **9**: 307; village, **7**: 235, 237, 239–40, 247, 284–85, 297, 299, **9**: 308n, 320n; rank, **7**: 242, 244; clothes, **7**: 249–50; visits, **7**: 261, 263, 331, 348–49; mentioned, **7**: 233n, 334n, **8**: 47, **9**: 307n

Broken Kettle (Prickley Pear) Creek, **3**: 355, 384

Broken Moccasin Indians. *See* Tukudika Indians

Brome, **7**: 335–36

Brome, California, **7**: 337n

Brome, fringed, **7**: 337n

Brome, smooth, **7**: 337n

Bromus carinatus, **7**: 337n. *See also* Brome, California

Bromus ciliatus, **7**: 337n. *See also* Brome, fringed

Bromus inermis, **7**: 337n. *See also* Brome, smooth

Bromus secalinus, **7**: 337n. *See also* Cheat

Brooches, **5**: 244, **8**: 318. *See also* Clothing

Broomrape, **7**: 335, 337, 338n

Brooms, **3**: 481

Broughton, William Robert, **5**: 301n, **6**: 14n, 29n, 47–48n, 115n, **7**: 61n, **9**: 249n, **10**: 166n, **11**: 382–83, 384n

Browne, Joseph, **8**: 362, 362n

Browns Island (Oreg.), **5**: 336n

Brown's Island (W. Va.), **2**: 72, 72n

Browns Lake, **8**: 94n

Brown's Ridge, **5**: 224n

Bruises. *See* Medical problems

Brule Island, **8**: 325–26n

Brulé Sioux Indians. *See* Sioux Indians, Brulé

Brunot, Felix, **2**: 66n

Brunot's Island, **2**: 65, 66n

Brush, bitter, **8**: 93, 94n

Brush, rabbit, **3**: 465, 470

Brush drag, **2**: 483, 484n, 485

Brush (Yellow Ochre) Creek, **2**: 350–51, 351n, **8**: 359n, **9**: 21, 21n

Brushy (Quawmash, Stony) Creek (Idaho), **5**: 204, 205n, 238, **6**: 452, 466, **8**: 61, 63, 64n, **9**: 223, 224n, 328, 328n, **10**: 142, 142n, **11**: 314–15, 316n

Bryan, Guy, **2**: 70, 70n

Bubo virginianus, **4**: 41n, **6**: 378n, **7**: 32n, **8**: 36on. *See also* Owl, great horned

Bubo virginianus occidentalis, **4**: 41n, **6**: 378n. *See also* Owl, Montana horned

Bubo virginianus saturatus, **6**: 378n. *See also* Owl, dusky horned

Bucephala albeola, **2**: 101n, **6**: 98n, **7**: 11n. *See also* Bufflehead

Buchloe dactyloides, **4**: 308n, **8**: 188n. *See also* Buffalograss

Buckbrush. *See* Coralberry

Buckets, **9**: 135

Buckeye, Ohio, **2**: 69n, **10**: 15n

Buckeye, western, **8**: 416, 418n, **9**: 20, 20n

Buckeye, yellow, **2**: 69n, **10**: 15n

Buckeyes, **2**: 69, **10**: 15

Buck (Full) Creek, **3**: 344, 383–84n

Buckshot. *See* Balls, bullets, and shot

Buckthorn, **8**: 12n. *See also* Ceanothus, redstem

Budge, George, **9**: 104, 104n

Buffalo: as trade item, **1**: 8, **3**: 392–437 passim, **4**: 35, **9**: 13, 83, 92, 100, 120, 352, **10**: 212, 270; and Indians, **2**: 277, 279, 399, 415–16, 423–24, 478–79, 482n, 490–92, 507, **7**: 145, 148; signs, **2**: 282–83, 350, **4**: 3, 285, 327–28, **5**: 32, **8**: 96, 118, 178, 182, **9**: 43, 336; grease, **2**: 294, 295n, **4**: 126, 155n, 334–36, 363; observed, **2**: 327, 369, **3**: 51–52, 57, 65, 79, 81–82, 87, 96, 99–100, 102, 107, 180, 182, 269, 294, **4**: 31, 33, 39, 44–46, 48, 51, 73–74, 90, 111, 113, 164, 186, 213–15, 218–19, 227, 232, 238, 250, 259, 285, 287, 309–10, 379, 382, **8**: 97, 112, 117–18, 194, 252, 308, 310, **9**: 18, 43–44, 56–57, 88–89, 103–4, 107, 131–32, 134–35, 137, 140, 142, 153, 157–58, 160, 162, 170–71, 175, 180, 343, 351, **10**: 37, 57, 80, 95, **11**: 62, 177, 184, 197, 208–9n, 210, 254; hunted, **2**: 502–3, 503n, **3**: 30, 48, 50, 55, 57–58, 61–62, 78, 83, 89–90, 133, 186–90, 192, 233–34, 238, 253–56, 257–59, 265, 267, 270, 272, 285, 292–93, 484–86, **4**: 36, 39, 48–49, 59n, 64, 66, 73–74, 96, 100, 113, 115, 121, 123, 130–31, 134, 136, 139–40, 151, 155, 157, 171, 176, 178, 189, 191, 193, 201, 205, 221n, 223, 228–29, 232, 242, 250, 252, 261–63, 280, 291–92, 306, 307–8, 317–18, 327–28, 333–34, 338–39, 341, 344, 356, 363–68, 374–76, 379, 386–87, **5**: 85n, 225n, **6**: 130n, 162–63, 448–49, 480, **8**: 99, 106, 108–9, 115, 121, 123, 131, 136, 141, 149, 151, 153–54, 189–90, 200, 202, 206, 209, 211–12, 218–19, 224, 237, 253, 268, 284, 325, 327–28, 344, **9**: 30, 38, 43, 50, 55–58, 60–62, 88, 97, 101–5, 108–9, 113, 135–38, 141, 143, 145–49, 152, 154–55, 159–65, 167–68, 170, 172–73, 175–76, 178–84, 312n, 337–43, 346–49, 354–55, 358, **10**: 30, 37–38, 40–41, 58, 62, 65–66, 65n, 69–70, 80, 82–83, 85, 87, 92–93, 96, 100, 104–6, 109, 111, 138, 251–52, 258–60, 262–63, 272–75, **11**: 60, 70–72, 76–78, 103, 108–11, 116–17, 120, 137–39, 142–43, 146, 148–49, 152–53, 156–59, 163–67, 169–70, 179–80, 182–84, 186, 188, 190–92, 196–97, 202–5, 207, 209–11, 214–21, 223–24, 228; abundance, **3**: 7, 11, 44, 57, 82, 93–94, 98–99, 104–5, 184–88, 190, 192, 255, **4**: 49, 53, 57–58, 60, 62, 67, 81–82, 85, 87, 103, 105–6, 108, 114, 124, 126, 128, 131–32, 134, 143, 151, 158, 165, 247, 256, 258, 280, 283, 291, 303, 305, 307–8, 310, 318, 324–25, 333–35, 339, 345–46, 363–66, 387–88, **5**: 4, 123, 178–79, **7**: 196, 198; skins, **3**: 22, 32, 77, 79, 115, 147n, 155, 209, 211, 232, 253, 270–71, 331n, 348, 489, **4**: 10, 38–39, 54, 306, 334, 338, 344, 354, 356, 363–67, 369, 371, 375, 379, 404, **5**: 126, 133, 139, 143, 150–51, 161, 258–59, **8**: 106, 111, 130, 190, 194, 217, 284, 313, 323, 419, **9**: 13, 64, 69–70, 83–84, 91–92, 95, 100, 107, 166, 180–81, 218, 240, 297, 306, 349, **10**: 32, 46, 51, 53, 55, 60–61, 65, 75, 109, 131, 138, 149, 212, 215, 231, 252, 259, 266, 270, **11**: 22–23, 64–65, 86–88,

Buffalo (*continued*)
96, 96n, 105–6, 111, 193–
94, 219, 273, 299–300, 329–
30, 353, 356–57, 393; behav-
ior, **3**: 46, 61–62, 256, **4**: 61–
63, 67, 108, 132, 280, 363, **8**:
104, 119, **10**: 83, **11**: 139,
205–8; food, **3**: 77, 309,
309n, 322, **4**: 66, 70, 142, **5**:
108n; as food, **3**: 116, 118,
321, 120n, 177, 227, 297,
321, 322n, 326, **4**: 55, 70,
111, 121, 130–32, 157–58,
224, 228–29, 280, 286–87,
289, 303, 307–8, 317–18,
327, 333–34, 336, 340, 354,
362, 374, 379, 386, **5**: 222, **8**:
2, 113–14, 150, 259, **9**: 67,
69, 95, 101, 116, 138, 170,
352, **11**: 100, 121, 139, 148–
49, 167, 199–200, 212, 217,
224–26; scarcity, **3**: 286, **4**:
159, 161, 184, 195, 354, 362,
366, 368–69, 403, 414, **5**:
91, **8**: 121, 123, 141, 146,
280, 321, **10**: 110, 122, 262,
11: 19, 159–60; habitat, **3**:
482, **5**: 164n; float, **4**: 31, 56,
74–75, 78, 156, 216–17,
219, 221n, 285, 303, 305,
337, **8**: 282–83; hair, **4**: 51,
5: 160, **8**: 97, 104, 106, 113,
115, 136, 139–40, 147–48,
150, 153, 195, 210, 219,
224–26, 232, 248, 255, 259,
268, 272–73, 318, 325–26,
328, **9**: 63–64, 87, 101, 132–
33, 135, 137–38, 140, 144,
146, 150, 169, 171–74, 176,
178, 337, 341, 343, 345–46,
354, **10**: 31, 38, 40, 64, 80–
81, 87, 94, 106, 109, 266, **11**:
102, 144–46, 148–53, 155–
57, 160–61, 185, 201–5,
207–8, 211–13; and Indians,
4: 216–17, 221n, 229n, **8**:
132, 180n, 182, 232, 309,
318, 350, **9**: 30, 69–70, 83–
84, 91, 209–10, 212, 214,
218–19, 228, 297–98, 306,
319, 391, 394, **10**: 46, 51, 53,
55, 60–61, 64, 70–71, 71n,
96n, 131, 138, 149, 215, 231,

11: 44–45, 50, 64–65, 86–
88, 96, 96n, 105–6, 122,
123n, 177–78, 178n, 179n,
283, 286–87, 292, 299–300,
303–4, 329–30, 356–57; attacked by, **4**: 294; dung, **4**:
403, 405, 423, **8**: 121–22;
use, **5**: 127, 150, **8**: 3, **9**: 349,
355, **11**: 129, 204–5, 207,
217; trails, **8**: 166, 181–86,
191–92; danger from, **8**: 258;
informed of, **8**: 327, **10**: 67;
mentioned, **2**: 283n, 259,
347, **3**: 35n, 109n, 131, 245,
368, **4**: 311, **5**: 149, 188n,
7: 303, 305, **8**: 106n, 108,
108n, 125, 135, 222n, 270n,
274, 277, 291, 314, 414, **9**:
18n, 149, 339, **10**: 30n, 66,
11: 6n, 47n, 60n. *See also*
Robes
Buffaloberry (graisse de boeuf,
rabbit berry, red berry): described, **2**: 498; abundance,
2: 504–5, **3**: 136, 150–51,
222, 481, **4**: 251, **5**: 39, **8**:
114, **9**: 43, 89, 136, 150, 195,
10: 30, 58, **11**: 104, 239; observed, **3**: 104–5, 107n, **4**:
94, 241, 388, **10**: 100, **11**: 61,
184–85; as food, **3**: 136;
name, **3**: 136, 138n; specimen, **3**: 464, 469, habitat, **4**:
26, 70, 73, 251, **8**: 117, 238;
mentioned, **2**: 498, 499n,
506n, **3**: 135, 138n, 153n,
223n, **4**: 28n, 397n, **5**: 40n,
8: 115n, 118n, 240n, **9**: 44n,
10: 30n, 58n, 101n, **11**: 61n,
104n, 186n, 239n
Buffalo Creek (Island Brook)
(Yellowstone County, Mont.),
8: 231, 234n, 390, 407
Buffalo Creek (W. Va.), **2**: 74,
74n
Buffalo fish, **2**: 432, 485–86
Buffalo fish, bigmouth, **2**:
432n
Buffalo fish, black, **2**: 432n
Buffalo fish, smallmouth, **2**:
432n
Buffalograss, **4**: 308n, **8**: 187,
188n

11: 44–45, 50, 64–65, 86–

Buffalo Medicine (Tar-ton-gar-
wa-ker), **3**: 108, 110n, 111,
113–14, 123–24, 126, 128–
30, 132, **8**: 331, 332n, **9**: 65,
66n, 67, 68n, **10**: 45, 45n,
47, 47n, 48n, 49, **11**: 85,
86n, 90, 91n
Buffalo Prairie, **10**: 30
Buffalo Rapids Ditch, **8**: 256n
Buffalo Shoals, **8**: 252–53,
255n, 256n, 390, 407
Buffington's (Emberson's) Island, **2**: 83, 83n
Bufflehead, **2**: 99, 101n, **6**: 98n,
383, 384n, 385, 397–98,
398n, 401n, **7**: 9, 11n
Bufo americanus, **7**: 312n. *See also*
Toad, American
Bufo boreas, **7**: 312n. *See also*
Toad, western
Bufo woodhousii, **7**: 312n. *See also*
Toad, Fowler's
Bug, melon, **7**: 76, 78n
Bug, tumble, **7**: 309, 311, 312n
Bullboats: use, **3**: 146–47, 149,
174, 232, 348, **8**: 156, 285,
285n, 289, 295, 334, 391,
414, **9**: 82–84, 349, **10**: 55,
265–66, **11**: 96; described, **3**:
155, **9**: 77, **10**: 51, 53; constructed, **8**: 3, 106, 284, **10**:
51, 252, 265n; and Indians,
8: 106, 106n, 285n, 297,
323; design, **8**: 106n, 284;
damaged, **8**: 290; mentioned,
3: 147n, **9**: 77n, **10**: 51n,
53n, 252n, **11**: 96n
Bull Creek (Beaverhead County,
Mont.), **8**: 171n
Bull Creek (Custer County,
Mont.), **8**: 248, 249n
Bull Creek (Shannon's River)
(Lyman County, S. Dak.),
3: 70, 73–74n, **8**: 328, 328n,
9: 59n, 60, 60n, 333n, 367n,
10: 39, 39n, 40n, **11**: 74–75,
75n, 76n
Bullet River. *See* Cannonball
River
Bullets. *See* Balls, bullets, and
shot
Bullhead, black, **2**: 433n
Bullion Creek, **8**: 408

Bullion Creek Formation, **4**: 47n, 50n, 63n, 75n, 76n

Bull Island, **8**: 417

Bull Mountains, **5**: 24, 29n, **8**: 225, 228n, **10**: 120, 120n

Bullsnake, **2**: 447, 449–50, 452n, **3**: 50, 51n, **4**: 425n, **9**: 34, 35n, 392

Bullwhacker (Softshell Turtle) Creek, **4**: 201–3, 207n, **6**: 448, 463, **9**: 155, 156n, **10**: 93, 93n, **11**: 169–70, 170n

Bulrush, western, **4**: 420, 422n, **5**: 21n, 326n, **10**: 160n

Bulrushes, **6**: 26, 29n, 305, 307, 307n, **7**: 159n, 191n, **10**: 160

Bunch (Budge), George, **1**: 8, 18n. 80, **3**: 258, 258n, 273n, 303, 307, 312n, **10**: 66, 66n

Bunchberry, **6**: 44–45, 45–46n

Bunchgrasses, **7**: 202–3, 204n

Bundleflower, **3**: 456–57, 463, 468

Bunks, **6**: 138

Bunting, lark, **4**: 329n

Burke Island, **6**: 23, 25n

Burlington Formation, **2**: 285n

Burning Bluffs, **8**: 379, 397

Burns (Samuel's) Creek, **8**: 270, 272–73, 274n, 275n, 389, 406

Burnt Fork (Scattered) Creek, **5**: 191n, **6**: 466, **8**: 393, 410

Burr, Aaron, **1**: 12, **8**: 347, 347–48n, 356n

Burr Canyon, **10**: 155n, **11**: 354n

Buteo jamaicensis, **5**: 76n, **6**: 94n. *See also* Hawk, red-tailed

Buteo swainsoni, **5**: 76n, **6**: 378n. *See also* Hawk, Swainson's

Butte Creek, **8**: 242, 244, 246n

Butter, **2**: 140–41, 173, 248, 395, **7**: 329

Butterbox. *See* Bufflehead

Butterflies, **7**: 46, 48n, 76, 309, 311

Butter Island, **2**: 395–96

Butternut, **2**: 80n, **9**: 8, 9n, 12, **10**: 10, 11n

Buttons, **6**: 187, 205, **7**: 38, 40, 153, 160, 274, 325, 328, **9**:

105, 302, 369n, **10**: 67, **11**: 113. *See also* Clothing

Buxus sempervirens, **4**: 29n. *See also* Box, common

Buzzard. *See* Condor, California

C

Cabaret Island, **2**: 129, 130n

Cabbage, skunk, **7**: 45, 47n

Cabin Creek (Custer County, Mont.), **8**: 251, 254, 256n

Cabin Creek (Oreg.), **5**: 357n

Cabin Creek (Yellowstone County, Mont.), **8**: 223, 227, 229n

Cabin (Gibson's) Creek (Prairie County, Mont.), **8**: 258–60, 261n, 262n, 389, 406

Cable. *See* Rope, tow; Ropes

Cabri (and similar spellings). *See* Pronghorn

Caches: at Marias River, **4**: 269, 271–72, 274, 274n, 275–76, 279, **8**: 138, 139n, **9**: 166, 342, 343n, **10**: 100–101, 100n, 101n, **11**: 191–93; at lower portage camp, **4**: 305–6, 309, 316, 334–35, 335n, 338–39, 362, **8**: 109, **9**: 170, 175–76, 340, 341n, **11**: 202; at upper portage camp, **4**: 334, 335n, 370–71, **8**: 2, 107–8, 108n, **9**: 338, **10**: 253, 253n; at Camp Fortunate, **5**: 125–26, 133, 141, **8**: 3, 172, 173n, **9**: 207, 333, **10**: 255, 255n, **11**: 278–79; at Canoe Camp, **5**: 247–48; on Clearwater River, **5**: 249–50, 257, **7**: 220, 222, 225n, 229; at Willow Ridge, **8**: 32–33, 34n, 52–53, 55n, **9**: 327, 327n; at Nez Perce village, **9**: 234, **11**: 339, 341–42; mentioned, **4**: 382, **8**: 1

Cactus. *See also* Prickly pear

Cactus, cochineal, **4**: 430, 433n

Cactus, pink pincushion, **5**: 78, 85n

Cactus, yellow pincushion, **4**: 430, 433n

Caddoan language, **3**: 127n, 153n, 167n, **10**: 274n, **11**: 126n

Caddo Indians, **3**: 447, 449

Cadotte Island, **3**: 95n

Cadotte's Pass, **8**: 104

Cahokia, Ill., **1**: 5, **2**: 127–28, 128n, 129n, 154n, 155, 166–67, 173–74, 180, 191, 197, 209, 221, 295n, **8**: 371, 371n, **10**: 4n

Cahokia Creek, **2**: 127–28

Cahokia Indians, **3**: 407

Cahokia Mounds, **2**: 153–54, 154n. *See also* Mounds, Indian burial

Cah-wah-na-hi-ooks River. *See* Lewis River

Cains Coulee, **8**: 267, 269, 270n

Caissee (and similar spellings). *See Cajeux*

Cajeux, **2**: 259–60, 260n, 266, 277, 279, 286–87, 294, 300. *See also* Canoes; Pirogues

Calamagrostis inexpansa, **5**: 60n. *See also* Reedgrass, northern

Calamagrostis stricta, **5**: 60n. *See also* Reedgrass, northern

Calamosopiza melanocorys, **4**: 329n. *See also* Bunting, lark

Calapooya Indians, **6**: 479, 487, 491. *See also* Kalapuya Indians

Calcarius mccownii, **4**: 257n. *See also* Longspur, McCown's

Calcium, **4**: 135n

Calcium carbonate, **3**: 285n

Calcium-magnesium, **8**: 120n

Caldwell, **2**: 74

Caldwell, D., **10**: 5n

Calico, **9**: 369n

Calico Island, **2**: 125, 125n

Calidris himantopus, **3**: 132n, **9**: 63n. *See also* Sandpiper, stilt

Calidris melanotos, **3**: 132n, **9**: 63n. *See also* Sandpiper, pectoral

California, Gulf of, **3**: 363, **7**: 41, 64, 83, 182, 185

Callallamet, **6**: 156, 161n, 427

Callamon, **6**: 156, 160–61n, 416, 416n, 427

Cal-lar-po-e-wah (and similar spellings) Indians. *See* Kalapuya Indians

Calliphoridae, **4**: 175n, **5**: 58n, **7**: 78n. *See also* Fly, blow

Calochortus macrocarpus, **7**: 190n. *See also* Lily, green-banded mariposa

Calomel, **2**: 86n

Calumet Bluff (Nebr.): arrive at, **3**: 1, 19–20, **8**: 342, 344n, **9**: 46, 357, 357n, **10**: 32, 275, 275n, **11**: 63; and Indians, **3**: 16–17, 123n; name, **3**: 21n, **9**: 51; astronomical observation at, **3**: 25; described, **3**: 37; distances, **3**: 372, **8**: 379, **10**: 172; listed, **3**: 379, **8**: 397, **9**: 367n; and mineralogical specimens, **3**: 475–76, 478; and species, **8**: 415–16, **9**: 52; depart, **11**: 67, 67n; latitude, **11**: 174; mentioned, **9**: 51n, 358

Camas (bread, passhico, quawmash, roots, squamash): discovered, **5**: 4, 224n; as food, **5**: 222–23, 232, 261–62; 318, **7**: 18–19, 238, 264, **8**: 17, 20, 21, **10**: 146–47; as trade item, **5**: 373, **7**: 30, 32, 35; described, **6**: 139, **8**: 14–16, 18–19, 22, **10**: 147, 237; and Indians, **6**: 193, **7**: 92, 205, 207, 234, 300, **8**: 14, 16–17, 20–21, 62–63, 167, **9**: 229, 287, **10**: 146–47, 218n, **11**: 326–28, 331, 344–45; as gift, **7**: 18–19, 237, 239, 339, 341, **11**: 326–27; observed, **7**: 55, 77, 200–201, 205, 207, 239, **10**: 246; habitat, **8**: 14, 168, 264; abundance, **8**: 20, 62–64, 90, 166, **9**: 308, 321, 331–32, **10**: 237; purchased, **9**: 228, 233, 235, 285, 300, **10**: 147, 159, 217, 225, **11**: 341–42; observed, **9**: 328; as bread, **11**: 329–30, 332, 337–38, 344–45; mentioned, **5**: 76n, **6**: 139n, 226–27, 227n, **7**: 21n, 237n, 241n, **8**: 12n, 21n, 26–27, 29, 38, 72, **9**: 228n, 287n, 310, **10**: 147n, 159n, 225n, **11**: 329n

Camas Prairie, **5**: 214n, **8**: 26, 27n, **9**: 226, 226n, **10**: 145, **11**: 321–22, 323n

Camassia quamash, **5**: 76n, **6**: 139n, **7**: 21n, **8**: 12n, **9**: 228n, **10**: 147n, **11**: 329n. *See also* Camas

Cambarus sp., **2**: 484n. *See also* Crayfish

Camden Bend, **11**: 28n

Cameahwait (Ka-me-ah-wah, Too-et-te-conl): relations with the party, **5**: 2–3, 79–81, 92, 102–4, 109, 111–12, 114, 128, 130, 131n, 148, 158–59, 165–66, 172–73, **9**: 205, 210, **11**: 277n; information from, **5**: 81, 88–91, 104–6, 124, 149, 171; gifts, **5**: 95–96, 117–18, 144, **11**: 286–87; name, **5**: 115, 116–17n, 159; mourning, **5**: 121–22; visits, **5**: 143; mentioned, **5**: 164, **5**: 86n, **9**: 206n, **11**: 288n

Camera obscura, **4**: 285, 288n

Cameron, Murdoch, **3**: 161, 166n, 305, 317, 356, 385n, 401, 412–13

Cameron Creek, **5**: 190n, **9**: 220n

Camomile. *See* Sage, long leaf

Campanula rotundifolia, **4**: 402n, **9**: 169n, **10**: 99n, **11**: 201n. *See also* Harebell, roundleaf

Campbell, **3**: 408, 410–11

Campbell, John, **1**: 16n. 32, **2**: 139n, 191, 191n, 510, 518, 522–23

Campbell Creek (Buffalo County, S. Dak.), **3**: 91n, 358, 372, 380, **8**: 380, 398, **9**: 62, 62n, **10**: 41, 41n, **11**: 78, 78n

Campbell Creek (Charles Mix County, S. Dak.), **3**: 60n, **11**: 71, 72n

Campbell Island, **3**: 60n

Camp Chopunnish (Idaho): and maps, **1**: 11; and journal-keeping methods, **2**: 28–29,

8: 376, **9**: xvi; name, **7**: 3, 259n, **9**: 310n, **10** 228n; arrive at, **7**: 255–56, 258, **9**: 310, 318, **10**: 227; location, **7**: 259n, **9**: 310n; depart, **8**: 1; and species, **8**: 12n, 13n, 30n; and members of the party, **8**: 14, 17, 45–46, **10**: 238; distances, **9**: 318n; and Indians, **10**: 227–28; and botanical specimens, **12**: 6; mentioned, **7**: 330n, 338n, **8**: 21n, 46n, **9**: 319n, **10**: 238n

Camp Creek (Prairie County, Mont.), **8**: 251–52, 255, 257n, 407

Camp Creek (Ravalli County, Mont.), **5**: 187, 187n, 188n, **8**: 165–66, 166n, 168n, **9**: 218, 218n, 219n, 331, 331n, 332n, **10**: 137, 137n, **11**: 301n

Camp Disappointment (Mont.), **8**: 2, 124n, 127, 293

Camp Dubois (Camp Wood, River Dubois) (Ill.): and maps, **1**: 4, 7; visits, **1**: 5, 7; arrive at, **1**: 5, **2**: 185; location, **1**: 16n. 31, **3**: 376; activities at, **2**: 6, 66n; and journal-keeping methods, **2**: 11–12, 16, 18, 40–41, 146n, 174n, 210n, 219n, 221n, 360n, 393n, 482n, 533, 537, 540–41; depart, **2**: 60, 177, 178n, 206–7, 215–16, 227, 242, **3**: 4; distances, **2**: 61, **3**: 2; name, **2**: 132n; constructed, **2**: 133–34, 133n, 140–42; discipline at, **2**: 200n; latitude and longitude, **2**: 215, 215n; and members of the party, **2**: 229n, 295n, 354n, 510, 514–15, 517, 519–20, 522–24, **9**: xiv, xvi, 3n, **11**: xiv; and species, **2**: 431n, 460. *See also* Dubois (Wood) River

Camp Fortunate (Mont.): and maps, **1**: 10–11; arrive at, **1**: 10, **8**: 172–73, 264, **9**: 205, **10**: 126, **11**: 272; name, **5**: 3; location, **5**: 109, 116n, **9**:

206n, **10**: 127n, **11**: 275n;
route to, **8**: 1, 3, 74, 166n,
172–73, 414, **9**: 334n; cache
at, **8**: 3, 74, 172–73, 264,
414, **9**: 332, **10**: 172, 174n,
255, 255n; depart, **8**: 174;
distances, **8**: 393, **9**: 231n,
10: 128; listed, **8**: 409; mentioned, **7**: 334n, **8**: 78n,
168n, 173n, **10**: 128n

Camphor, **4**: 35. *See also*
Medicine

Camps. *See individual states* (e.g.,
Missouri, camps in)

Camp White Catfish (Iowa): and
maps, **1**: 7, 9, **2**: 428; and
journal-keeping methods, **2**:
12, 15; arrive at, **2**: 60, 405,
407–8, **9**: 29, 360, **10**: 22,
277, **11**: 43–44; distances,
2: 407, 409, 487; latitude,
2: 407, 410, 413n, 416–18,
418n, 480, 487, **9**: 80; location, **2**: 413n, 416, **9**: 29,
29n, **10**: 22n; and species, **2**:
420; listed, **3**: 378, **11**: 174;
mentioned, **2**: 419, 421, **9**:
360n, **10**: 277n, **11**: 44n

Camp Wood. *See* Camp Dubois

Canada, **1**: 5–6, **2**: 3, 225n,
431n, 516, 526–29, **3**: 56n,
236n, **4**: 63n, 107n, 115n, **5**:
225n, **6**: 107n, 281–82, **8**: 3,
58, 123n, 132n, 356n, 367,
10: 6n, **12**: 4

Canadians, **5**: 4, 95n, **6**: 236, **8**:
280n. *See also* Traders

Canarygrass, reed, **2**: 304, 305n,
374–75, 487, **3**: 457, 467

Cancerroot, **7**: 338n

Candlefish, **6**: 346n. *See also*
Eulachon

Candles, **2**: 156, 181n, 203,
203n, 217, **5**: 211, **6**: 200–
201

Cane, **2**: 351, **7**: 335–36

Cane, large, **2**: 102, 104n

Cane, Mrs., **2**: 202

Canio. *See* Coboway

Canis latrans, **2**: 475n, **3**: 12n, **4**:
40n, **5**: 228n, **6**: 317n, **8**:
116n, **9**: 38n, **10**: 40n, **11**:
77n. *See also* Coyote

Canis lupus, **2**: 335n, **4**: 40n, **5**:
55n, **6**: 210n, **7**: 151n, **8**:
98n, **9**: 18n, **10**: 17n, **11**:
32n. *See also* Wolf, gray

Canis lupus fuscus, **6**: 317n. *See
also* Wolf, gray

Canis lupus nubilis, **2**: 399n, **3**:
57n, **4**: 116n, **6**: 317n. *See also*
Wolf, gray

Canisters, **2**: 6, 166, **4**: 309, **5**:
53, 232, 235, 248–50, 257,
271, **6**: 265, 272, **7**: 206–7,
220, 222, 236, **10**: 223, **11**:
192–93, 322–23, 341–42.
See also Arms and ammunition; Gunpowder

Cann (Cane, Carn, Carr), E.,
1: 17n. 73, **2**: 347, 476–77,
478n, 525, **3**: 7, 9, 12n, **9**: 38,
39n, 44, 45n, **10**: 28n, **11**:
62n

Cannon, swivel (bow piece),
2: 263, 264n, 347–48, 349n,
362–63, **3**: 125n, 261, 266,
275, **4**: 316, 334, **8**: 303–4,
305n, 330, 351, **9**: 3, 6, 20,
22, 33, 47, 68, 79, 91, 105,
126, 341, 349–50, 366, 386,
391, **10**: 8, 18, 60, 68, 268,
268n, **11**: 1, 4n, 11, 11n, 56–
57, 106, 113–15. *See also*
Arms and ammunition;
Blunderbusses

Cannonball (Bullet) River, **3**:
181–83, 183n, 286, 286n,
361, 363, 367, 373, 376, 381,
471, 473, 477, **7**: 343n, **8**:
310, 311n, 380, 399, 412,
416, **9**: 80–81, 82n, 86n, 87,
87n, 367n, **10**: 56n, 57, 57n,
11: 101n, 102, 102n, 172,
174

Cannon Beach Member, **6**:
179n, 185n

Cannons, **4**: 320, 321n, 361–62.
See also Arms and
ammunition

Canoe Camp (Idaho), **1**: 10, **5**:
234, 234n, 240, 242, **6**: 462,
7: 214n, 233, 236n, **9**: xvi,
230–31, 230n, **10**: 148,
149n, 173, **11**: 333–34,
334n, 339

Canoe Camp (Mont.), **8**: 208n,
215n

Canoe Creek. *See* White Salmon
River

Canoes: constructed, **1**: 10,
2: 30, **3**: 4, 227n, 304, 308n,
311, **4**: 3, 346n, 369, 371,
373–74, 376–77, 379, 389,
5: 4, 24n, 81, 113, 115, 145–
46, 162–63, 165, 233–36,
240, 242, 244–45, 247–48,
328n, 365, **6**: 262–63, 265,
267, 270, 272, **7**: 212, 232,
236, 236n, 275–77, 289–90,
8: 3, 106, 118, 184, 187,
189–91, 195, 204–5, 209,
211–12, 215, 217, 284, 305,
366, 391, 413–14, **9**: 182–
83, 182n, 205–6, 216, 229–
34, 308n, 314–15, 348–49,
10: 74, 110–11, 127, 148–
50, 231, 233, 266, **11**: 128,
128n, 221–24, 223n, 276,
332–39; problems with, **2**:
71–72, 83, **3**: 319–20, **4**: 13–
14, 22, 51, 53–56, 63, 77, 96,
98, 121, 378, 385, 393–94,
420, 437, **5**: 18, 24, 52–55,
93–94, 153, 155–56, 168,
173, 246, 249, 251, 253, 265,
272, 327, 329, 335, 377, **6**:
336, 432, 436, 440, 444, 448,
7: 94–96, **8**: 178, 332, **9**:
143, 185, 188, 195–97, 200,
203–5, 236–38, 243–45,
248, 256, 259, 266–67, 270,
276, 289, 320, 337, 340,
346–47, 356, **10**: 75, 131,
169–70, 176, 198, 210,
212, **11**: 272–73, 275, 341;
purchased, **2**: 71, **5**: 327–28,
6: 72, **9**: 278, 291, 299, **10**:
199, 210, **11**: 393n; loaded,
2: 84, **3**: 316, 332, **4**: 275–
77, 371, 378, 382, 394, **5**: 14,
56, 96, 249, 251, 255, 271,
275–76, 338, 346–47, **6**:
38–39, 49, 114, 126, **7**: 7–8,
78, 87, 96, 115–16, 136, **8**:
146, 174–75, 179, 268, 280,
286, 328, 349, **9**: 173–74,
182, 184, 191, 239, 244, 246,
253, 256, 258, 261, 291, 334,

Canoes (*continued*)
341, 347, **10**: 112, 151, 177,
180, 200, 208, **11**: 192–93,
212, 222–23, 225, 227, 232,
237–38, 242, 246–47, 251,
253, 256, 262, 266, 268, 339,
344, 354–55, 358, 369, 371,
375, 380, 391, 393, 398, 402,
405, 431; other, **2**: 191, 259–
60, 279, **3**: 134–35, 148,
155, 174, 181, 221, 230, 444,
5: 4, 359, 362–63, 366–67,
369, 371, **8**: 288, 362, **11**: 20,
93, 101; attention to, **3**: 279,
317–18, **11**: 202, 210, 371,
388, 391; repaired, **3**: 320–
21, **4**: 275–77, 324, 368,
371, **5**: 249–50, 252, 255,
340, 342–43, 367, 371, **6**:
49, 427, 429–30, **7**: 18–21,
23, 25, 112, 116–17, 214n,
8: 152–54, 174, **9**: 165, 181,
235, 278, 282, 336, 347, **10**:
152, 162, 196, 199, 203, 208,
11: 221, 344–46, 372, 426,
435; as trade item, **3**: 440,
443, **6**: 426, 428, **7**: 2, 7–8,
50, 53, 56, 115–17, 131, 146,
158, 162–64, **9**: 277, 295,
297, **11**: 427–29, 429n; portaged, **4**: 3, 286, 302–3, 319,
323–28, 330, 332–36, 338,
5: 266, 283, 326–27, 367,
369, **6**: 117–18, **7**: 136–37,
142–43, 152–54, **8**: 74, 110,
292, 412, **9**: 172–74, 176,
248, 294–95, 338–39, **10**:
105–8, 212, 214, 254, 256–
58, **11**: 201, 204, 206–7,
211, 213, 215, 256, 273, 275,
366–67, 379, 381; naviga-
tional problems, **4**: 24, 121,
123, 193, 295, 420, **5**: 2, 4,
17, 28–29, 37, 39, 42–43,
47, 55, 62, 66, 71, 75, 83–
84, 106, 249, 251, 253, 255,
258, 266, 268–69, 271, 276–
77, 282–83, 304–5, 336–38,
355, 357, 361, 377, **6**: 7–9,
30, 33, 35–36, 39, 43–49,
92–93, 108, 114, 272, 312,
314, 325–26, **7**: 39, 98, 100–
104, 108, 111, 136–37, **8**:

147, 185, 252–53, 258, 310,
384, **9**: 134–36, 141, 143–
44, 156, 166, 168–69, 193,
197, 236, 238, 245, 280, **10**:
77, 79, 81, 85–86, 93, 102–
3, 113, 119, 121, 151–52,
154–55, 162, 164–65, 180,
196, 207–9, 212, 234, 269,
11: 142, 148, 169, 174, 202,
221, 224–25, 229, 240, 253,
256–61, 264–66, 268–72,
339–40, 342, 351–55, 363,
370, 390; endangered, **4**:
121, 140, 213, 281, 295, 303,
6: 37–38, 40–41, **11**: 194,
290, 352; unloaded, **4**: 121,
375–76, 380, 435, **5**: 53,
111, 114, 250–52, 271, 276–
77, 283, 323, **6**: 39, 90–91,
8: 149, 152, 179, 182, 276, **9**:
168, 190, 245, 248, 252, 288,
294, 347, **10**: 110, 126, 164,
169, 178, 180, 207, 214, **11**:
184, 199, 221, 223–24, 226,
243–44, 258–59, 341, 343,
345–46, 352, 373, 391, 399;
sails, **4**: 332–34, **10**: 79, 86,
11: 210–11; oars and poles,
4: 379–80, **5**: 125, 272, **6**:
97, 180, 182, 186, 263, 270,
272n, 273n, **7**: 101, 115,
117, 151–52, **8**: 211–12, 141,
150, 152, 154, 297, 311, 323,
346, 365, 367, **9**: 14, 231,
234, 236, 345, 390, **10**: 14,
22, 214n, 264, **11**: 26, 36, 53,
79, 89, 232–33, 335, 339,
345–46, 427; cached, **5**: 55,
57–58, 148, **6**: 42–43, 88–
89, 97, 98n, 176, 180, 182,
186, 188, 194, 401, 451, 460,
494, **7**: 10–11, 39, 219, 222,
224, **8**: 3, 74, 167, 168n,
169–70, 172–73, 177, 177n,
414, **9**: 205, 209, 333–35,
10: 127, 247, **11**: 282; Indian, **6**: 1, 3, 12–18, 22–23,
26, 30–32, 34n, 35, 40–41,
44, 46, 53, 55, 65–66, 81,
88–89, 103, 105–6, 117,
122, 124–25, 135–36, 142,
146–47, 171, 201–2, 207–8,
210, 232–35, 243–44, 263,

265, 267, 270, 272, 336, 342,
346, 414–16, 418, 421, 423,
436, 440, 456, **7**: 7–9, 10,
11n, 12–13, 18–21, 23, 25,
29–30, 32–35, 38–40, 49,
52, 54–57, 59, 61n, 64, 66,
79–80, 82, 84, 98–99, 107,
111, 121, 178–79, 181, 183,
206, 208, 220, 222, 249, 252,
254, 258, 263–65, 271–72,
283, 285, 308, 310, **8**: 297,
369, **9**: 230, 234–35, 237,
241, 243, 245, 248–52, 258,
268, 273, 277–78, 280–84,
288, 300, 309, 314, 318, 365,
10: 11, 148, 150, 154, 158,
165–67, 170, 190, 199–201,
203–4, 217, 221, 227, 234,
11: 6n, 103, 332–34, 340–
43, 348–50, 356–57, 359–
61, 365–68, 379–88, 392,
399, 401, 403–6, 408, 415,
421–23, 425, 432–38; stolen,
6: 4, 426, 428, 428n, **7**: 9n,
10; carvings, **6**: 16, 18, 22–
23, 55, 246, 249, 263, 267,
271, 272n, 273n, 457; lost, **6**:
37, 198–99, 203–4, 265,
272, 401, 403, 406–7, 409,
411, 454, **7**: 210, 212, 308,
310, 314–15, **11**: 403, 413,
426–27; secured, **6**: 40, 171,
7: 22, 24; damaged, **6**: 42–
43, 46, 79, 90–91, 374, 376,
11: 397; found, **6**: 203–4,
278, 280, **11**: 403, 417;
sketches, **6**: 272n, 273n, **7**:
61n, 89n; as fuel, **7**: 137,
139, 141, 143, 146, 151; use,
8: 107, 111, 138, 139n, 140,
148, 156, 176n, 225, 251,
277, 289, 306–7, 325, 329–
30, 337, 351, 359, 393, 411–
12; sold, **10**: 213, 215; accidents, **11**: 251, 341, 343,
345; mentioned, **2**: 7, 25–26,
71n, 93, 187, 192–93, 257,
3: 47, 327, 327n, 350, 354,
361, **4**: 1, 7, 9, 11, 12n, 26–
27, 57n, 71, 87, 103, 106,
124, 151, 170, 189, 191, 196,
224, 228–29, 242, 247, 249,
251, 299–301, 324, 329,

331, 349n, 354, 356, 359, 363–66, 374n, 379n, 383, 398, 401, 414–18, 421, 423, **5**: 8, 105, 109, 112, 164n, 166, 229, 255–56, 285–88, 290–92, 296, 301, 303–5, 311, 315, 318, 321, 333, 341, 345–46, 348, 348n, 352, **6**: 68, 96, 101, 133, 158, 167–69, 181, 195–96, 215, 260, 275, 284–85, 290, 297, 351, 367, 381–82, 402, **7**: 9, 48, 51, 71, 74, 84, 105, 155, 157, 159, 161, 188, 322, 324, **8**: 1, 77, 109, 135, 137, 157, 176, 231, 238, 243, 272, 279, 280n, 290, 293, 295, 299, 303, 311, 318, 322, 327, 329, 338, 342, 345, 358, 360n, 409, **9**: xi–xii, 10–11, 86, 88, 96, 132, 137, 140–41, 147–48, 154, 159, 161, 170, 180, 182–84, 186–87, 196, 204, 238, 242, 253, 255, 257–59, 261–62, 265, 268–72, 274–75, 278, 285–86, 289–90, 296, 313, 330, 334–35, 342, 344–45, 351, 355–56, 359–66, 378, 380, **10**: xi–xii, xv, 12, 56, 77, 88, 91, 106, 108, 110n, 111, 115, 117, 120n, 122–23, 151, 154, 160, 166, 170, 170n, 178, 179n, 181, 183, 191–92, 197, 201–202, 204n, 205, 209n, 214–15, 223, 254n, 255–57, 262–63, 265–69, 271, 276, 279, **11**: xi–xii, xv, 86, 132, 156–57, 166–68, 219, 230–31, 233, 241, 245, 255, 292, 327–28, 331, 394, 400, 401n, 410, 414, 416, 418–19, 430. *See also* Cajeux; Pirogues
Canteens, **2**: 287, **4**: 343
Cantier (No Timber) Creek, **3**: 126, 127n
Cantonment Wilkinson-Ville, **2**: 86, 86n
Canvasback, **5**: 309, 312n, **6**: 35–36, 37n, 96, 161–62, 383, 385, 395, 397, **7**: 23, 25, 25n, **10**: 160, 160n
Canyon Creek (Canister Run)

(Idaho), **5**: 249, 250n, **6**: 453, 467
Canyon Creek (Mont.), **8**: 163, 164n
Canyon Creek (Oreg.), **6**: 176, 178n
Canzes (and similar spellings) Indians. *See* Kansa Indians
Cap-a-pie, **5**: 80, 86n
Cape Cinque Hommes, Mo., **2**: 114, 116n, 117
Cape Disappointment: name, **6**: 36n; located, **6**: 50, 109, 113–15, 188, 470, 493, **11**: 431; distances, **6**: 88, 458, **9**: 232, **10**: 173, 175; maps, **6**: 248n, 481n; arrive at, **9**: 254, 254n; mentioned, **6**: 47n, 49, 51n, 53, 59, 60–62, 66–67, 67n, 69–70, 71n, 182, 193, 201–2, **9**: 255, **10**: 173n, **11**: 395n, 396
Cape Flattery, **6**: 161n, 416n
Cape Girardeau (Jeradeau), Mo., **2**: 105–6, 108, 109n, 110, 113, 197, 516, **3**: 339, 446
Cape Horn, **6**: 9n, 29n, **7**: 14n, **10**: 202n, **11**: 434n
Cape La Croix (*La'crush*) Creek, **2**: 105, 109n
Cape (Lookout) Meares, **6**: 494
Cape Shoalwater, **6**: 459, 470
Cape Swells. *See* Grays Point
Capotes, **6**: 18, 20n, 123, 360, 407, **7**: 310, **8**: 329, **9**: 46, 102, 102n, 318. *See also* Clothing
Caprimulgus vociferus, **2**: 276n, **3**: 179n, **4**: 346n, **8**: 375n, **9**: 21n. *See also* Whip-poor-will
Caps, **3**: 256, 257n, **7**: 101–3. *See also* Clothing
Captain (Bealette's) Creek, **3**: 344, 383n
Carbondale Formation, **2**: 113n
Cardiidae, **6**: 120n, 409n. *See also* Cockles
Cardinal, northern, **2**: 276n, **7**: 339–40, 342n, 345
Cardinal-flower, blue, **6**: 240–41, 242n
Cardinalis cardinalis, **2**: 276n,

7: 342n. *See also* Cardinal, northern
Carduelis flammea, **4**: 269n. *See also* Redpoll, common
Carduelis pinus, **4**: 269n. *See also* Siskin, pine
Carduelis tristis, **4**: 269n. *See also* Goldfinch, American
Carejoe, Carkajeu (and similar spellings). *See* Wolverine
Carex filifolia, **4**: 145n, **5**: 21n. *See also* Sedge, thread-leaved
Carex sp., **6**: 217n, 307n. *See also* Sedges
Carex stenophylla, **5**: 21n. *See also* Sedge, needle leaf
Carey, Matthew, **10**: xvii
Car-gar-no-mok-she. *See* Raven Man Chief
Carlton Creek, **8**: 162n
Carmen Creek (Salmon Run), **5**: 141n, **6**: 451, 466, **9**: 215, 215n, **10**: 129, 129n
Carmen Formation, **5**: 141n, 148n
Carondelet (Viele Pauchr), Ill., **2**: 127–28, 128n
Carp Island, **3**: 176–77
Carpenters, **2**: 179
Carpinus caroliniana, **2**: 277n, **8**: 359n. *See also* Hornbeam, American
Carpiodes carpio, **2**: 433n. *See also* Carpsucker, river
Carpodacus mexicanus, **4**: 269n. *See also* Finch, house
Carpodacus purpureus, **4**: 269n. *See also* Finch, purple
Carps, **2**: 432, 433n
Carpsucker, river, **2**: 433n
Carriages, **8**: 74, 292. *See also* Wagons
Carrn. *See* Cann, E.
Carroll Creek, **4**: 187n, **9**: 153, 153n
Carrots, **6**: 74, 226–27. *See also* Tobacco
Carson, Alexander, **2**: 525
Carson, Christopher "Kit," **2**: 525
Cart. *See* Wagons
Cartarkah Indians. *See* Kiowa Apache Indians

Cartridges, **4**: 335. *See also* Arms and ammunition; Balls, bullets, and shot

Carya cordiformis, **8**: 355n. *See also* Hickory, bitternut

Carya illinoensis, **2**: 339n, **8**: 418n. *See also* Pecan

Carya ovata, **8**: 355n. *See also* Hickory, shagbark

Carya sp., **2**: 78n, 80n, **9**: 9n, 10n, **10**: 11n. *See also* Hickory

Cascade Indians, **6**: 10n, **7**: 114n

Cascades of the Columbia River. *See* Columbia River, Cascades of the

Cascade Range, **5**: 4, 277, 284n, 301n, 307n, 312n, 339, 340n, 353n, 362, 379, **6**: 3, 29n, 284n, 324, 325n, 370–71, 374n, **7**: 15n, 18, 20, 21n, 22n, 34, 37n, 48, 51, 53n, 70n, 114n, 121n, 194n, 195n, **8**: 73n, **9**: 241n, **10**: 164n, 209, 209n, **11**: 376, 377n

Cascara, **8**: 7, 11, 12n

Cash-hook Indians. *See* Cushook Indians

Casmerodius albus, **2**: 186n. *See also* Egret, great

Cassia fasciulata, **3**: 467. *See also* Pea, partridge

Castahana Indians, **8**: 232, 235n, 278

Castor canadensis, **2**: 420n, **6**: 77n, **8**: 95n, **9**: 20n, **10**: 22n, **11**: 45n. *See also* Beaver, American

Castoreum. *See* Beaver, American

Castostomus castostomus, **9**: 209n. *See also* Sucker, northern

Cat, tiger. *See* Bobcat, Oregon

Cataract (and similar spellings) River. *See* Klickitat River

Catbird, gray, **4**: 276, 277n

Catel, **6**: 416, 418, 420n, 425, 427, **9**: 277n, **10**: 198, 198n, **11**: 428n

Caterpillar, tent, **7**: 309, 311, 312n

Catfish: abundance, **2**: 71, 426–

27, 429–30, 432, 483, 485–86, **3**: 39, 480, **11**: 211–12; described, **2**: 89–90, 418, 426–27, **3**: 96, 98, **9**: 363; fishing for, **2**: 181, 388, 418, 426–27, 430, 472, 483, 485–86, **3**: 39, **4**: 180, 296–97, 309, 332, **8**: 248, **9**: 18, 31, 44–46, 55, 133–34, 163, 359, 363, **11**: 61, 187; observed, **4**: 278–79, 348, **11**: 41; mentioned, **2**: 237, **9**: 143, **10**: 28, 31–32

Catfish, blue, **2**: 72n, 90n, **3**: 40n, **9**: 18n, **10**: 279, 280n

Catfish, channel, **2**: 72n, 238n, 418n, 433n, 484n, **3**: 40n, **4**: 182n, 298n, 349n, **9**: 18n, **10**: 29n, 31n, **11**: 42n, 61, 62n, 187n

Catfish, flathead, **2**: 486n

Cathartes aura, **4**: 349n, **7**: 100n, **8**: 23n, **9**: 322n. *See also* Vulture, turkey

Catharus guttatus, **2**: 277n. *See also* Thrush, hermit

Cathead (Kakawissassa) Creek. *See* Fisher (Kakawissassa) Creek

Cathlahaw Indians. *See* Lakjalama Indians

Cath-lah-cam-mah-tup Indians, **7**: 26, 30, 31n, 34

Cath-lah-cum-up Indians, **7**: 26, 30, 31n, 32, 34

Cath-lah-nah-qui-ah Indians, **7**: 26, 30, 31n, 34, 36n

Cathlamet Bay, **6**: 36, 37n, 397n, **7**: 9, 11n, **10**: 201n, **11**: 433n

Cathlamet (Cath-lah-mah) Indians: canoes, **6**: 34n, 40–41, 88–89, 192, 263, 270, 421, 423, 436; clothes, **6**: 34n, 40–41, 89, 97, 192, 195–96, 432–36, 438–40; language, **6**: 34n, 41, 89, 192, 195–96, 236, 281, **7**: 17n, **10**: 178n, **11**: 399; lodges, **6**: 34n, 89n, 154, **10**: 202n; villages, **6**: 40, 41–42n, 58, 87–89, 89n, 154, **7**: 9–10, **8**: 387, 405, **9**: 257n, 274–75, 277, 280–81,

10: 178, 178n, 201, **11**: 399, 399n, 423, 426–28, 428n, 433–34, 433n; encountered, **6**: 40–41, **9**: 257, 277, **11**: 399; seamanship, **6**: 40–41, 41n; trade, **6**: 40–41, 87, 89, 199, 224, 401–2, 426, 428, **7**: 10, 11n, 18, 20, **10**: 199, 199n; historical sketch, **6**: 41–42n; located, **6**: 41–42n, 154, 201–2, 459, 471; food, **6**: 87, 89; customs, **6**: 88–89, 97–98, 435, 439, **7**: 9, **9**: 280; appearance, **6**: 89, 432–34, 437–38; artifacts, **6**: 90n, 97, 208, 210, **7**: 9–10; food, **6**: 154; chiefs, **6**: 155, 159n, 185n, **7**: 15–16, **9**: 266, **11**: 412n; visits, **6**: 192, 195–96, 409, 411, 429–30, **9**: 265, 266n, **11**: 411, 412n, 413; arms and ammunition, **6**: 206–10; relations with the party, **6**: 401, 403, **11**: 429; head deformation, **6**: 433, 437; departures, **6**: 436–40; numbers, **6**: 475, 485; fishing, **7**: 12–13, **11**: 434; gifts, **9**: 281; mentioned, **6**: 441, 474, 490, **9**: 277, **10**: 201n, **11**: 434n. *See also* Kathlamet language

Cathlamet Point (Point Samuel), **6**: 89, 90n, 459, 471, **9**: 232

Cathlapotle (Kalute, Quathlahpohtle) Indians: villages, **6**: 23, 457, 470, 477, 484, **7**: 27, 30, 31n, **9**: 282, **10**: 203, **11**: 387, 436, 436n; visits, **7**: 23, 25, **9**: 250; language, **7**: 24, 27, 30, 38, 54, 59, 65, 82; clothes, **7**: 24, 27, 38, 54, 59, 65, 82, 85, **11**: 436; lodges, **7**: 27; artifacts, **7**: 27–28, 36; trade, **7**: 28, **9**: 250, **11**: 387, 436; information from, **7**: 30; customs, **7**: 38; appearance, **7**: 54, 65; distances, **8**: 387; listed, **8**: 405; trade, **9**: 250; gifts, **9**: 282; mentioned, **6**: 24n, 474, **7**: 26n, **9**: 283n, **10**: 203n, **11**: 388n

Catholic Creek, **5**: 260n
Catlett (Catlate), Hanson, **2**: 168n, 186–87, 190n, 191, 213–14
Catlin, George, **2**: 496n, 499n, **3**: 190n, 214n
Catlinite, **2**: 497–98, 499n
Catoptrophorus semipalmatus, **4**: 135–36n. *See also* Willet
Catostomidae, **2**: 486n, **4**: 333n, **9**: 174n, **11**: 212n. *See also* Suckers
Catostomus catostomus, **5**: 39n, **6**: 409n. *See also* Sucker, northern
Catostomus platyrhynchus, **6**: 409n, **7**: 246n, **8**: 193n. *See also* Sucker, mountain
Catostomus sp., **5**: 13n, **7**: 177n, **9**: 298n. *See also* Suckers
Cat River, **2**: 458, 463n
Cats, **6**: 76
Cat-tail, common (flag): observed, **4**: 420, **6**: 26–27, **7**: 335, 337; abundance, **5**: 18; and Indians, **6**: 74, 76, 97, 135, 146–47, 186, 216–17, 366, 370, 435–36, 439–40, **9**: 229, 241, 243, **10**: 154, 160–61, **11**: 329, 331, 366; as trade item, **6**: 192, 196; mentioned, **4**: 422n, **5**: 21n, **6**: 29n, 77n, 307n, 368n, **7**: 159n, **9**: 229n, 241n, **10**: 160n, **11**: 331n
Cat-tarkah Indians. *See* Kiowa Apache Indians
Cattle. *See* Cows
Cattle Creek, **8**: 147n, **9**: 345n, **10**: 262n
Caulking, **9**: 122, 124, 181, 276
Causseu (and similar spellings). *See* Cajeux
Cave Gulch, **9**: 317n
Cayuse (Y-e-letpo, Wil-le-let-po) Indians, **5**: 307n, **9**: 320, 320n, **10**: 158n, **11**: 361n, **6**: 479, 482, 489, **7**: 172n, 341, 342n, 346
Ceanothus, redstem, **8**: 12n, 25, 26n
Ceanothus americanus, **8**: 12n. *See also* Redroot

Ceanothus sanguineus, **8**: 12n. *See also* Ceanothus, redstem
Cedar, dwarf. *See* Juniper, creeping
Cedar, eastern red, **2**: 110, 111n, 112, 275, 276n, 471–72, 475n, **10**: 30, 30n
Cedar, red, **3**: 46–47, 48n, 57, 61–62, 74–75, 79, 87, 92–93, 96, 98, 133, 135, 360, **9**: 38, 38n, 42, 53–54, 56, 60, 140, 394. *See also* Juniper, Rocky Mountain; Redcedar, western
Cedar, Rocky Mountain red, **4**: 17, 19n, 35, 140, 145, 147, 149, 157–58, 161–62, 178, 229, 284, 387, 402, 414, 419, 421, 430, **9**: 131n, 193, 194n, **10**: 88, 88n, 114, 114n, 117, **11**: 250–51, 251n. *See also* Juniper, Rocky Mountain
Cedar, western red. *See* Redcedar, western
Cedar, white. *See* Redcedar, western
Cedar (Catfish) Creek (Mont.), **8**: 258–60, 261n, 262n, 389, 406
Cedar Creek (Idaho), **5**: 216, 217n, 225, 227n, **8**: 26, 27n
Cedar Creek (Mo.), **2**: 275–76, 277n, **3**: 339–40, 370, 377, **8**: 377, 395, **9**: 10, 377, 378n
Cedar (Pape, Pappie) Creek (Kans.), **2**: 364–65, 365n, **9**: xviii, 23, 23n, 368n, 386
Cedar (Three Sisters) Creek (S. Dak.), **3**: 100, 102, 103n, **10**: 43, 43n
Cedar Fort. *See* Fort aux Cedres
Cedar Island (Mo.), **2**: 275, 276n
Cedar Island (S. Dak.). *See* Dorion Island No. 2
Cedar River (Elk Creek), **3**: 351–52, 384n
Cedars: observed, **5**: 39, 57, 355–56, **9**: 42–43, 131, 150–52, 160, 186, 190, 193, **10**: 30, 42, 117, **11**: 69, 152–53, 161–62, 180–81, 232–

33, 236–37, 242, 249–50; and Indians, **5**: 150, 359, 361, **7**: 93, 146, 254, **9**: 243–44, **10**: 167, 194, **11**: 365–66, 373; abundance, **5**: 379, **11**: 239, 241; use, **9**: 63–64; mentioned, **4**: 93, **10**: 35. *See also* Redcedar, western
Celilo (Great) Falls: arrive at, **5**: 4, 323, 326n, 376, **9**: 243; portage, **5**: 323, 326n, 327–29, 365, **7**: 1, 153–54, 155n, **9**: 243–44, **10**: 160, **11**: 366–68; maps, **5**: 326n; navigational problems, **5**: 331, 333; animals, **6**: 142, 144, 318, 320, 323, 328, 331, 340–41, 345, 347, 351, 354–55, 360, 390, 408, 411, 413–15, 421, 425, **7**: 282; and Indians, **6**: 201–4, 270, 313, 329, 334, 474, 478–79, 483, 486, **7**: 84, 123–24, 129, 130n, 132, 144–45, 162, **10**: 223; conditions, **6**: 315, 324, 370–71, 402; characteristics, **6**: 335–36, 338, **7**: 34; distances, **6**: 455, 461, 493, **8**: 385, **9**: 232, **10**: 153, 153n, 173, **11**: 364; located, **6**: 469, **7**: 18, 20; Indian name for, **7**: 162n; plants, **7**: 311; listed, **8**: 404, **10**: 174; described, **9**: 244–45, **10**: 161–62, **11**: 365–66, 368; latitude, **9**: 244, **11**: 367–68; mentioned, **2**: 28, **5**: 227, 228n, 230, 250, 318, 340n, 343, 345, 377, **6**: 40, 84, 86, 91–93, 136–37, 211–12, **7**: 49, 52–53, 56, 166, 168, 189, 206–7, 218, 229, 305, 330, **8**: 72, 73n, 384, 393–94, 413, **9**: 243n, 280, 286, 289n, 293, 295, **10**: 160n, 213, 213n, 224, **11**: 367n, 376, 382–84, 397
Celtis douglasii, **5**: 263n. *See also* Hackberry, netleaf
Celtis occidentalis, **2**: 315n, **8**: 418n, **9**: 54n. *See also* Hackberry
Celtis reticulata, **5**: 263n. *See also* Hackberry, netleaf

Cenas, Blaze, **2**: 54, 65, 138

Centrarchidae, **2**: 433n. *See also* Sunfish

Centrocercus urophasianus, **4**: 260n, **5**: 76n, **6**: 373n, **7**: 198n, **9**: 240n, **10**: 132n, **11**: 358n. *See also* Grouse, sage

Certificates and commissions, **3**: 23–24, 26–27, 31–32, 121–22, 123n, 210, **4**: 11

Cervis elaphus, **11**: 40n. *See also* Elk

Cervus dama, **3**: 79n. *See also* Deer, fallow

Cervus elaphus, **2**: 307n, **6**: 20n, **7**: 9n, **8**: 59n, **10**: 20n. *See also* Elk

Ceryle alcyon, **4**: 124n, **5**: 13n, **6**: 384n, **7**: 32n. *See also* Kingfisher, belter

Chaboillez, Charles, **3**: 201n, 220n, 257, 309n, 310, 492n, **10**: 66n

Chaffin Creek, **8**: 163, 164n

Chah-clel-lah Indians. *See* Watlala Indians

Chahulklilhum Village, **6**: 34n

Chah-wah-na-hi-ooks River. *See* Lewis River

Chain, surveyor's (two pole), **1**: 4, **2**: 92–93n

Chalcedony, **5**: 147n

Chalk, **9**: 45, 51, **11**: 63, 68

Chalk, Niobrara, **3**: 14, 15n, 16, 18n, 37–38, 39n, 45, 473

Challis Volcanics, **5**: 141n, 148n

Chambers, Ephraim, **8**: 419n

Chamomilla suaveolens, **4**: 262n. *See also* Pineapple weed

Chantier Creek, **3**: 126, 127n, **8**: 322, 323n, **9**: 73n, 354n, **10**: 48n, 272n, **11**: 92n

Chapelle Creek. *See* La Chapelle (Smoke) Creek

Chapellel (and similar spellings). *See* Cous

Char, red. *See* Salmon, sockeye

Charadrius montanus, **4**: 419n. *See also* Plover, mountain

Charadrius vociferus, **2**: 452n, **4**: 95n, **7**: 165n, **8**: 418n. *See also* Killdeer

Charbonneau, Jean Baptiste: leaves party, **2**: 8, **8**: 4, 305; fame, **2**: 509–10; birth, **3**: 3, 291, **10**: 72, 73n; listed, **3**: 4, **4**: 9, 11, **8**: 162n, 179, 277, **11**: 8n; biographical sketch, **3**: 291n; accidents, **4**: 2–3, 29, 341, 343, **6**: 1–2, 96–97, 172n; medical problems, **7**: 278, 280–82, 280n, 284–86, 289–91, 294, 296n, 297, 302, 304, 330–31, 334–36, 346–47, **8**: 281, **10**: 232–33; Pompeys Pillar named for, **8**: 3, 228n; as Clark's foster son, **8**: 305–6, 307n; clothes, **9**: 177; mentioned, **2**: 7, 512, **4**: 10, 52, 299, 343n, **8**: 161, 307n, **9**: 265n, 279, **10**: 77n, 105n, 108, 119n, 188n, 232n, 233n, 256n, 268n, **11**: 4n, 215–16, 216n, 410, 411n. *See also* Sacagawea

Charbonneau (Sharbono), Toussaint: joins party, **2**: 7, **3**: 3–4, 228, 316–317, 316n, **9**: 121–22; leaves party, **2**: 8, **3**: 312n, 313, 313n, **8**: 4, 305; fame, **2**: 509–10; biographical sketch, **3**: 228–29n; interpreter, **3**: 230n, 262, 262n, 327, 328n, **5**: 111, 122, 163, **6**: 428n, **7**: 129n, 242–44, **8**: 161, 162n, 302, **9**: 219n, 306n, **10**: 138n, **11**: 275, 309; wives, **3**: 232–33, 271, 272n, 277, 327, **10**: 68; sent out, **3**: 249, 293, **4**: 52, 81, 84n, 88–89, 128, 340, 342, 378, **5**: 14, 44, 129, 304, **6**: 60, **7**: 119, 121, 127–28, 137–39, 271–72, 289–90, 308, 310, **8**: 208–11, 298, **9**: 139, 176, 204, 265, 293, 320, **10**: 108, 119n, 127–28, 236, 255, **11**: 270, 272–73, 410; horse stolen, **3**: 259; information from, **3**: 272, 279, 310, 475, **5**: 165, **8**: 206, 302–3; returns, **3**: 290–91, 306, **5**: 145, **7**: 273, 297, 299, 322, 324, 345, **9**: 208, **10**: 69, 70n, 118, 233, **11**: 119, 243, 280–81, 396; and specimens, **3**: 475; accidents, **4**: 3, 29, 152–54, 341–43, **7**: 322, 324, **9**: 177, **11**: 215–16; listed, **4**: 9, 11, **8**: 74, 162n, 179, 277, **11**: 4n, 8n, 395n, 411n; creek named for, **4**: 36–37, 39, 41n; medical problems, **4**: 52, 427–28, 432, **5**: 18, 42, 44, **8**: 200, **11**: 119; cooking, **4**: 131, 332, 354; hunting, **4**: 232, **9**: 113, 172; and Sacagawea, **4**: 309, **5**: 93; and lower portage camp, **4**: 325–26; duties, **4**: 334–35, **5**: 158, 345, **6**: 157, **7**: 344; scouting, **4**: 417–18, **5**: 18, 24, **6**: 62, 65, 172n, **9**: 188, 193, 254, **10**: 116, 120–21, 175, **11**: 237–38, 249–50, 395; separated, **4**: 430, 432, 433n; visits whale site, **6**: 2, 168–69, 171, 172n; votes, **6**: 84; and species, **6**: 254–55; and Indians, **7**: 134, 162, 294, **10**: 68; and horses, **7**: 159, 161, 173–7; river named for, **8**: 261n; discharged, **8**: 305–6, 307n; visits, **9**: 95, 97, 109; collects food, **9**: 203; trading, **9**: 312, **10**: 212, 230, 233, **11**: 286; stays behind, **10**: 104, 268n; and saltmaking camp, **10**: 187; mentioned, **2**: 512, 522, **3**: 273n, 292, 312, **4**: 10, 298, 301, **5**: 17, 45, 52, 85n, 100, 109, 113–14, 116n, 118, 120, 131, 256, 268, 306, **6**: 73n, 137, **7**: 155–58, 180, 231, 265, 270, 278, 280, 302, **8**: 3, 167, 307n, **9**: 95n, 109n, 172, 172n, 188n, 255n, 265n, 279, 293n, 313n, 320n, **10**: 68n, 72, 78, 105n, 117n, 119n, 120n, 121n, 129n, 175n, 188n, 212n, 230n, 233n, 237n, 256n, **11**: 114n, 120n, 138, 207–8, 208n, 216n, 238n. *See also* Sacagawea

Charbonneau (Joseph Field's) Creek, **4**: 70n, 75n, **8**: 272–75, 274–75n, 279n, 295, 389, 406

Charbonnier Island, **2**: 229, 231–32n

Charbonnier Point, **2**: 230, 232–33, 232n, 234n

Charcoal, **4**: 324, 363, **9**: 111, 113, 120, **10**: 71, 110, **11**: 220–21

Char-cowah Indians. *See* Clowewalla Indians

Charette Creek, **2**: 252, 252n, **3**: 338, 370, 376, 8: 377, 395

Chariton (Charliton, Shariton) River: latitude, **2**: 291–92, 480, **3**: 370, **8**: 378, **11**: 171–72; described, **2**: 291–92, **3**: 342–43; distances, **2**: 405, 408, 487, **8**: 378, **9**: 81, 368n, **11**: 21; listed, **3**: 377, **8**: 395; conditions, **9**: 12, 379, **10**: 13, **11**: 22; mentioned, **2**: 293n, 296, 320n, **8**: 365, 365n, 366n, **9**: 12n, **10**: 13n, **11**: 21n, 22n. *See also* Little Chariton River

Charleston Creek, **2**: 363n, **9**: 22, 23n, 386

Charleston Museum, **12**: 6–8

Chawi Pawnee Indians. *See* Pawnee Indians, Grand or Chawi

Cheat, **7**: 335–36, 337n

Cheese, **2**: 141, **9**: 362

Chehalis (Chiltz) Indians, **6**: 51n, 73, 75, 77n, 154, 159n, 201–2, 437, 459, 475, 486, 491

Che-luc-it-te-quar (and similar spellings) Indians. *See* Wishram-Wasco Indians

Chen caerulescens, **2**: 186n, **3**: 146n, **4**: 18n, **6**: 10n, **7**: 11n, **9**: 143n, **10**: 167n. *See also* Goose, snow

Chenopodium album, **2**: 379n, **4**: 386n, **7**: 338n, **10**: 131n. *See also* Lamb's quarters

Chenopodium fremontii, **7**: 338n. *See also* Goosefoot, Fremont

Cherokee Indians, **3**: 446, 449

Cherries: abundance, **2**: 369–70, 380–81, **3**: 481, **4**: 251, **9**: 162, 309, **10**: 140, 227, **11**: 41, 196, 223; as food, **2**: 433, **9**: 27, **11**: 289–90, 299–

300; observed, **4**: 73, **7**: 112–13, **9**: 26, **10**: 129, 206; purchased, **5**: 261; listed, **8**: 417; and Indians, **9**: 208, 213, **10**: 130, 134, 141, **11**: 286–87, 299–300; mentioned, **2**: 30, **4**: 89, 93, 261, **6**: 139, 288–89, **9**: 28n, 163, 164n, **10**: 207n, 227n, **11**: 188. *See also* Plum, wild

Cherry, bitter, **7**: 114n, 344, 346n, **10**: 207, 207n

Cherry, black, **2**: 369–70, 373n, **8**: 158, 159n, 334, 336n

Cherry, choke: and Indians, **3**: 261, **5**: 142; habitat, **4**: 26, 70, 145, 247; observed, **4**: 28, 94, 236, 238, 241, 388, 396, 414, 429, **5**: 81, 218, 241, **7**: 188, 190, 192, 197, **8**: 7, 11, 79, **9**: 26, 161, 193, 215, 221, **10**: 118, **11**: 222–23, 249, 307; described, **4**: 145–46, **7**: 303, 305–6; use, **4**: 278, 279n, 372, 374, **8**: 208; abundance, **4**: 332, 392, 417, **8**: 320, **9**: 167–68, 174, 182, 216, 308, 388, **10**: 22, 100, 102, 118, 135, **11**: 184–85, 195, 198, 211–12, 250, 293–95, 308–11; as food, **5**: 81, 130, 137, 139, 156, 163; listed, **8**: 417; as food, **9**: 27; mentioned, **2**: 373n, **3**: 261n, **4**: 28n, 29n, 397n, **5**: 86n, 224n, **7**: 114n, 307n, 344, **8**: 158, 209n, 287, 418n, **9**: 28n, **10**: 22n, 101n, **11**: 42n, 186n

Cherry, mahaleb, **2**: 209n

Cherry, pin, **8**: 4, 158, 159n, 287–88, 288n, 334, 336n

Cherry, sour, **2**: 209n, **4**: 145, 148n

Cherry, sweet, **2**: 208, 209n

Cherry (Charbonneau's) Creek (Mont.), **8**: 257, 259–60, 261n, 390, 406

Cherry (Teel) Creek (S. Dak.). *See* Stove (Teel) Creek

Cherry Grows on a Bush (Caltarcota), **3**: 209, 212, 213n, 214n, 276n, 319n, **8**: 304, 305n

Chert, **2**: 111n, 285n, **4**: 405n, **5**: 147n. *See also* Flint

Chesley Island, **2**: 126, 127n

Cheyenne (Chien, Sharha) Indians: information about, **1**: 8; language, **2**: 438, 442n; encountered, **3**: 3, 163; and species, **3**: 85; numbers, **3**: 133; war, **3**: 133, 163; villages, **3**: 133, 175–76, 175n, 178n, **9**: 85; located, **3**: 134, 169, 180, 226; name, **3**: 136, 179n; listed, **3**: 136, 217n, 448; historical sketch, **3**: 167n, 420–21; adopted, **3**: 200–201n, 215; trade, **3**: 251–52, 403; appearance, **3**: 487, **8**: 318–19; and other Indians, **8**: 301, 312–14, 319, **9**: 352, **10**: 64, 270; relations with party, **8**: 312–14, 318–19, **9**: 100, **10**: 270; mentioned, **2**: 200, **3**: 138n, 235n, 400, 402, 416–17, 422, **8**: 317n, 320n, **9**: 85n, **10**: 64n, 270n

Cheyenne Creek, **3**: 176, **11**: 95n

Cheyenne Island, **8**: 322, 323n, **9**: 74n, **10**: 49n, **11**: 93n

Cheyenne (Pawnee) Island, **3**: 128–29, 130n, 132–33, 136n

Cheyenne River: information about, **1**: 8; characteristics, **2**: 401, **3**: 132–33, 135, 348, **4**: 69; listed, **2**: 485, **3**: 31, 373, 376, 380, 479, **8**: 380, 398, 412, **9**: 80–81, 367n, **11**: 174; arrive at, **3**: 132, **9**: 74, 353, **10**: 49, 271, **11**: 93; name, **3**: 137n, 171n, 222, 223n, **9**: 75n, **10**: 49n, **11**: 93n; described, **3**: 140, **8**: 322; Indians, **3**: 238, 258n, 413–17, 419, 421–26, 483, **8**: 321; and specimens, **3**: 470; animals, **3**: 482, **8**: 417; mentioned, **2**: 404n, **3**: 130n, 136n, 356, 358–60, **8**: 248, 250n, 323n, **9**: 74n, 354n, **10**: 271n

Chicago, Ill., **3**: 357

Chickasaw Bluffs, **2**: 147

Chickasaw Indians, **2**: 85n, **3**: 446, 449

Chickens (dunghill fowl), **5**: 74, 76n, 129, 131, **6**: 370–71, 373n

Chicot (Boat) Island, **3**: 55, 57n, 59, **9**: 56, 56n, **10**: 37, 37n, **11**: 71n

Chicot (Sheeco) Island. *See* Harrison (Sheeco) Island

Chief Joseph Pass, **5**: 186n

Chien, **3**: 137n. *See also* Cheyenne Indians; Cheyenne River

Chil-lar-la-wil. *See* Shelathwel

Chiltz Indians. *See* Chehalis Indians

Chiluckittequaw (and similar spellings) Indians. *See* Wishram-Wasco Indians

Chimnapam (and similar spellings) Indians. *See* Yakima Indians

Chimney Bluffs, **8**: 237, 240, 241n, 390, 407

Chimneys, **9**: 95–96, 98, 262, **10**: 184, **11**: 406–7

China Creek, **9**: 316, 317n

China Garden Creek, **9**: 317n

China Island, **5**: 233n, **9**: 229, 229n, **10**: 148, 148n, **11**: 331–32, 332n

Chin-ni-ni, **6**: 154, 159n

Chinookan Indians: canoes, **5**: 327–28, 328n; language, **5**: 346n, **6**: 34n, 61n, 82n, 91n, 98n, 115n, 120n, 162–63, 164n, 180, 184n, 198n, 317n, 340–41, 342n, 434, 496n, **7**: 21n, 61n, 65, 85, 145n; lodges, **6**: 34n, 221n, **7**: 64–65, 84; war, **6**: 155; head deformation, **6**: 159n; customs, **6**: 273–74, **7**: 85; medical problems, **6**: 286–87n, **7**: 65, 70n, 85–86, 89n; located, **6**: 457; villages, **6**: 470, **7**: 57, 61n, 64, 79, 84; numbers, **6**: 475, 478, 484, 486, **7**: 114n; clothes, **7**: 65, 85; appearance, **7**: 85; mentioned, **6**: 472n, 490, 492n

Chinookan language, **5**: 317, 319n, 326n, 329, 336n, 340n, 345, 346n, 347, 353n, 371, 380n, **6**: 34n, 45n, 76n, 77n, 154, 159n, 185–86n, **7**: 8n, 12, 14n, 22n, 25, 25n, 26n, 31n, 36n, 41n, 60n, 89n, 93n, 114n, 122n, **9**: 274n, 278n, 285n, 288n, 292n, **10**: 163n, 164n, 173n, 177n, 178n, 195, 195n, 199, **11**: 374n, 378n, 387n, 396n, 399n, 409n, 413n, 417n, 424n, 430n, 436n, 437n, **12**: 10n. *See also* Lower Chinookan language; Upper Chinookan language

Chinook Indians: canoes, **6**: 1, 98n, 270, 272n, 325, 327, 418, 436, **9**: 252; relations with the party, **6**: 18, 50, 60–61, 72, 82, 164–65, 194, 239, 241, 327, 330–31, **8**: 79, **10**: 171, 175–76, 188, 194, **9**: 253–54, **11**: 397–98; language, **6**: 34n, 50–51, 76n, 82, 89, 164–65, 180, 192, 194, 196, 236, 351, 353, **7**: 18, 20, 29, 35, 41n, 111, **10**: 173n; historical sketch, **6**: 51n; located, **6**: 51n, 70, 154, 201–2, 458, 470, **10**: 173n, 175; trade, **6**: 53, 61, 83, 164–65, 189, 221–22, 224, **9**: 252; villages, **6**: 59, 182, **9**: 252–53, **11**: 431; food, **6**: 60–61, 61n, 76, 188, **10**: 176; chiefs, **6**: 61n, 73n, 83, 85, 154, 159n, 330, 332, 416, 418, **7**: 7–8, **10**: 198, 198n, **11**: 428n; lodges, **6**: 65, 70, 154, 184, 218–21; medical problems, **6**: 65, 76, 239, 241, 286–87n, 416, 418; camps, **6**: 68n; customs, **6**: 75, 97–98, 98–99n, 142, 148n, 168–69, 182, 186, 190–91, 368n, 416, 418, 425, 427, **10**: 199, 200n; tattooing, **6**: 75, 435, 439; clothes, **6**: 75–76, 89, 97,

180, 192, 194, 196, 221–22, 325, 327, 432–36, 438–40, **7**: 8, 18, 20, 29, 35, **10**: 172, 175–76, 194, 199, **11**: 395; appearance, **6**: 75–76, 89, 168, 180, 190, 432–34, 437–38, **11**: 396, 431–32; pipes, **6**: 83, 179, 196; ceremonies, **6**: 85; artifacts, **6**: 97, 208, 211–14, 218, **11**: 397; war, **6**: 155; arms and ammunition, **6**: 206–10; fishing, **6**: 211–14; visits, **6**: 325, 327, **9**: 256, 277, 280, **10**: 184, 194, 199, **11**: 408, 428; head deformation, **6**: 435, 437; numbers, **6**: 475, 485; encountered, **7**: 7–8, 10, **11**: 395–96, 432; war, **7**: 18, 20; information from, **11**: 395; name, **11**: 398; mentioned, **6**: 474, 490, **7**: 8n, **9**: 256n, **11**: 398n, 439

Chinook jargon, **6**: 121, 122n, 164n, 178, 179n, 186n

Chinook Point, **6**: 51n, 73n, 115n, 470, **9**: 232, 254n, 255n, **10**: 171n, 174n, **11**: 394n

Chinook River, **6**: 62, 65, 67n, **9**: 232, 254, 255n, **10**: 173, 175, 175n. *See also* Wallacut River

Chionanthus virginica, **7**: 195n. *See also* Fringe-tree

Chip (Valley) Creek, **4**: 217, 221n, **6**: 449, 463, **9**: 157, 158n, **10**: 95, 96n, **11**: 177, 178n

Chipmunk, eastern, **6**: 347n

Chipmunk, Townsend's, **6**: 313, 315, 317n, 346, 347n, 348

Chippewa Indians, **2**: 132n, 223–24, 224n, 225n, **3**: 35n, 120n, 236, 236n, 305, 305n, 317, 406–15, 429, 433, 439–44, 449, 492n, **4**: 346n, **5**: 122, 157n, **6**: 240–41, **10**: 48n, 229n

Chippewa Island, **10**: 91, 91n

Chironomidae, **2**: 186n, **7**: 46n. *See also* Midges

Chisels, **4**: 275, 279, **6**: 265, 271

Chishuck, **6**: 461, 471

Chive, wild, **7**: 26, 31n, 46, 309, 311, 312n, **9**: 282, 283n

Chiwere language group. *See* Siouan language

Chloride, mercurous, **2**: 86n

Chocartooch. *See* Badger

Chocolate, **8**: 363. *See also* Medicine

Choctaw Indians, **3**: 446–47, 449–50

Chopunnish Indians. *See* Nez Perce Indians

Chopunnish River. *See* North Fork Clearwater River

Chordeiles minor, **4**: 346n. *See also* Nighthawk, common

Chordeiles minor hesperis, **4**: 346n. *See also* Nighthawk, Pacific

Chouteau, Auguste, **1**: 16n. 32

Chouteau, Brigitte Saucier, **2**: 240, 243n

Chouteau, Jean Pierre, **2**: 179, 180n, 206, 206n, 210n, 211, 211n, 237, 238n, 240, 243n, 266, 267n, 376n, **3**: 340, **8**: 346, 347n, 371–72, 371n, 372n, **9**: 373n, **11**: 22–23, 23n

Chouteau, Pierre Jr., **8**: 347n

Chouteau, Pierre, **1**: 16n. 32

Chouteau, René Auguste, **2**: 134n, 179, 180n, 234n, 237, 238n, 240, 243, 266, 267n, 376n, **8**: 351, 352n, 357, 371, 371n, **9**: 359, 359n, 361, **10**: 276, 276n, **11**: 22–23, 23n

Chouteau (Bourgeois), Marie Therese, **2**: 130n

Chouteau Bluffs, **3**: 51n

Chouteau (Goat) Creek, **3**: 49, 51n, **8**: 333n, **9**: 54, 54n, 357n, **10**: 35, 36n, 274n, **11**: 69, 70n

Chouteau Island, **2**: 130–31, 132n

Christy, William, **8**: 371, 371n, 372n

Christy's Tavern, **8**: 4

Chronometers: use, **1**: 4; prob-

lems with, **2**: 91, 97, 135, 139, 228, 381–82, 385–86, 388–89, 412–13, 506, **3**: 213, 260, 275, 275n, **4**: 372, **5**: 237, 366, **6**: 255, 257, 410, 417, **7**: 127, 340, 360, **8**: 127; described, **2**: 412–13; damaged, **7**: 266–68, 320, **8**: 82, 85; mentioned, **2**: 87n, 92n, **3**: 216, **5**: 56, **6**: 258n. *See also* Astronomical observations; Watches

Chrysemys picta, **4**: 333n. *See also* Turtle, painted

Chrysomelidae, **7**: 78n. *See also* Beetles

Chrysops sp., **5**: 58n, **7**: 312n, **8**: 144n. *See also* Fly, deer

Chrysothamnus nauseosus, **3**: 470, **7**: 172n, **10**: 218n. *See also* Rabbitbrush, rubber

Chrysothamnus viscidiflorus, **7**: 172n, **10**: 218n. *See also* Rabbitbrush, twisted leaf

Chub, Columbia River, **7**: 171, 173n

Chub, white. *See* Bass, striped; Sauger

Chucktins Creek, **6**: 461, 471

Churchhill River, **10**: 4n, 6n

Chymnappo (and similar spellings) Indians. *See* Yakima Indians

Cicely, sweet, **10**: 137n

Cicely, western sweet, **10**: 137n

Cicuta douglasii, **7**: 276n. *See also* Hemlock, water

Ci-in-twar, **6**: 154

Cinchona, **2**: 349n, **4**: 302n, **5**: 14n, **8**: 159n. *See also* Medicine, barks

Cincinnati, Ohio, **2**: 59, 85n

Cinnamon, **6**: 135, 174, 197

Cinquefoil. *See* Silver-weed

Cinque Hommes Creek, **2**: 116–17, 117n

Circumferenter, **2**: 87, 87n, 413, **4**: 341. *See also* Astronomical observations; Instruments, scientific

Circus cyaneus, **6**: 378n. *See also* Harrier, northern

Cirsium edule, **6**: 77n, **7**: 60n, **9**: 292n. *See also* Thistle, edible

Cirsium foliosum, **4**: 422n, **5**: 21n, **9**: 189n, **11**: 238n. *See also* Thistle, elk

Cirsium sp., **9**: 39n. *See also* Thistles

Cirsium undulatum, **5**: 21n. *See also* Thistle, wavyleaf

Cisco, **6**: 346n. *See also* Whitefish

Citadel Rock, **4**: 228, 234n

Citrullus sp., **2**: 437–38n. *See also* Watermelons

Citrullus vulgaris, **2**: 437n. *See also* Watermelons

Civet, **6**: 355n

CK (Teapot) Creek, **4**: 182n, 183–84, 186, 187n, **6**: 448, 463, **9**: 153, 153n, **10**: 91n, **11**: 165n

Clackamas (Clarkamos) Indians, **6**: 478, 486, 491, **7**: 59, 62n, 66, 70n, 81–82, 93, **9**: 285, 285n, **11**: 439, 440n

Clackamas (Clarkamos) River, **7**: 60n, 62n, 82, 92–93, **8**: 415, **9**: 285n

Clacks-star Indians. *See* Clatskanie Indians

Clahclellar (and similar spellings) Indians, **7**: 96–99, 100n, 101–2, 105, 108–9, **9**: 290, 290n, **10**: 208n

Clah-in-na-ta Indians, **7**: 26, 30, 31n, 34

Claiborne, Richard, **2**: 74, 74n

Clamorgan, Jacques, **1**: 8, **2**: 253n

Clams, **6**: 407, 409n, 420–21

Clan-nah-quah Indians, **7**: 32–35, 36n

Clan-nar-min-na-mun Indians. *See* Katlaminimin Indians

Clark, Frances, **6**: 29n, **7**: 17n, **9**: 281n

Clark, George Rogers, **2**: 1, 94n, 107, 109n, 119n, 139n, 240n, 244n, 295n, 513, **3**: 203, 205n

Clark, George Rogers Hancock, **1**: 4, **2**: 538

Clark, Jonathan, **1**: 18n. 93, **2**: 15–16, 240n, 541, **3**: 106n, 251n, 387, **8**: 372n

Clark, William: papers, **1**: 3–4, 7, 11; and maps, **1**: 3–4, 8–13, 19nn. 116–20, **2**: 114n, 116n, 132n, 134n, 149n, 153, 153n, 181n, 415–16, 417n, 418, 420, 428, 432, **3**: 39n, 76n, 99n, 114n, 178n, 227n, 260, 268, 268n, 270n, 275n, 303n, 308, 367, 369, 385–86n, **4**: 266, 336–37, 337n, 359, 362, 410n, **6**: 3, 307–9, 311n, **7**: 3, 74n, 219n, 233n, 315n, **8**: 94–95, 197n, 203n, 287, 344n, **12**: 1, 8; and geographical information, **1**: 6–8, 11, 13; and Nicholas Biddle, **1**: 12; journal-keeping methods, **1**: 16n. 30, 18n. 107, **2**: 128, 128n, 133, 133n, 150n, 168–69, 171n, 174n, 215, 215n, 229n, 232n, 318, 320n, 370, 373–74, 373n, 376n, 379, 382n, 444, 446n, 488, 490n, **3**: 22, 23n, 47, 78, 80n, 100, 103n, 104, 106n, 125, 127n, 134–35, 137n, 140, 140n, 169, 171–72n, 217, 220n, 224, 225n, 231, 231n, 253, 254n, 271, 271n, 285n, 293, 295n, 298, 298n, 327–29, 327–28n, 328n, 331n, 333–36, 383n, 386–87, **4**: 198, 200n, 228, 234n, 304, 305n, 309n, 317n, 321n, 349n, 350, 350n, 388, 391n, 425, **5**: 21–22n, 88, 92, 94n, 95n, 100, 156, 157n, 160, 162, 167, 173, 174n, 182n 197, 198n, 199, 199n, 205, 205n, 213–14, 214n, 226, 228n, 231n, 241, 243n, 277, 283n, 321, 326n, 345n, 346, 348n, **6**: 2–3, 7, 9n, 32, 34n, 59, 60n, 69, 71n, 88, 90n, 101, 104n, 112, 115n, 145–46, 146n, 148n, 153, 158n, 159–60n, 169, 172n, 229, 230n, 246, 248–49n, 257, 257–58n, 262n, 288, 290n, 309,

311n, 374n, 435, 440n, 445–46, 473–74, 477, 477n, 481n, 482, 488–89n, 492, **7**: 1, 8n, 35, 37n, 74, 74n, 76, 78n, 87, 89n, 127, 130n, 143, 145n, 178, 182–83, 187, 209, 299, 302n, 306, 307n, **8**: 3–4, 89, 90n, 92, 92n, 109, 111n, 153n, 158n, 167, 169n, 178, 180n, 198n, 201, 204, 207n, 215, 221n, 233, 235n, 263, 266n, 275, 277, 279n, 287, 288n, 295, 296n, 298–99, 299–300n, 300n, 372n, 376, 383, 387, 394, 410–11n, 411, 411n, 414n, 415, 415n, **9**: xii, xv, xvii, 373n, 382–83, 390, **11**: 4n, 6n; biographical sketch, **2**: 4, 513; scouting, **2**: 89, 93–94, 153–54, 154n, 168, 172, 269, 272n, 275–76, 286–87, 291–92, 298, 304, 317–18, 318n, 353, 366–67, 369–70, 374–75, 380–81, 394–398, 401–3, 421–24, 428–29, 447–48, 452, 454n, 457, 459, 464, 467–69, 503–5, **3**: 7–10, 37–39, 42, 46–47, 53, 55, 57–58, 66–67, 70–71, 74–75, 87, 89–90, 92–94, 100–102, 104–5, 144–45, 148–49, 179–80, 183–88, 208, 215, 219, 223, 225–26, **4**: 3–4, 15, 19, 27, 30, 32, 34, 38, 42–46, 48–49, 51–52, 57–59, 62, 64, 73, 81–82, 85, 87–90, 102–6, 108, 110, 112, 114, 118, 120, 123–25, 128, 134, 140, 143, 159, 161, 164–68, 176, 178, 180–81, 189, 191, 198, 200–201, 203, 211, 213, 215–17, 219, 225, 228, 230, 232, 238–40, 247, 250–53, 256, 259–61, 300, 302, 304, 307, 310, 319, 340, 342, 348, 366–68, 385, 396, 398–99, 401, 403, 407, 412, 414, 417–21, 423, 425–27, 430–31, 438, **5**: 3, 34, 37–38, 113, 115, 118, 131n, 152, 155, 162–63,181, 285, 287, 304–5, 321, 329, 335,

338, 355–56, 358, 360–62, **6**: 2, 12, 15, 17, 23–24, 44–45, 48–49, 62, 98, 116–17, 450, 458, **7**: 1, 17, 54, 56–59, 64, 79–86, 117, 117n, 119, 121, 157–58, **8**: 1–3, 38–39, 41, 164, 205, 230–32, 286, 297, 338, 353, 359, 361, **9**: 25, 28, 35, 37, 42, 44, 52, 55–58, 60, 62, 64, 92–93, 132–33, 138–39, 144–47, 151–54, 156, 161–63, 181, 186, 188–89, 194, 203, 211, 213, 229–30, 232, 240, 254, 255n, 259, 285, 292, 393–94, **10**: 20, 30–31, 36, 61, 61n, 81, 83, 90, 98–99, 114, 116, 127–28, 131, 147–48, 175, 176n, 181, 205, 206n, **11**: 60–61, 71, 78–79, 106, 139, 143–44, 152–53, 166–68, 184–87, 191, 195, 230–31, 234, 237–38, 252–53, 270, 332–33, 357–59, 395–96, 403–4, 438–39; medical problems, **2**: 101, 108, 154–55, 165–66, 168, 170, 172–73, 172n, 182, 272–73, 278, 282, 293, 306, **3**: 19–20, 89, 124–25, 155, 160–61, 191, 194–96, 198–200, 204, 230, 268, 293, 317, **4**: 332, 404–5, 409, 417, 427, 431–32, 433n, 436, 438, **5**: 1, 7, 9, 11, 13–14, 24n, 33, 35, 43, 46–47, 54–55, 59–60, 63, 177, 162–63, 219, 223, 227, 229–30, 232, 234, 246–49, **6**: 44, 105–7, 181, 450, **7**: 164, **8**: 55, 359, **9**: 190–91, **10**: 118–19, **11**: 243–46; receives messages, **2**: 137, 138n, 139, 139n, 145, 157, 167, 180, 205, 211, 211n, 212, 213n, 214, **4**: 295, **5**: 42–43, 175, **7**: 133–34; sends messages, **2**: 142, 155, 166, 180, 191–92, 201, 211, 214, 237, **3**: 121–22, 218, 224, **4**: 407, 427–28, **5**: 162–63, **7**: 126, 132–34, **8**: 3, 151n, 156, 179, 281, **9**: 187, 190, 196, 211, 228, 293, 346n, **10**: 115,

118, 132, 145, 263, 264n, **11:** 233–34, 241–42, 323–24; hunting, **2:** 153, 300, 317–18, 374–75, 377–78, 380, 397–98, 421–22, 447, 464, 502–5, **3:** 58, 65–66, 74–76, 78–79, 89–90, 100–102, 144–45, 179–80, 184–86, 188–89, 253–55, 257, 265, 266n, 285–86, 293–94, 306, **4:** 21, 30, 33, 36, 39, 45–46, 51–52, 57–58, 64, 73, 79, 82, 85, 87, 102, 105, 113–15, 118, 120–21, 123, 126, 128, 130, 134, 140, 143–44, 147, 149–51, 155, 159, 161, 164–68, 171, 174, 176, 178, 184–85, 189, 191, 193, 211, 213, 219, 281, 295, 338–39, 351, 354, 363–64, 399, 403, 405, 412, 414, 424, **5:** 27, 37–38, 93–94, 98, 100, 129, 131, 186, 191, 202–3, 209, 211, 216, 239, 242, 244, 288, 303, 305–6, 327, 337, 339, 366, 369, **6:** 22, 24, 103–4, 117, 119–21, 181, 449, 458, **7:** 91, 116, 278–79, **8:** 60, 80, 163, 178, 190, 206, 219, 225–26, 231–32, 238, 259, 268, 272, 276, 281–83, 286, 328–29, 333, 344, **9:** 12, 16, 24–25, 30, 35–37, 42–44, 56–57, 59–62, 64, 76–77, 86–88, 101–4, 112, 128–30, 132–33, 135–36, 139, 141–47, 149–54, 150n, 156, 158, 166, 178, 180–81, 186, 193–94, 202, 221, 225, 227, 247, 382–83, **10:** 26–27, 30, 38–39, 41–42, 52, 65–66, 72, 79–82, 143, 144n, 145, 210, 218, 274, 274n, **11:** 60, 71–78, 96–97, 110–11, 124–25, 137, 143–44, 147–56, 160–61, 163, 166–68, 176–78, 194–95, 218, 220, 227, 230–31, 233, 243–44, 249–50, 252–53, 266–68, 307, 318, 320–21, 377–78; medical practices, **2:** 165, 172–73, 336, 420, 420n, **3:** 279, 310, 317, **4:** 276–77, 279, 281,

287, 297, 301, 334–35, 365–66, 418, **5:** 232–34, **6:** 312, 315, 318–19, 324, 329, 333, 335, 376, 388, 390, 393–94, 396, 429–30, **7:** 2–3, 164, 178, 180, 186, 209–13, 215, 217, 243, 246–50, 252, 254, 269, 271–73, 278, 280–89, 291, 294, 297, 299, 302, 308, 310, 331, 334, 336, **8:** 46, 57–58, 59n, 162, 202, 204, 209, 290, 295, 300n, 319, 324, 359, **9:** 300, 309, 350, **10:** 148, 222; returns, **2:** 174n, 179, 180n, 201, 206, 318–19, **3:** 13, 285, 292–93, 306, **4:** 261, 318, 348, 436, **5:** 24, 24n, 177–78, 181–82, 182n, 229–30, 242, 286–87, **6:** 72, 73n, 122–22, 126, 151n, 192, 195–96, 262n, **7:** 62, 66, 86, 137, 139, 141, 342, **9:** 16, 53, 64, 114, 163, 170, 188, 190, 213, 228, 230, 260, 265, 285, 295, 320, **10:** 16, 31, 66, 104, 118, 132, 134, 146, 175, 181, 183, **11:** 188, 204–5, 236–37, 242–43, 289–90, 327–28, 332–33, 396, 404, 411; at St. Louis, **2:** 174n, 193, 206; listed, **2:** 194–95, 218, 242, 347; expedition finances, **2:** 201, 205, 239; receives commission, **2:** 213n; ecological observations, **2:** 286, 292, 306, 309, 313–14, 315n, 332, 346–47, 349n, 369–70, 373n, 380–81, 382n, 394, 398, 400n, 428–30, 431n, **3:** 10–11, 188, **4:** 42–44, 74, 123–24, 143, 204–6, 240, 363, **7:** 113, 114–15n, 120, 263, **8:** 210, 345; birthday, **2:** 433; and species, **2:** 435n, 471, 487, 498, **3:** 44, 53, 54n, 64–65, 70–72, 86–87, 317–18, 318n, **4:** 27, 140, 159, 161, **5:** 4, 98, 100, 286–87, 290n, 321, **6:** 139, 426–27, **7:** 201, 295–96, 304, **8:** 174, 200, 238, **9:** 158, 171, 203, **10:** 36, 92, 92n, **11:** 204–5,

269–70; and dispatches, **2:** 472; fishing, **2:** 483, **4:** 365, **5:** 153, 155, 174, 288, **6:** 42–43, 45, **7:** 227, 231, **9:** 40, 203, 395; accidents, **4:** 3, 341–43, **9:** 176–77, 335, **10:** 108, **11:** 215–16, 216n; loses notes, **4:** 310, **9:** 171, **11:** 204, 206; and upper portage camp, **4:** 325, 350, **10:** 108, **11:** 215; and lower portage camp, **4:** 327–28, 330, **9:** 173, **11:** 209, 210n; leads detachment, **4:** 370–77, **5:** 24n, **6:** 125, **7:** 104, 108, 125–34, 142–44, **8:** 74, 77, 83, 86n, **9:** 44, 46, 99, 122, 182–83, 182n, 243, 261, 265, 290, 293–94, 320, 330, 332, 332n, 334–35, 334n, 356–57, **10:** 61, 63, 110, 110n, 183, 187–88, 211–13, 212n, 247, 248n, 255, 266, **11:** 60, 108–10, 221–23, 226, 276–77, 288, 367, 405, 410; visits whale site, **6:** 2, 167–69, 171, 180, 183, 192, 262n; surveying, **6:** 60, **9:** 53, 53n, 169–71, **10:** 103, 107, 107n, **11:** 68, 68n, 201, 204–5, 209; votes, **6:** 84; gifts, **6:** 137, **10:** 184; separated, **9:** 16, **10:** 16, 31, **11:** 29, 74, 110–11, 403; clothes, **9:** 177, **10:** 28, **11:** 55–56, 269–70; collects food, **9:** 205; and botanical specimens, **12:** 1, 1on

Clark Canyon Creek, **9:** 204, 204n

Clark Creek, **10:** 80, 8on, **11:** 136, 136n

Clark Fork (Clark's, East Fork Clark's, Flathead) River: name, **1:** 10–11, **2:** 26, **7:** 216, 218, 219n, **10:** 157, 246n; and maps, **1:** 11, 13, 18n. 106; listed, **3:** 382; distances, **5:** 237, **6:** 308, 310, 493, **8:** 82; described, **5:** 192, 196, 199, **8:** 83, 100, 291, **10:** 246, 248; Indians, **6:** 480–82, 488, **8:** 65, 79, 85, 394; explored, **8:** 2; animals, **8:** 101,

Clark Fork (*continued*)
143; listed, **8**: 383, 401; mentioned, **3**: 298n, **5**: 185, 194, 198n, 231n, **6**: 311n, 325n, **8**: 26, 27n, 69n, 80n, 86n, 87–89, 87n, 89n, 90n, 104, **9**: 338, 338n, **10**: 157n, 247, 248–49n

Clarkia pulchella, **7**: 307n. *See also* Ragged robin

Clark-Maximilian maps. *See* Maps

Clarks Fork Yellowstone (Clark's Fork) River, **4**: 71, **8**: 212n, 216–17, 219–20, 221n, 277–79, 279n, 391–92, 408

Clark's map of 1805. *See* Maps

Clark's map of 1810. *See* Maps

Clark's Point of View. *See* Tillamook Head

Clark's River. *See* Bitterroot River; Clark Fork River; Deschutes River; Pend Oreille River

Clarksville, Ind., **2**: 6, 59, 85, 510

Clatskanie (Clacks-star, Claxtar) Indians, **6**: 155, 159n, 478, 484, 490, **7**: 26, 30, 31n, 32, 34

Clatskanie River, **7**: 14n, **9**: 281n, **10**: 202n, **11**: 434n

Clatsop Indians: information from, **1**: 11, **6**: 95–96, 141, 154, 302, 305, 336–37, 416, **11**: 404, 410; relations with the party, **6**: 4, 82, 87, 118–19, 167, 177, 275–76, 335, 344, 349, 384, 414, 416, 418–19, 426, 428, 444, **7**: 9n, 10, **9**: 257, 267, 274, 277–78, **10**: 194, 199n, **11**: 414–15, 419, 423–25, 429–30; located, **6**: 73, 75, 76–77n, 112, 154, 201–2, 459, 471; chiefs, **6**: 73, 118, 136, 154, 159n, 222–23, 342, 346, 420n, 428n, **9**: 260, 275, 275n, 278, **11**: 410n, 414n, 426; visits, **6**: 75, 81, 122–24, 135–36, 138–39, 147, 152–53, 162–63, 216, 218–19, 223–24, 232, 234,

299–300, 325, 327, 333, 335, 337, 342, 358, 381–82, 395–96, 443, **9**: 256, 260–62, 264, 264n, 267, 271, 273, 275–76, 275n, 277n, 278, **10**: 189, 196–97, 198n, 199, **11**: 404, 408–10, 414, 419, 421–23, 427–28, 430; historical sketch, **6**: 76–77n; language, **6**: 81–82, 164–65, 180, 184, 192, 194–96, 236, 243–44, 351, 353, 440n, **7**: 18, 20, 29–30, 35, 41n, 105, 109, **10**: 177n; trade, **6**: 81, 106, 123, 135–36, 144, 153, 161, 163–65, 189, 199, 221–22, 224, 336, 349, 360, 381–82, 409, 411, **7**: 18–20; canoes, **6**: 81, 117–18, 135, 235, 270, 285–86, 325, 327, 336, 342, 346, 414–16, 418, 436; medical problems, **6**: 81, 285–86, 286–87n, 444, **7**: 65, 86; movements, **6**: 87, 140, 143; villages, **6**: 117–18, 120n, 122, 136, 140n, 167, 171–72, 177, 182, 184n, 275, **8**: 387, **9**: 260, 277, **10**: 187, 187n, **11**: 404, 404n, 422, 424–25, 428; utensils, **6**: 118–19; customs, **6**: 118–19, 120n, 136, 137n, 142, 148n, 168–69, 186, 190–91, 233, 235, 285–86, 360, 365, 435, 439; lodges, **6**: 118–19, 167, 184, 218–21; food, **6**: 118, 136, 139, 163, 188; artifacts, **6**: 135, 208, 211–14; appearance, **6**: 142, 168, 180, 184, 190, 432–34, 437–38; pipes, **6**: 179, 196; clothes, **6**: 180, 184, 192, 194–96, 221–22, 223n, 235, 249, 251, 253n, 335–37, 342, 346, 381–82, 414–15, 434–36, **7**: 18, 20, 29, 35, **8**: 151, 152n, 419, **9**: 264, 267, 273, 277–78, **10**: 177, 194, **11**: 409, 414, 422–23, 430; arms and ammunition, **6**: 206–10, 233, 235; fishing, **6**: 211–14; departures, **6**: 235–36, 302, 305, 347, 349, 398,

400; head deformation, **6**: 433, 437; numbers, **6**: 475, 485; prisoners, **6**: 476; encountered, **7**: 12–13, **9**: 281, **10**: 177, 201, **11**: 433; name, **11**: 398; mentioned, **6**: 2, 119, 474, 490, **7**: 14n, **9**: 256n, 262, **10**: 188n, 196n, 202n, **11**: 398n, 409n, 422n, 425n, 428n

Clatsop River. *See* Necanicum River

Claxtar (and similar spellings) Indians. *See* Clatskanie Indians

Clay, **2**: 113, 300, 364–65, 394, 397–98, 440, 447–48, 452n, 471–72, 474, 502, 504–6, **3**: 16, 37–38, 42, 44, 46, 318, 340, 474, 477, **4**: 15, 18n, 47n, 73, 103, 106, 130, 135n, 140, 176, 208, 255, 262, 264n, 281, 283, 293, 296n, 298, 299n, 383, 419, **5**: 10n, 18, 45, 52n, 63n, 78, 85n, 196n, **6**: 66, 179n, 194, 230n, **8**: 114n, 118, 120n, 123, **9**: 23, 45, 139, 357, 388, **10**: 28, 92, 116, **11**: 70. *See also* Loess; Quaternary deposits

Clay Creek. *See* Whiskey (Fourth of July) Creek

Clayoquot Sound, **6**: 191n

Claystone, **8**: 261n

Claytonia lanceolata, **8**: 52n. *See also* Spring beauty, western

Cleaning and dressing. *See* Medicine

Clearwater Mountains, **5**: 94n, **8**: 27n

Clearwater (Flathead, Kooskooskee) River: arrive at, **1**: 10, **2**: 7, 25, 28, **5**: 3, 228n, **7**: 205, 252, 254, 330n, **9**: 228–29, **10**: 147n, **11**: 327–28, 329n, 331–34; maps, **1**: 11, **6**: 308–10; Indians, **4**: 13n, **5**: 289, **6**: 474, 479, 482, **7**: 50, 52, 209–11, 214n, 219, 320, 326, 341, 348n, **8**: 34; characteristics, **5**: 4, 227, 248–50, 256, **7**: 216, 218, 221, 223,

255, 257, 339, 345, **10**: 235–
36; name, **5**: 228n, 248n, **9**:
234n; conditions, **5**: 233, **7**:
318–19, 322n, 350, **8**: 70–
72, **9**: 230, 309, 320, **10**: 227,
234, **11**: 339–43, 345–46;
navigational problems, **5**:
249–51, **9**: 235; distances,
5: 256–58, **6**: 446, 453, 462,
493, **8**: 388, **10**: 173; plants,
6: 284–86, **7**: 266n, **8**: 174n,
11: 341–43, 345–46; ani-
mals, **6**: 331–32, 376–77,
387–88, 415, **7**: 320; located,
6: 467; explored, **7**: 2, 209n;
Indian name, **7**: 53n, **10**:
152, 174n, 222n; hunting
on, **7**: 269, 271, **8**: 45; described, **8**: 31–32, **9**: 228, **10**:
149, 222n, 232; decision at,
8: 46; listed, **8**: 384, 402; directions to, **10**: 132n, 135n,
140, 148; mentioned, **5**:
131n, 197, 198n, 205n, 232–
33, 234n, 237, 240, 249,
250n, 252n, 259n, 260n,
278, 287, 319, 353n, 365, **6**:
311n, **7**: 4, 174, 176, 177n,
190n, 196, 206–7, 212,
219n, 229, 233n, 236n,
255n, 258, 259n, 279, 286,
322, 325, 348–49, 350n, **8**:
1, 14, 21n, 73n, 88, 174n,
389, 412–13, **9**: xvi, 229n,
230n, 231, 234, 235n, 298,
300n, 304, 305n, 306n,
309n, 311–12n, 314n, 315,
318, 318n, 318n, 326, **10**:
148n, 149n, 151n, 152n,
157, 221–22, 222n, 223n,
226n, 227, 227n, 228n, 234,
11: 332n, 334n, 341n, 343n
Clearwater (Werner's) River
(Mont.), **8**: 90, 92, 92n, 101,
383, 401, **10**: 249, 249n
Cleome serrulata, **3**: 468, **12**: 10n.
See also Bee plant, Rocky
Mountain
Clinker, **8**: 250n, 253, 255n,
256n
Cloaks, **9**: 212, **11**: 286. *See also*
Clothing
Cloth, **3**: 310, 413, **5**: 89, 134,

226, 351, 361, **6**: 144n, 147,
187, 205, **7**: 28, 108, 116,
129, 158, 224, 253. *See also*
Clothing
Cloth, wiping, **5**: 230, 231n. *See
also* Arms and ammunition
Clothing: purchased, **2**: 6, **8**:
370–71; aired, **2**: 83, **3**: 313;
washed, **2**: 318, **9**: 24; and
skins, **3**: 76, **4**: 149, 248–
49, 272, 274, 365, **5**: 8, 9, 11,
13, 119, 121, 143, 231, 272,
288, **6**: 47, 93, 103–4, 186,
208, 218–19, 230, 381, 407;
mend, **3**: 76, **5**: 288, **6**: 103–
4; dried, **3**: 77, **4**: 156, **5**:
243, 272; gifts, **3**: 160, **9**: 92;
cached, **4**: 275, 279; portaged, **4**: 334–35; lost, **4**:
341, 343, **8**: 276, **9**: 197, **11**:
215–16, 258; making, **5**: 11,
121, **6**: 85, 339–40, **8**: 152–
53, 209, **9**: 191, **11**: 416–17,
423; wet, **5**: 272, **6**: 42, 47,
53–54; scarcity, **5**: 342–43,
6: 44, 84–86, 93, 130, **7**: 308,
310, **8**: 226, 238; attempted
theft, **6**: 181; as trade item,
6: 187, 205, **7**: 165, 167, **11**:
397; and Indians, **6**: 438;
repaired, **11**: 56, 411; mentioned, **2**: 108, 239, 443n,
3: 237, **4**: 165, 342, 408, **5**:
115, 218, 313n, **6**: 35. *See also
clothes of specific Indian tribes
and* Armbands; Beads; Belts;
Blanket-coat; Blankets;
Breechclothes; Breechcloths;
Breeches; Brooches; Buttons;
Capotes; Caps, Cloaks; Coats;
Combs; Drawers; Durant;
Earrings; Gloves; Gorgets;
Handkerchiefs; Hats; Ho-
siery; Indians; Leggings;
Linen; Moccasins; Overalls;
Plumes; Ribbons; Rings;
Robes; Scarlet; Shells; Shirts;
Shoes; Snowshoes; Socks;
Tippets; Trousers; Vests;
Waistcoats; Woolens
Cloudy. *See* Weather conditions
Clover, large-head, **10**: 216,
216n

Clover, longstalk, **5**: 60n, **8**: 79,
80n, **9**: 330, 330n
Clover, purple prairie, **3**: 456,
463, 467, 469
Clover, red, **5**: 98, 116, **8**: 143,
161, 263, **9**: 198, **10**: 127,
133, 133n, **10**: 216, 216n. *See
also* Thermopsis, mountain
Clover, small-head, **8**: 79, 80n
Clover, white prairie, **3**: 456,
463, 468
Clover, woolly, **8**: 80n
Cloves, **6**: 174, 197
Clowwewalla (Char-cow-ah,
Cush-hooks) Indians, **6**: 478,
486–87, 491, **7**: 60n, 66,
70n, 86
Clyster. *See* Medicine, enema
Coal: described, **2**: 103, 104n,
234n, **8**: 243; abundance, **2**:
112, 113n, 232–33, 321–22,
504–5, **4**: 81, **8**: 248, 266, **9**:
17; observed, **2**: 353, **3**: 204,
4: 17, 19–20, 34, 39, 45–46,
49, 52, 62, 70, 73, 82–83,
159, 161, 195, 198, 202, 205,
208–9, 216, 219, 229, 232,
239–40, 255, **8**: 150, 247–
49, 257–60, 267, 269, 378,
390, 396, 407, 414, **9**: 155,
160, 383, **10**: 60; scarcity, **4**:
103, 105, 107n, 117, 120–
21, 120n, 123, 140, 143,
144n, 227; use, **4**:, 364, 371,
7: 54, 56, 242, 244; mentioned, **2**: 230, 277n, 322n,
354n, 446–47n, **3**: 68n, 73n,
281, **4**: 15, 21n, 23, 63n,
163n, 200n, 207n, 210n,
234n, 257n, 282n, **8**: 151n,
153, 242–45, 246n, 250n,
255n, 256n, 261n, **9**: 111,
368n, **11**: 128–29
Coal, bituminous, **3**: 476, **4**: 198
Coal, lignite, **3**: 73n, 187–88,
189n, **4**: 18n, 41n, 47n, 50n,
84n, 85, 87, 88n
Coal, The (Sho-ta-harro-ra), **3**:
199–200, 200n, 208n, 211,
213n, 232n, 271, 288, 297,
300, 308, 310, 319
Coal Creek, **6**: 26, 28n, **8**: 247,
249, 249n, 250n

Coal Gulch, **5**: 186n

Coast Ranges, **6**: 25n, **7**: 37n, 53n, 70n, **10**: 226n

Coats: as gift, **6**: 72–73, **9**: 47, 67, 79, 123; as trade item, **6**: 187, 205, 346, 414, 416, 421, 423, 426, 428, **7**: 139, 141, 147–48, 325, 328, **9**: 205–6, **10**: 199, 199n, **11**: 276, 429n; making, **6**: 208, **11**: 429; mentioned, **4**: 56, 153, 257, **7**: 308, **8**: 419, **9**: 211. *See also* Clothing

Cobalt, **2**: 500–501, 504–5, **3**: 9, 16–17, 18n, 372, 481, **8**: 379

Cobbles, **5**: 17n, 86n, **8**: 114n, 119n, 124n, 188n, 203n, 240n, 280n

Coboway: biographical sketch, **6**: 123n; gifts, **6**: 123, 141–42, 163–64; visits, **6**: 138–39, 162–63, 214, 216, 232, 234, 342, 346, 384–85, 429, 430, **9**: 275; **10**: 182, 189, 194, **11**: 404, 407, 409, 414, 423, 426, 430; listed, **6**: 154; departures, **6**: 164–65, 235–36, 387, 390, 436, 440; trading, **6**: 336–37; certificate for, **6**: 432, 436; relations with the party, **6**: 444; mentioned, **6**: 112, 115n, 144n, 185n, 428n, **8**: 183n; **9**: 260n, 262n, 264n, 267n, 273n, 275n, 279n; **10**: 182n, 189n, 194n; **11**: 404n, 407n, 410n, 414n, 423n, 426n, 430n

Coccyzus americanus, **8**: 112n. *See also* Cuckoo, yellow-billed

Coccyzus erythropthalmus, **8**: 112n. *See also* Cuckoo, black-billed

Cock, mountain. *See* Grouse, sage

Cock, plains. *See* Grouse, sage

Cocklebur (Kuckould burr) River, **2**: 220

Cockleburs, **2**: 377–78, 379n

Cockles, **6**: 118–19, 120n, 407, 409n, 421

Cockspur thorn, **2**: 309n

Cod, Atlantic, **4**: 100, 102n

Codex journals: tin boxes for, **2**: 9, 11–12, 14, 21, 23–24, 26, 29, 32; discussed, **2**: 9–14, 16–35, 549, **3**: 23n, 78, 80n, 83, 86n, 115n, 137n, 140, 140n, 172n, 225n, 231n, 285n, 295n, 327–28n, 331n, 333–36, **4**: 12n, 135n, 156n, 192n, 350n, 396n, **5**: 29n, 51n, 86n, 102n, 117n, 141n, 146n, 147n, 157n, 174n, 195n, 196n, 198n, 199n, 210n, 214n, 231n, 240n, 245n, 248n, 260n, 263n, 290–91n, 300n, 307n, 325n, 326n, 328n, 336n, 340n, 344n, 346n, 364n, 380n, 381n, **12**: 2–4; Codex A begins, **2**: 215; Codex Aa begins, **2**: 229–30, 240–42; Codex B begins, **2**: 483; listed, **2**: 550–51, 553–62; Codex Ba begins, **3**: 76; Codex C begins, **3**: 135; Codex D begins, **4**: 7; Codex C ends, **4**: 11; Codex D ends, **4**: 185; Codex E begins, **4**: 188; Codex E ends, **4**: 387; Codex F begins, **4**: 391; Codex Fa begins, **5**: 24; Codex Fa ends, **5**: 44; Codex F ends, **5**: 145; Codex Fb begins, **5**: 148; Codex Fb ends, **5**: 173; Codex Fc begins, **5**: 191; Codex Fc ends, **5**: 197; Codex Fd begins, **5**: 211; Codex Fd ends, **5**: 229; Codex G ends, **5**: 259; Codex H begins, **5**: 261; Codex J discussed, **6**: 34n, 290n, 346n; Codex H ends, **6**: 71n; Codex I begins, **6**: 71n; Codex Ia begins, **6**: 94n; Codex Ia ends, **6**: 104n; Codex J begins, **6**: 158n; Codex I discussed, **6**: 160n, 172n, 445–46, 471n, 473, 477n, 481n, 488n, 495n, **8**: 411n; Codex P discussed, **6**: 232n; Codex I ends, **6**: 248n; Codex R discussed, **6**: 346n; Codex J ends, **6**: 442; Codex C discussed, **6**: 446; Codex N discussed, **6**: 446, 471n, **8**: 300n, 305n, 372n, 376–77, 410–11n, 418n; Codex G discussed, **6**: 493n; Codex J, **7**: 46n; Codex K discussed, **7**: 31n, 70n, 89n, 151n, 173n, 194n, 271n, 282n, 307n, 322n; Codex Q discussed, **7**: 31n, 173n; Codex L begins, **7**: 285n, 350n; Codex L discussed, **8**: 69n, 78n, 86n, 90n, 111n, 158n; Codex M discussed, **8**: 70n, 74n, 180n, 270n, 300n; Codex La begins, **8**: 86n; Codex La discussed, **8**: 90n; Codex La ends, **8**: 111n; Codex L ends, **8**: 153n; Codex Lb begins, **8**: 153n; Codex Lb ends, **8**: 158n; Codex M ends, **8**: 299n, 300n; Codex N begins, **8**: 303n; Codex N ends, **8**: 372n; Codex T discussed, **8**: 415n; mentioned, **2**: 225n, 226n, 229n, 231n, 239n, 251n, 261n, 264n, 266n, 269n, 272n, 274n, 281n, 283n, 293n, 299n, 307n, 311n, 312n, 314n, 318n, 320n, 321n, 322n, 325n, 326, 328n, 332n, 335n, 336n, 340n, 343n, 345n, 349n, 354n, 361n, 368n, 373n, 376n, 382n, 386n, 390n, 393n, 397n, 403n, 404n, 413n, 414n, 417n, 418n, 420n, 432n, 433n, 435n, 438n, 447n, 452n, 463n, 466n, 471n, 478n, 482n, 483n, 484n, 485n, 490n, 499n, 502n, 503n, 507n. *See also* Elkskin-bound Journal; Field Notes; First Draft; Voorhis journals

Coe, William Robertson, **1**: 4, 19n. 135

Coeur d'Alene Indians, **6**: 492, **8**: 48

Coeur d'Alene River, **7**: 219n

Coffee, **2**: 203, 217, 394, **4**: 332, **6**: 113

Coffee-tree, Kentucky (coffeenut), **2**: 429–30, 431n, **8**: 416, 418n, **9**: 32, 32n, 54

Coins, **2**: 106, 109n, **6**: 81, **9**: 316, 317n

Colaptes auratus, **4**: 96n, **5**: 223n, **6**: 381n, **7**: 297n, **8**: 78n. *See also* Flicker, common

Col-chote, **6**: 154

Cold. *See* Weather conditions

Colds. *See* Medical problems

Coldwater (Colewater) Creek, **2**: 215n, 227, 242, **8**: 370, 370n, **9**: 3n, **10**: 4n

Colic. *See* Medical problems

Colinus virginianus, **6**: 377n, **7**: 89n. *See also* Bobwhite, northern

Colles, Abraham, **7**: 181n

Collin, Joseph, **1**: 17n. 73, **2**: 256, 526–28

Collins, John: discipline, **2**: 60, 332, **8**: 153n; drunk, **2**: 143, 143n; listed, **2**: 148, 187–88, 194–95, 198–99, 255, **4**: 9, 11, **8**: 139n, 162n, **11**: 4n, 7n, 405n, 408n, 410n, 414n, 426n, 428n; hunting, **2**: 151, 152n, 166, 319, 457, 459, 502, **3**: 77, 79n, 271, 272n, **5**: 235, **6**: 8–10, 12, 40, 138, 140, 172n, 179, 186, 192, 198, 235–36, 290–91, 293, 295, 321, 324–26, 330–31, 333, 335, 356–58, 360, 366–67, 384–85, 387n, 391, 394, 409, 411, 414–16, 418, 420n, 443, **7**: 54, 56, 60n, 71, 74, 76–77, 95, 98, 100, 102–3, 226, 230, 256–60, 267–68, 271n, 274, 281, 284, 289, 297, 299, 326, 328, 336, **8**: 10–11, 38, 140, 146, 174, 176, 178, 322, 326–27, **9**: 30, 33, 36, 43, 52, 109, 249, 255n, 263, 263n, 265, 271, 274–75, 277, 284, 289, 307, 310–12, 311n, 315, 319, 321, 326, 334–37, 340, 343, **10**: 26, 33, 165, 184, 196, 198n, 199, 205–6, 208, 209n, 223, 227, 229–30, 232, 235, 237, 242, 247, 271, 273, **11**: 27–28, 44, 60, 67, 335, 382–83, 408–9, 411, 415, 421, 421n, 424–26,

428, 438; sent out, **2**: 153, 308, 309n, 315, **5**: 137, 139, 141n, **6**: 240, **7**: 269–70, 310, **8**: 170, 179, 180n, **9**: 268, 332, 335, 340, 345–46, **10**: 183, 198, 255, **11**: 75, 405; in permanent party, **2**: 229n; court-martialed, **2**: 235–37, 237n, 329, 518; scouting, **2**: 310, 315–16, returns, **2**: 315, **5**: 138–39, **6**: 126, 162, 164, 393, 396, **7**: 275–76, **9**: 157, **9**: 60, 264, 268, 276, 322, 329, 348, **10**: 195–96, 195n, 200, 207–8, 232–33, 236, 239, 266; duties, **2**: 357, 360, **5**: 116n, 315, 318; biographical sketch, **2**: 515; court-martial member, **3**: 170; information from, **5**: 140; creek named for, **5**: 224n, **10**: 146n; votes, **6**: 83; separated, **6**: 125, **7**: 101, 264, 266, 273–74, **8**: 147–48, 150, 153; and saltmaking camp, **6**: 223n, 235–38, 240; collects food, **6**: 330–32; and horses, **7**: 267–68; accidents, **7**: 308, **10**: 234; death, **8**: 316n; court-martialed, **9**: 18, 18n; lost, **9**: 261, **11**: 405; stays behind, **10**: 262–63; mentioned, **2**: 526, **6**: 221, **7**: 263n, 288, **8**: 328, **9**: 231n, 249n, 264n, 265n, 268n, 269n, 271n, 274n, 275n, 276n, 277n, 279, 285n, 290n, 307n, 310n, 312n, 315n, 320n, 332n, 336n, **10**: 26n, 34n, 150n, 166n, 183n, 184n, 189n, 196n, 198n, 200n, 205n, 206n, 208n, 224n, 228n, 229n, 230n, 232n, 233n, 234n, 235n, 236n, 238n, 239n, 242n, 247n, 255n, 262n, 263n, 264n, 266n, 271n, 273n, **11**: 27n, 68n, 336n, 384n, 411n, 415n, 424n, 440n

Collins, Zaccheus, **12**: 6–8

Collins Creek (Wash.), **7**: 117n, **9**: 291n, **10**: 210n

Collins's Creek. *See* Lolo Creek (Idaho)

Collot, Victor, **1**: 5, 7

Colorado Group, **8**: 119n, 208n, 221n, 234n, 279n

Colorado River, **2**: 327, 328n, **5**: 90, 95n, **6**: 312n, **10**: 206n

Colter, John: and maps, **1**: 12–13, 19n. 136, 138–39; hunting, **2**: 142, 153, 158, 307, 307n, 355, 356n, 436, **3**: 80, 82–83, 85n, 107, **5**: 235–36, **6**: 71, 215–16, 221, 223n, 228, 229n, 235–36, 444, **7**: 7–8, 95, 117, 273–74, 277, 279, 281, 289, 297, 299, 323, 325, 331, **8**: 23–24, 48, 140, 146, 177, **9**: 65, 132, 291, 315, 319, 322, 336–37, 344, **10**: 25, 43, 189, 210, 232, 235, 239, **11**: 26, 36, 49–50, 83, 335, 336n, 410, 414, 430–31; drunk, **2**: 143; listed, **2**: 148, 187, 189, 194, 196–97, 199, 255, **4**: 9, 11, **6**: 172n, **8**: 139n, 162n, **11**: 4n, 7n, 62n, 393n, 395n, 400n, 405n, 411n; returns, **2**: 157, 212, 213n, 436, **3**: 51–52, **5**: 173, 235, **6**: 46–47, 126, 167, 293, 295, **8**: 62, 64, 157, **9**: 55, 65, 253, 264, 267, 271, 313, 322, 348, **10**: 140, 149, 170, 200, 207–8, 230, 232–33, 236, 239, 266, **11**: 49–50, 70, 204–6, 393, 396; discipline, **2**: 179, 183, 194, 200n, 515, **7**: 216, 218; court-martialed, **2**: 182, 200n, 329–30; in permanent party, **2**: 229n; court-martial member, **2**: 329; sent out, **2**: 433–34, 435n, **3**: 7, 9, 20–22, 21n, **4**: 302, **5**: 162–63, 232, **6**: 44–45, 60, **7**: 155, 157, **8**: 62–63, 179, 180n, **9**: 46, 64, 229, 255, 261, 265, 328, 335, 345–46, **10**: 103, 147, 170, 183, 255, 258, **11**: 49, 61, 64, 331–32, 405, 410; one of "nine young men from Kentucky," **2**: 510; biographical sketch, **2**: 515;

Colter, John (*continued*)
separated, **3**: 40, 44–45, 48,
50, 51n, **6**: 125, **7**: 157–58, **8**:
47–48, 147–48, 150, 153; information from, **3**: 107–8;
and species, **4**: 308; and Indians, **5**: 10n, 196–97, 198n, **6**:
46–47, **7**: 96, 99, 334, 336,
9: 221, **11**: 308–9; duties,
5: 116n; creek named for, **5**:
252n, 258; scouting, **6**: 62,
65, 92, **9**: 44, 169, 253, 257,
10: 175, 178, **11**: 201, 393,
395, 400; votes, **6**: 83; and
saltmaking camp, **6**: 296–97,
10: 187, 193, 193n, **11**: 419;
discharged, **8**: 4, 158n, 302,
304; fishing, **8**: 35–36, 38;
accidents, **8**: 35–36, **9**: 324,
10: 241; explorations, **8**:
159n, 303n; information
from, **8**: 164, **9**: 211; leaves
party, **8**: 305, **9**: 351; horse
stolen, **10**: 43; stays behind,
10: 200, 262–63, 267–68,
267n; lost, **11**: 405; mentioned, **2**: 66n, 211n, 509–
10, 520, 523, **4**: 305n, **9**:
45n, 47, 50, 55, 169n, 222n,
229n, 231, 253n, 255n,
257n, 261n, 265n, 267n,
271, 271n, 278–79, 279n,
291n, 315n, 319n, 329n,
336n, **10**: 25n, 44n, 103n,
140n, 148n, 149n, 150n,
170n, 171n, 175n, 179n,
183n, 188n, 189n, 200n,
201n, 208n, 210n, 214,
214n, 230n, 232n, 233n,
235n, 236n, 239n, 241n,
255n, 258n, 262n, 263n,
264n, 266n, **11**: 202n, 310n,
332n, 410n, 414n, 419n,
430n, 432n
Colter Creek, **5**: 187n
Colter Falls, **4**: 290, 296n, 311,
315, **10**: 107
Colter's Creek. *See* Potlatch
River
Colt Killed Creek, **5**: 205, 205n,
228n, 238, **8**: 31, 33, 34n,
56–57, 59n, 67, **9**: 223,
224n, **10**: 142, 142n, **11**:
314–15, 316n

Coltsfoot, arrowleaf, **7**: 335,
337, 338n
Columba fasciata, **5**: 174n. *See also*
Pigeon, band-tailed
Columbia Basin, **7**: 172n, 190n
Columbian Plain. *See* Great Columbian Plain
Columbia Plateau, **5**: 266n,
307n
Columbia Rediviva, **6**: 36n, 160n
Columbia River: maps, **1**: 5, 9–
11, 13, **2**: 25–26, **5**: 263n,
272n, 296, **6**: 248n, 308–9,
430–31, 432n, **7**: 74n, 132;
arrive at, **1**: 10, **5**: 276–77,
283, **6**: 24, **9**: 239, **10**: 156;
explored, **2**: 2, **5**: 285, **6**: 86n,
87; and Indians, **3**: 435, 445,
4: 299, **5**: 289–90, 352, 373,
6: 41n, 61n, 75, 76n, 98n,
154–56, 195–96, 203–4,
214, 240–41, 246, 262, 267,
281, 313, 315, 368n, 438,
473–75, 477–78, 480–88,
7: 18–20, 23, 25, 37n, 41n,
65, 79, 86, 93, 99–100, 107,
115–16, 117n, 129, 133,
144, 149, 162n, 169n, 183,
185, 187n, 216, 224, 247,
251, 253, 329, **8**: 131, 278,
415, **11**: 349, 355–56, 360,
373, 374n, 392, 404, 426,
428, 431–32; affluents, **4**: 1,
71, 75n, 246, 270–71, 437,
11: 284–85, 286n, 332, 355,
365, 383, 384n, 432n, 440n;
head, **5**: 52n, 189; characteristics, **5**: 65, 286, 288, 312,
337–38, 363, **6**: 1, 34n, 35n,
36n, 46, 51n, 179n, 182,
335–36, 338, **7**: 26, 34, 37n,
40, 41n, 59–60, 66, 78, 78n,
81–83, 100n, 127, 173n,
182, 184, 187, 217–18,
219n, **11**: 358–59, 377–78,
398; conditions, **5**: 115, 294,
298, 300n, 301, 311, 315,
321, 331, 343, 354, 357n,
359–60, **6**: 2, 12, 14n, 19n,
98, 294, 310–11, **7**: 28, 30,
39, 120, 192, **8**: 113, 310,
384, **9**: 242–43, 243n, 244–
45, 257, 283, **10**: 153n,

157n, 161n, 180, 186n,
195n, 205, 205n, 206n,
226n, 246, **11**: 356–60, 374,
436; described, **5**: 215, 227,
230, 285–87, 292, **8**: 95, **9**:
240, 256, **10**: 157–58, 166,
177n, 203, 226n; naviga-
tional problems, **5**: 304–5,
315, 317–18, 337–38, **7**: 29,
41, **9**: 241–42, 251, 259,
273, 294, **10**: 208, **11**: 358–
60, 363, 377–78, 381, 438;
name, **6**: 36n, 184, **9**: 240,
10: 135n, **11**: 357; plants,
6: 77n, 229, 233, 282, 284,
284n, 295, **7**: 15n, 22n, 31n,
38, 40, 45, 104n, 114n, 188,
194n, 195n, 266n, 335, 337,
8: 14, 18, 79, 125, 132n;
traders, **6**: 85, 160n, 314,
316, 427, **7**: 106, 110n, **11**:
392, 392n; bearings on, **6**:
115n; animals, **6**: 131, 142,
144, 318, 320, 323, 340–41,
346, 349, 355, 360, 387–89,
395–97, 413, 415, **7**: 53n,
309, 311, **8**: 76, 125, 128;
fishing on, **6**: 351, 353; distances, **6**: 446, 454, 456–59,
461, **7**: 8n, **8**: 377, 385, 388,
412–13, **10**: 7n, 63n, 156n,
173, **11**: 398; located, **6**: 468;
latitude, **6**: 494, **8**: 387, **11**:
431; astronomical observa-
tions, **7**: 1, 50; hunting on,
7: 48, 51; listed, **8**: 403; mentioned, **2**: 3, 5, 7, 28, 328n,
525, **4**: 277n, **5**: 1–4, 52n,
59, 74, 76n, 90, 111, 113–
14, 122, 140, 155, 163, 165,
177–78, 181–82, 182n, 192,
197, 198n, 228n, 231n,
260n, 268n, 278, 284n,
290n, 319n, 325n, 340n,
365, **6**: 37n, 57, 71n, 94n,
276n, 337, 365, 371, 381–
82, 393, 451, 493n, **7**: 2, 53–
54, 56–58, 71, 74, 130n,
161, 174, 176, 177n, 186n,
202–3, 206–7, 305, **8**: 17,
102, 104, 358n, 364n, 368n,
382–83, **9**: xiii, 164, 190,
211n, 218, 232, 239n, 252n,

253, 257n, 258, 275, 280n, 285n, 286, 289, 293n, 300–301, 368n, **10**: xiii, 5n, 7n, 128, 135, 149, 149n, 155n, 156n, 157n, 158n, 163n, 167n, 171, 174n, 178n, 198–200, 200n, 206, 211, 212n, 215, 217n, 218n, 220, 222n, 226n, 246, 246n, 250, 272n, **11**: xiii, 5n, 6n, 190–91, 244n, 256, 290–93, 356n, 393, 394n, 395n, 399, 430, 433n, 434, 439. *See also* Celilo (Great) Falls

Columbia River, Cascades (Great Rapids, Great Shute) of the: maps, **1**: 10; arrive at, **5**: 4, 355–56, 358n, **10**: 164; portage, **5**: 4, 366–67, 369, 371, **6**: 7–8, 9n, **7**: 1, 111–12, **9**: 289–90, **11**: 379–81; characteristics, **5**: 360, 363, **6**: 335–36, 338, **7**: 34, 121n; and Indians, **6**: 10n, 203, 270–71, 475, 481, 483, **7**: 38, 40, 57, 64, 85, 88, 106, 113, 346–47, **11**: 378, 380–81; animals, **6**: 161–62, 318, 351, 354, 371, 402; plants, **6**: 285–86, 299–300, **12**: 8; distances, **6**: 456, 461, 493, **8**: 386, **9**: 232, **10**: 173; located, **6**: 469, **7**: 18, 20, 41n, 104n; conditions, **7**: 105, 108, 122n, **9**: 248, **10**: 209, **11**: 378; listed, **8**: 404, **10**: 174n; mentioned, **5**: 312n, 357n, 365, 379–80, 380n, **6**: 1, 29n, 73, **7**: 110n, 114n, 120, 193, 327, **9**: 247, 247n, 288, 289n, **10**: 164n, 185n, 209n, **11**: 377, 378n, 409n

Columbia River, Great Falls of the. *See* Celilo (Great) Falls
Columbia River, Southeast Fork of. *See* Salmon River; Snake River
Columbia River, The Dalles of the (Great Narrows): maps, **1**: 11; conditions, **5**: 328–29, **7**: 136, 144, 160, **9**: 244–45, **11**: 368–71; and Indians, **5**: 336n, **6**: 474–75, 483,

7: 123–24, 130n, 145n, 161, **11**: 374n; and species, **6**: 355, 360, 395–96, 402; listed, **6**: 469, **8**: 404, **10**: 174n; distances, **6**: 493; passed, **7**: 8, 9n; described, **10**: 161; mentioned, **5**: 312n, **6**: 405n, **7**: 120, 121n, 141n, 145n, 162n, 197, 267–68, **9**: 244n, 294n, **10**: 161n, 212n, 213n, **11**: 370n, 375n. *See also* Long Narrows; Short Narrows
Columbine, **3**: 460, 471
Columbine, red, **8**: 28, 30, 30n
Columbus, Christopher, **4**: 9, **10**: 34n
Colville (Whe-el-po) Indians, **6**: 480, 488, 491
Comanche (La Play, Nemousin) Indians, **3**: 328n, 395, 424–25, 437–38, 448, **8**: 235n, 364n
Combs, **4**: 194, 198, **5**: 341, **6**: 433, 437, **9**: 369n. *See also* Clothing
Comcomly, **6**: 60–61, 61–62n, 72, 73n, 154, 159n, 333n
Commissary. *See* Contractors
Commissions. *See* Certificates and commissions
Comowool. *See* Coboway
Compasses, **1**: 4, **2**: 92n, 97, 213n, 256, **4**: 201, 204, 320, 341–43, 345–46, 361, **5**: 230, **6**: 84, **7**: 58, 80, 242, 244, **9**: 177, **10**: 108, **11**: 215–16. *See also* Instruments, scientific
Condor, California: described, **5**: 354, 356, **6**: 66, 319–23, **9**: 247, 254, **11**: 377–78; observed, **5**: 365, **6**: 96, 162–63, **7**: 24–25, 26n, 76, 88, 90n, **11**: 377–78; hunted, **6**: 63, 66, 100, **9**: 272, **10**: 176, 198, **11**: 396; discovered, **6**: 67n; specimen, **6**: 69; sketches, **1**: 10, 18n. 104, **6**: 321n, 324n; Indian name, **6**: 495; mentioned, **5**: 357–58n, 366n, **6**: 379, 381, 381n, **9**: 247n, 255n, 272n, **10**: 176n, 198n, 203, **11**: 378n, 396n

Coneflower, narrow leaf purple, **3**: 258n, 304, 305n, 317, 318n, 325, 326n, 330, 331n, 460, 471
Conia. *See* Coboway
Conjunctivitis. *See* Medical problems
Conns Coulee, **8**: 261n
Conrad, John, **2**: 36–37
Continental Divide, **4**: 1–2, 234n, 282n, 339n, 381n, **5**: 2, 74, 76n, 85n, 164n, 177n, 186n, 198n, **6**: 473, **8**: 2, 43n, 96n, 102, 104, 124n, 166n, 168n, 393, 410, **9**: 217n, 332n, **10**: 127n, 128n, 137n, 154n, 206n, 226n, 250, 251n, 254n, **11**: 275n, 299n, 350n
Contractors, **2**: 139–40, 145, 150, 156, 166, 175, 187, 191–92
Conuropsis carolinensis, **2**: 325n, **8**: 418n. *See also* Parakeet, Carolina
Convolvulus sepium, **3**: 467. *See also* Bindweed, hedge
Con-year. *See* Coboway
Cook, James, **1**: 5, **2**: 1, 35, **4**: 9, 12n, **5**: 1, **6**: 36n, **7**: 10, 11n, **9**: xi, **10**: xi, 226n, **11**: xi, 384, **12**: 5
Cooke, Philip St. George, **3**: 291n
Coon (Nightingale) Creek, **2**: 275–76, 276n, **9**: 10, 10n
Coosan language, **6**: 237n
Coos (Cook-koo-oose) Indians, **6**: 237n, 432n, 476, 485, 491
Coot, American, **2**: 205n, **6**: 96–97, 98n, 398–400, 401n
Copaifera, **7**: 220n
Copalis (Pailsh) Indians, **6**: 472n, 476, 486, 491
Coppei Creek, **7**: 201n
Copper, **5**: 222, 289, 367, **6**: 15, 187, 205, 207, 210, 436, 440, **7**: 145, **9**: 42, 59, 237, 239, 369n, **10**: 30, **11**: 344–45, 355–56
Copperas, **2**: 500–501, 502n, **3**: 372, 481, **8**: 379, 397
Copperhead, **7**: 309, 311, 312n

Coppermine River, **10**: 6n
Coquille Indians, **6**: 491
Coralberry, **2**: 433–34, 435n, **3**: 468
Cordelle. *See* Rope, tow
Cordgrass, prairie, **2**: 373n, **3**: 167n
Cords. *See* Rope, tow; Ropes
Coregonus sp., **6**: 346n. *See also* Whitefish
Corks, **5**: 53
Cormorant, double-crested, **2**: 205n, **5**: 309, 311, 313n, 375, **6**: 13, 14n, 96, 161–62, 261, 383, 385, 387–89, **7**: 9, 11n, 45
Corn: purchased, **2**: 80, 248, **10**: 54, 61, 67, 71; loaded, **2**: 165, **3**: 199, **11**: 212; meal, **2**: 166, 181, 191, 201, 205, 218; parched, **2**: 181–82, 201, 205, 217, **3**: 313; listed, **2**: 200, 217–18; as food, **2**: 258, 347, **3**: 261, 313, **4**: 379, **5**: 133, 144, 147n, 148, 173, 186, 189, **8**: 285, 299, 301, 314–15, **9**: 72, 79, 92, 122–23, 218, 220, **10**: 137–38, 143, **11**: 209, 303–4; culti-vated, **2**: 302, 478–79, 482n, **3**: 32, 32, 48, 151–52, 161, 163, 197, 207n, 391–407, 410, 440, 483, **8**: 335, **9**: 22, 39, 78, 90, 93, 394–95, **11**: 91–92, 132; and Indians, **2**: 415–16, 489, **3**: 162, 201n, 201n, 272, 297, 320, 389, **8**: 285, 299, 301–3, 308, 315, 317, 330, 335, 338, 350, **10**: 32, 48, 53, 60, 67, 71, 267–68, **11**: 106; as trade item, **3**: 2–3, 121–22, 208, 216–19, 222–26, 235, 237, 239, 260–61, 264, 267, 275, 281, 284, 286, 288, 298, 308, 401–3, 484, 486, **5**: 112, 159, 171, **8**: 338, 349, 363, **9**: 93, 98, 103–6, 110–11, 113, 120, 129, 352, **10**: 270, 275, **11**: 113–15, 128–29; as gift, **3**: 21–22, 158–60, 162, **9**: 46, 50, 79, 82–83, 92, 97–98, 208, 211, 350, 357–58, 364,

11: 98, 122, 125, 280–81, 283–85; specimen, **3**: 330; damaged, **4**: 28; wet, **5**: 53, 55; cached, **10**: 101, **11**: 193–94; mentioned, **2**: 202n, **3**: 141, **5**: 140, **6**: 235n, **9**: xviii, 82n, 125n, 373n, **10**: 280
Corn de Cerf River. *See* Elkhorn River
Cornice Island, **2**: 125, 125n
Cornus canadensis, **6**: 45n. *See also* Bunchberry
Cornus florida, **7**: 78n. *See also* Dogwood, flowering
Cornus nuttallii, **7**: 78n, **9**: 287n, **10**: 207n. *See also* Dogwood, Nuttall's
Cornus sericea, **3**: 305n, **4**: 19n, **5**: 86n, **6**: 29n, **7**: 14n, **8**: 94n, **9**: 196n. *See also* Dog-wood, red osier
Cornus stolonifera, **6**: 29n
Corral (Turkey) Creek, **2**: 340–42, 343n, **3**: 378, **9**: 19, 19n, 384
Corrèa da Serra, José, **2**: 531
Corsica, **10**: 93n
Corvus, blue-crested. *See* Jay, Steller's
Corvus, parti-colored. *See* Mag-pie, black-billed
Corvus brachyrhynchos, **2**: 154n, **4**: 29n, **5**: 231n, **6**: 94n, **7**: 78n, **8**: 267n, **10**: 159n. *See also* Crow, common
Corvus brachyrhynchos hesperis, **5**: 231n, **9**: 242n, **10**: 159n, **11**: 362n. *See also* Crow, common
Corvus caurinus, **6**: 164n. *See also* Crow, northwestern
Corvus corax, **3**: 295n, **4**: 95n, **6**: 94n, **7**: 78n, **8**: 78n, **9**: 242n, **10**: 159n, **11**: 362n. *See also* Raven, common
Corvus corax principalis, **6**: 378n. *See also* Raven, common
Corvus corax sinuatus, **6**: 378n. *See also* Raven, common
Corvus Creek, **8**: 327n
Corylus americana, **2**: 293n, **8**: 418n, **11**: 261n. *See also* Hazelnut

Corylus cornuta, **5**: 326n, **6**: 347n, **7**: 122n, **10**: 164n. *See also* Hazelnut
Coryphantha missouriensis, **4**: 433n. *See also* Cactus, yellow pincushion
Coryphantha vivipara, **5**: 85n. *See also* Cactus, pink pincushion
Côte Noir, **9**: 75n. *See also* Black Hills
Cottle, Warren, **2**: 168n
Cottontail, eastern (rabbits), **2**: 156, 156n, 158, 164–65, **3**: 52, 54, 66, 73–75, 82, 87, **4**: 70, 75n, **6**: 317n, 362n, **9**: 17, 17n, 58, 60, 240, 383, **11**: 280–81, 357, 363–64
Cottontail, Nuttall's, **4**: 75n, **6**: 317n, 360, 362n, **8**: 166–67, 168n, **9**: 331, 332n
Cottonwood, black, **5**: 195n, 355–56, 358n, **6**: 7, 9, 11, 15, 17, 20n, **7**: 12, 14, 14n, 19, 21–22, 25, 32, 55, 77, 112–13, 188–89, 192, 197, 202–4, **8**: 79, 81n, 125, 126n, 128, 132n, **9**: 246–47, 247n, 287, 287n, **10**: 166, 166n, 219, 219n **11**: 376–77, 377n
Cottonwood, eastern, **9**: 8, 9n, 185n, **10**: 113n, **11**: 45, 46n
Cottonwood, narrowleaf, **4**: 2, 250, 253n, 280–81, 304–5, 324, 388, 391, 396n, 399, 401, 406, 417, 421, 435, **5**: 27, 30n, 36, 57, 58n, 71, 81, 195n, 255, **8**: 79, 81n, 98, 98n, 132n, 138, **9**: 163, 164n, 185, 185n, **10**: 113n, **11**: 188–89, 189n
Cottonwood, plains (wide or broad leaved), **4**: 17, 19n, 94, 96n, 100, 250, 253n, 280–81, 324, 391, 396n, 399, 414, **8**: 79, 81n, 99, 100n, 132n, 355n, **10**: 63n
Cottonwood Butte, **5**: 214n
Cottonwood Creek (Custer County, Mont., July 29, 1806), **8**: 248, 249n, 250n
Cottonwood Creek (Custer

County, Mont., July 30,
1806), **8**: 251, 254, 257n
Cottonwood Creek (Powell
County, Mont.), **8**: 92, 92n
Cottonwood Creek (Wibaux
County, Mont.), **8**: 268–69,
270n
Cottonwood Island, **6**: 28n
Cottonwoods: observed, **2**: 105,
428, 430, 465–66, 468, 470,
472, 474–76, **3**: 38, 57, 76,
80, 99, 104–5, 177, 182,
186, **4**: 17, 108, 146–48,
170, 184, 188, 191, 202, 205,
212, 214, 224, 233, 240, 242,
251, 280, 284, 291, 372, **5**:
253, 255, **8**: 207, 254, **9**: 12,
27–28, 30–32, 34–38, 42–
44, 46, 51, 60–61, 89, 93,
128, 130–31, 133, 137–38,
141–42, 151–52, 154, 167,
184, 190, 194, 198, 210, 216,
220, 249, 251, 301, 361,
380–82, **10**: 10, 15, 26, 32,
36, 85, 94, 105, 164, 218,
252, **11**: 45, 138, 140, 153,
162–64, 167, 179, 181–85,
192–98, 223, 227–30, 236–
37, 242, 246–56, 258–59,
261–62, 264–68, 270–71,
307, 340, 378, 384–89, 437;
discussed, **2**: 185, 209, 291,
313, 391–92; for keelboat
mast, **2**: 341; use, **3**: 4, 229,
231, 308n, 320–21, **4**: 3,
303, 325–26, 330, 334, 371–
72, **8**: 181, 184–85, 191,
209, 237, **9**: 93, 95, **10**: 62;
discovered, **3**: 39n; as food,
3: 69, 100–102, 232, 292,
320, **4**: 46, 125; leaves fall,
3: 131, 222; habitat, **3**: 354,
360–62, **8**: 82, 122, 186–87,
200, 203, 218, 231–32, 238,
243, 272, 293, 322, 343;
specimen, **3**: 452, 462, 466;
habitat, **4**: 26, 39, 54, 69, 73–
74, 88, 124, 176, 178, 216–
17, 261; as nest, **4**: 30, 33; for
lodges, **4**: 38, 378; abundance, **4**: 96, 170, 211, **8**:
103, 117, 128, 189–90, 192,
194, 219, **9**: 45, 53, 192, 214,

216, 306, 308, 338, **10**: 55,
58, 61, 94, 96–97, 102, 113,
118, 167, 227, 250, 258, **11**:
195, 241, 294–97, 304, 308–
9, 385; scarcity, **4**: 159, 161–
63, 165, 208, 210, 210n, 213,
222–23, 229, 332, 358, 388,
5: 36, 65, **9**: 146, 157, 159–
60, 201, 221, **11**: 159; and
Indians, **5**: 151, **9**: 127, **10**:
69, **11**: 116; and species,
6: 366, 368, **9**: 128, 196;
described, **8**: 79, 190, 205;
camped by, **9**: 53, 59, 129,
131–33, 136, 139, 141, 150,
155, 159, 166, 182, 190,
201–3; damaged, **9**: 195;
cache by, **9**: 197; mentioned,
2: 16, 292n, 315n, **4**: 33, 168,
210, 214, 292, **5**: 43, 75, 84,
98, 193, 258, 379, **8**: 22n, 86,
93, 99–100, 102, 114–15,
130, 132n, 133n, 138, 161,
182–83, 193, 195, 253, 259,
286, 359, **10**: 11n, **11**: 46n
Coturnicops noveboracensis, **3**:
12n. *See also* Rail, yellow
Coues, Elliott: edits Biddle's *History*, **1**: 4, **8**: 120n, 300n; editorial methods, **1**: 15n. 4, **2**:
11, 17, 22, 39, 42, 51–52,
431n, 532, 535, 537, 549, **3**:
268n; and maps, **1**: 15n. 9,
18n. 91, 19nn. 115, 135;
theory of journal composi-
tion, **2**: 9; examines journals,
2: 9, 38–39, 532–33, 536;
journal discoveries, **2**: 38;
character and training, **2**: 38,
40–41; emendations, **3**: 86n,
179n, **4**: 95n, 129n, **7**: 233n,
296n, 302n, **8**: 30n, 111n,
118n, 144n, 250n, 256n,
257n; marks, **5**: 52n, 189n,
6: 346n, **7**: 164n, 330n, **8**:
229n, 240n, 246n, 270n; notations, **5**: 147n, 170n, 190n,
263n, 381n, **8**: 158n; repairs
journals, **8**: 159n; mentioned, **1**: 11, **2**: 463n, **4**:
34n, 40n, 175n, 259n, 346n,
6: 29n, 362n, **7**: 259n, **10**:
228n

Cougar. *See* Mountain lion
Cougee, Charles, **1**: 17n. 73,
2: 347, 526
Council Bluff (Nebr.): arrive at,
2: 428–29, **8**: 353, **9**: 32,
391, **10**: 24, 277, **11**: 46; described, **2**: 429–30, 431n,
440–41, **3**: 353–54, **11**: 47n;
latitude, **2**: 480, 487, **3**: 94,
375, **9**: 32, 80, **10**: 25, **11**: 51,
67, 174; distances, **3**: 94, 371,
375, **9**: 81, 367n; as post site,
3: 353–54, 393–99, 414–17,
479, **9**: 34; location, **3**: 379,
10: 24n, 277n; and specimens, **3**: 457; listed, **8**: 379,
397, **11**: 171–72; name, **9**:
32, 32n, 391, **11**: 49–50;
mentioned, **2**: 60–61, 442n,
443n, 452–53, 465, 490, **3**:
355, **4**: 94, **8**: 354n, 416–17,
11: 67n
Counselor (Camel, Elm, Night)
Creek, **3**: 89–90, 91n, **10**:
41n, **11**: 78, 78n
Coup, counting. *See* Indians
Couplings. *See* Wagons
Courtin, Charles, **2**: 437n, **3**: 74,
75–76n, **8**: 158n, 288, 289n,
360, 360n, **10**: 279n
Courts-martial: of Newman, **2**:
13, 519, **3**: 2, 168–72, 171–
72n, 222, **9**: 84, 84n, **10**: 54,
55n; procedures, **2**: 163; of
Colter, Frazer, and Shields,
2: 182–83, 183n; of Collins,
Hall, and Werner, **2**: 235–
37, 237n; of Collins and Hall,
2: 329–30, 332, **9**: 18, 18n;
of Willard, **2**: 369–71, **9**:
24, 24n; of Reed, **2**: 488–
89, 520; of Howard, **3**: 290,
290n, **9**: 113–14, 114n; mentioned, **2**: 185, 200n, 518. *See
also* Discipline
Cous (chapellel, halse, shappa-
lell, uppah): and Indians, **5**:
371, **6**: 187, 205, **7**: 92, 98–
99, 234, 300, **9**: 288, 292,
294–97, 300, 312–15, 318–
19, **10**: 211, 214–15, 217,
222, 225; Indian name, **5**:
380n; discovered, **7**: 3; as

Cous (*continued*)
  trade item, **7**: 113, 119–20,
    132, 134, 146, 148, 158,
    160–61, 163, 181, 183, 205–
    8, 210–11, 213, 215, 217,
    235, 237, 272–75, 277, 284–
    85, 289, 291, 294, 297, 299,
    308, 322, 324, 326, 328–29,
    334, 336, 339, 341; as food,
    7: 239–40, 246, 264, 339,
    342, **8**: 52, 108, 125–26,
    163; cached, **8**: 32–33; use,
    8: 46; habitat, **8**: 167, **9**: 308;
    mentioned, **6**: 192n, **7**: 93n,
    190n, 209n, 275, 276n, 338,
    343, **8**: 12n, 46n, 59n, **9**:
    288n, 308n, 317n, **10**: 211n,
    225n
Cousin, Barthelemi, **2**: 107,
  109n
Cowbird, brown-headed, **8**: 108,
  108n
Cow Gulch (Hall's River, Little
  Wolf Creek), **8**: 229, 231,
  233, 234n, 235n, 390, 408
Cow Island, **2**: 343–44, 345n,
  8: 141n, **9**: 19, 20n
Cowlitz (Coweliskee) River, **6**:
  26, 28, 28n, 29n, 202, 346n,
  458, 470, 475, 477n, 484–
  85, **7**: 15n, 18, 20, 21n, 22n,
  70n, 130n, **8**: 387, 405, 415
Cowlitz Formation, **6**: 30n
Cowlitz (Hul-loo-et-tell) Indians,
  7: 18, 20, 21n, 26, 30, 346,
  9: 281, 282n, **10**: 202
Cowlitz language, **6**: 28n
Cow parsnip, **7**: 200–201, 201n
Cows, **2**: 102, 106, 145, 336,
  339, **3**: 82–83, **5**: 8, **6**: 302,
  305, 307n, **8**: 4, 214, 367
Cowslip, **2**: 209
Cowslip, American, **2**: 210n
Cowslip, Virginia, **2**: 210n, **7**:
  193, 195n
Cow (Windsor's) Creek, **4**: 202–
  3, 206, 207n, **6**: 448, 463,
  8: 141n, 382, 401, **9**: 155,
  156n, 344n, **10**: 92, 93n,
  260n, **11**: 169–70, 170n
Coxe, Anty, **2**: 166
Coyote (prairie wolf, small
  wolf): hunted, **2**: 471, 474,

3: 144–45, **4**: 65–66, **5**: 226,
  244, **9**: 61, 76, 233, **10**: 40,
  51, 82, **11**: 76–77, 95, 138;
  described, **2**: 471, 474, **11**:
  76–77; observed, **2**: 502–3,
  3: 7, 12n, 75, 86–87, 87–
  88n, **6**: 312–13, 315, **8**: 115;
  discovered, **3**: 1, 82, 85n, 87–
  88n; behavior, **3**: 181n, **8**:
  126, 356, **9**: 38, 56; specimen, **3**: 330; habitat, **3**: 482,
  6: 331, 335, **8**: 416; as trade
  item, **4**: 34; abundance, **4**:
  112; mentioned, **2**: 475n, **3**:
  76n, **4**: 40n, 116n, **5**: 228n,
  6: 317n, 333n, **8**: 116n,
  126n, 418n, **9**: 38n, **10**: 40n,
  82n, **11**: 77n, 138n
Coyote Creek, **5**: 76n, **6**: 465
Coyote Gulch, **7**: 214n
Crabapple, Oregon (wild crab),
  6: 3, 15–17, 19n, 98, 103,
  105n, 235, 237n, 243–44,
  244n, **7**: 15–16, 17n, **10**:
  196, 196n
Crabapple, western, **6**: 19n
Crabapple, wild, **2**: 321–22,
  323n, 369, **9**: 15, 15n
Cracker Box Creek, **8**: 258, 260,
  262n
Cracon du Nez, **4**: 257n, 279n
Cradleboard, **4**: 341, 343, 343n
Cranberries, **11**: 404
Cranberry, high bush, **3**: 481,
  492n, **5**: 354n
Cranberry, wild, **6**: 45–46n, 74,
  76, 77n, 103, 116–18, 235,
  237n, 243–44, 330–31
Cranberrybush, American, **5**:
  354n, **6**: 45n, **10**: 161, 161n,
  11: 369–70, 370n
Cranberry Island, **2**: 305n
Crane, blue. *See* Heron, great
  blue
Crane, sandhill: observed, **4**:
  408, **5**: 10–11, **7**: 23, 25, 320,
  8: 75; described, **4**: 411, **7**:
  275–76, **11**: 245; hunted, **5**:
  303, 305, 359, 362, **6**: 11, 13,
  14n, 21, 96, 161–62, 261,
  379–81, **7**: 286, 288, **9**: 220,
  321–22, 328, **10**: 139, **11**:
  304–5; as food, **5**: 303, 306;

abundance, **7**: 200–201,
  275–76, **8**: 10–11, 177; behavior, **9**: 191; mentioned, **4**:
  415n, **5**: 13n, 307n, **7**: 25n,
  8: 13n, **9**: 191n, **10**: 232n,
  11: 246n, 305n
Crane, The, **3**: 235n
Crane, white, **2**: 185, 186n
Crane, whooping, **2**: 186n,
  4: 22–23, 24n, **5**: 342–43,
  344n
Crane Meadows, **5**: 231n, **8**:
  23n, 25, 26n, 44–45, 45n, **9**:
  228, 228n, 322n, 326, 326n,
  10: 147n, 242, 243n
Cranes, **2**: 208, 459, **4**: 417, 420,
  423, **5**: 42–43, 59, 84, 194,
  6: 53–54, 73, **7**: 196, 198, **10**:
  166, 171, **11**: 411
Cranesbill (dove's foot), **2**: 209,
  210n
Crataegus calpodendron, **2**: 309n.
  See also Urn-tree
Crataegus columbiana, **5**: 164n,
  10: 130n, **11**: 329n. *See also*
  Hawthorn, Columbia
Crataegus crus-galli, **2**: 309n. *See
  also* Thorn, cockspur
Crataegus douglasii, **7**: 114n, **8**:
  13n **11**: 329n. *See also* Haw-
  thorn, black
Crataegus mollis, **2**: 309n. *See also*
  Haw, summer
Crataegus sp., **2**: 309n. *See also*
  Hawthorns
Crates Point, **5**: 348n, **9**: 246n,
  10: 163n, **11**: 375n
Crawford, Lewis, **1**: 16n. 32, **2**:
  191–92, 192n, **3**: 405, 415
Crayfish, **2**: 484n, **5**: 226, 228n,
  6: 396–97, 398n, **9**: 227,
  227n, **11**: 325–26, 326n.
  See also Silverfish
Crazy Mountains, **8**: 186–87,
  188n
Cree (Cristanoe, Knistanoe) In-
  dians, **3**: 3, 120n, 235–37,
  235n, 236n, 246, 317, 412–
  13, 430–34, 487, **4**: 35, **6**:
  235n, **10**: 43n, 60n
Creek Indians, **3**: 446–47, 449
Cress, Belle Isle, **7**: 195n

Cress, bog yellow, **2**: 281n, **3**: 466

Cress, sessile-flowered, **2**: 281n, **3**: 466

Cress, spreading yellow, **2**: 281n, **3**: 466

Cress, winter, **7**: 193, 195n

Cress, yellow, **2**: 281n

Cresses, **2**: 279

Cretaceous deposits, **2**: 103, 104n

Creve Coeur Creek, **2**: 244, 245n

Cricket, Mormon, **5**: 174n

Crickets, **5**: 11, 14n

Crims (Fanny's) Island, **6**: 27, 29n, 458, 470, **7**: 16–17, 17n, **8**: 387, 405, 411n, **9**: 281, 281n, **11**: 434, 434n

Cristanoe Indians. *See* Cree Indians

Croghan, John, **2**: 542, **9**: xvii

Cronin Point, **6**: 185n

Cronquist, Arthur, **12**: 7

Crooked Creek (Big Dry Brook) (Yellowstone County, Mont.), **8**: 223, 227, 229n, 391, 408

Crooked Creek (Garfield County, Mont.), **4**: 150, 150n, **9**: 147, 147n, **10**: 88, 88n, **11**: 155, 155n

Crooked Creek (Petroleum County, Mont.). *See* Sacagawea River

Crooked Creek (Prairie County, Mont.), **8**: 256n

Crooked Falls, **4**: 289, 296n, 305n, 307, 311, 314, **6**: 449, 464, **10**: 109, 109n

Crooked Fork (Glade, North Fork) Creek (Idaho), **5**: 204, 205n, 238, **6**: 452, 466, **8**: 61, 63, 64n, 383, 402, **9**: 223, 224n, 328, 328n, **11**: 314–15, 316n

Crooked (Panther, Tiger) River, **2**: 308, 309n, 310, 311n, **3**: 343, 370, 377, **8**: 378, 395, **9**: 15, 15n, 368n, **10**: 15, 15n, **11**: 28–29, 29n

Crooks, Ramsay, **1**: 19n. 139, **8**: 368n

Crosby, Betsey, **9**: xiv

Crossbars. *See* Boat, iron-frame

Crotalus horridus, **2**: 285n, **9**: 11n, **11**: 20n. *See also* Rattlesnake, timber

Crotalus viridis, **3**: 54n. *See also* Rattlesnake, prairie

Crotalus viridus oreganus, **7**: 169n. *See also* Rattlesnake, northern Pacific

Crotalus viridus viridus, **4**: 163n, **5**: 67n, **8**: 148n, **9**: 150n, **10**: 118n, **11**: 161n. *See also* Rattlesnake, prairie

Crow, common, **2**: 153, 154n, **3**: 82–83, 436, 487, **4**: 28, 29n, 93, 298, 407, **5**: 216, 229, 231n, **6**: 94, 94n, 96, **7**: 76, 78n, 259, 262, **8**: 180, 210, 266, 267n, **9**: 242, 242n, 267, **10**: 154, 159, 159n, **11**: 361–62, 362n, 411

Crow, northwestern, **6**: 162–63, 164n, 261, 375, 377, 378n

Crow, rain. *See* Cuckoos

Crowberry, **10**: 226n

Crow Coulee, **8**: 139n, **9**: 343n, **10**: 97, 97n, 260n, **11**: 183, 184n

Crow Creek (S. Dak.), **3**: 91n, 358, 372, 380, **8**: 380, 398, **9**: 62, 62n, **10**: 41, 41n, **11**: 78, 78n

Crow (Gass's) Creek (Mont.), **4**: 425n, 426–27, 429n, **6**: 450, 464, **10**: 117n

Crow Hills, **8**: 154, 156n, **10**: 265n

Crow (Paunch, Raven) Indians: war, **3**: 25–26, 161, 163, 234, 433, **8**: 132n, 195; located, **3**: 26n, 234, 386, **8**: 286n; prisoners, **3**: 163; language, **3**: 234, 490, **8**: 161, 162n; historical sketch, **3**: 234n, 427–29, 435; trade, **3**: 403–4, **8**: 278, 302; listed, **3**: 448–49; appearance, **3**: 487; relations with the party, **4**: 10–11, **8**: 3, 211, 284, 303n, **10**: 265n, 266; name, **7**: 342, 343n, **8**: 232, 235n, 309; forts, **8**: 198; signs, **8**: 201; lodges, **8**: 209, 210n, 218, 222n; ceremo-

nies, **8**: 210n; clothes, **8**: 211; speech to, **8**: 213–15, 215n; and plants, **8**: 218; and horses, **8**: 286n; origin story, **8**: 309, 309n; mentioned, **2**: 525, **3**: 242n, 402, 436, **5**: 80–81, 86n, 149, **7**: 245n, **8**: 302

Crow's Head (Car ka pá há), **2**: 490, 493, 493n

Crow Wing River, **3**: 409–10, 419, 440, 483

Cruciferae, **7**: 338n. *See also* Mustard

Cruzatte, Pierre: wounds Lewis, **1**: 9, **2**: 29, **8**: 3, 155–56, 157n, 287n, 290, **9**: 347, **10**: xvi, 265; river named for, **1**: 10, **5**: 357n, 379, **9**: 247n, **10**: 164n, **11**: 379n; listed, **1**: 17n. 73, **2**: 255, **4**: 9, 11, **8**: 139n, 162n, 180n, **11**: 4n, 8n, 187n; in permanent party, **2**: 229n, 510; duties, **2**: 258, 313, 364n, **4**: 269, **5**: 116n, 129–31, 132n, **9**: 377, 389, **10**: 100; lineage, **2**: 312, 347, 404, 415; hunting, **2**: 325, 326n, **3**: 186, 188, 188n, 222, **7**: 226, 230, 264–65, 268, 271n, 274, 281–82, 284, 285n, 286–87, 291, 294, **8**: 23, 38–39, 41, 155–56, 165, **9**: 17, 33, 88, 88n, 312, 314–15, 336–37, 341, 347, **10**: 223, 229, 232, 242, **11**: 103, 103n; sent out, **2**: 415–16, 476–77, **5**: 358, 360–61, **7**: 125, 129n, 133–34, 143–44, 260, 262, **8**: 179, 180n, **9**: 29, 38, 285, 335, 356, **10**: 22, 28, 204, 255, **11**: 44, 423, 423n; returns, **2**: 418–19, **5**: 138–39, **6**: 370, **7**: 131, **9**: 29, 325, **10**: 129, 195, 228, 232–33, 242, **11**: 44–45, 190–91, 424; and Indians, **2**: 445, **6**: 358, 360; biographical sketch, **2**: 516; interpreter, **3**: 111–12, 114n, 119, 121, 123, **8**: 329–30, 331n; information from, **3**: 121, 123, **5**: 140, **9**: 28, 34,

Cruzatte, Pierre (*continued*)
386, **11**: 43; medical problems, **3**: 198, 198n, **6**: 141–43; accidents, **4**: 2, 152–54; scouting, **4**: 250, 256, **7**: 54, 57, 60n, **10**: 98, **11**: 186–90, 438–39; opinion, **4**: 271, **5**: 333; and fiddle, **4**: 272, 332, **5**: 303, 306, 329, 335–36, 341, 343, **7**: 127–28, **10**: xii; separated, **5**: 137, 139, 141n, **7**: 273–74; votes, **6**: 84; fishing, **6**: 353, 355n, **10**: 194; loses horse, **8**: 7; collects food, **8**: 37; death, **8**: 364n; interpreter, **9**: 65, 66n, 67, **10**: 44, 44n, **11**: 88–89, 92; trading, **9**: 293–94, **10**: 212–13; and species, **10**: 57, 57n; stays behind, **10**: 129; and saltmaking camp, **10**: 187; mentioned, **2**: 190n, 511, 518, **6**: 172n, **8**: 43–44, **9**: xii, 29n, 34n, 39n, 68n, 265, 279, 285n, 293n, 294n, 312n, 314n, 315n, 336n, 356n, 377n, 386n, 389n, **10**: 23n, 28n, 98n, 100n, 129n, 130n, 188n, 195n, 206n, 212n, 213n, 224n, 229n, 230n, 232n, 233n, 242n, 255n, 265n, 274n, **11**: xii, 43n, 44n, 83, 84n, 93n, 411n, 425n, 440n

Cruzatte's River. *See* Wind River

Cuckoo, black-billed, **8**: 112n

Cuckoo, yellow-billed, **8**: 112n

Cuckoos, **8**: 112, 143

Cucumber, mock-, **4**: 383, 386n

Cucurbita maxima, **3**: 148n. *See also* Squash, hubbard

Cucurbita moschata, **3**: 154n. *See also* Squash, crookneck

Cucurbita pepo, **3**: 148n, **5**: 147n. *See also* Pumpkins; Squashes

Cuivre River, **3**: 338, 383n

Cul de Sac (Solitary) Island, **3**: 92, 94, 95n

Culho-mo (and similar spellings). *See* Lupine seashore

Cullaby Creek, **6**: 316n, **10**: 186n

Cul-te-ell, **6**: 155, 159n

Cummings (Cummuins), **2**: 166, 167n

Cups, **4**: 275, 279, **7**: 103, **9**: 166, 369n, **11**: 193–94

Curlander, Edward, **1**: 12

Curlew, Eskimo, **4**: 257n

Curlew, long-billed, **4**: 48–49, 50n, 94, 257n, 325, 326n, **5**: 37, 39, 39n, **6**: 382–83, 384n, **7**: 163, 165n, 167, 193, 196, 198, 200–201, **8**: 93, 94n, 117, 140

Curlews, **4**: 254, 349n, 380, 412, 415, 417, 423, **8**: 75, 117. *See also* Plovers

Currant, blood, **7**: 47n

Currant, buffalo, **3**: 12n, **4**: 57n, 89, 90–91n, **7**: 129n, **9**: 167–68, 167n, 182, **11**: 196n, 198, 222–23

Currant, garden, **4**: 392, 396n

Currant, golden (purple, yellow), **4**: 91n, 391–92, 396n, 406, 410n, 417, 419n, **5**: 31–32, 35n, 107, **7**: 126, 129n, 188, 190, 191n, **8**: 107, 107n, 173n, 200, 203n, 205, 264–65, 286, 287n, 320, **9**: 167n, 187, 187n, **10**: 115, 115n, **11**: 196n, 229–30, 230n, 233–34, 234n

Currant, purple. *See* Currant, wild black

Currant, red. *See* Currant, squaw

Currant, red flowering, **7**: 45, 47n, 55, 77, 112, 114n

Currant, squaw, **4**: 306, 308n, 364, 365n, 417, 419n, 427, 429, 429n, **5**: 31–32, 35n

Currant, sticky, **7**: 47n

Currant, swamp, **4**: 392, 397n, 436, 438n, **5**: 36, 39n

Currant, wild black (blue), **2**: 433, 435n, **3**: 12n, 454, 463, 468, **4**: 57n, 91n, 417, 419n, **5**: 31, 35n, **7**: 129n, **8**: 200, 203n, 205, 265, 320, 320n

Currants: observed, **3**: 8, **4**: 94, 238, 241, 247, 250–51, 287, 329, 364, 388, 396, **8**: 334, **9**: 185, 198, **10**: 118, 129, **11**: 259–60; gathered, **3**: 10; abundance, **3**: 481, **4**: 332,

391, 406, 414, 417, 428–29, 436, **9**: 187, 192–93, 195, 201–2, 204, **10**: 106, 114–15, 121, **11**: 196, 198, 211–12, 236–37, 239–40, 246–47, 249–50, 271; habitat, **4**: 54, 70, 324, 419; as food, **4**: 418; and Indians, **11**: 132; mentioned, **2**: 323n, **4**: 2, **5**: 28–30, 36, 39, 71, 83, 106, **8**: 100, **9**: 185n, **10**: 106n, 114n

Cushook (Cash-hook) Indians, **7**: 54–55, 59, 60n, 66, 82–83, 86, 89n

Cus-ka-lah (and similar spellings), **6**: 120–21, 120n, 135–36, 171, 358, 360, 365, 367

Custer Creek (York's Dry River), **8**: 252–53, 255, 255n, 256n, 257n, 390, 407

Cut Bank Creek (North Branch of Marias River), **8**: 2, 121–25, 121n, 122n, 123n, 124n, 125n, 128, 132n, 293, **9**: 341, 343n

Cutlasses, **5**: 347, **9**: 71. *See also* Arms and ammunition

Cut Nose (Neeshneparkkeook): and maps, **1**: 11; village, **7**: 211, 213, 215n; relations with the party, **7**: 221, 223, 247, 250, 326, 328, 333, 348–49, **8**: 21–22, **9**: 319; information from, **7**: 227; visits, **7**: 227, 346–47; and Twisted Hair, **7**: 228–32, 235, **9**: 307; rank, **7**: 242, 244; mourning, **7**: 329; hunting, **9**: 320–21; mentioned, **7**: 334n, **8**: 22n, 47, **9**: 307n, 319n, 326n

Cutright, Paul Russell, **12**: 7

Cuts-sâh-nim (and similar spellings) Indians. *See* Yakima Indians

Cutwhamo. *See* Lupine, seashore

Cyanea sp., **6**: 425n. *See also* Jellyfish

Cyanocitta cristata, **4**: 57n, **5**: 29n, **6**: 133n, **7**: 302n. *See also* Jay, blue

Cyanocitta stelleri, **5**: 214n, **6**: 94n, **7**: 78n. *See also* Jay, Steller's

Cyclopedia, **8**: 419n

Cygnus buccinator, **2**: 142n, **4**: 21n, **6**: 14n, **7**: 11n, **9**: 138n, **11**: 140n. *See also* Swan, trumpeter

Cygnus columbianus, **2**: 142n, **4**: 21n, **5**: 354n, **6**: 14n, **7**: 11n, **9**: 247n, **10**: 164n, **11**: 140n. *See also* Swan, tundra

Cynomys ludovicianus, **3**: 54n, **4**: 187n, **5**: 35n, **6**: 347n, **7**: 296n, **8**: 13n, **9**: 55n, **10**: 36n, **11**: 71n. *See also* Prairie dog

Cyperus esculentus, **7**: 297n. *See also* Nutgrass, yellow

Cypress, **11**: 316n

Cypripedium montanum, **8**: 69n. *See also* Lady's slipper, mountain

D

Daggers, **7**: 123–24, 125n, **8**: 137n. *See also* Arms and ammunition

Dakota Group, **8**: 351n

Dalles Indians, **5**: 353n

Dalles of the Columbia River. *See* Columbia River, The Dalles of the

Dame, John, **2**: 229n, 256, 415, 417n, 457, 457n, 460, 511, 516, **4**: 12n, **9**: 36, 36n, **10**: 26, 26n

Dancing, **7**: 127–28, 160–61, 162n, 166, 168, 178–81, 183, 186, 347. *See also* Balls; Indians; Members of the party; *specific Indian tribes; specific members of the party*

D'Anville, Jean, **1**: 5

Davidson, **6**: 156, 160n, 427

Davis, David, **10**: 229n

Day, John, **6**: 91n

Dead Horse Creek, **8**: 251, 254, 256n

Dead Indian Coulee, **8**: 120n, 174, 292

Deadman (Ash) Rapids, **4**: 216,

218–19, 221n, **6**: 449, 463, **8**: 382, 401, **9**: 157–58, 158n

Deadman Creek (Slate Run) (S. Dak.), **3**: 150–51, 153n, **9**: 77–78, 78n, **10**: 52, 52n, **11**: 97, 97n

Deadman Creek (Wash.), **5**: 264–65, 266n, 280

Dead River, **2**: 220

Deapolis site, **3**: 201n, **9**: 90n, **10**: 59n, **11**: 105n

Dearborn, Henry, **2**: 295, 299n, 513, 517, 519, **4**: 398, 401, 401n, **9**: 186n, **10**: 114n, **11**: 231n

Dearborn River: and maps, **1**: 11, **6**: 308–9; arrive at, **4**: 397–99, 401, **8**: 97, 103, **9**: 185, 186n, **10**: 114, 251, 251n, **11**: 230–31; described, **4**: 397; astronomical observation at, **4**: 400; listed, **6**: 449, 464, **8**: 383, 401; distances, **6**: 494–95; Indian name, **7**: 342, 343n; route to, **8**: 93, 104, 291; Indians, **8**: 109; mentioned, **4**: 397n, 401n, **8**: 98n, **10**: 113n, 114n, **11**: 230n

Deep Creek, **8**: 251, 254, 256n, **9**: 318, 318n

Deep River, **6**: 37n

Deepwater (Onion, Wild Onion) Creek, **4**: 30, 33n, **6**: 447, 462, **8**: 381, 399, **10**: 79, 79n

Deer: scarcity, **5**: 4, 45, 91, 115, **6**: 95, 186, **7**: 49, 52, 262, 269, 271, **8**: 123, 238, 325, 365, **9**: 388, **10**: 57, 125; hunted, **5**: 8–9, 27, 29, 31–32, 35–38, 43, 45, 47, 52–53, 55–57, 59, 63, 65–67, 71–72, 75–76, 84, 93–94, 98, 100, 103–4, 106, 112, 115, 117–19, 138, 140–41, 165–66, 174, 178–79, 183, 187, 191–94, 197, 203, 213, 226, 229–30, 232–33, 235–36, 337, 339–40, 342–45, 348, 354, 356, **6**: 12, 16, 19, 53–54, 60–61, 68–69, 73, 81, 91–93, 105, 108, 140,

163–64, 166–67, 188, 191, 232–36, 242–43, 326, 409, 411, 450, **7**: 25, 50, 53–56, 71, 74, 90, 92, 98, 103, 117–18, 120, 126, 132, 141, 196, 198, 201, 226, 230–31, 234, 236, 243–44, 258, 264–66, 273–74, 278–81, 286, 288, 291, 294, 297, 299, 308, 310, 313, 315, 331, 333–36, **8**: 10–11, 13, 17, 21–22, 24–26, 37–39, 41, 44–48, 48n, 50, 61, 63, 65, 68, 74, 77, 79–80, 82, 85, 90, 94–95, 98–99, 114, 116, 127–28, 141, 145–49, 152, 162–65, 174, 176–79, 181–82, 195, 202, 204, 206, 209, 224–26, 231–32, 238, 245, 273, 281, 283, 285–86, 290, 307–9, 320, 322–23, 327–28, 337, 356, 359–60, **9**: 8–12, 14–19, 22–24, 26–33, 35, 42–43, 47, 55–57, 60–65, 76, 86–88, 102–3, 108, 110, 112–13, 116–17, 126, 129–30, 133–36, 139, 141–42, 144–54, 150n, 162–68, 170, 172–73, 180–82, 184, 186–88, 190–203, 205–10, 213–16, 218–23, 225, 229, 231, 245–47, 249, 254–56, 258–59, 263–64, 268, 276, 278, 282, 284–86, 289, 291, 293–94, 301, 307–9, 311, 311n, 314, 319, 321–23, 325–33, 335–38, 341, 344–48, 351, 353–55, 360–62, 365, 375–83, 388, 391, **10**: 11–12, 15–17, 20–25, 25n, 30, 32, 35–38, 40–42, 52, 56–57, 62, 65–66, 65n, 69–72, 79, 81–82, 85, 87, 99–101, 104, 109, 115–18, 120, 122, 124–27, 130–31, 134–35, 137, 139–41, 148–50, 162–66, 171–72, 175, 177, 184, 189–90, 196–97, 199, 203–5, 208, 210–12, 210n, 215, 219, 223, 225, 229–31, 233–34, 234n, 236–39, 238n, 242–43, 246–51, 246n, 261–64, 268–69, 271, 278–

Deer (*continued*)
  79, **11**: 16–17, 20, 22–29,
  31–32, 34, 38–49, 49n, 52,
  59–60, 64–65, 69–73, 76–
  77, 79–81, 96–97, 101–3,
  108–11, 117, 121, 123–24,
  127, 137–39, 142–43, 145,
  149–55, 158–63, 165–66,
  176, 184, 186–91, 194–98,
  202–3, 207, 209–12, 220–
  21, 223–24, 227–28, 231,
  235–39, 241–47, 250–68,
  270–71, 273, 275–81, 283–
  84, 286–87, 289–95, 299–
  302, 304–9, 311–14, 318,
  327–28, 331–32, 335–36,
  372–75, 377–78, 382–85,
  394–96, 398, 401, 408, 410,
  414–15, 421n, 426–27, 430,
  435–38; skins, **5**: 9, 53, 61,
  63, 126–27, 133, 139, 143,
  286, 289, 309, 317, 350, 352,
  6: 76, 186n, 434, 438, **7**: 39,
  75–76, 101, 103, **8**: 83, 109,
  224, 226, 285, **9**: 186, 190,
  202, 207–8, 218, 229, 240,
  242, 297, 339, 344, 355, 376,
  10: 33, 114, 125, 158, 215,
  241, 264, **11**: 13, 129, 196,
  217, 231, 241–42, 261–62,
  269, 279–81, 329–30, 356–
  57, 363–64, 420; as food, **5**:
  11, 32, 40, 42, 74, 76, 98,
  100, 103–4, 197, 235, 337,
  341–43, 354–55, **6**: 84, 114,
  162, 215–16, 325–26, **7**:
  115, **8**: 23, 39, 52, 62, 64–
  65, 68, 75, 93, 127, 161, 163,
  178, 181, 202, 205, 307, **9**:
  77, 117, 199, 204, 245, 259,
  333, **10**: 165, **11**: 11, 28, 60,
  100, 121, 231, 263, 299,
  370–74, 389, 402–3; ob-
  served, **5**: 15, 19, 25–26, 37,
  39, 42–43, 71, 167, 169,
  244, **6**: 23, 70, 448, **7**: 16–17,
  33, 35, 200, 221, 223, 272–
  73, **8**: 71, 93, 180, 182, 297,
  321, 355, 361, 413, **9**: 54, 60,
  102, 153, 174, 199, 301, 316,
  330, 363, **10**: 235, **11**: 145,
  175; abundance, **5**: 31–32,

135, **7**: 174, 176, 297, 299,
  327, 329, **8**: 66, 68, 97–98,
  146–47, 175, 179, 219, 232,
  238, 245, 286, 326, 360, **9**:
  135, 138, 383, **10**: 82, 94,
  117–18, 226n, 238, 266, **11**:
  33, 76, 146, 160–61, 213,
  372–73; food, **5**: 98, **11**: 171;
  use, **5**: 127, **6**: 231, 351, 354,
  8: 226, **9**: 70, food, **9**: 11, 17,
  218; and Indians, **5**: 149,
  259, **6**: 19, 61, 74, 76, 206,
  208, 487, **7**: 18, 20, 38, 40,
  62, 65, 85, 128, 145–49,
  224, 227, 231, 261, 263,
  278–79, **9**: 70, 134, 209,
  212, 218, 229, 240, 242, 245,
  297, 308, 314, **10**: 215, **11**:
  282, 286–87, 356–57, 363–
  64, 370–71, 385–86, 389;
  signs, **5**: 203, 223, 355, **6**: 17,
  101, **7**: 33, 98, 100, 221, 223,
  8: 35–36, 356, **11**: 320; information about, **6**: 85; behavior, **6**: 403; as trade item, **7**:
  30, 112–13, 115–16, 183, **9**:
  376; mentioned, **5**: 246, **6**:
  71n, 83, 328, 405n, **7**: 80, 88,
  9: 155, **10**: 92
Deer, black-tailed. *See* Deer,
  mule
Deer, black-tailed fallow. *See*
  Deer, Columbian black-
  tailed
Deer, Columbian black-tailed, **6**:
  3, 68–70, 70–71n, 312, 315,
  317n, 328, 330n, 403–4,
  405n, **7**: 22, 24, 25n, 94,
  102–3, 116–17
Deer, Columbian white-tailed,
  6: 312, 315, 317n, 328,
  330n, **7**: 22, 24–25, 25n, 94,
  124–25
Deer, common. *See* Deer, white-
  tailed
Deer, common fallow. *See* Deer,
  Columbian white-tailed
Deer, eastern white-tailed, **5**:
  13n. *See also* Deer, white-
  tailed
Deer, fallow, **3**: 79n. *See also*
  Deer, white-tailed

Deer, long-tailed. *See* Deer, Columbian white-tailed
Deer, mule (black-tailed): discovered, **3**: 1, 48, 50, 50n,
  86n; hunted, **3**: 58, 148–49,
  4: 64, 136, 139, 143, 149–
  50, 164–5, 238, 240, 242,
  244, 255–56, 258, 280, 324,
  5: 10, 13n, 87, 134, 148–49,
  202, 209, **7**: 273–74, 314–
  15, **8**: 116–17, 247, 266,
  287, 326, 328, 331, **9**: 62, 77,
  136, 146, 160–61, 163, 165,
  209, 313, 355–56, **10**: 40–
  41, 82, 261, 273, **11**: 76–78,
  180–81, 188, 282–83; observed, **3**: 65, 82–83, 85n,
  86n, 87, **4**: 136–38, 227,
  229, 232, 256, 259, 280, **8**:
  56, 58, 119, 321, 323, **11**:
  152; abundance, **3**: 96, **4**: 81,
  126, 128, 143, **8**: 66, 68, 326;
  habitat, **3**: 183, 184n, 482,
  6: 331–32; scarcity, **3**: 222;
  specimen, **3**: 329–30, **8**: 326,
  327n, 419, **10**: 273; named,
  4: 65n, **10**: 40n; behavior,
  4: 136, 143, **6**: 404; skins, **4**:
  143, 150, 164–65; as food, **4**:
  255; described, **6**: 403–4, **9**:
  61; and Indians, **9**: 209; mentioned, **4**: 139n, **8**: 59n, 69n,
  328, 417, 418n, **6**: 312n,
  317n, 328, 403, 405n, **7**:
  274n, **9**: 61n, 146n, 209n,
  11: 77n, 152n, 283n
Deer, western white-tailed, **5**:
  10, 13n, 87, 149, **9**: 61, 61n,
  62, 209, 209n, **10**: 40, 40n,
  11: 282–83, 283n. *See also*
  Deer, white-tailed
Deer, white-tailed (common,
  fallow, long-tailed): hunted,
  2: 99, 142, 153, 158, 164–
  67, 239, 248, 250, 260–61,
  266, 269–70, 272–73, 275–
  76, 286–87, 291–93, 296,
  298, 300, 301n, 304, 307,
  313, 317–19, 323–25, 326n,
  327, 332–34, 354–55, 357,
  366–67, 369–70, 373n,
  388–89, 391–92, 395–96,

399, 402, 405, 408, 415–16, 418–23, 423n, 429, 431–35, 445, 500–504, **3**: 8, 9, 11, 22, 49–51, 55, 57–58, 65–66, 74–75, 78–79, 82–83, 86–87, 89–90, 94, 98, 100–102, 144, 169, 179–80, 182–86, 188, 238, 253, 255, 257, 263, 265, 269, 284–86, 292–94, 296, 299, 485–86, **4**: 23, 51–52, 54, 56–57, 65–66, 73, 82, 87, 100, 108, 111, 114, 126, 128, 130, 134, 136, 140, 149–50, 156, 164–65, 167–68, 171, 174, 176, 178, 180–81, 184–85, 250, 252, 255, 259, 263, 266, 281, 306, 327–28, 333, 366, 368, 374–77, 383, 385, 412, 415, 417–21, 423–25, 430, 432, 436, 438, **8**: 66, 68, **9**: 8, 146, **10**: 10, 40, 82, 273, **11**: 16; as food, **2**: 140, 227, 277, 294, 352, 394, 433, **3**: 8, 21–22, 50, 55, 86–87, **4**: 21–22, 55, 255, 263, 283, 379, 418, 424–25, 428, 431, **8**: 68, **9**: 134; signs, **2**: 254, **4**: 436; skins, **2**: 259, **3**: 79, 98, 390, **4**: 150, 165, 174, 261, 266, 365–66, 399, 404, 430, 436; abundance, **2**: 291–92, 301, 306, 308–9, 319–22, 333–334, 339, 340–41, **3**: 58, 76, 81, 184–86, 188, **4**: 53, 57–58, 60, 67, 75, 85, 103, 105–6, 126, 128, 184, 260, **8**: 66, 68, 326; behavior, **2**: 321–22, 334, **4**: 108, 137, 236, 348, **6**: 404, **8**: 325; scarcity, **2**: 351, 380, 418, 420, 432, **3**: 63, **4**: 161, 232; and Indians, **3**: 21, 116, 119, 199; as trade item, **3**: 27, 32, 390–444 passim; observed, **3**: 48–49, 78–79, 82, 93, **4**: 41, 45–46, 48, 81, 90, 108, 137, 151, 164, 186, 414, 428, **8**: 325; habitat, **3**: 58, 183, 482; food, **3**: 77, **4**: 70, 142; described, **6**: 403–4; mentioned, **2**: 101n, 224, 245–46, 285, 347, 395, **3**:

70, 79n, 184n, 260, **4**: 65n, 157–58, 193, 196–97, 411, **6**: 405n, **8**: 69n, 325n, **9**: 8n, **10**: 10n, **11**: 16n
Deer Creek (Idaho), **7**: 330n, **9**: 316, 316n, 318n
Deer (Grindstone, Panther) Creek (Mo.), **2**: 265, 266n, **9**: 8–9, 9n, 376, 376n, **10**: 10, 11n, **11**: 16, 16n
Deer (E-lal-lar) Island, **6**: 23, 25n, 458, 470, **7**: 19, 21–22, 22n, 24–26, 25n, 29, **8**: 387, 405, **9**: 282, 282n, **10**: 167, 167n, 202, 202n, 203n, **11**: 387, 388n, 435, 435n
Degie, Phillippe, **3**: 183n, **9**: 87n
D'Eglise, Jacques, **3**: 315n
Dejonah, Tice, **8**: 369
[Delash?], Silas, **9**: 3n
Delashelwilt, **1**: 19n. 126, **6**: 77n, 416, 418, 425, 427, 429–30, **7**: 7–8, 8n, **9**: 277n, 280n, **10**: 198, 198n, 200n, **11**: 428, 428n, 432n
Delassus, Don Carlos Dehault, **1**: 5
Delaunay, David, **2**: 243, 243n, **8**: 352n
Delaunay, Joseph, **8**: 352n
Delaunay, Pierre, **8**: 352n
De Laurier, **8**: 352n
Delaware Bar, **2**: 339n
Delaware Indians: **2**: 69n, 82n, 89, 90n, 107, 109n, 140, 174n, 182, 524, **3**: 391, 446, 449
Delaware River (Del.), **6**: 395, 397
Delaware River (Grasshopper Creek) (Kans.), **3**: 344, 384n
Delisle, Guillaume, **1**: 5
Del Nord River. See Rio Grande del Norte
Delorme, Jean Baptiste, **8**: 352n
Delorn, Henry, **8**: 351
Delphinium menziesii, **7**: 61n. See also Larkspur, Menzies's
Dendragapus canadensis, **5**: 204n, **6**: 377n, **8**: 55n, **10**: 136n. See also Grouse, spruce

Dendragapus fuliginosus, **7**: 130n. See also Grouse, sooty
Dendragapus obscurus, **4**: 415n, **5**: 29n, **6**: 377n, **7**: 130n, **8**: 55n, **9**: 307n, **10**: 136n. See also Grouse, blue
Dendrocopos villosus monticola, **8**: 27n. See also Woodpecker, Rocky Mountain hairy
Dentalium sp., **5**: 319n, **6**: 436, 439, 440n. See also Mollusks
Depression. See Medical problems
Dermacentor andersoni, **7**: 78n, **10**: 185n. See also Woodtick, Rocky Mountain
Dermacentor variabilis, **2**: 305n. See also Tick, American dog
Dermatitis. See Medical problems
Deroin Creek, **2**: 380, 382n, **9**: 25, 26n, **10**: 21n
Deschamps, Jean Baptiste, **1**: 17n. 73, **2**: 215n, 228–29n, 255, 258, 347, 362, 363n, 452, 454n, 526, **3**: 77, 79n, 227n, **4**: 12n, **9**: 60, 60n
Deschutes (Clark's, Towanahiook's) River: name, **1**: 10, **6**: 325n; maps, **1**: 10–12, 18n. 106, **7**: 132, 149; arrive at, **5**: 320–21, 376; characteristics, **5**: 325, **7**: 186n; Indian name, **5**: 326n, **7**: 216, 218, 219n; Indians, **6**: 13, 14n, 204, 314, 316, 317n, 480, 487, **7**: 122n, 152, 155, **10**: 160; conditions, **6**: 324; animals, **6**: 368; distances, **6**: 455, 493, **8**: 385; described, **7**: 127, 151n, 156, 158, 182, 184, **9**: 243, **10**: 160, **11**: 364–65; listed, **8**: 404, 415, **10**: 173, 174n; mentioned, **1**: 18n. 105, **5**: 319n, 320n, 323, 325n, 339, 377, 381n, **6**: 469, 472n, **7**: 130n, 153, 155n, 159n, **9**: 243n, 295, 295n, **10**: 160n, 214, 214n, **11**: 367n
Desks, **4**: 334–35, **5**: 206–7

Des Laurien's (Prospect) Island, **3**: 88–89, 91n, **10**: 41n, **11**: 78n

Desmanthus illinoensis, **3**: 468. *See also* Bundleflower

Des Moines (Dumoin, Demoin) River, **2**: 292, 293n, 296, 299n, 458, 463n, **3**: 17, 27, 32, 342–43, 346, 354–57, 406–8, 414–15, 419, 481, 483

Detachment Islands, **2**: 455–56, 456n

Detachment orders, **2**: 141n, 174–76, 178–79, 187–90, 190n, 196, 200n, 201n, 206, 212, 215n, 235–37, 254–58, 359–60, 502n, 511–12, 521, **3**: 14–15, 20–21, 152–53, 170–71, 290n, **6**: 156–58, **6**: 161n. *See also* Discipline; Orderly Book

Devil's club, **6**: 44, 45n

Dhegiha language group. *See* Siouan language

Diamond Island, **2**: 333–34, 335n, 336, 338–39, 339n, 479, 487, **3**: 386n, **9**: 80, **10**: 17n, **11**: 173, *See* Government Island

Diana Island, **2**: 284–85, 285n

Diarrhea. *See* Medical problems, dysentery

Dibblee Island, **6**: 28n, **7**: 17n, **9**: 281n, **10**: 202n, **11**: 434n

Dickson, Joseph: and Indians, **3**: 408, 410–11, **8**: 157; encountered, **8**: 3, 157, 288, **9**: 348, **10**: 266; and members of the party, **8**: 4, 158–59n, 302, 305, **9**: 351, **10**: 267–68; wounded, **8**: 157, 288, 330, 332n; biographical sketch, **8**: 158–59n; trapping, **8**: 158–59n; mentioned, **8**: 153n, 289n, 295, **9**: 349n, **10**: 266n, 267n. *See also* Hancock, Forrest

Dickson, Robert, **8**: 346, 347n, 368n

Dictionary, Owen's, **8**: 419n

Didelphis virginiana, **2**: 132n, **8**: 418n. *See also* Opossum

Diller, Aubrey, **1**: 5–6

Diospyros virginiana, **9**: 120n. *See also* Persimmon

Dirks, **2**: 205, **7**: 165, 169n. *See also* Arms and ammunition

Dirty Water River, **2**: 219–20

Discipline, **2**: 7, 60, 94, 140–41, 141n, 152, 156, 183, 183n, 194, 200n, 203, 211. *See also* Courts-martial; Detachment orders; *specific members of the party*

Dismal Swamp, **9**: 217n, **11**: 296–97

Distichlis spicata, **6**: 307n. *See also* Saltgrass, seashore

Diuretics. *See* Medicine

Divide (Willard's) Creek, **8**: 170–72, 171n, 173n, 393, 410, 415, **9**: 333n

Dixon Creek, **8**: 251, 254, 256n

Dock, Mexican, **4**: 383, 386n, **7**: 55, 61n, 77

Dock, seaside, **10**: 198n

Dock, western, **10**: 198n

Documents of Lewis and Clark, miscellaneous, **2**: 562–65

Dodecatheon meadia, **2**: 210n, *See* Cowslip, American

Dog. *See* Seaman

Dog, turnspit, **6**: 329, 330n, 334, 352, 357

Dogbane, hemp, **5**: 131n, **8**: 119, 120n, 190, 193n

Dogbane, spreading, **5**: 131n

Dogbane (silk grass), **5**: 131n, 135, 142, **6**: 211, 214, 216–17, 217n, 327, 434–35, 438–39

Dog (Bull) Creek (Mont.), **4**: 212–13, 214n, **6**: 448, 463, **9**: 157, 157n, **10**: 95n, **11**: 176n

Dog Creek (Wash.), **7**: 117n, **9**: 291n

Dog Mountain, **7**: 117n, **10**: 210n

Dogs: and Indians, **2**: 351, 507, **3**: 114n, 169, 228, 232, 255, 273, 410, 489, **6**: 196, 218–19, 274–75, 299–300, 312, 315, 318–19, 336–37, 395–96, 401, 403, **7**: 13, 49, 52, 188, 212, 220, 222, **10**: 32, 42, 43n, 46, 48, 79, 138; observed, **2**: 391, **5**: 77, **6**: 27; used for comparison, **2**: 471, 474, **3**: 53, 86–87; as food, **3**: 22, 116, 118–19, **5**: 256, 261–63, 278, 309, 311, 315, 318, 320, 327–28, **6**: 162–63, 166, **7**: 66, 88, 90, 92, 115, 117, 149, 152–53, 157, 170–71, 174, 176, 203–4, 210, 212–13, **8**: 319, 356–57, **9**: 69, 291, **10**: 32, 46, 152–53, 153n, 157, 161, 221, **11**: 86–88, 89n, 337–38; mad, **3**: 258, 304, 325, 489; and Indians, **4**: 23, 34, 38, 44, 54–56, 101, 136, 139, 211, 213, **9**: 27, 38, 70, 131, 157, 219, 306, 340, 388, **11**: 81, 86–87; as trade item, **5**: 255, 261–63, 277, 285, 287, 294, 296, 325, 346–47, 349, 350–53, **6**: 30–31, 33, 162–63, 192, 342, 346, 358, 360, 444, 456, 458, **7**: 9–10, 15–16, 28, 30, 66, 86, 97–100, 105, 109, 115, 117, 119–20, 123–24, 132, 134, 139, 141, 146, 148–49, 152–55, 157–61, 163–65, 167, 174, 176, 178–79, 181, 183, 187, 189, 205, 207, 209–11; purchased, **9**: 233, 235–37, 239–40, 244, 246–47, 249, 264–65, 278, 283, 285, 288, 291–92, 294–300, 304–5, 308, **10**: 153, 161, 163, 166, 168, 203, 205, 208, 210, 214–15, 217, 222, **11**: 341–42, 344–46, 348–49, 355–58, 367–70, 375–77, 385–86, 389, 410–11; mentioned, **4**: 84, **5**: 103, **6**: 321, 323, **7**: 262, **10**: 64n, **11**: 93n. *See also* Mastiff; Seaman; Spaniels

Dog's-tooth-violet, **8**: 28–29, 30n, 57–58, 59n, 72

Dog's-tooth-violet, white, **2**: 208–9, 209n

Dogwood, flowering, **7**: 76, 78n

Dogwood, Nuttall's, **7**: 76–77,

78n, **9**: 286, 287n, **10**: 207, 207n

Dogwood, red osier (red wood): and Indians, **3**: 305n, **7**: 15; observed, **4**: 17, 374, 388, 392, 429, **7**: 12–16, 112, 192, 197, 335, 337, **8**: 93, **9**: 196; habitat, **4**: 26, 54, 70, 73, 96, 176, 216, 324; scarcity, **4**: 358; abundance, **4**: 417, **6**: 26–27, **7**: 188–89; use, **5**: 81; mentioned, **4**: 19n, 28n, 57n, 429n, **5**: 86n, **6**: 29n, **7**: 14n, 17n, 194n, **8**: 94n, **9**: 196n

Dolichovespula maculata, **4**: 47n. *See also* Hornet, baldfaced

Dolichovespula sp., **7**: 312n. *See also* Hornets

Dollar Creek, **5**: 223n, 225, 227n, **8**: 37n, **9**: 227, 227n, 325n, **10**: 145n, 242n, **11**: 325n, 326n

Dolphees (Lahoocatt) Island, **3**: 143–44, 144n, 373, 380, **8**: 321, 321n, 323, 380, 398, **9**: 367n, **11**: 95, 95n

Dolphin, **2**: 418

Dominique, **6**: 373, 374n

Donation Book, **2**: 48n, 71, 563, **3**: 331n, 334, 450, 472

Donegan (Denegan), John, **2**: 146n

Donegany (Donegani), Joseph, **2**: 146n

Doniphan site, **2**: 349n

Donohoe's Landing, **2**: 117

Dorion, François, **10**: 29n

Dorion, Pierre, Jr., **2**: 493n, **3**: 21–24, 23n, 33, 34n, 36n, **8**: 338, 344n, 368n, **10**: 29n

Dorion, Pierre, Sr.: information from, **1**: 8, **2**: 497–98, **3**: 27, 34n, 36n, 41; interpreter, **2**: 60, 294, 295n, 347, **3**: 16–17, 41, **8**: 357, **9**: 13, 13n, 380, **10**: 13; sent out, **2**: 483, **3**: 16–17, 19, 21–24, 33; returns, **3**: 23; biographical sketch, **3**: 23n; duties, **3**: 26–27, 31–32, 116, 119; leaves party, **3**: 33, 37–38; and Indians, **3**: 33, **8**: 288, 338, 344n,

9: 40, 45, **10**: 31, 33, **11**: 63; mentioned, **2**: 493n, **3**: 29–30, 34, 121–22, 128–29, 139, **8**: 289n, 357, 358n, **9**: 40n, 45n, 50–51, 361, 362n, **10**: 14n, 29n, 32n, 33n, 278, 278n, **11**: 63n

Dorion Island No. 1 (Three Sisters Island), **3**: 100–103, 103n

Dorion Island No. 2 (Cedar Island), **1**: 8, **2**: 252, 253n, 295n, **3**: 31, 100–102, 103n, 104, 372, 375, 380, 415, 417, **8**: 324, 324n, 380, 398, **9**: 63–64, 64n, 354n, 367n, **10**: 42, 43n, 272n, **11**: 80–81, 81n, 172, 174

Dorosoma cepedianum, **4**: 279n. *See also* Shad, gizzard

Double Ditch site, **3**: 192n

Doubt Creek, **5**: 214n, 215, 217n

Douglas Creek, **10**: 78n, **11**: 134n

Dove, mourning (turtle), **4**: 235, 237n, 265, 378, **5**: 213, 214n, **6**: 379–80, 381n, **7**: 293, 296, 297n, 321, **8**: 75, 78n, 93, 107, 117, 143, 144n, 210, **10**: 111, 111n

Doves, **7**: 87, 90

Drag, **5**: 144

Dram. *See* Liquor

Draper, Lyman, **2**: 542–43, **9**: xvii

Draper Collection, State Historical Society of Wisconsin, **2**: 550

Drawers, **6**: 137. *See also* Clothing

Dress, hunting. *See* Shirts

Drewyer, Mr. **2**: 105, 109n

Drouillard (Drewyer), George: information from, **1**: 12, **3**: 63, 296n, **5**: 54–55, **7**: 40, 76, 243–44, 278, **8**: 31, 109, 125, **9**: 197, **11**: 257; and maps, **1**: 13, 19nn. 136–39, **3**: 309n, 385n; interpreter, **2**: 59, 85, 85n, 195, **3**: 327, 328n, **5**: 2, 78, 85n, 88, **7**: 129n, **8**: 130; returns, **2**:

139–40, 214, 235, 239, 251, 269–70, 304, 306, 418–19, 423–24, 435–36, **3**: 16, 236, 292, **4**: 73, 336, 419, **5**: 53–54, 113–14, 141, 159, **6**: 232–34, 275–76, 342, 346, 368, 370, 411, 414–15, **7**: 12, 71, 74, 92, 95, 127–28, 326, 328, **8**: 46–47, 109–10, 328, **9**: 27, 29–30, 33, 35, 40, 52, 54, 56, 64, 96, 198, 268–69, 272–73, 275, 277, 286, 291, 309, 326, **10**: 23, 28, 42, 106–7, 139, 185, 190–91, 195–97, 207–8, 210, 225, 225n, 229, 229n, 230–31, 233, 237, 239, 243n, 253, **11**: 44–45, 49–50, 57, 63, 190–91, 423–24, 428–29; hunting, **2**: 142, 153, 153n, 254, 260, 261n, 272, 283, 285n, 286, 288n, 293, 311, 313, 314n, 315, 319, 366–67, 369, 373n, 388, 391, 395, 429, 431–32, **3**: 13–14, 22, 38–40, 42, 57–58, 68–69, 77, 79n, 80, 85n, 89, 91n, 92–93, 95n, 98, 99n, 208, 294, **4**: 21, 23, 25, 27, 55, 57, 57n, 59n, 100, 102, 102n, 113–15, 193, 196, 227, 242, 255, 283, 296, 309, 328, 333, 336, 340, 344, 351, 354, 359n, 383, 386, 419, 421, **5**: 25–26, 35–36, 52, 56, 63, 74, 87, 97, 102–4, 118, 126, 133, 141–42, 191–92, 213, 235–36, 339, 340n, **6**: 101, 103, 117–18, 124, 135, 138, 140, 145, 161–62, 172n, 174, 179, 186, 192, 196, 198–200, 215–16, 228, 229n, 275, 277, 281–82, 290–91, 293, 307, 309, 312, 314, 323–24, 333, 335, 384–85, 387–88, 390–91, 393, 395–96, 398, 401–3, 401n, 409, 411, 430–31, 443–44, **7**: 7–8, 10, 16, 17n, 19, 24, 54, 56, 60n, 62, 66, 71, 75–76, 86, 88, 95, 106, 109, 118, 120, 124–25, 188–89, 196, 226, 228, 230,

Drouillard (Drewyer), George
(*continued*)

234, 243–44, 264–65, 268–
69, 271, 271n, 273–74, 278–
79, 282, 284, 285n, 286–87,
291, 294, 344–47, **8**: 23–24,
61, 63–66, 68, 87, 96, 99,
113, 116, 124–27, 144, 146,
152, 297, 323, 326, 328, **9**: 9,
12, 15–16, 23–25, 27, 29–
33, 35, 42, 45, 47, 52, 54, 56,
59–62, 64, 102, 128, 134–
36, 142, 170, 173, 179, 184,
184n, 198, 207–8, 231, 263,
263n, 265–66, 275–76, 278,
284–87, 293, 301, 309, 312,
314–15, 322, 344, 347, 361,
377–78, 388, **10**: 20–21,
23n, 24, 24n, 32–35, 34n,
37, 65, 65n, 105–6, 117n,
150, 181, 184, 192, 196–97,
200–201, 204–5, 207, 209,
211, 223–25, 228–30, 232,
239, 246, 248, 271, **11**: 19–
20, 22, 28–29, 31, 40–41,
43, 45–46, 49–50, 49n, 52,
64, 67–69, 71, 74, 76–78,
80, 143, 203, 209, 217, 227,
238, 259, 279–80, 306, 335–
36, 336n, 408, 411, 413, 415,
417, 420–21, 425, 427, 430,
432, 437–38; sent out, **2**:
142, 214, 237, 357, 380,
415–16, 433–34, 435n, 455,
488, **3**: 7, 9, 12n, 13–14,
294–95, 295n, **4**: 70, 75n,
339, 386, **5**: 53, 64, 68, 70,
73, 105, 109, 305, **6**: 242–
43, 336–37, 409, 411, **7**: 90,
92, 100, 125, 127–28, 129n,
228–29, 232, 260, 262, 322–
25, 339–40, **8**: 34–36, 51–
52, 107, 111, 114–16, 298,
371, **9**: 6, 25, 29, 33, 35, 44,
137, 166, 253, 273, 289–90,
320, 320n, 375, 389, 391, **10**:
9, 12, 16, 22, 24, 25n, 26, 41,
73, 101, 112, 170, 181, 212,
241, 243–44, 243n, 247,
252, **11**: 11, 44, 49, 52, 61,
78–79, 125, 193, 393, 423,
423n, 427–28; in permanent

party, **2**: 160, **3**: 4; listed, **2**:
194, 347, **4**: 9, 11, **8**: 74, 77,
86n, 110, **11**: 4n, 8n, 62n,
126n, 187n, 203n, 393n,
400n, 408n, 426n, 427n,
428n, 430n; duties, **2**: 214n,
258, **4**: 29, 152, 275, 277,
344, 349, **7**: 137, 139, 141,
257, 261, 272, 326, 328, **10**:
107, 253, **11**: 214; separated,
2: 228n, **4**: 327, 329–30,
418, **6**: 421, 423, **7**: 14, 98,
116, 237, 239, **8**: 39, 41, 44–
47, 108, **10**: 106, 106n; loses
letter, **2**: 239, 243; medical
problems, **2**: 397, **3**: 239,
281, **4**: 386, **5**: 45, 235, **6**:
429–30, **9**: 27, 29–30, 33,
35, 40, 52, 54, 56, 64, 96,
198, 268–69, 272–73, 275,
277, 286, 291, 309, 326; biographical sketch, **2**: 516; and
Indians, **3**: 295–96, 296n,
309, **5**: 141–42, 147n, 305,
6: 233, 235, 426, 428, 428n,
7: 163–64, 247, 250, 326,
328, 347, **8**: 51, **9**: 319, 326,
11: 280–81, 415; scouting, **4**:
66–69, 69n, 250, 256, 275,
277, **5**: 18, 24, 44, 61–62, **6**:
46–47, 92, 116, 117n, **8**: 2,
291–92, **9**: 193, 199, 257,
259, 338, 338n, **10**: 98, 107–
8, 116, 120–21, 120n, 123,
178, 254, **11**: 186–90, 249–
50, 261, 400, 403; and iron-
frame boat, **4**: 337; death, **5**:
10n; loses tomahawk, **5**: 138;
river named for, **5**: 268, 281;
accidents, **5**: 271; fishing, **6**:
351, 353, **10**: 194; discipline,
7: 216, 218; and horses, **7**:
264–65; and Blackfeet Indians, **8**: 2, 128–30, 133–35,
294–95; loses horse, **8**: 34–
35; and species, **8**: 52n, **9**: 67;
loses traps, **8**: 138; trading, **9**:
277, 293, 324, **10**: 199, 199n,
236, **11**: 429n; volunteers, **9**:
330, 330n; robbed, **11**: 125–
26; mentioned, **2**: 109n, 141,
141n, 147, 157, 211n, 300–

301, 317–18, 336, 340, 342,
355–56, 438, 510, 517, 523,
4: 10, **5**: 45, 69, 92, **6**: 137,
441–42, **7**: 197, 330n, **8**: 37,
9: 6n, 9n, 31, 39–40, 44n,
45, 99, 138n, 142n, 170n,
173n, 209n, 231n, 253n,
257n, 259n, 265n, 266n,
275n, 276n, 279–80, 279n,
284n, 285n, 286n, 293n,
302n, 312n, 314n, 315n,
375n, 377n, 388n, **10**: 9n,
12n, 16n, 20n, 21n, 23n,
26n, 29n, 32n, 34n, 36n, 38,
38n, 42n, 43n, 73n, 98n,
101n, 105n, 106n, 113n,
122n, 139n, 150n, 171n,
179n, 181n, 182n, 184n,
185n, 190n, 191n, 192n,
195n, 196n, 197n, 200n,
201n, 205n, 207n, 208n,
209n, 211n, 212n, 219n,
224n, 225n, 229n, 230n,
231n, 232n, 233n, 236n,
237n, 239n, 241n, 243n,
244n, 246n, 248n, 253n,
254n, 272n, **11**: xv, 11n, 20n,
41n, 48, 51, 52n, 58, 68n,
143n, 210n, 214n, 228n,
238n, 258, 282n, 307n,
403n, 411n, 413n, 415n,
417n, 420n, 421n, 425n,
433n, 437n, 440n

Droullard, Peter, **2**: 109n
Droulliez, Jean Baptiste, **2**: 109n
Drowned Man's Rapid. *See* Dead-
man Rapids
Drum, **5**: 340n, **9**: 48, 69
Drum, freshwater, **2**: 484n, **10**:
28, 29n
Drum (fish), **11**: 371–72
Drums (instruments), **11**:
65–66
Drunkenness. *See* Discipline
Dry Creek (Pryor's River), **8**:
219, 221, 222n, 391, 408
Dry (Deer, Short Leg) Creek,
3: 351–52, 384n
Dry Fork of Marias River, **8**:
119, 120n, 292
Dry (Goodrich's) Island
(Mont.), **4**: 200n, **6**: 448,

463, **8**: 141, 141n, 382, 401, **10**: 92, 92n, 260, 260n

Dry (Round) Island (S. Dak.), **3**: 70, 73n, **8**: 327–28, 329n

Dryobates villosus hyloscopus, **8**: 27n. *See also* Woodpecker, Cabanis's

Dryocopus pileatus, **5**: 195n, **6**: 381n, **7**: 78n, **8**: 27n, **9**: 221n, **11**: 308n. *See also* Woodpecker, pileated

Dubois Journal. *See* Field Notes (Clark's specific)

Dubois (Wood) Creek, **2**: 251–52, 252n, **9**: 7, 7n, 375, **10**: 9, 9n, **11**: 13, 13n

Dubois (Wood) River: arrive at, **1**: 5, **2**: 59, 131, **8**: 4, **9**: 366; name, **2**: 132n; hunting on, **2**: 153; conditions, **2**: 173–74; head of, **2**: 202; area described, **2**: 218; latitude and longitude, **2**: 228, 407, 479, **6**: 494, **11**: 4; distances, **2**: 486, **3**: 94, **9**: 200, **10**: 60, 124, **11**: 14, 264, 431; party leaves, **9**: xv, **10**: 1, **11**: 1; listed, **9**: 368n, **11**: 171–72; mentioned, **2**: 11, 173n, 178n, 210n, 229n, 252n, 382, 411–12, **3**: 251n, **9**: xi, 3, 233n, 279, 373, 374n, **10**: xi, xiv, **11**: xi, 8n. *See also* Camp Dubois

Dubuque, Julien, **1**: 16n. 32

Ducett. *See* Duquette

Ducharme, Jean Marie, **2**: 277n

Duck, black and white. *See* Bufflehead

Duck, fishing. *See* Mergansers

Duck, red-headed. *See* Mergansers

Duck, ring-necked, **7**: 23, 26n, 28, 31n

Duck, wood (summer), **2**: 99, 101n, 208, 210n, 336, 459, 485n, **4**: 310, 310n, **5**: 11, 13n, 42, **7**: 39, 41n, 46, 95, **10**: 208, 208n

Ducket Creek, **2**: 244, 245n

Duckinmallard. *See* Mallard

Ducks: observed, **2**: 177, 208, **3**:

147, 322, 325–26, **4**: 58, 90, 408, 420, **5**: 33, 35, 37, 39, 42, 59, 71, 84, 262, **6**: 161–62, 261, 385, **7**: 23, 25, 75–76, 196, 198, **9**: 128, 198, 200, 202, **10**: 154, **11**: 255, 260, 264–65, 267, 381–83; abundance, **2**: 208, 483, **4**: 49, 79, 103, 105, 298, **5**: 236–37, 242, **6**: 21–23, 35, 39, 88, 96, **7**: 28, 30, **8**: 10–11, 93, 119, 146, 148, 176, 350, **10**: 160, 164, 166, 168, **11**: 272–73, 378, 384, 386, 390–91, 399, 411; behavior, **2**: 222, **3**: 77, 232, 308, 457; hunted, **2**: 468, **5**: 15, 20, 43, 168, 193, 275, 279, 288, 303, 354, 356, **6**: 10–13, 16, 19, 38, 53–54, 60–61, 81, 93, 120–21, 188, **7**: 24–25, 33, 35, 94, 166, 168, 200, **9**: 44, 54, 145, 221, 227, 234, 238–39, 242, 251–52, 254–55, 257, 264, 288, 293, 299, 306, **10**: 146, 155, 166, 171, 177, 179, 203, 208, 212, 229, 243, **11**: 254, 266–67, 307–9, 325–26, 339, 352, 354, 361–62, 391, 394–96, 399–400, 405, 410; nests, **4**: 75, 78; as food, **5**: 15, 272n, 306, 312, **6**: 72; mentioned, **4**: 325n, **6**: 98n, 171, 383, **9**: 322, **10**: 160n, 179. *See also specific species*

Duck (Werner's) Creek (Valley County, Mont.), **4**: 133–35, 136n, **6**: 448, 463, **8**: 216, 220, 222n, 381, 400, **9**: 145, 145n, **10**: 87, 87n, **11**: 150–51, 151n

Duck (Whitehouse's) Creek (Broadwater County, Mont.), **4**: 419–20, 422n, **6**: 450, 464, **9**: 188, 188n, **10**: 116, 117n, **11**: 237–38, 238n

Dugout Coulee (Buffalo Creek), **8**: 115–17, 116n, 292

Dumetella carolinensis, **4**: 277n. *See also* Catbird, gray

Dump Creek, **5**: 157n, **10**: 131n

Dumpling, suet, **4**: 334, 362

Dunn Mountain, **8**: 225, 228n

Du Pratz, Antoine Simon Le Page, **2**: 351, 352n, **3**: 439

Duquette (Ducett, Ducete), François, **2**: 232–33, 234n, 235, 237, 244, 245n, **8**: 369, 369n

Durant, **2**: 167, 167n. *See also* Clothing

Durex (Troublesome) Island, **3**: 66, 67n

Durwain, Francis, **3**: 23n

Dutch. *See* Germans

Dysentery. *See* Medical problems

Dyssodia papposa, **4**: 262n. *See also* Marigold, fetid

E

Eagle, bald: observed, **4**: 31, 33, 93, 374, **5**: 63, 67n, **6**: 94, 96, 162–63, 363, **8**: 146, **9**: 202–3, **11**: 266–67; abundance, **4**: 78, 235; food, **4**: 121; described, **4**: 374, **7**: 15–17; and Indians, **8**: 218; use, **9**: 129; hunted, **9**: 129–30, 291; habitat, **9**: 133; mentioned, **3**: 482, **4**: 34n, 376n, **6**: 94n, 405–6, **7**: 17n, **8**: 147n, **9**: 129n, **11**: 267n

Eagle, golden (gray): and Indians, **3**: 117, 120n, 484, **4**: 93, **5**: 135, **7**: 348, **8**: 218; habitat, **3**: 184–85, 482, **6**: 404, 406, **11**: 252; observed, **4**: 93, 374, **6**: 94, 96, **8**: 146, **9**: 194, 203; described, **6**: 321, 323, 404–6, **7**: 15–17; hunted, **9**: 272, **11**: 421; behavior, **9**: 282; mentioned, **3**: 186n, **4**: 95n, **5**: 141n, **6**: 94n, 405n, **7**: 17n, **8**: 146n, **9**: 194n, **11**: 252n, 421n

Eagle Nose Butte, **3**: 186n

Eagle Nose site, **3**: 186n

Eagle Rock (Tower?), **4**: 387, 391n, 393, 401n, 433n, **9**: 190n, **10**: 118n, **11**: 242n

Eagles: habitat, **4**: 75, 78, 291, 295, **10**: 92, **11**: 167–68; observed, **4**: 94, **7**: 76, **8**: 148, 180, 210, 350, **9**: 128, **10**: 154; behavior, **7**: 24, 269, 271; hunted, **7**: 25, **9**: 288, **11**: 435; and Indians, **7**: 348–49, **9**: 320–21; mentioned, **4**: 296n, **6**: 321, 323

Eagle Sandstone, **4**: 233n, 234n, 257n, 386n

Eagles Feather (Piaheto), **3**: 155–56, 156n, 160, 162, 165–66, 167n, 172, 173n, 184–85, 187, 194–95, 199, 208–10, 219, 225–26, 230, 231n, **9**: 79, 82n, **10**: 55n. *See also* Arketarnarshar

Eagle (Stonewall) Creek, **4**: 228, 233, 234n, **6**: 449, 463, **8**: 382, 401, **9**: 160, 160n, 343, 343n, **10**: 96, 96n, **11**: 181n

Earbobs. *See* Earrings

Earrings, **6**: 139, 142, **11**: 276–77. *See also* Clothing

East Branch of Clark's River. *See* Clark Fork River

East Butte, **8**: 117, 118n

Eastern Journal, **2**: 18, 40, 42, 85n, 90n, 540–41, 544, 553, **9**: xvii

East Florida, **10**: 6n

East Fork Bitterroot River (Middle Fork Clark's River), **5**: 188n, 189, 190n, 193, **6**: 452, 466, **8**: 164–65, 165n, 166n, 393, 410, **9**: 220n, 331n, **10**: 138–39, 138n, 139n, 174n, **11**: 301n, 303–4, 304n, 305n

East Gallatin River (East Fork Gallatin's River), **8**: 181–83, 183n, 184–87, 193n, 392, 394, 409

East Indies, **6**: 314, 316, **10**: 5n

East Twin Creek, **8**: 90, 92n, 101

Echelute (and similar spellings) Indians. *See* Wishram-Wasco Indians

Echinacea angustifolia, **3**: 258n, 471. *See also* Coneflower, narrow leaf purple

Echinocystis lobata, **4**: 386n. *See also* Cucumber, mock-

Ecola Creek (McNeal's Folly), **6**: 180, 183–84, 185n, 284, 460, 471, **9**: 266, 266n, **10**: 188, 188n, **11**: 412, 413n

Ectopistes migratorius, **2**: 81n, **4**: 377n, **5**: 174n, **6**: 373n, **8**: 107n, **10**: 111n. *See also* Pigeon, passenger

Eel River, **3**: 406

Eggs, **2**: 181, 237, 252

Egregia menziesii, **6**: 423, 426, 428n, 431–32

Egret, great, **2**: 186n, 436–37, 438n

Egypt, **4**: 423

Eightmile Creek, **5**: 196n

Elaeagnus commutata, **8**: 94n. *See also* Silverberry

Elanus caeruleus, **5**: 217n. *See also* Kite, black-shouldered

Elder. *See* Elderberry

Elderberry, black, **10**: 142n

Elderberry, blue, **6**: 104n, 285–86, 286n, **7**: 197, 198n, 277, 280n, 337, **10**: 142n, **11**: 308–9, 310n

Elderberry, common, **6**: 286n, **8**: 79, 81n, 416, 418n

Elderberry, red, **6**: 103, 104n, **7**: 45, 47n

Eldorado Creek, **5**: 216, 217n, 219, 224n, 225, 227n, 239, **6**: 467, **8**: 25, 26n, 27, 29, 30n, 37n, 48, 50, 50n, 66, 384, 402, **9**: 323–24, 227n, 323n, 327n, **10**: 240–41, 240n, 242n, 243, 243n, **11**: 326n

Electricity. *See* Medicine

Elements of Botany (Barton), **2**: 79n; **12**: 8n

Eliatan Indians, **8**: 363, 364n

Elk: skins, **1**: 11, **2**: 259, **3**: 13–14, 21–22, 40, 42, 240, 285, 302–3, **4**: 26, 121, 149, 174, 211, 213, 242, 260–61, 278, 302, 306, 308, 323–24, 331, 333–34, 337–38, 344, 349, 354, 356, 363, 365–66, 369, 382, 407, **5**: 4, 126–27, 133–34, 230, 232, 258, 327, 341, 350, 352, **6**: 40, 74, 76, 85, 109, 114, 116–17, 126, 142, 144, 177, 186, 230–31, 328–29, 434, 438, **7**: 48, 51, 132, 141, 151, 322, 324, **8**: 51–52, 104, 140, 142, 149, 290, **9**: 46, 118, 156, 162, 169, 172, 187, 208, 229, 233, 240, 242, 250, 259, 267, 281, 289, 291, 245, 364n, **10**: 32, 105, 188, 192, **11**: 64, 129, 201, 203, 207, 220, 233–34, 329–30, 338, 353, 356–58, 363–64, 387, 414, 420, 430, 434; abundance, **2**: 306, 350, **3**: 7, 44, 58, 81, 126, 184–86, 188, **4**: 46, 49, 53, 57–58, 60, 62, 67, 75, 79, 81–82, 85, 103, 105–6, 114, 126, 128, 131–32, 143, 161, 165, 184, 250, 259, 421, **5**: 4, 135, **6**: 108, 184, **8**: 56, 99, 118, 121, 139–41, 146–48, 150, 154, 179, 184, 187, 189, 219, 225, 232, 237, 245, 259, 272–73, 280, 326, **9**: 72, 135, 138, 145, 149–50, 284, 336, 343, **10**: 57, 80, 94, 181, 261–62, 266, **11**: 145, 151, 159–61; signs, **2**: 351, 394, 432, 466, 500–501, **5**: 15, 31–32, 203, 342–43, **6**: 38, 42, 44–45, 61, 105, 116, 122, 134, 333, 335, **7**: 33, **9**: 25, 27, 30, 37, 42, 189, 388, **11**: 59, 239; observed, **2**: 369, 377, 464, 502–3, **3**: 61–62, 87, 93, 96, 98, 126, 182–83, **4**: 31, 33, 41, 44–46, 48, 57–58, 87, 90, 108, 111, 137–38, 151, 164, 186, 201–2, 205, 209, 227, 229, 232, 236, 247, 252, 256, 259, 277, 414, 420–21, 423, 428, **5**: 33, 35, 39, 167, 169, **6**: 17, 103–4, 448, **7**: 16–17, 33, **8**: 66, 68, 182, 191, 208, 255, 286, 310, 351, **9**: 25, 42, 129–30, 132–33, 135, 140, 142, 155, 166, 194, 332, 344, 353, 357, **10**: 20, 33, 276, **11**: 40, 146, 175–76, 181–82, 194–95, 252, 254, 400, 437; hunted, **2**: 377–78, 380, 423,

433–36, 457, 459, 463n, 504–5, **3**: 7–9, 11, 38–40, 42, 49–50, 55, 61–62, 65–66, 74–75, 89–90, 107–8, 146–47, 179–80, 182–86, 271, 238, 285, 292–94, 296, 299–300, 328, 485–86, **4**: 26, 39, 51–56, 65–66, 88–90, 96, 100, 102, 105, 113, 115, 118, 120–21, 123, 149, 159, 161, 167–68, 171, 174, 176, 178, 184–85, 208–9, 217, 219, 227, 229, 232, 242, 244, 250, 252, 258–59, 261–63, 278, 281, 308–9, 324, 327, 331, 333, 336, 362, 365–66, 382, 385, 387, 399, 403, 405–7, 417–18, **5**: 8, 25–26, 53, 55, 190–91, **6**: 53, 71, 96–97, 105–9, 116–18, 121–22, 124–27, 145, 151n, 152–53, 156, 161, 166–67, 171–72, 188, 191–92, 194–96, 200, 208, 215–16, 226–27, 232–34, 239–42, 244, 253, 255, 275, 279–80, 293, 295, 312, 314, 321, 323–24, 351, 353, 356–58, 360, 387–88, 390–91, 393–94, 396, 409, 411, 414–16, 418, 427, 430–32, 436, **7**: 7–8, 35, 50, 53–54, 56, 62, 66, 71, 74, 79, 95, **8**: 99, 104, 122, 141, 145, 149, 152–55, 184, 187, 189–90, 204, 206, 209, 232, 238, 276, 281, 286, 290, 295, 297, 309, 320, 325, 329, 342, 351, 353, 361, 374, **9**: 33, 36, 43–45, 52, 54–57, 60, 62, 65, 76, 78, 87, 97, 99, 109–10, 113–14, 116–17, 131, 133–34, 136, 140, 142–44, 147, 149–53, 156, 158, 160–64, 166, 169, 177–80, 184, 186–87, 191, 193, 197, 220, 258, 260, 263–65, 267–69, 271–80, 277n, 284–87, 311n, 336, 342, 344–49, 351, 353–55, 357, 359, 363, 391, 393, **10**: 23, 25–26, 30, 31, 33–35, 37–38, 43, 62, 69, 71–72, 81–82, 84, 95, 99–101, 104, 106–7, 115,

120, 139, 179, 181–82, 185–86, 188–93, 195–201, 204–6, 252, 261–62, 264–65, 269, 271–72, 274, 276, 279, **11**: 47, 49–50, 60, 67–73, 76, 83, 96, 102, 108–9, 119, 123–24, 127, 138, 141, 144, 146–48, 150, 154–55, 159–64, 177–80, 183–84, 186–91, 194–95, 203, 207, 217–18, 220, 227, 230–31, 233–34, 245, 250–51, 257–58, 305–6, 401, 404–5, 408–11, 413–21, 423–24, 426–30, 428n, 429n, 432, 438; scarcity, **2**: 397, **4**: 208, 306, 308, **5**: 87, 91, 115, **6**: 95, 242–43, 342, 344, 356, 381–82, **7**: 49, 52, 95, 127, 196, 198, **8**: 97, 106, 140, 195, **10**: 104, 106, **11**: 202–3, 209–11, 410; as food, **3**: 7–9, 11, 21–22, 40, 42, 49, 55, 81, 86–87, 90, 238, 272, 293, **4**: 26, 111, 120, 379, 382, 387, 405, **5**: 25, 27, **6**: 2, 84, 105–7, 116, 137–39, 142, 145, 152–53, 162, 177, 186, 200–201, 203–4, 210–12, 223–24, 245–46, 284–85, 287–88, 325–27, 368, 370, **7**: 8, 12–13, 75–76, 86–88, 90, 92, 115, 128, 170–71, **8**: 39, 150, 208, 286–88, **9**: 262, 270, 286–88, 298, **10**: 184, 186, **11**: 62, 123, 389, 401–3, 407, 409, 413–22, 424, 426, 428, 431, 433, 438; and Indians, **3**: 21, **6**: 19, 60–61, 66, 74, 76, 87, 89, 206, 208, 219–21, 231–33, 243–44, 274–75, 318–19, **7**: 18, 20, 38, 92, 128, 145–48, **9**: 30, 212, 229, 240, 242, 250, 391, **10**: 32, **11**: 356–57, 363–64; habitat, **3**: 58, 482, **6**: 315, 331, 333, 403; food, **3**: 77, **4**: 70, 142, **6**: 276–77, 287–88, **8**: 190–92, 276, **11**: 171; behavior, **3**: 131, **4**: 67, 136–37, 143, 237; specimen, **3**: 331; as trade item, **3**: 393–444 passim, **6**: 146–47, 180, 187,

205, 234, **7**: 10, 12–13, 53–56, 101, 103, 112–13, 115–17, 134, 139, 141, 248, **11**: 387, 434; horns, **4**: 57, 235, **7**: 43, **8**: 150, 319; use, **5**: 127, **6**: 202–4, 206–7, 209–10, 351, 354, 395–96, 407, 436, 440; teeth (tusks), **5**: 135, 145–46; antlers, **5**: 139, 149–50, 288; stolen, **6**: 4, 281–82, 299–300, 336, 426, 428; named, **6**: 20n; information about, **6**: 85, 92–93; marrow and tallow, **6**: 106–7, 201–2; spoiled, **6**: 109, 114, 125, 139, 142, 144, 287–88; sent for, **6**: 198–99, 262, 267, 325–26, 365, 367, 395–96; described, **6**: 404, 408, 410, **8**: 145; name, **8**: 59n; migration, **10**: 196; mentioned, **2**: 347, 307n, **3**: 135, 260, 488, **4**: 328, 423, 436, **6**: 317n, 405n, **7**: 9n, **8**: 3, 156, **9**: 116, 170, 173, 259, 261, 266–67, 269, 272–74, 278, 284, **10**: 20n, 195n, 197n, 198n, 199n, 252n, 264n, **11**: 6n, 40n

Elk Creek, **8**: 97, 98n, 103, **10**: 251, 251n

Elk Fawn Rapids, **8**: 150, 151n

Elkhorn (Corn de Cerf, Hart's Horn) River, **2**: 403, 404n, 419, 419n, 437n, **3**: 92, 95n, 350, 352–53, 355, 357–58, 384n, 395, 397

Elkhorn Mountains, **10**: 115–16, 115n, 116n, **11**: 235n

Elkhorn Point, **9**: 141n, **10**: 85n

Elk (Kid) Island, **4**: 166n, **10**: 90, 90n

Elk River, **10**: 43n, 67n

Elkskin-bound Journal: discussed, **2**: 9–10, 23–26, 34, 557, **5**: 210n, 214n, 228n, 260n, 263n, 284n, 319n, 340n, 343n, 344n, 348n, 380n, **6**: 158–59n; begins, **5**: 198, 199n; maps, **5**: 203n, 205n, 211n, 215n, 217n, 224n, 240n, 268n, 272n, 275n, 307n, 312n, 319n,

Elkskin-bound Journal
(*continued*)
353n, **6**: 68n, 127n; sketches, **6**: 67n; ends, **6**: 148n; mentioned, **2**: 33, 35, 538–39, 549, **5**: 245n, 248n, 290–91n, 300n. *See also* Codex journals; Field Notes; First Draft; Voorhis journals

Ellicott, Andrew, **1**: 5, **2**: 5, 87n, 93n, 122n, 411–12, **3**: 279, 301, 302n, **4**: 25

Elliott, Stephen, **12**: 6

Ellis, **7**: 241n

Elm, American, **3**: 182, 184n, **4**: 17, 19n, 26, 34, 39, 54, 69, 73–74, 93–94, 95n, **8**: 150, 151n, 273, 286, 354, 355n, 359, 359n, 417, 418n, **9**: 27, 27n, 31–32, 42–44, 51, 54, 61, 133, 138, **10**: 32, 32n

Elm, rock, **8**: 359, 359n

Elm, slippery, **2**: 349n, **8**: 345, 345n, 359, 359n, 373

Elms, **2**: 391–92, 407, 428, 430, **3**: 76–78, 222, 229, 361–62, **8**: 273

Elm (Wolf) Creek, **3**: 91n, 358, 372, 380, **8**: 380, 398, **9**: 62, 62n, **10**: 41, 41n, **11**: 78, 78n

Elute Indians. *See* Wishram-Wasco Indians

Elymus canadensis, **2**: 365n, **3**: 146n, 468, **5**: 60n, **7**: 338n, **8**: 222n, **9**: 23n, **11**: 38n. *See also* Wild rye, Canada

Elymus cinereus, **5**: 60n, **6**: 368n, **7**: 191n, **8**: 188n. *See also* Wild rye, basin

Elymus sp., **8**: 144n. *See also* Wild rye

Elymus villosus, **3**: 468. *See also* Wild rye, slender

Elymus virginicus, **3**: 468. *See also* Wild rye, Virginia

Emanuel (Plum) Creek, **3**: 44–45, 46n, 357, 379, **8**: 338, 344n, 379, 398, **9**: 53, 53n, **10**: 34, 35n, **11**: 68, 69n

Emetic. *See* Medicine

Emory, W. H., **3**: 291

Empidonax hammondii, **6**: 381n.

See also Flycatcher, Hammond's

Endeavour, **12**: 5

Enema. *See* Medicine

Eneshur (and similar spellings) Indians. *See* Tenino Indians

Engagés (French, French boatmen): information from, **1**: 8, **3**: 41, 136, 349, **4**: 137–38, 188–89, 204, 375, **8**: 357, **10**: 74n; listed, **1**: 17n. 73, **2**: 195, 255–56, 347, 349n, 512; recruited, **2**: 214, 214n, 510–11, **9**: 94; duties, **2**: 215n, 258, 264, 264n, 362, 504–5, **3**: 152, **9**: 45, 60, 375, **10**: 62; medical problems, **2**: 289, **3**: 99, 109; complain, **2**: 306, 307n, **3**: 99; return party, **2**: 511, **3**: 4, 227n, 230, 231n, 250n, 305n, 327, 333, **4**: 1, 7, 12n, **6**: 352, 357, 405–6, **8**: 318; biographical sketches, **2**: 516, 525–29; discharged, **3**: 2, 157–58n, 209–10, 226–27, 227n, 248, **9**: 93–94, **11**: 66, 67n; sent out, **3**: 16–17, 236, **9**: 125; damage pirogue, **3**: 19–20; and Indians, **3**: 114n, **7**: 17n, **8**: 318; interpret, **3**: 114n, **8**: 329–30, **9**: 65, 74; celebrate, **3**: 261; other, **4**: 35; tobacco, **4**: 324; and species, **7**: 302–5, **8**: 117, 286; encountered, **8**: 357; hunting, **9**: 112; mentioned, **2**: 149, 212, 228–29n, 237, 244–45, 259n, 261, 276, 286, 301n, 336, 338, 357, 427n, 430, 454n, 478n, 512, 516, **3**: 152, 181n, 464, **4**: 269, **9**: 8, 40, 41n, 45n, 60n, 119n, **10**: 62n, 152, 153n, 270n. *See also* Frenchmen

England, **6**: 187, 221, **12**: 3

English. *See* British

English River, **4**: 35, 40n

Engraulidae, **6**: 346n. *See also* Anchovies

Enhydra lutris, **5**: 328n, **6**: 86n, 166n, **7**: 9n, **9**: 243n, **10**:

162n, **11**: 367n. *See also* Otter, sea

Eoote-lash-Schute (and similar spellings) Indians. *See* Flathead Indians

Equipment, **2**: 6, **4**: 136, **4**: 152, 154, 156–58, 176, 178, 328, 333, 344–46, 354, 371n, 375, 420, **5**: 113, **6**: 96. *See also* Baggage; Instruments, scientific; *specific type of equipment;* Tools; Utensils, cooking

Equisetum arvense, **2**: 308, 309n, **3**: 468, **12**: 3. *See also* Horsetail, field

Equisetum hyemale, **2**: 104n, **5**: 10n, **9**: 191n. *See also* Rush, stout scouring

Equisetum sp., **2**: 309n, **4**: 381n, **8**: 120n, **9**: 9n, **10**: 11n. *See also* Horsetail; Rush

Equisetum telmateia, **6**: 225n, **7**: 47n, **9**: 287n. *See also* Horsetail, giant

Eremophila alpestris, **4**: 95n, **7**: 195n, **8**: 78n. *See also* Lark, horned

Erethizon dorsatum, **3**: 66n, **7**: 70n, **9**: 58n, **10**: 38n, **11**: 73n. *See also* Porcupine

Erethizon dorsatum epixanthum, **3**: 66n, **4**: 75n, **5**: 131n, **8**: 281n. *See also* Porcupine, yellow-haired

Eritettix simplex, **4**: 237n. *See also* Grasshoppers

Ermine. *See* Weasel, long-tailed

Erythronium albidum, **2**: 209n. *See also* Dog's-tooth-violet, white

Erythronium grandiflorum, **8**: 30n. *See also* Dog's-tooth-violet

Erythronium oregonum, **7**: 195n. *See also* Lily, fawn

Erythronium revolutum, **7**: 195n. *See also* Lily, fawn

Esox lucius, **2**: 72n, **9**: 40n, **10**: 29n, **11**: 56n. *See also* Pike, northern

Espontoon, **3**: 287, 287n, **4**: 104, 107n, 145, 202, 217, 219, 262, 289, 292, 294, **9**: 158, 158n, **11**: 177–78,

178n. *See also* Arms and ammunition

Estimate of Eastern Indians, **2**: 537–38, 541, 555, **3**: 334, 386–450, **5**: 86n

Estimate of Western Indians, **2**: 538, 560, **6**: 474–88

Eulachon (anchovy): discovered, **6**: 3; described, **6**: 342, 344, 349–51, 364–65, **10**: 194–95; fished for, **6**: 346, 351, 353, **10**: 195; sketch, **6**: 346n, 351n; habitat, **6**: 346n, **7**: 44; and Indians, **6**: 358, 360, 378–80, **7**: 12–13, 14n, 18, 27–28, 36, 98–99, **9**: 278, 282, **10**: 194, 197, 197n, **11**: 424, 429–30, 430n; as food, **6**: 368, 370, 379, 384–85, 402–3, **7**: 18, 28, **9**: 275, 278, 282, **11**: 423; as trade item, **6**: 444; mentioned, **7**: 47n, **9**: 275n, 278n, **10**: 194n, **11**: 423n, 425n

Euphagus carolinus, **4**: 237n, **6**: 378n, **8**: 78n, **9**: 181n, **10**: 106n, **11**: 222n. *See also* Blackbird, Rusty

Euphagus cyanocephalus, **4**: 237n, **6**: 378n, **7**: 32n, **8**: 78n, **9**: 181n, **10**: 106n, **11**: 222n. *See also* Blackbird, Brewer's

Euphorbia marginata, **3**: 468. *See also* Snow-on-the-mountain

Eutamias townsendii, **6**: 317n. *See also* Chipmunk, Townsend's

Evans, John Thomas, **1**: 5–7, 12, 16n. 46, 17n. 56, 18n. 82, **2**: 2–3, 6, 60, 155n, 478n, 507, 508n, **3**: 73n, 108–9, 177, 183, 184n, 186–87, 201n, 205n, 237, 241n. *See also* Mackay, James

Evans Bend, **10**: 101n

Evil Spirit Creek. *See* Blackbird Creek

Ewan, Joseph, **12**: 5

Ewen, **6**: 155–56, 160n, 427

Exogonium jalapa, **2**: 86n, **5**: 235n. *See also* Jalap; Medicine

Eyedaggs, **8**: 135, 137n. *See also* Arms and ammunition

Eyes. *See* Medical problems

Eye water. *See* Medicine

F

Fabaceae, **7**: 338n. *See also* Peas

Factory (Sand) Creek, **2**: 277, 279, 281n

Fagus grandifolia, **2**: 80n, **5**: 358n. *See also* Beech

Falco sparverius, **4**: 34n, **6**: 378n. *See also* Kestrel, American

Fallawan. *See* Callamon

Fall Indians. *See* Atsina Indians

Falls Mountain. *See* Mount Hood

Falls of St. Anthony, **3**: 409–11, 480

Fanny's bottom (valley), **7**: 16, 17, 17n

Farfonge (Fairfong, Faufong), **2**: 435–36, 437n, 439, 442n, 492, 494–95, **10**: 29n

Farm (Horse) Island, **3**: 107, 109n

Fascine, **4**: 102, 105, 107n

Fatigue. *See* Medical problems

Feathers, **3**: 24, 28, 120n, 481, 484, **5**: 140, 150, 161, 259, 289, **6**: 207, 209, **7**: 267, **8**: 295, **9**: 67, 79, 92

Feet. *See* Medical problems

Feldspar, **5**: 157n

Felis concolor, **2**: 309n, **4**: 158n, **5**: 39n, **6**: 136n, **9**: 149n, **10**: 148n, **11**: 159n. *See also* Mountain lion

Felon. *See* Medical problems, fingers

Femme Osage (Osage Woman's) River, **2**: 246n, 248, 249n, **3**: 338, 369, 376, 446, 451, 476, **8**: 377, 394, **9**: 7, 7n, 368n, 375, **10**: 9, 9n

Fennel, sweet, **7**: 266n

Fern, Christmas, **6**: 303, 305, 307n

Fern, deer, **6**: 303–4, 306, 307n

Fern, western bracken, **6**: 193, 224, 224n, 228–29, 230n, **7**:

33, 37n, 55, 61n, 77, **9**: 287, 287n

Fern Glen Formation, **2**: 285n

Ferns, **5**: 356, **6**: 44–45, 45n, 276–77

Ferret, **6**: 355n

Fescue, Idaho, **5**: 228n, **7**: 204n, **8**: 38n

Festuca idahoensis, **5**: 228n, **7**: 204n, **8**: 38n. *See also* Fescue, Idaho

Fever. *See* Medical problems, ague and fever

Fiddle, **2**: 516, **4**: 70, 272, 332, 362, **5**: 173, 303, 306, 329, 336, 341, 343, 350, 353, **7**: 127–28, 160–61, 166, 168, 178–80, 347, **9**: xii, 83, 107, 138, 165, 179, 296–97, 299, 308–9, 320, **10**: xii, **11**: 114, 191, 344–45. *See also* Cruzatte; Gibson

Fiddle (Little Quiver) Creek, **2**: 249–50, 251n

Fiddlers Creek, **9**: 39n

Fidler, Peter, **1**: 5, 16n. 28, **3**: 365, 385n, **4**: 266, 269, 269n, 270–71, **7**: 216, 218, 219n

Field (Fields), Joseph: listed, **2**: 148, 187, 189, 194, 197, 199, 255, **4**: 9, 11, **8**: 74, 77, 86n, 110, **11**: 4n, 7n, 62n, 187n, 210n, 393n, 395n, 408n, 424n, 427n, 430n; returns, **2**: 154, 248, 431–32, **3**: 19–20, 57–58, **4**: 70, 250, 295, 297, 336, **6**: 411, **7**: 12, 14, 199–200, 272–73, 289–90, 308, 310, **8**: 150, **9**: 109, 258, 269, 272, 274, 286, 291, 319, **10**: 24, 105–7, 118, 125, 179, 195, 197, 210, 230–31, 233–34, 236, 239, 253, **11**: 48–49, 188, 197, 204–6, 236–37, 396, 401, 416, 420; in permanent party, **2**: 229n; hunting, **2**: 327, 328n, 366, 398–99, 429–30, 502–3, 503n, **3**: 89, 91n, 257, 271–72, 271n, 286, 286n, **4**: 100, 102n, 277, 283, 331, 333,

Field (Fields), Joseph
(*continued*)

336, 412, 415, 431, **5**: 27, 29, 45, 47, 66–67, 93–94, 359, 362, **6**: 8–9, 40–41, 68, 71, 105, 106n, 177, 188, 190–91, 253, 255, 351, 353, 358, 360, 365, 368n, 391, 393, 395–96, 398, 401–3, 401n, 409, 411, 414–16, 418, 420n, 430–31, 443–44, **7**: 7–8, 8n, 10, 16, 17n, 24, 33, 35, 54, 56, 60n, 62, 66, 71, 74–76, 86, 88, 96, 99, 106, 109, 268, 271, 271n, 273–74, 278–79, 284, 286–87, 289–90, 297, 299, 308, 310, 313, 315, 326, 328, 331, **8**: 35–38, 44–45, 48, 50–51, 62, 64–65, 68, 87, 98, 124–27, 140, 146, 148, 150, 320, 322, 326, 328, 331, 337, 361, **9**: 18, 23, 28, 30, 32–33, 42, 54, 61–62, 103, 258, 269, 276–78, 278n, 280, 284, 287–88, 290, 312, 315, 322, 324, 343–48, **10**: 20, 24–25, 30, 30n, 35, 66, 106, 179, 187, 191, 197, 199, 207, 209, 212, 229, 232–35, 241–42, 244, 246, 248, 262, 264, 271, 274, 277, **11**: 32, 47–48, 60, 77, 268, 401, 416n, 424, 426–30, 429n, 432, 438; accidents, **2**: 345, 347, **9**: 20, 163, 178, 385, **10**: 18, 98, 106; sent out, **2**: 488, **3**: 7, 9, 16, **4**: 289, 297–99, 327, 329, 348, **5**: 305, 358, 360–61, **6**: 60, 262, 267, 403, **7**: 90, 92, 100, 139, 258, 271–74, **8**: 46–47, 62–63, 107, 115–16, 153, **9**: 26, 28, 166, 168, 253, 289, 329, **10**: 101–2, 105, 114, 170, 191, 220, 227, 252, **11**: 48–49, 61, 193, 198, 393, 407, 417; biographical sketch, **2**: 517; one of "nine young men from Kentucky," **2**: 529n; and Indians, **3**: 271–72n, **5**: 305, **7**: 289–90, **9**: 342, **10**: 259; medical problems, **3**: 294, **4**:

109–10, 111n, 118, **6**: 122, **7**: 261–63, 265, 269, 271, **9**: 143, **10**: 85–86, 86n, **11**: 146, 147n; scouting, **4**: 66–69, 69n, 250, 252, 256, 275, 277, 398, 401, 417–18, **6**: 46–47, 62, 65, **8**: 2, 291–92, **9**: 44, 137, 186, 188, 254, 338, 338n, **10**: 98, 116, 175, 254, **11**: 186–89, 201, 230–31, 237–38, 395; information from, **4**: 70–71, 250, 320, **10**: 102; and species, **4**: 71, 74, 75n, 256, 331, 351, **7**: 126, 131, **10**: 212n, **11**: 188–89, 214–15; discovers creek, **4**: 74; duties, **4**: 275, 277, 279, 349, **5**: 252, **7**: 66, **8**: 113–14, **10**: 105, **11**: 209, 214; and iron-frame boat, **4**: 323, 337, 343–44; separated, **4**: 430, 432–33, 433n, **7**: 98, 116, **8**: 107, 149, 323, 329, 351–52; votes, **6**: 83; and gifts, **6**: 136, 138; and salt-making camp, **6**: 138, 140, 166, 172n, 297, 321–22, 324, **9**: 263, 263n, **10**: 184, 191, 193, 193n; and Blackfeet Indians, **8**: 2, 128–30, 133–35, 294–95; death, **8**: 364n; volunteers, **9**: 330, 330n; mentioned, **2**: 154n, 200n, 346, **4**: 257n, 305n, **5**: 256, **6**: 441, **8**: 97, 111, 147, **9**: 44n, 103n, 109n, 138n, 168n, 169n, 185n, 188n, 253n, 255n, 258n, 269n, 272n, 274n, 276n, 277n, 279, 285n, 286n, 312n, 315n, 319n, 327n, 329n, 373–74n, 395n, **10**: 18n, 20n, 24n, 25n, 36n, 66n, 98n, 99n, 101n, 102n, 103n, 106n, 107n, 114n, 117n, 119n, 125n, 171n, 175n, 179n, 184n, 187n, 191n, 193n, 195n, 197n, 199n, 207n, 209n, 211n, 212n, 220n, 228n, 230n, 231n, 232n, 233n, 234n, 235n, 239n, 242n, 243n, 244n,

246n, 248n, 253n, 254n, 260n, 262n, 264n, 271n, 274n, 277n, **11**: 32n, 49n, 60n, 198n, 199n, 202n, 214n, 232n, 238n, 268n, 401n, 417n, 421n, 426n, 428n, 433n, 440n

Field (Fields), Reubin: listed, **2**: 147, 187, 189, 194, 197, 199, 255, **4**: 9, 11, **6**: 172n, **8**: 74, 77, 86n, 110, **11**: 4n, 7n, 187n, 203n, 393n, 395n, 400n, 408n, 411n, 419n, 427n, 430n; hunting, **2**: 153, 165, 183, 205, 239, 248, 261, 319, 327, 328n, 388, 397, 402, 421–22, 429–30, 502–3, 503n, **3**: 8–9, 11, 40, 42, 51, 57–58, 93–94, 104, 106, 271–72, 271n, **4**: 309, 332–33, **5**: 27, 29, 37–39, 45, 47, 59, 93–94, 211, 214n, 229, **6**: 8, 35, 138, 140, 227, 229, 239–40, 275–76, 278–80, 284–85, 296–97, 351, 353, 356, 358, 360, 366–67, 391, 393, 409–11, 414–15, 443–44, 450, **7**: 7–8, 8n, 10, 16, 17n, 54, 56, 60n, 62, 66, 71, 86–88, 90, 96, 99, 106, 109, 129n, 260, 262, 268–69, 271, 271n, 273–74, 278–79, 284, 286–87, 289–90, 297, 299, 308, 310, 313, 315, 326, 328, 335–36, **8**: 22–23, 25–26, 35–39, 41, 44–45, 48, 50–51, 61, 63, 87, 95, 97, 99, 116–17, 127–28, 140, 146, 148, 320, 322, 326, 337, 361, **9**: 8–9, 12, 16–18, 32–33, 52, 54–55, 62, 64, 170, 173, 194, 198, 226, 255, 255n, 263, 263n, 268, 270–71, 274, 276, 280, 284, 287–88, 290, 310, 312, 315, 322–25, 329, 343–47, 383, **10**: 10, 24, 30, 30n, 33–34, 34n, 35–37, 41, 43, 105, 143, 184, 191–92, 197–98, 207, 209, 229, 232–35, 239, 241–42, 244, 246, 248, 262, 264, 271, 273–74, 276, **11**: 16,

32, 59, 67, 71, 76, 79, 82, 203, 209, 252–53, 260, 268, 320–21, 408–9, 414, 419–20, 424, 426–27; shooting match, **2**: 157; discipline, **2**: 178, 194; in permanent party, **2**: 229n; court-martial member, **2**: 236; returns, **2**: 248, 377, 431–32, **3**: 57, 77–78, **4**: 328, 330, **5**: 58, 60, 228, **6**: 162, 164, **7**: 12, 14, 158, 188, 190, 272–73, **8**: 64, 150, **9**: 56, 65, 109, 172, 228, 264, 270, 272, 276, 291, 296, 320, 325, **10**: 24, 28, 31, 106, 106n, 118, 125, 195–96, 210, 228, 230–31, 233–34, 236, 242, **11**: 48–49, 57, 59, 60n, 75–76, 188, 209, 260, 326–27, 396, 417; sent out, **2**: 357, 455, 488, **3**: 74–75, 76n, **4**: 104, 106, 252, **5**: 55, 57, 226–27, 230, 242, 305, **6**: 60, 72, 281–82, **7**: 90, 92, 100, 159, 161, 271–72, 289–90, 293, **8**: 46–47, 111, 113–14, 153, 327, 329, **9**: 25, 28, 35, 253, 265, 289, 322, 325, **10**: 26, 170, 192, **11**: 48–49, 52, 72–73, 75–76, 393, 410, 418; duties, **2**: 376n, 499n; biographical sketch, **2**: 517; one of "nine young men from Kentucky," **2**: 529n; creek named for, **3**: 104, 106, 107n, **4**: 250, 333, **5**: 27–29, 29n, 48, **11**: 251n; medical problems, **3**: 196, 198, **6**: 35; and Indians, **3**: 272n, **5**: 305, **7**: 289–90, 347, **9**: 342, **10**: 259; scouting, **4**: 250, 256, 417–18, 432, 433n, **6**: 46–47, 62, 65, 92, **8**: 2, 291–92, **9**: 188, 254, 257, 338, 338n, **10**: 39, 98, 116, 175, 178, 254, **11**: 186–89, 237–38, 395, 400; separated, **4**: 327, 329–30, **7**: 98, 116, 157, 159n, **8**: 149, 323, 331, 351–52; and species, **6**: 62–63, 66, 67n, 69, 100, 320, 390, 398, 400, 401n, **7**:

126, 129n, **9**: 255n; votes, **6**: 83; information from, **6**: 280; and Blackfeet Indians, **8**: 2, 129–30, 132–35, 136n, 294–95; river named for, **9**: 194n, **10**: 120n; volunteers, **9**: 330, 330n; trading, **10**: 146; and saltmaking camp, **10**: 187; mentioned, **2**: 157n, 200n, 375, 426–27, 503n, **5**: 256, **6**: 38, 287–88, 401, 403, 441, **8**: 126, 133, 147, **9**: xiv, xvi, 109n, 170n, 173n, 188n, 226n, 253n, 257n, 264n, 265n, 268n, 270n, 271n, 272n, 274n, 276n, 279, 285n, 311n, 312n, 315n, 320n, 327, 395n, **10**: 10n, 24n, 26n, 29n, 31n, 36n, 37n, 40n, 42n, 43n, 98n, 105n, 117n, 119n, 125n, 144n, 147n, 171n, 175n, 179n, 184n, 188n, 191n, 192n, 193n, 195n, 196n, 197n, 198n, 207n, 209n, 211n, 214, 214n, 229n, 230n, 231n, 232n, 233n, 234n, 235n, 236n, 239n, 240n, 242n, 243n, 244n, 246n, 248n, 254n, 260n, 262n, 264n, 271n, 273n, 274n, 277n, **11**: 32n, 49n, 60n, 68n, 210n, 238n, 268n, 321n, 410n, 414n, 418n, 421n, 424n, 426n, 433n, 440n

Field Notes (Clark's specific): and maps, **1**: 7–8, 16n. 30, 17nn. 65, 68, **2**: 92n, 94n, 134n, 276n; discussed, **2**: 12–17, 32, 41, 92n, 94n, 133n, 541–42, 553; journal-keeping methods, **2**: 94n, 174n, 232n, 249n, 259n, 307n, 326n, 339n, 340n, 379n, 393n, 397n, 403n, 427n, 443n, 482n, 486n, 490n, 493n, 506n, 507n, 527, **3**: 80n, 86n, 91n, 115n, 127n, 172n, 231n, 263n, 271n, 285n, 327n, 328n, 331n, 335–36; Biddle's nota-

tions, **2**: 228n, 274n, 283n, 292n, 303n, 306n, 332n, 333n, 343n, 351n, 354n, 375n, 386n, 404n, 431n, 444n, 465n, 474n, 506n, **3**: 238n; editorial procedure, **2**: 229n, 335n, 349n, 379n, 427n, 442n, 471n, 494n, 508n, 549; calculations, **2**: 287n, 292n, 294n, 308n, 393n, 413n; loss, **2**: 373–74, 376n, 404n; notations on, **3**: 23n, 251n; sent to Jefferson, **3**: 333; mentioned, **2**: 20, 33, 42, 49, 51, 88, 215n, 268n, 314n, 320n, 328n, 363n, 466n, 503n, 512, 520, 528, **3**: 106n, 171n. *See also* Codex journals; Elkskin-bound Journal; First Draft; Voorhis journals

Field notes (general), **2**: 9–10, 12–13, 17–18, 21–22, 32–33, 41

Fields Creek, **8**: 178

15 July Island, **3**: 386n

Filberts. *See* Hazelnuts

Files, **2**: 157, 157n, 167, **3**: 268, **4**: 275, 279, **6**: 134–36, 153, 173n, 176–77, 181, 187, 265, 271, **7**: 343–44, **8**: 157, **9**: 369n

Fincastle, Va., **1**: 12, **2**: 37, 530, 532, 534, 539–41

Finch, house, **4**: 269n

Finch, purple, **4**: 269n

Findley, Charles, **2**: 101, 104n

Fingers. *See* Medical problems

Fir, balsam. *See* Fir, grand

Fir, Douglas: observed, **4**: 181, 396, 402, 405n, **5**: 191, 195n, 209, 210n, 215, 238, **6**: 3, 19n, 45n, 124n, **7**: 121n, **8**: 7, 11, 79, 86, 89, 92, 101, **9**: 185–86, 185n, **10**: 207, 207n, **11**: 171, 175, 229, 232–33, 235; abundance, **5**: 215, 238; described, **6**: 282–83, 290–92; mentioned, **4**: 184, 187n, **5**: 202n, **6**: 284n, 293n, **7**: 37n, 114n, **8**: 12n, **11**: 175n, 230n

Fir, European, **5**: 195n

Fir, grand (balsam): observed, **5**: 4, 209, 210n, 215, 238, **6**: 65, **7**: 234, **8**: 7, 11, **9**: 211, 212n, 216–18, 225, 259, 259n, **10**: 144, 144n, **11**: 285, 286n, 296–300, 318, 320, 322; habitat, **6**: 45n; use, **6**: 124, **10**: 182, 182n; described, **6**: 281–83, **11**: 298; abundance, **7**: 205, 207; mentioned, **6**: 3, 26, 28n, 124n, 279–80, 284n, **7**: 37n, 208–9n, **8**: 12n

Fir, Pacific silver, **6**: 284n

Fir, subalpine, **5**: 202n, 204–5, 205n, 209, 210n, 215, 238

Fir Bluff, **10**: 223n

Fire Heart Butte, **3**: 173n, **10**: 55n

Fire (Little Fire, Fire Prairie) Creek, **2**: 316n, **9**: 16, 368n, 382

Fire-on-the-mountain, **3**: 464, 470

Fire Prairie, **11**: 28

Fire Prairie Creek, **3**: 370, 377, **8**: 378, 396

Fires, prairie, **2**: 362, 398, 400n, 415–16, 482, 487–88, **3**: 8, 11, 16–17, 48n, 77, 80–81, 104, 209–11, 309, 309n, 322, 401, 465, 478, **4**: 19–20, 21n, 237, 407–10, 410n, 427–28, **5**: 42, 48, 148, 179

Fir Island, **7**: 220n

Firs: observed, **5**: 185, 201, **6**: 116, **7**: 55, 77, 79, 97, 110, 112–13, 120, **8**: 7, 11, 28, 30, **9**: 321–22, **10**: 226, 249; abundance, **6**: 183, 194, 312, 314, **7**: 33, **8**: 25, **10**: 190; and Indians, **6**: 262, 267, **7**: 84; described, **6**: 276–77, 390, **9**: 286; and species, **6**: 373, 375, **8**: 60–61; and fires, **7**: 98, **8**: 50–51; mentioned, **6**: 280, **7**: 83, **8**: 14, 18

First Draft: January 6–10, 1806, **2**: 26–27, 558–59, **6**: 172n, 178n, 446; April 16–21, 1806, **2**: 560, **7**: 130n, 142n,

155n; July 13–19, 24–August 3, 1806, **2**: 561, **8**: 180n, 197n, 203n, 207n, 221n, 279n. *See also* Codex journals; Elkskin-bound Journal; Field Notes; Voorhis journals

First Island, **2**: 126, 127n

Fish: fished for, **2**: 181, **4**: 278, 280, 286, 296, 318, 331, 365, 371, **5**: 119, 144–46, 153, 155, 162, 169, 174, 274, 288, **6**: 46, 105, 451, **8**: 57, **9**: 37, 130, 132, 137, 146, 163, 166, 180, 276, 395, **10**: 28, 131–33, 170, **11**: 29, 55–56, 64, 187, 193–94, 277–81, 401n; abundance, **2**: 246, 348, **3**: 38, 480, **5**: 265, 287, 294, **9**: 21–22, 138, 174, **10**: 135, 155, **11**: 273; and Indians, **3**: 368, **5**: 91, 138–40, 145–46, 149, 175, 177, 240, 271–72, 286–87, 290, 298, 301, 304, 306, 309, 311–12, 315, 317–18, 320–21, 323, 329, 331, 335, 347–48, 350, 352, 355, 359, 362–63, 366–67, 371, 374–76, **6**: 7–8, 32, 60–61, 74, 76, 87, 89, 121, 154, 168, 180, 184, 190, 201–2, 214–17, 219, 221, 224, 248–49, 307, 436, 440, **7**: 8, 12–13, 49, 52, 82, 86, 93, 99, 127, 129, 131, 133–34, 145–147, 149, 153, 182, 184, 230, **8**: 182, **9**: 211, 266, 275–76, 280–81, 317, **10**: 128, 130, 134, 146, 148, 155, 196; as food, **4**: 121, 283, **5**: 145, 163, 167, 228, 230, 235, 243, 245–46, 256, 278, 294, 311, 315, 317–18, 320, 348, 351, 357, 371, **6**: 2, 30–31, 39–40, 44–45, 65, 67, 87, 91–93, 97, 103–5, 118–19, 121, 137–38, 320, 322, 334, 387–88, 399, 401, **7**: 126, 152, 154, 275–76, 284, **8**: 35–38, **10**: 130–31, 146, 150, 152, 154, 196, **11**: 393, 404, 408, 423, 431; scarcity, **4**: 180, 332, 358, 371, **5**: 174, 194, 205, 296, 327, **11**: 277–78;

dried, **4**: 309; roe, **5**: 177; as trade item, **5**: 182, 228, 232, 244–46, 251–52, 255–56, 261–64, 306, 311, 314, 317–18, 325, 349, 351, 371, **6**: 30–31, 33, 35, 85, 89, 124, 126–27, 134–36, 146–47, 181, 204, 349, 351, 353, 381–82, 401–2, **7**: 18–20, 129, 148, 239, **11**: 379–80, 433, 438; information about, **5**: 219, **6**: 302, 305, 406–7; as gift, **5**: 348, 371, **7**: 15–16, **9**: 245, 308, **11**: 404, 425; habitat, **5**: 262–63, 266, 268, 280; purchased, **5**: 285, 309, 311, 317, 325, 349, 351, **6**: 395–96, **7**: 128, **9**: 251, 274–75, 304, **10**: 133, 147, 153, 161–62, 168, 202–3, 217, **11**: 364, 388–89, 408, 410, 423, 425–27, 429–30, 436; spoiled, **5**: 285, **6**: 48–49, **7**: 327, 329; observed, **6**: 116, **11**: 146–47; mentioned, **4**: 111, 376, **5**: 287, **9**: 206, 245, 245n, **10**: 133n, **11**: 372n. *See also specific species*

Fish, white. *See* Sauger; Goldeye

Fish Camp, **2**: 476, 480, 485–86, 488n

Fish (Council) Creek (Nebr.), **2**: 445–46, 446n, **9**: 34, 34n, 392, 392n, **10**: 25, 25n

Fish Creek (Idaho County, Idaho), **5**: 216, 217n, 218, 223n, **8**: 27, 29, 30n, 37n, 384, 402, **9**: 323n, **10**: 240n

Fisher, **3**: 35n, 408–35 passim, **6**: 313, 315, 317n, 329, 330n, 333–35, **9**: 242, 242n, **11**: 362–63, 364n

Fisher, blue crested. *See* Kingfisher, belted

Fisher Island, **6**: 28n

Fisher (Kakawissassa) Creek, **3**: 152, 154n, 160n, **9**: 83, 83n, **10**: 53, 54n, **11**: 97n, 99, 99n

Fishhook (Bason) Rapids, **5**: 275, 276n, **6**: 454, 467, **8**: 384, 403, **9**: 239n, **10**: 155n, **11**: 354n

Fishhooks: as trade item, **3**: 174,

290, **5**: 177, **6**: 25, 27, 30–31, 35, 40, 72, 89, 106, 120–21, 123, 134–36, 139, 146–47, 161–62, 168, 175, 177, 181, 187, 196, 205, 221–22, 358, 360, **7**: 32, 35, **9**: 83, 85, 369n; and Indians, **5**: 122, **6**: 134, 190, 211, 213–14, **7**: 171; as gift, **5**: 197, **6**: 65; use, **6**: 423, **9**: 31, **10**: 31, **11**: 267, 277–78; mentioned, **6**: 172n

Fishing. *See* Members of the party; *specific members of the party*

Fishing Camp, **8**: 350n

Fishing (Fire Prairie River) River, **2**: 315–16, 316n, 318n, 341–42

Fishing River Island, **2**: 318n

Fish Island, **5**: 228n

Fish (Night, Prickly Pear) Creek (S. Dak.), **3**: 89–90, 91n, **10**: 41n, **11**: 78, 78n

Fishstack Rapid, **8**: 385, 404

Fivemile Creek (Kans.), **2**: 339n, 340n, **9**: 384, 384n

Five Mile (Rock) Creek (Mont.), **8**: 223, 226, 229n, 391, 408

Five-Mile (Discharge, Portage) Rapids, **5**: 277, 283n, **6**: 454, 467, 472n, **8**: 384, 403

Flag, cooper's. *See* Cat-tail, common

Flag, sweet, **9**: 27, 28n

Flag, western blue, **8**: 93, 94n

Flags: purchased, **2**: 182; displayed, **2**: 201, 415–16, 428, **3**: 23, 203, 261, **4**: 420, **5**: 71, 77, 79, 104, **8**: 128, 214, 342, **9**: 66–67, 73, 188, 212–13, 219, 362, 390, **10**: 23, 68, **11**: 63–64, 90, 105, 113–14, 238, 286–88, 301–2; as gift, **2**: 408, 439–40, 477, **3**: 23–24, 27, 30, 156, 210–11, 215, 252, 272, 310–11, **5**: 231, **6**: 72, 173n, **7**: 215, 217, 232, 236–37, 239, 247, 250, **8**: 130, 135, 294, 304, 312, 314, 317n, **9**: 47–48, 50, 79, 92, 219, 229, 240, 283, 299, **10**: 23, 50, 53, **11**: 99, 106,

286–87, 301–2, 329–30, 357–58; and Indians, **2**: 467–69, **3**: 123–25, 208n, 272, **8**: 295, 312, 314, **9**: 37, 73, 308, **10**: 27, 53, **11**: 99, 436; other, **3**: 116, 118, 242; use, **6**: 421, 423, **8**: 214; as guides, **11**: 210; mentioned, **2**: 471n, **8**: 164

Flannel. *See* Medicine

Flasks, powder. *See* Horns, powder

Flatbacks, **2**: 485–86, 486n, **4**: 332, 333n

Flatboats, **9**: 366

Flathead (Eoote-lash-schute, Oote-lash-schute, Tushepah) Indians: war, **3**: 207n, **7**: 251n, **8**: 48, 66, 68, 131, 132n, 364n, **11**: 302; located, **3**: 368, 386, **8**: 65; historical sketch, **3**: 444–45; listed, **3**: 449, **6**: 474, 480, 488–89, 492, 494–95; encountered, **5**: 3, 185, 187, 189, **7**: 151n, **8**: 166n, 167, 413, **9**: 215, 218, 331, **10**: 137, **11**: 293, 299–300; bands, **5**: 123, 179, **6**: 482; located, **5**: 157, 157n; ceremonies, **5**: 187; food, **5**: 187; historical sketch, **5**: 187–88n; clothes, **5**: 187–89, **11**: 299–300; councils, **5**: 188, **11**: 301–2; lodges, **5**: 189; language, **5**: 189n, 222, 225n, 345, **8**: 90n, **9**: xv, 218–19, 240n, **10**: 138, **11**: 301–3, 302n, 374n; information from, **6**: 310; trade, **7**: 136, **8**: 132n, 364n, 388–89, **11**: 302; relations with the party, **7**: 148, 339, 341, **8**: 109, **9**: 218–19, **11**: 300, 302; name, **8**: 48n, 55n, **11**: 293, 350n, 374n, 429n; visits, **8**: 53–54; trails, **8**: 62, 165, 180n; search for, **8**: 66, 68, 79, 87–88, 291; camps, **8**: 77; signs, **8**: 83, 86; scouts, **8**: 86, 87n; artifacts, **8**: 86n; villages, **9**: 218–19, **11**: 299–300; appearance, **11**: 299; hunting, **11**: 303; mentioned, **4**: 13n,

5: 196, 198n, 205, 205n, 289, **7**: 331–32, 332n, **9**: 215n, 219n, 331n, 338n, **10**: 138n, 140, 140n, 248, **11**: 294n, 301n, 304n, 310n. *See also* Nez Perce Indians

Flathead Pass, **8**: 180, 180n, 185

Flathead River. *See* Bitterroot River; Clark Fork River; Clearwater River; Pend Oreille River

Flax, **2**: 374–75, 487, **3**: 457, **9**: 186, 188, 192, 202, **10**: 127, 249, **11**: 199, 237–38, 248, 267. *See also* Canarygrass, reed

Flax, blue, **4**: 398, 402n, 420, 422n, **5**: 18, 21n, 58, **9**: 169, 169n, **10**: 99, 99n, 133, 133n, **11**: 201n, 231, 232n

Flax, common, **4**: 398, 402n

Fleas, **5**: 327, 344n, 357, 361, **6**: 26–27, 29n, 35–36, 48, 50, 118, 120, 122–23, 138, 142, 144, 161–62, 188, 191, **7**: 59, 82, **11**: 367–68, 368n, 439. *See also* Lice

Fleury, Francis, *dit* Grenier, **3**: 183n, **8**: 311, 316n, **9**: 87n, 352n, **10**: 56, 57n, 269, 270n, **11**: 101, 102n, 104

Flicker, common, **4**: 93, 96n, **5**: 217, 223n, **6**: 379–80, 381n, **7**: 293, 296, 297n, **8**: 75, 78n

Flies, **2**: 421, **3**: 326, **6**: 132, 259, 365, **7**: 192, 312n, **9**: 198, 200, 243, 337, 339, **11**: 264–65

Flies, crane, **2**: 186n, **10**: 185, 185n

Flies, sand, **6**: 259

Flint, **2**: 111n, 114, 154, 284, 285n, **3**: 473–75, **4**: 27, 60, 405, 406n, 407, **5**: 140, 143, 149, 154, 235, 290, **7**: 225n, **9**: 134, 235, **10**: 152, **11**: 344–45

Flintlocks, **2**: 214n. *See also* Arms and ammunition

Flints, **2**: 166, **5**: 146–47n, 198, 209, 210n, 230, 231n, **6**: 146–47. *See also* Arms and ammunition

Floods. *See* Weather conditions

Flora Americae Septentrionalis (Pursh), **12**: 4, 7–8, 9n

Flora of the Great Plains (Barkley), **12**: 7

Flora of the Pacific Northwest, An Illustrated Manual (Hitchcock and Cronquist), **12**: 7

Flounder, starry, **6**: 63, 67, 67n, 407, 410, 412, 414n, **10**: 175, 175n, **11**: 395, 395n

Flour, **2**: 75, 165, 181, 191, 198–200, 202, 217, 258, 436, **4**: 131, 275, 279, 334–35, 338–39, 379, **5**: 75, 87–88, 95–97, 143, 148, 189, **6**: 96–97, **8**: 138, 349, 367, **9**: 166, 176, 208, 358, 365, **10**: 67, 101, 136–37, **11**: 113, 193, 249–50

Floyd, Charles: death, **1**: 8, **2**: 7, 13, 61, 495, 496n, 511, **9**: 41, **10**: xii, xiv, 31n, **11**: 58; journal, **2**: 40–41, 301n, 314n, 316n, 484n, 513, 542–45, 565, **9**: xvii–xviii, 10n, 13n, 14n, 17n, 23n, 26n, 40n, 373–74n, 377n, 378n, 388n, 392n, 394n, 395n, **10**: xii–xiii, 12n, 13n, **11**: xii–xiv; sent out, **2**: 134, 139, 205, 286, 319, 380, **9**: 25, 40, 395, **10**: 28; returns, **2**: 137, 211; listed, **2**: 147, 189, 194, 197, 199, 254, 347, **9**: 279, **11**: 4n, 7n; duties, **2**: 175, 179, 193, 212, 256; in permanent party, **2**: 187, 215n, 229n; appointed sergeant, **2**: 188; medical problems, **2**: 429, 431n, 492–95, **9**: 33, 33n, 41, 391, **10**: 28–29, 29n, **11**: 57–58, 59n; fishing, **2**: 483, **10**: 28; river named for, **2**: 495, 496n, **3**: 355, **9**: 41, **10**: 29, **11**: 58; grave, **2**: 495, 496n, **8**: 4, 349, 349–50n, **9**: 359n, **10**: 276n; biographical sketch, **2**: 513, **9**: xvii–xviii; one of "nine young men from Kentucky," **2**: 529n; tomahawks, **7**: 326, 328, **9**: 319, 319n; hunting, **9**: 36;

mentioned, **2**: 176n, 200n, 218n, 254, 329, 357, 359, 393n, 472, 474, 475n, 484n, 497, 514, 544, **3**: 14–15, **11**: 28n, 30n, 39n, 47n

Floyd, Nancy, **9**: xvii

Floyd, Nathaniel, **9**: xvii

Floyd River, **2**: 61, 495, 496, 496n, 497, 513, **3**: 94, 355, 372, 379, 388, 480, **8**: 349, 349n, 379, 397, **9**: 41, 41n, 367n, **10**: 29, 29n, **11**: 58, 58n

Floyd's Bluff, **2**: 495–96, 496n, **8**: 349

Flume Ripple, **4**: 411, 415n

Fly, black, **10**: 244, 244n

Fly, blow, **4**: 170, 173, 175n, 365, 366n, **5**: 56, 58n, **7**: 76, 78n, 309, 311

Fly, crane, **6**: 94, 96, 139n, 145, 147

Fly, deer, **5**: 56, 58n, **7**: 309, 311, 312n, **8**: 143, 144n

Fly, ear. *See* Greenhead

Fly, horse, **5**: 56, 58n, 92, 95n, **7**: 309, 311, 312n, **8**: 143, 144n, **11**: 259, 259n

Fly, house, **7**: 44, 47n, 309, 311

Fly, March, **7**: 44, 47n

Flycatcher, Hammond's, **6**: 379, 381, 381n

Fly Creek (Bighorn County, Mont.), **8**: 284, 285n

Fly Creek (Shannon's River) (Yellowstone County, Mont.), **8**: 225–26, 228, 228n, 229n, 391, 408

Flynn Creek, **8**: 183, 186, 188n

Foeniculum vulgare, **7**: 266n. *See also* Fennel, sweet

Fog. *See* Weather conditions

Fomalhaut, **5**: 343n

Food. *See* Provisions

Football, **11**: 176

Forge, iron, **3**: 262–63, 262n, 281n

Forks, **2**: 360, **9**: 355. *See also* Utensils, cooking

Formicidae, **7**: 194n. *See also* Ants

Fort Abraham Lincoln (N. Dak.), **3**: 188n

Fort Alexandria (Coude de l'homme, Man's Elbow) (Canada), **2**: 225, 226n

Fort Assiniboine (Canada), **3**: 197, 220n, 224n, 241, 257

Fort Atkinson (Nebr.), **2**: 443n, **3**: 491n, **8**: 316n

Fort aux Cedres (S. Dak.), **3**: 88n, 100–102, 103n, **8**: 324, 324n, **9**: 63, 64n, 80–81, 354, 354n, **10**: 42, 43n, 272, 272n, **11**: 80–81, 81n, 174

Fort Bellefontaine (Mo.), **8**: 370n, **9**: 3n, 366, 366n

Fort Berthold Reservation (N. Dak.), **3**: 154n, 201n, 207n

Fort Buford (N. Dak.), **4**: 8on

Fort Camp. *See* Fort Rock Camp

Fort Chaboillez (Canada), **3**: 491

Fort Charles (Nebr.), **1**: 6, **2**: 446n, 475–76, 478n

Fort Chepewyan (Canada), **10**: 6n

Fort Churchhill (Canada), **10**: 4n

Fort Clatsop (Oreg.): and maps, **1**: 9–12, 18n. 104, 19n. 126, **8**: 299n; conditions at, **2**: 7, **6**: 2, 161–62, 273–74, 284–85, 288, 312, 314, 353, 374, 376, 382–83, 441–42, **11**: 431; and journal-keeping methods, **2**: 26–28, 34, **4**: 13n, **6**: 133n, 158n, 172n, 445–46, 473, 488, 492, **8**: 376, 411, 414–15n, **9**: xv, 232n, **10**: xv, **11**: xvi; constructed, **6**: 2, 121–24, 126–27, 130, 133–36, 138, 140, 143, 145–47, 152–53, **9**: 260–62, **10**: 281–84, **11**: 403–6, 408, 431; and Indians, **6**: 77n, 195–96, 299, 330–32, 425, 427, **10**: 194, **11**: 407–10, 414, 422–23, 425–26, 430; location, **6**: 9on, 112, 115n, 172n, 243–44, 383, 471, **8**: 388, **9**: 258n, 259n, **10**: 180, 181n, **11**: 401, 402n, 403n; depart, **6**: 123n, **7**: 1, 7–8, **9**: 279, **10**: 201, **11**: 432; and species, **6**:

131n, 194, 363, 378n, **7**: 23, 25, 33, 46, 61n, 94, 298, 304, **11**: 411; guarding, **6**: 156–58, 179, **9**: 264, **11**: 409; distances, **6**: 189, 193, 459, **8**: 387, **11**: 428, 431; and members of the party, **6**: 200, **10**: 232n, **11**: 410–11, 413–31; astronomical observations at, **6**: 257, 347, 349, 495n, **11**: 431; listed, **8**: 406; name, **9**: 262, **10**: 185, **11**: 407; visits, **9**: 262–65, 267–69, 271, 273, 275–78, **10**: 181–85, 189–90, 194, 196–98, **11**: 406–11, 413–14, 422–23, 426, 428, 430; mentioned, **6**: 104n, 127n, 233–34, 278, 280, 293, 295–97, 362n, 428n, 496, 496n, **7**: 3, 9n, 259n, 275, **8**: 1, 432n, **9**: 310n

Fort Crevècoeur (Ill.), **2**: 128n, 147, 150n

Fort Dauphin (Canada), **2**: 226n

Fort de Cavagnial (Kans.), **2**: 341–42, 343n, **9**: 384, 385n, **10**: 18, 18n

Fort de Chartres (Ill.), **2**: 121, 122n, 123–24, 130n

Fort de la Reine (Queen's Fort) (Canada), **2**: 225, 226n

Fort des Prairies (Canada), **3**: 236, 236n, **4**: 211, 214n, 216, 222, 224, **9**: 159, 159n

Fort Don Carlos (Mo.), **2**: 147, 150n

Fort Esperance (Canada), **2**: 226n

Fort Fincastle (Henry) (W. Va.), **2**: 74, 74n

Fort George (Elk?) Island, **3**: 106n, **11**: 82

Fort George (Oreg.), **6**: 94n

Fortifications, **3**: 40–43, 172–73, 173n, 372, 379

Fort Island, **4**: 179, 182n

Fort Jefferson (Ky.), **2**: 93, 94n

Fort Kaskaskia (Ill.), **2**: 510

Fort Mandan (N. Dak.): and maps, **1**: 4–10, 12, 18nn. 87, 91–93, **3**: 234n, 492n, **4**:

337, 337n, 359, 362, **6**: 307; and Indians, **1**: 5, 8, 10, **2**: 7, **3**: 235, 237–39, 249, 253–54, 256, 261, 265, 270, 277, 289, 294, 310, 322, 332, 400, 402–3, 429–30, 432, **4**: 129n, 267, **5**: 158, 160, **8**: 96n, 193n, 261n, **11**: 109, 111, 113–14, 129, 132; visits, **1**: 8–9, 18n. 81, **3**: 158n, 179n, 241, 252n, 257–58, 261–62, 265, **8**: 212n, **9**: 93–125 passim, **10**: 63–64, 67, 69–70, 74; and members of the party, **1**: 12, **2**: 511–12, 521–24, 526, **3**: 230n, 244, 247, 253, 257, 270, 293, 305n, 313n, 316n, 317, **8**: 307, 358n, **9**: 84n, 119n, **10**: 74n, **11**: 116–21, 123–27; and journal-keeping methods, **2**: 9, 17, 26, 32, 41, 220n, 403n, **3**: 285n, 333–36, 383n, 385n, 388, 450–51, 479, 491n, **6**: 445–46, 473, **8**: 376, **9**: xi, xiii, xv, xvii, 82n, **10**: xi, xiii, xv–xvi, 73n, **11**: xi, xiii, xv, xvii, 4n; discussed, **2**: 11–16, 18–21, 36, 28; depart, **2**: 511, **3**: 328–29, 328n, 331–32n, 333–35, **4**: 1, 9, 42, 95n, 213, 236, 344, **6**: 86n, 492, **10**: 77, **11**: 131–32; location, **3**: 2–3, 199, 200n, 225–26, 225n, 226n, **6**: 71n, 462, 494, **8**: 307n, 412, **9**: 93, 93n, **10**: 61, 61n, **11**: 108n, 174; and live specimens, **3**: 67n; name, **3**: 226; constructed, **3**: 226, 227n, 232, 237, 240–41, 261, 265, **9**: 93–100, 105–6, **10**: 61–62, 64, **11**: 107–8, 112–13; described, **3**: 227n, **10**: 62, **11**: 110, 115; and species, **3**: 258n, **4**: 93; longitude, **3**: 275n, 280, **6**: 71n, 494; distances, **3**: 298n, 348, 373, 376, 487, 491, 492n, **4**: 3, **6**: 447, **9**: 81, **10**: 83, **11**: 139, 172; latitude, **3**: 376, **6**: 447, **9**: 80, **10**: 63, 63n; listed, **3**: 381, **8**: 381,

399; and botanical specimens, **3**: 450, 464, 471, **4**: 334, **12**: 2–3, 9n, 10n; and mineralogical specimens, **3**: 474–78; mentioned, **2**: 264n, **3**: 183n, 286, 295n, 320, 481, **4**: 20–21, 36, 44, 261, 270, 274, **6**: 2, 496, 496n, **7**: 259n, **8**: 288, 327n, **9**: 157, 310n, **10**: 91, **11**: 107n, 115n, 125n, 150n

Fort Maneury Bend, **9**: 130n, **10**: 79, 79n

Fort Manuel (S. Dak.), **3**: 171n, 229n

Fort Massac (Ill.), **2**: 59, 85–86, 85n, 86n, 105, 109n, 141n, 510, 516

Fort McKenzie (Mont.), **8**: 280n

Fort Mountain. *See* Square Butte

Fort Mountain Creek, **4**: 380, 381n, 384, **10**: 112, 112n

Fort Orleans (Mo.), **2**: 150n, 304, 305n, 352n, **3**: 342, 370, **8**: 378

Fort Osage (Mo.), **2**: 291n, 318n, **8**: 370n, **11**: xv

Fort Point, **3**: 377, **8**: 378, 396

Fort Prudhomme (Miss.), **2**: 147, 150n

Fort Raymond (Mont.), **8**: 279n

Fort River. *See* Lewis and Clark River

Fort Rock Camp (Oreg.), **5**: 337, 339, 340n, **7**: 123–24, 125n, 134, 141, 188–89, 193, 319, **9**: 245, 245n, 292, 293n, **10**: 162, 162n, 211, 211n, **11**: 371–73, 372n

Fort Union (N. Dak.), **4**: 80n

Fort Union Formation, **4**: 75n, 84n, 88n, 135n, 163n, **8**: 151n, 246n, 250n, 255n, 256n, 261n, 262n, 270n, 275n, 279n

Fort William (N. Dak.), **4**: 80n

Fossils, **8**: 226, 228–29n

Fountain. *See* Giant Springs

Fountain (Eagle) Creek, **2**: 124–26, 125n, 126n

Four Bears Creek, **9**: 77, 77n, **10**: 51, 51n, **11**: 96, 96n

Fourchette (Weiser's) Creek, **4**: 163–66, 166n, **6**: 448, 463, **8**: 382, 400, **9**: 150, 150n

Four Mile Creek, **3**: 174, 175n, 178n, **9**: 85, 85n

Four o'clock, wild, **3**: 464, 469

Fourth of July Creek, **5**: 144, 146, 147n, **10**: 18n

Fowl, dunghill. *See* Chicken

Fowl, prairie. *See* Grouse, sharp-tailed; Prairie-chicken, greater

Fowls. *See* Birds; Waterfowl

Fox, cross. *See* Fox, red

Fox, gray, **3**: 86–87, 405–6, 408, 482

Fox, red, **3**: 65–67, 66n, 297, 297n, 330–31, 408–10, 482, **4**: 227, 229–30, 234n, **5**: 141n, **6**: 187, 192n, 313, 315, 317n, 329–30, 330n, 334

Fox, swift (kit), **4**: 35, 40n, 364, 365n, 366–67, 368n, **6**: 313, 315, 317n, 329, 330n, 334, **8**: 128, 132n, **9**: 181, 181n, **10**: 109–10, 110n, **11**: 220–21, 221n

Fox Creek (Mont.), **8**: 272, 274n

Fox (Sentinel) Creek (S. Dak.), **3**: 133, 136n

Foxes, **3**: 485, **4**: 38, 229, 256, 258, **5**: 122, 350, 352, **6**: 76, 205, 208, 210, 315, **7**: 124–25, 253, 255, **9**: 108, 160, **10**: 93n

Fox Hills Formation, **3**: 181n

Fox Hills Sandstone, **4**: 107n, 120n, 135n, 145n, 148n, 163n, 179n

Fox (Renar) Indians, **2**: 181n, 299n, 524, **3**: 136, 340, 394–95, 408–17, 439, 448, 483. *See also* Sauk Indians

Foxtail, **5**: 60n, **7**: 335–36, 337n

Fragaria vesca, **4**: 237–38n, **5**: 364n, **6**: 9n, **7**: 61n, **8**: 73n, **10**: 102n, **11**: 199n. *See also* Strawberry, woodland

Fragaria virginiana, **2**: 217n, **4**: 237–38n, **7**: 61n, **8**: 73n, **10**: 102n, **11**: 38n, 199n. *See also* Strawberry, wild

Frame (Ash) Creek, **2**: 259–60, 261n, **9**: 8, 8n, 375, **10**: 9, 10n, **11**: 14, 14n

France, **1**: 5, **2**: 1, 4, 122, 130n, 174n, 244n, 343n, 512, **6**: 51n, **10**: 76, 76n

Franchère, Gabriel, **7**: 17n, 61n

Franklin, Benjamin, **7**: 288n

Fraser, Simon, **5**: 198n, **10**: 157n

Fraser (Tacoutche-Tesse) River, **5**: 196, 198n, 286, **10**: 156n

Fraxinus americana, **2**: 314n, **8**: 345n, **10**: 11n. *See also* Ash, white

Fraxinus latifolia, **5**: 358n, **6**: 20n, **7**: 14n, **9**: 287n, **10**: 164n. *See also* Ash, Oregon

Fraxinus pennsylvanica, **2**: 314n, **3**: 184n, **4**: 28n, **8**: 151n, 345n, **9**: 130n, **10**: 11n. *See also* Ash, Green

Fraxinus quadrangulata, **2**: 315n. *See also* Ash, blue

Fraxinus sp., **9**: 10n. *See also* Ash

Frazer (Frasure), Robert: and maps, **1**: 12; listed, **2**: 148, 187, 189, 194–95, 198–99, 256, **4**: 9, 11, **8**: 74, 77, 86n, 110, 139n, **11**: 4n, 7n, 62n, 393n, 411n, 420n; shooting match, **2**: 157, 157n; court-martialed, **2**: 182; return party, **2**: 188, 198, 229n, 415, 417n; in permanent party, **2**: 190n, 511, **3**: 152–53; discipline, **2**: 194; hunting, **2**: 205, **4**: 287, **5**: 168, **6**: 317–18, 321, 324, 391, 393, 398, 401–3, 401n, 409, 411, **7**: 88, **8**: 326, **9**: 131, 272, 276, 341, 343, **10**: 197, 252, **11**: 420, 426–27, 427n; duties, **2**: 212, **7**: 177–79, 274, **8**: 99, 291, **10**: 107, 254, **11**: 214; medical problems, **2**: 355–57, **7**: 261–63, 265; biographical sketch, **2**: 517; journal, **2**: 544–45; scouting, **3**: 7, 9, **4**: 417–18 432, 433n, **6**: 46–47, **9**: 44, 188, **10**:

116, **11**: 237–38; sent out, **3**: 295–96, **4**: 331, **6**: 195, 403, **7**: 125, 127–28, 129n, 137, 139, 291, 296n, 327, 329, **8**: 46–47, **9**: 233, 253, 265–66, 293, 315, 338, **10**: 73, 106, 170, 248, **11**: 61, 125, 336–37, 393, 410; and iron-frame boat, **4**: 330, 333, 336–37, 343, 349; creek named for, **5**: 28, 30n, 48, **9**: 194n, **11**: 251n; horse, **5**: 215; trading, **5**: 244–45, **9**: 316, 317n, 320, **10**: 150, 212, 233n, 235, 235n, 237, 237n; votes, **6**: 83; visits whale site, **6**: 169, 172n; discipline, **6**: 195, 198n; and species, **6**: 390, 398, 400, 401n; returns, **7**: 274, 326, 329, 338, **8**: 48, 50, **9**: 266, 276, 320, **10**: 106, 118, 188, 196, 212, 235, 243, **11**: 338, 413; and Indians, **7**: 327, 329, 337, 342, 344–45; information from, **8**: 37; volunteers, **9**: 330, 330n; journal, **10**: xiii, xvi; and saltmaking camp, **10**: 187; robbed, **11**: 125–26; mentioned, **2**: 200n, **3**: 296n, **9**: xiii, 45n, 188n, 226n, 233n, 253n, 265n, 266n, 272n, 276n, 279, 293n, 320n, 338n, **10**: 73n, 106n, 107n, 117n, 119n, 145n, 150n, 171n, 188n, 196n, 197n, 212n, 243n, 248n, 252n, 254n, **11**: xiii, 126n, 214n, 238n, 323n, 337n, 413n, 426n, 428n

Fred Burr Creek, **8**: 161, 162n

Freestone, **4**: 60, 233n, **8**: 65n, 117, 118n, 121, *See* Granite; Limestone; Sandstone

Freestone, white. *See* Sandstone

Frémont, John C., **3**: 291n, **7**: 42n

French language, **1**: 3–4, **2**: 118n, 128n, 130n, 144n, 223, 225n, 232–33, 277n, 281n, 283n, 314n, 363n, 386n, 390, 392, 395, 404n, 431n, 458, 511–12, 527, **3**: 15n, 21n, 25n, 32, 35n, 48n,

136, 137n, 179n, 184n, 234n, 236n, 261n, 278n, 316n, 383n, **4**: 33n, 257n, **5**: 80, 86n, 164n, 224n, **7**: 242, 244, 307n, 343n, **8**: 93, 94n, 117, 118n, 200, 203n, 288n, **9**: 29, 29n, 32, 32n, 45, 45n, 47, 48n, 75n, 92n, 137, 137n, 219n, 306n, 353n, 365, 386, 394, **10**: 16, 16n, 22n, 24, 24n, 36, 36n, 49, 49n, 60, 61n, 64, 64n, 70, 83, 83n, 270, 270n, **11**: 48n, 62n, 71n, 93n, 133n, 137n, 138n, 239n, 276–77

Frenchman Creek, **2**: 123, 124n

Frenchman Springs Member, **5**: 319n, 326n, 336n, 348n

Frenchmen: information from, **2**: 99, 108, **3**: 85, 114n, 270n, 304, 358, 445, **9**: 126; settlers, **2**: 123, **8**: 366–67, 368n, **9**: 6; visits, **2**: 173, 187, 214, **3**: 151, 304, 305n, 309, **9**: 9, 13, 51; at St. Charles, **2**: 232–33, 234n, 241; customs, **2**: 246, 248; at La Charette, **2**: 252, 252n, **3**: 338; trade, **2**: 439, **4**: 20, 30, 36, **8**: 294, 355, **9**: 20, 96–97, 359–63; and Indians, **2**: 444n, **3**: 192–93, 209–10, 217–19, 395, **5**: 95n, **9**: 391, **10**: 58, 69; encountered, **3**: 134–35, 221, 223n, 286, 286n, 290, **8**: 311, **9**: 10–11, 22, 96–97, 128–30, 352, 359–63, 365, 378, 380, **10**: 12, 14, 31, 79, 79n, 269, 270n; interpreters, **3**: 151; mentioned, **3**: 273n, **5**: 161, **9**: 143, 348, **10**: 31, 32n, 62, 62n, 74n, 92. *See also* Engagés; Traders

Frene (Ash) Creek, **2**: 261n, **9**: 8n, **11**: 14n

Friendly village, **5**: 353n, **6**: 456, 469

Fringe-tree, **7**: 195n

Fritillaria lanceolata, **12**: 10n

Frizzen, **5**: 209, 210n. *See also* Arms and ammunition

Frog, chorus, **7**: 309, 311, 312n

Frog, green, **7**: 309, 311, 312n

Frog, Pacific tree, **7**: 28, 32n, 46, 48n, 309, 311, 312n

Frog, striped chorus, **2**: 185, 186n, **4**: 41, 44n

Frogs, **2**: 436, **3**: 52–53

Frost. *See* Weather conditions

Frostbite. *See* Medical problems

Frows, **6**: 113, 115n

Fulica americana, **2**: 205n, **6**: 98n. *See also* Coot, American

Fulmar, northern, **6**: 3, 386–88, 387n, 391n

Fulmarus glacialis, **6**: 387n. *See also* Fulmar, northern

Furze, **5**: 291n

Fusils, **3**: 23–24, 25n, 117, 296, 484–85, **4**: 343, 418, **5**: 178, **6**: 60–61, 74, 450, **8**: 329, 338, **9**: 177, **11**: 215–16. *See also* Arms and ammunition; Muskets

G

Gadus morhua, **4**: 102n. *See also* Cod, Atlantic

Galena, **2**: 277n, **3**: 475. *See also* Lead ore

Gallagher Creek, **5**: 98, 102n, **9**: 203, 204n, **10**: 126n, **11**: 270–71, 270n, 272n

Gallatin, Albert, **4**: 437, 438–39n, **5**: 7, **8**: 180n, **9**: 191n, **11**: 246n

Gallatin Range, **8**: 185, 187, 188n

Gallatin (South, Southeast Fork) River: listed, **3**: 382, **6**: 450, 465, **8**: 392–93, 409, 412, 415; name, **4**: 4, **5**: 1, 7, **9**: 200, **10**: 123, **11**: 263; latitude, **4**: 4, **6**: 450, **8**: 413, **9**: 191, **11**: 246; arrive at, **4**: 4, **9**: 335, **10**: 255, 266, **11**: 242–44; described, **4**: 428, 434, **5**: 8, **8**: 179, 181–82, **9**: 191, 348, **10**: 118, **11**: 245–46; distances, **6**: 450, **8**: 178–80, 185; and Indians, **8**: 40, 42; animals, **8**: 179–80;

camped on, **9**: 191, 191n; mentioned, **4**: 75n, **5**: 10n, 150, **8**: 175, 180n, 183n, 414, **9**: 190n, **10**: 118n, **11**: 244n, 246n

Gallinago gallinago, **6**: 383n. *See also* Snipe, common

Galusha, Elijah, **2**: 156n

Game, four-stick, **7**: 138–39, 140–41, 142n, 154

Game, hand, **7**: 137–38, 140, 142n, 154, 249, **9**: 212, 213n, 295, 295n, 309n

Game, hoop and pole, **9**: 104, 104n

Games, **9**: 306, **11**: 286–88, 288n. *See also* Indians, feasts and games; *specific games; specific Indian tribes*

Garden Book (Jefferson), **12**: 1

Garden Creek, **10**: 80, 81n, **11**: 136, 136n

Garden Gulch, **4**: 430, 433n, **10**: 118n

Garlic, **4**: 420, 422n, **9**: 188, 192

Garreau, Joseph, **1**: 18n. 81, **3**: 154n, 313–15, 315–16n, 318n, **8**: 317, 319n, **10**: 52n, **11**: 98n

Gasconade River: camped on, **2**: 260, **9**: 375, **10**: 10, **11**: 14; described, **2**: 261–62, **3**: 338, 383n; distances, **2**: 405, 408, 486, **3**: 94, 370, 375, **9**: 81, 368n, **11**: 171; latitude, **2**: 407, 479, 486, **3**: 94, 375, **9**: 80, **11**: 173; listed, **3**: 376, **8**: 377, 395, **11**: 171; name, **3**: 383n; arrive at, **9**: 8, 375, **10**: 9–10, **11**: 14; mentioned, **2**; 238n, 260n, 261n, 263, 264n, **3**: 452–53, **8**: 366, 367n, **9**: 8n, **10**: 10n, 11, **11**: 14n

Gass, Patrick: and maps, **1**: 9; journal, **2**: 7, 12, 36–37, 40–41, 253n, 311n, 471n, 486n, 513, 542, 544–45, 566, **3**: 99n, 103n, 120n, 136n, 140n, 166n, 227n, **4**: 299n, 374n, 410n, **5**: 152, 157n, 188n, **6**: 59n, 86n, 130n, 384n, **8**: 141n, 157n, 316n,

Gass, Patrick (*continued*)
327n, 362n, **9**: 9n, 93n,
104n, 115n, 168n, 179n,
217n, 315n, 317n, 344n,
345n, **10**: xii–xvii, 8n, 14n,
16n, 22n, 24n, 31n, 36n,
52n, 54n, 55n, 56n, 61n,
62n, 64n, 70n, 71n, 72n,
73n, 77n, 78n, 85n, 87n,
93n, 96n, 97n, 99n, 102n,
105n, 106n, 107n, 109n,
114n, 115n, 117n, 118n,
119n, 120n, 121n, 123n,
132n, 135n, 140n, 144n,
153n, 154n, 157n, 160n,
163n, 164n, 168n, 172n,
175n, 180n, 188n, 195n,
199n, 200n, 204n, 214n,
216n, 220n, 222n, 224n,
226n, 229n, 231n, 252n,
256n, 260n, 262n, 268n,
272–73n, 273n, 274n, 275n,
276n, 280n, **11**: xiii, 15n,
16n, 34n, 35n, 42n, 49n,
55n, 59n, 94n, 96n, 97n,
115n, 123n, 144n, 183n,
199n, 217n, 234n, 288n,
297n, 350n, 390n, 393n,
394n, 403n, 421n, 424n,
428n, 430n; listed, **2**: 148,
187, 189, 194, 197, 199, 255,
4: 9, 11, **8**: 74, 77, 86n, 110,
11: 4n, 7n, 187n, 210n,
419n; becomes sergeant, **2**:
218n, 500–501, 511, **3**: 14,
10: xii, 31n; in permanent
party, **2**: 229n; court-martial
member, **2**: 329, **3**: 170; biographical sketch, **2**: 513, **10**:
xiv–xvii; duties, **3**: 15, 153, **4**:
333–34, 371, **5**: 252, **7**: 126,
8: 156, 291, **9**: 275, 293, 339,
10: xiv–xv, 62, 107, 254, **11**:
111, 209, 214, 426; sent out,
3: 74–75, 76n, 296, 297n, **4**:
327, 331, 359, 376, **5**: 44, 52,
56, 175, 177n, **6**: 253, 257n,
262, 267, 278–79, 281–82,
325–26, 358, 360, 365, 367,
401, 403, **7**: 159, 161, 308,
310, **8**: 46–47, 99, 299, **9**:
58, 104, 112, 179, 270, 276,
320, 341, **10**: 73, 187n, 191–

92, 247, 258, **11**: 75–76,
403, 409, 417–18, 421, 424,
427–28; returns, **3**: 77–78,
5: 175, **6**: 200, 275–76, 287–
88, 328–29, **7**: 158, **8**: 48,
50, 107, 138, **9**: 122, 213,
272, 286, 296, **11**: 75–76,
184, 186, 188, 288–89, 413,
418, 424, 427, 440n; hunting, **3**: 286, 286n, **4**: 331,
334, **6**: 296–97, 323–24, **7**:
54, 56, 60n, 71, 74, 76–77,
8: 44–45, **9**: 269, 271–72,
274, 284, 326, 342, **10**: 205,
242, 243n, **11**: 73, 76, 156,
217, 416, 419–20, 438; and
mineralogical specimens, **3**:
474; scouting, **4**: 247, 250,
252n, 256, **5**: 24, 116n, **9**:
115, 161, 162n, 193, **10**: 39,
97–98, 120–22, **11**: 184–89,
186n, 249–50; information
from, **4**: 249–50, 252, **9**: 70;
and iron-frame boat, **4**: 323,
330, 336, 343–44, 349, 351;
creek named for, **4**: 425n,
426, **10**: 117n; medical problems, **5**: 18, 24; accidents,
5: 251, **10**: xv, 120n; votes,
6: 83; and saltmaking camp,
6: 162–64, 172n, 177, 179,
194–95, **9**: 264, 266, **10**:
185, 186n; separated, **6**:
284–85, 318, 321, **7**: 71, 74,
157, 159n, **8**: 107; and Indians, **7**: 343–45, **10**: 195,
195n, 197, 197n, 200, 200n,
228, 229n, 247, 248n, 249,
250n; leads detachment,
8: 2, 239n, **9**: 270n, 272n,
274n, 276n, 338, 338n; and
species, **8**: 99, **9**: 28n, **10**:
135–37, 135n, 136n, 137n,
198n, 206n, 235n; trading, **9**:
93; volunteers, **9**: 330, 330n;
book, **10**: xiii, xv–xvii, 4n, 5n,
172n; and French language,
10: 16, 16n, 24, 24n, 31,
32n, 36, 36n, 49, 49n, 64,
64, 64n, 270, 270n; and geo-
logic phenonmenon, **10**: 34,
34n; stays behind, **10**: 122,
122n, 131n, 132n, 134, 192,

192n; mentioned, **2**: 74n,
509, **5**: 32, 45, 202n, **9**: xii,
xiii, xvi, 266n, 270n, 271n,
279, 285n, 320n, 373n,
395n, 396n, **10**: 73n, 98n,
107n, 191n, 192n, 193n,
195n, 205n, 248n, 254n,
258n, **11**: xii, xiv, 155, 214n,
413n, 418n, 427n
Gates of the Rocky Mountains,
1: 10, **4**: 4, 381n, 402–4,
405n, 408, **5**: 192, **6**: 450,
464, **9**: 186, 186n, 336,
337n, **10**: 114, 114n, **11**:
232–33, 233n
Gaultheria shallon, **6**: 120n, **7**:
60n. *See also* Salal
Gavia arctica, **6**: 391n. *See also*
Loon, arctic
Gavia arctica pacifica, **6**: 391n, **9**:
247n, **10**: 174n, **11**: 378n. *See
also* Loon, Pacific
Gavia immer, **2**: 205n, **6**: 391n,
9: 247n, **10**: 174n, **11**: 378n.
See also Loon, common
Gavia stellata, **6**: 391n, **9**: 247n,
11: 378n. *See also* Loon, red-
throated
Gayfeather, rough, **3**: 465, 469
Gayfeather, tall blazing star, **3**:
464, 469
Geese: observed, **2**: 177, 231,
291, 336, 445, **3**: 147, 221,
319, 326, **4**: 17, 19–20, 36,
90, 94, 111, 184, 204–5,
236, 287, 291, 420, 423, **5**:
33, 35, 37, 39, 42, 59, 71, 84,
262, **6**: 161–62, 171, 261, **7**:
23, 25, 75–76, **8**: 117, 119,
146, 180, 189, 349, 350, **9**:
20, 54, 128, 130, 144, 166,
198, 200, **10**: 154–55, **11**:
159–60, 177–78, 194, 260,
264–65, 382–83, 394; be-
havior, **2**: 208, **7**: 193, **8**: 210,
266; and species, **2**: 222;
hunted, **2**: 315, 374–75,
429–30, 502, **4**: 22–23, 41,
43, 55–56, 77, 82, 90, 426,
5: 43, 61, 152, 155, 179, 275,
279, 337, 339, 341, 363, **6**: 8,
10, 35–36, 53–54, 91, 93, **7**:
24, **8**: 176–78, **9**: 16, 24, 55,

129, 133–34, 136–37, 140–41, 189, 195, 220–21, 239, 242, 245, 247–48, 251, 254–55, 286, 334, **10**: 81, 131, 140, 155, 165, 171, 198, 203, 205, **11**: 142, 178, 240–41, 249–50, 254, 304–5, 307–9, 354, 361–62, 372–73, 381, 383–85, 390, 400, 405, 410; abundance, **2**: 346–48, 350, 364–65, 395–96, **4**: 23, 30, 33, 46, 49, 58, 79, 103, 105, 298, 411, 417, **6**: 9, 11, 13, 21–23, 35, 88, 96, **7**: 28, 30, 193, **8**: 112, 148, 177, 190, **9**: 21, 23, 249–51, 385, **10**: 160, 164, 166, 168, **11**: 195, 255, 372–73, 377–78, 381, 384–86, 390, 399, 411, 436; described, **2**: 432; scarcity, **2**: 459, **6**: 73, **7**: 45; migrations, **3**: 131, 230, 232, 249, 322; food, **3**: 457, **4**: 36; nests, **4**: 40, 75, 78, 104; as food, **4**: 78, 90, **5**: 191, 337, **10**: 165, 198; mentioned, **2**: 186n, 316n, **4**: 429n, **6**: 287, **8**: 264, **9**: 135. *See also* Goose, Canada

Geneva, Switzerland, **12**: 4

Gens de Soulier. *See* Hidatsa Indians, Awaxawi

Geomys pinetis, **4**: 18n. *See also* Gopher, southeastern pocket

George III, **12**: 5

Georgetown, Pa., **2**: 70–71, 71n, 72n, 81

Georgia, **7**: 335

Geranium carolinianum, **2**: 210n. *See also* Cranesbill

Germans, **2**: 108, 110n

Giant Springs, **4**: 307, 308n, 312, 315, 339–40, 368, **9**: 171, 171n, 175, 179, 181, **10**: 108–9, 108n, 109n, **11**: 204, 206, 206n, 213, 220–21

Gibbons Pass, **8**: 168n, 169n, 410, **9**: 332n

Gibson, George: shooting match, **2**: 144; listed, **2**: 148, 187–88, 194, 197, 199, 255, **4**: 9, 11, **8**: 162n, 179, 277,

11: 4n, 7n, 408n; returns, **2**: 157, 434, **7**: 102–3, 273, 291, 294, **8**: 206, 295, **9**: 289, 322, **10**: 188, 230–33, 239, **11**: 49, 413; hunting, **2**: 158, 165–66, **4**: 149–50, 283, **6**: 105–6, 106n, 177, 190, 194–95, 253, 255, **7**: 19, 48, 51, 53n, 71, 74, 87, 268, 271n, 272–73, 275–76, 278–79, 284, 286, 288, **8**: 13, 17, 177, 179, 255, 283, 285–86, 290, 326, 360n, **9**: 33, 57, 61, 258, 258n, 312, 315, 321–22, 335, 360, 362, **10**: 24, 179, 187, 204–5, 229, 231, 238, 273, **11**: 401, 416n, 437–38; in permanent party, **2**: 229n; duties, **2**: 377, **5**: 252, **7**: 98, 102, **10**: 208; sent out, **2**: 434, 435n, **3**: 48, 50, **6**: 42–43, **7**: 116, 262, **8**: 170, 205, **9**: 57, 166, 286, 289, 332, 391, **10**: 101, **11**: 49, 193, 407–8; biographical sketch, **2**: 517–18; one of "nine young men from Kentucky," **2**: 529n; scouting, **4**: 275, 277, **6**: 43; and fiddle, **5**: 306; votes, **6**: 84; medical problems, **6**: 122, 135, 239, 241, 242n, 293, 295–97, 307, 309, 311n, 312, 314–15, 316n, 318–19, 321, 324, 330, 332–33, 335–37, **8**: 3, 198n, 202–5, 209, 255, **9**: 260, 271–73, **10**: 192–93, 192n, **11**: 168, 404, 406, 419–20, 419n; and saltmaking camp, **6**: 138, 140, 166, 172n, 195, **9**: 263, 263n, 266, **10**: 184; separated, **7**: 101, **8**: 21–22, 290; fishing, **8**: 35–36, 38, **9**: 325; river named for, **8**: 261n; creek named for, **9**: 148n, **10**: 89n, **11**: 157n; accidents, **10**: 92; mentioned, **2**: 153n, 194, 289, 500–501, **3**: 309n, **8**: 151, 302, **9**: 58n, 266n, 279, 286n, 290, 312n, 315n, 332n, 373–74n, 391n, **10**: 25n, 38n, 92n, 101n, 179n,

184n, 187n, 188n, 193n, 204n, 206n, 209n, 230n, 231n, 232n, 233n, 238n, 239n, 255, 256n, 273n, **11**: 401n, 413n, 419n, 420n, 438n

Gigs, **4**: 420, **5**: 122, 138–39, 141n, 145–46, 177, 183, 233, 290, 315, 321, 341, 343, 376, **6**: 44–47, 76, 118, 206, 208, 210–11, 213–14, 421, 425, **7**: 245, 343–44, **8**: 35–38, 41, **9**: 212–14, 231, 234, 240, 245, 325, 369n, **10**: 170, 242, **11**: 267, 286–88, 295, 332–33, 335, 339, 348–49, 392

Gilbert, **2**: 134, 134n

Ginger, long-tailed wild, **8**: 57–58, 59n

Ginger, wild, **3**: 453–54, 463, 467, **8**: 205, 208n

Gingras Creek, **2**: 129, 130n

Ginseng, American, **7**: 234, 236–37n, 300

Gird Creek, **5**: 191n

Girty, Simon, **2**: 181–82, 182n

Glade Creek, **7**: 169n, **9**: 297n, **10**: 216n

Glaize Creek, **2**: 126, 127n

Glass, **6**: 113

Glass, black. *See* Obsidian

Glass, Hugh, **4**: 69n

Glass, looking (burning), **2**: 490, 492, 493n, **3**: 161, 163, 290, **5**: 69–70, 78, 112, **6**: 113, **7**: 54, 57, 60n, **9**: 105, 301

Glass, spy. *See* Telescopes

Glass Bluffs, **4**: 69n, **11**: 138n

Glaucoma. *See* Medical problems, eyes

Gleditsia triancanthos, **8**: 418n, **9**: 20n. *See also* Locust, honey

Glendive Creek, **8**: 270n

Gloves, **3**: 256, 257n, **6**: 385. *See also* Clothing

Gluts, **6**: 243–44, 244n

Glycyrrhiza glabra, **4**: 129n, **6**: 61n, 230n. *See also* Liquorice

Glycyrrhiza lepidota, **4**: 129n, **6**: 230n, **8**: 120n. *See also* Liquorice

Gnat, buffalo, **4**: 377, 377n, **5**: 8, 10n, 56, 58n

Gnats, **2**: 317–18, **3**: 326, **4**: 376–77, 379, 381, 394, 415, 417, 423, 427, **10**: 242, **11**: 222–23, 223n

Goat, common, **4**: 193–94, 196–97, **6**: 307n

Goat, mountain: described, **5**: 4, 160, 350, 352, **6**: 337, **10**: 148–49, 208; and Indians, **5**: 160, 350, 352, **6**: 195, 336, 434, 438, **7**: 101–3, 112, **8**: 56, **9**: 289; observed, **6**: 313, 315; habitat, **6**: 338; abundance, **8**: 56, 58, 74–75; as specimen, **8**: 418; mentioned, **5**: 164n, **6**: 317n, 339n, **7**: 103–4n, **8**: 58n, **9**: 290n, **10**: 149n, 209n

Goat Island, **3**: 100–102, 103n, 104–5, **5**: 294, 300n, 307n

Goats. *See* Pronghorn

Goatsucker, **4**: 346n

Goiter. *See* Medical problems

Gold, **8**: 363, **9**: 364, **10**: 280

Gold Butte (Tower Mountain), **8**: 117, 118n

Gold Creek, **8**: 90, 92n, 101

Goldenrod, Missouri, **9**: 198, 199n, 210, 210n

Golden seal, **3**: 453, 462–63, 467

Goldeye, **2**: 484n, **4**: 2, 278, 279n, 309, 332, 347, **9**: 40, 40n, 166, 166n, **11**: 193, 194n, 199–200

Goldfinch, American, **4**: 265, 269n

Goldsmith, Oliver, **10**: 93n

Gonorrhea. *See* Medical problems, venereal disease

Good Island, **3**: 386n. *See also* Sun (Fair Sun, Good Sun) Island

Good Mans Island, **3**: 379

Goodrich (Guterge, Guterich, Guthrege, Gutrich), Silas: listed, **2**: 148, 187, 189, 195, 198–99, 255, **3**: 170, **4**: 9, 11, **8**: 74, 77, 86n, **11**: 4n, 7n; returns, **2**: 181, 377, **3**: 296, **5**: 245, **7**: 277, 279, **10**: 237,

11: 338; in permanent party, **2**: 229n; sent out, **2**: 357, **3**: 295, **5**: 244, **7**: 125, 127–28, 129n, 297, 299, **9**: 166, 320, 330, 338, **10**: 73, 101, 236, 247, **11**: 125, 193, 336–37; duties, **2**: 376n, **4**: 296, **7**: 139, 141, **8**: 139n, 291, **10**: 254; fishing, **2**: 387–88, 418, **4**: 2, 278, 280, 286, 296, **5**: 126, 159, **9**: 55, 163, **11**: 187; biographical sketch, **2**: 518; scouting, **4**: 275, 277; and lower portage camp, **4**: 325–26; votes, **6**: 84; gifts, **6**: 137; medical problems, **6**: 239, 241, 242n, 356–57, 391, 393, **8**: 79; and Indians, **7**: 275–76, 286–87, 312, 314, 343–45; information from, **7**: 286–87; trading, **9**: 233, 293, 313, **10**: 150, 212, 234; island named for, **10**: 92n; stays behind, **10**: 104; creek named for, **11**: 96, 97n; robbed, **11**: 125–26; mentioned, **2**: 375, **3**: 296n, **4**: 283, **9**: 172, 172n, 233n, 279, 293n, 313n, 320n, 330n, 338n, **10**: 73n, 101n, 105n, 150n, 212n, 234n, 237n, 248n, 254n, **11**: 126n, 207–8, 208n, 337n

Goodrich's Island. *See* Dry (Goodrich's) Island

Goods. *See* Provisions

Good Soldier (Elm) Creek, **3**: 90, 91n, **10**: 41n, **11**: 78, 78n

Goose. *See* Geese

Goose, cackling, **4**: 115n

Goose, Canada: observed, **2**: 229, **3**: 88n, **4**: 20, 204, **6**: 383, 385, **7**: 9, **9**: 128, **10**: 79; nests, **4**: 30–31, 33, 33–34n, 104; described, **4**: 411; abundance, **4**: 411, 415n, **11**: 140; hunted, **6**: 8, **7**: 15–16; mentioned, **2**: 186n, 232n, **4**: 21n, 111–12, 115n, **6**: 9–10n, 384n, 391–394, 394n, **7**: 11n, **9**: 128n, **10**: 79n, **11**: 140n. *See also* Geese

Goose, greater white-fronted, **6**: 3, 417–20, 420n

Goose, Hutchins's, **4**: 115n

Goose, lesser Canada, **4**: 115n, 204–5, **6**: 8, 10n, **7**: 9, 11n

Goose, snow (white brant): observed, **3**: 144–45, 222, **4**: 14–15; migration, **4**: 31, 9, **6**: 16, 18–19, 161–624; described, **4**: 111–12, 204–5, **6**: 391–93; hunted, **4**: 114, **6**: 22–23, 53–54, **10**: 167; abundance, **6**: 9, 21–23, 73, 96, **9**: 143; island named for, **6**: 20n; behavior, **6**: 75; mentioned, **2**: 186n, **3**: 146n, 223n, **4**: 18n, 115n, **6**: 10n, 60n, 228, 261, 383, 385, 394n, 418, 420, 457, **7**: 9, 11n, **9**: 143n, **10**: 167n

Gooseberries: observed, **2**: 209, 377–78, 433, **4**: 94, 247, 329, 388, 414, **5**: 36, **7**: 13–14, 112, 188, 190, 337, **8**: 10–11, 71, 334, **9**: 162, 202, **10**: 238; abundance, **2**: 308, 381, **4**: 251, 287, 332, 406, 417, 436, **8**: 100, **9**: 167–68, 174, **10**: 102, 110, **11**: 184,- 85, 195–96, 198, 211–12; habitat, **4**: 54, 70, 73, 251, 324; as food, **5**: 31–32, **8**: 286; and Indians, **11**: 132; mentioned, **4**: 2, 308n, 365n, 397n, 429n, **5**: 39n, **7**: 114n, **8**: 23n, 100n, **11**: 133n, 186n

Gooseberry, bristly, **4**: 57n, 392, 397n, **8**: 100n, 287n, **10**: 100, 101n

Gooseberry, canyon, **7**: 15n, 114n

Gooseberry, garden, **2**: 210n

Gooseberry, hawthorn, **4**: 57n, **8**: 287n

Gooseberry, Hudson, **5**: 75, 76n, **7**: 47n

Gooseberry, Idaho, **8**: 13n

Gooseberry, Missouri, **2**: 210n, 309n, **9**: 15, 15n

Gooseberry, redshoot, **8**: 100n

Gooseberry, snow, **8**: 13n

Gooseberry, straggly, **7**: 15n, 45, 47n, 114n

Gooseberry, whitestem, **8**: 100n

Goose Egg Lake, **4**: 30–31, 33, 33n

Goosefoot, Fremont, **7**: 335, 337, 338n

Goose River, **2**: 219

Gopher, northern pocket, **4**: 18n, **7**: 221, 223, 225n

Gopher, southeastern pocket, **4**: 18n

Gorgets, **3**: 311, 311n, **5**: 246, 341, **6**: 254, 256, 257n. *See also* Clothing

Gorse, **5**: 291n

Goshen, **11**: 1, 4n

Gosling Lake, **2**: 347–48, 349n, 350

Government (Diamond, White Goose, Swan) Island: camped on, **6**: 13, **10**: 166, **11**: 384–85; described, **6**: 15–16, 55; distances, **6**: 457; listed, **6**: 470, **8**: 386, 405; and Indians, **6**: 478, 484, **7**: 56–57, 79, **9**: 285, **10**: 205; arrive at, **7**: 39, **11**: 384n; mentioned, **6**: 14n, 20n, **7**: 41n, 84, 89n, 97, 107, 110, **9**: 249n, 286n, **10**: 166n, 167n, 206n, **11**: 387n, 440n. *See also* McGuire Island

Governor Creek, **8**: 171n, **9**: 333n

Grackle, common, **4**: 237n, **5**: 24n, **7**: 28, 32n, **9**: 181n, **10**: 106n, **11**: 222n

Graine de volaille (pois de shico-riat), **2**: 144, 144n, 223. *See also* Lotus, American

Graisse de boeuf (and similar spellings). *See* Buffaloberry

Grama, blue, **4**: 308n, **8**: 187, 188n

Grampus, **6**: 62, 67n

Grampus griseus, **6**: 67n. *See also* Grampus

Grand Detour. *See* Missouri River, Big Bend of the

Grande Ronde River, **5**: 255, 26on, **7**: 186n

Grand Falls Formation, **2**: 285n

Grand Fork River, **2**: 219

Grand (Ibex) Island, **6**: 448, 463, **8**: 382, 401

Grand Natural Wall, **4**: 228, 234

Grand Osage Indians. *See* Great Osage Indians

Grand Osage River. *See* Osage River

Grand Pawnee Indians. *See* Pawnee Indians, Grand or Chawi

Grand River (Mo.): camped on, **2**: 296, **9**: 13, **10**: 14, **11**: 23–24; latitude, **2**: 298, 480, 487, **3**: 94, 370, 375, 377, **9**: 80–81, **11**: 173; distances, **2**: 405–6, 409, **8**: 378, **9**: 81, 368n, **11**: 172; discussed, **3**: 342–43, 345–46; listed, **3**: 390, **8**: 395; and Indians, **3**: 391, 395; hunted on, **8**: 364–65; conditions, **9**: 380; mentioned, **2**: 299n, 305n, 357, 498, **8**: 365n, **9**: 13n, 364n, **10**: 14n, 280, 280n, **11**: 22, 24n

Grand (We-tar-hoo and similar spellings) River (S. Dak.): described, **3**: 150–52; distances, **3**: 152, **8**: 380, 367n, **9**: 80, 82n; latitude, **3**: 153, 373, 376, **11**: 174; discussed, **3**: 360–61; listed, **3**: 380, **8**: 399; arrive at, **8**: 318; mentioned, **3**: 153n, **8**: 316n, 317n, 319n, **9**: 78n, 352n, 353n, **10**: 52n, 270n, 271n, **11**: 97n

Grand Tower, **1**: 5. *See also* Tower Rock

Grand View Island, **2**: 79, 79n, 8on

Granite (freestone), **4**: 60, 125, 200n, 391n, 397n, 405n, **5**: 2on, 3on, 157n, 203n, 218, 223n

Granite Range, **8**: 203n

Grant Creek, **8**: 82, 86n, **10**: 248n

Grape, choriser, **3**: 135

Grape, concord (purple), **2**: 452n

Grape, dull Oregon, **6**: 3, 26, 28n, 299, 301, 302n, **7**: 6on, 112, 114n, 193

Grape, fall, **2**: 351

Grape, grayback, **2**: 379n

Grape, Oregon, **6**: 3, 26, 28n, 297–300, 298n, 302n, **7**: 55, 6on, 77, 112, 114n, 193

Grape, Oregon creeping, **10**: 135, 135n

Grape, river-bank, **2**: 373n, 452n, **8**: 238, 240n, 324, 324n, 359n, 416, 418n, **9**: 8, 9n, **10**: 10, 11n, **11**: 68, 68n

Grape, summer, **2**: 351, 378, 379n, 452n

Grape, winter, **2**: 452n

Grapes: abundance, **2**: 292, 336, 338, 350, 369–70, 375, 380–81, 434, 447–48, **3**: 75, 222, 481, **4**: 89, **8**: 320, 326, 335, 338, 359, 416, **9**: 24, 26, 29, 35, 38–39, 53, 73; observed, **2**: 366, 428–29, **3**: 8, 10, 44–45, 87, 104–5, 131, 168, **8**: 265, 416, **9**: 12, 36, 44, 58–60, 64, 361; as food, **2**: 369, 433, **3**: 14, 65–66, 71, 74, 169, **5**: 54, **9**: 58, **10**: 20, 38, **11**: 72–73; and Indians, **8**: 308; mentioned, **8**: 266n, 417, 418n

Grass: observed, **2**: 185, **3**: 71, 148–49, **4**: 93, 108, 170, 176, 178, 254, 256, 291, 307, 332, 340, 358, 380, 383, 385, 396, 399, 411–12, 428, 430, **6**: 54, 63, 67, 88, 116, 122, 240, 242, 276–77, 313, 316, **7**: 46, 131, 170–71, 221, 223, 234, 267–68, 300, 305, 327, 329, **9**: 37–38, 43, 60, 78, 132, 149, 152, 163, 174, 183, 185, 192, 195, 198, 200–201, 203, 210–11, 257, 282, 306, 323, 328, 332, 354, **10**: 85, 98, 112, 240, 245, **11**: 59, 111, 171, 175, 188–89, 211–12, 226–27, 229–30, 235–36, 238, 251–54, 260, 266–67, 269–70, 275, 307, 314, 326, 340, 389; prairie, **2**: 292, 349n, 369–70, 375, 394–95, 397, 428–30, 380, 394–95, 397, 400n, 428–30, 434, 502–3, **3**: 80, 456, 465;

Grass (*continued*)
 and fires, **2**: 400n, **3**: 77, 81,
  209, 211, 231–32, 309,
  309n, 322; and species, **3**: 73;
  use, **3**: 161, 231–32, 457,
  489, **5**: 139, 259, 323, 361, **6**:
  77n, 96–97, 360–61, 366–
  67, 391, 393, 398, 400, **9**: 95,
  10: 228, 231; and Indians,
  3: 461, **11**: 98, **9**: 264, 315;
  specimens, **3**: 463; as food,
  4: 17, 19, 36, 46, 194, 198,
  8: 10, 24, 28–29, 34, 48, 50,
  69, 76, 201, 265; scarcity, **4**:
  140, 179, 181, 189, **5**: 45, 89,
  97, 205, 218, **8**: 56, 58, 69,
  205, 325, **9**: 152, 327, **10**: 81,
  92, **11**: 171, 175; abundance,
  5: 8, 27, 30–31, 37, 54, 62,
  71, 135, 171, 227, 356, 359,
  362, **8**: 38, 53–54, 59–60,
  179–80, 185, 338, **9**: 89, **10**:
  127, 245, **11**: 203, 249; habitat, **5**: 18, 21n, 228n; and
  horses, **5**: 178, 209, 214; described, **6**: 304, 307, **8**: 61,
  97, 103, 113, 310, 342, **10**:
  94; grazing, **7**: 158, 166, 167,
  256, 258, 292, 295–96, 302;
  lodges, **7**: 158, 239–40, 261–
  63, 275–76, 285; fuel, **7**:
  163; informed of, **7**: 174,
  176, 248; discussed, **7**: 335–
  37; damaged, **9**: 187, 206;
  mentioned, **2**: 380, **3**: 73n, **4**:
  36, 141, 297, 328, 331, 356,
  358, 411, 418, **5**: 10n, 70, 80,
  222, **7**: 349, **8**: 15–18, 20,
  26–27, 32, 55n, 72, 87, 95,
  102, 104, 107, 109, 161,
  174–75, 187, 192, 211, 225,
  264, 326, **10**: 13n, 203,
  211n. *See also specific species*
Grass, basket. *See* Beargrass
Grass, corn. *See* Grass, Johnson-
Grass, Johnson-, **7**: 191n, 335–
  36, 337n
Grass, needle and thread, **4**:
  430, 433n, **5**: 19, 21n, 36,
  45, 65, 67n, 78
Grass, plaited. *See* Sweetgrass
Grass, silk. *See* Dogbane
Grass, tongue, **2**: 279, 281n

Grasshopper, migratory, **8**:
  208n
Grasshoppers, **4**: 235, 255,
  237n, 278, 306, 308n, 380,
  5: 11, 14n, 286–87, **8**: 205,
  265
Grasshopper (Willard's) Creek,
  5: 98–99, 102n, 115, **6**: 451,
  465, **8**: 171–72, 173n, **9**:
  203, 203n, 333, 333n, **11**:
  269, 270n
Gratiot, Charles, **1**: 16n. 32, **2**:
  139, 139n, 180, 240, 243
Grave Creek, **2**: 77, 78n, **5**: 201,
  201n, 237, **6**: 452, 466, **8**: 65,
  68, 69n, 383, 402, **9**: 222,
  222n, 329n, **10**: 141, 141n,
  246, 246n, **11**: 311–12, 312n
Grave Creek Mound, **2**: 77, 78n
Gravel, **5**: 8, 10n, 16, 17n, 18,
  31–32, 37, 40–41, 45, 52n,
  53, 78, 81, 85n, 86n, 137,
  192, 196n, 294, **6**: 93–94,
  94n, 206, 208, 230n, **7**: 182,
  184, 186n, **8**: 88, 97–98,
  98n, 103, 113–14, 114n,
  118, 119n, 122, 123n, 124n,
  187, 188n, 200–201, 203n,
  210n, 231, 238, 248, 250n,
  277, 280n
Gravelines, Joseph: encoun-
  tered, **1**: 8, **8**: 357, **9**: 78, 361,
  10: 278, 278n, **11**: 98; interpreter, **3**: 151–52, 154n, 179,
  181n, 230, 313n, 332, 332n,
  4: 12n, **8**: 357, **9**: 94, 125,
  126, **10**: 52n, 76n; biographical sketch, **3**: 154n; returns,
  3: 157–58n, 304, 305n, 307,
  9: 119; information from, **3**:
  180, 305, **10**: 278, **11**: 105,
  126; sent out, **3**: 230–31, **9**:
  352; duties, **3**: 231n, 248–
  49, 252, **4**: 7, **8**: 357–58,
  358n, **10**: 74n; and Indians,
  3: 309, **10**: 52, **11**: 98, 98n,
  126; joins party, **4**: 7, **8**:
  358n, **9**: 121; robbed, **9**: 115,
  11: 101–2; mentioned, **3**:
  157, 182, 183n, **8**: 316n, **9**:
  78n, 86, 94n, 125n, 353n,
  10: 57n, **11**: 98n, 102n, 126n
Gravelly Range, **5**: 58, 60n

Gravey Creek, **5**: 211n, **8**: 58n
Graveyard (Mar-Shas-kap)
  Creek, **8**: 242–43, 245,
  246n, 390, 407
Gray, Robert, **2**: 2, **6**: 36n, 37n,
  51n, 160n, **10**: 186n
Grays Harbor, **6**: 77n, **7**: 110n,
  130n, **10**: 200n
Grays (Mast) Creek, **2**: 275–76,
  277n, **9**: 377, 377n
Grays Point (Cape Swells), **6**:
  35, 37n, 493, 493n, **10**: 168–
  69, 169n, **11**: 391n
Grays River, **6**: 37n, **10**: 168,
  169n
Grays (Shallow) Bay, **6**: 35–36,
  37n, 51n, 86–87, 87n, 112,
  458–59, 470, 493, **9**: 232,
  251, 251n, 256, **10**: 168,
  169n, 173, 174n, 178, 178n,
  11: 391n, 399, 399n
Grease, **4**: 324, 331, 344, 349,
  363–64, 371, 382, **8**: 37,
  38n, 125, **11**: 222. *See also*
  Bear; Buffalo; Tallow
Greasewood, **4**: 142, 145n, 146,
  189, 417, **5**: 45, 52n, 65, 67n,
  6: 370–71, 373n
Greasing. *See* Medicine
Greasy (Rest, Rush) Creek, **2**:
  264–65, 266n, **9**: 8, 8n, 376,
  10: 10, 10n, **11**: 15–16, 16n
Greasy Head, **3**: 310
Great Basin, **5**: 85n, **6**: 312n, **7**:
  42n, 130n, **10**: 206n, 226n
Great Bend of the Missouri
  River. *See* Missouri River,
  Great Bend of the
Great Columbian Plain, **4**: 198,
  200n, **5**: 4, 227, 228n, 263,
  265, 266n, 268, 275, 277,
  288, 339, 342–43, **6**: 211,
  213, 311, 313, 315, 318, 324,
  331–32, 335–36, 346, 348,
  352, 355–57, 359–60, 366–
  70, 382–83, **7**: 131, 188,
  326, 329, **8**: 88, 93, 102, 113,
  10: 153, 156, 207, 212, 215,
  219, 226n
Great Falls of the Columbia
  River. *See* Celilo (Great)
  Falls
Great Falls of the Missouri

River. *See* Missouri River, Great Falls of the

Great Father. *See* Jefferson, Thomas

Great (Grand, To-pah-cass) Osage Indians, **2**: 259–60, 266, 266–67n, 302–3, **3**: 136, 138n, 217n, 390–93, 437–38, 447, **8**: 367, 367n, **9**: 381n. *See also* Little Osage Indians; Osage Indians

Great Lakes, **1**: 5, **6**: 344, 346n, 351, 392, 394, **8**: 368n

Great Osage River. *See* Osage River

Great Plains, **2**: 346–47, 349n, 369–70, 373n, 380–81, 382n, 394, 398–99, 400n, 428–30, 431n, **3**: 8, 10, 44–45, 70–71, 77, 80–81, 89, 96, 188, 396–97, 401, 414, 418, 481, **4**: 19, 26, 35–36, 42–46, 69–71, 74, 76–77, 88, 96, 104, 121, 123–25, 130, 143, 158–59, 170, 176, 189, 201–2, 204–6, 238, 240, 254, 283–85, 363, **8**: 114n, 132n, 270n, **10**: 94. *See also* Clark, William, ecological observations; Lewis, Meriwether, ecological observations

Great Rapids. *See* Columbia River, Cascades of the

Great River of the West. *See* Columbia River

Great Saline River, **3**: 391

Great Shute. *See* Columbia River, Cascades of the

Great Slave Lake, **10**: 6n

Grebe, horned, **6**: 399, 401, 401n

Grebe, pied-billed, **6**: 399–400, 401n

Grebe, red-necked, **6**: 399, 401, 401n

Grebe, western, **6**: 98n, 391n

Greece, **10**: 93n

Greenbriar, bristly, **8**: 416, 418n

Green Creek, **10**: 250, 251n

Greene, Griffin, **2**: 81, 81n

Greenhead, **7**: 309, 311, 312n

Green Lake, **6**: 21n

Green River, **5**: 95n, **6**: 312n

Greenshield site, **3**: 198n, **9**: 90n

Greensward, **5**: 58, 60n, 109–11, **6**: 304, 307, 307n

Greenville, Treaty of, **2**: 107, 109n, 140, 140n

Greenwich, **10**: 6n, 63n

Gregoire, Charles, **2**: 183, 183n

Grenier, Francis Fleury *dit*. *See* Fleury, Francis, *dit* Grenier

Greybull River, **8**: 235n

Grey Eyes, **8**: 312–14, 316–17n, 317

Griffith, **3**: 474

Griffith, Samuel, **2**: 134, 134n, 140

Grimes Creek, **5**: 76n

Grindelia squarrosa, **3**: 468. *See also* Gumweed, curly-top

Grindstone, **4**: 370

Griping. *See* Medical problems, bowels

Grog, **4**: 153, 250, 266, 337, 343, **8**: 139n, **9**: 163, 177, **10**: 98, 99n, **11**: 188, 189n

Grog Spring, **4**: 256, 282, 282n, **8**: 137–38, 139n, 292, 295, **11**: 188, 189n

Gros Ventres Indians, **3**: 198n. *See also* Atsina Indians; Hidatsa Indians

Gros Ventres of the Missouri, **3**: 206n, **4**: 214n. *See also* Hidatsa Indians

Gros Ventres of the Prairie, **3**: 206n, **4**: 214n. *See also* Atsina Indians

Groundhog, **2**: 429–30. *See also* Woodchuck

Groundnut. *See* Potato, Indian

Ground squirrel. *See* Squirrel, ground

Grouse (pheasant, prairie hen): hunted, **2**: 151, 158, **5**: 162–63, 186, 189, 194, 197, 201–3, 207, 210–11, 216, 226, 197, 288, 341, 343–45, **7**: 234, 236, 257, 259–60, 262, 264, 282, **9**: 217, 217n, 220–22, 227, 231, 310, 312, 321, **10**: 132, 135, 142, 146, 148, 218, 223, 228, 230, 243, **11**: 296–300, 304–5, 307, 311–12, 322–26, 336; observed, **3**: 98, **4**: 28, 90, **5**: 213; abundance, **3**: 148–49, 150n, 294; behavior, **4**: 70, **7**: 282n; described, **5**: 217–18, 223n; mentioned, **4**: 236, **10**: 218n, 243n, **11**: 299n, 305n, 356. *See also* Prairie-chicken, greater

Grouse, blue (black pheasant, brown pheasant): observed, **4**: 412, 415n, **5**: 26–27, 29n, 217, 223n, **7**: 193, 259; described, **7**: 126, 130n; hunted, **7**: 257, 259, 281–82, 282n, **8**: 52, 54, 55n, 60, 63, **9**: 306–7, 307n, **10**: 135, 136n, 232n; mentioned, **6**: 377n

Grouse, Columbian sharp-tailed (prairie hen), **6**: 366–67, 368n

Grouse, Oregon ruffed (pheasant), **5**: 218, 223n, **6**: 22, 24, 24n, 279–80, 280n, 375–76, 377n, **8**: 28, 30, 30n, **10**: 136n

Grouse, ruffed (pheasant), **2**: 134, 134n, 419, 419n, **4**: 42, 45n, 412, 417, **5**: 26–27, 29n, 218, 223n, **6**: 374, 377n, **7**: 43, 46n, **8**: 53–54, 55n, 80

Grouse, sage (cock of the plains, mountain cock): observed, **4**: 258, 260n, 347, **5**: 74, 129, 167, **7**: 198n, **10**: 157, 157n; hunted, **5**: 131, 162–63, 181, 286–88, 291, 296, **10**: 131, 132n, 157, 157n, **11**: 356–59, 358n; described, **5**: 287, **6**: 368–71; specimen, **5**: 290n; discovered, **6**: 3, 373n; abundance, **6**: 368, 370, **9**: 240, 240n; sketch, **6**: 370, 373n, 374n; mentioned, **5**: 76n, 132n

Grouse, sharp-tailed (prairie hen): observed, **3**: 48, 50n, 67, 67n, **4**: 93, 95n, 179, 182n, **8**: 75, 78n; described, **3**: 133, 137n, **6**: 366–67,

Grouse (*continued*)
368n; abundance, **3**: 147,
148n, **4**: 42; behavior, **4**: 42,
176; hunted, **5**: 179, 191,
193, **8**: 86, **9**: 129, 221; habitat, **8**: 416–17; as specimen,
9: 123, 123n, 126, 127n;
mentioned, **3**: 150n, **4**: 44–
45n, **5**: 74, 76n, **8**: 418n
Grouse, sooty, **7**: 130n
Grouse, spruce (black and white
pheasant, small speckled
pheasant), **5**: 203, 204n, 217,
223n, **6**: 371, 373–76, 377n,
8: 52, 54, 55n, **10**: 136n
Grouseberry, **8**: 60–61, 61n
Grouse Island, **8**: 320n
Grows. *See* Grouse
Grus americana, **2**: 186n, **4**: 24n,
5: 344n. *See also* Crane,
whooping
Grus canadensis, **4**: 415n, **5**: 13n,
6: 14n, **7**: 25n, **8**: 13n, **9**:
191n, **10**: 139n, **11**: 246n.
See also Crane, sandhill
Guard, trigger, **8**: 111n. *See also*
Arms and ammunition
Guard Lake, **8**: 351n, **10**: 27n
Guinea pig, **8**: 75
Guitard, Vincent, **2**: 482n
Gulf of California, **1**: 3, **5**: 1, 90,
95n, **6**: 316, **10**: 6n, 205
Gulf of Mexico, **1**: 3, 5, **4**: 248,
5: 1, 65
Gull, Bonaparte's, **6**: 387n, **8**:
151n
Gull, glaucous-winged, **6**: 387n
Gull, herring, **3**: 132n
Gull, ring-billed, **3**: 132n
Gull, sea, **10**: 169, 169n
Gull, western, **6**: 383, 384n,
385–88, 387n
Gulls: abundance, **3**: 128, 130–
31, **6**: 9, 11, 13, 39, 42, 88,
96, **10**: 166; observed, **3**: 141,
147, 221, **4**: 23, 94, **6**: 383,
385, **8**: 150, 266, **9**: 252,
10: 159–60, 166, **11**: 391;
hunted, **5**: 309, 312, **6**: 181;
described, **6**: 388, **8**: 150;
mentioned, **3**: 132n, **4**: 24n,
5: 312n, **6**: 387n, **8**: 267n,
9: 252n

Gulo luscus, **4**: 296n, **5**: 76n. *See
also* Wolverine
Gum. *See* Pitch
Gum, black, **2**: 69, 69n
Gumbo, **4**: 264n
Gumbo Point site (Little Zoe
Prairie), **2**: 299n, 303n, **9**:
14n, 381n, **10**: 14n, **11**: 24–
25, 25n
Gumbo-till, **8**: 114n
Gumweed, curly-top, **3**: 459,
464, 468
Gunpowder: purchased, **2**: 6;
distributed, **2**: 166, 201, **3**:
79, **8**: 80, 157, 302, 305–6,
311; packed, **2**: 214, **4**: 334–
35, **6**: 265, 272, **11**: 212,
322–23; wet, **2**: 327, **4**: 13–
14, 22, 156–57, 341, 343, **5**:
53, 115, 271–72, 275, **6**: 138,
8: 146, **10**: 77, **11**: 257–58;
and Indians, **2**: 438, **3**: 28–
31, 34, 142–43, 166, 246–
47, 356, 402, **5**: 142, 146–
47n, 178, 198, **6**: 15, 74, 76,
187, 205–6, 208–9, 233,
235, **8**: 294, 305–6, 317,
330, **9**: 48, 50, 76, 248, 306;
as medicine, **3**: 297n; as gift,
3: 310, **7**: 196, 198, 247, 256,
258; cached, **4**: 269, 274–76,
279, **5**: 248–50, **7**: 220, 222,
232, 235–36, **8**: 138, **9**: 165–
66, 234, **10**: 101, 224, **11**:
192–93, 341–42; as trade
item, **5**: 178, **7**: 177, 179,
248, 250, **9**: 300, 348, 369n;
described, **6**: 265, 273n;
found, **7**: 137, 139, 161;
damaged, **9**: 127; lost, **9**: 177,
197; mentioned, **3**: 125n, **4**:
309, **5**: 210n, **7**: 89n, **8**: 359,
9: xviii, 174, 351, 393. *See also*
Arms and ammunition;
Canisters
Guns: contests and practice, **2**:
144, 156–57, 175, 202, 205,
211–12; lost, **2**: 424–27, **3**:
188, 188n, 222, **4**: 342–43;
Indian, **3**: 122, 130, 139,
165, 223n, 237, 246–47,
356, 401, 428, 484, **5**: 86n,
160, 179, 355, 357, **6**: 13,

15, 76, 206, 208–9, **7**: 247,
251n, **8**: 132n, 135, 295,
312, 317, 330, 337, **9**: 205,
221, 341–42, 357, 391, **11**:
94, 272, 276; damaged, **3**:
296, **4**: 331, **6**: 416, 418, **10**:
170, 254; fired, **3**: 311, **4**:
242, **5**: 15, 53, 172, **6**: 186,
278, 279, **8**: 135, 137, 318,
329, 349–50, 352, 367, 370,
9: 107, 197, 262, 374, **11**:
114, 258; and Indians, **4**: 11,
398, 407, 412, **5**: 3, 104–5,
125, 142, **7**: 3, 94, 99, 149, **8**:
280n, 306, 312, 331, **10**: 259,
260n; repaired, **4**: 27, **6**: 147,
441–42, **7**: 91–92, 95, **8**: 74–
75, 79; signaling with, **4**: 70,
152–54; hunting with, **4**:
151, 293–94, **7**: 98, 177,
179, 275, **8**: 38, 145, 155,
281, **11**: 357; wet, **4**: 256,
261; carrying, **4**: 330; hid,
4: 341–42; as trade item, **5**:
80, 91–92, 95n, 111, **6**: 187,
205, 360, 405–6, **7**: 146,
229, 248, 250, **8**: 1, 35–36,
47, 75, 80, 214, 294, **9**: 302,
318, 369n, **11**: 290–91, 387;
problems, **5**: 209, 210n, **8**:
99; stolen, **6**: 48–50, **8**: 2,
129, 133–34, 294, **9**: 87,
208, 253–54, **11**: 281, 282n,
394; other, **6**: 156; mentioned, **2**: 7, 83, 90, 105, 264,
270, 301, 318, 374, 423, 502,
506, 525, **3**: 80, 112, **4**: 215,
263, 289, **5**: 68–69, 78–79,
146–47n, 163, 196, 213,
222, 244, 329, 333, **6**: 47,
113, 456, **7**: 109, **9**: 387. *See
also* Arms and ammunition;
Muskets; Pistols; Rifles
Gunshot wound. *See* Medical
problems
Gurnett Creek. *See* Duck (Whitehouse's) Creek
Guterge, Guterich, Guthrege,
Gutrich (and similar spellings). *See* Goodrich
Gutierrezia sarothrae, **3**: 469. *See
also* Snakeweed, broom
Gymnocladus dioica, **2**: 431n, **8**:

418n, **9**: 32n. *See also* Coffee-
tree, Kentucky
Gymnogyps californianus, **1**: 10,
  5: 357–58n, **6**: 67n, **7**: 26n,
  9: 247n, **10**: 176n, **11**: 378n.
  See also Condor, California
Gymnorhinus cyanocephalus, **5**:
  29n, **6**: 131n. *See also* Jay,
  pinyon
Gypsum, **3**: 51n, 69n, 473, 476,
  478, **4**: 135n

H

Hackberry, **2**: 313, 315n, **8**: 416,
  418n, **9**: 53, 54n
Hackberry, netleaf, **5**: 261,
  263n, 265, 274, 279
Hackmatack, **8**: 12n. *See also*
  Larch, western
Hadrosaurus, **8**: 229n
Hague, Arnold, **1**: 9. *See also*
  Maps, Clark's map of 1805
Hail. *See* Weather conditions
Hairy Horn, **3**: 288
Haley. *See* Hill, Samuel
Haley, Gertrude, **2**: 543, **11**: xvi
Haley's Bay. *See* Baker Bay
Half-Breed (Pine) Island, **4**:
  392, 395–96, 396n, 397n
Half-Breed (Pine Island) Rap-
  ids, **4**: 387, 391n, 393, **6**:
  449, 464, 473n, 494, **8**: 291,
  9: 185, 185n, 337, 337n, **10**:
  113, 113n, **11**: 229, 230n
The Half Man, (Ane, a, wish, a
  Shaddie La, dom, Anchas,
  week, achappa, Arcawechar-
  chi), **3**: 30–31, 34, 37n, **9**:
  49, 51, 51n
Haliaeetus leucocephalus, **4**: 34n,
  5: 67n, **6**: 94n, **7**: 17n, **8**:
  147n, **9**: 129n, **11**: 267n.
  See also Eagle, bald
Haliotis sp., **5**: 140n. *See also*
  Abalone
Hall, Hugh: drunk, **2**: 143,
  143n; listed, **2**: 148, 187,
  189, 195, 198–99, 255, **3**:
  170, **4**: 9, 11, **6**: 83, **8**: 162n,

179, **9**: 279, **11**: 4n, 7n; hunting, **2**: 158, **7**: 262; returns,
  2: 214, **8**: 283; in permanent
  party, **2**: 229n; discipline, **2**:
  235, 332; court-martialed, **2**:
  235–37, 329–30; **9**: 18, 18n,
  11: xv; biographical sketch,
  2: 518; lake named for, **4**: 50;
  accidents, **6**: 384–85; sent
  out, **7**: 271–72, **8**: 208, 219,
  9: 312, 313n, **10**: 230, 230n,
  255, 256n; river named for,
  8: 231, 233, 234n, 235n;
  mentioned, **2**: 139n, **7**: 167,
  10: 265, 265n
Hall's Strand Creek, **11**: 136n
Halters, **5**: 160–61
Hamilton, Alexander, **8**: 347,
  348n
Hamilton Creek, **6**: 7, 9n, 54
Hamilton (Strawberry) Island,
  5: 359, 362, 364n, **6**: 7, 8–9,
  9n, 54, 493, **7**: 100, 101n,
  102, **9**: 232, 248, 248n, 288,
  289n, **10**: 173, 174n, 208,
  208n
Hammerean Creek, **5**: 185n,
  9: 216, 217n
Hammers, **4**: 275
Hammond, John Henry, **2**: 41,
  541
Hancock, Forrest: encountered,
  8: 3, 157, 288, **9**: 348, **10**:
  266; and Indians, **8**: 157;
  biographical sketch, **8**: 158–
  59; trapping, **8**: 158–59n;
  and members of the party,
  8: 4, 158–59n, 302, 305, **9**:
  351, **10**: 267–68; mentioned,
  8: 153n, 289n, 295, **9**: 349n,
  10: 266n, 267n, 268. *See also*
  Dickson, Joseph
Hancock, George, **2**: 142, 142n
Hancock, Julia, **2**: 37, 142n,
  4: 2, 220n, **9**: 158n, **10**: 96n,
  11: 178n
Handkerchiefs: as gift, **3**: 240,
  242, 268, **5**: 77, 112, 197,
  219, 227, 231, 278, 301, 303,
  341–42, **6**: 136–37, **7**: 256,
  258, **8**: 83, 88, 130, 294, **9**:
  206, 262, **10**: 184, **11**: 407; as
  trade item, **5**: 117–18, 158,

166, 244, **6**: 81, 281, **7**: 12–
  13, 147–48, 212, 326, 328,
  11: 276, 434; and Indians, **8**:
  329; mentioned, **6**: 421, 423,
  7: 27, 35. *See also* Clothing
Hands. *See* Medical problems
Handsome Falls. *See* Rainbow
  Falls
Hanley, Samuel, **2**: 173, 173n
Hard Scrabble Creek, **8**: 96n
Hardy Creek, **9**: 337n
Hare. *See* Jackrabbits; Jackrabbit,
  white-tailed
Harebell, roundleaf, **4**: 400,
  402n, **9**: 169, 169n, **10**: 99n,
  11: 201n
Harley Canyon, **7**: 159n
Harnesses, **5**: 125, 133, **11**: 210
Harp, Jew's, **9**: 48n, **11**: 65–66
Harper, Francis P., **2**: 38
Harpers Ferry, W. Va., **4**: 370,
  371n, **6**: 441–42, **7**: 169n
Harrier, northern, **6**: 375, 377,
  378n
Harris Creek, **8**: 251, 254, 256n
Harrison, William Henry, **1**: 6–
  7, **2**: 182, 183n, **8**: 371, 371n
Harrison (Sheeco) Island, **2**:
  291–92, 293n
Harrodsburg, Ky., **2**: 434, 435n
Hart's Horn River. *See* Elkhorn
  River
Hassler, Ferdinand Rudolph,
  1: 12, 19n. 134, **2**: 533–34
Hatchet Creek, **8**: 257, 260,
  262n
Hatchets, **3**: 279, 281, 284,
  492n, **5**: 150, 328, **7**: 123. *See
  also* Arms and ammunition
Hat Rock, **5**: 301, 307n, 374,
  6: 454, 468
Hats: accidents, **2**: 65; as signal,
  5: 68; and Indians, **5**: 104,
  346–47, 351, **6**: 187, 205,
  221–22, **7**: 9, 8; 152n, **9**: 267,
  273, 277; purchased, **5**: 371,
  6: 74, 76, 335, 337, **7**: 9, 8:
  152n, **9**: 267, 273, 278; as
  gift, **6**: 139, **9**: 47, 67, 79, 92;
  sketch, **6**: 249n, 253n; as
  trade item, **6**: 421, 423, **8**:
  351, **9**: 359, **10**: 194, **11**: 414,
  422–23, 430; found, **8**: 151;

Hats (*continued*)
listed, **8**: 419; mentioned, **2**: 238, **6**: 78n. *See also* Clothing
Hatwai Creek, **5**: 253, 258, 259n
Hatwai site, **5**: 259n
Hatwai village, **7**: 214n
Haw, black, **2**: 309n, **3**: 223n, **8**: 359, 359n, 416, 418n
Haw, crimson. *See* Hawthorn
Haw, southern black, **2**: 309n, **3**: 223n
Haw, summer, **2**: 309n
Hawaiian Islands, **6**: 192n, 307n
Hawk, Cooper's, **6**: 375, 378n
Hawk, fishing. *See* Osprey
Hawk, red-tailed, **5**: 76n, **6**: 94, 94n, 96, 375, 377, 378n
Hawk, sparrow. *See* Kestrel, American
Hawk, Swainson's, **5**: 76n, **6**: 375, 377, 378n
Hawks: abundance, **3**: 80, **6**: 96, **8**: 117; observed, **4**: 93, **5**: 73, 76n, 216, **7**: 76, **8**: 75, 93, 180, 210, 350, 359, **10**: 154; hunted, **6**: 96–97, 101, **7**: 269, 271, **9**: 220, 312, **10**: 175, **11**: 304–5; mentioned, **3**: 82, 85, **4**: 95n, 276, **6**: 321–23. *See also* Kestrel, American
Haws, **10**: 141, **11**: 348. *See also* Hawthorn, Columbia
Hawthorn, black (purple haw, white thorn), **7**: 112–13, 114n, 188–89, 191n, 197, **8**: 10–11, 13n, 183, 186, **11**: 326, 328, 329n
Hawthorn, Columbia, **5**: 156, 162–63, 164n, 219, 232, **7**: 319, **10**: 130, 130n, **11**: 326, 328, 329n
Hawthorns, **2**: 309, 309n, **11**: 348
Hay, **2**: 304, 305n, 346, **5**: 8, **9**: 111
Hay (Pocasse), **3**: 155–56, 156n, 158, 160, 162, 164–65, 168–69, 171n
Hay, John, **1**: 5, 7, 16nn. 32, 37, **2**: 126, 127n, 167, 167–68n, 168n, 172, 174, 183, 191,

206–7, 211, 219, 220n, 225–26n, **8**: 371, 371n
Hay Creek (Custer County, Mont.), **8**: 251, 254, 256n
Hay Creek (Treasure County, Mont.), **8**: 237, 239, 241n
Hayden (Image Canoe) Island, **6**: 16–17, 20n, 23, 55, 457, 470, **7**: 33–35, 36n, 41, 54, 56, 58–60, 81, 83, **10**: 166, 167n, **11**: 384–85, 387n, 440n
Hayden Creek, **5**: 88, 94n
Hays, John, **1**: 16n. 32, **2**: 167, 168n, 172, 191, 208, 209n
Haystack Butte, **7**: 159n, **8**: 96–97, 98n, 103
Haystack Rock, **6**: 185n
Hazelnut, **2**: 291–92, 293n, 381, 428, 433, **5**: 323, 326n, 348, 351, 353n, 358n, **6**: 345, 347n, 348, **7**: 119–20, 122n, **8**: 416, 418n, **10**: 164, 164n, **11**: 260, 261n
Headaches. *See* Medical problems
Head deformation. *See* Cathlamet Indians; Chinook Indians; Clatsop Indians; Indians
Hearne, Samuel, **10**: 6n, 7n
Heart (Ches-che-tar and similar spellings) River: and Indians, **3**: 189, 207n, 294, 298n, 312n; arrive at, **3**: 189, **9**: 88, **11**: 103; described, **3**: 362; distances, **3**: 373, 376, **8**: 380, **9**: 367n, **11**: 172; listed, **3**: 381, **8**: 399; name, **7**: 343n; camped on, **8**: 308, **10**: 58, **11**: 125n; mentioned, **3**: 186, 188n, 190n, 295n, 361, **8**: 309n, **9**: 88n, 351n, **10**: 58n, 73n, 269n, **11**: 103n
Heat. *See* Medicine; Weather conditions
Hébert, Charles (Chalo?), **1**: 17n. 73, **2**: 255, 347, 526
Heceta, Bruno de, **6**: 36n
Hedysarum boreale, **7**: 338n. *See also* Vetch, sweet
Helianthus annuus, **4**: 386n, **7**: 122n, **8**: 120n, **9**: 39n,

10: 131n. *See also* Sunflower, annual
Helianthus cusickii, **7**: 122n. *See also* Sunflower, Cusick's
Helianthus laetiflorus, **8**: 120n. *See also* Sunflower, stiff
Helianthus nuttallii, **5**: 60n, **8**: 52n, 120n, **9**: 212n, **10**: 131n, **11**: 261n. *See also* Sunflower, Nuttall
Helianthus petiolaris, **8**: 120n. *See also* Sunflower, plains
Helianthus rigidus, **8**: 120n. *See also* Sunflower, stiff
Helianthus sp., **8**: 73n
Helianthus tuberosus, **3**: 327n, **4**: 18n, **5**: 147n, **8**: 52n. *See also* Artichoke, Jerusalem
Hell (Stick Lodge) Creek, **4**: 151, 153–54, 155n, **9**: 148n, **10**: 88, 89n, **11**: 155–56, 158n
Hell Creek Formation, **4**: 107n, 120n, 135n, 145n, 148n, 163n, **8**: 228n, 229n, 234n, 235n, 240n, 246n
Hellgate River. *See* Clark Fork River
Hematite, **8**: 27n
Hemlock, mountain, **5**: 209, 210n, 215, 238
Hemlock, water, **7**: 275, 276–77n
Hemlock, western, **6**: 3, 19n, 45n, 279–80, 280n, 284n, **7**: 37n, 60n, 114n, **10**: 206n
Hemp, Indian, **6**: 217n. *See also* Dogbane
Hen, heath, **2**: 90n. *See also* Grouse, sage
Hen, Indian. *See* Prairie-chicken, greater
Hen, prairie. *See* Grouse, Columbian sharp-tailed; Grouse, sharp-tailed; Prairie-chicken, greater
Henderson, George, **1**: 8, **3**: 251, 251–52n, **9**: 100, 100n, **10**: 64, 64n
Hendry, Anthony, **8**: 132n
Heneberry, Patrick, **2**: 144, 144n

Heney, Hugh: and maps, **1**: 8–9; information from, **3**: 176, 179n, 304, 317, 386n, 492n; visits, **3**: 254, 257–59, 265; biographical sketch, **3**: 258n; as trader, **3**: 417, **9**: 104, 104n, **10**: 66, 66n; letter for, **8**: 3, 74, 77, 212, 212n; meets Lewis and Clark, **8**: 78n, 212n; services sought, **8**: 156, 212, **10**: 265n; mentioned, **2**: 253n, **11**: xiii, 111n

Henry, Alexander (younger), **3**: 201n, 205n, 213n, 276n, 311n, **8**: 317n

Henry, Andrew, **1**: 19n. 139, **5**: 10n

Henshaw, Henry, **2**: 39

Heracleum lanatum, **7**: 201n. *See also* Parsnip, cow

Herbs. *See* Medicine

Hermaphrodite Creek, **8**: 399, **9**: 84n, **11**: 100n

Heron, black-crowned night-, **3**: 13n

Heron, great blue, **2**: 177, 178n, 468, 470, 471n, **6**: 96, 98n, 383, 385, 388, **9**: 50, 51n

Heron, white. *See* Egret, great

Herpestes sp., **6**: 355n. *See also* Mongoose

Herring, **6**: 302, 305, 336–37, 344, 346n, 349. *See also* Eulachon

Heterodon nasicus, **4**: 422n, **8**: 266n. *See also* Snake, western hog-nosed

He-that-looks-at-the-calf, **8**: 134, 136n

Hibbard Creek, **8**: 230–31, 233, 234n

Hickory, **2**: 78–79, 78n, 80n, 112, 275, 286, 429–30, **4**: 374, **8**: 354, 355n, 359, 416, 418n, **9**: 8, 9n, 10, 10n, 12, 31–32, **10**: 10–11, 11n

Hickory, bitternut, **8**: 355n, 418n

Hickory, shagbark, **8**: 355n, 418n

Hidatsa (Big Belly, Gros Ventres, Minitari) Indians: trade, **1**: 3, **3**: 137n, 220n, 228n, 251, 262, 331n, 400, 421–22, 425–29, 433, 484, 487, **5**: 95n, **7**: 247, **9**: 104, 306, **11**: 121; villages, **1**: 6–9, 12, **2**: 7–8, **9**: 90n, 91n, 98, 98–99n, 103, 110, 122, 127, 127n, 349–50, **3**: 2–3, 137n, 193–94, 194n, 198n, 204, 205–6n, 217n, 227n, 229n, 230, 237, 242n, 258n, 362, 275n, 362, 373, 376, 385n, 483, **5**: 86n, **8**: 78n, 298, 300n, 381, 399, **10**: 70, 77, 78n, 267, 273n, **11**: 133, 134n; chiefs, **1**: 8, **2**: 264n, **3**: 208–12, 213n, 226, 235n, 249, 272, 275, 294, 303, 307, 310–11, 311n, 318–19, 319n, 325, **5**: 160, **8**: 4, 289, 299, 300, 302–3, 305–6, **9**: 91, 98, 98–99n, 109–10, 121, 121n, **10**: 61n; information from, **1**: 8–9, **3**: 298n, 444–45, **4**: 2–4, 170, 173, 198, 246, 248, 250, 253n, 296n, 320, 374–75, **5**: 1, 187–88n, 195, 195n, 196, **8**: 96n, 193n, 208n, 221n, 232, 246n, 250n, 256n, 259, 261n, **9**: 145n, **11**: 374n; language, **2**: 438, 442n, **3**: 153n, 205–6n, 228, 234, 234n, 258n, 284n, 365, 385n, 490, **4**: 124, 128, 175n, 246, 252n, **7**: 242, 244, **8**: 162n, 205, 208n, 235n, 243, 246n, 248, 250n, 259, 261n, **9**: 219n, 306n, **11**: 302n; distances, **2**: 485, **3**: 31; establish peace, **3**: 2, 156n, 234, 304, 485, **4**: 9–10, **5**: 91, 130, 160, **8**: 303; name, **3**: 37n, 206–7n, 250n, **8**: 65n, **9**: 91n, 92n, 306n, 343n, 350n, **10**: 61n, 260n; located, **3**: 154n, 312, 362, **4**: 222, **6**: 447, 462; war, **3**: 196–97, 233–34, 244, 246, 267, 276, 309, 317, 330–31, 416–17, 485, **4**: 159–61, **5**: 9, 106, 109, 116n, 120–21, 168, 173, **8**: 195, 302–3, 306, 311–13, 330, **9**: 110n, 190, 191n, 192, **10**: 74, 119, **11**: 108–9, 242–43, 244n, 246–47; and Mandan Indians, **3**: 201n; historical sketch, **3**: 206–7n, 403–5; councils, **3**: 207, 209–12, **8**: 4, 300–301, **9**: 91, **10**: 60, **11**: 106; relations with the party, **3**: 207–12, 216, 240, 245–46, 272, 274, 276, 286, 303, 307, 313, 318, 319n, **8**: 304, 306, **10**: 75–76, 268; medical problems, **3**: 207n, 312, 324n, 405, **10**: 76; gifts, **3**: 209, 211, **9**: 350; prisoners, **3**: 229n, 485, **5**: 9; encountered, **3**: 238, **4**: 19, 23, **8**: 298, **11**: 105; visits, **3**: 238, 240–41, 265, 274–75, 277, 284, 297, 303, 307–9, 318–19, 325, **9**: 120–21, 122–23; camps, **3**: 259, 278, **4**: 16–18, 28, 161; hunting, **3**: 265, 310, 482, 484–85, **4**: 26, 31, **8**: 297, **9**: 128, **10**: 78, **11**: 134; food, **3**: 272, 273n, 326, 489; and animals, **3**: 292, 489, **8**: 319; customs, **3**: 299, 485–86, 488, **4**: 55, **5**: 120, **6**: 169, 191, 273–74, 405–6, **8**: 317n, **10**: 76; clothes, **3**: 330, 488, **5**: 133; listed, **3**: 448; tobacco, **3**: 466, **5**: 81; character, **3**: 483; lodges, **3**: 489, **4**: 16, **11**: 105; artifacts, **4**: 211, 430, **8**: 106n; arms and ammunition, **5**: 150; origin story, **8**: 308–9, 309n; mentioned, **2**: 486n, **3**: 424, **4**: 1, 22, 214n, **6**: 172n, **7**: 245n, 343n, **8**: 316n, **9**: 92, 97, 129, **10**: xvii, 267n, **11**: 105n, 110n, 208. *See also* Mandan Indians

Hidatsa Indians, Awatixa (Black Moccasins, Maharhas), **3**: 206n, 234n, **8**: 298–99, 303n, 313, 319

Hidatsa Indians, Awaxawi (Ahna haways, Watersoons): name, 2: 486n, 3: 205–6n, 247n, 9: 92n, 121n, 11: 105n; villages, 3: 193–94, 194n, 300, 362, 376, 8: 298–99, 302; historical sketch, 3: 205–6n, 206–7n, 403–4; councils, 3: 207, 9: 91, 10: 60, 11: 105–6; war, 3: 207, 244, 246, 267, 304, 11: 108–9; chiefs, 3: 209, 213n, 216, 303, 307, 311, 9: 121; trade, 3: 256, 400, 422, 428, 483; customs, 3: 405, 483, 485–86, 6: 169, 191; listed, 3: 448; tobacco, 3: 466; appearance, 3: 487; language, 3: 490; and other Indians, 4: 9, 8: 313; mentioned, 6: 172n, 9: 91n, 10: 61n, 78n

Hidatsa Indians, Hidatsas proper, 3: 206–7n, 234n

Hierochloe odorata, 4: 57n, 5: 141n, 8: 222n. See also Sweetgrass

Higgins, 2: 151, 182

Highland Mountains, 8: 178, 178n, 10: 120, 121n

Highwood (South) Mountains, 4: 200n, 241n, 247, 252n, 253, 257n, 268, 282n, 312–13, 316, 8: 115, 116n, 9: 165n, 10: 98, 99n, 11: 181–84, 182n, 184n, 186n, 188–89, 189n

Highwood (Strawberry) Creek (Shields's River), 4: 298, 299n, 6: 449, 464, 8: 382, 401, 9: 168, 168n, 10: 102, 102n, 11: 198, 199n

Hill, Alfred J., 2: 39

Hill, Samuel, 1: 19n. 126, 6: 27, 29n, 48n, 86n, 155–56, 160n, 416, 416n, 427, 432n, 9: 252n, 277n, 11: 392, 392n

Hillsboro soil, 7: 37n

Hinges, 2: 181

Hiodon alosoides, 2: 484n, 4: 279n, 9: 40n, 11: 194n. See also Goldeye

Hiodon tergisus, 2: 484n, 9: 40n. See also Mooneye

Hips. See Medical problems

Hirundo pyrrhonota, 4: 233n, 11: 182n. See also Swallow, cliff

Hirundo rustica, 3: 132n, 8: 267n. See also Swallow, barn

Historie de la Louisiane (Du Pratz), 2: 352n

History of the Expedition under the Command of Captains Lewis and Clark (Biddle), 2: 37, 544, 3: 184n, 268n, 324n, 4: 155n. See also Biddle, Nicholas

Hitchcock, C. Leo, 12: 7

Hocking River, 2: 82, 82n, 83n

Hoes, 3: 264

Hog Island, 5: 253, 258, 259n

Hogs, 2: 151–53, 203, 218, 224, 333, 429–30, 5: 37, 6: 185, 8: 145, 214

Hogthief Island, 2: 386n, 10: 21, 21n. See also Bald (Chauvin) Island

Hoh (Ca-last-ho-cle) Indians, 6: 476, 486, 491

Hoh-host. See Bear, grizzly

Hohots Ilppilp: and maps, 1: 11; relations with the party, 7: 238, 240, 256–59, 290, 294, 314, 322, 324, 326, 328, 333, 344–45, 9: 319, 319n, 320n, 10: 228, 229n, 233n, 236, 237n; visits, 7: 238, 261–65, 289–90, 339, 342, 348–49; sister, 7: 241n; rank, 7: 242, 244; father, 7: 247, 251; clothes, 7: 253–55; mentioned, 7: 241n, 334n, 8: 48n, 9: 318n

Holly, mountain, 6: 297, 298n, 299, 302, 302n. See Grape, dull Oregon; Grape, Oregon

Holmes Island. See Vingt-un Island

Holy Rainbow, 8: 344n

Hominy, 3: 19, 116, 119–20, 208, 6: 235n

Honey, 2: 181

Honeysuckle, California, 7: 114n

Honeysuckle, western trumpet, 5: 191, 195n, 218, 224n, 6:

284–86, 286n, 7: 114n, 8: 28–29, 30n, 71, 128, 187, 263, 266n

Honeysuckle, white berry. See Snowberry, common

Honeysuckle, wild, 4: 57n

Honeysuckles, 2: 435n, 3: 457–58, 463, 4: 70, 108, 176, 216, 324, 417, 7: 45, 47n, 112, 193, 197, 335, 337. See also Wolfberry; Snowberry, common

Hononquise, 8: 348n

Hood, Samuel, 5: 301n, 9: 249n, 10: 166n, 11: 384n

Hood (Labiche's) River, 5: 350, 352, 354n, 378, 6: 456, 469, 472n, 475, 483, 7: 118, 120, 121n, 122n, 8: 386, 404, 9: 291, 292n, 11: 376, 377n, 378, 379n

Hooker, William Jackson, 12: 5

Hop-hornbeam, 8: 416, 418n

Hordeum jubatum, 4: 333n. See also Barley, foxtail

Hornbeam, American, 2: 277n, 8: 359, 359n, 416, 418n

Horned Weasel (Maw-pah'-pir-re-cos-satoo), 3: 212, 213n, 214n, 241

Hornet, baldfaced, 4: 45–46, 47n

Hornets, 7: 309, 311, 312n

Horns, powder (powder flasks), 4: 341, 343, 5: 53, 147n, 6: 138, 206, 208, 8: 80, 311, 359, 9: 177, 197, 248, 10: 122, 268, 11: 165–66, 215–16, 257–58, 352–53, 381. See also Arms and ammunition; Gunpowder

Horns, tin (trumpets), 2: 72, 72n, 105, 5: 53, 9: 83, 107, 115–16, 197, 10: 55, 11: 257–58

Hornworm, tobacco, 8: 264, 266n

Horse Coulee, 8: 117n

Horse Creek (N. Dak.), 8: 275n, 406

Horse Creek (Table River) (Mont.), 8: 242–44, 245n, 390, 407

Horse (Graveley) Creek
(Nebr.), **3**: 351–52, 384n
Horse Heaven Hills, **5**: 276–77,
284n, 286, 288, 290n, **7**:
182, 184, 186n
Horse Island, **2**: 117, 117n
Horse Prairie, **9**: 334n
Horse Prairie Creek (West Fork
Jefferson River), **1**: 10, **5**: 64–
65, 67n, 102n, 108n, 163n,
170n, **6**: 465, 118, **8**: 172,
173n, **9**: 203, 204n, 209–10,
210n, 211n, 334n, **10**: 126–
27, 127n, 128n, **11**: 272,
275n, 283, 284n
Horses: as trade item, **1**: 8, **2**: 7,
106, **3**: 199, 277, 296, 309, **5**:
106, 109, 113, 117–18, 129–
31, 137, 144, 148, 158, 162–
63, 328, **6**: 421, 423, **7**: 2, 54,
56, 123–28, 131–34, 136,
139–45, 152–53, 155, 157,
166, 168, 177, 179, 183, 185,
187, 189, 209–10, 212–13,
215, 217, 275–76, 346–349,
8: 14, 17, 23, 35–36, 132,
285, 363, 389, **9**: 100, 208,
219, 292–93, 309, 319, **11**:
276–77, 337; Indian, **2**: 16,
306, 343–44, 348, 366–67,
489, 493, **3**: 30, 100–102,
109n, 114n, 125, 135, 191,
196–97, 204, 228, 231–32,
235, 238, 244–46, 250n,
254–55, 261–62, 276, 292,
298n, 322, 356, 369, 395–
438 passim, 484, 489, **4**: 23,
55, 211, 221n, 386, 437, **5**:
2–4, 68–70, 79, 83, 85n, 87–
89, 91–92, 96–97, 103, 111–
12, 120–21, 123, 129–31,
135, 139–40, 142–42, 146,
148–49, 151, 155, 159–62,
171–73, 188, 196–98, 225n,
229–30, 232, 234, 239, 242,
256, 259, 268, 290, 300, 306,
323, 329, 338, 343, 347, 377,
6: 3, 312–16, 317n, 336,
338, 405–6, 455, **7**: 3, 49,
52, 119–21, 127, 129, 132,
137, 146–48, 152–54, 160–
61, 163, 165–68, 169n, 170–
71, 176, 188, 190, 219n, 222,

224, 231, 233, 252, 254,
260n, 261, 263–65, 272,
278–79, 280, 307, 308n, 326,
328–29, **8**: 44, 46–47, 53–
55, 79–80, 93, 96n, 128–29,
132n, 135, 168n, 214, 218–
19, 222n, 293, 295, 312,
315–17, 319, **9**: 41, 50, 99,
108, 142, 204–5, 209, 214,
218–19, 229–30, 238, 240–
41, 243, 245, 292–94, 297,
300, 305–6, 314, 320, 342,
355, 369n, 385, 390, **10**: 55,
64, 69, 126–29, 131, 140,
149, 158, 167, 200, 210–
211, 215–16, 218, 224–25,
224n, 231–32, 235–37, 239,
259, **11**: 66–67, 107–9, 116,
133, 273–78, 280–84, 287,
290–92, 299–303, 308–9,
331, 333–34, 344–45, 351,
356–60, 365–66, 370; problems, **2**: 23, 275, 428–29,
3: 65, **5**: 144, 152–53, 155,
178–79, 183, 185–86, 190,
201, 204, 206–7, 211, 215–
16, 229, **7**: 2, 50, 52, 143,
164, 178–80, 190, 205–7,
228, 230, 232, 235–37, 261,
277, 307, 309, 311, 322, 324,
326–28, 331–32, **8**: 31, 33,
43–44, 82, 85, 104, 118,
122–23, 162, 164, 179, 187,
189, 200, 218–19, 284, **9**:
215–17, 224, 226, 309, 319–
20, 324, 387, **10**: xii, 38, 131,
135, 142, 144, 213, 217, 223,
227, 229, 234, 241–45, 249,
257, **11**: 21–22, 39, 293–98,
316–17, 319, 321–24, 323n;
hired, **2**: 68, 73, **3**: 227, **4**: 4,
299, 398, **5**: 166; use, **2**: 70,
3: 254–56, 285–86, 290–91,
295, 410, **5**: 133, 233, 244,
7: 142, 152, 154, 166, 220,
267–68, **8**: 7, 10, 24, 39, 41,
56, 58, 77, 126–27, 130,
136, 138, 161, 166, 173–74,
176n, 190, 194, 204–5, 212,
292, 412, **9**: 32, 109–10,
112, 114, 116, 209–10, 212,
214, 216, 233, 295, 312, 334,
339, 341, **10**: 65, 70–73,

132, 136, 216, 234, 254, 256,
11: 49, 73, 81, 120–21, 123,
125, 272, 277–79, 282–84,
286–88, 292, 296, 303, 312,
316–18, 324, 327, 330–31,
336, 338, 341–42, 365–66;
sought, **2**: 73, 184, 205, 431–
34, **3**: 1, 13–14, 16, 19–20,
5: 73, 173, 202–3, 211, 218,
232, **7**: 3, 54, 255, 257, 262,
289–90, 293, **9**: 33, 45–46,
54, 110, 223, 225, 228–30,
294, 296, 321–22, 331–32,
334, 342, 391, **10**: 24, 28, 36,
133, 140–43, 215, 218, 220–
21, 224, 227, 238, 241, 244,
252–53, 256, **11**: 63–64,
302–3, 310–14, 319–21,
323–27, 329–34; food, **2**:
102, **3**: 457, 459, **5**: 8, 104,
171, 178–79, 203, 205, 209,
214, 218, 225, **6**: 211, **7**: 158,
166, 168, 195, 221, 223,
248–49, 252, 254, 256, 302,
335–37, **8**: 10, 24, 26–29,
31–36, 38, 40, 42, 44–45,
48, 50, 53–54, 59–61, 65,
69, 115, 122, 125, 128, 136,
161–64, 170, 172, 175, 179,
184, 186, 190, 195, 201–2,
205, 284, **9**: 221, 318, 321,
324, 327–28, **11**: 293, 305–
6, 312–13, 318, 321–22, 326;
found, **2**: 306, 343–44, 351,
435–36, **5**: 191, 202, 216,
230, 235, **7**: 156, 162–64,
235–37, 243–44, 248–50,
252, 254, 264–65, 313, 315,
8: 21–22, 64, 111, 174, **9**: 20,
24, 33, 220–21, 230, 304,
309, 321, 327, 381, 385, **10**:
15, 18, 20, 25, 139–43, 145–
46, 213, 218, 220, 224–25,
227, 230, 237, 242, 252, 254,
259, **11**: 34–35, 38–39, 50,
306, 315–16, 323, 326, 335;
lost, **2**: 431–32, **5**: 173, 190,
199, 202, 211, 218, 230, **8**:
10, 37, 41, 43, 63, 107, **11**:
48, 304, 313, 320–21; stolen,
3: 107–8, 133, 135, 260,
295–97, 305–7, 329, **5**: 159,
7: 153, 155, **8**: 2–3, 109–10,

Horses (*continued*)
113, 132, 134, 156, 169, 209–11, 213–14, 215n, 291, 294, 301, 304, **9**: 35, 65, 114–15, 294, 338, 348–49, **10**: 73–74, 140, 222, 253, 259, 265–66, **11**: 66–67, 83–84, 108–9, 125, 308–9, 326–27; returned, **3**: 108, 279; observed, **4**: 423–25, 430, **5**: 190, **6**: 450, **9**: 139, 190; signs, **4**: 427–28, **5**: 45, 64, 71, 78, **8**: 82–83, 109, 165, 210–11, **9**: 54, 190, **11**: 241–43; as food, **3**: 66, **5**: 3–4, 163, 204–7, 209–11, 216, 218, 226–27, 230, 238–40, 242, 243n, 244–45, 277–78, **6**: 166, 452–53, **7**: 54, 56, 90, 92, 115, 215, 217–18, 221–24, 226–27, 230, 237–40, 275–77, 279, 290, 293, 322n, **8**: 28–29, 30n, 69, 413, **9**: 223, 225, 227, 233, 305–6, 310–11, 323n, **10**: 129, 142–43, 145, 150, 222, 225, 231, 233, **11**: 319, 323–24, 337; needed, **5**: 59, 70, 115; loaded, **5**: 164, 166, 190, **8**: 83, 88, 98, 135, 137; rested, **5**: 192, 206, 209; strayed, **5**: 210, 225, 228–29, 232, 235, **7**: 151–52, 154–55, 161, 173–74, 181, 187–88, 199–200, 212, 216, 218, 233, 264–65, 267, 277, 279, 308, 310, **9**: 58, 223, 225–26, 229, 296, 303, 324–25, 339, 391, **10**: 24, 139–43, 215, 220, 241, 252, **11**: 310, 312, 319–25, 327, 329, 331–32; hobbled, picketed, and spanceled, **5**: 226, 228, **7**: 143, 146, 153, 155, 158–60, 162–64, **8**: 24, 170, **9**: 294, 295n, 303, 321, 333, **10**: 237, 237n; branded, **5**: 246, **10**: 151, **11**: 338; English, **6**: 313, 315; as gift, **7**: 186, 230, 232, 237–39, 242–44, 247, 249–50, 256, 258, 285, 301, 339, 342, 344–45, **8**: 47, 48n, 75,

78, **10**: 236–37; castrated, **7**: 257–59, 261, 263, 272–73, 281–82, 328, 330, **8**: 23; accidents, **8**: 3, 25–26, 35–36, 65–66, 80, 110, 120, 163, 200, 202, **9**: 31, **10**: 24; hair, **8**: 41, 43n, 318; searched for, **8**: 14, 17, 25, 34–35, 38, 51–52, 62, 107, 111, 169–70, 189, 210–11; wild, **8**: 90, 101; unloaded, **8**: 106; purchased, **8**: 305, **9**: 206, 209–10, 212–14, 219–20, 294, 296, 309, **10**: 127, 133, 135, 138, 212–18, 239, **11**: 273, 275–77, 280–83, 286–92, 301–3; scarcity, **10**: 200; shoed, **11**: 125; mentioned, **2**: 24, 30, 72, 108, 139, 166, 172, 212, 212n, 214, 254, 270, 308, 317, 339, 347, 350, 355, 377, 421, 441, 494, 497, 499, 499n, 501–3, 524, **3**: 82, 92–93, 137n, 281, 288, 294, **5**: 164n, 170, 188n, 213, 222, 312, **6**: 404, **7**: 88, 126, 145n, 197, 266, 299, 303, 305, **8**: 57, 68, 74, 99, 115, 216–17, 221, **9**: xii, 20, 21, 26, 28, 30, 32, 42, 55, 60–62, 64, 102–3, 110, 112, 114, 207–8, 214, 221, 295, 298, 300, 304, 307–8, 310, 315, 315n, 317–18, 323, 328–30, 333–34, 375, 377, 385, **10**: 9, 11, 21, 24n, 25n, 41, 43, 131n, 134–35, 145n, 212n, 214n, 224n, 228, 228n, 239–41, 247, 249, 257–58, 279, **11**: xii, 11, 45–46, 59–60, 60n, 71–72, 75, 78, 80, 290–91, 294. *See also* Appaloosas; Bridles; Halters; Saddles
Horseshoe Bend Creek, **5**: 74, 76n, **9**: 211, 211n, **11**: 284–85, 286n
Horseshoe Creek, **8**: 58n
Horseshoe Hills, **8**: 180n
Horseshoe Point, **8**: 145n, **9**: 344n, **10**: 261n
Horsesteak Meadow, **8**: 30n, **9**: 323, 323n

Horsetail, field, **2**: 308, 309n, **3**: 459, 464, 468, **4**: 381n, **7**: 191n
Horsetail, giant, **6**: 224, 225n, 230–31, 232n, **7**: 44, 47n, 55, 61n, 77, **9**: 287, 287n. *See also* Rushes
Horsetail Creek, **7**: 100n
Horsetail Falls, **7**: 100n
Hosiery, **6**: 137, 138n. *See also* Clothing
Hospitality (Wethaa), **2**: 439, 441, 443n
Hot Island, **2**: 114, 116n
Hot Springs Island, **3**: 64n, **8**: 331, 332n, **9**: 356n, **10**: 274n
Hounds. *See* Wagons
Howard, J., **9**: 3n
Howard, Thomas P.: listed, **2**: 148, 187–88, 194, 197, 199, **4**: 9, 11, **6**: 83, **8**: 139n, 162n, 180n, **9**: 279, **11**: 4n, 7n; sent out, **2**: 166, **8**: 179, **9**: 285, 335, **10**: 205; in permanent party, **2**: 229n; duties, **2**: 256, 259n, 521; biographical sketch, **2**: 518; hunting, **3**: 40, 42, **7**: 71, 74, **9**: 52, 286, 341, **10**: 34, 34n; court-martialed, **3**: 290, 290n, **9**: 113–14, 114n; medical problems, **3**: 297, **7**: 261, 263, 265; creek named for, **4**: 430, 433n, 450, 465, **10**: 118n; and saltmaking camp, **6**: 230–31, 237, **9**: 268, **10**: 189, **11**: 414, 414n; returns, **6**: 242–43, **9**: 269, **10**: 190, 255, **11**: 416, 416n; scouting, **7**: 54, 57, 60n, **11**: 438; accidents, **8**: 178; mentioned, **2**: 139n, 200n, **9**: 268n, 269n, 285n, 286n, 336n, **10**: 189n, 190n, 206n, 255n, **11**: 440n
Howard Creek, **8**: 56, 58, 58n
Howell Island, **2**: 246n
Howels, **4**: 275, 279
Huckleberries, **6**: 276–77, 373, **7**: 112–13, **8**: 72
Huckleberry, evergreen, **6**: 237–39, 239n, 297, 298n, **7**: 45, 47n, 55, 60n, 77, 114n

Huckleberry, mountain, **5**: 224n, **6**: 285–86, 286n, 444, 444n, **8**: 28–29, 30n
Hudon, **9**: 3n
Hudson's Bay, **3**: 17, 27, 297n, **6**: 481, **8**: 412, **10**: 4n, 6n, 67n
Hudson's Bay Company: traders, **1**: 8, **2**: 168n, 525, 529, **3**; 3, 199, 201n, 231, 238, 242n, 251, 251–52n, 254, 258, **9**: 100n; posts, **2**: 225–26n, 226n, **3**: 198n, **9**: 100; headquarters, **2**: 226n; relations with the party, **3**: 3, 199, 231, 238, 254, 258, 272, 303, 307, 312, 312n, 487, **9**: 100, **10**: 64n, 66n; and Indians, **3**: 120n, 402–4, 429–32, **4**: 40n, **7**: 215n, **8**: 132n; employees, **4**: 269n, **10**: 6n; blankets, **5**: 131n; mentioned, **10**: 7n, 67n. *See also* North West Company; Traders; Trading establishments
Hughes, Thomas, **9**: 3n
Hughes Point, **5**: 187n
Hull Creek, **5**: 182, 183n, **10**: 135n, **11**: 296n
Hul-loo-et-tell (and similar spellings) Indians. *See* Cowlitz Indians; Watlala Indians
Hummingbird, black-chinned, **7**: 47n
Hummingbird, broad-tailed, **8**: 27n
Hummingbird, calliope, **7**: 47n
Hummingbird, rufous, **7**: 47n
Hummingbirds, **7**: 45, 75–76, **8**: 25
Hump (Weasel) Creek, **8**: 197, 197n, 198n, 391, 408
Humus, **5**: 21n, 35n, 52n, 223n
Hungery Creek: name, **5**: 213, 214–15n; arrive at, **5**: 213, 215, 239, **8**: 27, 51, **9**: 327, 327n, **10**: 144, 145n, 240–41, 240n, 241n, **11**: 322–23, 323n; camped on, **5**: 213, **9**: 323–24, 323n, 324n, **10**: 244, 244n; distances, **5**: 239, **6**: 453; listed, **6**: 467, **8**: 383–84, 402; described, **8**: 28–30;

conditions, **8**: 31, 66–67, 383; accidents on, **8**: 36, 42; hunting on, **8**: 38, 48, 50; and Indians, **8**: 48, 51; mentioned, **5**: 217n, 223n, **8**: 30n, 32, 34–35, 34n, 39, 52–53, 52n, 411n, **9**: 226n
Hunkpapa (Pocasse) Creek, **3**: 168–69, 171n
Hunkpapa Sioux Indians. *See* Sioux Indians, Hunkpapa
Hunt, Thomas, **8**: 370, 370n
Hunt, Wilson Price, **1**: 19n. 139, **2**: 525, **8**: 316n, 368n
Hunters Island, **11**: 30, 30n
Huntley Creek, **8**: 203n
Hurricane (Deer, Deer Lick) Creek, **9**: 12, 12n, 379, **10**: 13, 13n
Hyacinth, wild, **7**: 132, 135n, 190n, 193
Hyacinths, **8**: 15, 18
Hyalite Creek, **8**: 181, 185, 188n
Hydrangea arborescens, **8**: 12–13n. *See also* Sevenbark
Hydrastis canadensis, **3**: 467. *See also* Golden seal
Hydrogen sulfide, **8**: 171n
Hyla regilla, **7**: 32n. *See also* Frog, Pacific tree
Hyssop, **4**: 35, 40n. *See also* Sagebrush, big
Hyssop, giant-, nettle-leaved, **7**: 283, 285n, 286, 335, 337
Hyssopus officinalis, **4**: 40n. *See also* Hyssop

I

Ibex. *See* Sheep, bighorn
Ice. *See* Weather conditions
Ice, glacial, **4**: 29n, 63n, 76n, 129n, 233n, 257n
Ice House Lake site, **7**: 114n
Ictalurus furcatus, **2**: 72n, **3**: 40n, **9**: 18n, **10**: 280n. *See also* Catfish, blue; Catfish, channel
Ictalurus melas, **2**: 433n. *See also* Bullhead, black

Ictalurus punctatus, **2**: 72n, **3**: 40n, **4**: 182n, **9**: 18n, **10**: 29n, **11**: 42n. *See also* Catfish, channel
Icterus sp., **3**: 86n. *See also* Oriole
Ictiobus bubalus, **2**: 432n. *See also* Buffalo fish, smallmouth
Ictiobus cyprinellus, **2**: 432n. *See also* Buffalo fish, bigmouth
Ictiobus niger, **2**: 432n. *See also* Buffalo fish, black
Idaho, camps in: Lemhi County, **5**: 76n, 86n, 125n, 132n, 141n, 147n, 157n, 164n, 178n, 179n, 183n, 185n, 186–87n; Idaho County, **5**: 203n, 205n, 207n, 210n, 211n, 214–15n, 217n, 223n, **7**: 259n, **8**: 26n, 30n, 34n, 37n, 50n, 52n, 55n, 58n, 61n; Clearwater County, **5**: 224n, 227n, 228n, 231n, 232n, 233n, 234n, **7**: 233n, 237n, **8**: 12n, 21n, 45n, 58n; Nez Perce County, **5**: 250n, 252n, **7**: 214n, 219–20n, 224–25n; Lewis County, **7**: 241n, 255n. *See also* Camp Chopunnish
Ignimbrite, **5**: 147n
Ile aux Cedres. *See* Cedar Island (S. Dak.)
Ilex montana, **6**: 302n. *See also* Holly, mountain
Illinois, **9**: 348, **11**: 5n
Illinois, camps in: Massac County, **2**: 85n; Alexander County, **2**: 86n, 94n, 97n, 101n, 104n; Union County, **2**: 111n; Randolph County, **2**: 119n; Monroe County, **2**: 126n; Saint Clair County, **2**: 128n, 129n; Madison County, **2**: 130n, 132n
Illinois Indians, **2**: 128n, **3**: 407, 446, 449
Illinois River, **2**: 245, **3**: 338, 407
Illnesses. *See* Medical problems
An Illustration of the Sexual System of Linnaeus (Miller), **2**: 79n, **12**: 8n

An Illustration of the Termini Botanici of Linnaeus (Miller), **2**: 79n, **12**: 8n
Image Canoe Island. *See* Hayden Island; Tomahawk Island
Immell, Michael, **8**: 198n
Impostumes. *See* Medical problems, abscesses
Independence Creek, **2**: 346–48, 349n, 487, **3**: 94, 345, 371, 375, 378, **8**: 378, 396, 416, **9**: 20, 20n, 368n, 385, **10**: 18, 18n, **11**: 34–35, 35n
Index specula, **2**: 412, 414n
Indiana Territory, **1**: 6, **8**: 371n
Indian (Berry) Creek (Idaho), **5**: 152, 155, 157n, 162, 164n, 168, 170
Indian (Turf) Creek (Mont.), **5**: 55–57, 58n
Indian Grave Peak, **5**: 211n, **6**: 467, **8**: 58n, **9**: 225n, **10**: 143n, **11**: 320n
Indian Knob Creek. *See* Pigeon (Indian Knob) Creek
Indian Office map. *See* Maps
Indian Post Office, **5**: 210n, 188n, **9**: 225n, **10**: 143n, **11**: 319n
Indians: trade, **1**: 3, **2**: 5–6, 28, 94, 252, 404n, 439–42, 510, 514, 516, 519, 566, **3**: 27, 32, 163, 201n, 235, 238, 251, 308, 311n, 312n, 308, 331n, 365, 387, 389–444 passim, 479, 486, **4**: 38, 40n, 306, **5**: 94n, 95n, 114, 135, 140, 197, 284n, 294, 296, 312–13n, 315, 357, 359, 363, 367, 369, 371–73, **6**: 30–31, 35–36, 66, 73, 88, 90, 106, 126–27, 133–34, 144, 164–65, 175, 187, 201–6, 215, 221, 229, 234, 237–38, 302, 305, 314, 316, 427, 431, **7**: 11, 19–20, 27–28, 36, 50, 53, 76–77, 127, 134, 139, 245n, 251n, **8**: 213, 388–89, **9**: 248, **10**: 159, 165; and maps, **1**: 4, 10–11, 18nn. 107, 109; information from, **1**: 6, 10–11, 13, **2**: 328n, **3**: 3–4, 25n, 136n, 333, 335, 348, 358,
362, 364, 367, 369, 426, 476, 492n, **4**: 42, 48, 63n, 71, 73, 75n, 129n, 170, 258, 267, 269n, 270, 295, 354, **5**: 66, 318, **6**: 67, 85, 154–55, 160n, 204–5, 211, 213, 290–91, 305, 308, 340, 382–83, 404, 406, 413, 415, 459, 461, 473, **7**: 13, 14, 18, 20, 26, 39, 41, 48, 51, 55, 82, 92–93, 184, 256, **8**: 2, 58n, 277, 394; villages, **1**: 8, **3**: 136n, 184n, **5**: 252n, 276n, 300n, 356–60, 357n, 362, 364n, **6**: 26, 30–31, 35, 48, 50, 53–55, 57, 59, 87–88, 113, 460, **7**: 15–16, 17n, 22, 24, 123, 125n, **11**: 62, 62n, 124, 125n, 126n, 376, 433n, 438–39; relations with the party, **2**: 7, 181, 206, 245–46, 477–78, 488–90, 492–93, 513, **5**: 69, 320, 375, **6**: 4, 31, 48–49, 53, 58, 60, 72, 79, 81, 84–85, 90–91, 134, 153, 156–57, 181, 189, 234, 314, 316, 331–32, 421, 425, 428n, 444, 444n, **7**: 1, 2, 33, 35, 50, 53, 55, 57, 62, 79, 82, 87, 94, 96, 99–100, 132, 142, 146, 152–54, 156, 159, 163, 170–71, 202, 204, 238, 240, **8**: 2, 69, 215, **10**: 165, 170, 223, **11**: 11, 361, 388, 394, 394n; clothes, **2**: 25, **3**: 24, 27–28, 32, 34, 107–8, 115, 117, 156, 160–62, 164, 196, 210, 215, 217–18, 222, 246, 253, 260, 270–71, 297, 310–11, 318, 330–31, 436, 486–88, **4**: 216, 219, **5**: 319n, 341–42, 346–47, 367, 371, 373, **6**: 15–17, 30, 74, 78n, 85, 88, 97, 144, 144n, 186, 221, 246, 262n, 334, 336, 338, 347, 405–6, 409n, **7**: 27, 54, 62, 123–25, 138–39, **8**: 232, **9**: 157, 267n, 369n, **11**: 380; councils, **2**: 31, 438–42, 488–93, **5**: 112; gifts, **2**: 71, 181, 206, 215, 438–39, 441, 443n, 455–56, 477, 490, 492–93, **3**: 21, 23–
24, 26, 107–8, 112, 162–63, 166, 208–10, 235, 240, 242, 261–62, 268, 290, 310–11, 318, 493–505, **4**: 29, 152, 154, 156, 306, 334–35, **5**: 2, 53–54, 115, 166, 178, 188, 244, 339, **6**: 421, 423, 426, 428–29, 441–42; encountered, **2**: 133–34, **5**: 2–3, **6**: 22, 36, 106, 176, 178, **10**: 11; war, **2**: 141, 180, 185, 235, 273, 278–79, 295–96, 302–3, 306, 327, 348, 350, 362–63, 419, 479, 487–89, 491, 507, **5**: 122, 160, 188n, 318, 320, 325, 328–29, **8**: 131; artifacts, **2**: 154, **5**: 348n, 361, 367, 369, 371, **6**: 77n, 97, 211–14, 296n, 305, **8**: 196, **9**: 157, **10**: 142n, **11**: 176, 82n; food, **2**: 222–23, **3**: 272, 273n, 321, 322n, 326, **4**: 126, 128, 146, 391, 403, **5**: 4, 76n, 91, 147n, 149, 201, 224n, 239, 317, 349, 351, 373, **6**: 74, 104, 136, 162–63, 226–29, 233, 236, 238–39, 245–46, 251, 253, 285–87, 297, 303, 305, 342, 370, 378, 388, 410, 412, 420–21, **7**: 3, 44, 49, 52, 77, 132, 188–89, 190n, 205, 207, 234, 300, **8**: 14, 16–18, 20–21, 32, 174, 282, 288; customs, **2**: 246, 248, 370, 504–5, **3**: 28, 34, 116, 118–19, 121–22, 167n, 168–69, 180, 189–90, 190n, 198–99, 201n, 208–9, 211, 216, 233, 239, 240n, 259–60, 261n, 268–69n, 272n, 285, 330, 355, 482–83, 485–86, 488–89, 492n, **4**: 54–56, 93, 100–102, 105, 211, 213, 214n, 320, 378, 379n, **5**: 83, 159, 164n, 201, 237, 263, 264n, 268–69, 269n, 272n, 281–82, 309, 311–12, 320, 325, 347, 349, 353n, 358–62, 367, 371, 375, 380, **6**: 73–74, 97–98, 99n, 119, 136, 137n, 168–69, 172n, 176, 182, 185n, 186–87, 190–91,

193, 365–67, 368n, 425–28, 436, 440n, 460, **7**: 10–11, 41n, 61n, 145n, 190n, 235, 241n, 249, 291, 294, **8**: 55n, 225, 291, 394, 414, **9**: 37, 43–44, 141, 213n, 241, 289, 292, 369n, **10**: 85, 199, **11**: 142–43, 310–11, 360–61, 433; hunting, **2**: 261, 416, **3**: 176–77, 254, 484–85, **4**: 31, 45, 85, 113–14, 216–17, 221n, **5**: 129, 275, 307n, 320, 325, 340, 362, **6**: 105, 336, 338, 344, 347, **10**: 95; signs, **2**: 272, **3**: 99, 104, **4**: 48–49, 126, 128, 379, 414, 421, 424, 428, 432, 436, 438, **5**: 2, 37–38, 42–43, 45, 73, 78, 153, 155, 157; pictographs, **2**: 283–84, 369–70; peace, **2**: 497–98, 499n, **3**: 218, 485, **5**: 160, 268; sign language, **2**: 516, **6**: 46, 118, **8**: 130, 132n, **10**: 149; relations among, **3**: 16–17, 161, 191, 217, 219, 224, 233, 236, 238, 243–46, 262, 267, 275, 304–5, 317, 332, 332n, 423, 428, 483, 485, **5**: 231, 312–13n, 317, **8**: 214; languages, **3**: 56n, 136, 144n, 184n, 319, 328n, 383n, 490, **4**: 188, 204, 214n, 439n, **6**: 30, 91, 164–65, 316, 430–31, **7**: 27, 30, 54; camps, **3**: 100, **4**: 38, 49, 53–54, 58, 127, 159, 161, 211, 213, 216–17, 219, 222, 224, 287, 387, 394, 403, 405, **5**: 206, 238, **6**: 58, 115n; lodges, **3**: 139, 147n, 163, 489, **4**: 38, 88, 108–10, 202, 206, 211, 213, 216, 222, 239, 241, 256, 258, 263, 284, 378, 386–88, 394, **5**: 32, 92, 98, 121, 199, 224n, 266, 268, 269n, 271–72, 275, 282–83, 314–15, 317, 320–21, 323, 333, 356–61, 367, 369, 371, 374, 376, **6**: 15, 17, 48, 50, 57, 66, 72, 93, 133, 184, 188, 191, 218–19, 221, 221n, 243–44, **7**: 27, 60, 83, 93, 151n, 203–4, **8**: 90, 92–94,

98, 102, 109, 125, 127–28, 130, 133n, 141, 144, 216, 253, **9**: 155–57, **11**: 51, 159–60, 167, 169–70, 175, 181, 360–61; medical problems, **3**: 167n, 260, **5**: 367, 373, **6**: 74, 77n, 239–41, 286–87n, **7**: 70n, 86, 95, 139, 181n, 186, 212–13, 215, 217; tools and utensils, **4**: 194, 198, **6**: 97, 215–17, 231–32, 234, 243–44; danger from, **4**: 309, **5**: 337, 339, **8**: 108; roads, **4**: 387, 399, 401, 403, 405, 405–6n, 407, 409, 420–21, 423, 425, 431–32, **5**: 55, 63–64, 68, 73, 75–78, 99, 107, 140, 145, 148n, 152, 154, 156–57, 162, 167–68, 192, 355–56, 360–62, **6**: 169, 171, 178, **7**: 195–97; appearance, **5**: 122, 367, 369, 373, **6**: 74, 144, 168, 190, 433, 437, **7**: 54, 96, **11**: 65n; fishing, **5**: 152–53, 240, 284n, 315, 317, 321, 375, **6**: 105, 204, 211–14, 407, 409n 410–11, **7**: 34, 95, 104n; head deformation, **5**: 187–88n, 291n, 345, 345–46n, 369, 373, **6**: 3, 15, 159n, 253n, 368n, 433, 437, 440n, 476, **7**: 166–67, **10**: 162–63, 163n; visits, **5**: 341, **6**: 43, 81, 86, 124, 133–34, 145, **7**: 16–17, 71, 74–76, 88, **9**: 293, **10**: 8; numbers, **6**: 481, **8**: 23; and horses, **7**: 143, 188, 190, **8**: 168n, 218–19, 222n; forts, **8**: 194–96, 197–98n, 200, 202–4, 203–4n, 206, 207n, 208n, 220; mentioned, **1**: 3, **2**: 3, 8, 16, 26, 36, 161, 233, 242, 288n, 290n, 294n, 301, 301n, 343, 343n, 347, 352n, 403, 442n, 454n, 452–53, 507n, 525, **3**: 24, 26n, 166n, 196n, 223n, 229, 338, 353, 368, **4**: 1–2, 18n, 22, 36, 85, 129n, 141, 276, 287, 386–87, 416, 439n, **5**: 90, 103, 177, 264, 275n, **6**: 86n, 267, 272, 302n, 329, 436, 492n,

7: 3, 19, 21, 28, 35, 144, 162n, **8**: 62, 123, 155, 362, **9**: 7, 17, 56, 58, 75, 286, 388, 391368n, **10**: xiii, 1, **11**: xiii, 5n, 29, 51n, 87n, 393n, 394n, **12**: 3. *See also* Estimate of Eastern Indians; Estimate of Western Indians; *specific Indian tribes*

Indigestion. *See* Medical problems, bowels

Indigo, **3**: 454, **8**: 193n

Indigo, false, **3**: 451–52, 462, 466, **8**: 193n

Indigo, wild, **8**: 190, 264

Indigo, wild false, **8**: 193n

Indigoifera sp., **8**: 193n. *See also* Indigo

Infectious conjunctivitis. *See* Medical problems

Influenza. *See* Medical problems

Injuries. *See specific members of the party*

Ink, **4**: 222, **5**: 133, **6**: 173n, **7**: 80, **8**: 352, **9**: 207, **11**: 279. *See also* Pens, ink

Insects, **3**: 10, 330, 466, **4**: 276, **5**: 35, **6**: 94, 96, 132, 145, 147, 259–60, 358, 363–67, **7**: 43–44, 46, 76, 83, 293, 296, 298, 304, **10**: xii. *See also specific species*

Instruments, scientific, **1**: 4, **2**: 92n, 122n, 410–13, 414n, **4**: 29, 152, 154, 156, 323, 365, 393, **8**: 31–33, 120–21, 129, **9**: 83, **11**: 138, 185, 340–41, 350–51. *See also* Chain, two pole; Chronometer; Compasses; Quadrants; Reel, log line; Sextants; *specific scientific instruments*

Interpreters: listed, **2**: 149, 160, 163, 194–95; Sioux, **3**: 111–13; Arikara, **3**: 152, 174–80, 181n; Mandan, **3**: 195, 199–200, 203–4, 208, 217, 227, 233, 236, 239–42, 245, 255, 266–68, 277–78, 289; Hidatsa, **3**: 245, 255, 260, 262, 277–78, 289, 293, 310, French, **3**: 316, **6**: 158; mentioned, **2**: 163. *See also* Char-

Interpreters (*continued*)
bonneau; Cruzatte; Dorion;
Drouillard; Farfonge; Gravelines; Jusseaume; Labiche;
Old Toby; Sacagawea; Ta-
beau; Tetoharsky; Twisted
Hair
Ionia volcano, **1**: 7, 17n. 62,
2: 504–6, 506n, **3**: 73n
Iowa, camps in: Fremont
County, **2**: 397n; Mills
County, **2**: 413n, **8**: 354n;
Pottawattamie County, **2**:
413n, 425n, 428n, **8**: 354n;
Harrison County, **2**: 442n,
447n, 452n, 454n, 456n,
465n, **8**: 352n, 353n; Mon-
ona County, **2**: 462n, 467n,
471n, 475n, **8**: 351n; Wood-
bury County, **2**: 475n, 478n,
496n, **8**: 350n
Iowa (Aiaouez, Aieway, Ayauwa)
Indians: speech for, **2**: 191–
92; historical sketch, **2**: 192n,
3: 405–6; language, **2**: 192n,
437n, 438, 442n, **3**: 490; villages, **2**: 292, 422, 424–25,
425n, 495–96, 502n, **3**: 353,
371, 379, **8**: 379, 397; war, **2**:
306, 327, **3**: 340, 406, 409–
10, 439; graves, **2**: 372n;
located, **3**: 407, 483; listed,
3: 448; trade, **3**: 483; mentioned, **2**: 293n, 354n, **3**:
414–15
Irish, **3**: 201n, **10**: xiv
Iris missouriensis, **8**: 94n. *See also*
Flag, western blue
Iron articles, **3**: 262, 286, 288,
300, 436, **5**: 359, **6**: 207, 210,
436, 440, **7**: 28, 36, 146,
151n, 160, 343–44, **8**: 37,
10: 213. *See also* Branding
iron; Forge, iron
Iron Eyes (Sarnánone), **2**: 490,
493, 494n
Iron ore, **2**: 391–92, 394–96,
3: 473, **4**: 41n, 208, 210n,
233n, 300, 332, 333n, **9**: 27–
28, 388, **10**: 21, **11**: 41, 41n
Iron wood. *See* Hop-hornbeam
Iroquois Indians, **2**: 69n
Island a la Merde, **2**: 117, 117n

Island (Biscuit) Creek, **2**: 336,
338, 339n, **9**: 19, 19n, 384
Isle à Berger, **2**: 253–54, 259n
Ives Island, **7**: 98, 100, 101n
Ivy, poison, **5**: 85n, **8**: 12n
Ivy Station site, **7**: 9n
Ixodes pacificus, **7**: 78n, **10**: 185n.
See also Woodtick, Rocky
Mountain
Ixoreus naevius, **5**: 223n, **6**: 257n.
See also Thrush, varied

J

Jackass Bend, **2**: 317, 318n
Jackrabbit, white-tailed (hare):
discovered, **3**: 1, 73n; described, **3**: 70–73, **4**: 207, **6**:
359–62, 362n, **9**: 59, **10**: 79,
79n, **11**: 169–70; observed,
3: 83, 93–94, 107–8, **4**: 201,
5: 167, 170n, 174, **6**: 313,
315, 317n; hunted, **3**: 267,
4: 27, 29n, 207, **9**: 59, 59n,
109–10, 109n, 111n, 130,
10: 39, 39n, 69, 69n, 79,
79n, **11**: 74–75, 75n, 116–
17, 169–70; specimen, **3**:
330; as trade item, **3**: 402–37
passim; behavior, **4**: 70, 75n,
146; abundance, **10**: 69, 157;
mentioned, **3**: 74n, 482, **4**:
207n
Jacks Creek (Canister Run),
5: 250n, **7**: 225n, **10**: 151n,
11: 341n
Jackson, **6**: 155–56, 427
Jackson, Donald, **1**: 7, **2**: 3, 8,
19, 42, 543–44, **9**: xi, **10**: xi,
11: xi, xvi
Jackson Creek (Middle Branch
of East Fork of Gallatin's
River), **8**: 187n, 392, 409
Jackson Hole, **8**: 303n
Jackson Hot Spring, **8**: 170,
171n, 264, 393, 410, 415,
9: 333, 333n, **10**: 255, 255n
Jalap, **2**: 86n. *See also* Medicine
James (Jacque) River (S. Dak.):
arrive at, **3**: 1, 17, **8**: 344,

345n, **9**: 45, 45n, 357, 358n,
11: 63, 63n; observed, **3**: 7,
11; listed, **3**: 16–17, 379,
409, 413, **8**: 397, 411; and
Indians, **3**: 18n, 19–20, 22,
27, 32, 180, 412, **9**: 46, **10**:
31–32, 32n; described, **3**:
22–23, 356; latitude, **3**: 95;
distances, **3**: 372, 480, **8**: 379,
9: 367n; and species, **6**: 395,
397, **8**: 416; and traders, **8**:
351; mentioned, **3**: 23n, 41,
43, 146, 169, 171n, 176, 358,
361, 385–86n, 481, **4**: 324,
10: 275n
James River (Va.), **5**: 92
James's Bay, **10**: 43n
James site, **2**: 373n
Jarrett Creek, **8**: 409
Jarrot (Garroes), Nicholas, **1**: 5,
2: 127n, 191, 191n, 208
Jasper, **5**: 147n
Jay, blue, **3**: 85, **4**: 56, 57n, 407,
5: 27, 29n, 216, **6**: 132, 133n,
7: 298, 304
Jay, gray, **5**: 223n, **6**: 130–31,
131n, 162–63, 164n, 379–
80, 381n, **7**: 298, 302n, 304
Jay, pinyon, **5**: 27, 29n, 214n,
6: 131n
Jay, scrub, **5**: 214n
Jay, Steller's, **5**: 214n, 217,
223n, **6**: 94, 94n, 131–32,
131n, 133n, 162–63, 261,
379–80, 381n, **7**: 76, 78n
Jefferson, Thomas: and Lewis,
1: 3, 5, 12, **2**: 3–5, 75, 75n,
80n, 81, 122n, 242, 243n,
413n, 418n, 442n, **6**: 86n, **9**:
xi, **11**: xi, 5n; and western exploration, **1**: 3, **2**: 1–3, 6–7;
and maps, **1**: 6–7, 9, 12, 18n.
88, **2**: 415–16, **3**: 268n, **4**:
269n, 337n; and journals, **2**:
9–10, 12, 31–32, 35, 37–38,
40, 530–39, 541, **3**: 328,
333–34, **9**: xi, xvii–xviii,
10: xi, **11**: xi; and specimens,
2: 210n, 431n, 523, **3**: 54n,
67n, 79n, 257n, 329–31,
331n, 333–34, 472, **4**: 1, 7,
199n, **5**: 85n, 131n, **8**: 327n,
10: 75, **12**: 3–4; and Indians,

2: 294, 3: 26, 28, 156n, 160, 162, 164–66, 242, 246–47, 332, 4: 11, 8: 4, 215, 298, 300–302, 304, 306, 312, 315, 357, 358n, 9: 41, 48, 68, 10: 268n, 11: 280–81, 12: 1–3; dispatches, letters, and reports to, 3: 328n, 387, 4: 1, 7, 8: 369n, 371, 414n; river named for, 4: 437, 5: 7, 9: 191n, 10: 123, 123n; and Indian peace medals, 5: 112, 7: 238, 242, 245n, 9: 34n, 10: 50n, 11: 50, 51n; as naturalist, 12: 1–2; mentioned, 2: 8, 14–16, 18, 20–21, 36, 75n, 78, 79n, 80n, 94, 510, 512, 3: 2, 4, 205n, 210, 212, 214n, 4: 12n, 386n, 401n, 438n, 5: 198n, 6: 445, 7: 11n, 169n, 8: 213–14, 314, 319, 346, 348n, 355n, 363, 372n, 9: 184n, 186n, 10: 112n, 114n, 11: 7n

Jefferson Canyon, 5: 29–30n
Jefferson River (North, Southwest Fork): arrive at, 1: 10, 4: 4, 427–28, 5: 1, 9: 190, 191n, 10: 118, 11: 242–46, 244n, 247n, 249n, 250, 256n, 259, 259n, 261n, 263, 277; listed, 3: 382, 8: 393, 412; described, 4: 427–28, 431–32, 434–35 5: 8, 10n, 18, 21n, 27, 30–31, 35–36, 9: 191–92, 10: 118; affluents, 4: 433n, 5: 18, 9: 331, 333; name, 4: 437, 438n, 9: 191n, 200, 10: 123, 123n, 11: 246, 246n; conditions, 5: 2, 30–31, 36–37, 9: 192–94, 10: 121, 121n, 133; characteristics, 5: 7, 17n, 18, 29n, 30n, 39n, 57, 65, 84; navigational problems, 5: 34, 37, 39, 42–43, 45, 47; forks, 5: 43n, 52, 55, 64, 66, 138, 181, 195, 9: 196n; plants, 5: 57; and maps, 6: 307–11; distances, 6: 450, 473n, 493–94; and Indians, 6: 459, 8: 51; latitude, 6: 492, 8: 413; men-

tioned, 4: 429n, 5: 9, 10n, 20n, 35n, 43n, 54, 55n, 56, 61, 96, 202n, 6: 465, 7: 304, 334, 334n, 8: 1, 74, 77, 176n, 177n, 178n, 180n, 299n, 9: 334n, 335n, 10: 118n, 119n, 120n, 122n, 247, 255, 266

Jellyfish, 6: 423, 425n, 426
Jerky, 2: 277, 279, 279–81n, 294, 307, 307n, 319, 352, 360, 3: 8, 11, 13–14, 40, 42, 49–50, 55, 81, 86–87, 92, 4: 317, 377, 382, 5: 164n, 6: 186, 200, 203–4, 290, 293, 295, 302, 305, 365, 367, 7: 54, 56, 62, 67, 71, 74, 75–76, 79, 86–88, 90–92, 94–95, 275, 8: 23, 108, 152, 211, 9: 267, 271, 10: 16, 34, 41, 11: 60. *See also* Pemmican
Jersey Creek, 2: 328, 332n, 9: 18, 18n
Jim Ford (Village) Creek, 5: 224n, 231n, 239, 6: 453, 467, 8: 12n, 9: 228n, 10: 147n, 237n, 11: 326, 328, 328n
Joachim (Swacken) Creek, 2: 124–25, 125n
John Coulee, 8: 124n
John Day (Kekemarque) River (Clatsop County, Oreg.), 6: 91, 91n, 105, 7: 7–8, 9n, 162n, 9: 280n, 10: 201, 201n, 11: 433n
John Day (Lepage's) River (Sherman-Gilliam counties, Oreg.), 1: 10, 5: 312n, 315, 317–18, 319n, 320n, 376, 6: 91n, 455, 468, 480, 483, 487, 7: 162n, 182, 184, 8: 385, 404, 415, 10: 215n, 11: 363–64, 364n
Johnson Slough (Killamalk-ka Creek), 6: 125, 126n, 10: 181, 181n
Jonah, 6: 184, 193
Jones, Robert, 8: 198n
Jones Creek, 8: 251, 254, 256n
Journals, 2: 8–42, 459–67, 530–47. *See also* Astronomy Notebook; Clark; Codex

journals; Eastern Journal; Elkskin-bound Journal; Field Notes; First Draft; Floyd; Frazer; Gass; Lewis; Members of the party; Orderly Book; Ordway; Pryor; Voorhis; Voorhis journals; Weather Diary; Whitehouse; Willard
Juan de Fuca, Strait of, 7: 130n
Judith (South) Mountains, 4: 2, 189, 191, 192n, 198, 200n, 8: 115, 116n, 9: 154, 154n
Judith River, 4: 2, 215–17, 220n, 221n, 6: 449, 463, 8: 382, 401, 9: 157, 158n, 10: 95, 96n, 11: 177, 178n
Judith River Formation, 4: 129n, 179n, 200n, 207n, 210n, 8: 240n
Juglans cinerea, 2: 80n, 9: 9n, 10: 11n. *See also* Butternut
Juglans nigra, 2: 80n, 8: 350n, 9: 10n, 10: 11n. *See also* Walnut, black
Juneberry, 4: 57n, 392, 396n
Juniper. *See* Cedar, Rocky Mountain red
Juniper, common, 5: 28, 30n, 9: 193, 194n, 11: 250–51, 251n
Juniper, creeping, 3: 460, 464, 470–71, 4: 17, 19n, 27, 28n, 35, 53, 140, 143, 145n, 170, 176, 189, 191, 208, 8: 150, 151n, 270n, 9: 131n, 146, 154
Juniper, Rocky Mountain, 3: 465, 470, 5: 28, 30n, 107, 108n, 8: 195, 197n, 218, 270n
Juniperus communis, 3: 471, 5: 30n, 9: 194n, 11: 251n. *See also* Juniper, common
Juniperus horizontalis, 3: 470, 4: 19n, 8: 151n, 9: 131n. *See also* Juniper, creeping
Juniperus scopulorum, 3: 470, 4: 19n, 5: 30n, 8: 197n, 9: 131n, 10: 88n, 11: 251n. *See also* Juniper, Rocky Mountain
Juniperus virginiana, 2: 111n, 3: 48n, 9: 38n, 10: 30n. *See also* Cedar, eastern red
Juno, 6: 432n

Jusseaume, René: recruited, **1**: 8, **3**: 203–4, 226–27, 248–49, **9**: 94; interpreter, **3**: 203–4, 227, 230n, 231, 253, 486, **8**: 298, 306, **10**: 68, 68n, 268, 268n, 274n, **11**: 114n; biographical sketch, **3**: 205n; family, **3**: 241, 277, **9**: 95, 95n, 350–51, 351n, 356n; sent out, **3**: 249, 259; medical problems, **3**: 279–81, 284; information from, **3**: 291, 386n; and Indians, **3**: 300, **8**: 304–5; returns, **3**: 302; encountered, **9**: 91, 91n; and members of the party, **9**: 99, 99n; mentioned, **3**: 239, 241n, 318, **8**: 300n, 310, 331n, **9**: 94n

K

Kaiser Creek, **8**: 229, 231, 233, 234n
Kakawissassa. *See* Lighting Crow
Kakawita. *See* Raven Man
Kalama (Cath-la-haw's) River, **6**: 23, 25n, 57, 457, 470, **8**: 387, 405, **9**: 282n, **11**: 435, 435n
Kalapuya (Cal-lap-no-wah) Indians, **7**: 66, 70n, 86, 93, **9**: 285, 285–86n, **11**: 439, 440n
Kalapuyan language, **7**: 70n, **9**: 286n
Kale, **3**: 466
Kalispel (Coos-pel-lar) Indians, **5**: 189n, **6**: 481, 488, 491
Kalmia latifolia, **6**: 28n. *See also* Laurel, mountain
Ka-me-ah-wah. *See* Cameahwait
Kamiłpᵘ village, **5**: 319n
Kanasisi (Sho-to) Indians, **7**: 33, 35, 36n
Kane, Lucile M., **2**: 41
Kannuck Creek, **9**: 153n, **11**: 165n. *See also* CK Creek
Kansa (Kanza, Kaw) Indians: listed, **2**: 195, **3**: 448; hunting, **2**: 277, 279; historical sketch, **2**: 281n, 327, **3**: 392–93; language, **2**: 281n, 438,

442n, **3**: 27, 32, 34n, 490; villages, **2**: 327, 328n, 336, 341–42, 343n, 346, 348, 349n, 351, 354n, 406, 409, 479, 487, **3**: 94, 344–45, 371, 384n, 386n, **8**: 378, 396, 416–17, **9**: 19–20, 19n, 80–81, 362, 362n, 368n, 384–85, **11**: 31–32, 34, 35n, 172, 174; trade, **2**: 344; war, **2**: 348, 350, **3**: 393, 395, 406, 437–38, 445, 482, **6**: 405; appearance, **3**: 487; relations with the party, **8**: 360, 360n, **11**: 31–32; latitude, **9**: 80–81, **11**: 174; mentioned, **3**: 394, **8**: 362n, **10**: 279n, **11**: 25, 25n, 32n
Kansas, camps in: Wyandotte County, **2**: 324n, 335n; Atchison County, **2**: 345n; Doniphan County, **2**: 349n, 352n, 354n, 356n, 363n, **8**: 359n; Leavenworth County, **2**: 340n, **8**: 360n
Kansas (Decaugh, Kaw) River: arrive at, **2**: 60, 323–25, **8**: 361, 361n, **9**: 17, 17n, 363n, 384, **10**: 279, 279n, **11**: 31, 31n; and traders, **2**: 277, 279, **9**: 10, 10n, 378; described, **2**: 286, 327, 332, **3**: 343–44, **11**: 32; astronomical observation at, **2**: 317, 325–26; distances, **2**: 341–42, 406, 409, **3**: 343–44, 348, 370, 480, **8**: 378, **9**: 81, 368n; latitude, **2**: 406, 479, 487, **3**: 94, 375, **11**: 173; forts on, **3**: 41, 43, **9**: 80; listed, **3**: 378, 479, **8**: 396, 411, **11**: 171–72; and Indians, **3**: 396–98, 406, 437, 439; hunted on, **9**: 18; camped on, **9**: 383, **10**: 17, 17n; mentioned, **2**: 324n, 325n, 329, 333–34, 333n, 342, 343n, 348, 351, 354n, 362–63, 369–70, 372n, 401, 409, 429, 438, 439, 442n, **3**: 336, 339, 345–46, 350, 383n, 391–92, 457–59, 465, 481–83, **4**: 188, 204, 277n, **8**: 288

Karlson (Seal) Island, **6**: 395, 397, 397n, 471, **7**: 9–10, 11n, **8**: 405, **9**: 280, 281n, **11**: 433, 433n
Karok Indians, **6**: 432n
Kartesz, John T., **12**: 7
Kaskaskia, Ill., **2**: 18, 101, 112, 116, 118–19, 118n, 119n, 121, 125, 197, 221, 514, 518, 524, **9**: xiv, **11**: xiv, 5n
Kaskaskia Island, **2**: 119n
Kaskaskia River, **2**: 59, 117, 118n, 245
Kathlamet language, **6**: 34n, 41n. *See also* Cathlamet Indians
Katlaminimin (Clan-nar-min-na-mun) Indians, **6**: 477, 484, 490, **7**: 26, 29, 31n, 32, 34, **10**: 204n, **11**: 437, 437n
Katydid, **2**: 462, 463n
Keelboat: constructed, **2**: 6, 66n, 104n, 163, 164n; returns, **2**: 7, 14–16, 511, 533, **3**: 4, 227n, 304, 327, 333, **9**: 126, **11**: 132; navigational problems, **2**: 65, 67–68, 80, 83, 229, 231, 249–50, 275, 278, 289–90, 296, 300–301, 304–6, 306–7n, 313, 319, 328–29, 350–51, 377–78, 379n, 383, 459, **3**: 56, 98, 124, 128, 130, 133–34, 147, 179–80, 222, **9**: 14, **10**: 9, 13, 17, 39, **11**: 27–28, 33–34, 46, 73; masts, **2**: 66n, 73, 127, 163, 205, 275, 278–79, 281–82, 334, 340–42, 485–86, **3**: 48, 50, 111, 113, 141, 142n, 243, **9**: 9–10, 19, 40, 53–54, 99, 377–78, **10**: 12, 17, 28, 35, **11**: 33–34, 69; other, **2**: 101–2, 211, 235, 237–38, **3**: 9, 66, 74, 89–90, 106n, 151, 204, 250n, **9**: 359, 361–63; attention to, **2**: 139–40, 152–55, 177, 180–81, 211, 237, 315, 327, 420–21, 486, **3**: 86–87, 111–12, 115, 117, 154, 278–81, 284–85, 302–3, 307, **9**: 98–99, 111–12, 117–18, **10**: 71–72, 74, **11**: 123, 128; personnel,

2: 149, 160, 214, 215n, 227, 347, 3: 8, 11, 20, 80, 152, 160, 199–200; oars and poles, 2: 161, 213, 214, 257–58, 302, 304–7, 312–13, 340, 342, 415–16, 421, 3: 12, 7: 136, 151–52, 8: 289n, 288, 368n 2, 9: 29, 55, 361, 381, 11: 44, 81; sketches, 2: 162, 164n; provisions, 2: 165, 166n; loaded, 2: 212–13, 242, 9: 29, 125, 10: 75, 11: 31, 60, 131; sails, 2: 302, 307, 3: 128–29, 130n, 9: 73–74, 11: 1, 24–25, 40, 147–49, 167; windows, 2: 312–13; anchors and cables, 2: 377, 11: 88–89; unloaded, 3: 76, 78–79, 235, 4: 1, 7, 9, 11, 12n, 66n, 95n, 124; and Indians, 3: 113–14, 116, 119, 121–23, 156, 163, 177, 195, 207–8, 218, 9: 68, 71, 126, 11: 90–92, 99–100; accidents, 3: 302, 9: 70, 11: 23–24, 88–89; repairs, 3: 302, 321, 9: 124; endangered, 3: 249, 278, 280–81, 284–85, 302–3, 9: 17, 21, 25, 58–60, 74, 11: 39; set out, 9: 3, 44, 57, 373, 11: 1; mentioned, 2: 59–60, 70, 71n, 108, 114n, 117, 118n, 287, 317, 361, 380, 384, 394, 398, 464, 499, 3: 55, 57–58, 94, 156, 159, 340, 358, 361, 9: 3n, 22, 45, 55, 58, 374, 10: 1, 75, 77, 279, 11: 4n, 15, 20, 82, 84, 87, 104, 107, 130

Keep Cool Creek, 8: 95, 96n, 102

Kegs, 2: 165, 199–200, 202, 205, 211, 217–18, 286, 4: 34–35, 38, 115, 141, 275, 279, 334–35, 339, 354, 5: 53, 6: 321, 324, 333, 335, 8: 338, 9: 42, 127, 166, 176, 178, 197, 310, 357, 364, 10: 33, 280, 11: 193, 216

Ke-ke-mar-que River. See John Day River

Kelly Creek, 8: 182, 183n, 187n, 409

Kenney Creek, 5: 132n, 10: 134n, 11: 286n

Kentucky, 3: 453, 462, 9: xvii

Kentucky, camps in, 2: 86n

Kenvill River. See Vermillion (White Stone) River

Keokuk Formation, 2: 285n

Kestrel, American (sparrow hawk), 4: 31, 33, 34n, 6: 375, 377, 378n

Kettles, 2: 189, 3: 21–22, 30, 33, 37–38, 356, 401, 403, 413, 428, 4: 102, 105. 152–53, 5: 144, 149–50, 346–47, 359, 361, 371, 6: 113, 139–40, 187, 205, 275–76, 322, 324, 7: 141–42, 144, 147–48, 152–55, 177, 179, 246, 253–54, 300, 9: 51, 106, 180, 228, 237–38, 242, 246, 263, 272, 289, 299, 302, 369n, 10: 193, 11: 209, 219, 329–30, 348–49, 352–53, 361–62, 369–70, 375, 407, 420–22. See also Teakettles; Utensils, cooking

Kettles, glacial, 8: 115n

Kew Gardens, London, 12: 5–8

Kickapoo (Bear Medicine, Ordway's, Wau-car-ba war-con-da) Island, 2: 340–42, 343n, 3: 371, 378, 11: 33–34, 34n

Kickapoo Indians, 2: 144, 144n, 174n, 180, 180n, 185, 207, 212, 221, 224, 235, 237, 238n, 245, 246n, 3: 338, 391, 446, 449, 8: 348n, 369, 369n

Kilchis River, 6: 185n, 471

Kil-her-hurst, 6: 461, 471

Kil-her-ner, 6: 461, 471

Kilhow-a-nah-kle River. See Youngs River

Killamox (and similiar spellings) Indians. See Tillamook Indians

Killdeer, 2: 451, 452n, 4: 93, 95n, 7: 163, 165n, 167, 8: 416, 418n

Killdeer (Turtle) Mountains, 3: 189, 190n, 272, 273n, 305n, 362–63, 405, 487, 491, 4: 26–27, 28n, 9: 130n

Kiln, 4: 351, 354, 6: 229, 233, 238–39, 9: 111, 111n, 179. See also Tar

Kimooenem (and similar spellings) Creek. See Tucannon River

Kimooenem (and similar spellings) River. See North Fork Clearwater River; Snake River

King, Nicholas, 1: 5, 9, 12, 16n. 25, 19nn. 129, 133. See also Maps

Kingbird, eastern, 4: 238n, 277n, 6: 130, 131n, 8: 78n

Kingbird, western, 4: 277n, 8: 25, 27n, 75, 78n, 93, 108

Kingbirds, 4: 276

Kingfisher, belted, 4: 121, 124n, 236, 376–77, 377n, 5: 11, 13n, 6: 383, 384n, 385, 388, 7: 28, 32n, 45, 193

King Hill, 2: 401–2, 404n

King's map of 1803. See Maps

Kinnikinnick, 3: 120n, 305n, 5: 188n, 353n, 7: 17n, 9: 134, 134n. See also Bearberry

Kiowa Apache (Cartarkah) Indians, 3: 136, 138n, 217n, 403, 439, 449

Kiowa (Kiawa, Wetepahato) Indians, 3: 136, 138n, 167n, 217n, 387, 403, 421–22, 439, 448

Kipps Coulee, 8: 133n

Kite, black-shouldered, 5: 216, 217n

Kitkahahki Pawnee Indians. See Pawnee Indians, Republican or Kitkahahki

Kittita Indians, 6: 491, 7: 142n, 151n. See also Klickitat Indians

Klaskanine River, 6: 384n

Kleinschmidt Lake, 8: 93, 94n, 10: 249, 250n

Klickitat (Cataract) River, 5: 349, 352, 353n, 363, 378, 6: 112, 294–95, 296n, 456, 469, 479, 487, 493, 7: 120, 122n, 123–24, 125n, 129, 142n, 151n, 162n, 8: 356, 386, 404, 9: 232, 246, 247n,

Klickitat (Cataract) River
(*continued*)
   292, 293n, **10**: 173, 174n,
   211, 211n, **11**: 376, 377n
Klickitat (Shan-wap-pom, Shal-
   lât-to, Skâdât, Squân-nar-oo)
   Indians, **1**: 11, **5**: 349–53,
   353–54n, **6**: 479, 487, 491,
   7: 122n, 137–41, 142n,
   146–49, 151–52, 151n, 154,
   8: 385, **10**: 164n, **11**: 376–
   77, 377n
Klikitat (*xla tixat*) village, **5**:
   353n
Knapsacks, **4**: 250, 253n, **9**:
   xviii, 197, 393, **11**: 257–58
Knats (and similar spellings). *See*
   Gnats
Knees. *See* Medical problems
Knife River: source, **3**: 190n; arrive at, **9**: 127, **11**: 133, 133n;
   and Indians, **3**: 194n, 206–
   7n, 312, 312n, 404, **9**: 127,
   127n, **10**: 77, 78n, **11**: 134n;
   camped on, **3**: 203; and
   North West Company, **3**: 364;
   distances, **3**; 373, 376, **6**: 447,
   8: 381; listed, **3**: 381, **6**: 462,
   8: 399; and maps, **4**: 26, 28n;
   name, **7**: 342, 343n; mentioned, **3**: 3, 189, 204, 362–
   63, 487, **4**: 18n, 44, **5**: 9, **10**:
   265n,
Knistanoe Indians. *See* Cree
   Indians
Knives: damaged, **2**: 83; distributed, **2**: 192; as gift, **2**: 237, **3**:
   34, 128, 130, **5**: 90, 112, 231,
   246, 341–42, **6**: 191, **9**: 67,
   74, 123, 206, 289, 301, 303;
   use, **2**: 248, **4**: 263, 334, **9**:
   xvi, 342; and Indians, **3**:
   165–66, 310, 356, 413, 462,
   484, **5**: 90, 112, 117, 139,
   144, 149, 231, 246, 341–42,
   6: 246–51, **9**: 48–49, 205;
   stolen, **3**: 296, **6**: 31, 33, 46,
   7: 146, **9**: 106, 266; as trade
   item, **5**: 105, 117, 158, 178,
   231, **6**: 74, 165, 187, 205,
   214, 216, 221–22, **7**: 101–3,
   129, 147–48, 152, 253–54,
   9: 302, 369n; lost, **6**: 195,

198n; sketch, **6**: 249n, 253n;
   payment, **7**: 102–3; for de-
   fense, **7**: 105, 109; returned,
   7: 196, 198, **8**: 23, 35–36,
   134, 138, 294, 302, 359;
   making, **9**: 355; accidents, **9**:
   324, 340; left, **9**: 34, 393, **10**:
   67, 107, 241, 257, 259, 268,
   11: 50–51, 113, 125, 276,
   329–30, 362; mentioned, **5**:
   230, **6**: 172n, 427, 432. *See
   also* Arms and ammunition;
   Daggers; Dirks
Koehn (Kane, Cane), Francis,
   2: 172–73, 172n
Kohokia (and similar spellings).
   See Cahokia
Kooskooskee (and similar spell-
   ings) River. *See* Clearwater
   River
Kootenai Creek, **8**: 161, 162n,
   9: 330n
Kootenai Formation, **4**: 288n,
   299n, 333n, 337n, **8**: 120n
Krohn Lake, **10**: 250, 251n
Kun-na-nar-wesh (and similar
   spellings) Indians. *See*
   Arapaho Indians
Kusis village, **5**: 284n
Kuske-lar. *See* Cus-ka-lah
Kutenai (Cat-tanahaw) Indians,
   3: 434–35, 449, **7**: 251n
Kwahari Comanche Indians. *See*
   Comanche Indians

L

Labbadie, Sylvester, **2**: 243,
   243n
Labeaume, Louis, **1**: 16n. 32
Labiche, François: listed, **1**: 17n.
   73, **2**: 255, **4**: 9, 11, **6**: 172n,
   8: 162n, 179, 277, **11**: 4n,
   8n, 62n, 395n, 400n, 408n,
   411n, 414n, 419n, 420n,
   426n; in permanent party, **2**:
   229n, 510–11; duties, **2**: 258,
   347, **9**: 377; lineage, **2**: 404n;
   sent out, **2**: 455, 456n, 487–
   88, **3**: 7, **6**: 391, 393, **7**: 143–

44, 159, 161, **8**: 164, 170,
   208, 211, 231, **9**: 35, 255,
   265, 276, 332, 356, **10**: 26,
   255, **11**: 52, 61, 410, 426;
   and Indians, **2**: 492, 494n;
   biographical sketch, **2**: 518–
   19; interpreter, **3**: 316n, **5**:
   111, **8**: 329–30, 331n, **9**: 65,
   66n, **10**: 44, 44n, 138n, **11**:
   58; and species, **4**: 157, **6**:
   319, 321–23, **7**: 282; hunting, **5**: 275, 356, **6**: 8–10, 12,
   38, 62, 66, 71–72, 138, 140,
   221, 226–27, 229, 239–40,
   275–76, 279–80, 287–88,
   317–18, 321, 324, 328–29,
   342, 344, 384–85, 387–88,
   387n, 390, 415–16, 418,
   420n, **7**: 126, 196, 198, 257–
   60, 262, 264, 266, 268, 271n,
   273–74, 281–82, 285n,
   286–87, 291, 294, 335–36,
   8: 13, 17, 23, 38–39, 41,
   162, 184, 189–90, 212, 245,
   266, 276, 282, 290, 326–27,
   342, **9**: 33, 255, 255n, 263,
   263n, 267–68, 272–73,
   273n, 275, 301, 310, 312,
   314–15, 319, 321, **10**: 184,
   189, 192, 198, 219, 227–29,
   232, 238, 242, 273, **11**: 396,
   408, 414, 420, 423, 423n,
   425–26, 428, 428n; river
   named for, **5**: 352, 354n,
   378, **8**: 237, **9**: 247n, **11**:
   377n; scouting, **6**: 62, 65, 92,
   9: 44, 254, 257, **10**: 175, 178,
   11: 395, 400; votes, **6**: 83; information from, **7**: 156, **8**:
   211, 328, **9**: 28, 386; separated, **8**: 190; returns, **8**: 328,
   9: 40, 267, 270, 277, 313,
   322, 325, **10**: 28, 196, 229,
   232–33, 236, 239, 242, **11**:
   56, 396, 418; trading, **9**: 294,
   10: 213; and saltmaking
   camp, **10**: 187; mentioned, **2**:
   144n, 364n, 516, **8**: 187n, **9**:
   29n, 45n, 255n, 257n, 265n,
   268n, 271n, 272n, 275n,
   276n, 277n, 279, 293, 294n,
   302n, 310n, 312n, 314n,
   315n, 320, 332n, 356n,

377n, 386n, 396n, **10**: 26n, 29n, 175n, 179n, 184n, 188n, 189n, 192n, 196n, 198n, 213n, 219n, 228n, 229n, 230n, 232n, 233n, 236n, 238n, 239n, 242n, 256n, 273n, 274n, **11**: 43n, 52n, 56n, 58n, 84n, 396n, 414n, 426n

Labrador, **10**: 6n, 43n

Lace, **9**: 369n

La Chapelle (Smoke) Creek, **3**: 105, 106n, **8**: 324, 324n, **9**: 64, 65n, **10**: 43, 43n, **11**: 82, 82n

La Charette (St. John's), Mo., **1**: 8, **2**: 251–52, 252n, **3**: 452, **8**: 4, 366–67, 366n, 368n, **9**: 7, 7n, 365, 365n, 368n, 375, **10**: 9, 9n, **11**: 13, 13n, 29

Lacomb, **8**: 367

La Croix, Joseph, **8**: 355, 356n, 360, **10**: 277, 277n

Lacroy, **10**: 279n

Lady's slipper, mountain, **8**: 66, 69n, 80

Lady Washington, **6**: 155–56, 160n, 427

Lady (White Brant) Island, **6**: 11, 14n, **7**: 39–40, 41n

La Fallowoine Lake, **3**: 409–11

La Fass, Alexander, **8**: 355, **9**: 360n, **10**: 277, 277n

Lafayette Formation, **2**: 104n

Lafferty Island, **8**: 398, **11**: 95, 95n

La Framboise (Good Humored) Island, **3**: 107–8, 109n

Lafrance, Baptiste, **1**: 8, **3**: 241, 241n, 259

Lagopus leucurus, **3**: 86n. *See also* Ptarmigan, white-tailed

La Grue (Chechark), **3**: 235, 235n

Lahocatt village, **3**: 143–44, 144n

Laird Creek. *See* Warm Springs Creek

La Jeunesse, Jean Baptiste, **1**: 17n. 73, **2**: 255, 347, 452, 454n, 526, 528, **3**: 227n, 230–31, 231n, 249, 250n, **9**: 94, 94n, 250n, 396n

Lake Athabaska, **4**: 35, 40n, 103

Lake Coeur d'Alene, **7**: 217, 219n

Lake Creek, **8**: 170, 171n

Lake (Quever) Creek, **2**: 250–52, 252n

Lake d'Esprit, **2**: 485, **3**: 354

Lake Dubois, **3**: 440–41

Lake Goodenough, **11**: 59n

Lake Huron, **3**: 206n, 305, 305n

Lake Manitoba, **3**: 442–43

Lake Michigan, **3**: 206n, 407

Lake of the Hills, **10**: 43n

Lake of the Woods, **3**: 367, 388, 440–43

Lake Pend Oreille, **5**: 198n, **6**: 480, 488, **7**: 216–18, 219n

Lake River, **6**: 24n

Lake Superior, **3**: 305n, 440, **10**: 4n, 48n, 67n

Lake Walula, **10**: 217n

Lake Winnipeg (Winnepique, Osnehuger), **2**: 220, 225, 226n, **3**: 17, 23, 32, 175, 178n, 356, 363, 400, 419, 421, 441–43, 481, 484, **4**: 43, 76n, 107n, **6**: 245, 248n, 251, **8**: 381, 412, **10**: 43n

Lakjalama (Cathlahaw) Indians, **6**: 25n, **8**: 387, 405

La Liberté: listed, **1**: 17n. 73; deserts, **2**: 61, 441, 452–53, 455–56, 487–88, **9**: 31n, 391n, **10**: 24n, 28, 29n, **11**: 47n, 57; listed, **2**: 347; sent out, **2**: 426, 427n, 435n, **9**: 390, **11**: 47; biographical sketch, **2**: 526–28; and Indians, **9**: 31, 33, 35, 40, **10**: 23, **11**: 48–49; mentioned, **2**: 54, 349n, 429, 434, 438, 512, **10**: 25n

La Loutre (L'outre, Luter) Island, **2**: 254, 259n, 259–60, 261n

Lambert, Aylmer Bourke, **12**: 3–5, 7–8

Lamb's quarters, **2**: 377–78, 379n, **4**: 383, 385, 386n, **7**: 335, 337, 338n, **10**: 130, 131n, 134. *See also* Goosefoot, Fremont

Lame. *See* Medical problems

Lamine (Mine) River, **2**: 277, 279, 281n, 286–87, 288n, 313, 323, 324n, 405, 408, 486, **3**: 43, 94, 341–43, 370, 377, **8**: 365, 365n, 377, 395, **9**: 11, 11n, 81, 364n, 368n, 378, 379n, **10**: 12, 13n, 280n, **11**: 20, 20n, 172

Lance Formation. *See* Hell Creek Formation

Lances, **5**: 122, **7**: 211, 213. *See also* Arms and ammunition; Spears

Lancing. *See* Medicine

Landers Fork Blackfoot River, **8**: 94–95, 95n, 96n, 102, **10**: 250, 250n, 251n

Languages, Indian. *See* Indians, languages; *Indian language families* (e.g., Siouan language); *specific Indian languages*

Lanius ludovicianus, **4**: 277n. *See also* Shrike, loggerhead

Lanius ludovicianus excubitorides, **4**: 277n. *See also* Shrike, white-rumped

La Perouse, Jean-François de Galaup, Comte de, **6**: 36n, 50, 51n

La Play Indians. *See* Comanche Indians

Lapwai (Cottonwood) Creek, **5**: 253, 255, 258, 259n, 260n, **7**: 214n, **9**: 305, 305n, **10**: 222n

Larch, western, **5**: 204–5, 206n, **6**: 28n, **7**: 205, 208n, 234, **8**: 7, 11, 12n, 25, 28, 30, 79, 86, 92, 101

Lard, **7**: 215n

Larix occidentalis, **5**: 206n, **6**: 28n, **7**: 208n, **8**: 12n. *See also* Larch, western

Lark, horned, **4**: 95n, **7**: 195n, 198n, **8**: 75, 78n

Lark, prairie, **3**: 8, 11, 12n, 13n, 98

Lark bunting. *See* Bunting, lark

Larks, **4**: 28, 93, 349n, **7**: 196, **8**: 117, 210. *See also* Meadowlark, western

Larkspur, Menzies's, **7**: 55, 61n,
193
Larocque, François-Antoine: information from, **1**: 8–9, **3**:
227n, 252n, 258n, 275n,
278n, 312n, 492n, **11**: 121,
121n; and the party, **1**: 8–9,
3: 241–42, 250, 258, 281,
281n, 284; visits, **1**: 18n. 79,
3: 265, 277, 281, 308, 318–
19, 325, 329, 332, **9**: 123;
trader, **3**: 238, 259, 262n;
biographical sketch, **3**: 241–
42n; exploration, **8**; 159n,
228n; and North West Com-
pany, **9**: 104, 104n, 110,
110n, 121, 121n, 123, **10**:
66, 66n, 70, 70n, **11**: 121,
121n; mentioned, **1**: 18n. 80,
3: 234n, 279, 284, 311n
Larus argentatus, **3**: 132n. *See also*
Gull, herring
Larus delawarensis, **3**: 132n. *See
also* Gull, ring-billed
Larus glaucescens, **6**: 387n. *See
also* Gull, glaucous-winged
Larus occidentalis, **6**: 384n. *See
also* Gull, western
Larus philadelphia, **6**: 387n, **8**:
151n. *See also* Gull, Bona-
parte's
Larus sp., **4**: 24n, **6**: 385, 387n,
388, **8**: 267n, **9**: 252n, **10**:
169n, **11**: 392n. *See also* Gulls
La Salle, Sieur de (Robert Cave-
lier), **2**: 147, 150n
Lassoes, **7**: 307, 308n, 326. *See
also* Ropes
Lastaro (and similar spellings)
River. *See* Pend Oreille River
Lastaw (and similar spellings)
River. *See* Pend Oreille River
Lathyrus sp., **7**: 61n, 338n. *See
also* Pea, sweet
Latourell Falls, **7**: 89n, **9**: 287n,
10: 207n
Latrines (sinks), **9**: 94, 94n,
263, 263n, **11**: 409, 409n
Laudanum. *See* Medicine
Laurel. *See* Rhododendron,
California
Laurel, mountain, **6**: 28n
Lauren soil, **7**: 37n

Lava, **3**: 95, 96n, **4**: 15, 23, 48–
49, 60, **5**: 94n, 266n, **6**:
131n, 179n, **8**: 414
Lava, breccias, **4**: 397n
Lawler, **2**: 138
Lawyer (Commearp) Creek, **1**:
11, **7**: 237–38, 240, 241n,
252, 255n, 259n, 289, 327,
329, 330n, 339, 341, 342n,
343, **9**: 308–9, 308n, 309n,
310n, 315, 315n, **10**: 225n,
227, 227n, 228n
Lax. *See* Medical problems,
bowels
Laxative. *See* Medicine
Lead, **2**: 80, 106, 201, **4**: 269,
274–75, 279, 334–35, **5**: 53,
6: 113, 205, 265, 272, **7**: 90,
92, 196, 235–36, 248, **8**:
157, 294, 302, 306, 311, **9**:
50, 166, 174, 351, **10**: 101,
11: 192–93, 212. *See also*
Arms and ammunition
Lead acetate, **10**: 230n. *See also*
Medicine
Leadbetter Point, **6**: 470
Lead Mine Hill, **3**: 370, 377, **8**:
377, 395, **9**: 368n
Lead ore, **2**: 275–76, 277n,
286, **3**: 475, 481, **9**: 10, **10**:
12
Leaf River, **2**: 220, 220n
Leagle Creek. *See* Fountain
(Eagle) Creek
Leakens, **2**: 143, 143n, 148–
49, 173
Leander, **8**: 346, 348n
Leary site, **2**: 372n
Leavenworth, Henry, **8**: 317n
Leavenworth Island (Field Is-
lands, Green, Isles des
Parques), **2**: 336, 338–39,
340n, **8**: 360, 360n, **10**: 18,
18n, **11**: 33, 33n
Leavenworth site, **3**: 156n
Le Baume, Louis, **2**: 221, 221n
Lebo Member, **8**: 261n, 262n
Le Borgne (One Eye), **2**: 264n,
3: 209, 211, 214n, 215n,
235n, 272, 273n, 310–11,
311n, 319, 319n, 325, **8**:
299, 300n, 301, 303–4, 306,
9: 121, 121n, **10**: 268n

Ledyard, John, **2**: 1, **7**: 11n
Lee, Jason, **7**: 215n
Leech Lake, **3**: 409–11, 439
Lee Island, **2**: 123, 124n
Leggings, **2**: 157, **4**: 165, 174,
430, **5**: 8, 119, **7**: 249, **8**: 219,
9: 151, 163, 206, **11**: 276. *See
also* Clothing
Legs. *See* Medical problems
Leguminosae, **7**: 338n. *See also*
Peas
Lelia Bird, **6**: 29n
Lemhi (East Fork Lewis's) River:
listed, **3**: 382, 465, **10**: 172;
arrive at, **5**: 2, 76–77, 85n,
130, 132n, 141n, 177, **10**:
126, 127n; described, **5**: 78,
81–82, 85n; characteristics,
5: 81, 86n, 140; and maps, **5**:
88; distances, **5**: 169, **6**: 451,
493, 495, **8**: 172, **9**: 231, **10**:
128–29; and Indians, **6**: 479,
482, **8**: 40, 42, 48, 182, **9**:
190, 204–6, **11**: 243–44,
244n, 272–76, 275n;
camped on, **9**: 215n; mentioned, **3**: 98n, **5**: 76n, 94n,
178, 179n, 260n, **6**: 493n,
8: 43n, 173n, 388, 413, **9**:
191n, 11n, **10**: 129n, 133,
133n, 134n, 135n, 152n,
160n, 174n, **11**: 85, 86n,
288, 289n, 292n, 294n, 347n
Lemhi Pass, **1**: 10, **5**: 2, 76n,
177n, **8**: 173n, **10**: 128, 128n
Lemhi Range, **5**: 76–77, 83,
85n, 86n
Lemhi Shoshone Indians. *See*
Shoshone Indians, Lemhi
Lemon, **6**: 156
Lepage, Jean Baptiste: joins
party, **2**: 511, **3**: 3, 226, **9**: 94,
94n; biographical sketch, **3**:
227n; listed, **4**: 9, 11, **6**:
172n, **8**: 139n, 162n, **11**:
187n, 411n; information
from, **4**: 27, 28n, 29n, **6**:
337–38; scouting, **4**: 250,
256, **10**: 98, **11**: 186–90;
medical problems, **4**: 378, **6**:
337, 357, 374, 376, **9**: 183,
11: 225; sent out, **4**: 382,
386, **5**: 218, **7**: 289, 308, 310,

8: 34–35, 179, 180n, **9**: 265, 335, **10**: 112, 145, 241, **11**: 410; river named for, **5**: 319n, **10**: 215n, **11**: 364n; votes, **6**: 84; hunting, **6**: 215–16, 217n, 228, 229n, 242–43, 276, **7**: 268–69, 271, 271n, 274, 281, **9**: 312, **10**: 190, 229–30, **11**: 415, 417; returns, **6**: 232, 234, 275, **7**: 297, 299, 322, 324, **8**: 37–38, **9**: 268–69, **10**: 191, 230, 232–33, 242, 255, **11**: 190–91; and Indians, **7**: 294; accidents, **7**: 322–24; and saltmaking camp, **10**: 187; mentioned, **2**: 512, **4**: 36, **8**: 331n, **9**: 183n, 265n, 270n, 312n, 336n, 356n, **10**: 98n, 113n, 145n, 188n, 190n, 191n, 230n, 232n, 233n, 241n, 242n, 255n, 274n, **11**: 225n, 415n, 417n

Lepage River. *See* John Day River (Sherman-Gilliam counties, Oreg.)

Lepidium sp., **8**: 94n. *See also* Mustard

Lepidium virginicum, **7**: 338n, **8**: 94n. *See also* Peppergrass, tall

Lepoy, **3**: 460

Lepus townsendii, **3**: 73n, **4**: 29n, **5**: 170n, **6**: 317n, **9**: 59n, **10**: 39n, **11**: 75n. *See also* Jackrabbit, white-tailed

LeRaye, Charles, **8**: 159n

Letart's Falls, **2**: 84, 84–85n

Lettuce, **11**: 132

Level, spirit, **2**: 94n, 412–13, **4**: 304. *See also* Instruments, scientific

Lewis, Lucy. *See* Marks, Lucy Meriwether Lewis

Lewis, Meriwether: and maps, **1**: 4–5, 7, 9–13, 16n. 23, 18n. 87, **4**: 415–16, 435, 438n, **8**: 92–93n, 139n; journal-keeping methods, **1**: 16n. 14, 18n. 107, **2**: 85, 85n, 117, 118n, 168–69, 171n, 317–18, 318n, 320n, 370, 373n, 376, 376n, 379, 379n, 382n, 398, 399n, 400, 403–4n, 418,

418n, 424–26, 425n, 427n, 428n, 430, 431n, 444, 446n, 452n, 463, 464n, 488, 490n, 504, 507n, **3**: 2, 54, 56n, 76, 79n, 284, 285n, 313, 315n, 333–36, 383n, **4**: 7, 12n, 12–13n, 95n, 120, 121n, 134, 136n, 166, 166n, 179n, 220n, 241n, 257n, 261, 262n, 266, 269n, 279, 279n, 298, 299n, 301, 302n, 313, 317n, 318, 321n, 327, 394, 397n, 407, 410n, 415n, **5**: 29n, 61, 63n, 94n, 140, 173, 174n, 181, 182n 197, 198n, 241, 243n, 262, 263n, 268, 327, 328n, 366n, **6**: 2–3, 22, 24n, 32, 34n, 60–61, 101, 104n, 131, 131n, 133n, 257, 257–58n, 262n, 406, 440, 442n, 443, 443n, 445, 473–74, 477n, 487, 489n, 492, **7**: 1, 8n, 318, 322n, **8**: 3–4, 82, 86n, 89, 90n, 108, 111n, 158–59, 158n, 159n, 160n, 277, 279n, 385, 411, **9**: xi–xii, 390, **10**: 123n; biographical sketch, **2**: 3, 512; leaves Pittsburgh, **2**: 65; ecological observations, **2**: 67–69, 68n, 78, 78n, **3**: 81–82, **4**: 19, 26, 35–36, 42, 69–71, 76–77, 88, 96, 104, 121, 124–25, 130, 158–59, 170, 176, 189, 201–2, 221–22, 224n, 225–27, 238, 254, 283–85, **5**: 65, 67n, 85n, **7**: 55, 60n, 112, 114n, 118, 121–22n, 126, 131, 188, 190n, 202, 204n, 205, 208n, 262, **8**: 79, 81n, 128, 132n; scouting, **2**: 77, 89, 93–94, 103, 115, 168, 172, 245, 248–49, 266, 273, 283–87, 291, 298, 315–16, 319, 346–47, 386–88, 395, 401–3, 428–29, 467–69, 504–5, **3**: 7–10, 37–39, 53, 74–75, 79–83, 104, 106, 143, 147, 176–77, 208, 232, 296–97, 307, **4**: 3–4, 9, 13, 36, 39, 41, 43, 51, 54–56, 59–60, 62, 66–68, 76–79, 84, 88, 90, 106, 108, 111,

114, 124, 130, 145, 147, 157–58, 179–81, 201, 205, 215, 218–19, 227, 229–30, 232, 247, 250–58, 260–63, 265–66, 275, 277, 279–81, 283, 289–92, 339, 347, 380, 382, 385–87, 416, **5**: 1–2, 14, 17–18, 20, 24–25, 59, 61–62, 274–75, 321, 328, 331, 338, **6**: 1, 46–47, 91n, 92–93, 101, 105, 450, **7**: 33, 35, 94, 107–8, **8**: 1–2, 39, 41, 113, 353, 361, **9**: 11, 37, 44, 52, 55, 58, 60, 134, 137, 147, 152, 155, 157, 160–62, 164–66, 168, 183–84, 186, 191, 193, 197, 199, 203–4, 207, 253, 257, 257n, 292, 385, 394, **10**: 31, 36, 83–84, 98, 101–3, 107–8, 112, 119–21, 119n, 123, 125, 170, 173n, 178, **11**: 19, 61, 138, 186–87, 193, 197, 199–200, 227, 246–47, 249–50, 261–62, 278–79, 393–95, 395n, 400–401; medical problems, **2**: 82n, 86, 86n, 500–501, 502n, **3**: 7, 9, 19–20, **4**: 271, 274–75, 277–78, 280, **5**: 25–26, 31–32, 226, 232–36, 243, 243n, 245–46, 253, **7**: 163, **8**: 3–4, 156, 300n, 309, 316n, 319–20, 324–25, 329, 345, 347, 350, 354, **9**: 350, **10**: 148, 265–66, 269; hunting, **2**: 83, 272, 291–92, 319, 355, 356n, 364–65, 398, **3**: 55, 58, 76, 78–83, 104, 253–55, 265, 296, 299, **4**: 36, 39, 41, 43, 48–49, 54, 56, 66, 77–78, 84, 86–88, 90, 111, 114, 118, 121, 130–32, 134, 141, 151, 155, 157–58, 167–68, 180–81, 201, 205, 227, 230, 232, 242, 244, 292, 340, 351, 354, 382, 402, 416, **5**: 15, 20, 25–26, 61, 226, **6**: 11, 13, **7**: 98, 278–79, **8**: 63, 97, 99, 126–27, 144, 154–55, 290, **9**: 9, 9n, 12, 16–17, 23, 27, 56, 60–63, 77, 85, 101–2, 131, 133–34, 137, 140, 150, 152, 155, 161, 175, 178,

Lewis, Meriwether (*continued*)
186, 227, 344, 347, 377, 379,
383, 388, **10**: 12, 37, 40–42,
56, 64–65, 84, 252, 252n,
265, **11**: 36, 76–79, 110–11,
141, 161–62, 169–70, 180,
190–91, 227, 232, 250–51,
325–26; medical practices,
2: 86, 173, 173n, 345, 347,
349n, 356, 500–501, **3**: 191,
260, 279, **4**: 109, 138, 271,
274, 278–79, 300–301, 303,
306, 309, 334, 365, 436, **5**:
25–26, 158, **6**: 239, 242n,
312, 315, 318–19, 321, 324,
333, 335, 374, 388, 391, 394,
396, **7**: 2–3, 163, 178, 180,
210–13, 243, 269, 272, 278,
280–84, 286, 288–89, 291,
297, 302, 308, 310, 331, 334,
336, **8**: 35, 36, 46n, 57–58,
59n, 156, 157n, 158, **9**: 324,
10: 69, 69n, 106, 148, 222,
11: 58, 118; and species, **2**:
99, 110, 111n, 210n, 431n,
450, 457–60, 471, **3**: 54n,
69, 178, **4**: 27, 51, 53, 60,
62–63, 84–85, 88n, 108,
132, 134–35, 141, 259, 292–
93, 297, 344, 378–79, 423,
427, **5**: 58, **7**: 3, 19, 55, 126,
129n, 170, 172n, 200, 265,
292–93, 306, **8**: 12n, 13n,
21n, 28, 30, 30n, 50, 52n,
53, 55n, 79, 80n, 80–81n,
87, 89, 93, 94n, 140–41,
174n, **9**: 32, 36, 160, 293,
343, **10**: 26, 36, 40–41, 84,
84n, 260–61, **11**: 52–53, 70,
141, 141n; returns, **2**: 108,
171, 174n, 182, 185, 207n,
240–43, 387–88, **3**: 296,
299, 307, **4**: 70, 74, 266–67,
5: 52, 55, **6**: 47n, 60–61,
108, 149, 151n, **7**: 137, 139,
141, **9**: 6, 86, 164, 168, 254,
258, 341, 374, **10**: 8, 31, 65,
83, 100, 103, 105, 141, 172,
180, 210, 259, **11**: 10, 128,
139, 199–200, 229, 313–14,
395, 401; at Kaskaskia, **2**:
118n; at St. Louis, **2**: 118n,

126, 127n, 128n, 129, 167n,
174n, 180, 187, 193, 205–6,
208, 214, 227, 240, 243n, **11**:
1, 9–10; at Cahokia, **2**: 118n,
145, 155, 166–67, 167n,
186n; sends messages, **2**:
137, 138n, 139, 139n, 145,
157, 167, 211n, 239, 472, **3**:
219, **4**: 70, 280, 289, **5**: 2–3,
40, 42, 46, 52, 54, 64, 105, **7**:
131, 156, **8**: 150, **9**: xi, 195,
197n, 213, 293–94, 346, **10**:
102, 121, 122n, 263, **11**: 254,
257, 258n, 288–89; expedition finances, **2**: 182–83; at
St. Charles, **2**: 185, 186n;
listed, **2**: 194–95, 218, 347;
fishing, **2**: 485–86, **4**: 280,
309, 331–32, 37, **9**: 40, 137,
395, **10**: 28, **11**: 561; birthday, **2**: 488, **3**: 118; and
Floyd's death, **2**: 495, **9**: 41;
leads detachment, **2**: 502–3,
6: 200–201, **7**: 111, 115–16,
8: 74, 77, 83, 86n, 104, 290,
9: 43–44, 115–16, 141, 172,
267, 290–91, 329–30, 338,
338n, **10**: 30n, 73, 247,
248n, 253–54, **11**: 60, 126–
27, 413; accidents, **4**: 262, **8**:
65–66, 80, 82–83, 85; and
upper portage camp, **4**: 325,
9: 172, **10**: 107, 107n, 111,
11: 207–10, 213–14, 214n,
225; receives messages, **4**:
407, 430, 435, **5**: 173, 218, **7**:
126, 131, **8**: 3, 150, 156, **10**:
263, 264n; votes, **6**: 84; gifts,
6: 137, **10**: 184; and Blackfeet Indians, **8**: 2, 128–35,
132–33n, 139n, 293–95,
414, **9**: 341–42, **10**: 259; Cruzatte shoots, **8**: 3, 155–56,
287n, 290, **9**: 347; separated,
9: 164, 185, 192, 196, **10**: 1,
31, 99–100, 105, 119, 122,
11: 127, 139, 188–90, 229,
232–33, 246–48, 400–401;
and botanical specimens, **12**:
2–7, 8–9n, 9n, 10n; species
named for, **12**: 7
Lewis, Reuben, **2**: 211n

Lewis, Samuel, **1**: 13, **6**: 90n, **8**:
275n
*Lewis and Clark, Pioneering Natur-
alists* (Cutright), **12**: 7
Lewis and Clark (Fort, Netul)
River: and Fort Clatsop, **6**: 2,
90n, 242–44, **8**: 388, 406,
9: 258, 258n, **11**: 401, 403n,
431; arrive at, **6**: 95, 109,
114, **10**: 180; animals and
plants, **6**: 108, 277, 390;
party at, **6**: 221–22; hunting
on, **6**: 241–43, 262, 267,
275–76, 287–88, 290, 296–
97, 312, 314, 325–26, 328–
29, 351, 353, 356, 360, 382,
388, 390–91, 393, 398–99,
406–7, 409, 411, 443–44,
9: 270, 271n, 276n, **10**: 191,
11: 405, 418, 427n; name, **6**:
243, **9**: 274, 274n, **10**: 195,
195n, **11**: 424, 424n, 427n;
conditions, **6**: 253, 255, 363;
located, **6**: 459, 471, described, **11**: 402; frozen, **11**:
416; mentioned, **6**: 89, 98n,
115n, 171, 223n, 230n, 278–
79, 400–401, 403, **10**: 181,
181n, 186n, 197n, **11**: 402n,
417, 432n
Lewis and Clark Pass, **8**: 95,
96n, 383, 401, **9**: 338, 339n,
10: 250n
Lewis and Clark's map of 1806.
See Maps
Lewis and Clark's map of 1814.
See Maps
Lewis (Cahwahnakiooks) River,
6: 24n, 457, 470, 472n, 477,
484, **7**: 22n, 25–26, 26n, 30,
31n, 77, **8**: 387, 405, 415, **9**:
250n, 282, 283n, **10**: 203n,
11: 388n, 436, 436n. *See also*
Salmon River; Snake River
Lewisia rediviva, **5**: 147n, **8**: 80n.
See also Bitterroot
Lewis Range, **9**: 171, 171n,
176n, 338, 339n, 342, **11**:
204, 206, 206n
Lewis (Snowy) Range, **4**: 277,
282n, 310, 338–39, 339n,
351, 358–59, 381n
Lexington Island, **2**: 310, 312n

Liatris aspera, **3**: 469. *See also* Gayfeather, rough

Liatris pycnostachya, **3**: 469. *See also* Gayfeather, tall blazing star

Library Company, **2**: 352n

Library of Congress, **1**: 12, 19n. 125, **2**: 536, 539, 543

Lice, human body, **5**: 342–43, 344n, 357, **10**: 211, 211n, **11**: 368n

Lichen, **7**: 227, 230, 233n

Licorice. *See* Liquorice

Licorice-root, **8**: 28–30, 31n

Liffecue Rocks (Devil's Race Grounds), **2**: 249–50, 251n

Lighting Crow (Kakawissassa), **3**: 152, 155–56, 156n, 158–60, 166, **4**: 12n, **8**: 312, 317n, **9**: 79, 82n

Lignite Creek, **8**: 247, 249, 249n, 250n

Liguest, Pierre Laclede, **2**: 130n

Ligusticum verticillatum, **8**: 31n. *See also* Licorice-root

Ligustrum vulgare, **2**: 499n. *See also* Privets

Like-a-Fishhook village, **3**: 154n, 207n

Lilac, **2**: 209, 2lon

Lilies, **8**: 15, 18

Lily, fawn. *See* Dog's-tooth-violet

Lily, green-banded mariposa, **7**: 190n

Lime, **3**: 473–78, **4**: 340

Limestone, Cambrian Pilgrim, **8**: 18on

Limestone, Devonian Jefferson, **8**: 18on

Limestone, Girardeau, **2**: 110–11, 111n, 113n

Limestone, Grand Tower, **2**: 113, 114n

Limestone, Jefferson City, **2**: 277n, **8**: 374, 375n

Limestone, Meagher, **8**: 18on

Limestone, Plattsmouth, **2**: 401–2, 404n

Limestone, Saint Louis, **2**: 227, 228n

Limestone, Sexton Creek, **2**: 110–11, 111n, 113n

Limestone, Spring Branch, **2**: 401–2, 404n

Limestone (freestone), **2**: 115, 276, 284, 373n, 393n, 467n, 471–72, 474, 475n, **3**: 339, 341, **4**: 27, 60, 71–72, 76n, 104, 106, 107n, 195, 200n, 233n, 405n, 406n, 426, 429n, 433–34, 436, 438n, **5**: 18, 2on, 27, 29n, 3on, 61n, 83–84, 87n, 97, 99, 102n, 157n, **8**: 65n, 124n, 171n, 179, 18on, 185, 188n, **9**: 28

Limonite (ocher), **2**: 350–51, 352n, **8**: 417, 418n

Linden, **2**: 313, 314n, 429–30, **8**: 345, 345n, 373, 415, 418n, **9**: 31–32, 31n

Lindera benzoin, **2**: 186n. *See also* Spice bush

Lindsey Creek, **5**: 357n

Line, tow. *See* Rope, tow

Line (Wolf) Creek, **11**: 32, 32n

Linen, **2**: 211, 212n, **4**: 408, **9**: 369n. *See also* Clothing; Medicine

Liniment. *See* Medicine

Linnaean system, **2**: 79n, **6**: 346n, **12**: 1

Linnet, **4**: 269n

Linseed, **4**: 402n

Lint. *See* Medicine

Linum perenne, **4**: 402n, **5**: 21n, **9**: 169n, **10**: 99n, **11**: 201n, 232n. *See also* Flax, blue

Linum usitatissiumum, **4**: 402n. *See also* Flax, common

Linwood site, **2**: 400n, 444n

Liquor: and members of the party, **2**: 142, **4**: 70, 153, 217, 219, 225, 228, 230, 250, 252, 329, 338–39, 342–43, 350, 362, **8**: 359n, **9**: 73, 137, 143, 158–59, 162, 164–65, 176, 179, 262, **10**: 109, 184, **11**: 115, 145–46, 156, 177–78, 180, 184–86, 191–92, 218, 407; supplies, **2**: 256; and Indians, **3**: 157, 157n, 166n, 183, 441, 443–44, 461–62, 484, **4**: 34, 38, **6**: 179, 196, **8**: 131, **9**: 67; and traders,

8: 338, 360, **9**: 360, **10**: 276; freezes, **10**: 65. *See also* Alcoholic beverages; Medicine, alcohol

Liquorice, **4**: 125, 128, 129n, **6**: 60–61, 61n, 229, 230n, 233. *See also* Lupine, seashore

Liquorice, wild, **6**: 229, 230n, 233, **8**: 119, 120n

Liriodendron sp., **3**: 307–8n. *See also* Poplar, tulip-

Liriodendron tulipifera, **2**: 78n. *See also* Tulip tree

Lisa, Manuel, **1**: 12–13, 16n. 32, **2**: 211, 211n, 379n, 515–16, 520, 523, 528, **3**: 88n, 171n, 228n, **8**: 197n, 279n, 316n, 358n

Lisbet, Thomas, **2**: 116, 144, 144n

Litters, **8**: 204–5

Little Bason, **4**: 20–21, **8**: 297, 298n, 381, 399

Little Beaver Creek (Mercer County, N. Dak.), **4**: 21n

Little Beaver Creek (Ohio), **2**: 72n

Little Beaver (Kee-tooch Sar-kar-nar) Creek (Emmons County, N. Dak.), **3**: 175–77, 178n, 361, 381, 470

Little Belt Mountains, **4**: 234n, 247, 252n, 26on, 282n, **8**: 115, 116n, **9**: 163, 164n, 166, 180, **10**: 99, 99n, 112, 112n

Little Bighorn River, **8**: 232, 235n, 245n, 25on

Little Blue River (Hay Cabin Creek), **2**: 319–20, 320n, **3**: 317, 318n, 343, 370, 377, **8**: 361, 361n, 378, 396, **9**: 16, 16n, 363n, 368n, 383, **10**: 16, 16n, 279n, **11**: 29, 3on

Little Bowl, **3**: 19

Little Bow (Petite Arch) village, **3**: 13–14, 15n

Little Canyon Creek, **7**: 225n, 233n, 236n, **9**: 307n, **10**: 224n

Little Cedar (Cedar) Island, **3**: 61–63, 63n, 372, 380, **8**: 332, 333n, 380, 398, **9**: 367n

Little Chariton (Shariton)
River: described, 2: 291–92,
3: 342; latitude, 2: 291–92, 3:
370, 8: 378, 11: 171–72; distances, 2: 405, 408, 8: 378,
9: 81, 368n; listed, 3: 377, 8:
395; conditions, 9: 12, 379,
10: 12, 11: 22; mentioned,
2: 293n, 9: 12n, 10: 13n, 11:
21, 22n. *See also* Chariton
River

Little Cheyenne (Hidden) River
(Hidden Creek), 3: 144–45,
146n, 10: 51, 51n, 11: 95,
95n

Little Crow (Ka-goh-ha-me), 3:
209, 211, 213n, 214n, 218,
226–27, 261, 268, 270, 275–
76, 298, 317, 8: 302, 303n,
304, 9: 350n

Little Ducket Creek. *See* Ducket
Creek

Little Fox (Oh-harh), 3: 209,
211, 213n, 309, 10: 61n

Little Gate of the Mountain,
4: 426, 429n, 6: 450, 465,
11: 240, 241n

Little Grave Creek, 2: 77, 78n

Little Heart River, 3: 187, 188n,
9: 88, 88n, 10: 57, 57n, 11:
102, 103n

Little Hocking River, 2: 82, 82n,
83n

Little Horsetail Ripple, 2: 67,
68n

Little Kanawaha River, 2: 82,
82–83n

Little Knife River (Goat Pen
Creek), 4: 18n, 42, 44, 45n,
6: 447, 462, 8: 3, 159n, 289,
289n, 381, 400, 9: 132,
132n, 349n, 10: 80, 80n,
266n, 11: 135, 135n

Little Lake Creek, 8: 170, 171n

Little Missouri (E-mâh-tark',-
Ah'-zhah) River, 3: 110n,
226, 227n, 363, 373, 381,
431, 4: 23–28, 28n, 29n, 30,
32, 34, 39, 44, 6: 337–38,
447, 462, 496, 7: 342, 343n,
8: 152, 297, 381, 399, 412, 9:
129, 129n, 130n, 138, 10:
78n, 79, 79n, 83, 267, 11:
134–35, 134n, 135n

Little Muddy Creek, 4: 81, 83,
84n

Little Muddy (White Earth)
River, 4: 58–60, 59n, 62,
63n, 69, 107n, 6: 447, 462,
8: 123, 124n, 152–54, 153n,
154n, 158, 282, 282n, 283n,
381, 400, 412, 9: 135, 135n,
10: 82, 82n, 264, 264n, 11:
137, 137n

Little Narrows. *See* Short (Little)
Narrows

Little Nemaha River, 2: 380–
81, 382n, 3: 347, 371, 378,
8: 378, 396, 416–17, 9: 26,
26n, 367n, 388, 10: 21, 21n,
11: 40, 40n

Little Osage Indians, 2: 266–
67n, 277n, 286, 288n, 302–
3, 303n, 3: 370, 377, 390–
93, 437–38, 447, 457, 8: 362,
364n, 378, 395, 9: 368n. *See
also* Great Osage Indians;
Osage Indians

Little Platte River. *See* Platte
River (Mo.)

Little Porcupine (Table) Creek,
8: 242–44, 245n

Little Prickly Pear (Ordway's)
Creek, 4: 398–401, 401n,
402n, 6: 450, 464, 9: 186,
186n, 336, 337n, 10: 114,
114n, 11: 230–31, 232n

Little Raven. *See* Little Crow

Little Rocky (North) Mountains, 4: 2, 167, 169n, 189,
191, 192n, 198, 200n, 9:
153n, 154, 160, 11: 163–66,
164n, 166n

Little Sandy Creek, 10: 96, 97n,
11: 181–82, 182n

Little Sandy Island, 11: 39

Little Sheep Mountain, 8: 258,
261n

Little Shoal Creek (Sharriton-
Cartie), 2: 319–20, 320n

Little Sioux (Ye-yeau War-da-
pon) River, 2: 454n, 456n,
457–60, 462, 463n, 475n,
480, 485, 487, 3: 94, 354,
371, 375, 379, 386n, 409,
414, 483, 8: 311n, 351–52,
352n, 379, 397, 411, 416, 9:

35n, 36, 36n, 80–81, 359n,
367n, 393, 10: 26, 26n, 11:
172, 174

Little Sni a Bar Creek, 9: 15,
15n, 368n, 382, 10: 16n

Little Tarkio Creek, 2: 361–62,
363n, 366, 368n, 9: 22–23,
23n, 24n, 387, 10: 20, 20n

Little Tavern Creek (Callaway
County, Mo.), 2: 264–65,
266n, 276n, 9: 8n

Little Tavern Creek (Franklin
County, Mo.), 2: 246, 249n

Little Thief (Petit Voleur, Wa-ar-
ruge-nor), 2: 439, 441, 443n,
490, 492, 9: 40–41, 41n, 11:
56–57, 56n

Little Timber (Small, Grape)
Creek, 8: 189–90, 192, 193n

Little White Salmon River
(Little Lake Creek), 5: 353n,
6: 469, 8: 386, 404, 9: 247n,
10: 164n, 11: 377n

Little Wolf Mountain, 8: 224–
25

Little Wolfs Medicine (Shhakó-
hopinnee), 3: 212, 213n

Littorina sp., 6: 409n. *See also*
Periwinkles

Livingston Formation, 8: 188n,
193n, 203n

Lizard, black. *See* Lizard, western fence

Lizard, brown. *See* Lizard, western fence

Lizard, eastern short-horned, 5:
174, 174n, 7: 307n

Lizard, pigmy horned, 7: 3, 166,
168, 169n, 302–5, 307n,
309, 311

Lizard, western fence, 6: 405n,
7: 163, 165n, 166–68, 169n,
302, 305, 309, 311, 312n

Lizards, 3: 53, 6: 94, 96, 402,
408, 7: 309, 311

Loam, 4: 130, 140, 146, 159,
225, 230, 257, 412, 5: 18,
30–31, 7: 78n, 205, 207,
221, 223

Lobelia siphilitica, 6: 242n. *See
also* Cardinal-flower, blue

Lochsa (Upper Kooskooske)
River, 5: 204–6, 205n, 207n,

228n, 238, **6**: 452, 466, **8**: 31, 33, 34n, 53–54, 55n, 56–57, 59n, 61, 61n, 63, 67, 383, **9**: 223, 224n, 328n, **10**: 142, 142n, 143n, 245n, 246n, **11**: 315–16, 316n, 318n

Locke (Stinking Cabin) Creek, **8**: 192n, 391, 409. *See also* Mission Creek

Locoweed, purple, **8**: 193n

Locust, honey, **8**: 416, 418n, **9**: 20, 20n, 54, 361

Locust, Rocky Mountain, **8**: 208n

Lodgepole Formation, **5**: 20n, 29n

Lodgepole Limestone, **4**: 405–6n, 429n, 438n

Lodges. *See* Indians, lodges

Loess, **2**: 356, 356–57n, 386n, 404n

Logtown Riffle, **2**: 68, 69n

Loins. *See* Medical problems

Loisel, Régis, **1**: 8, **2**: 221, 221n, 252, 253n, 294, 295n, **3**: 88n, 100–102, 103n, 136n, 154n, 155–56n, 258n, 415–17, 420, **8**: 324, 324n, 380, **9**: 63, 64n, 81, 354, 354n, **10**: 42, 43n, 272n, **11**: 80–81, 81n, 93

Loiselle Creek, **9**: 64, 64n, **10**: 43n, **11**: 82n

Lolo (Collins's) Creek (Idaho): arrive at, **5**: 219, 224n, 225, 227n, **8**: 7, 10–11, 25–26, **10**: 146, 146n, **11**: 325–26, 326n; distances, **6**: 453; listed, **6**: 467, **8**: 384, 402; informed of, **7**: 264, 266; hunting on, **7**: 269, 271, 273–74, 282, 284, 286, 289–91, 294, 297, 299, 323, 325–26, 328, 331–32, 344–45, **8**: 22, 44; explored, **7**: 277, 279; camped on, **7**: 308, 310, **9**: 227, 227n, 313, 314n, **11**: 325–26, 326n; plants, **8**: 28; rendezvous at, **8**: 35–36; and Indians, **8**: 43, 83; party at, **8**: 48, 50; mentioned, **7**: 266n, 332n, 342, **8**: 12n, 26n, 45–

46, 45n, **9**: 321, 322n, 323, 325–26, 326n

Lolo (Travelers' Rest) Creek (Mont.): arrive at, **1**: 10, **5**: 192–94, 242, **8**: 66–68, **9**: 328–29, 329n; location, **5**: 195, 197, **6**: 466, 492, **8**: 413; and Indians, **5**: 196, **7**: 331, **8**: 54; distances, **5**: 198–99, 202, 237, **6**: 308–10, 452, 473n, 493–95, **9**: 231, **10**: 173, **11**: 174n; guides to, **8**: 36; conditions, **8**: 62, 64–65, 68; camped on, **8**: 80, 85, **9**: 221–22, 221n, 222n, **10**: 140, 140n, 246, 246n, **11**: 307–8, 308n; listed, **8**: 383, 394, 402, 410; mentioned, **5**: 196n, 199n, 203, **6**: 311n, 495n, **8**: 65n, 69n, 100, 172, 388, 393, **7**: 332, 339, 341, **10**: 141, 141n, **11**: 310–11, 311n, 312n. *See also* Travelers' Rest

Lolo Hot Springs, **5**: 202–3, 202n, 203n, 237, 242, **6**: 452, 466, **8**: 62–64, 65n, 67, 383, 402, **9**: 222n, 223, 223n, 328, 329n, **10**: 141, 141n, 246n, **11**: 312, 312n, 314, 314n

Lolo Mountains, **5**: 199, 201n

Lolo Pass, **5**: 203n, **9**: 223n, **10**: 141n, **11**: 314n

Lolo Trail: arrive at, **1**: 10, **5**: 199n; conditions, **2**: 23, 28, 32, **5**: 201, 203–7, 209–10, 213, 215–16, 218–19, 225, 227, 229, 238–39, **7**: 1, 3–4, **8**: 1, **11**: 310–11, 322; plants, **6**: 286n, **12**: 6; mentioned, **2**: 24, **5**: 3, 90, 131n, 164n, 205n, 207n, 225n, **8**: 55n, 61n, **9**: xv, 222n, 224n, 328n, **10**: 132n, 135n, 140n, 143n, 245n, **11**: 311n, 318n

Lomatium, big seed, **7**: 190n

Lomatium, ternate, **7**: 190n, **8**: 174, 174n

Lomatium, Watson's, **7**: 190n

Lomatium cous, **5**: 380n, **6**: 192n, **7**: 93n, **8**: 12n, **9**: 288n, **10**: 211n. *See also* Cous

Lomatium macrocarpum, **7**: 190n. *See also* Lomatium, big seed

Lomatium triternatum, **7**: 190n, **8**: 174n. *See also* Lomatium, ternate

Lomatium watsonii, **7**: 190n. *See also* Lomatium, Watson's

Lombard thrust fault, **4**: 425, 425n, 427, 429n

London, **10**: xvii, 4n, 63n, 226n, **12**: 5–6

Lone Pine Rapids. *See* Half-Breed Rapids

Lone Ridge, **6**: 383, 384n

Lone Tree Creek, **8**: 272, 274n

Long, Stephen H., **3**: 228n

Long Gulch Creek, **5**: 98–99, 102n

Long Knife Creek, **3**: 182, 184n

Long Lake (Fish, Chewah) Creek, **3**: 182, 184n, 361–62, 373, 381, **9**: 367n, **11**: 102, 102n

Long Narrows, **5**: 336n, 337, 340n, 350, **6**: 462, 469, 487, 493, **9**: 232, 280, **10**: 212, 213n, **11**: 370n, 374, 431. *See also* Columbia River, The Dalles of the

Long Point, **10**: 90n

Long Soldier (Sharhá) Creek, **3**: 174–75, 175n, 178n, **9**: 85, 85n, **10**: 56, 56n, **11**: 101, 101n

Longspur, McCown's, **4**: 254, 257n

Lonicera ciliosa, **5**: 195n, **6**: 286n, **7**: 114n, **8**: 30n, **12**: 5. *See also* Honeysuckle, western trumpet

Lonicera dioica, **4**: 57n. *See also* Honeysuckle, wild

Lonicera hirsuta, **12**: 6

Lonicera hispidula, **7**: 114n. *See also* Honeysuckle, California

Lonicera sp., **2**: 435n, **7**: 47n. *See also* Honeysuckles

Looking Glass, **7**: 204–5n

Lookout Bend, **3**: 136n, **8**: 321, 322n, **9**: 353n, **10**: 271n

Lookout Mountain, **2**: 361–62, 363n

Loon, arctic, **6**: 391n

Loon, black, **2**: 205

Loon, common, **2**: 205n, **6**: 391n, **9**: 247n, **10**: 174n, **11**: 378n

Loon, Pacific, **6**: 391n, 438, **9**: 247n, **10**: 174n, **11**: 378n

Loon, red-throated, **6**: 391n, **9**: 247n, **11**: 378n

Loon, speckled. *See* Loon, Pacific

Loons, **6**: 11, 74, 98n, 261, 383, 385, 389–90, **9**: 247, **10**: 172, **11**: 377

Loose (Beaver, Bear) Creek, **2**: 267, 269n, **9**: 9, 9n, 376, **10**: 11, 11n, **11**: 16–17, 17n

Lord Island, **7**: 17n

Lorimier, Agatha, **2**: 108, 109n

Lorimier, Auguste, **2**: 108, 109n

Lorimier, Louis, **2**: 105–8, 109n, 237, 238n

Lorimier, Louis, Jr., **2**: 108, 109n

Lorimier, William, **2**: 108, 109n

Lost Boy Creek, **8**: 257, 259, 262n

Lost (Paint, White Lime) Creek, **3**: 46–47, 47–48n, **9**: 53, 54n, **10**: 35, 35n, **11**: 69, 69n. *See also* Bazile Creek

Lost Horse Creek, **5**: 190n, 194, **8**: 163, 164n, **11**: 304–5, 305n

Lost Trail Pass, **1**: 10, **5**: 186n, **9**: 217n, **10**: 137n, **11**: 299n

Lotus, American, **2**: 144, 144n, 221–23, 224n

Louisiana, **10**: 6n, 79n, 63–64n, 272n, **11**: 4n, 5n, 8n, 432n

Louisiana Purchase, **1**: 3, **2**: 1, 3–4, 6, 59, 90n, 145n, 379n, **4**: 63n, **5**: 76n, **8**: 1, 348n, 368n, **10**: 226n, **12**: 3

Louisiana Territory, **1**: 5, 7, **2**: 6, 36, 59–61, 266, 512, **3**: 491n, **8**: 346, 347n, 348n, 363, 368n

Louis veneri (and similar spellings). *See* Medical problems, venereal disease

Louisville, Ky., **2**: 15, 18, 84, 101, 108, **8**: 418, 419n

Loupes Branch, **2**: 285–86, 288n, **9**: 11, 11n

Loup Indians. *See* Pawnee Indians, Loup or Skiri

Loup (Wolf) River, **2**: 363n, **3**: 348, 350–52, 384n, 397–98, 422, 424–27, **10**: 277n

Louservia (and similar spellings). *See* Lynx, Canada

L'outre Island. *See* La Loutre Island

Loutre River (Otter Creek), **9**: 7, 7n, 375, **10**: 9, 9n, **11**: 13–14, 14n

Lower Chehalis Indians, **6**: 28n, 77n, **10**: 199, 200n

Lower Chinookan language, **7**: 21n, 61n, **9**: 260n, 270, 270n, **10**: 202n. *See also* Chinookan language; Upper Chinookan language

Lower Chinook Indians, **6**: 34n, 76n, 77n, 78n, 185n, 218n, **7**: 41n

Lower Deer Creek (Beaver River), **8**: 194–96, 197n, 198n, 391, 408

Lower Memaloose Island (Sepulcher Rock), **7**: 118–21, 121n, 123–24, **8**: 386, 404, **9**: 292, 293n

Lower Oven Island, **2**: 393n. *See also* Oven Islands

Lower portage camp, **4**: 299, 301, 302n, 305, 319, 321, 329, 327–29, 331–34, 336, 338, 344, 350, **9**: 168–70, 169n, 172–74, 341n, **10**: 255, 255n, 257, 258n, **11**: 201n, 203, 203n, 208n, 210n

Lower Umpqua (Kil-la-wats) Indians, **6**: 476, 485, 491

Ludlow Member, **8**: 261n, 262n, 270n

Lues venerea (louis veneri), **5**: 122, 125n. *See also* Medical problems, venereal disease

Lukens, Isaiah, **2**: 66n

Lunch Creek, **8**: 26n, **9**: 323n, **10**: 240n

Lupine, seashore (cul-wha-mo), **6**: 60–61, 61n, 74, 76, 118, 133, 135, 139, 153–54, 224, 229, 230n, 233, 495

Lupines, **7**: 338n

Lupinus littoralis, **6**: 61n. *See also* Lupine, seashore

Lupinus sp., **7**: 338n. *See also* Lupines

Luscinia megarhynchos, **2**: 276n. *See also* Nightingale

Lutra canadensis, **3**: 35n, **4**: 40n, **5**: 20n, **6**: 162n, **7**: 190n, **8**: 120n, **9**: 88n, **10**: 58n, **11**: 103n. *See also* Otter, river

Luzula hitchcockii, **8**: 61n. *See also* Woodrush, smooth

Lydia, **6**: 29n, 86n, 432n, **9**: 252n, **11**: 392n

Lye, **6**: 230–31

Lyle site, **5**: 353n

Lynx, Canada, **3**: 27, 32, 35n, 256, 256n, 330, 426–44 passim, 482, **5**: 350, 352, 354n, **6**: 124, 124n, 327, 328n, 334

Lynx canadensis, **3**: 35n, **5**: 354n, **6**: 124n. *See also* Lynx, Canada

Lynx rufus, **2**: 167n, **3**: 256n, **6**: 328n, **8**: 267n. *See also* Bobcat

Lynx rufus fasciatus, **6**: 77n, **7**: 26n, **9**: 260n, **11**: 405n. *See also* Bobcat, Oregon

Lyon, Matthew, **2**: 237, 238n

Lysichitum americanum, **7**: 47n. *See also* Cabbage, skunk

M

McCarthy Creek, **7**: 26, 31n, 34, 37n

McClain, **2**: 201, 202n, 207

McClellan, Robert, **8**: 288, 289n, 344, 345n, 349–50, 350n, 356n, 357–59, 358n, 364n, 368n, **9**: 361–62, 362n, **10**: 278, 278n

McClallen (McClellan), John, **2**: 516–17, 522, **8**: 363, 364n, 365, **9**: 364, 364n, **10**: 279, 280n

McCoy Creek, **5**: 190n, **11**: 304–5, 305n

McCracken, Hugh, **1**: 8, **3**: 199, 201n, 218, 224, **9**: 90, 90n, **10**: 59, 59n, **11**: 104, 105n

McDonald Creek, **8**: 181, 185, 188n

McDuff Rapids, **9**: 317n

Mace, **6**: 175, 178n, 197

Mace (Ordway's) Creek, **2**: 357–58, 360n, 361n, **9**: 22, 22n

McFarlane, Andrew, **2**: 138

McGarry Bar, **9**: 156n

McGee, **6**: 155–56, 160n, 427

McGuire (Diamond, Swan, White Goose) Island: and Indians, **6**: 13; camped on, **6**: 13, 14n, **9**: 249, **10**: 166, **11**: 384; described, **6**: 16; hunted on, **6**: 16, **11**: 385; arrive at, **7**: 39, **10**: 166; distances, **8**: 386; listed, **8**: 405; mentioned, **6**: 15, 20n, **7**: 44n, **9**: 249n, 285, 286n, **10**: 166n, 167n, 205, 206n, **11**: 384n, 387n, 438–39, 440n. See also Government Island

McIntosh, Pa., **2**: 70, 70n, 81

Mackay, James, **1**: 5–7, 12, 16n. 46, 17nn. 51, 55–56, 62, **2**: 6, 60, 154, 154–55n, 225n, 304, 305n, 336, 446n, 460, 475–76, 478n, **3**: 70–71, 73n, 184n, **8**: 354n, **10**: 78n. See also Evans, John Thomas

Mack Creek, **8**: 251, 254, 257n

McKeehan, David: as Gass's editor, **2**: 12, 36, 542, **10**: xvi–xvii, 4n, 9n, 61n, 70n, 73n, 76n, 114n, 123n, 135n, 138n, 144n, 157n, 160n, 172n, 174n, 199n, 200n, 226n; notes, **2**: 32, **10**: 4n, 9n, 13n, 16n, 21n, 34n, 43n, 48n, 51n, 60n, 63–64n, 66–67n, 70n, 78n, 79n, 91n, 93n, 155n, 156n, 177n, 204n, 206n, 211n, 226–27n, 229n, 248n, 252n, 270n, 272–73n; and Lewis, **2**: 36, **10**: xvi–xvii

McKees Rocks, **2**: 65, 66n

Mackenzie, Alexander, **1**: 5, **2**: 3, **5**: 1, 4, 198n, **6**: 107n, **8**: 58n, **10**: 4n, 6n, 43n, 48n, 60n, 63n, 78n, 155n, 156–

57n, 177n, 204n, 206n, 211n, 226n

McKenzie, Charles, **1**: 8, **2**: 518, **3**: 238, 241, 242n, 276n, 277, 290, 297–98, 306–7, 312n, 313, 316n, 318–19, 329, 332, 492n, **4**: 95n, **8**: 289, 289n, **9**: 110, 110n, 115, 121n, 123, **10**: 70, 70n, **11**: 121, 121n

McKenzie Head, **6**: 63, 67n, **9**: 255n

McKenzie (Lookout, Sentinal) Creek, **3**: 133–34, 136n

Mackenzie River, **10**: 6n

Mackey. See McGee

Mackinac, **8**: 346, 347n

Mackinac, Mich., **2**: 192, 192n

Mackinac, Straits of, **3**: 206n

McKissock Island, **2**: 386n, **10**: 21, 21n. See also Bald (Chauvin) Island

Maclura pomifera, **2**: 210n. See also Osage orange

McMahon, Bernard, **2**: 210n, **12**: 3, 9n

McNairy Formation, **2**: 104n

McNeal, Hugh: listed, **2**: 148, 187, 189, 195, 197, 199, 254, **4**: 9, 11, **8**: 74, 77, 86n, 139n, **11**: 4n, 7n, 405n, 411n; separated, **2**: 155, **6**: 125; in permanent party, **2**: 229n; biographical sketch, **2**: 519; sent out, **4**: 359, **7**: 125, 129n, 133–34, 325, 328, **8**: 109, **9**: 179, 199, 265–66, 320, 330, 338, 338n, **10**: 108, 183, 236, 247, 253, **11**: 410; scouting, **5**: 61–62, **10**: 123, **11**: 261; creek named for, **5**: 67n, 76n, 83–84, **9**: 202n, 266, **10**: 125n; duties, **5**: 71, 88, 95, 103, 109, **8**: 291; medical problems, **6**: 35, 242n, 254–55, 330, 332, 333n, 336–37, 356–57, 391, 393, **8**: 79; votes, **6**: 84; returns, **6**: 126, **7**: 345; visits whale site, **6**: 169, 172n; and Indians, **6**: 181, 189, 194, **7**: 277, 279, 343–44, **9**: 266, **11**: 412;

loses horse, **7**: 162, 164; and species, **8**: 2, 110, 111n; lost, **9**: 261, **11**: 405; and saltmaking camp, **10**: 187; trading, **10**: 212; hunting, **11**: 217; mentioned, **5**: 68–69, 74, **9**: 179n, 265n, 279, 320n, 330n, 373n, 395n, **10**: 109n, 123n, 183n, 188n, 212n, 237n, 248n, 254n, **11**: 217n

McTavish, Simon, **3**: 308, 308n

Madison, James, **4**: 437, 439n, **5**: 1, 7, 10n, **9**: 191n, **11**: 246n

Madison, Wis., **9**: xvii

Madison Group, **5**: 61n, 87n, **8**: 180n

Madison Mountains, **4**: 434–35, 438n, **11**: 241–42, 242n

Madison Plateau, **5**: 157n

Madison River (Middle Fork): name, **1**: 10, **4**: 4, **5**: 1, 7, **9**: 191n, 200, **10**: 123, **11**: 263; distances, **3**: 382, **4**: 437, **6**: 450, **8**: 393; arrive at, **4**: 427–28, **8**: 179, 180n, **10**: 118, 119n, **11**: 242–43, 244n, 245–46, 246n; described, **4**: 428, 435, **5**: 7, **8**: 183, 412, **9**: 191, **10**: 118, 118n; and Indians, **5**: 150; listed, **6**: 465; latitude, **8**: 413; mentioned, **4**: 75n, 427, 431, 434–36, 438, **5**: 10n, 18, 58–60, 60n, 157n, **6**: 308, 310, **8**: 40, 42, 175, 182

Madisons Cave, **6**: 356, 358n

Madrone, Pacific, **6**: 103, 105n

Magnesia, **6**: 178, 193

Magnesium sulphate, **4**: 23n, 120n, **5**: 39n

Magnets, **7**: 58, 80

Magnolia, **6**: 105n

Magpie, black-billed, **2**: 484n, 523, **3**: 1, 76, 79n, 82–85, 85n, 104, 146–47, 293, 330–31, 331n, 482, **4**: 27–28, 29n, 36, 40, 41n, 75, 78, 93, 348, **6**: 379–80, 381n, **7**: 131, 135n, 193, 320, **8**: 146, 146n, 326, 327n, 417, 418n, **9**: 61, 61n, 123, 123n, 126, 127n, **10**: 40–41, 41n, 238, **11**: 76–77, 76n, **12**: 3

Maha (and similar spellings) In-
dians. *See* Omaha Indians
Mahaha (and similar spellings)
Indians. *See* Hidatsa Indians,
Awaxawi
Mahawha (Marharha) village, **3**:
203, 205n, 209, 211–12, 309,
311–12, 403, **9**: 91, 91n, 127,
127n, **10**: 78n, **11**: 133, 134n
Mahhaha site, **3**: 312n
Mahonia repens, **12**: 6
Major Creek, **7**: 119, 122n, **9**:
292n, **10**: 210, 211n
Makah (Quin-ne-chart) Indians,
6: 161n, 416, 416n, 472n,
476, 486, 491
Makes-Tracks-Far-Away (Big
Track, Big Foot), **2**: 267n
Malacosoma disstria, **7**: 312n. *See
also* Caterpillar, tent
Malaria. *See* Medical problems
Ma-laŭgh, **6**: 73, 77n
Malboeuf (Mabbauf), Etienne,
1: 17n. 73, **2**: 255, 526, 528,
3: 227n, **4**: 12n
Malheur River, **7**: 182, 184,
186n
Mallard, **3**: 221, 223n, **4**: 23,
24n, 46, 436, 438n, **5**: 11,
13n, 33, 309, **6**: 96, 98n,
161–62, 383, 385, 395–98,
400, **7**: 9, 11n, 23, 166, 168,
193, 226, **10**: 160, 160n
Mallets, **5**: 288, **6**: 113
Malnutrition. *See* Medical
problems
Maloney Creek, **9**: 318n
Malta Bend, **9**: 364n, **10**: 280n
Malus diversifolia, **6**: 19n, **7**: 17n,
10: 196n. *See also* Crabapple,
Oregon
Mammoth, **3**: 340
Mandan Indians: trade, **1**: 3, **2**:
482n, **3**: 137n, 201n, 315n,
331n, 422–23, 425–29,
483–84, 487, **9**: 100; villages,
1: 5–9, 12, **2**: 2–3, 7–8,
144n, 154–55n, 478n, **3**: 2–
3, 37n, 56n, 127n, 184–87,
186n, 188n, 189–96, 198n,
201n, 203–4, 205n, 207n,
212, 213n, 214n, 225n,
227n, 236, 250n, 270–71,

270n, 275n, 277–78, 290,
295, 295n, 298, 312, 373,
381, 385n, 404, **4**: 9, 11, 14,
5: 86n, **7**: 343n, **8**: 3–4, 74,
77, 78n, 112, 139n, 159n,
209–10, 212, 219, 265, 286,
295, 298, 300n, 303, 306,
308–9, 309n, 311, 357, 380–
81, 399, 412, 414, 417, **9**: 81,
88–91, 90n, 93, 98, 104,
106–8, 126–27, 127n, 129–
30, 172, 279, 306, 348–52,
361, 366n, **10**: 59n, 60–61,
60n, 61n, 63, 63n, 64, 66,
68, 70n, 76–77, 77n, 79n,
124, 124n, 125n, 266–67,
267n, 272n, 273n, **11**: xi,
105–7, 109, 132–33, 133n,
172, 208, 208n, 250; located,
1: 7, **3**: 166, 187, 193, 206n,
312, 362, 419, 462, 482, 496,
10: 63n, 79n, 272n; information from, **1**: 8–9, **3**: 137n, **4**:
2, 248, 251, 253n, **5**: 1, 187–
88n, **8**: 193n, 207n, 208n,
221n, 235n, 246n, 256n,
261n, **9**: 100, 145n, **10**: 64,
67, **11**: 108, 111, 143, 374n;
and members of the party, **1**:
9, **2**: 144, 511–12, 514–15,
526, **3**: 241; chiefs, **2**: 10, **3**:
160, 194–96, 197, 200n,
205n, 207, 208n, 213–14n,
215, 225–26, 252, 256, 261,
269, 275, 300, 308–10, 317,
8: 4, 212, 298, 301–2, 306,
314–16, 326, 338, **9**: 91–93,
95–96, 95n, 99–101, 115,
350–51, 350n, **10**: 60, 64,
267–68, **11**: 106–7, 133;
distances, **2**: 159, 485, **3**: 31;
listed, **2**: 195, **3**: 448; language, **2**: 438, 442n, **3**: 136,
138n, 153n, 200n, 201n,
205n, 206n, 208n, 234,
234n, 251, 251n, 257n,
261n, 385n, 490, **8**: 250n,
253, 256n, 259, 261n; peace,
3: 2, 156n, 159–60, 162,
165, 218, 239, 304, **4**: 10, **5**:
91, 130, **8**: 313–14, 316, **9**:
83, 125–26, **11**: 131; war, **3**:
159–61, 191–92, 234, 243–

44, 246, 251, 276, 284, 292,
296–97, 331, 412–13, 416–
17, **8**: 289, 303, 311–13, 315,
330, **9**: 99, 115, 119, 352, **10**:
74, **11**: 108–10; name, **3**:
163; and traders, **3**: 181–82,
220n, 241–42n, **9**: 86–87,
11: 101–2; customs, **3**: 189–
90, 190n, 197–98, 201n,
208–9, 211, 233, 234n, 239,
260, 268, 268–69n, 271,
272n, 298, 298–99n, 299,
313–14, 330, 331n, 404–5,
485–86, 488, 492n, **4**: 13,
55, **5**: 120, **6**: 191, 405–6, **8**:
308, 309n, **9**: 91, 104, **10**: 60,
71, 72n, 76n, **11**: 105–6,
122, 123n, 133; medical
problems, **3**: 191, 201n, 233,
273, 279, 281, 295, 297, 312,
324n, **8**: 308–9, **10**: 76n;
camps and lodges, **3**: 192,
193n, 199, 200n, 222, 229,
232, 489, **9**: 113; encountered, **3**: 194–95, 197, 199,
4: 13, **9**: 89–90, **10**: 58–59,
267, **11**: 104; historical
sketch, **3**: 201n, 401–3; relations with the party, **3**: 201n,
207–12, 216, 219 223, 227n,
238n, 239, 242, 245–47,
250, 252–54, 256, 261, 264,
266–70, 273–75, 279, 281–
82, 284, 286, 288–90, 293,
296–98, 308–9, 313, 317,
319, 327–28, 332, 486, **9**:
93–94, 98, 102–9, 111, 115,
120, 344–50, 358, **10**: 61,
63, 66, 68–69, 73, 75n, 77n,
267–68, war, **11**: 106–7,
114–16, 120, 133; councils,
3: 204, 207–12, 217–18, 288,
8: 300–302, **9**: 91–92, **10**:
60, 267; gifts, **3**: 215, 218–
19; and horses, **3**: 232, 259,
292, 320, 331, 489, **8**: 319,
10: 6, **11**: 116; hunting, **3**:
233, 243–44, 254, 265, 271–
72, 321, 326, 328, 362, 484–
85, **9**: 101, 103, **10**: 58–59,
64, 69, 73, **11**: 104, 111, 118,
120; clothes, **3**: 253, 488, **5**:
133–34, **8**: 307, 338, 418, **9**:

115; food, **3**: 272, 272n, 489, **5**: 144, **8**: 285, 335, **9**: 106–7, **11**: 132; visits, **3**: 276–77, **10**: 64, 66, 67; arms and ammunition, **3**: 329–30, **5**: 150; and specimens, **3**: 460, 466, 481; tobacco, **3**: 466, **5**: 81; appearance, **3**: 487, **5**: 121, **8**: 307, 318, **11**: 133, 277; artifacts, **4**: 430, **8**: 3, 106, 106n, 284, 285n; mentioned, **2**: 486n, **3**: 154n, 421, 424, 433, 436, **4**: 1, 17, 108, 171, 180, 201, 212, 278, **7**: 264n, **8**: 316n, 332, 352, 355, **9**: xi, 3n, 60, 92, 219n, **10**: xi, xvii, 53–54, 58, 59n, 60n, 73, 267n, **11**: 4n, 7n, 20, 20n, 98–99, 103, 137–38, 175, 304n, 397. *See also* Hidatsa Indians

Mandan Island, **3**: 293, 295n, 373, **10**: 72n

Manduca sexta, **8**: 266n. *See also* Hornworm, tobacco

Manitou Creek. *See* Moniteau Creek

Man-nes-surree (and similar spellings). *See* Tail of Calumet Bird

Man Wolf Chief (Ar-rat-toe-no-mook-gu), **3**: 208, 210, 212, 213n, 214n, 276n, 319n

Maple, bigleaf, **6**: 15, 17, 19n, 103, 104n, 294–95, 296n, **9**: 287, 287n, **10**: 166, 166n, 207n, **7**: 12–14, 14n, 19, 21, 32, 55, 77, 110, 111n, 112–13, 193

Maple, Rocky Mountain, **5**: 77, 85n, **8**: 28–29, 30n, **10**: 207n

Maple, silver, **2**: 78n, **9**: 377n, **10**: 15n

Maple, sugar, **2**: 78, 78n, 177, **8**: 416, 418n, **9**: 377, 377n, **10**: 15n

Maple, vine, **6**: 294–95, 296n, **7**: 112–13, 114n, **10**: 207n

Maple, white, **6**: 294–95

Maples, **6**: 7, 26, 96, 98n, **9**: 42, 42n, **10**: 15, 167, 207

Maps: mapmaking, **1**: 3–4; route maps, **1**: 4, 7–11, **4**:

337n, **6**: 47n; Lewis and Clark's map of 1814, **1**: 4, 12–13, 19nn. 129, 133, 135–36; Clark's map of 1810, **1**: 4, 12–13, 19nn. 133, 135–36, 139, **4**: 220n, **7**: 219n; King's map of 1803, **1**: 5, 16nn. 23, 25, **5**: 95n; Indian Office map, **1**: 6–7, 17n. 53; Clark-Maximilian maps, **1**: 7–11, 17n. 72, 18n. 99; Lewis and Clark's map of 1804, **1**: 7, 17n. 65, **2**: 153, 153n; Clark's map of 1805 (Hague's copy, State Department copy, War Department copy), **1**: 9, 12, 18nn. 84, 87, 91–92, 19nn. 128–29; Lewis and Clark's map of 1806, **1**: 12, 18n. 93, 19nn. 128–29, 133, **6**: 307, 309, 311n; Frazer's map of 1807, **1**: 12, 19nn. 124–25; Fort Clatsop map, **1**: 12, 19nn. 126, 133; Clark's map of 1814, **2**: 5, 38; in Elkskin-bound Journal, **2**: 23–25; in Field Notes, **2**: 134n; Clark's map of 1805, **3**: 3, 268n, 275n, 303, 303n, 308, 335, **4**: 26, 28n, **5**: 95n; from Heney, **3**: 258, 259n; Indian, **3**: 258, 276, 333, **5**: 88, 157, 231, 296, **6**: 181, **7**: 54, 56, 62, 66, 86, 92, 132, 135n, 149; Clark preparing, **3**: 268–69, 302n, **4**: 266, 336–37, 362; Big White's, **3**: 270n; cached, **4**: 336–37, 359, 362, **8**: 107; Arrowsmith's of 1802, **4**: 266–67, 269n, **7**: 219n; Lewis's, **4**: 435, 438n; Nez Perce, **7**: 3, 227, 231, 315n, 318n; Yelleppit's, **7**: 177n; for Nez Perces, **7**: 242, 244; sketch, **8**: 92n, 197n, 203n; lost, **8**: 108n, 288n; Lewis carrying, **8**: 139n; mentioned, **2**: 7, 12, 28, 36, 211, 415–16, 417–18n, 423n, 428, **6**: 3, **7**: 70n, 74n, 104n, 141n, 151n, 168n, 169n, 172n, 190n, 233n, 315n, 318n, 342n, **8**: 281n, 299n,

372n, 376, 415n, **11**: 5n, **12**: 1, 3. *See also* Arrowsmith, Aaron; Clark, William; Drouillard, George; Evans, John Thomas; Frazer, Robert; King, Nicholas; Mackay, James; Maximilian, Alexander Philip; Soulard, Antoine

Marais des Cygnes River, **2**: 324n

Marcasite, **2**: 234n, 500, 502n

Margaret, **6**: 160n

Margaritanidae, **2**: 484n, **4**: 333n, **9**: 174n, **11**: 175n. *See also* Mussels

Marharha (and similar spellings). *See* Mahawha village

Marias River: and maps, **1**: 9, 11; explored, **2**: 8, **8**: 1–2, 74, 86n, 121, **9**: 162, 330, 330n, 341, **10**: 247, 253, 259, **11**: 184–87; arrive at, **4**: 2, 242–43, 245–47, 245n, 252n, **8**: 138, **9**: 342, **10**: 97, 259, **11**: 183; decision at, **4**: 2, 251, 256–58, 260–61, 265–66, 271, 274, **8**: 126, **9**: 161–62, **11**: 183–88, 190; name, **4**: 220n, 266, **7**: 342, 343n, **9**: 161n, **10**: 97n, 100; conditions, **4**: 247, 249, 257n, 265–66, **8**: 139, 147; described, **4**: 248–49, 255, 267, **8**: 115, 118–19, 119n, 120, 124n, **9**: 162, 164, **11**: 184–85, 190–91; animals and plants, **4**: 253n, 276, 347, **8**: 118–19, 139, **9**: 161–62, **11**: 184–85, 188, 191; characteristics, **4**: 254, **8**: 121n; deposit at, **4**: 275–76, **7**: 93n, **8**: 106, 138, 295, 349, **9**: 164–65, 338, 338n, 342, 343n, **10**: 101, 259, 260n, **11**: 192–93; distances and latitude, **4**: 276, **5**: 195, **6**: 449, 492, 493n, 496, **8**: 77, 116–17, 119, 292, **9**: 162, **11**: 174; listed, **6**: 464, **8**: 382, 401, 412; Indians, **7**: 333, **8**: 109, 125, 127, 131, 135, 137, 139n, 280n, 294, 388, 414, **10**: xv, 98n; accidents on,

Marias River (*continued*)
8: 109–10, 113; hunting on,
8: 115, 9: 161, 164–65, 11:
183–88, 190–92; camped
on, 8: 116n, 117n, 9: 161n,
162n, 10: 98, 99n, 254,
259n, 11: 183; mentioned, 4:
124, 129n, 260n, 272, 277–
78, 324, 5: 196n, 8: 37, 104,
112, 117, 118n, 120n, 123n,
128, 132n, 278, 291, 293,
9: 334, 334n, 10: 258, 11:
175n, 184n, 186n, 187n, 191
Marietta, Ohio, 2: 80–81, 81n
Marigold, fetid, 4: 262n
Marion (Bad Humored) Island,
3: 109n, 112, 114, 114n, 9:
68n, 10: 45, 45n, 11: 85–86,
86n
Marks, Lucy Meriwether Lewis,
2: 173n, 12: 1
Marl. *See* Niobrara Chalk
Mar-lock-ke, 6: 77n, 154
Marmot, yellow-bellied, 5: 126,
131n, 7: 163, 165n, 167, 10:
131, 132n
Marmota flaviventris, 5: 131n, 7:
165n, 10: 132n. *See also* Mar-
mot, yellow-bellied
Marmota monax, 5: 131n, 7:
165n, 9: 32n. *See also*
Woodchuck
Mar-noh-tah. *See* Big Stealer
Maropa River. *See* Rampart
Creek
Marshall, Moses, 2: 1, 2
Marshall Creek, 8: 87, 89n, 100
Marsh (Seal) Island, 6: 395,
397, 397n, 7: 9–10, 11n, 9:
280, 281n, 11: 433, 433n
Marten, 3: 2, 27, 32, 34n, 330,
331n, 409–44 passim
Martes americana, 3: 34n. *See also*
Marten
Martes pennanti, 6: 317n, 9:
242n, 11: 364n. *See also*
Fisher
Martha's Island, 3: 60n
Martin. *See* Swallow, cliff
Martin, bee. *See* Kingbird
Martin, brown, 3: 10, 13n
Martin, purple, 4: 110, 111n,
235, 7: 76, 78n

Martin Island, 6: 23, 25n
Martin site, 6: 70n
Mary, 6: 160n
Marystown Creek, 2: 123, 124n
Mastiff, 6: 339–40
Masts. *See* Keelboat; Pirogue,
white
Matootonha (and similar spellings). *See* Mitutanka village
Matricaria discoidea, 12: 10n
Matricaria matricarioides, 4:
262n. *See also* Pineapple weed
Mats, 5: 250, 285–88, 290, 305,
311, 325, 361, 371, 6: 33, 61,
74, 76, 77n, 90, 97, 118–20,
133–36, 146–47, 153, 186,
192, 196, 216–17, 219–20,
305, 307, 307n, 378, 380,
434–35, 438–39, 7: 38, 54,
56, 59, 82, 129, 145, 147,
149, 151n, 158, 159n, 210,
216, 218, 233, 235, 239–40,
242, 244, 10: 160n, 170
Maxent, Laclede, and Company,
2: 130n
Maximilian, Alexander Philip,
Prince of Wied-Neuwied, 1:
7–11, 18n. 99, 2: 471n,
494n, 3: 74n, 91n, 106n,
114n, 153n, 205n, 228n,
229n, 297n, 307n, 4: 19n,
8: 245n
Mayapple, 2: 208, 209n
Mayfield Creek, 2: 93, 94n
Maysville (Limestone), Ky., 2:
81, 81n, 515, 521
Mdewakanton Sioux Indians. *See*
Sioux Indians, Mdewakanton
Meadowlark, eastern, 4: 325–
26, 326n, 6: 379–80, 381n
Meadowlark, western, 3: 12n, 4:
29n, 325–26, 326n, 6: 379–
80, 381n, 7: 195n, 196, 198,
198n
Meadow Portage (Source at
Lake Manitou), 2: 225, 226n
Meadow (Zoncar, Zon Cau)
Creek, 2: 275–76, 277n, 9:
10, 10n, 377, 11: 18, 18n
Meal, parched, 3: 232, 292, 313,
4: 28, 275, 279, 287, 334–
35, 379, 5: 53, 75, 87, 8: 138,
146, 9: 166. *See also* Corn

Meares, John, 6: 36n, 191n, 11:
395n
Mears, James A., 12: 6
Meat. *See* Jerky; Pemmican;
Provisions
Medals, 3: 24, 29, 31, 210, 242
Medals, Indian peace, 2: 439–
41, 443n, 492, 494n, 3: 24,
30, 107–8, 111–12, 121–22,
209, 212, 214–15n, 215,
310, 318, 4: 11, 5: 112, 115,
188, 226–27, 231, 252n,
269n, 278, 291, 301, 303,
307n, 335, 337, 339, 341–
42, 6: 72–73, 75, 123, 142,
144, 172n, 192, 196, 198n,
330, 332, 432n, 7: 15–16,
17n, 28, 30, 106, 109, 165,
167, 173, 176, 177n, 183,
185, 211, 213, 215n, 238,
240, 241n, 242–43, 245n, 8:
77, 78n, 79, 130, 133, 135,
294, 312–15, 316n, 317n,
338, 9: 33, 34n, 41, 49, 67,
79, 121, 123, 205, 208, 219,
229, 240–41, 246, 281, 283,
290, 297, 299–300, 10: 50,
50n, 149, 158, 162, 175, 259,
270, 270n, 11: 50, 51n, 57–
58, 66, 85, 301–2, 357–58,
360, 370–71, 374, 396, 434,
436
Mede,thunk,a, 9: 49, 51, 51n,
67, 68n
Medical problems: abscesses
and boils, 2: 60, 149, 306–7,
307n, 336, 357, 378, 388,
399, 415–16, 417n, 420,
420n, 426, 429–30, 3: 99,
109, 119, 260, 481, 4: 138,
168, 287, 295, 5: 1, 17–18,
20, 33, 35, 43, 46, 59, 63, 6:
122, 135, 7: 2, 210–13, 215,
217, 245n, 280n, 294, 296n,
297, 302, 330–31, 334–36,
346–47; dysentery, 2: 60,
306–7, 307n, 4: 109–10,
111n, 118, 271, 274–75,
277–78, 280, 5: 25–26, 31–
32, 215, 6: 122; goiter, 2: 81;
ague and fever, 2: 81–82,
82n, 86, 99, 278, 4: 309,
310n, 317–18, 365, 436,

438, **7**: 186, 278, 289, 297, 302, **10**: 152; malaria, **2**: 82n, 86n; unidentified, **2**: 101, 108, 154–55, 165–66, 170, 172–73, 172n, 182–83, 190–92, 242, 248, 289, 397, 426, **3**: 19–20, 204, 233, 268, 277, 279–81, 317, **4**: 52, 271, 274, 333–35, 337, 365–66, 378, 386, **5**: 1, 4, 7, 9, 11, 13–14, 24n, 219, 223, 227, 229, 232–34, 233n, 243, 243n, 245–46, 249, 253, **6**: 96, 105–7, 121, 293, 295–97, 307, 309, 311n, 312, 314, 321, 324, 330, 332–33, 339–40, 342, 344, 347, 349, 356–57, 368, 370, 374, 376, 384–85, 393, 416, 419, 429–30, 450, **7**: 10, 30, 104, 213, 246–47, 272–73, **8**: 359, **9**: 28, 33, 33n, 143, 165–67, 170, 174–75, 183, 190–91, 229, 260–61, 271–74, 273n, 313, 330, 387, 391, **10**: 85–86, 107, 110, 113, 131, 192–93, 192n, 203, 203n, 232–33, **11**: 47, 146, 147n, 194–97, 203, 211–13, 225, 343n, 367, 400, 404, 406, 419–20, 422, 424; headaches, **2**: 168, 282, 357–58, **4**: 287, 289n, **6**: 332, 337, **8**: 55; colds and sore throats, **2**: 272–73, 282, 293, 306, 429, **3**: 240, **6**: 53–54, 122, 140–43, 312, 314–15, 336–37, 444, **7**: 186; eyes, **2**: 310, **3**: 297, 297n, 453, 460, 462, **4**: 65, 66n, 138, 168, **5**: 289, 291n, 367, 373, **7**: 2, 85, 95, 178, 181n, 186, 215, 217, 243–45, 249, 269, 271–72, **8**: 4, 366, **9**: 313, 365, **10**: 229; sunstroke, **2**: 355–57; fingers, **2**: 377–78, **4**: 281, 374n, 375, 376n, **5**: 45; appendicitis, **2**: 431n, 496n, **10**: 29n, **11**: 59n; colic, **2**: 492–93, **6**: 125, **7**: 261, 263, 265, **9**: 209, **10**: 28–29, 29n, **11**: 57–58, 283, 340–41; smallpox, **2**: 467, 469, 478–79,

482n, **3**: 161, 167n, 191, 201n, 207n, 233, 277n, 295, 312, 395, 398–403, 405, 440, **5**: 122, **6**: 81, 285–86, 286–87n, **7**: 65, 70n, 86, **8**: 308–9, **9**: 38, 358, 394; bowels, **2**: 494–95, **4**: 332, **5**: 3, 232, 235–36, 242, 244–48, **6**: 97, 98n, 105, 125, **7**: 269, 271, 278, **9**: 230, **10**: 147–48; peritonitis, **2**: 496n; poisoning, **2**: 500–501, 502n, **3**: 9; venereal disease, **3**: 3, 153n, 233, 234n, 273, 277, 277n, 322, 324, 324n, **4**: 66n, 302n, **5**: 122, 125n, 291n, **6**: 3, 65, 74, 76, 77n, 239–41, 242n, 254–55, 330, 332, 333n, 356–57, 391, 393, 416, 418, **7**: 89n, 181n, **8**: 79; hands, **3**: 89, 239, **6**: 44, **8**: 285, **9**: 383, **11**: 196–97; feet, **3**: 89, 293, 309, 309n, **4**: 249, 251, 328–29, 404–5, 407, 409–10, 414, 417, 427, 432, **5**: 42–43, 46–47, 60, **6**: 384–85, **7**: 163–64, **10**: 135, **11**: 120, 184–85, 240–41, 416; pleurisy, **3**: 155, 278–79, 281, 481; rheumatism, **3**: 160–61, 191, 194–96, 198–200, 198n, 230, 240, 481, **4**: 96, 98, **6**: 395, 443, **7**: 2, 178, 215, 217, 243–45, 249–50, 269, 271–72, **10**: 207; frostbite, **3**: 254–56, 265, 266n, 270–71, 273, 275, 276n, 279, 294, 297, 486, **9**: 101, 109, **10**: 65, 65n, 69, **11**: 119–21, 416; snakebites, **3**: 258n, 325, 489; teeth, **3**: 258n, **4**: 281, 294–95, **5**: 367, 373; sweat baths, **3**: 279; rabies, **3**: 325, 489, **8**: 286n; diarrhea, **3**: 481, **5**: 3, **6**: 97, 98n, 105, **11**: 334; lame, **4**: 11; scurvy, **4**: 139n; malnutrition, **4**: 139n, **5**: 177, 215, 226, 230, **6**: 181, 441–42; abdomen, **4**: 267–77, 279, 281, 287, 294, 297–301, 303, 306, 309; pelvis, **4**: 302n; fatigue, **4**: 329, 334,

336, 350, 412, 423, 431–33, 433n, **5**: 38, 43, 46–47, 54, 75–76, 84, 98, 100, 107, 201, 204–6, 215, 230, **6**: 181, 188, 194, **9**: 273, 387, **11**: 241, 368; bruises, **4**: 342–43, 345, 349n, **5**: 18, 162–63, **6**: 135, **8**: 200; legs, **4**: 350, **5**: 42, 44–45, 54, **6**: 443, **7**: 163–64, **8**: 35–36, 45–46, 57–58, 59n, 138, 162, **10**: 241, 257, **11**: 257–58; shoulders, **4**: 376–77, **5**: 17, **6**: 122, **11**: 168; ankles, **4**: 427–28, 432, **5**: 18, 54–55, **6**: 384–85, **7**: 163; back, **5**: 18, 24, **6**: 318, 329–30, 332, 337, 388, 390–91, 393–96, 443, **7**: 3, 104, 139, 146, 152, 154, 249–50, 282–86, 285n, 302, 304, 330–31, 346, **9**: 314, **10**: 232; skin, **5**: 215, 259, 260n; hips, **5**: 230, 232; sea sickness, **6**: 35–36; knees, **6**: 122, 293, 295, **7**: 178, 180, 212, **10**: 192–93, 192n, **11**: 419n; strains, **6**: 126–27, 140; fevers, **6**: 312, 314–15, 316n, 318–19, 321, 324, 332, 336–37, **8**: 159n; bile, **6**: 318–19; influenza, **6**: 335–37, **11**: 423, 423n; thighs, **6**: 443, **7**: 212, **8**: 3, 198n, 202–5, 209, 255; paralysis, **7**: 3, 243–45, 283–86, 288–89, 291, 294, 297, 299, 302, 304, 308, 310, 330–31, 334, 336, 346–47, **10**: 232, 232n; trachoma, **7**: 89n, 181n; arms, **7**: 178, 186; glaucoma, **7**: 181n; loins, **7**: 186, 249, 272; nose, **7**: 211; ulcers, **7**: 243–44; scrofula, **7**: 243–44, 245n; swelling, **7**: 250, 278, 280–82, 284–86, 289–91, 294, **8**: 281; headache, **7**: 261–63, 265, **11**: 196; depression, **7**: 273n; mumps, **7**: 280n; tonsillitis, **7**: 280n; wounds, **8**: 3–4, 156, 300n, 309, 316n, 319–20, 324–25, 329, 345, 347, 350, 354, **10**: 265–66; sunburn, **8**:

Medical problems (*continued*)
365–66; dermatitis, **8**: 366n,
9: 365n; infectious conjunctivitis, **8**: 366n, **9**: 365n; gunshot wound, **9**: 347, 350;
snake-bite, **10**: 18; syphilis,
10: 76, 76n. *See also specific Indian tribes; specific members of
the party*; Indians; Members
of the party
Medicine: supplies, **2**: 6, **4**: 29;
Rush's pills, **2**: 86, 86n, 496n,
3: 310, **4**: 436, 438, **5**: 232–
33, **6**: 318–19, 321n, **10**:
148; laxative, **2**: 86n, 165,
165n, 173n, **3**: 186n, 279n,
460, **7**: 212; unidentified, **2**:
172, 336, **3**: 260, 317, **4**: 281,
298, 303, 30, **5**: 7, **6**: 254–55,
7: 2, 139, 180, 186, 215, 283,
9: 299–300, 305, 309, **10**:
222, 225, 230, **11**: 335;
barks, **2**: 173, 173n, 345,
347, 349n, **4**: 297, 300–301,
302n, **5**: 11, 14n, **6**: 318, 321,
321n, 324, 333, 335, **8**: 158,
159n; bleeding, **2**: 356,
357n, 496n, **3**: 278–79, 281,
4: 276–77, 279, 302n, 334,
6: 429–30, **10**: 107, **11**: 212;
saltpeter, **2**: 356, 357n, **4**:
309, 310n; lancing, **2**: 420,
420n; salts, **2**: 500–501,
502n, **3**: 280, **4**: 22, 52, 271,
274, 287, 334–35, **5**: 234,
243; heat, **3**: 191; roots and
herbs, **3**: 258n, 304, 325,
330, 453, 460, 462, 464–65,
489, **6**: 105n, 120n, 239–41,
286n, 302n, 307n, 315, **7**:
277, 280n, **9**: 385; tea, **3**:
277, 281, **7**: 283, 286; amputations, **3**: 279, 281; baths, **3**:
279, 460, 488–89; greasing,
3: 279n; rattlesnake rattle, **3**:
291; steam, **3**: 297, 297n; diuretics, **3**: 460; poultices, **3**:
460, **4**: 138, 302n, **7**: 278,
280–82, 284, 287, 289–90,
331, 334, **8**: 46, 57–58, 59n,
205; laudanum, **4**: 109,
111n, 300–301, 302n, 309,
5: 158, 163n, **6**: 312, 315,

316n, 388, 390, **7**: 272–73,
273n, 284–85, 291, 294, **8**:
107; lead acetate, **4**: 138,
139n, **7**: 181n, 186, 187n;
zinc sulphate, **4**: 138, 139n,
7: 181n, 186, 187n; endangered, **4**: 152, 154; wet or
spoiled, **4**: 156–58, **5**: 52,
54–55, **8**: 164. **11**: 156–57;
astringent, **4**: 278, 279n,
308n; mineral water, **4**: 300,
306; sulphuric acid, **4**: 306,
308n; emetic, **4**: 365–66,
366n, **5**: 234; cached, **5**: 126;
essence of peppermint, **5**:
158, 163n; jalap, **5**: 234,
235n; mercury, **6**: 239, 241,
242n, 333n, 391, 393, **8**: 79;
potassium nitrate, **6**: 312,
315, 316n, 318–19; Scott's
pills, **6**: 329, 330n, 333, 335,
374, 376; alcohol, **6**: 388,
390, 390n; soap, **6**: 388, 390,
390n; liniment, **6**: 388, 390,
395–96, **7**: 209, 212, 272–
73; camphor, **6**: 388, 390, **7**:
139, 142n; flannel, **6**: 395–
96, **7**: 139, 186; sweat baths,
7: 3, 33, 283–86, 288, 290–
91, 294, 297, 299, 302, 304,
308, 310, 334, 336; eye water, **7**: 178, 180, 181n, 186,
209, 212, 215, 217, 246,
248–51, 269, 271–73, 281,
325, 328, **10**: 229, 230n; basilicon, **7**: 210, 213, 215n,
325, 328, 334, 336; tents,
7: 210, 213, 215n, **8**: 156,
157n, 319, 324; potassium
bitartrate, **7**: 211, 213, 215n,
269, 271, 278, 280, 282,
282n, 284–87, 289–90; sulphur, **7**: 211, 213, 215n, 269,
271, 278, 280, 282n, 284–
85, 289–90; Castile soap,
7: 212, 215n; cleaning and
dressing, **7**: 212, **8**: 35, 202,
204, 209, 295; linen, **7**:
215n; salve, **7**: 215n, 336;
balsam copaiba, **7**: 217,
220n; opium, **7**: 273n, **8**:
162; soup, **7**: 284–85, 289–
90; electricity, **7**: 286, 288n;

enema, **7**: 286, 288n, 289;
phosphorus, **7**: 325; lint, **8**:
156, 157n; chocolate, **8**: 359;
listed, **8**: 419; sweating, **9**:
313–14, **10**: 232–33; mentioned, **2**: 53
Medicine (Reubin's) Creek, **3**:
104, 106, 107n
Medicine (Tylor's, Turkey)
River, **3**: 96, 98, 99n, 359,
372, 380, **8**: 324–25, 324–
25n, 335, 380, 398, 417, **9**:
63, 63n, 354, 354n, **10**: 42,
42n, 272n, **11**: 80, 80n
Medicine River. *See* Sun River
Medicine Rock Coulee, **8**: 120n
Mediterranean Sea, **8**: 346
Meehan, Thomas, **12**: 6–8
Megginson Gulch, **7**: 208n
Melanerpes erythrocephalus, **4**:
238n, **5**: 195n, **7**: 297n, **8**:
144n, **9**: 221n, **10**: 239n, **11**:
308n. *See also* Woodpecker,
red-headed
Melanerpes lewis, **4**: 410n, **5**: 35n,
7: 266n, **8**: 78n, **10**: 239n. *See
also* Woodpecker, Lewis's
Melanoplus saguinipes, **8**: 208n.
See also Grasshopper, mi-
gratory
Melanoplus spretus, **8**: 208n. *See
also* Locust, Rocky Mountain
Melanterite, **2**: 502n
Meleagris gallopavo, **2**: 132n, **3**:
86n, **8**: 325n, **9**: 15n, **10**:
27n, **11**: 28n. *See also* Turkey,
wild
Melgares, Facundo, **8**: 364n
Melica bulbosa, **7**: 297n. *See also*
Oniongrass
Melica spectabilis, **7**: 297n. *See also*
Oniongrass, showy
Melons, **3**: 396, 399, 407
Melospiza melodia, **6**: 383n. *See
also* Sparrow, song
Memaloose (Sepulcher) Island,
5: 349, 352, 353n
Members of the party: and
maps, **1**: 9–13; recruits, **2**: 6,
59–60, 85n, 510; return
party, **2**: 7, 14, 18, 190n,
215n, 229n, 347, 415, 510–
11, 514, 516–17, 519–24,

526, 529, 529n, 533, **3**: 2, 4,
19, 21n, 78, 79n, 327, 328n,
331n, 333–34, **4**: 1, 7, 11,
12n, 359, **8**: 288, 289n, **10**:
77, 77n; permanent party, **2**:
14, 214, 215n, 509–11, 515–
17, 519–20, 522–23, 533, **3**:
327, 333, **4**: 1, 9, 11, 12n, **10**:
77, 77n; journals, **2**: 21,
229n, 237n, 374, 542–45,
565–67, **11**: vi, vii, xii, 14n,
16n, 19n, 23n, 25n, 27n,
28n, 30n, 38n, 40n, 41n,
47n, 97n, 138n, 319n; hunting, **2**: 23, 101, 131, 134,
141, 151, 155–56, 158, 165,
167, 175, 202, 230, 248, 254,
261–62, 270, 272, 275–76,
284–87, 289–90, 293, 296,
298, 307, 324–25, 327, 332–
34, 352, 354, 369, 380, 415,
418–19, 428–29, 432, 435,
457, **3**: 48–50, 55, 63, 66, 77,
79, 80–83, 87, 89–90, 96,
100–2, 147–48, 169, 176–
77, 179–80, 182–86, 188,
192, 226, 233, 238, 248–49,
253–57, 259, 261, 265, 267–
73, 278, 281, 284–86, 292–
93, 297, 300, 306, 486, **4**: 3,
22–25, 30–34, 36, 40, 45–
46, 48–58, 60, 62, 65–67,
70, 73–74, 81–82, 84–87,
96, 100, 108, 113, 115, 118,
121, 126, 128, 136, 141,
143, 149, 150–51, 154–59,
161, 165–68, 170, 174, 176,
181, 184–85, 202, 205, 208–
9, 217, 219, 227, 229, 232,
238, 240, 242, 244, 250, 252,
258–63, 266–67, 277, 280,
286, 302, 306–8, 310, 317–
18, 324, 327, 336, 344, 350–
52, 354, 356, 362–68, 373–
77, 379, 385, 387, 403, 406,
411–12, 414, 417–18, 420,
423, 426, 431–33, 435–36,
5: 7–8, 10, 18, 20, 31, 35–
39, 42–43, 45, 47, 52–53,
55–56, 58–59, 62–63, 65–
67, 71–72 75–76, 83–84,
87, 106–7, 112, 115, 117–
19, 123, 125–26, 133, 138,

140, 148–49, 152, 155, 162–
63, 165–67, 169, 173–75,
178–79, 183, 186–87, 189–
92, 196–97, 199, 201, 207,
211, 213, 216, 219, 223,
226–27, 229, 232–33, 235,
239, 242–44, 246, 274, 287,
291, 337, 339–45, 363, **6**: 3,
11–14, 22–23, 26–27, 36,
42, 53–54, 60–62, 69, 73,
81–83, 85, 91–93, 96–97,
101, 103–4, 108, 116, 140–
41, 145, 152–53, 166, 171–
72, 188, 192, 196, 199–200,
210, 222, 235–36, 239, 242–
43, 253, 255, 312, 314, 323–
24, 344, 351, 353, 381–82,
384, 398–400, 406–7, 444,
7: 16, 18, 21–25, 48, 50–51,
53–56, 62, 71, 74, 79, 87, 94,
116–17, 124–27, 130, 132,
141, 166, 168, 196–97, 199–
200, 221, 223, 226, 230,
232–36, 255, 260, 262, 264,
267–68, 270, 278–79, 314–
15, **8**: 10–11, 13–14, 17, 21–
25, 35–39, 41, 44–47, 52–
54, 62, 64–65, 68, 74, 77,
79–80, 82, 85, 87–88, 90,
93, 95, 99, 104, 106, 108,
111–15, 121–23, 126, 136,
138–41, 145–51, 154, 163,
165, 176, 179, 200, 206, 209,
224, 253, 259, 268, 282–83,
286–87, 307–9, 318, 321–
23, 325, 327–29, 338, 344,
351, 353, 355–56, 358–59,
364–65, **9**: 8–9, 12, 14, 19,
22–24, 27, 44, 54, 96, 101–
3, 105, 107–8, 112, 116,
136, 147–48, 161, 165, 167,
173, 179, 180, 187–88, 191,
209, 225, 245, 249, 251,
256–57, 261, 272, 274–76,
278, 284, 286, 303, 307, 312,
323, 326–28, 331, 337, 375–
76, 379, 382, 384, **10**: xii, 12,
24, 65–66, 72, 72n, 109,
132–33, 138–39, 141, 143,
194–98, 200, 207, 227, 238;
numbers, **2**: 59–60, 160–63,
164n, 218, 227, 228–29n,
3: 4, 327; unknown corporal,

2: 76–77, 76n; fishing, **2**: 89,
483, 485–86, **5**: 98, 106,
118–19, 138, 144–46, 152,
162–63, 167, 174–75, 183,
341–43, **6**: 42–43, 105, 344,
351, 384, **7**: 249, 275–76, **8**:
37, 39, 41, 125, **9**: 44–45,
10: 195–96; duties, **2**: 133–
34, 139–42, 151–52, 165,
175, 180–82, 206–7, 237n,
256–58, 262, 306–7, 315,
327, 332, 336, 407, 421,
428–29, **3**: 19–22, 40, 42,
76, 87, 96, 98, 109, 114,
121–23, 127, 139, 151–52,
230, 237, 251, 278, 289,
292–93, 300, 308, 310, 313,
317–18, 320–21, **4**: 3, 67,
113, 141, 248–49, 260, 269,
272, 274, 286, 289, 296, 300,
302, 304–6, 309, 323–24,
327, 338–40, 342, 344–46,
351–52, 354, 356, 365, 368,
370–71, 375–77, 379, **5**:
25–26, 119, 125, 133, 143,
158, 163, 174, 198, 216,
235–36, 244–45, 251–52,
288–89, 336–39, 366, **6**: 2–
3, 93, 96–97, 103, 121–23,
125, 127, 133–36, 138–43,
146–47, 179, 181, 186, 203–
4, 218–19, 230–31, 245–46,
265, 272, 290, 293, 328–29,
7: 48, 51, 54, 56, 79, 86, 90–
92, 98, 102, 104, 108, 115,
126, 128, 130, 142–44, 146,
164, 195, 236n, 267–68,
272–73, 275–76, 308, 310,
344–45, **8**: 32–33, 77, 106,
109, 146, 152–54, 156, 170,
173–74, 209, 211, 226, 272,
283, 290, 311, 328, 332, **10**:
xii, 264; sent out, **2**: 134,
180, 184, 187, 193, 205, 211,
214, 230, 283, 285, 306, 415,
452, 455–56, 456n, 469,
471–72, 478, 483–86, 488,
490, 497, 499, 502–4, **3**: 1,
9, 38, 107–9, 115, 117, 143,
151–52, 215, 219, 222, 225,
237, 239–40, 243, 245, 250,
266, 291, 294, 296, 304, 307,
317, **4**: 69, 84, 86, 174, 189,

Members of the party
(*continued*)

203, 222, 224, 228–29, 262, 286, 289, 296, 298–99, 301, 309, 318, 344–45, 359, 364, 366–67, 370, 373, 375–76, 378–79, 387, **5**: 14, 24n, 141, 152, 155, 173, 177, 182, 185, 202–3, 209, 218, 229, 244, 323, 331, 335, 338, 340, 342, **6**: 2, 4, 8, 46, 95, 105, 107–8, 122–25, 126, 133–34, 145, 161, 163, 167–68, 181, 189, 198–201, 203–4, 226–27, 239, 253, 255, 262, 262n, 267, 276–82, 287–88, 296–97, 325–26, 336, 358, 360, 365, 367, 381–82, 391, 393–94, 396, 401, 403, 406–7, 409, 411, 414–16, 418, 432, 436, **7**: 1, 9–10, 22, 24, 48, 50–51, 53, 62, 66, 75–76, 79, 86–87, 104–5, 108–9, 111–12, 115–17, 126–28, 137, 142, 151, 156, 162, 181, 183, 187, 189, 197, 199–200, 233, 255–56, 260, 293, 339–40, **8**: 1–3, 74, 77, 106, 111, 163–65, 166n, 169, 175, 205, 208, 210, 299, 328, 332, 337, 349, 352–53, 414; medical problems, **2**: 214, 365, 484, **3**: 322, 324, **4**: 10, 70, **5**: 209, 235–37, 244–45, 320, **6**: 42–43, 125, 162–63, 336–37, **8**: 4, 21, 366, 366n, **9**: 191, 209, 229–30, 260–61, 271–74, 314, 330, 383, 387, 391, **10**: 18, 28–29, 85–86, 107, 113, 131, 147–48, 152, 192, 232–33, 257, **11**: 196–97, 340–41, 367–68, 400, 422–23; pay and allowances, **2**: 239, 240n; recreation, **2**: 239, 293, 488–89, **3**: 215–16, 218–19, 241, 261, 266–67, 318, 322, 324, **5**: 173, 329, 336, 342–43, **7**: 127–28, 160–61, 166, 168, 178–82, 185, 347, 349, **8**: 80, **9**: 40, 107; separated, **2**: 263, **4**: 96, 100n, **6**: 161, 284–85, 307, 309, 318, 321,

395–96, **7**: 23, 25, 71, 74, 116, 153, 157–58, 323, 325; scouting, **2**: 275, 277–79, 287, 317, 321–22, 355, 423–24, **3**: 150, **4**: 1, 3–4, 66–68, 74, 136, 139, 170, 189, 191, 247, 249, 251–58, 260–63, 265–67, 302, 310, 347, 419, **5**: 1–3, 20, 25, 113, 115, 116n, 117, 285, 287, **6**: 1, 91n, 93, 101, 105, 116–17, **7**: 79, **8**: 39–42, 74, 77, 104, 114, 414, **9**: 115; morale, **2**: 292–93, 319–20, 430, **3**: 3, 40, 127, 208, 239, 261, 318, 322, 324, **4**: 10, 70, 153, 217, 219, 225, 230, 249, 271–72, 274, 298, 319, 328–29, 332–33, 345, 359–62, 382, 412, 416, **5**: 75–76, 100, 113, 163, 175, 213, 215, 235, 252–53, **6**: 38, 65, 67, 106, 108, 211–12, **7**: 222, 224, 239–40, 349, **8**: 24, 32, 34, 141, 146, 354, 360, 365–67, 369; return, **2**: 323, 478–79, 483, 488, **3**: 271, 275, 292, 318, **4**: 152, 193, 196, 261, 266–67, 289, 300–301, 318, 345, 351, 363, **5**: 179, 182–83, 190, 357, **6**: 60, 106, 108–9, 114, 121–22, 127, 192, 195, 199–200, 227, 229, 242–43, 275–76, 287–88, 312, 314, **7**: 24–25, 39–40, 54, 56, 86, 88, 118, 120, 139, 152, 272, **8**: 107, 174, 179, 338, 342, 368; collect food, **2**: 433, **4**: 416, 420, **5**: 106, **8**: 288, 326, 361; biographical sketches, **2**: 509–29; and Indians, **3**: 174, 203–4, 221, 260, 266–67, 271, 282, **5**: 83, 121, 232, **6**: 3, 73–75, 85, 148n, 331–32, 416, 418, 425–28, 428n, **7**: 9n, 10, 12–13, 33, 79, 94–95, 99, 105–6, 152, 158, 239–40, 249, 274–76, 284–85, 287, 289–91, 339, 341–42, 348–49, **8**: 14, 17, 23, 79–80, 302; accidents, **3**: 232, **4**: 29, 152–54, 160–62,

5: 251, 271–72, **8**: 83, 85, **9**: 324, 340, 385, **10**: 63, 120n, 257; and species, **4**: 132, 215, 218, 281, 367, **6**: 130, 351, 354, **7**: 77, 275–76, 282, 298, 309, 311, 320, **8**: 2, 190, 226, 280–81; and iron-frame boat, **4**: 324, 333, 350–51, 354, 359, 362–63, 365, 371; and upper portage camp, **4**: 325, 329–30, 334, 350; and lower portage camp, **4**: 327, 331–32, 336–37; information from, **4**: 369–71, **6**: 383, **7**: 55, 246–47, 301, 345, **8**: 33, 39, 41; and saltmaking camp, **6**: 140n, 171, 175, 177, 188, 190, 192, 195, 235–36, 242–43, 253–55, 275–76, 321–22, 324–26, 328–29, 333, 335; and liquor and tobacco, **8**: 172, 348, 351, 355, 358, 359n, 360, 367; mentioned, **2**: 65, 66n, 206, 242–43, 300, 310, 338, 353, 401–3, 405, 436, **3**: 4, 8, 10, 111, 119, 124, 128, 130, 140, 144–45, 200, 223, 227, 299, 304, 306–7, 454, **4**: 101, 105, 201, 212–13, 246, 265, 294, 320, 342–43, 349n, 394, 407, **5**: 18, 77–80, 92, 95–97, 104, 106, 170, 172, 201, 228, 317, 327, 329, 333, **6**: 18, 37, 40–41, 49–50, 66, 76, 151, 193, 223–24, 281–82, 339–41, 347, 349, 374, 376, 429–31, 432n, **7**: 15, 30, 57, 64, 78, 148–49, 174, 176, 216, 218, 237, 248, 276–77n, 288, 332, **8**: 7, 21, 63, 97, 137, 155, 157, 161, 177n, 293, 295, **11**: xiii–xiv. *See also En-gagés;* Medical Problems; *specific members of the party*

Memoranda of Lewis and Clark, miscellaneous, **2**: 563–65

Ménard, Pierre, **3**: 196–97, 198n, 234, 270n, 492n, **5**: 10n

Menetarra village, **3**: 249, 318, 404, **8**: 305n, **9**: 127, 127n, **10**: 77, 78n, **11**: 133, 134n

Mentha arvensis, **4**: 333n, **7**: 285n, **10**: 106n, **11**: 175n. *See also* Mint, field

Mentha pulegium, **7**: 338n. *See also* Pennyroyal

Mephitis mephitis, **3**: 85n, **4**: 200n, **5**: 140n, **6**: 317n, **7**: 70n, **9**: 155n. *See also* Skunk, striped

Meramec River, **2**: 126–27, 127n, 128n, **3**: 338, 475

Merchandise. *See* Indians, gifts; Provisions

Mercury. *See* Medicine

Mercury (planet), **2**: 299n

Merganser, common, **4**: 324, 324–25n, 425n, **5**: 35n, **6**: 384n, **7**: 47n

Merganser, red-breasted, **4**: 324, 324n, 425n, **5**: 35n, **6**: 384n, **7**: 47n

Mergansers (red-headed fishing duck), **4**: 408, 423, **6**: 383, 385, 396–97, **7**: 45

Mergus merganser, **4**: 325n, **5**: 35n, **6**: 384n, **7**: 47n. *See also* Merganser, common

Mergus serrator, **4**: 324n, **5**: 35n, **6**: 384n, **7**: 47n. *See also* Merganser, red-breasted

Meriwether's Bay. *See* Young's Bay; Youngs Bay

Mertensia paniculata, **8**: 30n. *See also* Bluebells, tall

Mertensia platyphylla, **7**: 195n. *See also* Bluebells

Mertensia virginica, **2**: 210n, **7**: 195n. *See also* Cowslip, Virginia

Meship, **6**: 155, 427. *See also* Winship, Jonathan

Message from the President (Jefferson), **2**: 538

Metaharta (Metehartar) village, **3**: 3, 206–7n, 209, 211–12, 214n, 215n, 229n, 249, 311, 404, **8**: 298, 303, 303n, **9**: 98, 99n, 127, 127n, **10**: 77, 78n, **11**: 133, 134n

Met-cow-we Indians, **7**: 163–65

Methow Indians, **5**: 317, 319n, **7**: 164n, **10**: 159, 159n

Metolius River, **7**: 151n, 156, 159n, 182, 184, 186n

Mexico, **4**: 381n, **6**: 160n, **8**: 356n

Miami (Maumie) Indians, **2**: 174, 174n, **3**: 391, 446, 449

Miami River, **6**: 355

Mice, **3**: 141, 142n, 330, **4**: 15, 18n, 28, **6**: 313, 315, 317n, **11**: 217

Michaux, André, **2**: 2–3

Michilimackinac Island, **3**: 203, 206n, 389, 405–6, 408, 410–12, 483–84

Micropterus dolomieui, **2**: 72n, **9**: 40n. *See also* Bass, small-mouth

Micropterus salmoides, **2**: 72n, **9**: 40n. *See also* Bass, large-mouth

Microtus pennsylvanicus, **3**: 160n, **4**: 18n, **6**: 355n. *See also* Mouse, meadow

Middle Chinook language, **6**: 34n

Middle Fork Clearwater River, **7**: 290n, 325n

Midges, **2**: 186n, **7**: 46n

Mikey Butte, **4**: 169n

Miles Creek, **5**: 224n

Milk, **2**: 173, 237, 252, **9**: 365

Milk (Ah-mâh-tâh ru-shush-sher, River Which Scolds at All Others) River, **3**: 365, 367, 374, 382, **4**: 124–25, 127–28, 129n, 200n, 248, 251, 253n, **6**: 448, 463, **8**: 120n, 123, 123n, 147, 148n, 150, 151n, 381, 400, **9**: 144, 145n, **10**: 86, 262, **11**: 149–50, 150n

Milk River Hills, **4**: 125, 129n

Milkvetch, **8**: 193n

Milkvetch, Canada, **3**: 464, 469

Milkvetch, Missouri, **3**: 464, 469

Mill, corn, **9**: 82, 92, **10**: 60, **11**: 106, 193–94

Mill Creek (W. Va.), **2**: 71, 72n

Mill (Que-nett) Creek (Oreg.), **5**: 337, 339, 340n, 345, 377, **7**: 123–24, 125n, **9**: 245, 245n, 292, 293n, **10**: 162, 162n, 211n, **11**: 371–72, 372n

Mill (Scattered) Creek (Mont.), **5**: 191n, **6**: 466, **8**: 393, 410

Mill Creek Island, **2**: 79, 79n, 80n

Miller, John, **12**: 8n

Miller Creek, **8**: 82, 85, 86n, 100

Miller Island, **5**: 321, 326n, **7**: 155n, **9**: 243, 243n, **10**: 214, 214n

Mills, **3**: 199–200, 201n, 209–10, 213n, 221, 345, 357

Mimulus lewisii, **12**: 7

Mimus polyglottos, **2**: 276n, **4**: 163n. *See also* Mockingbird

Mine Hill, **2**: 275–76

Mineralogical Collections, **3**: 472–78

Minerals, **5**: 126. *See also specific minerals*

Miner Creek, **8**: 183, 186, 188n

Mine River. *See* Lamine River

Minetare (and similar spellings) Indians. *See* Hidatsa Indians

Minetares of Fort de Prairie Indians. *See* Atsina Indians

Miniconjou Sioux Indians. *See* Sioux Indians, Miniconjou

Minitari (and similar spellings) Indians. *See* Hidatsa Indians

Mink, **3**: 405–44 passim, **6**: 313, 315, 317n, 340–41, 355n, **7**: 62, 70n, **9**: 45, 45n

Minnesota Historical Society, **2**: 41

Minnesota River (St. Peters), **2**: 219, 497–98, 499n, **3**: 17, 18n, 23, 27–28, 32–33, 36, 47, 161, 166n, 169, 171n, 355, 357, 385n, 386n, 401, 408–13, 418–19, 480

Minnows, **2**: 486n

Mint, field, **4**: 331, 333n, **7**: 285n, **10**: 106, 106n, **11**: 171, 175, 175n. *See also* Peppermint

Mirabilis nyctaginea, **3**: 469. *See also* Four o'clock, wild

Mission Canyon Formation, **5**: 20n, 29n

Mission Canyon Limestone, **4**: 405–6n, 429n, 438n

Mission Range, **10**: 249, 249n

Mission (Stinking Cabin) Creek, **8**: 192n, 391, 409. *See also* Locke Creek

Mississippi River: and maps, **1**: 4–5, 7–9, 12, **10**: 273n; arrive at, **2**: 86–87, **9**: 366; conditions, **2**: 87, 93, 101, 114–15, 173, 173n, **3**: 347–48, **8**: 374; described, **2**: 99, 112, 218; affluents, **2**: 127n, **10**: 42, **11**: 79; inhabitants on, **2**: 147; navigational problems, **2**: 229–30; Indians, **3**: 27, 33, 406, 412, 419, 483, **8**: 347n; distances and latitudes, **3**: 337, 343, **8**: 377, 388–89, 414, **9**: 368n, **10**: 4n; trade on, **3**: 411; and specimens, **3**: 451–72; animals, **4**: 22, 31, **6**: 392, 394, 399–400, **8**: 416; plants, **7**: 200, **8**: 79, **10**: 279; mentioned, **2**: 2–3, 101n, 213, 213n, 292, 325n, 400, 436, 437n, 483, 513–14, **3**: 18n, 258n, 357, 362, 385n, **4**: 281, **5**: 65, **8**: 355, 355n, 370, 370n, 417, **9**: 366n, **10**: 1, 6, **11**: 4n, 8n

Missouri, camps in: Mississippi County, **2**: 90n, 94n, 101n; Cape Girardeau County, **2**: 109n, 111n; Perry County, **2**: 114n, 116n, 117n; Sainte Genevieve County, **2**: 122n; Jefferson County, **2**: 124n; Saint Louis County, **2**: 127n, **8**: 370n; Saint Charles County, **2**: 224n, 228n, 231n, 234n, 244n, 246n, 249n, **8**: 369n; Franklin County, **2**: 251n, 259n; Warren County, **2**: 252n, **8**: 368n; Gasconade County, **2**: 259n, 260n, 264n; Osage County, **2**: 264n, 266n, 269n; Cole County, **2**: 274n, 277n, **8**: 366n; Boone County, **2**: 281n, 283n; Howard County, **2**: 285n, 290n; Saline County, **2**: 288n, 293n, **8**: 365n; Cooper County, **2**: 288n, **8**: 365n; Chariton County, **2**: 295n, 299n; Carroll County, **2**:

299n, 301n, 307n, **8**: 362n; Lafayette County, **2**: 309n, 312n, 314n, 316n; Ray County, **2**: 315n; Jackson County, **2**: 316n, 318n, 321n, 323n, **8**: 361n; Platte County, **2**: 332n, 343n; Buchanan County, **2**: 356n, **8**: 357n, 358n, 359n; Andrew County, **2**: 361n, **8**: 357n; Holt County, **2**: 365n, 368n, **8**: 356n; Atchison County, **2**: 386n, **8**: 355n; Clay County, **8**: 361n

Missouri, State Historical Society of, **2**: 542

Missouri Company, **1**: 6, 8, **2**: 253n

Missouri Fur Company, **2**: 211n, 515, **3**: 88n, 228n, **5**: 10n, **8**: 198n, 279n, 316n

Missouri Historical Society, **1**: 4, **2**: 40, 538, 541, **3**: 336, 383n, 388, 479, 492n, **6**: 473, 496n. *See also* Voorhis Collection

Missouri Indians: councils, **2**: 60, 435–36, 438–41, **8**: 354n, **9**: 390–92, **10**: 25; located, **2**: 266n; trade, **2**: 277n, **3**: 483; villages, **2**: 295–96, 302–3, 303n, 304n, 351, 405, 408, 487, **3**: 370, 377, **8**: 378, 395, **9**: 81, 380–81, 380n, **10**: 14, 14n, **11**: 25n, 172; historical sketch, **2**: 296, 299n, 437n, **3**: 394–95; language, **2**: 299n, 425n, 437n, 438–39, 442n, 443n, 493–94, **3**: 490; encountered, **2**: 423–24; 488–89, 491–93; speech for, **2**: 456; clothes, **2**: 492; peace, **3**: 26, 30, 32; medical problems, **3**: 395; war, **3**: 398–99, 406–7, 482; listed, **3**: 448; appearance, **3**: 487; visits, **9**: 33n; relations with party, **9**: 40–41, 41n, 390–91, **11**: 57; gifts, **11**: 50–51; mentioned, **2**: 352n, **9**: 50, **10**: 23n, 29n, 277n, **11**: 47n, 67n, 107n. *See also* Oto Indians

Missouri River: and maps, **1**: 4–13, **6**: 308–10, 430–31, **7**: 74n, 315n; exploration, **1**: 5–6, **11**: 184–88; distances, **1**: 6, **2**: 231, 405–10, 413, **5**: 71–72, **6**: 59, 446, 493, 493n, 495, **8**: 277, 291, 359, 377, 388–89, 412, 415–17, **9**: 18, 80–82, 91, 144, 166, 170, 200, 231, 366–68n, 373, **10**: 63n, 79n, 94, 124, 172, **11**: 9, 62, 65, 105, 139, 149 171, 175, 194, 203, 264–65, 285; conditions, **2**: 7, 252, 291, 301–2, 305, 317, 327, 375, 389, 472, **3**: 2, 4, 13, 17, 67, 69, 135, 145, 155, 219, 240–43, 249, 250n, 252–53, 255–57, 260, 265, 278, 283–85, 294, 300, 302–3, 309, 313, 316, 319–22, 348, 353, 355, 368, 476, **4**: 1, 20, 32, 35, 39, 71, 73, 110, 132, 139, 143, 149, 159, 161, 168, 170–71, 174, 176, 178–79, 181, 186, 191, 193, 198, 208–9, 211, 222, 228, 232, 247, 256, 267, 270–71, 291, 297, 327, 340, 338, 356, 378, 383, 402–3, 412, 415–16, 422, 426, 433, **7**: 320, 343n, **8**: 71, 140–41, 146, 298, 352, 354, 414, **9**: 13, 26, 28, 37n, 39, 43n, 46, 52–53, 60, 93n, 130, 138, 138n, 152, 155, 157; characteristics, **2**: 213, 235, 260, 269–70, 354n, 356, 358, 400–401, 404n, 408–9, 471n, **3**: 104, 106, 146, 365–67, **4**: 18n, 30, 42, 47n, 148n, 163, 257n, 267, 313, 316, 380, 393, **5**: 37, 65, 81, 114, 192, **8**: 114, 120n, 147, 232, 238, 243, 252, 310–11, 322, 323n, 362–63, 364n, 365n, **10**: 22n, 61n, 82, 86, 94, 98, 99n, 103, 103n, 104n, 108–109, 113n, 133, 226n, 252n, 279, **11**: 1, 17, 79, 127, 137, 139, 155, 161–62, 182–85, 225, 233, 238, 241–42, 272, 274, 284–85; arrive at, **2**:

215–16, **8**: 106, 334, **11**: 1;
plants, **2**: 225n, 339n, 431n,
4: 75n, 91n, 129n, 280–81,
392, **5**: 21n, 78, 83, **7**: 14n,
126, 129n, 292, 296, **8**: 79,
151n, 162n, 287n, 322,
345n, 349, 350n, 354, 355n,
417, **11**: 195, 198; navigational problems, **2**: 229–30,
246, 248–51, 278–79, 286,
289–90, 296, 300, 302, 304,
308, 312–13, 323–24, 328–
29, 340, 342, 352–53, 355,
395–96, 457–59, **3**: 19, 67,
96, 98, 134, 142n, 326, **4**: 4,
139–40, 193, 202, 210–11,
213, 222–25, 228–29, 295,
297, 301, 422, **7**: 1, 50, 52, **8**:
278, 411, **9**: 26, 36, 55, 58,
74, 96, 123–24, 156, 158–
59, 167–69, 189, 345, 345n,
381, 388, **10**: 17–19, 36, 39,
49–50, 56, 78, 153, **11**: 27,
31, 46, 64, 198–200, 235,
239–40, 242, 246–47, 265;
and Indians, **2**: 238n, 277,
286, 305n, 352n, 470n,
478n, 482n, **3**: 27, 206n,
213n, 233, 238, 276, 386,
388, 489, **4**: 20, **5**: 69, 83,
290, **6**: 190–91, 474, 480,
482, **7**: 145, 248, 250–51,
291, 294, 296, 301, 343n, **8**:
52, 74, 88, 157, 213–14, 278,
280n, 289, 291, 298, 301,
314, 316n, 323, 360, 362,
412, **11**: 5n, 6n, 65n, 86, 91–
92, 105–6, 133, 179, 283,
286–87, 292, 303–4, 309,
329–30; affluents, **2**: 261n,
274n, 277n, 360n, 376n,
379n, 390n, 397n, 428n,
503n, 507n, 533, **3**: 298,
298n, 335–86, **4**: 103, 170,
176, 178, 416, **8**: 328n,
343n, 347n, 361, 361n,
367n, **11**: 76n, 93, 139n,
141, 145, 149, 151, 203n,
231, 244, 286; animals, **2**:
456, **3**: 147, **4**: 22, 31, 33,
114, 279, 376–77, 411, **5**:
11, 123, 126, **6**: 131, 161,
329, 331–32, 336, 338, 352,

354–55, 357, 359–60, 366–
67, 368n, 371, 379–80, 382–
83, 396, 402, 404, 406–7,
413–14, **7**: 126, 196, 198,
256, 260–61, 282, 287–88,
291–92, 294–95, 296n, 302,
304, 308, 310, 313–14, **8**: 97,
106, 112, 125, 128, 139, 141,
276, 278, 321, 374, 414, **11**:
74–75, 207, 231, 265; latitudes, **3**: 94–95, 375–76,
386n; trade on, **3**: 365, **11**:
13; and specimens, **3**: 451–
72; described, **3**: 480–90, **4**:
28, 132, 168, 248–49, 259,
267, 383, 387, 394, 396, 415,
8: 111–12, 114, 118, 140,
183, 186, 248, 277, 343, 353,
365, **9**: 9, 27–28, 31–32, 72,
130, 138, 150–51, 155, 159,
164, 184, 360, 377, 389, **10**:
4n, 11, 14, 26, 39, 41, 48,
63n, 83–84, 89–90, 95, 99–
100, 113, 272–73n, 273;
head, **5**: 2, 51n, 67n, 74, 170,
177, 189; cache on, **6**: 275–
76, 321, 441–42; hunting
and fishing on, **8**: 146, 157,
276, 280, 290, 356, **11**: 52,
64; mentioned, **1**: 3, **2**: 1–3,
5, 14, 29, 211n, 213n, 214,
215n, 221, 229n, 231n, 233,
242, 253n, 267, 299n, 301n,
314n, 322, 325, 332, 335n,
344–45, 357, 363n, 364n,
380, 388, 402, 403, 421,
442n, 446n, 454, 457–58,
465n, 467n, 500–501, 506n,
511–12, 521, 523, 537, 541,
3: 30, 46–47, 48n, 56n, 57n,
69n, 74–75, 76n, 77–78,
79n, 120n, 148n, 152–53,
155n, 167n, 188n, 201n,
204, 226n, 227n, 229n,
230n, 232, 237, 258n, 295n,
4: 58, 59–60, 62, 68–69,
69n, 72, 77–79, 118–19,
130, 201, 204, 246, 260n,
269, 272, 274–75, 277, 299,
5: 7, 54, 90–91, 115, 127,
140, 145–46, 147n, 148n,
158, 162–63, 164n, 165,
178–79, 183–84, 194–95,
195n, 196, 198–99, 237,

259, **6**: 311n, 462, 494, **7**:
182–83, 222, 224, 323, 325,
333, **8**: 1–4, 43n, 85, 87n,
93, 95, 96n, 98n, 102, 104,
106n 107, 107n, 108n, 111n,
112n, 137, 139n, 140n,
147n, 148n, 154, 157–58,
158n, 168, 180n, 183n,
188n, 191, 275, 279n, 280n,
281n, 282n, 286, 289n,
303n, 346, 349n, 352n,
353n, 357n, 358n, 359n,
362n, 368n, 370, 378, 382–
83, 392–93, 418n, **9**: xiii, xv–
xvi, 3, 13, 17–20, 22–23,
24n, 25–27, 27n, 28, 29n,
31, 35, 37–38, 40, 44, 46,
60n, 71, 82n, 83, 93–94, 98,
118, 122, 131n, 137n, 157n,
161, 162n, 164, 170n, 184n,
199–200, 204, 207, 209–11,
211n, 212, 214, 219–20,
227n, 228, 296, 299, 305–6,
313, 330, 334n, 336n, 337n,
343n, 350n, 354n, 357n,
358n, 360n, 363n, 364n,
366, 369n, 380, 393, **10**: xiii,
1, 4n, 5n, 6n, 7n, 31–32, 39,
51n, 72, 75–76, 79–80, 87n,
91n, 92n, 97n, 98, 98n, 100,
112n, 113n, 114n, 115n,
116n, 118, 123, 127–28,
128n, 138, 149, 171, 176,
193, 200, 247, 248n, 250,
251n, 252n, 253n, 255n,
257, 257n, 259, 259n, 260n,
262n, 264n, 265n, 266,
267n, 270n, 271n, 272n,
274n, 275, 277, 277n, 279n,
280n, **11**: xiii–xiv, 4n, 8n, 14,
19, 21, 23–24, 29, 37, 40,
42–43, 61, 83, 100, 103,
107–9, 108n, 115, 126, 132,
134–36, 138, 140–42, 153–
54, 156, 173, 184n, 186n,
187n, 189n, 191, 201n, 222–
23, 261–63, 277–78, 325. *See
also* Missouri River, Big Bend
of the; Missouri River, Breaks
of the; Missouri River, Great
Falls of the; Missouri River,
Three Forks of the; Missouri
River, White Cliffs of the

Missouri River, Big Bend of the (Grand Detour), **2**: 354n, **3**: 2, 31, 33, 89–90, 92–96, 95n, 98, 99n, 359, 372, 380, 415, 464, 476, **8**: 311, 323, 325, 325n, 380, 398, 417, **9**: 62–63, 63n, 354n, 367n, **10**: 41, 42n, 272, 272n, 273n, **11**: 79, 80n, 172

Missouri River, Breaks of the, **4**: 2, 195, 198, 200n, 207–9, 210n, 233n, **9**: 159–60, 160n, **10**: 94, 95n, 96n, **11**: 171, 175n, 179n

Missouri River, Great Bend of the, **1**: 3, 5, **2**: 354n, **10**: 273n

Missouri River, Great Falls of the: portage, **2**: 22, **4**: 299–305, 305n, 307–8, 310–17, 317n, 318, 335, 348, **10**: 105, **11**: 197, 199–201, 204; cache at, **2**: 264n, **8**: 108, 305n, **11**: 202; and maps, **3**: 269, 270n, **4**: 305n; distances, **3**: 348, 374, **6**: 449, **8**: 114, 291–92, 296n, 382, 384, 388, 394, 413, **11**: 236–37; and Indians, **3**: 433–35, 444, **5**: 86n, **8**: 280n; listed, **3**: 382, **6**: 464; arrive at, **4**: 3, 283–86, 348, **8**: 2, 104, 111, **10**: 102, **11**: 198; described, **4**: 270, 283–86, 288n, 297, 362, 368, **8**: 110, 112, **9**: 168, 175, **10**: 103, 107–9, **11**: 197, 200, 204–6, 225; animals and plants, **5**: 11, 119, 125n, **7**: 303, 305, **8**: 173n, 412, **9**: 171, **11**: 207–8; minerals, **5**: 39n; latitude, **5**: 195, **6**: 492, **8**: 413; route, **6**: 309–10, **8**: 1, 3, 74, 85, 100, 372n, 411–12, 414, **9**: 330, **10**: 247, 248n, 266; guides to, **8**: 21–22, 35–36, 46–47, 53–54, 77; drawing, **8**: 112, 114n; mentioned, **2**: 7, 23, **3**: 367, 491n, **4**: 3, 200n, 270, 289, 295, 297, 309, 319, 320–21, 323–26, 332, 335, 337, 340, 342, 349n, 350–51, 359, 359n, 362–64, 366, 383,

385, 396n, 401n, **5**: 23, 115, 126, 164n, 248, **6**: 3, 446, **7**: 333, 339, 341, **8**: 79, 86n, 87n, 112n, 115n, 131, 137–38, 139n, 180n, 293, 358n, **9**: xvi, 169–70, 169n, 174, 179–81, 330n, 334, 339, 339n, **10**: xv, 103n, 105, 256n, **11**: 200n, 206n, 208n, 213, 218, 220–21

Missouri River, middle fork. *See* Madison River

Missouri River, north or southwest fork. *See* Jefferson River

Missouri River, south or southeast fork. *See* Gallatin River

Missouri River, Three Forks of the: and maps, **1**: 10–11; leave, **2**: 30, **5**: 14, 16, 24, **9**: xvi, **10**: 119; post at, **2**: 211n, 516, **5**: 10n; and members of the party, **2**: 515–16, 520, 523, **3**: 229n; and Indians, **3**: 369n, **7**: 334, **8**: 280n, **9**: 188, 188n, **11**: 236–38, 242–43; distances, **3**: 374, **6**: 450, 494–95, **8**: 178–79, 185, 207n; listed, **3**: 382, **6**: 465; arrive at, **4**: 4, 427–28, 434, **5**: 1, **9**: 190, 191n, 335, 336n, **11**: 242; animals and plants, **4**: 427–28, 435–36, **7**: 129n, 297, **8**: 412, **10**: 118, **11**: 242–43; described, **4**: 434–36, **8**: 394, **9**: 191, **11**: 242; name, **5**: 7, 10n; characteristics, **5**: 7, 18, 150, 157n; latitude, **6**: 450, **8**: 413, **9**: 191; mentioned, **3**: 364, 445, **4**: 425n, 429n, 431, **5**: 9, 30, 123, 162, 189, 194, 199, **7**: 334n, **8**: 1–3, 74, 139n, 175, 183n, 188n, 360n, 364n, 392–93, 412–14, **9**: 334, 348, **10**: 118, 118n, 123, 254n, 255, 255n, **11**: 242n, 244n, **12**: 6

Missouri River, White Cliffs of the, **4**: 2, 225–31, 233n, **6**: 329, 330n, 334, **8**: 140, 140n, **9**: 159–60, 160n, 343, 343n, **10**: 96, 96n, 260, 260n, **11**: 179–81, 179n

Missouri River Miscellany, **3**: 479–92

Mistletoe, **2**: 97, 101n

Mitchell, David D., **6**: 148n

Mitchell, John, **1**: 5

Mitchell Creek, **9**: 316n

Mitutanka (Matootonha) village, **3**: 199–200, 201n, 203–4, 209, 211, 213n, 214n, 223, 225n, 233, 248, 254, 266, 268–69, 275, 275n, 376, 401, **4**: 12n, **8**: 298, 300n, 305n, 306, 307n, **9**: 90, 90n, 95, 95n, 126, 127n, 350, 350n, **10**: 59n, 60–61, 60n, 61n, 77, 77n, 267, 268, **11**: 105, 105n, 107n, 110, 115, 116n, 122, 132–33, 133n

Moccasin Mountains, **4**: 192n, **9**: 154n

Moccasins: purchased, **2**: 294; problems, **3**: 100–102, 103n, 294, **4**: 225, 228, 230, 249, 254, 325, 430, **5**: 78, 209, **6**: 130, **7**: 259, **9**: 147, 159, 217, **11**: 155–56, 299–300; and Indians, **3**: 290, **4**: 14, **5**: 80, **6**: 438, **7**: 148, **10**: 188n, **11**: 113, 278; making, **4**: 165, 366, **5**: 8–9, 119, 198, **6**: 3, 186, **8**: 190, **9**: xii, 151, 163, 179, 191, 208, 267, **10**: xii, 104, 188, **11**: xii, 187, 189–90, 280–81, 411, 415, 417, 420, 425; repairing, **4**: 309, 327–28, 404, **5**: 174, **9**: 173, 207, 225, **11**: 129, 318; gifts, **6**: 137, **8**: 219, **10**: 243; abundance, **6**: 339–40, 407, **9**: 278; lost, **9**: 197, 219, **10**: 138, **11**: 257; as trade item, **9**: 350, 352, **10**: 67, **11**: 22–23; counted, **10**: 197–98, **11**: 430; mentioned, **4**: 3, 263, **7**: 346n, **11**: 34–35, 210–11, 425. *See also* Clothing

Moc-cup-pin. *See* Water lily, white

Mockingbird, **2**: 276n, **4**: 162, 163n, 236

Mock Island, **3**: 96, 99

Mock orange, Lewis's. *See* Syringa, Lewis's

Molander site, **3**: 194n, 312n

Molasses, **3**: 58, 247n

Molasses Spring, **3**: 60n

Mole, eastern, **6**: 355–56, 355n

Mole, western, **6**: 355–56, 355n

Moles, **6**: 313, 315, 317n

Mollusks, **5**: 319n, **6**: 440n

Molothrus ater, **8**: 108n. *See also* Cowbird, brown-headed

Monadenia fidelis, **6**: 405n, **7**: 46n. *See also* Snails

Monbrains (Monbrun, Montbrun's) Tavern, **2**: 264–65

Mongoose, **6**: 352, 354, 355n, 434, 438

Moniteau (Big Devil, Big Monitu) Creek (River) (Howard-Boone county line, Mo.), **2**: 283–84, 285n, **3**: 341, 370, 377, **8**: 377, 395, **9**: 11, 11n, 368n, 378, **10**: 12, 12n, **11**: 19, 20n

Moniteau (Little Manitou) Creek (Cole County, Mo.), **2**: 277, 279, 281n, **3**: 341, 370, 377, **8**: 377, 395, **9**: 368n

Monongahela River, **2**: 82, 82n

Mono-Paviotso (Sho-bar-boo-be-er) Indians, **6**: 314, 316, 317n, 479, 487, 491

Mons veneris, **7**: 27, 31n, 35–36

Montagne à la Bosse (Hump Mountain Fort), **2**: 225, 226n, **8**: 212n

Montana, camps in: Roosevelt County, **4**: 80n, 88n, 100n; Richland County, **4**: 84n, 91n, 102n, **8**: 149n; McCone County, **4**: 107n, 116n, 121n, 124n, **8**: 148n; Valley County, **4**: 124n, 130n, 136n, 139n, 156n, **8**: 147n, 148n; Garfield County, **4**: 139n, 145n, 148n, 150n, 158n, 163n, 166n, 169n, 175n; Phillips County, **4**: 158n, 169n, 193n, **8**: 142n, 145n; Petroleum County, **4**: 175n, 179n, **8**: 145n; Fergus County, **4**: 187n, 193n, 200n, 207n, 210n, **8**: 142n; Chouteau County, **4**: 214n, 221n, 224n, 234n, 241n, 245n, 252n,

257n, 260n, 279n, 282n, 289n, 296n, **8**: 111n, 115n, 137n, 139n, 140n; Cascade County, **4**: 288n, 298n, 302n, 305n, 309n, 374n, 386n, 391n, **8**: 98n, 99n, 100n, 106n, 107n, 108n, 122n; Lewis and Clark County, **4**: 397n, 402n, 405n, 406n, 410n, 415n, **8**: 95n, 96n, 98n; Broadwater County, **4**: 411n, 415n, 419n, 422n, 425n, 429n; Jefferson County, **4**: 429n, **5**: 17n, 29n, **8**: 178n; Gallatin County, **4**: 433n, 438n, **8**: 180n, 183n; Gallatin or Madison counties, **5**: 21n; Madison County, **5**: 30n, 35n, 39n, 44n, 52n, 55n, 58n, 61n, 63n, **8**: 178n; Jefferson or Madison counties, **5**: 40n; Madison or Beaverhead counties, **5**: 43n, 67n; Beaverhead County, **5**: 63n, 67n, 72n, 73n, 76n, 87n, 95n, 102n, 108n, 116n, 119n, 164n, 170n, **8**: 169n, 171n, 173n, 176n, 177n; Ravalli County, **5**: 186n, 187n, 188n, 190n, 191n, **8**: 162n, 164n, 166n; Missoula County, **5**: 196n, 199n, 202n, **8**: 65n, 69n, 86n, 90n; Powell County, **8**: 92n; Liberty County, **8**: 116n; Toole County, **8**: 117n, 120n; Glacier County, **8**: 122n, 124n; Pondera County, **8**: 133n; Blaine County, **8**: 141n; Park County, **8**: 188n; Sweet Grass County, **8**: 193n, 197n; Stillwater County, **8**: 203n, 208n; Yellowstone County, **8**: 222n, 229n; Treasure County, **8**: 234n; Rosebud County, **8**: 240n, 246n; Custer County, **8**: 250n; Prairie County, **8**: 256n, 262n; Dawson County, **8**: 270n

Monters Creek, **2**: 361–62. *See also* Charleston Creek; Mosquito Creek (Kans.)

Montgomery, Samuel, **2**: 81

Monticello, **12**: 1

Montreal, Canada, **3**: 155n, 220n, **12**: 4

Monture (Seaman's) Creek, **8**: 92–93, 92–93n, 94n, 101, 383, 401, **10**: 249, 249n

Monument Butte, **8**: 200, 203n

Monumental Rock, **5**: 269, 271, 272n, 281

Moonax. *See* Marmot, yellow-bellied

Moon Creek (Idaho), **5**: 210n, **6**: 466, **8**: 56, 58, 58n, **9**: 225, 225n, **10**: 143, 143n, **11**: 319n

Moon (Turtle Dry, Turtle) Creek (Mont.), **8**: 247–49, 249n, 250n, 390, 407

Mooneye, **2**: 484n, **9**: 40, 40n

Moore, Hugh, **6**: 155–56, 160n, 302, 305, 307n, 416, 416n, 427

Moore, T., **2**: 65, 66n, 67, 83, 102

Moose, **3**: 432–35, 438, **6**: 405n, **7**: 326, 329, 330n, **8**: 95, 96n, **11**: 152n

Moose Creek (Lemhi County, Idaho) (August 23, 1805), **5**: 157n, **10**: 131n

Moose Creek (Lemhi County, Idaho) (September 3, 1805), **5**: 186n

Moose Creek (Mont.), **8**: 167–68, 169n, 174, 174n, **9**: 332, 332n

Moose Deer Mountain, **3**: 487, 492n

Morchella angusticeps, **8**: 38n. *See also* Morel, black

Moreau (Murrow) River (Mo.), **2**: 272–73, 274n, **3**: 340–41, 370, 377, **8**: 377, 395, **9**: 9, 9n, 368n, **10**: 12, 12n, **11**: 17n

Moreau (Sur-war-kar-ne) River (S. Dak.), **3**: 31, 37n, 148–49, 150n, 360, 373, 376, 380, **8**: 320, 320n, 380, 399, **9**: 77, 77n, 81, 353n, 367n, **10**: 51, 52n, 271n, **11**: 96–97, 97n

Morel, black, **8**: 37, 38n

Morgan Creek, **8**: 270n

Morgan, Daniel, **2**: 138, 138n

Morgan Island, **2**: 379, 381, 382n, 479

Mormon Creek, **8**: 162n

Morone chrysops, **2**: 486n. *See also* Bass, white

Morone saxatilis, **4**: 279n. *See also* Bass, striped

Morparperyoopatoo, **4**: 14

Morrison, William, **2**: 140, 140n, 144n, 182

Morus alba, **2**: 217n. *See also* Mulberry, white

Morus rubra, **2**: 217n, **8**: 359n, **9**: 12n, **10**: 14n. *See also* Mulberry, red

Mosquito Creek. *See* Big Canyon (Mosquito) Creek

Mosquito Creek (Iowa), **2**: 407, 413n, **3**: 353, 371, 378, **8**: 379, 397, **9**: 29, 29n, 367n, **11**: 43–44, 44n

Mosquito Creek (Kans.), **2**: 363n, **9**: 22, 23n, 386

Mosquitoes, **2**: 60, 181, 185, 216, 261, 272, 304, 305n, 306–8, 310–11, 317–18, 420–22, 430, 432–34, 438, 440, 447–48, 455, 457, 459, 464, 466, 470, 472, 474, 485–86, **3**: 14, 15n, 68–69, 102, **4**: 17, 19, 19n, 20, 93, 184, 186, 333, 350–51, 354, 365, 367, 372, 374, 376–77, 379, 381, 387, 394, 401–3, 405, 409, 412, 415, 417–18, 423, 427, 429, **5**: 8, 10n, 15, 27, 56, 58n, 62, 181, **6**: 139, **7**: 46, 48n, 76–77, 192, 221, 223, 319, **8**: 3, 21–22, 22n, 37–38, 72, 79–80, 82, 85, 86n, 93, 107–8, 110, 112, 119, 125, 143, 150, 152, 162, 175, 178, 263–64, 266n, 272–73, 275–76, 280–83, 289, 297, 299, 311, 320, 326, 331, 334, 337, 342, 345, 348–51, 353–54, 356, 361, 374, **9**: 15, 15n, 22, 29n, 34–35, 37–38, 44, 59, 128, 153, 178, 180–81, 183, 199, 288, 324–25, 329, 336–39, 347, 349, 352, 354–55, 357–60, **10**: 26–27, 39, 106, 106n, 111, 116, 198, 238–39, 241–42, 244, 247, 250–51, 253–56, 264, 266, 269, 274–76, 278, **11**: 21–22, 53, 74, 216, 222–23, 225–26, 229–30, 237, 261–62, 265

Moss. *See* Lichen

Mounds, **2**: 422, 423n, 424, 425n. *See also* Mounds, Indian burial; Spirit Mound

Mounds, Indian burial, **2**: 77–78, 269–70, 272n, 275–76, 277n, 369–70, 372n, 479, **10**: 34n. *See also* Cahokia Mounds

Moundsville, W. Va., **2**: 77, 78n

Mount Adams, **5**: 301, 304, 307n, **6**: 21n, **7**: 59, 61n, 81, 89n, **9**: 241, 241n, **11**: 360–61, 361n

Mountain beaver (sewelel), **6**: 3, 76, 78n, 208, 210n, 313, 315, 317n, 351–54, 355n, 434, 438, **9**: 260, 260n, **10**: 174n, **11**: 405n

Mountain lion, **2**: 309n, **4**: 157–58, 158n, **5**: 37–39, 39n, 53, 55, 139, **6**: 114, 135, 136n, 313, 315, 317n, 355–56, 356n, 434, 438, **9**: 149, 149n, 194, 336, **10**: 148, 148n, **11**: 29n, 158–59, 159n, 252–53

Mount Coffin, **6**: 27, 29n, **7**: 18, 20, 21n

Mount Hood (Timm, Falls Mountain): **5**: 298, 301n, 318, 319n, 339, 342, 345, 350, 352, **6**: 11–13, 14n, **7**: 33–34, 41, 48–49, 51–52, 59, 62, 81, 118, 120, 127, 130n, 149, 151n, 156–58, 163, 167, 182, 184, 216, 218, **9**: 232, 249, 249n, 253n, 283, 292, **10**: 163, 164n, 165, 166n, **11**: 361n, 382–83, 384n, 385–86, 392, 392n, 437

Mount Jefferson, **6**: 478, 486, **7**: 36, 38n, 59, 66, 81–82, 92–93, 93n, 149, 151n, 156–58, 182, 184, 216, 218, **8**: 415, **9**: 284, **11**: 438, 438n

Mount Rainier, **6**: 87, 87n, 112, **7**: 59, 81, **9**: 250n, 283, **10**: 167n, **11**: 387n, 437n

Mount St. Helens, **5**: 307n, **6**: 16, 18, 20n, 21n, 56, 87, 112, **7**: 33–34, 59, 81, 93, 93n, **9**: 250, 250n, **10**: 166, 167n, **11**: 385–86, 387n, 437, 437n

Mouse, deer, **7**: 129, 130n, 141

Mouse, meadow, **3**: 158, 160n, **4**: 18n, **6**: 355–56, 355n

Mouse River. *See* Souris River

Moxostoma macrolepidotum, **2**: 484n. *See also* Red horse, shorthead

Mud Creek, **9**: 10n, **10**: 12, 12n, **11**: 18n, 19n

Mud (Lead, Big Rock) Creek, **2**: 277, 279, 281n

Muddy Creek, **3**: 339, 376, **9**: 8, 9n, 376, **10**: 10, 10n, **11**: 16, 16n

Muddy (Little Miry) Creek (Muddy River), **2**: 265, 266n, 267, 269–70

Mudstones, **6**: 179n, 185n, **8**: 261n

Mufflon, **10**: 93n

Muggins (Windsor's) Creek, **8**: 236–37, 239, 240n, 245n, 390, 407

Muhlenberg, Gotthilf Heinrich Ernst (Henry), **12**: 6, 9n

Mulberry, red, **2**: 185, 216, 217n, 313, 319, 388, 391–92, 428, 430, **8**: 359, 359n, 416, 418n, **9**: 12, 12n, 27, 377, 377n, **10**: 14, 14n

Mulberry, white, **2**: 217n

Mulehead Point, **10**: 37, 38n

Mules, **3**: 392, 394, 401, 426, 428, 435–38, **5**: 89, 92, 120–21, 123–24, 135, 158, **6**: 314, 316, 317n, 404, 451, **8**: 37, 43–44, 302, 303n, 363, **9**: 208, **10**: 134, **11**: 280–81

Mulford (Milford, Minford), Clarence, **2**: 240, 243n

Mullan Road, **8**: 89n

Mullets. *See* Suckers

Multnomah Creek, **7**: 100n

Multnomah Falls, **7**: 89n, 100n, **9**: 248n, **11**: 382n

Mult-no-mah Indians, **7**: 32, 34, 36n

Multnomah-Latourell soil, **7**: 78n

Multnomah River. *See* Willamette River

Mumps. *See* Medical problems

Munsell, John, **9**: 3n

Murray, William A., **2**: 66n

Murrow Creek, **2**: 272–73. *See also* Moreau River

Musca domestica, **7**: 47n. *See also* Fly, house

Musket, North West, **8**: 136n. *See also* Arms and ammunition

Musket, U. S. Model 1795, **8**: 111n. *See also* Arms and ammunition

Muskets, **2**: 213, 213–14n, **3**: 25n, 144n, **4**: 275, 279, 364, 416, **5**: 23, 168, 178, 346–47, **6**: 17, 121, 122n, 146, 187, 205–6, 208, 265, 272, **7**: 248, 251n, **8**: 2, 110, 177n, 289n, **9**: 131, 246, 248, 250, 309, 341, 369n, **11**: 375, 381, 385–87. *See also* Arms and ammunition; Fusils; Guns; Pistols; Rifles

Muskingum River, **2**: 80–81, 81n, 99

Muskrat, **2**: 205, 205n, **3**: 393–444 passim, **4**: 52, 53n, 436, **5**: 57, 58n, 59, **6**: 402, 408, **9**: 131, 131n, 190, **10**: 172, 174n, **11**: 243–44

Mussels, **2**: 483, 484n, **4**: 332, 333n, **5**: 301, 304, **6**: 120n, 407, 409n, 420–21, **9**: 174, 174n, 205, **11**: 171, 175, 175n, 179, 276–77

Musselshell (Mah-tush,-ah-zhah, Shell) River, **1**: 9, **3**: 364, 367, 374, 382, **4**: 168, 169n, 170–76, 175n, 178–80, 215, 363, 370, **5**: 162, **6**: 448, 463, **7**: 342, 343n, **8**: 144–45, 145n, 382, 400, **9**: 150n,

151, 152n, 344n, **10**: 90, 90n, 261, 261n, **11**: 162–63, 163n

Musselshell Rapids, **5**: 303, 307n, **6**: 18, 454, 468, 474, 483, **7**: 131, 174, **8**: 385, 403, 415

Mustard, **6**: 174, 197, **7**: 335, 337, 338n, **8**: 94n, **11**: 132

Mustela, **6**: 355n

Mustela frenata, **3**: 232n, **5**: 95n, **6**: 138n, **7**: 135n, **9**: 206n, **11**: 277n. *See also* Weasel, long-tailed; Weasels

Mustela vison, **6**: 317n, **7**: 70n, **9**: 45n. *See also* Mink

Muster (Dry) Creek, **8**: 251–52, 254, 255n, 256n

Mustin, E. Clarence Lighthall, **2**: 543

Mustin, George S., **2**: 544

Mycteria americana, **6**: 14n. *See also* Stork, wood

Mylocheilus lateralis, **7**: 173n. *See also* Chub, Columbia River

Myristica fragrans, **6**: 178n. *See also* Nutmeg

Myrrhis odorata, **10**: 137n. *See also* Cicely, sweet

Mytilidae, **6**: 409n. *See also* Clams

Mytilus sp., **6**: 409n. *See also* Mussels

N

Nacogdoches, **8**: 348n

Nahpooitle Village, **6**: 24n, **7**: 31n, **9**: 282, 283n, **10**: 203, 203n, **11**: 436, 436n

Nails, **5**: 125, **8**: 138, 177, **9**: 333, 342, **10**: 259

Nannyberry, **3**: 222, 223n, 492n

Nar-nis, **3**: 135, 138n

Narrows of the Columbia River. *See* Columbia River, The Dalles of the

Nasomah (Shal-la-lah) Indians, **6**: 476, 486, 491

Natchez Indians, **3**: 447, 450

Natchitoches, La., **3**: 446–47, **8**: 346, 348n

Natural History Museum, **12**: 5

Nautical Almanac and Astronomical Ephemeris, The (Kelly), **2**: 87n

Nayakxa tcix village, **5**: 348n

Neacoxie (Neercawanaca) Creek, **6**: 171–72, 173n, 175, 177, 194, 459, 471

Nebraska, camps in: Richardson County, **2**: 376n, 379n, **8**: 356n; Nemaha County, **2**: 379n, 382n, 386n, **8**: 355n; Otoe County, **2**: 393n; Cass County, **2**: 400n; Sarpy County, **2**: 404n; Douglas County, **2**: 423n; Washington County, **2**: 431n, 442n, 447n, **8**: 352n, 353n; Burt County, **2**: 462n, **8**: 352n; Dakota County, **2**: 478n, **8**: 347n, 350n; Dixon County, **2**: 503n, **3**: 12n; Cedar County, **3**: 12n, 21n, **8**: 345n; Knox County, **3**: 39n, 46n, 48n, 51n; Boyd County, **3**: 54n

Necanicum (Clatsop) River, **6**: 120n, 154, 159n, 175, 177, 178n, 184n, 193–95, 198n, 460, 471, **10**: 187, 187n, **11**: 404n

Ne-cha-co-lee or Neech-e-coke village, **7**: 57, 61n, 64, 70n, 79, 84, 86, 89n, **9**: 285, 286n

Needles, **3**: 119, 290, **4**: 354, 363, **6**: 173n, 333, 335, **7**: 275–76, **8**: 299, **9**: 369n

Ne-er-cho-ki-oo Indians. *See* Watlala Indians

Ne-er-cho-ki-oo village, **7**: 57, 61n, 64, 79, 83

Neesh-nah-ba-to-na River. *See* Nishnabotna (Neesh-nah-ba-to-na) River

Neeshneparkkeeook (and similar spellings). *See* Cut Nose

Nehalem Bay, **6**: 185n

Nehalem River (Ni-e-lee Creek), **6**: 461, 471

Neighing Horse (Manresse-sar-ra-ree), **3**: 211–12, 213n

Nelumbo lutea, **2**: 144n, 224n. *See also* Lotus, American

Nemaha River, **8**: 418n. *See also* Big Nemaha River; Little Nemaha River

Ne-mal-quin-ner Indians, **7**: 83, 89n

Nemousin Indians. *See* Comanche Indians

Neotoma cinerea, **4**: 354n, **6**: 355n, **9**: 179n. *See also* Woodrat, bushy-tailed

Neotoma floridana, **2**: 267n, **6**: 355n, **10**: 19n. *See also* Woodrat, eastern

Nereocystis leutkeana, **6**: 423, 426, 428n, 431–32

Nestucca Indians, **6**: 490

Nets, **5**: 118–19, 290, 311, 321, **6**: 76, 192, 211, 213–14, 216, 346, 349, **7**: 133–34, 146–47, 149, 182, 184, 236n, 245, 245n, 269, 271n, 320, **8**: 38, 41, **9**: 206, 317, 325, **10**: 28, **11**: 277–78, 348–49, 364–65

Nets, mosquito (bier), **2**: 6, **4**: 379, 387, 412, **5**: 27, 106, **8**: 80, 108, 110, 275, 280–81, **9**: 15, 15n

Nettle, horse-, **7**: 285n

Nettle, stinging, **4**: 380, 381n, 385, **6**: 26–27, 29n, **7**: 45, 47n, **10**: 202, 202n

Nettle, tall, **2**: 276, 277n

Nettles, **6**: 217n

Netul River. *See* Lewis and Clark River

Nevada (Prairie of the Knobs) Valley, **8**: 93, 94n, 101

Neville Island, **2**: 68n

New Archangel, Alaska, **6**: 432n

Newberry Library, **2**: 543, **11**: xvi

Newfound (New) Island, **2**: 367, 368n, 370

New Hampshire, **9**: xiv, xvi

New Madrid, Mo., **2**: 197, **3**: 446

Newman, John: court-martialed, **2**: 13, 190n, **3**: 2, 168–71, 171–72n, 222, **10**: 54, 55n, **9**: 84, 84n; listed, **2**: 147,

189, 191n, 194, 197–99, 255, **9**: 395n; sent out, **2**: 180, **10**: 73, 73n; returns, **2**: 181; in permanent party, **2**: 187, 229n, **9**: 373–74n; discipline, **2**: 194, 520, **3**: 167, 172–73, 222, 227n, **9**: 84, **10**: 54n; hunting, **2**: 205, 283, **3**: 40–42, **9**: 52, 54, 57, **10**: 34, 34n, 38–39, 39n, **11**: 19–20n, 73, 125, 126n; court-martial member, **2**: 329; return party, **2**: 511, **4**: 12n; biographical sketch, **2**: 519; information from, **3**: 92; and Indians, **3**: 295–96, 296n; mentioned, **2**: 259n, **3**: 3, **9**: 58, 94n

New Mexico, **3**: 137, 137n, 435–38, 484, **5**: 94n, **6**: 311, 314, 316, 317n, **7**: 308n, **8**: 277, 279n, 303n, 356n, 363, 364n, **9**: 205, 213, 316, 317n, 364, **10**: 6n, 231n, 235, 280, **11**: 273, 275, 275n, 288–89. *See also* Spanish

New North Wales, **10**: 6–7n

New Orleans, La., **2**: 102, **9**: 361, **10**: 4n

New South Wales, **10**: 6n

Newt, rough-skinned, **6**: 402, 405n, 408

New York, **8**: 347, 348n, **12**: 3

New York Botanical Garden, **12**: 6

New York Historical Society, **2**: 543, **11**: xvi

Nez Perce Creek (Beaverhead County, Mont.), **5**: 43n, **10**: 121n

Nez Perce (Blue Mud, Chopunnish, Ki-moo-e-nim, Pel-lote-pal-lah, Wil-le-wah) Indians: villages, **1**: 10, **5**: 222, 224n, 228n, 229, 231n, 232, 232n, 239, 242, 263n, **6**: 453, **7**: 50, 52, 205–7, 208n, 214n, 220, 225n, 241n, 289–90, 310, 322, 325n, 346, 348n, **8**: 12n, **9**: 228, 238, 305, 305n, 308n, 315, 315n, 324, **10**: 147n, 150–51, 153, 173, 222, 222n, **11**: 326, 328; and

maps, **1**: 11; information from, **1**: 11, **5**: 89–90, 197, 198n, 226, 230, 235, 250, 255–56, 260n, 265n, 271, **7**: 2–3, 52, 157–58, 195–97, 206–7, 221–22, 233n, 264, 278, 301–2, 320, 331–32, 347–48, **8**: 40, 42, 43n, 53–54, 57, 59–60, 68, 71, 74–75, 77, 83, 115n, **9**: 298, 317, 319–20, **10**: 218, 223, 236, 236n; chiefs, **1**: 11, **5**: 226–27, 231, 246, 256, 271, **7**: 202–3, 204n, 208n, 209n, 211, 215, 215n, 228–29, 231–32, 235, 240, 241n, 242, 244, **9**: 234, 234n, 304, 305n, 306–7, 307n, 318, 320, 320n, 326, **10**: 151, 151n, 154, 221, 221n, 222n, 224, 224n, 229n, 233n, 237n, **11**: 329–30, 331n, 332–33, 338, 358–59; encountered, **2**: 7–8, 24, **5**: 3, 196–97, 219, 222, 229, 242, 262, 268, 281, **7**: 206, 274, 299, **8**: 7, 43, 53–54, 87, **9**: 221–22, 230, 237, 321n, **10**: 140, 147n, 237, 237n, **11**: 308–9, 326, 328, 374n; located, **2**: 28, **6**: 313, 315, 467, **7**: 206, 343n, **10**: 132n, 154n, **11**: 350n; language, **2**: 29, **4**: 13n, **5**: 224n, 228n, 248n, 260n, 268–69n, 284n, 287, 307n, **6**: 148n, **7**: 21n, 53n, 158, 160, 162, 177n, 204n, 216–17, 241n, 242, 244, 245n, 312, 314, 315n, 330n, 342, 342n, 343n, 348n, **8**: 14, 17, 39, 41, 43n, 79, 82, 86n, 90n, **9**: 234n, 301n, 304n, 306n, 308n, 310n, 318n, **10**: 200n, 221n, 225n, 248n, 250n, **11**: 374n; listed, **3**: 435, 449; food, **5**: 4, 219, 224n, 319, **7**: 3, 205, 207, 227, 231, 239–40, 243, 245, 257, 265, 330, **8**: 14, 18, 20, **9**: 321, **11**: 326–29, 331; relations with the party, **5**: 4, 197, 219, 222, 226, 228–30, 232, 234–35, 245–46, 251–

53, 256, 259, **6**: 3, **7**: 2–3, 50,
139, 154, 160–61, 163–64,
167, 197, 199–200, 208–14,
209n, 216–18, 220, 222,
228, 230–32, 237–40, 241n,
242, 244, 246–50, 252, 256–
57, 269–71, 275, 277, 279–
81, 283, 288, 290, 294, 297,
300–301, 304, 324–26, 328,
330n, 332n, 333–34, 341–
42, 347, **8**: 7, 10–11, 14, 17,
23, 32–34, 36–37, 46–47,
48n, 50–52, 78–79, 82, 85,
88, 290, **9**: 229–30, 297,
304, 306, 308–9, 316, 318–
20, 326, 330, **10**: 146, 150–
151, 154, 215, 222, 224–25,
232–33, 233n, 235–37,
237n, 242–43, 243n, 247–
48, **11**: 308–9, 326–30, 332,
338, 343–45, 349; name, **5**:
94n, 205n, 222, **9**: 325n, **10**:
228, 228n, **11**: 333n; guide,
5: 196–97, 199; appearance,
5: 197, 222, 258–59, **7**: 3,
158, 216–17, 243, 245, 252–
54, **11**: 341–42; gifts, **5**: 197–
98, 219, 222, 227, 231, 246,
7: 196, **8**: 75,78; lodges, **5**:
199, 232, 250, 256–57, 261–
65, 279–80, **7**: 3, 158, 210,
213, 218, 233, 235, 239–40,
330, **9**: 305, 308n, **10**: 154,
222, 229n; and Lolo Trail,
5: 199n; fishing, **5**: 204–5,
233–34, 238, 251, 256, 259,
263, **7**: 217–18, 230–31,
245, 269, 271, 320, 327,
329–30, **8**: 56–57, **11**: 342,
349, 351; customs, **5**: 222–
23, 252–53, 253n, 255, 259,
262, 263, 263n, 264n, **7**: 4,
144, 187, 189, 206, 208,
209n, 215n, 219, 220n, 222,
224–25, 233, 235, 236n,
241n, 246–47, 249–50,
253–54, 256, 258, 291, 294,
300–301, 326, 328–29, **8**:
80, **9**: 235–36, 306, 309,
313, 320, **10**: 152, 200, **11**:
344–45; historical sketch, **5**:
224–25n; trade, **5**: 226, 231,
243, 255, 264–65, **7**: 129,

163, 242, 246, 248, 251n,
253, 301, **9**: 229, 369n, **10**:
149n, **11**: 329, 349; ceremonies, **5**: 227, **8**: 50–51, 55–
57, 63–64; clothes, **5**: 231,
258–59, **7**: 3, 119–20, 124–
25, 145, 148, 158, 160, 216–
17, 224, 249–50, 253, 255, **8**:
51–52, **9**: 228–29, **10**: 149,
11: 329–30; camps, **5**: 251,
253, 255–56, 258, 278–79,
7: 221, 223, **8**: 1, **11**: 341–42,
348, 349n; medical prob-
lems, **5**: 259, 260n, **7**: 2–3,
210–13, 215, 217, 243–47,
245n, 249–50, 269, 271–73,
273n, 283–86, 288–89, 291,
294, 297, 299, 302, 304, 308,
310, 330–31, 334, 336, 346–
47, **9**: 313, **10**: 222, 225,
229–30; hunting, **5**: 259,
262–63, **7**: 224, 261, 263,
265, 278–81, **8**: 13–14, 17,
46–47, 75, **9**: 314, **10**: 231–
32; war, **5**: 259, **7**: 247, 250–
51, 251n, 278, 301, **8**: 40, 42,
132n, 169n, **9**: 222, 313,
317n, 329, **10**: 228, 235,
11: 308–10; bands, **5**: 263n,
264n, 292, **8**: 89n; peace, **5**:
335, **7**: 301, 334, 341, **9**: 329;
and animals, **6**: 313, 315,
317n; numbers, **6**: 474, 479,
482, **7**: 239–40; and horses,
7: 3, 227, 250, 257–59,
260n, 261, 278, 307, 308n,
328, 330, **10**: 224, 224n, 227,
231n, **11**: 331; artifacts,
7: 230, 245, 253–54, 269,
8: 83, **10**: 228, 231, 231n,
11: 351, 354; visits, **8**: 21–22,
10: 239; mentioned, **4**: 207n,
5: 237, 243n, 268n, **6**: 284,
286, 328, 331–32, 480, 489,
7: 49, 53–54, 56, 88, 90, 92,
152, 165, **8**: 48, **9**: 222n,
228n, 237n, 304, 314, **10**:
140n, 153n, 215n, 221, 243,
248n, **11**: 310n, 328n, 350
Nez Perce Indians, Almotipu,
5: 264n
Nez Perce Indians, Alpaweyma,
5: 263n

Nez Perce Prairie, **5**: 214n, **8**:
26, 27n, **9**: 226, 226n, **10**:
145, 145n, **11**: 321–22, 323n
Nez Perce Trail, **5**: 199n, **7**:
225n, 241n
Niagara Falls, **11**: xv
Niangua (Ne Angua Ne unguh)
River, **2**: 181n, **3**: 390–92
Nickwall (Indian Fort) Creek,
4: 110–11n, **6**: 447, 462, **9**:
142, 142n, **10**: 86n, **11**: 145,
145n
Nicotiana quadrivalvis, **3**: 166n,
470–71, 472n, **4**: 57n, **5**:
86n, **9**: 82n, **10**: 53n. *See also*
Tobacco; Tobacco, Indian
Nicotiana rustica, **3**: 471, 472n.
See also Tobacco
Nighthawk, common, **4**: 344,
346n, 347, 349n
Nighthawk, Pacific, **4**: 346n
Nightingale, **2**: 276n, **9**: 10
Ninebark, **6**: 103, 104n, 285–
86, 286n, **7**: 12–14, 14n,
188, 190, 335, 337, **8**: 12n
Ninemile Creek, **2**: 339n, 340n,
9: 384, 384n
Ninemile Prairie, **8**: 90, 92n,
101, **10**: 249, 249n
Niobrara Formation, **3**: 18n,
21n, 48n, 51n, 52n
Niobrara (Quicurre, Rapid)
River, **1**: 6, **3**: 16, 18n, 46–
47, 48n, 75, 95, 350, 357–
58, 372, 375, 380, 398–99,
419, 464, 474–75, **8**: 4,
208n, 221n, 337, 342, 343n,
377, 379, 398, 411, 416, **9**:
53, 54n, 56n, 357, 357n,
367n, **10**: 35, 35n, 37n, **11**:
69, 69n, 71n, 172
Nishnabotna (Neesh-nah-ba-to-
na and similar spellings)
River, **2**: 376, 378, 379n,
386, 388, 390n, **3**: 346–47,
353, 371, 378, **8**: 378, 396,
9: 25–26, 25n, 367n, 387,
10: 20, 20n, **11**: 40, 40n
Niter, **2**: 356. *See also* Medicine,
saltpeter
Nodaway Island, **2**: 357–62,
361n, 363n, 479, **8**: 356,
357n, **9**: 22, 361n, **10**: 278,
278n

Nodaway River, **2**: 357–59, 361n, 365n, 375, 406–7, 409, 423–24, 452–53, 487, **3**: 94, 345–46, 371, 375, 378, **8**: 356, 357n, 378, 396, 418n, **9**: 22, 22n, 24, 35, 80–81, 367n, 386, **10**: 19, 19n, **11**: 36–37, 37n, 47n, 172, 174

No Heart (Lookout) Creek, **3**: 133–34, 136n

Nohly Lake, **4**: 76n, **10**: 83, 83n

Nonius, **2**: 411, 414n

Noo-tar-wau Indians, **3**: 136

Nootka Indians, **6**: 272n, 416n

Nootka Sound, **1**: 4, **3**: 386n, **6**: 187, 191n, 205, 302, 305, 307n, **7**: 11n

Nopalea cochinillifera, **4**: 433n. *See also* Cactus, cochineal

No Preserve Island, **3**: 49–50, 95, **8**: 333, 333n

Nor-car-te, **6**: 154, 159n

North Blackbird Creek, **3**: 379, 384n

North Dakota, camps in: Emmons County, **3**: 173n, 175n; Sioux County, **3**: 178n, 181n; Morton County, **3**: 184n, 186n, 188n, 190n; Oliver County, **3**: 192n, 193n, 198n, 295n, **8**: 307n; McLean County, **3**: 195n, 198n, 205n, 225n, 226n, 295n, **4**: 12n, 14n, 19n, 21n, 24n, **8**: 298n; Mercer County, **3**: 201n, **8**: 300n; Burleigh County, **3**: 295n, **8**: 309n, 310n; Dunn County, **4**: 28n; Mountrail County, **4**: 34n, 41n, **8**: 157n, 289n, 296n; McKenzie County, **4**: 45n, 47n, 50n, 59n, 63n, 75n, **8**: 154n, 275n, 279n, 281n, 282n, 283n, 287n, 296n; Williams County, **4**: 53n, 57n, 69n, **8**: 152n, 153n, 281n

Northern Lights. *See* Aurora borealis

Northern Paiute (Snake) Indians, **5**: 94n, 318, 320–21, 320n, 325, 339, 342–43,

349, 351–52, **6**: 479–80, 487, 491

North Fork Big Hole River, **8**: 169n, **9**: 332n

North Fork Blackfoot (Cohahlarishkit) River, **8**: 93, 94n, 383, 401, **10**: 250, 250n

North Fork Clearwater (Chopunnish) River, **5**: 227, 228n, 230, 231n, 233–34, 234n, 240, 365, **6**: 387–88, 453, 462, 467, 482, **7**: 209, 212, 214n, 220–22, 229, 236n, 322, 325, **8**: 26, 27n, 31–32, 53–54, 55n, 67, 384, 402, **9**: 230, 230n, 232, **10**: 148, 148n, 149n, **11**: 332–34, 333n, 334n

North Fork Salmon River (Fish Creek), **1**: 10, **5**: 144, 146, 147n, 148n, 162, 164n, 167, 169, 182–83, 183n, 184, 186n, 223n, **6**: 451, 466, 493, **8**: 167, 169n, **9**: 216, 216n, 231, **10**: 130, 130n, 132, 132n, 134–35, 135n, 173, 174n, **11**: 295–97, 296n, 297n

North Gabourie Creek, **2**: 123, 124n

North Loup (Deep Water) River, **3**: 351–52, 384n

North Platte River, **8**: 235n

North Saskatchewan River, **8**: 133n

North Spring (Scattered) Creek, **5**: 191n, **6**: 466, **8**: 393, 410

North Table Creek, **2**: 394–96, 397n, **9**: 27n, 388n, **11**: 42n

Northwest Coast, **10**: 163n

North West Company: traders, **1**: 5, 8, **2**: 167n, 192n, 225n, 522, 525, 527–28, **3**: 199, 201n, 218–19, 220n, 228n, 238, 241, 241–42n, 250n, 257–58, 258n, 308n, 309n, **4**: 42, **6**: 329, **8**: 316n, **9**: 90, 90n, 104–5, 104n, **10**: 59, 66, 70, **11**: 121; employees, **2**: 3, **3**: 308; relations with the party, **2**: 192n, **3**: 3, 238,

253–54, 262, 272, 281n, 284, 290, 297, 304, 308–9, 313, 318, 329, 332, **9**: 104–5, 104n, 110, 110n, 121, 121n, **11**: 125; posts, **2**: 220, 226n, **3**: 198n, 236n, 272, 363–64, 492n, **4**: 214n, **6**: 94n, **8**: 77, 133n, 212, 212n, **9**: 100, 159n; and Indians, **3**: 120n, 259, 262, 310, 318, 363–64, 402–5, 429–32, 439–44, 487, **4**: 40n, **5**: 80, **6**: 333n, **7**: 123–24, **8**: 289, 289n, **9**: 110–11, 115, **11**: 104, 104n; mentioned. **3**: 205n, 208n, 251n, **4**: 103, **6**: 236, **9**: 351, **10**: 6–7n, 59n, 63n, 64, 64n, 66–67n, 265n, 269, 272–73n. *See also* Hudson's Bay Company; Traders; Trading establishments

Northwest Passage, **1**: 3, 13, **5**: 1, **10**: 5n

Northwest Plateau, **10**: 224n

Northwest Territory, **8**: 358n

North Winnipeg River, **3**: 386n

Nose. *See* Medical problems

Notebook journals. *See* Codex journals; Voorhis journals

Notes on Virginia (Jefferson), **12**: 1

Noturus flavus, **2**: 484n, **10**: 29n. *See also* Stonecat

Nowater Creek, **8**: 232, 235n

Nucifraga columbiana, **5**: 147n, **7**: 302n. *See also* Nutcracker, Clark's

Numenius americanus, **4**: 50n, **5**: 39n, **6**: 384n, **7**: 165n, **8**: 94n. *See also* Curlew, long-billed

Numenius borealis, **4**: 257n. *See also* Curlew, Eskimo

Nut, ground. *See* Potato, Indian

Nutcracker, Clark's, **5**: 4, 145–46, 147n, **7**: 297–98, 302n, 304

Nutgrass, yellow, **7**: 297n

Nutmeg, **5**: 143, **6**: 174, 178n, 197

Nuts, **5**: 349, 355, 357, 371

Nuttall, Thomas, **12**: 6

Nyctea scandiaca, **3**: 492n. *See also* Owl, snowy

Nycticorax nycticorax, **3**: 13n. *See also* Heron, black-crowned night-

Nymphaea tuberosa, **2**: 225n. *See also* Water lily, white

Nyssa sylvatica, **2**: 69n. *See also* Gum, black

O

Oak, bur, **3**: 76–77, 79n, 464, 469, **8**: 345, 345n, 354, 355n, 417, 418n

Oak, Garry, **11**: 389n

Oak, green, **8**: 354

Oak, Oregon white, **5**: 309, 312n, 317, 318, 338–39, 342–43, 349, 351–52, 355–56, 358n, 377, 379, **6**: 15, 17, 19n, **7**: 16–17, 17n, 19, 21, 33, 194, **10**: 159n, 202, 202n, **11**: 374, 389, 389n, 437

Oak, red, **2**: 78, 78n, **8**: 416, 418n

Oak, white, **2**: 77–78, 78n, 102, 222, **6**: 3, 17, 345, 347–48, **8**: 345n, **9**: 32, **10**: 164

Oak (Maropa) Creek, **9**: 78, 78n, **10**: 52, 52n, **11**: 97, 97n

Oak Point, **6**: 41n

Oaks, **2**: 112, 218, 275, 286, 314, 315n, 388, 407, 429–30, **3**: 189, **8**: 354, 365, 416, **9**: 10, 10n, 20, 20n, 31, 42, 46, 51, 54, 61, 89, 245, 249–50, 283, **10**: 10–11, 11n, 32, 162, **11**: 63–64, 362, 371–72, 376, 382, 385–86, 435

Oars, **4**: 66, 68, 101–2, 178, 183, 185, 200, 236, 398, 403, 429. *See also* Boat, iron-frame; Canoes; Keelboat; Pirogues

O'Brien Creek, **8**: 272, 274n

Obsidian, **5**: 143, 147n

Obstetrics. *See* Medicine

O'Cain, **6**: 16on

O'Cain, Joseph, **6**: 16on

Ochre, yellow. *See* Limonite

O-co-no, **6**: 154, 495

Octants, **2**: 121, 122n, 134–35, 134n, 137, 139, 410–11, **4**: 25, 250, **6**: 317, **7**: 349. *See also* Instruments, scientific

Oddawey, Odderway, Odeway (and similar spellings). *See* Ordway

Odocoileus hemionus, **3**: 50n, 86n, **4**: 65n, **5**: 13n, **7**: 274n, **8**: 59n, **9**: 61n, **10**: 40n, **11**: 77n. *See also* Deer, mule

Odocoileus hemionus columbiana, **6**: 70n, **7**: 25n. *See also* Deer, Columbian black-tailed

Odocoileus virginianus, **2**: 101n, **3**: 79n, **4**: 65n, **5**: 13n, **6**: 405n, **8**: 69n, **9**: 8n, **10**: 10n, **11**: 16n. *See also* Deer, white-tailed

Odocoileus virginianus dacotensis, **3**: 79n, **5**: 13n, **9**: 61n, **10**: 40n, **11**: 283n. *See also* Deer, western white-tailed

Odocoileus virginianus leucura, **6**: 317n, **7**: 25n. *See also* Deer, Columbian white-tailed

Odway (and similar spellings). *See* Ordway

O'Fallon, Benjamin, **1**: 7, **8**: 261n

O'Fallon (Coal, Oke-tar-pas-ah-ha) Creek, **3**: 364–65, 374, 382, **8**: 257, 259–60, 261n, 262n, 390, 406

Office of Indian Affairs, **1**: 6

Oglala Sioux Indians. *See* Sioux Indians, Oglala

Ohio, camps in: Jefferson County, **2**: 73n; Belmont County, **2**: 76n; Washington County, **2**: 80n, 81n, 82n; Meigs County, **2**: 84n

Ohio River, **1**: 4, **2**: 6, 18, 59, 65, 66n, 67–69, 68n, 70–71, 83–84, 87, 93, 103, 104n, 120, **3**: 386n, 475–76, 485, **4**: 20, 35, 39, **6**: 392, 394, 397, 399–400, **7**: 200–201, **10**: xv

Ohio River, Falls of the, **9**: xvii

Oil, **8**: 61, **9**: 153, 227, 266, 273, 273n, 310, 344

Oil, bear's, **11**: 146–47, 164–65, 215–16, 323–24, 344–45, 371. *See also* Bear, grizzly; Bears

Oil, fish, **6**: 215, 217

Oil, olive, **7**: 215n

Oil, train. *See* Whales

Ojibway Indians. *See* Chippewa Indians

Okanogan River, **5**: 319n

Okobojo Creek, **3**: 127n

Okobojo Island, **3**: 127n

Old Baldy (Dome), **3**: 54n, 372, 380, **8**: 333, 333n, 380, 398, 417, **9**: 55, 55n, 367n, **10**: 36, 36n

Old Toby: hired, **5**: 3, 128, 130, 163, 164n, 173, **10**: 128; relations with the party, **5**: 138; information from, **5**: 145, 152–54, 156–57, 162–63, 168, 170, 173, 192, 215, **9**: 214, **10**: 132, **11**: 291–92, 296–97, 309; sent out, **5**: 155, 173, **10**:131; duties, **5**: 169, 173; family, **5**: 178; guide, **5**: 178, 203, 205n, **6**: 452, **8**: 96n, **9**: 214, **10**: 137, 141, **11**: 339–40; interpreter, **5**: 196, **11**: 313, 315; and horses, **5**: 230, **7**: 248, 313, 315, **10**: 222, 230, 234; leaves party, **5**: 252–53, **9**: 236, 236n, 305n, **10**: 152, **11**: 345–46; village, **10**: 129; son joins party, **10**: 136; mentioned, **5**: 131n, 146, 167, 183, 235, **7**: 251n, 315n, **9**: 275n, **10**: 129n, 138n, 152n, 222n, 230n, **11**: 292n, 299–300, 341n

Oldtown Bar, **2**: 83, 84n

Old Woman at a Distance (Lo-tong-gar-tihar), **3**: 212, 213n

Olive Creek, **6**: 468

Olivine, **8**: 26n

Ollicutt. *See* Yelleppit

Omadi Creek, **8**: 350, 350n

Omaha (Mahar) Creek, **3**: 355, **9**: 38–40, 38n, 39n, 395n, **10**: 28, 29n

Omaha (Mahar) Indians: villages, **1**: 6, **2**: 452, 472, 476–78, 478n, 480, 483, 486–87, 497–98, 499n, **3**: 11, 13–14, 15n, 65, 94, 354, 372, 459, 464, **8**: 338, 344n, 347n, 349, 350n, 356n, 357, 379, 381, 397, 416–17, **9**: 36, 38, 39n, 80–81, 358, 367n, 394, **10**: 28, 247, 248n, 275–76, 276n, **11**: 55, 55n, 172; listed, **2**: 195, **3**: 448; trade, **2**: 259–60, 286–87, 445, 475, **3**: 353, 482, 484, **8**: 338, 355, 360, 362, **9**: 34, 358, 361–62, **10**: 278; and members of the party, **2**: 312, 516, 518; language, **2**: 343n, 376, 378, 399n, 404n, 438, 442n, 471n, 482n, 502n, **3**: 27, 32, 34, 48n, 50n, 114n, 121, 384n, 394, 490, **8**: 329–30, **9**: 65, 66n, **11**: 84n, 93n; located, **2**: 440–41, 458, **3**: 13–14, 166, 358, 483, **8**: 329; war, **2**: 440, 488–89, 507, **3**: 116, 119, 121–22, 416–17, 484, **9**: 69, **10**: 46, **11**: 56–57, 88–89; and Oto Indians, **2**: 455–56; chiefs, **2**: 466–67, 470n, 494n, **9**: 37, 37n, 394, **10**: 27, 27n, **11**: 54, 54n, 174; diseases, **2**: 469; gifts, **2**: 474, **3**: 493–94; historical sketch, **2**: 482n, **3**: 398–99; distances, **2**: 485; customs, **2**: 504–5, **9**: 37, 394; peace, **3**: 2, 26, 32, **9**: 40, 48–49, **11**: 57; encountered, **3**: 16–17, 19, 116, 118–19, **9**: 45, **10**: 31; prisoners, **3**: 114n, 115, 118–19, 121–23; food, **3**: 148n; medical problems, **3**: 398–99, **9**: 38; character, **3**: 482–83; hunting, **3**: 484–85; appearance, **3**: 487; signs, **8**: 350; mentioned, **2**: 490, 494n, **3**: 395, 400, 481, **8**: 331n, **10**: 28, 32, **11**: 56n, 107n

Omete (Ameat) Creek, **2**: 116–17, 117n

On-a-Slant village, **3**: 188n, **9**: 88, 88n, **4**: 288n, **5**: 13n, **8**: 126n, **9**: 169n, **11**: 201n

Oncorhynchus clarki (formerly *Salmo clarkii*), **4**: 288n, **5**: 13n, **6**: 409n, **8**: 126n, **9**: 169n, **10**: 125n, **11**: 201n. *See also* Trout, cutthroat

Oncorhynchus kisutch, **5**: 290n, **6**: 409n, **7**: 47n, **10**: 157n, **11**: 358n. *See also* Salmon, coho

Oncorhynchus mykiss, **6**: 409n, **7**: 241n, **8**: 37n, **9**: 209n, **10**: 242n, **11**: 374n. *See also* Trout, steelhead

Oncorhynchus nerka, **5**: 290n, **6**: 41n, **10**: 157n, **11**: 358n. *See also* Salmon, sockeye

Oncorhynchus sp., **5**: 86n, **9**: 206n, **10**: 130n. *See also* Salmon

Oncorhynchus tshawytscha, **6**: 414n. *See also* Salmon, king

Ondatra zibethicus, **2**: 205n, **4**: 53n, **5**: 58n, **9**: 131n, **10**: 174n. *See also* Muskrat

One Arm, **8**: 315

One Eye. *See* Le Borgne

One Horse Creek, **8**: 162n

Oneota village, **2**: 349n, 369, 372n

On His Guard (War-chapa), **3**: 121–22, 123n

Onion, Douglas's, **7**: 312n

Onion, Geyer's, **4**: 418n, **7**: 264–65, 266n, 309, 311, 312n, **10**: 116n

Onion, nodding, **4**: 418n, **10**: 116n

Onion, Tolmie's, **7**: 312n

Onion, white wild, **4**: 25–26, 28n, 30, 32

Oniongrass, **7**: 292, 295, 297n

Oniongrass, showy, **7**: 292, 295, 297n

Onion Island, **4**: 416–17, 418n

Onions, **2**: 153, **4**: 420, **5**: 18, 21n, 167, 170n, 219, 222, **7**: 127–28, 278, 280–82, 284, 287, 289–90, 331, **8**: 14, 17–18, 20, 360, **9**: 130, 189, 192, 198, 210, 292, 306, 308, 362, **10**: 116, **11**: 238. *See also*

Chive, wild

Opheodrys vernalis, **8**: 375n. *See also* Snake, smooth green

Opium, **5**: 163n. *See also* Medicine, laudanum

Oplopanax horridum, **6**: 45n. *See also* Devil's club

Opossum, **2**: 131, 132n, **8**: 416, 418n

Opuntia fragilis, **3**: 91n, **5**: 85n, **8**: 100n. *See also* Prickly pear, brittle

Opuntia macrorhiza, **3**: 91n. *See also* Prickly pear, bigroot

Opuntia polyacantha, **3**: 91n, **4**: 175n, **5**: 21n, **8**: 100n, **9**: 152n, **10**: 99n, **11**: 189n. *See also* Prickly pear, plains

Orderly Book, **2**: 234n, 237n, 259n, 332n, 520, 539–40, 558, **3**: 15n, 121n, 154n, 172n, **6**: 152–53, 158n, 161n, 198n, **9**: 18n, 24n, 114n, 264n, **11**: 409n. *See also* Detachment orders

Ordway (Odway, Ordeway), John: journal, **1**: 7, **2**: 8, 37, 40–42, 249n, 295n, 301n, 311n, 314n, 316n, 326n, 328n, 354n, 423n, 482n, 510, 513–14, 520, 527, 529, 531, 540–41, 544–45, 565–66, **3**: 66n, 79n, 91n, 95n, 99n, 103n, 114n, 120n, 125n, 130n, 136n, 142n, 157–58n, 171n, 181n, 240n, 255n, 270n, 271–72n, 274n, 290n, 297n, 305n, 313n, 322, 324n, **4**: 12n, 57n, 59n, 69n, 84n, 299n, 359n, 368n, 379n, 390n, 410n, **5**: 76n, 177n, 189n, **6**: 59n, 229n, 244n, 257n, 327n, 408n, 428n, **7**: 11n, 159n, **8**: 139n, 141n, 157n, 176n, 300n, 316n, 319n, 327n, 331–32n, 360n, 362n, 364n, 371n, **9**: 3n, 9n, 10n, 12n, 14n, 15n, 17n, 18n, 20n, 21n, 23n, 24n, 26n, 27n, 28n, 29n, 32n, 35n, 36n, 44n, 45n, 48n, 51n, 58n, 82n, 84n, 85n, 86n, 92n, 95n, 98n,

106n, 119n, 124n, 125n, 127n, 128n, 131n, 139n, 146n, 148n, 151n, 154n, 159n, 160n, 162n, 163n, 164n, 201n, 203n, 217n, 231n, 232–33n, 239n, 247n, 269n, 278n, 279n, 280n, 281n, 285n, 290n, 295n, 305n, 310n, 311–12n, 313n, 317n, 333n, 335n, 336n, 337n, 338n, 339n, 344n, 350n, 351n, 354n, 356n, 359n, 362n, 364n, 366n, 368n, 386n, **10**: xiii, 11n, 12n, 13n, 17n, 23n, 24n, 25n, 29n, 51n, 56n, 62n, 74n, 84n, 85n, 102n, 109n, 157n, 172n, 181n, 189n, 190n, 194n, 195n, 197n, 199n, 201n, 214n, 232n, 235n, 237n, 238n, 239n, 241n, 242n, 243n, 244n, 247n, 255n, 256n, 258n, 260n, 261n, 262n, 263n, 264n, 270n, 273n, 274n, 275n, 276n, 279n, 280n, **11**: xiii, 15n, 16n, 21n, 34n, 38n, 44n, 47n, 49n, 74n, 96n, 97n, 111n, 126n, 144n, 152n, 189n, 195n, 199n, 212n, 217n, 234n, 237n, 244n, 277n, 284n, 297n, 325n, 378n, 394n, 403n, 405n, 413n, 414n, 415n, 420n, 421n, 426n, 427n, 428n, 429n, 430n, 432n, 433n; returns, **1**: 9, **2**: 145, 173, 357, **4**: 380, **6**: 126, 227, 284–85, **7**: 139, 141, 277, 279, 326, 329, **8**: 174, 332, 353, **9**: 57, 59, 77, 89, 175, 184, 270, 270n, 313, **10**: 192, 235, **11**: 74, 422, 396; sent out, **2**: 142, 212, 476–77, **3**: 7, 9, 296, 297n, **4**: 366, 371–73, 378, 386–87, 416, **5**: 158, **6**: 198, 199n, 281, 287–88, 406, 409, 411, **7**: 9, 71, 74–76, 291, 293, **8**: 151, 170, 174, 176n, 311, 332, 352, **9**: 15, 21–22, 25, 38–39, 39n, 43–44, 44n, 57, 78–79, 99, 108, 115–16, 143,

176, 188, 211, 254, 259, 268, 270, 270n, 276–77, 280, 286, 332–33, 335, **10**: 30, 73, 183, 192, **11**: 61, 213, 237n, 403, 416, 416n, 418, 421–22, 421n, 426–27, 426n, 427n, 428n, 433, 433n; listed, **2**: 148, 187, 189, 194, 197, 199, 255, 347, **4**: 9, 11, **8**: 162n, **11**: 4n, 7n, 62n, 395n; separated, **2**: 155, **6**: 125, **7**: 323, 325, **10**: 104, 262, 276; duties, **2**: 174–76, 174n, 176n, 178–79, 190, 193, 206, 212, 256, 258, 371, **7**: 116–17, **9**: 40, 71, **10**: xii, xv; appointed sergeant, **2**: 188; in permanent party, **2**: 215n, 229n; court-martial member, **2**: 236, **3**: 170; hunting, **2**: 313, 314n, 315, 316n, 380, 382n, **3**: 66, **8**: 147, **9**: 18, 57–59, 77, 89, 149, 175, 261, **10**: 38–39, **11**: 72–74, 74n, 158, 164; biographical sketch, **2**: 513–14; information from, **3**: 21n, 313n, **4**: 158n, 383, **7**: 327, 330, **8**: 148, 151, 175; and Indians, **3**: 239, 266, 267n, 270, **7**: 275–76, 327, 329, **9**: 51n, 95, 104, 218, 219n, 280, 282–83, 285n, 289, 296n, 343n, 357n, **10**: 68; scouting, **4**: 66–68, 69n, **6**: 62, 65, **9**: 38, 39n, 44, **10**: 175, **11**: 395; and lower portage camp, **4**: 325–26; creek named for, **4**: 398, **9**: 22, 22n, **10**: 114n, **11**: 232n; votes, **6**: 83; medical problems, **6**: 135, 336–37, 339, **9**: 261, 273–74, 273n, **11**: 406, 422–23, 423n; and species, **6**: 325, **9**: 20, 20n, 25, 25n, 43, 44n, 57, 58n, 127n, 129, 131n, 135, 160, 167, 178, 187n, 197n, 199n, 224n, 260n, 286–87, 287n, 325n; and saltmaking camp, **6**: 325–26, 328–29, 333, 335, **9**: 272, **10**: 193–94; leads detachment, **7**: 327, 329, 330n,

8: 2–3, 74, 139n, 179, 180n, **9**: 182n, 332–33, 335–41, **10**: 28, 110, 181, 201, 255; accidents, **8**: 147–48, **9**: 238, 259, **11**: 352–53; clothes, **9**: 57, 112; trading, **9**: 104, 313, 315–18, **10**: 212, 233; loses axe, **9**: 184, **11**: 228; in Bissell's company, **10**: xiv; island named for, **11**: 33–34, 34n; lost, **11**: 405; mentioned, **2**: 143n, 193n, 206n, 212n, 218n, 234n, 237n, 243n, 254, 360, 360n, 363n, 373n, 374, 376n, 463n, 522, **5**: 157n, **9**: xiv–xvii, 16n, 22n, 44n, 59n, 172n, 211n, 255n, 257, 257n, 279, 313n, 334n, 336n, **10**: 28n, 30n, 38n, 39n, 68n, 73n, 105n, 110n, 131n, 175n, 183n, 190n, 192n, 193n, 201n, 212n, 233n, 235n, 255n, 262n, 277n, **11**: xii, xiv, 207–8, 208n, 418n

Ordway's Creek, **4**: 422n. See also Little Prickly Pear Creek

Oreamnos americanus, **5**: 164n, **6**: 317n, **7**: 103n, **8**: 58n, **9**: 290n, **10**: 149n. See also Goat, mountain

Oregon, camps in: Morrow County, **5**: 307n; Wasco County, **5**: 340n, 348n, **7**: 125n; Multnomah County, **6**: 10n, 14n, **7**: 62n, 89n, 101n; Columbia County, **6**: 24n, 30n, **7**: 14n, 17n, 22n, 25n; Clatsop County, **6**: 90n, 91n, 94n, 115n, **7**: 9n, 11n. See also Fort Clatsop

Oregon Historical Society, **4**: 277n

Oreortyx pictus, **7**: 89n, **9**: 287n, **10**: 207n. See also Quail, Mountain

Oriole, **3**: 86n

Orobanche sp., **7**: 338n. See also Broomrape

Orofino (Rock Dam) Creek, **5**: 233, 234n, **6**: 453, 467, **8**: 384, 402, **9**: 230, 230n, **11**: 333–34, 334n

Orthocarpus tenuifolius, **8**: 81n.
See also Owl-clover, thinleaf
Osage (Osarge) Indians: information from, **1**: 7; war, **2**:
141, 174n, 180, 235, 279,
306, **3**: 340, 395, 406, 483;
language, **2**: 181n, 267n,
425, 425n, 438, 442n, **3**: 27,
32, 34n, 394–95, 398–99,
402, 446, 473, 490; trade, **2**:
260n, 343n, 379n, 514, **3**:
483; historical sketch, **2**:
266–67n, **3**: 390–93; villages, **2**: 304n, 305n, **3**: 340,
383n, **10**: 11; located, **3**: 483;
customs, **3**: 483, 486, **6**: 405–
6; appearance, **3**: 487, **10**:
11; and animals, **6**: 405–6;
hunting, **9**: 376, 376n; mentioned, **2**: 180n, 374, 352n,
3: 393, 396. See also Great
Osage Indians; Little Osage
Indians
Osage orange (apple), **2**: 208,
210n
Osage (Osarge) River: and
maps, **1**: 5, 7, 16n. 39, **2**:
269n, 274n, 276n; arrive at,
2: 267, **8**: 366, 366n, **9**: 9, 9n,
365, 365n; latitude and lon-
gitude, **2**: 269, 407, 479, 486,
3: 94, **9**: 80, **11**: 173; described, **2**: 270, **3**: 339, **8**:
411, **10**: 11, 11n, **11**: 17, 17n;
and Indians, **2**: 323, 324n, **3**:
391, 483, **8**: 348n; distances,
2: 405, 408, 486, **3**: 94, 339–
40, 370, 375, **8**: 377, **9**: 81,
368n; fortifications on, **3**: 43;
listed, **3**: 376, 390, 479, **8**:
395, 411, **11**: 171–72; specimens, **3**: 453–54, 478; animals and plants, **4**: 276,
277n; camped on, **9**: 376–
77, **10**: 11, 11n, **11**: 17, 17n;
mentioned, **2**: 260n, 278,
286, 302, 304n, 401, **3**: 341–
42, 348, 480, **9**: 376n
Osage Woman's River. See
Femme Osage River
Osgood, Ernest S., **2**: 13, 41–
42, 52

Osmaronia cerasiformis, **7**: 195n.
See also Plum, Indian
Osmorhiza occidentalis, **10**: 137n.
See also Cicely, western sweet
Osmorhiza sp., **10**: 137n. See also
Cicely
Osprey, **4**: 121, 124n, **5**: 63,
67n, **6**: 383, 384n, 385, 388,
8: 264, 266n
Ossiniboin (and similar spellings) Indians. See Assiniboine
Indians
Ostrya virginiana, **8**: 418n. See
also Hop-hornbeam
Otis Creek, **4**: 81, 83, 84n, **9**:
139n, **10**: 84n, **11**: 140n
Oto (Otteau, Zoto) Indians:
councils, **2**: 60, 415–16, 428,
432–33, 435–36, 438–41,
488–93, **3**: 23n, **8**: 354n,
9: 33, 41, 392, **10**: 25, 277,
277n, **11**: 44–51 passim, 56–
57, 56n, 67n; language, **2**:
192n, 299n, 368n, 379n,
399n, 404n, 437n, 438–39,
442n, 443n, 493–94n, 527,
3: 405, 490, **9**: 31; listed, **2**:
195, **3**: 448, **8**: 397; villages,
2: 296, 302–3, 403, 407,
372n, 399, 400n, 407, 418–
19, 418n, 422–24, 423n,
426, 434, 444n, 446n, 478,
485, **3**: 94, 350, 352, 371,
379, **9**: 29–30, 35, 393; hunting, **2**: 366–67, 399, **9**: 33;
trade, **2**: 377–78, **3**: 353,
483, **9**: 25, 25n, 34; historical
sketch, **2**: 437n, **3**: 393–94;
war, **2**: 440, 488–89, **3**: 398–
99, 406, 408, 482, **9**: 395; located, **2**: 440, **3**: 166, **9**: 389,
10: 22, 22n; speech for, **2**:
455–56, **3**: 156–57; clothes,
2: 492; chiefs, **2**: 494n, **9**:
40–41, 41n, 395; customs, **2**:
504–5, **3**: 92, 486; relations
with the party, **2**: 526, **10**: 26,
28, 29n, **11**: 44–51 passim,
44n, 47n, 56–57; peace, **3**:
26, 30, 32, **9**: 40, 48, 50; and
mineralogical specimens,
3: 474; appearance, **3**: 487;

gifts, **3**: 493; distances, **8**:
379; search for, **9**: 29, 391;
encountered, **9**: 31, 33, 391;
mentioned, **2**: 435n, 443n,
483–84, 486–87, **3**: 395–96,
8: 362–63, 367, **9**: 31, 33n,
363, 389n, **11**: 107n. See also
Missouri Indians
Ottawa Indians, **2**: 132n
Otter, river: as trade item, **3**: 27,
390–444 passim, **6**: 30, 187,
205, 444; hunted, **3**: 190, **4**:
34, 356, 358, 376–77, 383,
385, 403, 416, 436, **6**: 161–
62, 174, 196, 430–31, **7**:
188–89, **9**: 88, 131, 179,
184, 186, 190, 264–65, 269,
284, 301, **10**: 58, 199, 220,
11: 217, 227–28, 232–33,
243–44, 264–65, 410–11,
416, 438; abundance, **3**: 482,
4: 403, 428, 433, **7**: 200–
201, **9**: 189, 337, **10**: 125,
266, **11**: 232–34, 239–40;
observed, **4**: 420, 422, 430,
438, **9**: 135, 202, **11**: 266;
signs, **4**: 436, 281; and Indians, **6**: 208, **7**: 224, 253, 255,
9: 206, **11**: 280–81; habitat,
6: 313, 315; skins, **9**: 233,
309, 369n, 378, **10**: 201, **11**:
338, 362–63; mentioned, **3**:
35n, 191n, **4**: 40n, **6**: 162n,
317n, 337–38, **7**: 190n, **9**:
88n, 242n, **10**: 58n, 91n,
11: 103n, 364n
Otter, sea: abundance, **6**: 11;
skins, **6**: 72, 74, 76, 194–95,
354, 434, 438, **9**: 255–56,
271, 273, 280–82, 369n; as
trade item, **6**: 73, 81, 83, 85,
121, 123–25, 165, 180, 187,
205, 221–22, 325, 327, 346;
and Indians, **6**: 208, 210,
214, 216, 395–96, 416, 418,
11: 419, 423, 432, 434, 436;
habitat, **6**: 313, 315, **7**: 7–8,
9n, 12–13, 28, 30, **8**: 164; described, **6**: 339–42; name, **6**:
342n; observed, **9**: 250, 252,
11: 365; scarcity, **9**: 256;
purchased, **9**: 280, **10**: 162n,

169, 176, **11**: 419, 423, 434, 436; mentioned, **6**: 86n, 160n, 166n, 317n, **9**: 242n, 243n, **11**: 367n. *See also* Seal, harbor

Otters, **5**: 18, 20n, 39, 43, 57, 59, 71–72, 84, 92, 121, 127–28, 135, 139, 151, 188, 259, 350, 352, **8**: 119, 120n, 175, 179–80, 278, 318, 414, **9**: 242

Ottertail Lake, **1**: 5, **2**: 219

Ouabesca, **8**: 348n

Ouifumcaka, **8**: 348n

Oven, Dutch, **9**: 166, **11**: 193–94

Oven Islands, **2**: 392, 393–94n, 394–95

Overalls, **3**: 310, **6**: 20n, 407, **9**: 208, 209n, 303, **10**: 193, **11**: 280–81, 282n. *See also* Clothing

Ovis ammon, **3**: 120n. *See also* Argali

Ovis canadensis, **3**: 120n, **4**: 75n, **5**: 21n, **7**: 114n, **8**: 69n, **9**: 127n, **10**: 84n, **11**: 141n. *See also* Sheep, bighorn

Ovis canadensis auduboni, **4**: 75n. *See also* Sheep, Audubon's mountain

Owl, dusky horned, **6**: 378n

Owl, great gray, **7**: 282, 282n, 298–99, 302n

Owl, great horned, **4**: 41n, **6**: 376–77, 378n, **7**: 28, 32n, **8**: 359, 360n, 374

Owl, long-eared, **4**: 175n

Owl, Montana horned, **4**: 2, 41n, 175n, **6**: 378n

Owl, snowy, **3**: 482, 492n

Owl-clover, thinleaf, **8**: 81n

Owls, **4**: 36, 40, 171

Owyhee River, **5**: 89, 94n, 95n, **7**: 182, 184–85, 186n

Ox, **4**: 336

Oxalis, Oregon, **7**: 44, 47n

Oxalis oregana, **7**: 47n. *See also* Oxalis, Oregon

Oxen, **2**: 67–68, 72–73, 142

Oxford, **12**: 4

Oxytropis lambertii, **8**: 193n. *See also* Locoweed, purple

Oysters, **5**: 89, 128, 134–35

P

Pacific Coast, **1**: 4–6, 10–11, **5**: 4, 114, 224n, 313n, **9**: 254n, **11**: 395n

Pacific Fur Company, **6**: 94n

Pacific Ocean: route to, **1**: 3, 9; and maps, **1**: 13, **6**: 309; arrive at, **2**: 7, 24–25, **5**: 83, **6**: 51n, 58–59, **9**: 254, 256, **10**: 171, 181, **11**: 394; distances, **2**: 159, **5**: 373, **6**: 458–59, **8**: 377, 388, **10**: 173; tides, **6**: 8–10, 15–16, 27, 30, 32–33, 34n, 35–46, 48, 50, 60–61, 73, 75, 107–9, 114, 175, 181, 196, 199, 203, 275–76, 278, 280; observed, **6**: 48–49, 61, 182, 193; conditions, **6**: 50, 103–4, 194, **10**: 226n; animals and plants, **6**: 131, 134, 315, 318, 324, 327, 333, 335, **7**: 221, 223, **8**: 416; traders, **6**: 187, 314, 316; islands, **6**: 205; mentioned, **2**: 1–2, 8, 26, 35, 229n, **3**: 4, 23n, 368, **4**: 1, 12n, 201, 204, 250, 260, **5**: 1, 4, 65, 90, 92, 95n, 111, 135, 365, **6**: 31, 35n, 65–67, 71n, 95, 107n, 117–18, 140, 151n, 168, 171–72, 177, 183, 263, 270, 282, 308, 311–12, 331, 366–67, 384n, **7**: 66, 81, **8**: 131, 213–14, 305, 368n, 376, 387, **9**: xiii–xiv, 94n, 233n, 260, 279, **10**: xiii, 4n, 6–7n, 63n, 77n, 155n, 156n, 172, 186n, 187n, 206n, 228, 246, **11**: xiii–xiv, 1, 4n, 5n, 6n, 8n, 132, 290–91, 403–4, 431

Pack (Glade) Creek, **5**: 202–3, 203n, 238, **6**: 466, **8**: 62–63, 65n, 67, **9**: 223, 223n, 328, 329n, **10**: 141, 141n, 246, 246n, **11**: 314n

Packer Meadows (Quawmash Glades), **5**: 203n, **6**: 452, 466, **8**: 56–57, 58n, 62–63, 65n, 67, 383, 402, **9**: 223n, 329n, **10**: 141, 141n, 246, 246n, **11**: 314n

Packs, **5**: 61, 77, 97, 209, 210n, 218, **8**: 56, 58, 135

Packsaddles. *See* Saddles

Paddles, **8**: 177, **9**: 334–35, **10**: 159, **11**: 361–62. *See also* Canoes, oars and poles

Paden Island, **2**: 79, 79n

Padouca Indians. *See* Plains Apache Indians

Padoucan language, **3**: 424–25

Padoucas Fork, **3**: 351, 422–23, 439

Pads, saddle. *See* Saddles, pads

Pah-kee (and similar spellings) Indians. *See* Atsina Indians

Paint, **3**: 240, 242, 484, **5**: 70, 78–79, 112, 158, 259, 341–42, **6**: 172n, **7**: 147–48, 276, 322, 324, **9**: 79, 83, 103, 134, 329n, 369n. *See also* Vermillion

Painted Woods Lake, **3**: 194–95, 195n, **9**: 89n, 117n, **10**: 59n

Painter Creek, **5**: 76n

Paints, **8**: 184, 191, 237, 318

Paiute (Snake, Towanahhiook) Indians, **5**: 326n, **6**: 13, 14n, **7**: 119, 121, 122n, 129, 218, **10**: 160, 160n, 214n

Paiute Indians, Northern. *See* Northern Paiute Indians

Palmer Creek, **2**: 295–96, 298, 299n, **9**: 380, 380n, **10**: 14, 14n

Palmer site, **2**: 444n

Palouse (Drouillard's) River, **5**: 266, 268, 269n, 281, **6**: 454, 467, **8**: 384, 403

Palouse (So-yen-now) Indians, **5**: 263n, 264n, 268, 269n, 275–77, 276n, 281–83, 284n, 291n, **6**: 482, 489, **7**: 348n, **8**: 89n, **9**: 237n, 324, 325n, 369n, **10**: 153–54, 153n, 154n, 158n, **11**: 349n, 350n, 356n

Palouse silt, **7**: 236n

Pamphlin, William, **12**: 5

Pan, **5**: 142, 146–47n. *See also* Arms and ammunition

Panax quinquefolius, **7**: 236n. *See also* Ginseng, American

Pan-dan-apappy (variously spelled). *See* Struck by the Ree

Pandion haliaetus, **4**: 124n, **5**: 67n, **6**: 384n, **8**: 266n. *See also* Osprey

Pania (and similar spellings) Indians. *See* Pawnee Indians

Pania Island, **3**: 46, 48n, 49

Pans, **5**: 359, 361, **9**: 369n

Panther. *See* Mountain lion

Panther Creek, **5**: 155, 157n

Papillion (Butterfly, Pappeo) Creek, **2**: 402–3, 404n, 407, 413n, 419, **3**: 353, 371, 378, **8**: 379, 397, **9**: 28, 29n, **10**: 22, 22n, **11**: 43, 43n

Papoose Creek, **5**: 157n

Papoose Saddle, **8**: 61n, **9**: 328n, **10**: 245n

Parakeet, Carolina, **2**: 323–24, 325n, **8**: 416, 418n

Paralysis. *See* Medical problems

Parhelion, **3**: 255n

Paris, **10**: xvii

Parker, Thomas, **2**: 92n

Parnarne Arparbe. *See* Struck by the Ree

Parsley, **7**: 277n

Parsnip, cow. *See* Cow parsnip

Partisan (Torto-hongar), **3**: 110n, 111–13, 114n, 122–26, 131, 132n, **9**: 67, 68n, **10**: 45, 45n, **11**: 85, 86n

Partridges, **3**: 11, 12n, 13n

Pascal Creek, **3**: 144n

Pascal (Good Hope) Island, **3**: 141–43, 142n, 144n, **8**: 321, 321n, **9**: 75n

Pashaquaw (and similar spellings). *See* Camas

Passerella iliaca, **6**: 164n. *See also* Sparrow, fox

Passhico (and similar spellings). *See* Camas

Pataha Creek, **7**: 202–4, 204n, 205n, **9**: 304, 304n, **10**: 221, 221n

Patit Creek, **7**: 199–201, 201n, 204n, **9**: 303, 303n, **10**: 220, 220n

Patroon. *See* Deschamps

Pattee Creek, **5**: 77, 85n, 97, 102n, 125n, **10**: 128n

Patterson, Robert, **2**: 5, 75, 75n, 87n, 93n, 122n, 412, 542, **3**: 301, 302n

Patterson, William Ewing, **2**: 75–76, 75–76n

Paunch Indians. *See* Crow Indians

Pawnee (Pania) Indians: trade, **2**: 259–60, 300, 377–78, 439, 445, **3**: 353, 483, **9**: 13, 25, 25n, 34, 363; villages, **2**: 369–70, 372–73n, 399, 400n, 403, 444n, 485, **3**: 348, **9**: 29, **10**: 22, 22n; councils, **2**: 415–16; language, **2**: 431n, 429–30, 438, 442n, **3**: 127n, 138n, 167n, 247n, 490, **10**: 274, 274n; located, **2**: 440, **3**: 395, **9**: 389; war, **2**: 440, **3**: 406, 437–38, 445; hunting, **2**: 488; peace, **3**: 16–17, 26, 32, **9**: 49; historical sketch, **3**: 395–98; listed, **3**: 448; character, **3**: 482; appearance, **3**: 487; gifts, **3**: 493; visits, **11**: 44–45, 44n; mentioned, **2**: 301n, **3**: 48n, 55, 401, **4**: 375, **8**: 308, 357, 362–63, **9**: 13n, 380, 381n, 389n, **10**: 14, 14n, 279–80, **11**: 126, 126n

Pawnee Indians, Grand or Chawi, **2**: 195, 200–201n, 400n, 438, 444n,**3**: 350, 352–53, 395–96, 398, 437–38

Pawnee Indians, Loup or Skiri, **2**: 195, 200–201n, 438, 440, 442, 444n, 489, 492, **3**: 26, 128n, 153n, 352–53, 395–97, 416–17, 437–38, 482–83, 490, **8**: 355, 355n, **10**: 22, 22n, 277, 277n

Pawnee Indians, Republican or

Kitkahahki, **2**: 195, 200n, 438, 440, 442, 443n, 444n, **3**: 350, 353, 395, 397–98, 437–38, 482–83, 490

Pawnee Indians, Tappage or Pitahawirata, **2**: 373n

Pawnee (Ponceras) Island, **8**: 337, 343n

Pawnee Pick Indians. *See* Wichita Indians

Pawnee Proper Indians. *See* Pawnee Indians, Grand or Chawi

Pawpaw, **8**: 7, 11, 12n, 357, 359, 361, 365–66, 366n, 416, 418n, **9**: 361, 361n, 363–64, 365n

Pawpaws, **10**: 279–80, 280n

Pea, common, **4**: 51

Pea, golden, **4**: 51, 53n, 108

Pea, partridge, **3**: 458, 464, 467

Pea, scurf. *See* Breadroot

Pea, sweet, **7**: 55, 61n, 77, 338n

Peace River, **10**: 6n, 156n

Peaches, **2**: 208, 209n, **9**: xvi

Peacock, **3**: 84

Peale, Charles Willson, **2**: 78, 78n, 531, **6**: 68n, 144, 145n, **7**: 89n, **12**: 6

Peale's Museum, **2**: 78, 78n, **6**: 66, 144, 145n

Peanut, hog, **2**: 380, 382n, **3**: 160n, **4**: 18n, 146, 148n, **8**: 338, 344n, 359, 360n, **9**: 227, 227n, **10**: 54n, **11**: 92n, 323–24, 325n

Pearls, **7**: 224, 253

Peas, **2**: 217, **7**: 335, 337, 338n, **11**: 91–92

Pease, Seth, **1**: 7

Pease Creek, **3**: 60n, **10**: 37, 37n, **11**: 71, 72n

Pease Island, **3**: 60n

Peat bogs, **5**: 37, 39n, 55, 57, 57n, 62, 63n, 71

Pebbles, **8**: 98, 103, 114n, 240n, 250n, 278. *See also* Gravel

Pecan, **2**: 336, 339, 339n, **8**: 416, 418n

Pediculus humanus, **5**: 344n, **10**: 211n, **11**: 368n. *See also* Lice

Peebles, John J., **1**: 4

Pekan (and similar spellings). *See* Fisher

Pelecanus erythrorhynchos, **2:** 209n, **3:** 66n, **4:** 96n, **5:** 313n, **8:** 149n, **9:** 36n, **10:** 26n, **11:** 53n. *See also* Pelican, American white

Pelican, American white, **2:** 208, 209n, 310, 336, 455, 457–62, 463n, 516, **3:** 66, 66n, 183, 185, **4:** 94, 96n, **5:** 309, 311, 313n, 375, **8:** 148, 149n, 194–96, 335, 349–50, 352, **9:** 36, 36n, 87, 242, 359, 393, **10:** 26, 26n, 57, 159, 276, **11:** 52–53, 53n, 102, 361–62

Pelican Island, **2:** 229–30, 231n, 232n

Pelican (Pelecan, Pillacon) Rapid, **5:** 311, 313n, **6:** 454, 468, **8:** 385, 403

Pelvis. *See* Medical problems

Pembina, **3:** 492n

Pembina (Pembenar) River, **2:** 220, **3:** 419, 441–43

Pemmican, **2:** 295n, **3:** 118–19, 120n, 252–53, 429–31, **4:** 40n, 354, 356, 379, **9:** 69, 70n, **10:** 47n, **11:** 89n. *See also* Jerky

Pemmican River, **2:** 220

Penawawa Creek, **5:** 264, 266n, 280

Pend d'Oreille (La-han-na) Indians, **5:** 189n, **6:** 480, 487, 491

Pend Oreille (Clark's, Flathead, Lastaro, Lastaw) River, **1:** 10–11, 18nn. 106, 107, **2:** 26, **5:** 198n, 230, 231n **6:** 325n, 480, 482, 487–88, **7:** 216–18, 219n, **10:** 157, 157n, 246, 246n

Pennsylvania, **10:** xiv

Pennsylvania, camps in: Allegheny County, **2:** 67n, 68n, Beaver County, **2:** 69n, 70n

Pennycress, field, **3:** 451, 462, 466

Pennyroyal, **7:** 338n, **9:** 166, 166n, **11:** 194–95, 195n

Pennyweight, **6:** 187, 192n, 205

Pens, ink, **5:** 133, **6:** 173n, 349, **9:** 207, **11:** 279. *See also* Ink

Penutian language, **6:** 432n

Peoria Indians, **2:** 150n, **3:** 407, 446, 449

Pepper, **4:** 131, 303, **8:** 37, **10:** 67, **11:** 113

Peppergrass, **7:** 335, 337, 338n, **8:** 93, 94n

Peppergrass, tall, **8:** 94n

Peppermint, essence of. *See* Medicine

Peramyscus maniculatus, **7:** 130n. *See also* Mouse, deer

Perca flavescens, **2:** 433n. *See also* Perch, yellow

Perch, **2:** 432, 483, 484n, **8:** 364n

Perch, yellow, **2:** 433n

Perchee (Split Rock) Creek, **2:** 281–83, 283n, 480, **3:** 341, 370, 377, **8:** 377, 395, **9:** 10, 11n, 368n, 378

Perideridia gairdneri, **5:** 174n, **7:** 266n. *See also* Yampah, Gairdner's

Perisoreus canadensis, **5:** 223n, **6:** 131n, **7:** 302n. *See also* Jay, gray

Peritonitis. *See* Medical problems

Periwinkles, **6:** 407, 409n, 420–21

Permian Admire Group, **2:** 386n

Peromyscus sp., **3:** 142n. *See also* Mice

Perrin du Lac, François-Marie, **1:** 7

Perry (Willow) Creek, **2:** 496–98, 499n, **10:** 29n

Persimmon, **9:** 120, 120n

Petalostemum candidum, **3:** 468. *See also* Clover, white prairie

Petalostemum purpureum, **3:** 467. *See also* Clover, purple prairie

Petasites sagittatus, **7:** 338n. *See also* Coltsfoot, arrowleaf

Peter, George, **8:** 370, 370n, 419, 419n

Peter's (Whip-poor-will) Creek, **2:** 354n, **9:** 21n, 386, **10:** 19, 19n, **11:** 36n

Petit, Salomin (Solomon), **2:** 365n

Petite Saline (Saline) Creek (Saline or Salt River), **2:** 282–83, 283n, **3:** 340–41, 347, 370, 377, **8:** 374, 375n, 377, 395, **9:** 11, 11n, 368n, 378, **10:** 12, 12n

Petites Côtes, Les. *See* Saint Charles

Peucedanum simplex, **7:** 190n. *See also* Lomatium, ternate

Phalacrocorax auritus, **2:** 205n, **5:** 313n, **6:** 14n, **7:** 11n. *See also* Cormorant, double-crested

Phalaenoptilus nuttallii, **3:** 179n, **4:** 237n, **8:** 148n. *See also* Poorwill, common

Phalaris arundinacea, **2:** 305n, **3:** 467. *See also* Canarygrass, reed

Phaseolus vulgaris, **5:** 147n. *See also* Beans

Pheasants, **5:** 153. *See also* Grouse

Philadelphia, Pa., **1:** 5, 13, **2:** 1, 5, 11, 36–38, 146n, 352n, 493n, **3:** 201n, 386n, 472, **6:** 330n, **7:** 187n, 328, **9:** 175n, **10:** xvii, 4n, 6n, 142n, 156n, 226n, 272n, **11:** xvi, 316n, **12:** 2, 5–6

Philadelphia, University of, **2:** 75

Philadelphus lewisii, **5:** 73n, **8:** 13n, **12:** 6. *See also* Syringa, Lewis's

Philanthropy River. *See* Ruby River

Phleum alpinum, **10:** 138n. *See also* Timothy, alpine

Phleum pratense, **2:** 305n, **10:** 138n. *See also* Timothy

Phoca Rock, **6:** 9, 10n, 457, 469, **8:** 386, 405

Phoca vitulina richardii, **5:** 328n, **6:** 10n, **7:** 41n, **9:** 243n, **10:** 162n, **11:** 367n. *See also* Seal, harbor

Phocoena phocoena, **6:** 414n, **9:** 252n, **10:** 169n, **11:** 392n. *See also* Porpoise, harbor

Phoebe, Say's, **7:** 193, 195n

Phoenix, **6:** 160n

Phoradendron flavescens, **2**: 101n.
See also Mistletoe
Phosphorus. See Medicine
Phragmites communis, **7**: 337n. See
also Reedgrass, common
Phrynosoma douglassi brevirostre,
5: 174n, **7**: 307n. See also Lizard, eastern short-horned
Phrynosoma douglassi douglassi, **7**:
169n. See also Lizard, pigmy
horned
Physic. See Medicine, laxative
Physocarpus capitatus, **6**: 104n, **7**:
14n, **8**: 12n. See also Ninebark
Physocarpus opulifolius, **6**: 104n.
See also Ninebark
Piaheto. See Eagles Feather
Pica pica, **2**: 484n, **3**: 79n, **4**:
29n, **6**: 381n, **7**: 135n, **8**:
146n, **9**: 61n, **10**: 41n, **11**:
76n. See also Magpie, black-billed
Picea engelmannii, **4**: 397n, **5**:
195n, **6**: 19n, **8**: 12n, **9**:
154n, **10**: 114n, **11**: 318.
See also Spruce, Engelmann
Picea sitchensis, **5**: 358n, **6**: 19n,
7: 78n, **9**: 259n, **10**: 189n,
11: 403n. See also Spruce,
sitka
Pickets, **6**: 139–41, 143, See
Horses, hobbled, picketed,
and spanceled
Picoides pubescens, **4**: 95n, **7**: 78n.
See also Woodpecker, downy;
Woodpecker, hairy
Picoides villosus, **4**: 95n, **7**: 78n,
8: 27n. See also Woodpecker,
downy; Woodpecker, hairy
Picou (and similar spellings). See
Lynx, Canada
Piegan Indians. See Blackfeet Indians, Piegan
Pierced Nose Indians. See Nez
Perce Indians
Pierced Wood River, **2**: 219
Pierce Island, **7**: 98, 100, 101n
Pierre Fresne (Arrow) Creek,
2: 288–89, 290n, **9**: 12, 12n,
379, **10**: 13, 13n
Pierson Formation, **2**: 285n
Pigeon, band-tailed, **5**: 174n
Pigeon, passenger, **2**: 80, 81n,

177, **3**: 8, 13n, 77, 82–83,
4: 377, 377n, 378, 379n, **5**:
174n, **6**: 369, 371, 373n,
385, 388, 425–26, **8**: 107,
107n, 117, 126–27, 143,
150, 210, **10**: 111, 111n
Pigeon (Beaver, Indian Knob,
Round-knob) Creek (Iowa),
2: 423–27, 425n, **3**: 353,
379, **9**: 30, 31n, 390, 390n,
10: 23, 23n, **11**: 46, 47n
Pigeon Creek (Nebr.), **2**: 484n
Pigeons, **5**: 174, 191, 217
Pike, northern, **2**: 71, 72n, 362,
363n, 432, 433n, 483, 485–
86, **9**: 40, 40n, **10**: 28, 29n,
11: 56, 56n
Pike, Zebulon Montgomery, **1**:
4, 12, 19nn. 133, 139, **2**: 183,
183n, 514, **3**: 114n, 166n, **8**:
355, 355–56n
Pike's Peak, **8**: 356n
Pilea pumila, **2**: 373n, **8**: 344n.
See also Richweed
Pillar Rock, **6**: 33, 34n, 87n, **9**:
251n, 256n, **10**: 168n, 178n,
11: 390n, 399n
Pills, Rush's. See Medicine
Pilot. See Old Toby
Pilot's village, **8**: 384, 403
Pinaut, Peter (Charles Pineau?),
1: 17n. 73, **2**: 255, 528, **4**:
12n
Pinch, **8**: 364n
Pine, limber, **4**: 227, 229, 232,
233–34n, 253n, **5**: 18, 21n,
35, 39n, 106–7, 108n, 202n,
8: 195, 197n, 268, 270n, **9**:
160, 160n, 193, 193n, **11**:
230–31, 232n
Pine, lodgepole, **5**: 4, 201,
202n, 204–5, 205–6n, 209,
210n, 215, 238, **8**: 10–11,
13n, 25, 28, 30, 102, 161,
162n, 163, **9**: 205, 210–11,
212n, 215, 218, 221–22,
224, 224n, 228, 230, 306,
310, 321, 330, **10**: 137, 138n,
142, 144, 224, 224n, **11**:
284–85, 286n, 293–94,
296–97, 300–301, 304–9,
311–12, 326, 331–32, 335,
374

Pine, long-leafed. See Pine,
ponderosa
Pine, pitch-, **2**: 111n, **4**: 140,
144n, 176, 227, 232, 396,
401, 403, 405n, **5**: 205–6n,
8: 10–11, 13n, **9**: 212n. See
also Pine, lodgepole; Pine,
ponderosa
Pine, ponderosa (long-leafed):
observed, **3**: 78, 79n, **4**: 2,
140, 143–44, 144n, 403,
405n, **5**: 191, 195n, 201,
202n, 228n, 233–34, 234n,
355–56, 358n, **6**: 3, **7**: 118,
120, 199, 201, 218, 221, 223,
227, 256, 299, 335, 337, **8**: 7,
11, **9**: 146–47, 146n, 149–
51, 185, 185n, **10**: 88, 88n,
114, 114n, **11**: 153–55, 159–
62, 164–68, 171, 175, 229–
32, 269–70; habitat, **7**: 121–
22n, 216, 218, 233–34, **8**:
28, 30, 81n, 82, 86, 89, 92,
100–101, 161; abundance,
7: 205, 207, **8**: 25, 79; bark,
7: 227; seeds, **7**: 227; use,
7: 336; mentioned, **5**: 21n,
210n, **6**: 19n, **7**: 233, **11**:
153n, 230n, 232n, **8**: 12n,
162n. See also Pine, pitch-
Pine, shore, **6**: 45n
Pine, spruce. See Spruce, Sitka
Pine, western white, **5**: 210n, **6**:
3, 207, 209, 279–80, 282–
84, 284n, **7**: 33, 37n, 102,
104n, **8**: 25, 26n, 28, 30
Pine, whitebark, **5**: 209, 210n,
215, 238
Pine, yellow, **2**: 110, 111n, 112
Pineapple weed, **4**: 262n
Pineau, Charles (Peter Pinaut),
3: 227n
Pine Creek, **7**: 219–20n, 224n,
9: 306n, **10**: 223n
Pine Island Rapids. See Half-
Breed Rapids
Pine Ridge, **8**: 225, 228n
Pines: use, **3**: 133, 136, **4**: 330,
356, 369, **5**: 150, 162, 234,
6: 68–70, 106–7, 119, 124,
172, 180, 219–20, 230–31,
243, 249, 251, **7**: 102, 217,
261, 327, 329, **8**: 56–57, **10**:

106n, **11**: 334; observed, **3**: 357–59, 368, **4**: 140, 144, 147, 157–58, 176, 178, 181, 184, 189, 191, 195, 203, 392, 394, 398–99, 402, 404, 406, 411, 421, **5**: 28, 36, 39, 48, 57, 77, 97, 140, 145–46, 154, 168, 170, 177, 190, 194, 203, 219, 222, 226–27, 239–40, 249–50, 315, 318, 338–39, 342–43, 349, 351–52, 360, 376–77, **6**: 8–9, 11, 15, 27, 31, 45, 65, 68, 96, 98, 116, 183, 448, 452–53, **7**: 60, 79, 217–18, **8**: 141, 167, 194, 197–98, 201–2, 225, 231, 238, 277, 384, 390, 414, **9**: 20, 152, 154, 160, 172, 186, 188, 190, 194, 201, 220–21, 229, 235, 242, 246, 248–50, 307, 321–22, **10**: 89–90, 92, 115, 123, 127, 129, 132, 136, 147, 151, 163, **11**: 163–64, 166, 169–70, 232–33, 235, 238, 248–50, 266–67, 296–97, 305–7, 310–16, 322, 324–25, 331–32, 340, 344, 363–64, 371–72, 376–78, 381–82, 384–86, 388–91, 402, 404; scarcity, **4**: 149–50, 161–62, 170, 201, 205, 209, 387, **5**: 346, **10**: 96; abundance, **4**: 181, 396, 414, **5**: 156, 167, 169, 184–85, 193, 204, 207, 209, 215, 218, 229, 237–38, 379, **6**: 7, 22–26, 42–44, 55–57, 59, 89, 114, 117, 183, 194, 237, **8**: 38, 224, **9**: 195, 216, 257–58, 306, **10**: 88, 135, 162, 226n, 238, **11**: 235, 241, 249–52, 294–96, 304, 376, 385; habitat, **4**: 419, **6**: 70, **8**: 82, 93, 100, 102, 186–87, 195, 200, 205; as food, **5**: 146, **8**: 60–61; and Indians, **5**: 201, 232, 288, 347, 359, 361, 369, **7**: 93, 230, 257, 259, **9**: 222, **10**: 154, **11**: 310–11; described, **6**: 183, 184; seeds, **6**: 348, 373, 375, **7**: 298, 304; damaged, **9**: 195; camped by, **9**: 225; mentioned, **5**: 210n,

6: 19n, 131, 177, 245, 261, 279–80, 298, 302, 345, 347, 379, **8**: 14, 18, **9**: 20n, **10**: 136n, **11**: 406

Pine Tree (Cave) Rapids, **5**: 272n, **6**: 454, 467, **8**: 384, 403

Pinhooks. *See* Fishhooks

Pinkerton's Geography, **10**: 64n

Pins, **5**: 296, **6**: 181, **7**: 271–72, 275–76

Pinus albicaulis, **5**: 210n. *See also* Pine, whitebark

Pinus contorta, **5**: 202n, **6**: 45n, **8**: 13n, **9**: 212n, **10**: 138n, **11**: 286n. *See also* Pine, lodgepole; Pine, shore

Pinus echinata, **2**: 111n

Pinus flexilis, **4**: 233–34n, **5**: 21n, **8**: 197n, **9**: 160n, **11**: 232n. *See also* Pine, limber

Pinus monticola, **5**: 210n, **6**: 284n, **7**: 37n, **8**: 26n. *See also* Pine, western white

Pinus ponderosa, **3**: 79n, **4**: 144n, **5**: 21n, **7**: 121n, **8**: 12n, **9**: 146n, **10**: 88n, **11**: 153n. *See also* Pine, ponderosa

Pinus rigida, **2**: 111n, **4**: 144n, **5**: 205–6n, **8**: 13n. *See also* Pine, pitch-

Pioneer Mountains, **5**: 52n, **8**: 169n

Piper, James, **2**: 229, 231n

Piper's Landing, **2**: 229–31

Pipes, **2**: 433, 498, **3**: 21n, 24, 28–29, 31, 33, 116, 118, 120n, 130, 195, 204, 208–9, 216–18, 224, 238, 251–52, 267–68, 274–75, 305, 311, 317, 321n, 355, 484–85, **4**: 13, 93, **5**: 79–81, 86n, 96–97, 112, 115, 128, 130, 165, 187, 227, 249, 305, 338, 349, 351, **6**: 83, 147, 179, 196, 223–24, 405–6, **7**: 58, 81, 148–49, 232, 238, 247–48, 251, 257, 341, 343n, **8**: 56–57, 88, 130–31, 298, 300, 302–3, 306, 313, 316, 338, **9**: 34n, 93, 126, 250, **10**: 50n

Pipestone. *See* Catlinite

Pipestone (Red Pipe Stone) Creek, **3**: 355, 384n

Pipit, Sprague's, **6**: 382–83, 383n

Piranga ludoviciana, **7**: 342n. *See also* Tanager, western

Pirogue, red (French, large): personnel, **2**: 214, 215n, 227, 256, 347, **3**: 171; accidents, **2**: 408, 452–53, **3**: 19, 307, **4**: 24, 108, 110; loaded, **3**: 76, **9**: 60; navigational problems, **4**: 24, **11**: 27; rudders, **4**: 108, 110, **9**: 142, **11**: 144–45; cached, **4**: 269, 274–76, **9**: 164–65, 342, **10**: 100, 100n, 259, 260n, **11**: 192–93; problems, **8**: 138, 295, **9**: 46, **10**: 259; repaired, **9**: 17; mentioned, **2**: 71n, 261, 263, 264n, 362, 415, 452n, **3**: 8, 76, 79n, 109, **9**: 8, 8n, 18n, 168, **10**: 10, 10n, **11**: 15

Pirogue, white (poplar, soldier's): illustration, **2**: 196, 201n; personnel, **2**: 214, 215n, 227, 248–49, 256, 347; accidents, **3**: 300, 307, **4**: 29–30, 55, 111, 152–56, 215, 225, 330, **9**: 46, 157–59; sails, **4**: 29–30, 152, **11**: 156–57; rudders, **4**: 111, 152; halyards, **4**: 152; unloaded, **4**: 153, 302, 304, **9**: 347; loaded, **4**: 156, **11**: 192; endangered, **4**: 230; cached, **4**: 300, 305, **9**: 170, 340–41, 341n, **10**: 103, 104n, 258, 258n, **11**: 202; mast, **4**: 303, 325, **11**: 156–57; navigational problems, **9**: 42, **11**: 20; repaired, **9**: 165, 347; awning, **11**: 156–57; mentioned, **2**: 71n, **3**: 109, 302n, 307–8n, **8**: 138, **9**: 31, 44–45, 348, **11**: 22, 29–31

Pirogues: other, **1**: 6, 8, **2**: 134, 140, 142, 144, 212, **3**: 29, 182, 226, 340, 350, **8**: 355, 357, 362, **11**: 16, 22–23; accidents, **2**: 19, **3**: 19–20, 96, 98, 121–22, 326, **4**: 2, 93, 114, 152–55, **7**: 111, 115,

Pirogues (*continued*)
11: 24, 63–64, 88–89, 144;
loaded, **2**: 70, 213, 237, 242,
261–62, 421, **3**: 57, 76–79,
107–8, 316, 332, **7**: 115–16,
8: 144, 146, 349, **9**: 46, 51,
57, 60, 62, 125, **10**: 62, **11**:
131, 139, 141, 158–59, 193;
articles damaged, **2**: 70–71,
76, 230, **3**: 19, 141, **4**: 153,
156; described, **2**: 71n; purchased, **2**: 75; personnel, **2**:
149, 160–61, 218, **3**: 20,
79n, 106n, 151–52, 171,
333, **7**: 115, **11**: 138; repaired, **2**: 325, 327, **3**: 20, 40,
42, 237, 320–21, **7**: 112, **8**:
152–54, 324, **9**: 46, **10**: 264,
11: 64; sent out, **3**: 22–24,
107–8, 111, 113, 126–27,
129, 215, 231, 239, 244,
248–49, **7**: 54, 111, **11**: 22,
106; constructed, **3**: 227,
227n, 304, 308–12, **9**: 94,
118–22, **11**: 129; attention
to, **3**: 278, 284–85, 300,
302–3, **4**: 51, 141, 193, 375,
11: 123, 128; endangered, **3**:
284–85, **4**: 140, 213, 218,
225, 295, **11**: 177, 250; problems with, **4**: 55–56, 63–64,
77, **9**: 96, 111–12, 117–18,
122–23, 142, 156, 159, 347,
10: 32, 47, 71–72, 74; rud-
ders, **4**: 114; sails, **4**: 154, **9**:
41, **10**: 88; navigational problems, **4**: 193, **8**: 252, 332,
9: 25, 41, 70, 96, 127, 134,
136–37, 148, **10**: 88, 102,
11: 20–21, 27, 144, 171; and
Indians, **7**: 53, **8**: 360, **11**:
85–86, 90–91, 99; un-
loaded, **7**: 94, 136, **8**: 152,
11: 157; use, **7**: 137, **8**: 138,
156, 325, 342, 412; cached,
8: 109, **9**: 164–65, 170,
341n, **10**: 100, 253; awnings,
8: 149; oars and poles, **8**:
324, **9**: 71, 123–24, 152,
156, 186; set out, **11**: 1; mentioned, **2**: 7, 18, 60, 206, 212,
229n, 257, 279, 282, 286,
290, 306, 357–58, 366, 369,

377–78, 402, 418, 457, **3**: 8–
10, 16–17, 111, 114, 135,
238, 327, 327n, 338–361
passim, 452, **4**: 1, 9, 11, 22,
44, 48, 55, 64, 68, 71, 73, 85,
93, 103, 105–6, 124, 168,
224, 228–29, 242, 281, 301,
310, 316–17, **5**: 226, **8**: 150,
155, 157, 232, 278–79, 280n,
290, 297, 303, 366, **9**: xi, 3,
3n, 9, 22–23, 45, 51, 57, 60,
65, 67, 92, 96–98, 125, 129,
137, 146, 157, 165, 363, 373,
386, **10**: xi, 1, 11, 13, 38, 43,
45, 47, 51, 54, 62, 75, 77, 95,
255, 257, 265, 277–79, **11**:
xi, 4n, 8n, 30–31, 59, 65–
66, 82–83, 87, 95, 104, 107–
9, 128n, 130, 147, 152–53,
167, 174, 199. *See also Cajeux;*
Canoes
Pish-quit-pah (and similar spellings) Indians. *See* Yakima
Indians
Pismire, **7**: 192, 194n
Pisquow (Pish-quit-pah) Indians, **7**: 142n, 151n, 165–67,
168n. *See also* Klickitat Indians; Umatilla Indians
Pistols, **2**: 183, **3**: 237, **5**: 178,
6: 16–17, **7**: 183, 185, 186n,
8: 134–35, 155, 294. *See also*
Arms and ammunition;
Guns; Muskets; Rifles
Pitahawirata Pawnee Indians. *See*
Pawnee Indians, Tappage or
Pitahawirata
Pitch, **4**: 324, 330, 359n, 369,
6: 124n, **7**: 18, 20, 23, 25, **8**:
153, **9**: 181, 181n, 289, 336,
10: 106n, 208, 209n, **11**:
221–22, 221n, 372–73, 427
Pittsburgh, Pa., **2**: 6, 18, 40, 59,
65, 66n, 81, 306, 514, **10**:
xv–xvi, 229n
Pittsburgh *Gazette*, **10**: xv, xvi
Pituophis melanoleucus deserticola,
7: 266n. *See also* Snake, Great
Basin gopher
Pituophis melanoleucus sayi, **2**:
452n, **3**: 51n, **4**: 425n, **9**:
35n. *See also* Bullsnake
Plains. *See* Great Plains

Plains Apache (Padouca) Indi-
ans, **3**: 136, 395, 403, 422–
26, 438–39, 449
Planes, **4**: 275, 279, **9**: 166, **11**:
193–94
Plantain, **7**: 338n
Platanus occidentalis, **2**: 314n, **8**:
355n, **9**: 9n, **10**: 11n. *See also*
Sycamore
Plates, **6**: 187, 205, 216–17. *See
also* Utensils, cooking
Platichthys stellatus, **6**: 67n, **10**:
175n, **11**: 395n. *See also*
Flounder, starry
Platte (Little Platte) River
(Mo.), **2**: 179, 180n, 333–34,
335n, **3**: 371, 378, **8**: 378,
396, **9**: 18, 19n, 368n, 384
Platten (Platt) Creek, **2**: 121,
124–25, 125n
Platte River (Nebr.): and maps,
1: 7; described, **2**: 20, 400–
403, **11**: 43; arrive at, **2**: 60,
8: 354n, **9**: 28–29, 29n, 389,
10: 22, 22n, 277, **11**: 43–43,
43n; Indian name, **2**: 404n;
distances, **2**: 406, 409, **8**: 353,
357, 361, 378, 414, **9**: 367n,
10: 94, **11**: 172; latitude, **2**:
407, 480, 487, **9**: 80–81; astronomical observation at, **2**:
410; fortifications on, **3**: 41,
43; used for comparison, **3**:
75, **4**: 167–68, **9**: 389; listed,
3: 94, 371, 375, 378, **8**: 396,
11: 171; affluents, **3**: 344,
347–52, 384n, **4**: 71, 73;
conditions, **3**: 348–49, 457,
8: 354; and Indians, **3**: 350,
352, 393–99, 414, 422–23,
435–39, 445, **8**: 355, **9**: 363–
64, **10**: 279–80; and specimens, **3**: 474, 478, 480–82;
traders on, **3**: 484; animals
and plants, **4**: 112, **8**: 416,
10: 279; hunting on, **8**: 363;
navigational problems on,
8: 411; mentioned, **2**: 180n,
296, 300, 302–3, 395–96,
399, 415, 416, 418, 432,
437n, 494n, 496, 498, **3**: 47,
335–36, 480–82, **4**: 188,
204, **6**: 11–12, **7**: 243, **8**: 232,

234n, 277, 374, **9**: 19n, 31–32, 74, 360, **10**: 17n

Platters, **6**: 119

Plattner site, **2**: 288n

Pleasant (Plum) Camp (S. Dak.), **3**: 79n, 83, **8**: 326, 327n, **10**: 273, 273n, **11**: 76–77, 76n, 77n

Plesiosaur, **3**: 61–62, 63n, **9**: 57, 57n, **10**: 37–38, 38n, **11**: 72, 72n

Pleurisy. *See* Medical problems

Plover, black-bellied, **2**: 485n, **4**: 93, 95n

Plover, lesser golden-, **2**: 485n, **4**: 97, 100, 100n, 132, 135, 135–36n

Plover, mountain, **4**: 419n

Plovers, **2**: 483, **3**: 96, 98, 131, 147, **4**: 417, **6**: 9, 13, 62, 66, 383, **8**: 93. *See also* Curlews

Pluck, **6**: 416, 418, 420n

Plum, big-tree, **3**: 8, 12n, 14, **11**: 62, 62n

Plum, Chickasaw (Osage), **2**: 208, 2l0n, 291–92, 293n, 370

Plum, damson, **2**: 504–5, 506n

Plum, ground, **3**: 454, 463, 467

Plum, hortulan, **2**: 293n

Plum, Indian, **7**: 193, 195n

Plum, Osage. *See* Plum, Chickasaw

Plum, wild goose, **2**: 293n

Plum, wild, **2**: 322, 323n, **3**: 8, 12n, 14, 15n, 85n, **4**: 52, 53n, 54, 94, **8**: 308, 324, 324n, 326, 327n, 329, 335, 417, 418n, **10**: 273, 274n, **11**: 62, 62n

Plum Camp. *See* Pleasant Camp

Plum (Caution) Island, **3**: 138, 140, 140n, **8**: 321, 321n, **9**: 75, 75n, **10**: 50n, **11**: 94n

Plumes, **7**: 147–48, 158. *See also* Clothing

Plum (Falling) Creek (Gosper County, Nebr.), **3**: 351–52, 384n

Plum (Mustle Shell) Creek (Nance County, Nebr.), **3**: 351–52, 384n

Plums, **2**: 369, 377–78, 380–81, 428–29, 433–34, 498, **3**: 10, 14, 15n, 19, 44–45, 78, 80, 82, 87, 131, 481, **9**: 12, 12n, 44–45, 51, 53–54, 59–60, 65, 355, **11**: 68–69

Pluvialis dominica, **2**: 485n, **4**: 100n. *See also* Plover, lesser golden-

Pluvialis squatarola, **2**: 485n, **4**: 95n. *See also* Plover, black-bellied

Poa glaucifolia, **8**: 222n. *See also* Bluegrass, fowl

Poa palustris, **8**: 222n. *See also* Bluegrass

Poa secunda, **4**: 41n, **7**: 190n, 337n, **10**: 218n. *See also* Bluegrass, Sandberg's

Pocahontas Island, **3**: 64n, **8**: 331, 332n, **9**: 57, 57n, **10**: 38, 38n, **11**: 72n

Pocasse, **9**: 79, 82n. *See also* Hay

Podiceps auritus, **6**: 401n. *See also* Grebe, horned

Podiceps grisegena, **6**: 401n. *See also* Grebe, red-necked

Podilymbus podiceps, **6**: 401n. *See also* Grebe, pied-billed

Podophyllum peltatum, **2**: 209n. *See also* Mayapple

Poggamoggan, **5**: 122, 151, 157n, **10**: 228–29, 229n. *See also* Arms and ammunition

Pogonomyrmex occidentalis, **5**: 14n. *See also* Ant, western harvester

Pogonomyrmex sp., **3**: 12n, **9**: 45n. *See also* Ant, harvester

Poinsett, Joel, **2**: 38

Poinsettia cyathophora, **3**: 470. *See also* Fire-on-the-mountain

Point Adams, **6**: 49–51, 53–54, 59, 62, 65, 67, 76n, 88, 95, 104n, 109, 114–16, 115n, 133n, 138, 140n, 177, 188–89, 192–93, 221–22, 228–29, 233–36, 275, 276n, 312, 321, 324, 351, 353, 356, 382, 391, 393, 409, 411, 459, 471, 475, 485, 494, **7**: 8, **8**: 387,

406, **9**: 279, 280n, **10**: 186, 186n, **11**: 394n, 431

Point Ellice (Point Distress), **6**: 40n, 48–50, 51n, 53, 59, 458, 470, **9**: 252n, **10**: 169, 169n, 171n, 173, 174n, **11**: 392n, 394n

Point Lewis, **6**: 458, 470

Point Meriwether. *See* Astoria

Point Samuel, **8**: 275n

Point Vancouver, **6**: 14n

Point William. *See* Tongue Point

Poisoning. *See* Medical problems

Po-kish'-a-co-mah, **2**: 144n, 221

Polanisia dodecandra, **12**: 10n

Polecat. *See* Skunk

Poles, **5**: 2, 70, 139, 340, 361, 369, **11**: 382. *See also* Travois

Poles, flag, **5**: 71, **9**: 37, 78, 91, 390

Poles, lodge, **4**: 378, 405, **5**: 333, 335, **8**: 125, 218, **9**: 157, **11**: 179

Poles, setting, **3**: 455, **4**: 171, 178, 202, 205, 210, 213, 222, 380, 398, 403, 406, 411–12, 414, 420, 423, 429, **5**: 33, 59, 71–72, 94, 233, 248. *See also* Canoes; Keelboat; Pirogues

Polistes sp., **7**: 312n. *See also* Wasps

The Polsey. *See* The Shake Hand

Polygala senega, **7**: 285n. *See also* Snakeroot, seneca

Polygonatum biflorum, **6**: 242n. *See also* Solomon's seal

Polygonum sp., **8**: 418n. *See also* Smartweed

Polystichum munitum, **6**: 307n. *See also* Fern, Christmas

Pomme blanche. *See* Breadroot

Pomme de terre. *See* Potato, Indian

Pompeys Pillar Creek, **8**: 224–25, 227, 228n, 408

Pompeys Pillar (Pompy's Tower), **3**: 291n, **8**: 3, 224–27, 228n, 229n, 284–85, 391, 408

Ponca (Pania, Poncar) Creek, **3**: 48–49, 50n, 95, 358, 372, 380, 400, **8**: 343n, 380, 398, **9**: 54, 54n, 367n, **10**: 35, 36n

Ponca (Poncar) Indians: listed, **2**: 195, **3**: 448; located, **2**: 252, **3**: 399; trade, **2**: 365n, **3**: 76n, 353, 484; language, **2**: 438, 442n, 482n, **3**: 27, 32, 34n, 490, **8**: 330, **9**: 356, **10**: 274; peace, **3**: 26, 30, 32, 353; villages, **3**: 46–49, 48n, 358, 400, **9**: 53, 54n; historical sketch, **3**: 50–51n, 399–400; distances, **3**: 95; medical problems, **3**: 400; war, **3**: 416–17, 482; character, **3**: 482–83; hunting, **3**: 484–85; gifts, **3**: 493; relations with the party, **9**: 50; mentioned, **2**: 301n, **3**: 398, **8**: 329, 331n, 360n, **9**: 38, 39n

Pondera Creek, **8**: 117, 118n

Pond River, **2**: 219–20

Poorman Creek, **8**: 94–95n, **10**: 250n

Poorwill, common, **3**: 178–80, 179n, 181n, **4**: 236, 237n, 344, 346n, **8**: 147, 148n, 417, 418n

Poplar, lombardy, **3**: 452, **10**: 63n

Poplar, tulip-, **3**: 307–8n

Poplar (Porcupine) River, **4**: 103, 105–6, 107n, 109, 222, **6**: 447, 462, **8**: 149, 149n, 151n, 381, 400, 412, **9**: 142, 142n, **10**: 85, 85n, **11**: 144, 144n

Poplars, **3**: 221, 307n, **5**: 355

Pop-pank, **5**: 109, 116n

Populus angustifolia, **4**: 253n, 396n, **5**: 30n, 195n, **8**: 81n, **9**: 164n, 185n, **11**: 189n. *See also* Cottonwood, narrowleaf

Populus augustifolia, **10**: 113n. *See also* Cottonwood, narrowleaf

Populus deltoides, **2**: 292n, **3**: 39n, 466, **4**: 19n, 396n, **8**: 81n, **9**: 9n, 185n, **10**: 11n, 113n, **11**: 46n. *See also* Cottonwood, plains

Populus nigra, **10**: 63n. *See also* Poplar, Lombardy

Populus sp., **3**: 307n. *See also* Poplars

Populus tremuloides, **4**: 96n, **8**: 81n. *See also* Aspen, quaking

Populus trichocarpa, **5**: 195n, **6**: 20n, **7**: 14n, **8**: 81n, **9**: 247n, **10**: 166n, **11**: 377n. *See also* Cottonwood, black

Porcupine, **3**: 23–24, 65, 66n, 69, 69n, 82, 87, 117, 482, **6**: 353, 358, **7**: 62, 70n, 124–25, 129, 145, 148, **9**: 47, 57, 58n, 59, 109, 110, 355, **10**: 38–39, 38n, 70

Porcupine, yellow-haired, **3**: 66n, **4**: 39, 70, 75n, 103–6, **5**: 122, 126–27, 131n, 134–35, 150, **8**: 281, 281n, 328, **11**: 72–73, 73n, 120

Porcupine Creek (Mont.), **4**: 125, 129n

Porcupine (Sharhá, So-harch, Girl) Creek (S. Dak.), **3**: 174–76, 175n, 178n, **9**: 85, 85n, 86n, **10**: 56, 56n, **11**: 101, 101n

Porcupine River. *See* Poplar River

Pork, **2**: 165, 191, 198–200, 202–5, 211, 217, 258, 436, **4**: 275, 279, 334–35, 338–39, **5**: 74–75, 131, 133, **6**: 113, 166–67, **8**: 138, 360, 367, **9**: 42, 67, 166, 174, 176, 208, 217, 365, **10**: 101, 136, 278, **11**: 193, 212

Porpoise, harbor, **6**: 407, 410–11, 414n, **9**: 252, 252n, **10**: 169, 169n, **11**: 391, 392n

Portage. *See* Missouri River, Great Falls of the

Portage des Sioux, **2**: 166, 166n, 180, 180n, 218, 230–31, 232n

Portage la Prairie, **3**: 442–43

Porter, **2**: 166, 167n. *See also* Alcoholic beverages

Portfire, **3**: 124, 125n, **7**: 58, 80, 89n. *See also* Arms and ammunition

Portland Island, **2**: 265, 266n

Portmanteau, **8**: 164

Post Office Lake, **6**: 21n

Potassium bitartrate. *See* Medicine

Potassium nitrate, **2**: 357n. *See also* Medicine; Medicine, saltpeter

Potato. *See* Wapato; Camas

Potato, Indian, **2**: 223, 224n, 364–65, 365n, **3**: 117–19, 120n, **8** 359, 360n, **9**: 23, 23n, **11**: 89n, 92n

Potato, sweet. *See* Cous

Potatoes, **2**: 80, 166

Potawatomi Indians, **2**: 131, 132n

Potentilla anserina, **7**: 61n. *See also* Silver-weed

Potentilla sp., **7**: 61n

Potlatch River (Colter's Creek), **5**: 251, 252n, 258, **6**: 453, 467, 482, **7**: 210, 212, 214n, 215n, 216–18, 221, 223, 226, **8**: 384, 402, **9**: 235n, 305, 306n, **10**: 151n, 222, 222n, **11**: 343n

Potoash Indians. *See* Salishan Indians

Potomac River, **4**: 278, 291, 324, **6**: 388, 395, 397

Pots, **5**: 10n, 150, **6**: 187

Potts, John: recruited, **2**: 139n; listed, **2**: 148, 187, 189, 195–96, 198–99, 255, **4**: 9, 11, **6**: 83, 172n, **8**: 139n, 162n, **11**: 4n, 7n, 411n; discipline, **2**: 150, 194, 523; in permanent party, **2**: 229n; court-martial member, **2**: 236, 329; biographical sketch, **2**: 520; hunting, **4**: 57, 59n, **5**: 162, 164, **9**: 133, 135, **10**: 229, **11**: 409; sent out, **4**: 382, 386, 398, **7**: 155, 157, 268–72, **8**: 179, 180n, **9**: 265, 285, 335, **10**: 112, 114, 205, 258, **11**: 410; medical problems, **4**: 386, **8**: 35–36, 45–46, 57–58, 59n, 162, 365; scouting, **4**: 398, 401, **7**: 54, 57, 60n, **9**: 186, **11**: 230–31, 438–39; creek named for, **4**: 407–8, **11**: 47, 48n; death, **5**: 10n; separated, **7**: 157–58; returns, **7**: 273, **9**: 264, **10**: 255, **11**: 236–37; accidents, **7**: 308, 310, **9**: 324, **10**: 234,

241; trading, **9**: 312, **10**: 230; and canoes, **9**: 340; and salt-making camp, **10**: 187; mentioned, **2**: 211n, **9**: 133n, 186n, 264n, 265n, 279, 285n, 313n, 336n, **10**: 113n, 114n, 188n, 206n, 214, 214n, 230n, 234n, 241n, 255n, 258n, **11**: 232n, 410n, 440n

Pouch, shot, **2**: 497, **4**: 151, 153, 341, 343, **5**: 53, 69, 230, 231n, 271–72, **8**: 134–35, 295, 359, **9**: 177, 197, **10**: 122, 268, **11**: 165–66, 215–16, 257–58, 352–53. *See also* Arms and ammunition

Poucon Indians. *See* Winnebago Indians

Poultices. *See* Medicine

Powder. *See* Gunpowder

Powder, ink, **2**: 6

Powder (Wah-har-sah, Red-stone) River, **1**: 11, **3**: 234n, 365, 374, 382, **4**: 76n, **8**: 252–53, 255, 256n, 261n, 258–59, 390, 406–7

Powell Junction, **8**: 61n

Powers Island, **2**: 104n

Pox. *See* Medical problems, venereal disease

A Practical Introduction to Spherics and Nautical Astronomy . . . (Kelly), **2**: 87n

Prairie-chicken, greater (Indian hen, prairie fowl, prairie hen), **2**: 90, 90n, 101, 153, 154n, 462, 463n, **4**: 98, **6**: 366, 367, 368n,**8**: 148, 149n, 345, 345n, 373, 416, 418n

Prairie dog (barking squirrel): specimen, **2**: 523, **3**: 4, 330–31, 331n, **8**: 327, 419, **9**: 123n, 126, 127n, **12**: 3; discovered, **3**: 1, 52–53, 54n; hunted, **3**: 55, 58, **8**: 329, 331, 333, **9**: 55–56, 182; observed, **3**: 64–65, 67, 82–83, **4**: 39, 112, **5**: 33, 35n, **8**: 333; abundance, **3**: 78–80, 87, **4**: 256, 280, **8**: 326; habitat, **3**: 482, **6**: 346, 347n, 348, **8**: 380; behavior, **4**: 36, 112,

183–84, 187n, **8**: 76; villages, **4**: 36, 189–91, **9**: 55–56, 58, 154, 182, **10**: 36, 91n, **11**: 70, 71n, 222–23; described, **8**: 75–76, **9**: 55, 55n, **11**: 70, 71n; mentioned, **2**: 439–30, **3**: 372, **4**: 15, 17, 259n, **6**: 352, 354, **7**: 296n, **8**: 13n, 78n, 97, 326, 327n, 332n, 333n, 417, 418n, **10**: 36n

Prairie du Chien, **2**: 191, 191n, 208, 458, **3**: 27, 32–33, 406, 408, 414, 480, **8**: 346, 347n

Prairie du Rocher Creek, **2**: 123, 124n

Prairie Elk Creek (Little Dry River), **4**: 117, 119, 120n, **6**: 447, 463, **8**: 148, 148n, 381, 400, **9**: 144, 144n, 346n, **10**: 86n, 263n

Prairie fires. *See* Fires, prairie

Prairie of the Arrows. *See* Arrow Prairie

Prairie of the Knobs. *See* Nevada Valley

Prairie turnip. *See* Breadroot

Prarow. *See* Badger

Precambrian Belt Group, **5**: 141n, 148n, 203n

President, **8**: 346, 348n

Prickly pear, **3**: 90, 93, 99, **4**: 3, 176, 178, 181, 238–39, 241, 247, 251, 254, 256, 294, 325, 327–28, 352, 383, 385, 404–5, 407, 410, 423, 427–28, 430, 432, **5**: 301, **6**: 370, **8**: 116–17, 136, 143–44, 202, 210, 264, 416, 418n, **9**: 161–63, 173, 187, 189, 210, 210n. *See also* Cactus

Prickly pear, bigroot, **3**: 91n

Prickly pear, brittle, **3**: 91n, **5**: 78, 85n, 191, 191n, 241, 278, **8**: 99, 100n, 204n

Prickly pear, plains, **3**: 91n, **4**: 170, 175n, **5**: 18, 21n, 36, 45, 65, 67n, 78, 85n, **8**: 99, 100n, 204n, **9**: 152, 152n, **10**: 98, 99n, **11**: 184–85, 188–89, 189n, 234, 239

Prickly Pear (Pryor's) Creek, **4**: 405, 406n, 410n

Pries, **9**: 111, 111n, 118

Priest Rapids Member, **5**: 340n

Primeau, Paul, **2**: 255, 347, 526, 528, **3**: 230–31, 231n, 249, 250n, **9**: 94, 94n

Prince of Wales' Fort, **10**: 6n

Prince William Henry, **6**: 160n

Prisoner's base, **7**: 347, 348n, 349, **9**: 320, 320n

Privets, **2**: 498, 499n, 505, **3**: 456, **5**: 73n

Procyon lotor, **2**: 166n, **6**: 211n, **8**: 356n, **9**: 242n, **10**: 159n, **11**: 364n. *See also* Raccoon

Progne subis, **4**: 111n, **7**: 78n. *See also* Martin, purple

Pronghorn (antelope, cabri, goat): discovered, **3**: 1, 70–72, 73n, 74n; observed, **3**: 44, 46n, 48–52, 51n, 77–79, 87, 93–94, 131, 144–45, 176–77, 186, 222, **4**: 19–20, 48–49, 57–58, 82–83, 103, 108, 111, 151, 164, 186, 237, 247, 251, 256, 258–59, 280, 403, 414, **5**: 15, 19, 25–26, 37, 39, 42–43, 45, 71, 84, **7**: 127, 171, **8**: 93, 115, 117–18, 179, 182, 189, 210, 255, **9**: 54, 78, 89, 130–31, 137, 143, 153, 166, 174, 195, 332, **10**: 35, 67, 251, **11**: 112, 145–46, 184, 194–95, 210–13, 242–43, 266; hunted, **3**: 55, 58, 70–72, 82–83, 104, 106, 144, 176–77, 182–83, 229, 256, 288, 485, **4**: 31–33, 42, 44–46, 45n, 96, 113, 115, 157–58, 266, 280, 287, 356, 358, 363–64, 366, 368, 374–75, 402, 417, 421, 423, 426, **5**: 55, 59, 62–63, 72, 93–94, 104, 112, 115, 129–30, 149, 164, 262–63, 275, **8**: 90, 93, 98, 116, 172, 204, 206, 238, 245, 255, 287, 326, **9**: 59, 61–62, 65, 76, 87–88, 113, 132, 149, 163, 172–73, 178, 181, 186, 189, 198, 201–2, 205, 210, 333, 335–36, 339, 342, **10**: 39, 42–43, 51, 56–57, 80, 109, 116, 122–25, 131, 249, 251, 258, **11**: 74–76, 79, 82, 95, 101–

Pronghorn (antelope, cabri, goat) (*continued*)
3, 139, 158–59, 188, 211, 216, 220–21, 232, 240, 243–44, 260–62, 266, 268, 273; abundance, **3**: 81–83, 90, 96, 98, 133, 179–80, 184, 186, 188, 256, **4**: 53, 57, 60, 62, 67, 75, 79, 81–83, 85, 87, 90, 105, 126, 128, 134, 143, 184, 421, 436, **5**: 31–32, 135, **7**: 174, 176, **8**: 97–98, 112–13, 148, 187, 189–90, 219, 232, 259, 326, 417, **9**: 101, 139–40, 190, **10**: 40, 56–57, **11**: 146, 185, 189, 211–12; and Indians, **3**: 116, 119, 257n, **4**: 114, 126, 128, 237, **5**: 87–88, **7**: 128, 263, **8**: 232, **9**: 85, 103, 132n, 205, **10**: 56, 131, **11**: 276–77; skins, **3**: 161–62, 164, 253, 270–71, 488, **4**: 126, 128, 137, 266, 364–66, **5**: 80, 126–27, 134, 139, 151, 188, 286, 289, 309, 317, **9**: 126, 189, 205, **10**: 264, **11**: 239; specimen, **3**: 329–30, 465, **8**: 327n, **10**: 273; as trade item, **3**: 390–444 passim; food, **3**: 464–65, **4**: 35, 70, 146; habitat, **3**: 482; behavior, **4**: 16–17, 67, 87, 113, 143, 236–37, 334, 426, **6**: 328, **8**: 112; as food, **4**: 111, 157, 198, 280, **5**: 62, 83, **9**: 199–200, 333, **11**: 263; scarcity, **4**: 227, 229, 232, **5**: 91, **7**: 49, 52, **8**: 123, 128, **9**: 160, **10**: 125; listed, **6**: 313, 315; described, **6**: 336, 338, **8**: 112, 175, **9**: 59, **10**: 40, 258; use, **7**: 147, 297, 308, 310; mentioned, **4**: 21n, 194, 197, 429n, **5**: 17n, **6**: 317n, 339n, 403, **7**: 53n, **8**: 92n, 237, 245, 327, 328, 418n, **9**: 54n, 127n, **10**: 36n, 80n, 258n, 273n, **11**: 6n, 75n
Prophet Dance, **7**: 162n
Proulx, Basil, **8**: 369–70, 369n
Provisions: packing, **1**: 5, **2**: 191, 193, 214–15, **3**: 316; purchased, **2**: 6, 80, 230; wet, **2**:

83, 215, 230, 261, 408, 415–16, **3**: 82–83, **4**: 55–56, 65–66, 156, **5**: 53, 319, **6**: 83–85, 196; delivered, **2**: 125–26, 137, 156–57, 187, 201–5; stored, **2**: 142, **5**: 367; listed, **2**: 165, 198–204, 217–18, 443n; and Indians, **2**: 181, 245, 435–36, 489, **3**: 21–22, 32, 148, 173–74, 176–77, 226–27, 255, 303, 309, **7**: 238–39; examined, **2**: 211, 293; obtained, **2**: 235, **3**: 155, 238, 293–96, 308; issued, **2**: 258, **5**: 133; spoiled, **2**: 327, 333, **4**: 156–57; orders concerning, **2**: 332, 357–60, 474; damaged, **3**: 140–41, 299, **5**: 53, **6**: 259; low, **3**: 285–86, 298; seeking, **3**: 288, 291–92, 306, **5**: 164n, 211; transported, **3**: 312, **4**: 323; loaded, **3**: 332, **5**: 96, **7**: 345; endangered, **4**: 2; portaged, **4**: 3; dried, **4**: 156–57, 267, 356, **5**: 55, 57; cached, **4**: 274; scarcity, **5**: 148, 159, 213, **6**: 81, 223–24, 351, 381–82, 441–43, **7**: 177, 179, 209–10, 211–12, 230; exhausted, **5**: 152–53, 244; need, **5**: 156, 163; as trade item, **5**: 227, 231–32, 242–43, 262, 265, 278, 296, **6**: 167–68, 353, **7**: 123–24, 126, 128, 133–34, 137, 141; lost, **5**: 272, **7**: 310; secured, **7**: 149; mentioned, **4**: 306, **6**: 211. *See also specific food items*
Prunus americana, **2**: 323n, **3**: 12n, **4**: 53n, **8**: 324n, **10**: 274n, **11**: 62n. *See also* Plum, wild
Prunus angustifolia, **2**: 210n. *See also* Plum, Chickasaw
Prunus avium, **2**: 209n. *See also* Cherry, sweet
Prunus cerasus, **2**: 209n, **4**: 148n. *See also* Cherry, sour
Prunus emarginata, **7**: 114n, 346n, **10**: 207n. *See also* Cherry, bitter

Prunus hortulana, **2**: 293n. *See also* Plum, hortulan
Prunus insititia, **2**: 506n. *See also* Plum, damson
Prunus mahaleb, **2**: 209n. *See also* Cherry, mahaleb
Prunus mexicana, **3**: 12n, **11**: 62n. *See also* Plum, big-tree
Prunus munsoniana, **2**: 293n. *See also* Plum, wild goose
Prunus pensylvanica, **8**: 159n. *See also* Cherry, pin
Prunus persica, **2**: 209n. *See also* Peaches
Prunus serotina, **2**: 373n, **8**: 159n. *See also* Cherry, black
Prunus sp., **9**: 13n, **10**: 227n. *See also* Cherries; Plums
Prunus spinosa, **7**: 346n. *See also* Sloe
Prunus virginiana, **2**: 373n, **3**: 261n, **4**: 28n, **5**: 86n, **7**: 114n, 307n, **8**: 12n, **9**: 28n, **10**: 22n, **11**: 42n. *See also* Cherry, choke
Pryor, Nathaniel Hale: separated, **2**: 103, 105, **6**: 307, 309, 395–96, **7**: 264, 266, **8**: 177, 285n, **10**: 265; returns, **2**: 110, 157, **3**: 21–22, **6**: 109, 114, 281–82, 287–88, 312, 314, 401–3, **7**: 48–49, 51, 102–3, 118, 120, 267–68, 278, 291, 294, **8**: 156, 179, 206, 218, 283–85, 334, **9**: 46, 57, 59, 270, 276, 291, 314, **10**: 197, 210, 233, **11**: 64–65, 74, 184, 186, 190–91, 396, 402, 418, 420, 424, 427; listed, **2**: 148, 187–88, 194, 197, 199, 255, 347, **4**: 9, 11, **8**: 162n, 179, **11**: 4n, 7n, 187n, 395n, 411n, 419n; sent out, **2**: 155, 306, **3**: 16–17, 19, 21–23, 117, 120n, 239, **4**: 260, 373, 375, **5**: 115, 116n, **6**: 60, 107, 133, 181, 189, 275–77, 296–97, 336, 381–82, 409, 411, **7**: 48, 51, 62, 66, 100, 102, 116–17, 143–44, 277, 279, 293, **8**: 175, 205, 208, 210–12, 222n, 285, 303, **9**: 28, 45,

58–59, 265, 277, 285, 291, 313, 349, **10**: 110, 255, **11**: 63, 401, 410, 417, 419, 419n, 424, 426; duties, **2**: 175, 212, 256, **3**: 8, 11, 12n, 99n, **5**: 252, **6**: 429–30, **7**: 75–76, 112, 126, 308, 310, **8**: 170, 209–10, **10**: xv, 31, 31n, 180, 193n, 195, 198, 209; medical problems, **2**: 183, 190, 192, **3**: 243, 243n, **4**: 333–35, 337, 376–77, **5**: 17–18, 17n, 157n, **6**: 122, **8**: 285, 286n, **9**: 174, **10**: 63, 131, **11**: 211; appointed sergeant, **2**: 188; in permanent party, **2**: 215n, 229n; court-martial member, **2**: 329; hunting, **2**: 398–99, **3**: 66, 66n, 273, **6**: 105–6, 106n, **7**: 267–68, 280–81, **8**: 182, 326, **9**: 110, 144, 258, 258n, 270, 274, 311, **10**: 38–39, 179, 229, 231, 273, **11**: 72–74, 74n, 401, 438; biographical sketch, **2**: 514; journal, **2**: 514, 544–45, **8**: 212, 212n, 286n, **10**: xiii; one of "nine young men from Kentucky," **2**: 529n; information from, **3**: 63, 64n, **4**: 249, 251, 267, **7**: 49, 51–52, 267–68, **9**: 46; later career, **3**: 154n, 316n; scouting, **4**: 247, 250, 252n, 256, **6**: 62, 65, **9**: 161, 162n, 254, 284, **10**: 97–98, 175, **11**: 184–90, 186n, 395, 437; and iron-frame boat, **4**: 351; creek named for, **4**: 405, 412, 415n, 417, **8**: 219, 222n, 229n, 285, 286n, **10**: 115n, **11**: 235n; accidents, **5**: 276; votes, **6**: 83; visits whale site, **6**: 169, 172n; and species, **7**: 77; and Indians, **7**: 289–90, **9**: 348, **10**: 31; leads detachment, **8**: 3, 74, 77, 212, 218–19, 265, 285n, 286n, **9**: 270n, 271, 274n, **10**: 97; trading, **9**: 98, 275, 294, **10**: 213, 233; stays behind, **10**: 131n; and saltmaking camp, **10**: 187, 193n;

fishing, **10**: 197; mentioned, **2**: 218n, 254, 357, 360, 497, 517, 521, **6**: 426, 428, 436, 440–42, **7**: 148, **8**: 176, 316n, 332, **9**: xiii, xvii, 58n, 255n, 265n, 271n, 279, 294n, 312n, **10**: 32n, 38, 38n, 39n, 63n, 98n, 110n, 131n, 175n, 179n, 180n, 188n, 195n, 197n, 198n, 209n, 211n, 213n, 229n, 232n, 233n, 256n, 265n, 273n, **11**: xiii, 63n, 401n, 417n, 424n

Pryor Creek, **8**: 223, 227, 229n, 285, 286n, 391, 408

Pryor Mountains, **8**: 198, 203n, 205, 208n, 228n, 286n

Pryor's Valley Creek. *See* Spokane Creek

Pseudacris triseriata, **2**: 186n, **4**: 44n, **7**: 312n. *See also* Frog, striped chorus

Pseudotsuga menziesii, **4**: 187n, **5**: 195n, **6**: 19n, **7**: 37n, **8**: 12n, **9**: 185n, **10**: 207n, **11**: 175n. *See also* Fir, Douglas

Psoralea argophylla, **3**: 471. *See also* Scurf pea, silver-leaf

Psoralea esculenta, **3**: 37n, **4**: 129n, **8**: 283n, **9**: 70n, **10**: 47n. *See also* Breadroot

Psoralea lanceolata, **3**: 469. *See also* Scurf pea, lemon

Ptarmigan, white-tailed, **3**: 86n

Pteridium aquilinium, **6**: 224n, **9**: 287n. *See also* Fern, western bracken

Pteridium aquilinum, **7**: 37n. *See also* Fern, western bracken

Ptychocheilus oregonensis, **7**: 135n. *See also* Squawfish, northern

Pudding, **5**: 95

Pudding, white, **4**: 131, 195, 354, 423

Puget (Sea Otter, Sturgeon) Island, **6**: 29n, 33n, 41n, 458, 470, **7**: 12, 14, 14n, **9**: 281, 281n, **10**: 202n, **11**: 434, 434n, **8**: 387, 405

Puget Sound, **7**: 130n

Pulicidae, **6**: 29n, **11**: 368n. *See also* Fleas

Pumice, **2**: 286–87, 445, 446n, **3**: 317–18, 318n, 478, **4**: 15, 23, 34, 39, 48–49, 52, 60, 81–82, 103, 117, 120–21, 140, 143, 195, 198, 202, 205, 208–9, 227, **8**: 414, **10**: 21, 78, 81, 176

Pumpkin Creek, **8**: 248, 250n

Pumpkins, **3**: 148n, 154n, 252–53, **8**: 350, **9**: 78–79, 82n, **11**: 132

Puncheons, **6**: 126–27, 130n, 133–36, **10**: 62, 182–83, **11**: 390

Purdy, Robert, **2**: 520

Purge. *See* Medicine

Pursh, Frederick, **2**: 531, **4**: 129n, 402n, **5**: 21n, 73n, 147n, **7**: 129n, 307n, **8**: 13n, 21n, 80n, **12**: 3–8, 9n

Purshia tridentata, **8**: 94n. *See also* Antelope brush

Pylodictis olivaris, **2**: 486n. *See also* Catfish, flathead

Pyrenees, **10**: 93n

Pyrite, **2**: 234n, 500–501, 502n, **3**: 372, 476–78, 481, **8**: 379

Pyrus coronaria, **2**: 323n. *See also* Crabapple, wild

Pyrus fusca, **6**: 19n. *See also* Crabapple, western

Pyrus ioensis, **2**: 323n, **9**: 15n. *See also* Crabapple, wild

Pyrus malus, **2**: 209n. *See also* Apples

Q

Quadrants, **1**: 4, **9**: 121, 121n. *See also* Octant

Quaife, Milo Milton, **2**: 40–42, 540, **9**: xvii

Quail, mountain, **7**: 87–88, 89n, 90n, 90–91, **9**: 287, 287n, **10**: 207, 207n

Quamash (and similar spellings). *See* Camas

Quannio. *See* Coboway

Qu'Appelle (Catapie, Cappell) River, **2**: 225, 226n, **3**: 429–32

Quarie or Querie, **8**: 369

Quartz, **3**: 475, **4**: 135n, 144n, 195, 207n, 232, 233n, **5**: 157n, **6**: 94n, 179n. *See also* Selenite

Quartz Creek, **5**: 185n

Quartzite, **5**: 147n, **8**: 124n

Quaternary deposits, **2**: 103, 104n

Quathlahpohtle (and similar spellings) Indians. *See* Cathlapotle Indians

Quawmash (and similar spellings). *See* Camas

Quawmash (and similar spellings) Grounds. *See* Weippe Prairie

Quebec, Canada, **3**: 155n, 241n

Quechua Indians, **2**: 281n

Queet (Qui-eet-so) Indians, **6**: 472n, 476, 486, 491

Quercus alba, **2**: 78n, **8**: 345n. *See also* Oak, white

Quercus borealis, **2**: 78n, **8**: 418n. *See also* Oak, red

Quercus garryana, **5**: 312n, **6**: 19n, **7**: 17n, **10**: 159n, **11**: 389n. *See also* Oak, Oregon white

Quercus macrocarpa, **3**: 79n, 469, **8**: 345n. *See also* Oak, bur

Quercus sp., **9**: 10n, **10**: 11n, **11**: 64. *See also* Oaks

Quicksand River. *See* Sandy River

Quicurre (and similar spellings) River. *See* Niobrara River

Quileute (Chil-late) Indians, **6**: 472n, 476, 486, 491

Quill wood. *See* Holly, mountain

Quinault (Qui-ni-ilt) Indians, **6**: 221n, 459, 475–76, 486, 491

Quinn Creek, **8**: 186, 188n

Quinnette Creek. *See* Mill Creek

Quioo, **6**: 155, 159n

Quiscalus quiscula, **4**: 237n, **5**: 24n, **7**: 32n, **9**: 181n, **10**: 106n, **11**: 222n. *See also* Grackle, common

Quivers. *See* Bows and arrows

Quivre River, **2**: 252n

Quoits, **7**: 349, 350n

Rabbit, white. *See* Jackrabbit, white-tailed

Rabbitbrush, **7**: 204n

Rabbitbrush, rubber, **7**: 172n, **10**: 218n

Rabbitbrush, twisted leaf, **7**: 172n, **10**: 218n

Rabbit Island, **3**: 74, 76n, **5**: 294, 300n

Rabbits. *See* Cottontails

Rabies. *See* Medical problems

Raccoon, **2**: 165, 166n, 298, **3**: 390–444 passim, **6**: 162, 208, 210, 211n, 313, 315, 317n, 334, 344, 347, 434, 438–39, **8**: 355, 356n, 416, 418n, **9**: 242, 242n, 360, **10**: 159, 159n, 199, **11**: 362–63, 364n, 378

Raccoon River, **3**: 343

Rafts, **4**: 260–61, 327, **5**: 234–35, 287, **6**: 72, 116–18, **7**: 277, 279, 322, 324, **8**: 82–83, 86n, 137, 290, 323, **9**: 54, 230, 234, 238, **10**: 148, 187, 231, 247

Ragged robin, **7**: 3, 306–7, 307n, 323–24, 325n

Rail, yellow, **3**: 12n

Rain. *See* Weather conditions

Rainbow (Handsome, Beautiful) Falls, **4**: 290, 296n, 307, 311, 315, 368, **6**: 449, 464, **8**: 111, 112n, **10**: 107

Rainier, Peter, **6**: 87n

Rainy Lake, **3**: 443, **4**: 35, 40n

Raja binoculata, **6**: 178n. *See also* Skate, big

Ram. *See* Sheep, bighorn

Ramey, **2**: 142, 153, 156

Ramey, Matthew, **2**: 143n

Rampart (Maropa) Creek, **3**: 150–53, 153n, 154n, 360–61, 373, 380, 400, **8**: 318, 319n, **10**: 52, 52n, **11**: 97n

Ramsay, Jack, **6**: 147–48, 148n, **10**: 177, 177n

Ramy, William, **2**: 143n

Rana clamitans, **7**: 312n. *See also* Frog, green

Randolph, Ellen Wayles, **2**: 531

Rankin, James, **2**: 243, 243n

Rape, **3**: 466

Raspberries, **2**: 286, 288n, 308, 322, 335–36, 338, 433–34, **3**: 481, **5**: 242, 243n, **7**: 19, 21, 92, 94, 96n, 335, 337

Raspberry, black, **2**: 286, 288n, **7**: 338n, **9**: 15, 15n

Raspberry, red, **7**: 96n, 338n

Rat. *See* Woodrat, eastern

Rat, pack. *See* Woodrat, bushy-tailed

Rat River, **2**: 220

Rats, **6**: 313, 315, 317n, 345, 348, **8**: 75, **11**: 217

Rattles, **9**: 48n, 69

Rattlesnake, northern Pacific, **7**: 166, 168, 169n, 308, 310–11

Rattlesnake, prairie, **3**: 52–53, 54n, 82–83, 181, 291, 341, 465, 482, **4**: 2, 159, 161, 163n, 201–2, 281, 297–98, 319, **5**: 64, 67n, **8**: 147, 148n, 266, 267n, **9**: 149, 150n, 345n, **10**: 117, 118n, **11**: 160, 161n, 223–24, 224n

Rattlesnake, timber, **2**: 283–84, 285n, **9**: 11, 11n, **11**: 19, 20n

Rattlesnake Cliffs, **5**: 61n, 63–64, 66, 67n, 93, 99–100, 102n, 105, **6**: 451, 465, 496, **8**: 175–76, 176n, 299n, **10**: 126, 126n, **11**: 269, 270n

Rattlesnake Creek (Missoula County, Mont.), **8**: 86–87, 87n, 89n, 100

Rattlesnake (Track) Creek (Beaverhead County, Mont.), **5**: 92–93, 95n, **8**: 175, 176n, **9**: 202, 202n, **10**: 125, 125n, **11**: 268, 268n

Rattlesnakes, **2**: 323–24, 447–48, **5**: 33–34, 98, 100, **6**: 402, 408, 451, **7**: 265, **8**: 175–76, 238, **9**: 166, 171, 181–82, 203, 336, 345, 363, 378, **10**: 212, **11**: xv, 194–95, 204, 206, 220–22, 269–70

Raven, common, **3**: 85, 293,

R

295n, **4**: 93, 95n, **5**: 216, **10**: 159, 159n, 198, **6**: 94, 94n, 96, 181, 261, 375, 377, 378n, **7**: 76, 78n, **8**: 75, 78n, 93, 117, 210, **9**: 242, 242n, 264, 267, 322, **11**: 361–62, 362n, 410–11

Raven Indians. *See* Crow Indians

Raven Man (Kakawita), **4**: 10–11, 12n, **9**: 126, 127n, **11**: 132, 133n

Raven Man Chief (Car-gar-no-mok-she), **3**: 209, 211, 213n, 216, 308, 328, **9**: 120, 120n

Razor Creek, **8**: 223, 227, 229n

Razors, **6**: 141–42, **9**: 316, 317n, **10**: 175, 235, **11**: 396

Reaume, J., **2**: 220n

Reaume's Fort, **2**: 220, 220n

Recurvirostra americana, **4**: 100n, **8**: 114n. *See also* Avocet, American

Red Butte, **3**: 85n, **10**: 127n

Redcedar, western (arborvitae, white cedar): described, **5**: 218, 224n, 226; and Indians, **5**: 333, 347–48, 348n, **6**: 30, 32, 74–75, 77n, 97, 144n, 180, 186, 206, 209, 211, 214–16, 218, 220–22, 246, 249, 262, 267, 279, 325, 327, 335, 337, 434–36, 438–40, **7**: 64, 83–84, 93, 107, 110, **10**: 175, **11**: 369, 395; observed, **5**: 358n, **6**: 25–27, 176, 183, 194, 284, **7**: 33, **8**: 28, **9**: 224, 224n, **10**: 145, 145n, **11**: 315–17, 316n, 324–25, 325n; abundance, **6**: 26, **8**: 25, 26n, **9**: 286, 322, **10**: 206, 206n, **11**: 389, 389n; habitat, **6**: 45n, **7**: 77, 97, 112–13, 114n, 118, 120; mentioned, **5**: 201n, **6**: 28n, 284n, 293n, **7**: 37n, 121n

Red Cedar River, **3**: 342

Red Hand, **3**: 19

Red horse, shorthead, **2**: 483, 484n, 485–86

Red Lake, **3**: 439–41

Red Lake River, **2**: 219, **3**: 441

Redpoll, common, **4**: 269n

Red River, **3**: 438, 445, 447, **8**: 355n, **9**: 361

Red River of the North, **1**: 5, **2**: 144, 144n, 219–20, 220n, 225, 226n, **3**: 17, 18n, 23, 27, 32, 169, 171n, 175, 178n, 180, 198n, 356, 363, 385n, 386n, 400, 412, 419, 421, 431, 441–43, 481

Red Rock (East Fork Jefferson) River, **1**: 10, **5**: 64, 67n, 108n, 148, **6**: 451, 465, **9**: 203, 204n, **10**: 126, 127n, **11**: 275n

Redroot, **8**: 7, 11, 12n

Red Shield (Warherassa), **3**: 212, 213n, 215n, 240, 240n, 311n

Red Water (2,000 Mile) Creek, **4**: 104–7, 107n, **6**: 447, 462, **9**: 142, 142n, 346, 346n, **10**: 85, 85n, **11**: 144, 144–45n

Reed, **8**: 367, 368n

Reed, Moses B: deserts, **2**: 60, 190n, 445, 447, 447n, 449, 452–53, 455, 456n, 484, 487, 527, **9**: 34–35, 393, **10**: 25, 25n, **11**: 51–52, 52n; drunk, **2**: 144; listed, **2**: 148–49, 189, 191n, 195, 198–99, 255; duties, **2**: 152; hunting, **2**: 167; in permanent party, **2**: 187, 229n; return party, **2**: 188, 190n, 511, **11**: 132; sent out, **2**: 201, 212, 213n; returns, **2**: 205, **9**: 40, **10**: 28, 29n, **11**: 56–57; court-martialed, **2**: 488–89, 490n; discipline, **2**: 488–89, **3**: 171n, **9**: 84; biographical sketch, **2**: 520; mentioned, **2**: 259n, 517, 519, **3**: 198n, **4**: 12n, **9**: xvi, xviii, 84n, **10**: 26n, 54n

Reedgrass, common, **7**: 335–36, 337n

Reedgrass, northern, **5**: 60n

Reed Island, **6**: 14n

Reeds, **2**: 351

Reeds Spring Formation, **2**: 285n

Ree Indians. *See* Arikara Indians

Reel, log line, **1**: 4

Reeveys Prairie, **2**: 352–53

Refraction, **3**: 282–83, 284n

Renar Indians. *See* Fox Indians

Republican Pawnee Indians. *See* Pawnee Indians, Republican or Kitkahahki

Republican River, **3**: 302, 344–45, 381, 384n, 397

Reservation Creek (Custer County, Mont.), **8**: 248, 249–50n

Reservation Creek (Rosebud County, Mont.), **8**: 237, 240, 241n, 407

Resin, **7**: 98, 102, 116–17, 215n, 336

Reubens (Ragid) Rapids, **5**: 255, 260n

Rezanov, Nicolai, **6**: 432n

Rhamnus purshiana, **8**: 12n. *See also* Cascara

Rheumatism. *See* Medical problems

Rhododendron, California (laurel), **6**: 26–27, 28–29n, 97–98, 98n, 117, **7**: 113, 115n

Rhododendron macrophyllum, **6**: 28n, **7**: 115n. *See also* Rhododendron, California

Rhtarahe village, **3**: 156n, 160, 162, 166n, **10**: 54, 54n

Rhue, **3**: 40, 42, 43n

Rhus aromatica, **3**: 470, **8**: 240n. *See also* Sumac, aromatic

Rhus copallina, **6**: 242n. *See also* Sumac, drawf

Rhus glabra, **3**: 43n, **4**: 391n, **7**: 191n, **8**: 12n. *See also* Sumac, smooth

Rhus radicans, **5**: 85n, **8**: 12n. *See also* Ivy, poison

Rhus trilobata, **4**: 391n, **5**: 85n. *See also* Sumac, skunkbush

Rhyolite, **5**: 67n, 102n, 148n

Ribbons, **5**: 197, 219, 222, 244, 288, 341, 348, 351, **6**: 74, 76, 139, 142, 144, 172n, 421, 423, **7**: 147–48, 249–50, 275, 341, **8**: 78, 314, 338. *See also* Clothing

Ribes americanum, **2**: 435n, **3**: 12n, 468, **4**: 57n, 91n, 419n, **5**: 35n, **7**: 129n, **8**: 203n. *See also* Currant, wild black

Ribes aureum, **4**: 91n, 419n, **5**:
    35n, **7**: 129n, **8**: 107n, **9**:
    167n, **10**: 115n, **11**: 196n.
    See also Currant, golden
Ribes cereum, **4**: 308n, 419n, **5**:
    35n. *See also* Currant, squaw
Ribes divaricatum, **7**: 15n. *See also*
    Gooseberry, straggly
Ribes grossularia, **2**: 210n. *See also*
    Gooseberry, garden
Ribes hudsonianum, **5**: 76n, **7**:
    47n. *See also* Gooseberry,
    Hudson
Ribes inerme, **8**: 100n. *See also*
    Gooseberry, whitestem
Ribes irriguum, **8**: 13n. *See also*
    Gooseberry, Idaho
Ribes lacustre, **4**: 397n, **5**: 39n. *See
    also* Currant, swamp
Ribes menziesii, **7**: 15n. *See also*
    Gooseberry, canyon
Ribes missouriense, **2**: 210n, **9**:
    15n. *See also* Gooseberry,
    Missouri
Ribes niveum, **8**: 13n. *See also*
    Gooseberry, snow
Ribes odoratum, **3**: 12n, **4**: 57n,
    91n, **7**: 129n, **9**: 167n, **11**:
    196n. *See also* Currant,
    buffalo
Ribes oxyacanthoides, **4**: 57n, **8**:
    287n. *See also* Gooseberry,
    hawthorn
Ribes rubrum, **5**: 35n. *See also*
    Currant, red
Ribes sanguineum, **7**: 47n. *See also*
    Currant, red flowering
Ribes sativum, **4**: 396n. *See also*
    Currant, garden
Ribes setosum, **4**: 57n, **8**: 100n,
    287n, **10**: 101n. *See also*
    Gooseberry, bristly
Ribes sp., **2**: 309n, **11**: 133n. *See
    also* Gooseberries
Ribes viscossisimum, **7**: 47n. *See
    also* Currant, sticky
Ricara (and similar spellings)
    Indians. *See* Arikara Indians
Rice, wild, **3**: 440–41, 465, 469,
    11: 37–38, 38n
Rice Creek, **11**: 102n
Richard, **8**: 346–47, 348n

Richardson, **9**: 311n
Richland (Blackbird) Creek, **2**:
    289–90, 290n, **9**: 12n, 379,
    379n, **10**: 13, 13n, **11**: 21n
Richweed, **2**: 373n, 377–78,
    380, 382n, **8**: 338, 344n
Rickaree Indians. *See* Arikara
    Indians
Rifle, Kentucky, **2**: 66n, 213–
    14n, 459, 463n, **3**: 189,
    190n, **7**: 92, 93n, 95. *See
    also* Arms and ammunition
Rifle, Model 1803, **2**: 213–14n,
    7: 111–12, 114n, **8**: 156,
    157n, **9**: 324, 325n. *See also*
    Arms and ammunition
Rifles, **2**: 213, 213–14n, 428n,
    489, **4**: 145, 215, 218, 292,
    294, **5**: 53, 77, **6**: 50, 119–
    21, 181, 206, 208, 224, 233,
    235, **8**: 27, 29, 34, 36, 80,
    137n, 138, 155, 289n, **9**: 31,
    57, 157, **11**: 165–66, 177,
    339, 350–51, 387, 400. *See
    also* Arms and ammunition;
    Guns; Muskets; Pistols; *specific
    rifles*
Rings, **3**: 253, 484, **5**: 197, 244,
    6: 74, 79, **8**: 318. *See also*
    Clothing
Rio de los Apostolos, **5**: 90, 95n
Rio Grande del Norte, **1**: 12,
    2: 327, 328n, **3**: 349, 363,
    6: 311n, 316, **7**: 183, 185,
    186n, **8**: 277, 279n
Riparia riparia, **2**: 386n, **3**: 13n,
    7: 47n, **8**: 210n, **9**: 35n, **11**:
    244n. *See also* Swallow, bank
Rising (Cupboard) Creek, **2**:
    272–73, 274n
River au Boeuf (Beef River)
    (Mo.), **2**: 253–54, 259n, **11**:
    13, 13n
River au Boeuf (Minn.), **2**: 219
River des Peres, **2**: 127–28,
    128n
River Journal. *See* Field Notes
    (Clark's specific)
River of No Return. *See* Salmon
    River
River Which Scolds at All Oth-
    ers. *See* Milk River

Rivet, François, **1**: 17n. 73, **2**:
    255, 347, 528–29, **3**: 183n,
    198n, 227n, 266, 267n, **4**:
    12n, **8**: 311, 316n, **9**: 87n,
    98, 107, 107n, 123, 123n,
    352, 352n, **10**: 68, 68n, 269,
    270n
Rivière à Dubois. *See* Dubois
    River
Rivière à la Loutre (Otter
    River), **2**: 259–60, 261n
Roaring Lion Creek, **8**: 163,
    164n
Robertson (Robinson), John, **2**:
    141, 141n, 148, 150, 151n,
    179, 188–89, 190n, 194,
    197–98, 229n, 295, 511–12,
    520–21, **4**: 12n, **11**: 23n
Robes: as carrier, **3**: 22, 23n,
    117–18, **5**: 114; Indian, **3**:
    22–24, 23n, 115, 117–18,
    159–61, 164–65, 199, 253,
    267–68, 270–71, 288, 356,
    361, 413, 488, **6**: 30, 32, 40,
    72, 74–76, 90, 142, 144,
    248–49, 262n, 327, 334,
    336, 338, 345, 348, 351, 354,
    360, 434, 438, 440, 480, **7**:
    27, 35, 39–40, 65, 85, 112,
    123, 125, 128–29, 133, 145,
    147–49, 160, 166–67, 183,
    185, 244, 253, 255, **8**: 51–52,
    288, 318, **10**: 158, 172, 174n,
    177, 199, 270, **11**: 299–300;
    as gift, **3**: 160, 219, 253, 267,
    8: 51–52, **10**: 259, 270; as
    trade item, **3**: 221, 226–27,
    5: 339, 367, 371, **6**: 49, 72–
    73, 123–25, 206, 208, 327,
    358, **7**: 30, 113, 115, 117,
    139, 141, 147–48, 162, **8**:
    302; sent back, **3**: 330–31,
    8: 418–19; as signal, **5**: 69;
    as clothes, **5**: 122, 126, 134,
    139, 187, 189, 258–59, 289,
    303, 306, 309, 317, 350, 352,
    367, 373; in huts, **5**: 286;
    burial, **5**: 311, **6**: 97, 186, **7**:
    108, 219; rotten, **6**: 33, 42–
    43, 47, 91; infested, **6**: 122–
    23; gamble with, **7**: 137–38;
    lost, **7**: 155–57; found, **7**:

156–57; mentioned, **6**: 31, 421, 423. *See also* Clothing

Robidoux, Joseph, **8**: 362, 362n, **9**: 363, 363n, **10**: 279, 279n

Robin, American, **4**: 94, 96n, 265, **5**: 27, 29n, 145–46, 217, **6**: 254, 256, 257n, 363–64, 379–80, **7**: 44, 47n, **8**: 75, 78n, 93, 419

Rochejhone (and similar spellings). *See* Yellowstone (Rochejhone) River

Rocher Island. *See* Terrapin Island

Rock Creek (Beaverhead County, Mont.), **8**: 170, 171n

Rock Creek (Jefferson County, Mo.), **2**: 126, 127n

Rock Creek (Klickitat County, Wash.), **5**: 319n, **6**: 468, **7**: 160, 162, 162n, **8**: 403

Rock Creek (Lewis and Clark County, Mont.), **4**: 402n

Rock Creek (Ravalli County, Mont.), **5**: 190n, 194, **8**: 163, 164n, **11**: 304–5, 305n

Rock Creek (Skamania County, Wash.), **5**: 356, 358n, **9**: 296, 296n, **10**: 215, 215n

Rock Creek (Yellowstone County, Mont.), **8**: 408

Rock (Lead, Big Rock) Creek (Cole County, Mo.), **2**: 277, 279, 281n, **9**: 10, 10n, 378, **10**: 12, 12n, **11**: 18, 18n, 19, 19n

Rock (North Mountain) Creek (Phillips County, Mont.), **4**: 187n, 189–91, 192n, **6**: 448, 463, **8**: 142, 142n, 382, 400, **9**: 154, 154n, 344n, **10**: 91, 91n, 261n, **11**: 166–67, 166n, 167n

Rock-flour, **7**: 236n

Rock Island, **2**: 105, 109n

Rock Prairie, **11**: 35

Rock River, **3**: 355, 384n, 407–8

Rocky Creek, **8**: 181–82, 183n, 185, 392, 409

Rocky Mountain House, **8**: 133n

Rocky Mountains: and maps, **1**: 5–6, 11, **2**: 29, **4**: 266–67, **6**:

308–9, **7**: 315n; described, **1**: 13, **3**: 486–87, **4**: 247, 259, 267, 280, 320, 361, 380, 381n, 388, 392, 405, 407, 411, 414–15, 430, 434, **8**: 122–23, 392, **9**: 171, 171n, 185, 306, **10**: 1, 226n, **11**: 229, 240; and traders, **2**: 3; and Indians, **2**: 5, **3**: 3, 207n, 208, 210, 229n, 232, 234, 310, 334, 414, 445, 475, 488, **5**: 69, **6**: 313, 433, 437, 445, 473–74, 482, 488, **7**: 92, 153, **8**: 14, 18, 23, 131, 278, 388, **9**: 157, 298, **11**: 119, 373; route through, **2**: 7, **7**: 251, **8**: 88, 377, 384, 388; distances, **2**: 159–60, **3**: 374, **6**: 446, 472n, 492, **8**: 383; and members of the party, **2**: 510, 514, 516–17, 522, 525, **8**: 303n; name, **3**: 48n, 136n, **4**: 320, 361; animals, **3**: 120n, 330, 482, **5**: 11, 123, **6**: 131, 131n, 254–55, 315, 318, 324, 328, 331–32, 336, 338, 345, 348, 354, 356, 371, 374, 376–77, 379–80, 396–97, 404–6, 408, 413, **7**: 113, 260n, 293, 296–98, 304, 309, 311, **8**: 89, 112, 112n, 145, 238, 332n, **9**: 184, 298, 337, **11**: 141, 228; rivers, **3**: 349, 351, 363–65, 368, **7**: 186n, 217–18; listed, **3**: 382, 424–26, 434–37, 444; plants, **4**: 91n, 253n, **5**: 21n, 78, 195n, **6**: 104n, 240, 245, 251, **7**: 45, 47n, **8**: 13n, 14, 18, 30n, 126n, 132n, 270n, 416, **12**: 6; observed, **4**: 201, 203–4, 280, 282n, **7**: 221, 223, 268, **8**: 26, 201, 205, 224–25, 227; sounds from, **4**: 320, 321n, 361–62, 374–75; conditions, **4**: 379, 401, **5**: 4, 65, 157n, 218, **6**: 2–3, 445, **7**: 222–23, 233, 262–63, 276, 299–300, 321, **8**: 414, **10**: 156n; arrive at, **4**: 388, 393, 395, 396n, 426, **10**: 113; crossing, **5**: 1, 3,

173, 229, **6**: 84, 211, 213, 310–11, **7**: 1, 39, 50, 52, 126, 128, 238, 240, 271, 273, 275, 277, 325, 331–32, 328, 344, 347–48, **11**: 222, 321; mentioned, **1**: 3, 10, **2**: 27, 404n, **3**: 26n, **4**: 1, 71, 73, 76n, 89, 132, 170, 173, 187n, 188, 192n, 197, 216, 223, 246, 248, 258, 267n, 270, 344, 380, 382, 386, 390, 425n, 428, **5**: 59, 85n, 94n, 192, 196, 225n, 373, **6**: 105, 285–86, 346, 355, 358, 360, 366–67, 402, 481, **7**: 11, 34, 42n, 215, 270, 333, 343n, **8**: 66, 69, 73n, 87, 96n, 97, 103, 114, 119, 152, 159n, 162, 183, 185–86, 188n, 232, 234n, 252, 277, 291, 357, 412–13, **9**: 176n, 240n, 328, 339n, **10**: 6n, 34n, 67n, 69, 78n, 84, 93n, 157n, 177n, 200, 223, 225n, 237, 248n, **11**: 6n, 206n. *See also* Gates of the Rocky Mountains

Rocky Point, **9**: 328n

Rocky Rapids, **6**: 455, 468, **8**: 385, 403

Rod, ram, **4**: 374. *See also* Arms and ammunition

Rod, wiping, **4**: 341, **5**: 231n. *See also* Arms and ammunition

Rodney, Caesar, **2**: 74n

Rodney, Ceasar Augustus, **2**: 74, 75n

Rodney, Thomas, **2**: 74–75, 74n, 75n

Rogers, George A., **12**: 6

Roi (Roie, Rokey), Peter, **1**: 17n, 73, **2**: 256, 347, 529, **3**: 77, 79n, 158n, 198n, 305n, **8**: 318, 319n, **9**: 60, 60n, 119, 119n, 352, 353n, **10**: 74n, 270, 270n

Roloje Creek. *See* Aowa Creek

Rooptahee (and similar spellings). *See* Ruptáre village

Roots: as food, **5**: 3–4, 89, 143, 188, 219, 222–23, 230, 235, 245–46, 256, 315, 341–42, 348–51, 353, **6**: 2, 106, 118–

Roots (*continued*)

19, 137–38, 188, 358, 391, 393, **7**: 8, 88, 90, 92, 152, 154, 222, 224, 236–37, 239–40, 261, 264, 276, 279, 288, 292, 295, 302, 304, 334, 339, 342, 349, **8**: 57–58, 61, 63, **9**: 218, 242, 280, 292, 298, 304, 306, **10**: 150, 221, 242, 245, **11**: 431; and Indians, **5**: 71, 73, 85n, 91, 115, 120, 142, 239, 321, 355, 357, 359, 362, 371, 373, **6**: 32, 53, 60–61, 74, 76, 89, 121, 123, 154, 168, 190, 205, 214, 216–17, 224, 307, 360, 436, 440, **7**: 44, 57, 82, 86, 93, 107–8, 110, 121, 131, 134, 174, 176, 221, 223, 243, 245, 284, 286–87, 327, 330, 339, **8**: 44–45, **9**: 208, 218–19, 242, 244, 249, 251, 264, 292, 298, 304–5, 312–13, **10**: 138, 176, 224–25, 226n, **11**: 272, 274, 281, 286–87, 389, 392, 438; observed, **5**: 143, **9**: 307; as trade item, **5**: 226–28, 231–32, 242, 244–46, 251, 314, 317, 346–47, **6**: 16, 18, 61, 74, 76, 85, 90, 120–21, 123–24, 134, 136, 142, 145, 152–53, 161–65, 195, 358, 398, 400, 414–15, **7**: 18–20, 58, 81, 113, 119–20, 147, 209, 211, 236, 271–72, 274–77, 284–85, 289–91, 294, 308, 310, 325–26, 328, 336, 341, **11**: 404; dried, **5**: 252; lost, **5**: 271–72, **7**: 322, 324; wet, **5**: 275, **8**: 7, 164; as gift, **6**: 137, 139, **7**: 18–20, 333–34, **11**: 299–300, 326, 399, 404; described, **6**: 228, 233, **8**: 11; as bread, **9**: 242, 244, 304–5, **11**: 327, 334, 362–64, 366, 369–71, 375; purchased, **9**: 244, 249, 251, 304, 313, **10**: 175, 221–22, 230, 233–36, **11**: 388–89, 399, 410, 429; abundance, **10**: 226n; mentioned, **5**: 96, **6**: 225n, **7**: 21n, 47n, 338, 343, 345. *See also* Bread;

Camas; Cous; Medicine; Spring beauty, western; Wapato

Rope, tow, **2**: 302, 305–8, 306–7n, 312–13, 324, 355, **3**: 13–14, 21–22, 111–13, 121–24, 237, 240, 285, 302–3, 308, **4**: 24–25, 51, 59, 62, 158, 161, 163, 165–66, 168, 170, 173, 176, 178–79, 188, 193, 200–202, 205, 207, 210–11, 213, 215, 222–23, 225, 228, 230, 238–39, 241, 251, 297–99, 398, 403, 406, 411, 420, 429, **5**: 4, 15, 28, 33, 42, 153, 156, 161, 327, 336, 338, **11**: 31, 34–35, 85–86, 89–90, 169, 171, 179, 183, 195, 229, 245, 250–51, 253–54, 367–68. *See also* Ropes

Ropes, **5**: 125, 135, 227, 325, 327, 361, **6**: 97, 203–4, 217n, 296n, 336, 433, 437, **7**: 48, 51, 59, 64, 82–83, 89n, 101–3, 105, 111–12, 136, 141, 143, 151, 155n, 165, 167, 182, 184, 202–3, 216, 218–19, 277, 294, 343, 345, **8**: 30, 284, **9**: 17, 46, 55, 68, 70, 98, 156, 158–59, 162, 165, 168, 289–90, 295n, 321, 381, 386, **10**: 16–17, 47, 62, 163, 213, **11**: 26, 32, 129, 191–92, 210–11. *See also* Lassoes

Ropewalk, **2**: 305, 306–7n
Rope Walk Camp (Mo.), **11**: 25–26, 26n
Rorippa islandica, **7**: 61n. *See also* Watercress
Rorippa nasturtium-aquaticum, **7**: 61n. *See also* Watercress
Rorippa palustris, **2**: 281n, **3**: 466. *See also* Cress, bog yellow
Rorippa sessiliflora, **2**: 281n, **3**: 466. *See also* Cress, sessile-flowered
Rorippa sinuata, **2**: 281n, **3**: 466. *See also* Cress, spreading yellow
Rorippa sp., **2**: 281n. *See also* Cresses

Rosa, Salvator, **4**: 285, 288n
Rosa acicularis, **8**: 118n. *See also* Rose, prickly
Rosa arkansana, **3**: 471. *See also* Rose, prairie wild
Rosa nutkana, **7**: 338n, **8**: 13n. *See also* Rose, nootka
Rosa sp., **5**: 243n, **7**: 47n, **9**: 150n, **11**: 38n, 161n. *See also* Roses
Rosa woodsii, **4**: 53n, **5**: 39n, **7**: 338n, **8**: 13n. *See also* Rose, western wild
Rose, Nootka, **7**: 335, 337, 338n, **8**: 10–11, 13n
Rose, prairie wild, **3**: 465, 471
Rose, prickly, **8**: 118n
Rose, western wild, **4**: 51, 53n, 54, 57n, **5**: 36, 39n, **7**: 335, 337, 338n, **8**: 10–11, 13n, 118n, 232, 234n, 238
Rose, white, **3**: 458
Rose, wild, **5**: 243n, **7**: 47n
Rose, Wood's, **7**: 338n, **8**: 13n
Rosebud (Little Horn River, Mar-Shas-kap) Creek, **3**: 365, 374, 382, **8**: 208n, 242–44, 246n, 390, 407
Rosebud Mountains, **8**: 235n
Roses, **2**: 350–51, **4**: 39, 70, 73, 96, 108, 176, 178, 184, 216, 236, 238, 241, 247, 250, 256, 266, 324, 414, 417, 419, **5**: 59, 191, 242, **6**: 96, 98, **7**: 188, 190, 197, **8**: 71, 79, 117, 128, 187, **9**: 150, 150n, 152, 161, 196, **11**: 38, 38n, 160, 161n, 175, 254–55
Rosin, **5**: 252, 340, 342, **6**: 212, 214–15, 277–83. *See also* Resin
Ross, Alexander, **7**: 17n
Ross's Hole, **5**: 188n, 301, 301n, **8**: 165, 166n, 168n, 393–94, 410, **9**: 218, 219n, 331n, **10**: 138n, **11**: 299
Round Island, **9**: 355n, **10**: 274n
Rover, **6**: 160n
Roy, Pierre, **2**: 529
Royal Botanic Gardens. *See* Kew Gardens

Roys Creek, **2**: 369, 372n

Rubus idaeus, **7**: 96n. *See also*
Raspberry, red

Rubus leucodermis, **7**: 338n. *See
also* Raspberry, black

Rubus occidentalis, **2**: 288n, **9**:
15n. *See also* Raspberry, black

Rubus parviflorus, **7**: 96n. *See also*
Thimbleberry

Rubus sp., **2**: 288n, **7**: 15n, 47n,
96n. *See also* Blackberries;
Raspberries

Rubus spectabilis, **6**: 104n, **7**: 15n.
See also Salmonberry

Rubus ursinus, **6**: 20n, **7**: 14n. *See
also* Blackberry, Pacific

Ruby Creek, **8**: 167, 169n

Ruby (Philanthropy) River, **1**:
10, **5**: 39n, 40–41, 43n, 44n,
47, 51, 52n, 54, 57n, 58–60,
61n, 100, **6**: 451, 465, 494, **8**:
172, 175, 176n, 177, **9**: 197–
98, 197n, 199n, 200, **10**:
121, 121n, 122n, 123, 123n,
11: 258n, 259–61, 261n,
263–64

Ruby Range, **5**: 67n, 86n

Rudders. *See* Pirogues

Rum, **3**: 34, and Indians, **4**: 35,
8: 139n, **9**: 100n, **10**: 99n. *See
also* Tafia

Rumex acetosa, **10**: 198n. *See also*
Sorrel, garden

Rumex maritimus, **10**: 198n. *See
also* Dock, seaside

Rumex mexicanus, **4**: 386n. *See
also* Dock, Mexican

Rumex occidentalis, **10**: 198n. *See
also* Dock, western

Rumex salicifolius, **4**: 386n, **7**:
61n. *See also* Dock, Mexican

Ruminantia, **6**: 405n

Rumsey (Runsey), Nathan, **2**:
156, 156n, 184, 193, 201,
205, 211–14

Ruptáre (Rooptahee) village, **3**:
201n, 203, 205n, 208n, 209,
211, 214n, 216, 223, 238–
39, 267, 289, 296, 311, 328,
401, **8**: 298, 300n, 301, **9**: 91,
91n, 120n, 127n, 350, 350n,
10: 60, 60n, **11**: 106, 107n,

109–10, 116, 116n, 133,
133n

Rush, Benjamin, **2**: 6, 86n,
496n, **4**: 139n, **6**: 321n, **7**:
288n

Rush, sand, **4**: 380, 381n, 383

Rush, scouring, **2**: 309n, **4**:
381n, **8**: 119, 120n. *See also*
Sandrush

Rush, stout scouring, **2**: 102,
104n

Rush Creek, **2**: 321n, **9**: 383,
383n, **10**: 16n

Rushes, **2**: 275–76, 281, **5**: 10n,
60n, 288, 290, 323, **6**: 26,
29n, 76, 77n, 97, 119, 135,
146–47, 186, 188, 192–93,
196, 216–17, 276–77, 436,
439–40, **7**: 188, 190, **8**: 187,
211, 359, **9**: 8, 9n, 18, 21, 89,
292, 361, **10**: 10, 11n. *See also*
Bulrushes; Horsetail

Rush's pills. *See* Medicine

Russians, **6**: 2, 432n

Ryan (Teapot) Island, **4**: 183,
185, 187n, **10**: 91

Rye. *See* Wild rye, Canada

S

Sabine River, **8**: 348n

Sacagawea: joins party, **2**: 7, **3**:
3–4, 228, 228n, **2**: 8, **8**: 4,
305, **10**: 77–78; fame, **2**:
509–10; death, **3**: 171n; captured, **3**: 207n, **5**: 9, 14, 16,
106; biographical sketch, **3**:
229n; pregnant, **3**: 272n;
gives birth, **3**: 291, **10**: 72;
interpreter, **3**: 327, 328n,
5: 94n, 111, 122, **6**: 13, 14n,
7: 178, 180, 231, 242–44,
8: 161, 162n, **9**: 219n, 299,
306n, **10**: 138n, 223, **11**:
275, 309; accidents, **4**: 2–3,
29–30, 154, 157, 341–43, **9**:
177, **11**: 215–16; listed, **4**: 9,
11, **8**: 74, 162n, 179, 277, **11**:
4n, 8n, 411n; collects food,

4: 15, 128, 129n, **7**: 264–65,
270, **9**: 203, **11**: 270–71; sent
out, **4**: 52, 88, 340, 342, **5**:
14, 129, 304, **7**: 125, 156, **9**:
176, 183, 204, 265, 293, **10**:
108, 119n, 127–28, **11**: 225,
272–73, 410; information
from, **4**: 89, 91n, 216, 219,
221n, 403, 416, 422, **5**: 2, 59,
72n, 165, **8**: 167, 180, 180n,
182, 195, 197n, 235n, **9**:
157, 188, 190, 331, **10**: 116–
17, 119, **11**: 138, 141, 236–
37, 240; river named for,
4: 171, 174, 175n, **9**: 152n;
medical problems, **4**: 276–
77, 279, 281, 287, 294, 297–
301, 302n, 303, 306, 309,
317–18, **6**: 35, **9**: 165–67,
170, **11**: 194–95, 197, 203;
and lower portage camp, **4**:
325; duties, **4**: 326; and Toussaint Charbonneau, **5**: 93;
and Cameahwait, **5**: 109,
114, 144; returns, **5**: 143, **9**:
208, **11**: 280–81; and Indians, **5**: 268, 306, **6**: 1; visits
whale site, **6**: 2, 168–69, 171,
172n; votes, **6**: 2, 84, 86n;
gifts, **6**: 96–97, 137; cooks, **6**:
106–7; and Shoshone Indi-
ans, **8**: 43n; and species, **8**:
51, 52n, 174, 286; visits, **9**:
95; and beads, **9**: 256, **10**:
176, **11**: 397; stays behind,
10: 104, 268n; and saltmaking camp, **10**: 187; trade, **10**:
212; mentioned, **2**: 512, **3**:
206n, 312, **4**: 1, 4, 10, 13n,
302n, 330, 343n, 378, **5**: 1,
85n, 98, 100, 113, 116n,
118, 120, 131, 158, **6**: 44,
72–73, 172n, **7**: 162, **8**: 3,
307n, **9**: xii, 95n, 172, 172n,
191n, 206n, 265n, 279,
293n, 300n, **10**: xii, 68n,
105n, 120n, 129n, 188n,
212n, 256n, **11**: xii, 114,
114n, 138n, 207–8, 208n,
216n, 242–43, 244n, 246–
47, 288n, 374n. *See also*
Charbonneau

Sacagawea River, **4**: 171, 175n, **9**: 151, 152n

Sacagawea Springs, **11**: 201n

Saccacommis. *See* Bearberry

Sac Indians. *See* Sauk Indians

Sacrifice (Yellow) Cliff, **8**: 223n, 391, 408

Sacrophagidae, **4**: 175n, **5**: 58n. *See also* Fly, blow

Saddle Mountain (Idaho), **5**: 186n, 187, 187n, **6**: 452, 466, **8**: 166, 168n, **9**: 217, 218n, **10**: 137, 137n

Saddle Mountain (Oreg.), **6**: 127, 127n, 383, 384n

Saddle Peak, **8**: 188n

Saddles, **5**: 68, 119, 124–25, 133, 160–61, 177–78, 247–48, **7**: 126, 128, 130, 132, 141, 155, 157, 159, 163–64, 165, 167, 188, 190, 228–29, 232–33, 235–36, 250, 297, 299, 308, 310, 344–45, **8**: 83, 88, 111, 128–29, 135, 137, 172, 204, 285, 295, **9**: 207, 213, 219, 234, 293, 296, 307, 342, **10**: 134, 151, 212, 223–24, 231, 231n, **11**: 277–78, 301–2, 339

Sagamity, **6**: 233, 235n

Sage, garden, **4**: 35, 40n

Sage, long leaf, **3**: 465, 470

Sage, white, **3**: 458–59, 464, 467

Sagebrush, **4**: 2, 40n, 417, 419n, **7**: 202–3, 204n, 338n, **10**: 81, 81n

Sagebrush, big (hyssop, south-ernwood, whins, wild sage), **4**: 35, 39, 41n, 54, 70, 141–42, 146, 189, 419n, **5**: 65, 67n, 286–88, 290n, 291n, **7**: 146, 151n, 172n, 173, 175, **8**: 93, 94n, 172, 173n, **9**: 139, 140n, 146, 210, 210n, 301, 301n, **10**: 133, 133n, 217–18, 217n, 218n, **11**: 153, 154n, 171, 175, 307

Sagebrush, black, **4**: 145n

Sagebrush, silver (southern-wood), **3**: 465, 470, **4**: 35, 41n, 189, 419n

Sagebrush Creek, **8**: 406

Sage Creek, **4**: 149n

Sagewort, prairie, **3**: 464–65, 469–70

Sagittaria cuneata, **5**: 326n. *See also* Wapato

Sagittaria latifolia, **5**: 326n, **6**: 19n, **7**: 11n, **9**: 250n, **10**: 167n, **11**: 387n. *See also* Wapato

Sagittaria sagittifolia, **6**: 20n, **7**: 32, 36n, 38. *See also* Arrow-head. *See also* Wapato

Sah-hah-woh-cap, **7**: 15–16, 17n

Sails, **4**: 96, 119, 130, 158, 188, 365, **5**: 111, **6**: 91, **7**: 147, 262, **10**: 228. *See also* Canoes; Keelboat; Pirogues; Pirogue, white

Saint Aubert Island, **2**: 265, 266n

Saint Charles, Mo., **1**: 6, **2**: 17, 19–20, 60, 179, 185, 207, 216, 218, 227, 229n, 231n, 232–33, 234n, 240–42, 244, 405, 408, 480, 486, 512, 518, 523, 526, **3**: 94, 335, 337–38, 369, 375–76, 383n, 451, **8**: 4, 369, 369n, 374, 376–77, 394, **9**: 6, 6n, 13, 80–81, 132, 365, 368n, 374, **10**: 8n, **11**: 1, 9, 9n, 11, 22, 171, 173

Saint Charles Island, **2**: 244, 244n

Saint Clair, Arthur, **8**: 371n

Sainte Genevieve, Mo., **2**: 118, 119n, 123–25, 124n, 197, **3**: 446, **9**: 75n

Saint Ferdinand de Florissant, Mo., **2**: 130–31, 131–32n

Saint Francis (Tanslagrass) River, **2**: 99, 101n, 108, 112, 113n, 116, 124, **3**: 338

Saint John's Island, **2**: 251, 253n

Saint Joseph, Mich., **3**: 203, 206n

Saint Joseph (Grand Detour, Great Bend) Bend, **2**: 352–53, 354n

Saint Joseph River, **3**: 206n

Saint Josephs Island, **2**: 374–75

Saint Laurent Creek, **2**: 119n

Saint Lawrence River, **10**: 43n

Saint Louis, Mo.: and traders, **1**: 3, 6, **8**: 346, 347n, 348, 351, 355, 357, 360, 362n, **9**: 352, 359, 361–62, 363n, **11**: 22–23; arrive at, **1**: 4, **2**: 60, 129, **8**: 4, 302, 370, 374, 376, 411, **9**: 366, **10**: 280; balls at, **1**: 5, **2**: 174, 193; and maps, **1**: 10; return to, **2**: 8, 10–11, 28, 30, 34, 240, 509, 520, 523, 532–33, **6**: 432n, 445, **9**: xiii, xv–xvi, 125, **10**: xiii, 270, **11**: xiii, xv; leave, **2**: 17, **7**: 1, **11**: 8n; capital of Upper Louisi-ana, **2**: 36; trade from, **3**: 32, 155, 270n, 386–421 passim, 483–84; garrison at, **3**: 357; as post site, **3**: 479; keelboat returns to, **4**: 1, 7, 11, 319, 359, **9**: 125, **10**: 75, **11**: 132 ; located, **10**: 4n; and Indians, **10**: 77; mentioned, **1**: 6–8, 12–13, **2**: 6, 16, 18, 31, 118n, 130n, 181, 187, 192, 205, 210n, 211–13, 213n, 216, 220n, 227, 229n, 237, 239, 240–43, 266, 293n, 482, 512, 516, 521, 526, 536, 539, 540, **3**: 4, 56n, 183n, 214n, 291n, 446, 450, 464, **6**: 148n, **7**: 36n, 221, 223, 308, 311, **8**: 152, 303n, 358n, 369n, 371–72, 371n, 412, 414, 419n, **9**: 20, 25, **10**: 7n, 8, 138n, **11**: 1, 4n, 7n, 9–10, 432n, **12**: 3

Saint Louis River, **3**: 440

Saint Marys River Formation, **8**: 126n

Saint-Mémin, Charles B. J. F. de, **5**: 131n

Saint Michael's Prairie, **2**: 355–56, **3**: 371, 378, **8**: 357, 358n, 378, 396, **9**: 21, 362n, 368n, **10**: 278n

Saint Paul, Minn., **2**: 41

Saint Peter's River. *See* Minne-sota River

Sakakawea site, **3**: 3, 206n, 229n, **9**: 99n, **10**: 78n, **11**: 134n

Salal, **6**: 3, 119, 120n, 139, 235–

36, 237n, 239n, 276–77, 278n, 287–90, 290n, 297, 495, **7**: 55, 60n, 77

Salamander. *See* Gopher, northern pocket

Saline Creek, **2**: 116, 118, 119n

Saline (Little Salt) River, **3**: 345, 383–84n

Salishan Indians, **6**: 489–91

Salishan language, **1**: 11, **5**: 188–89, 189n, 222, 225n, 317, 319n, **6**: 77n, 184n, 186n, 237n, 432n, 490, **7**: 21n, 168n, 219n, **9**: 219n, 240n, **10**: 188n, **11**: 302n, 374n, 412n

Salish Indians. *See* Flathead Indians

Salix amygdaloides, **2**: 368n, **3**: 467, **4**: 75n, **7**: 14n, **8**: 162n. *See also* Willow, peach-leaved

Salix babylonica, **2**: 210n. *See also* Willow, weeping

Salix bebbiana, **8**: 81n. *See also* Willow, Bebb

Salix exigua, **2**: 368n, **3**: 467, **4**: 28n, **5**: 39n, **7**: 194n, **8**: 81n. *See also* Willow, sandbar

Salix fluviatilis, **7**: 194n. *See also* Willow, Columbia River

Salix lasiandra, **6**: 29n, **7**: 14n, **8**: 162n, **9**: 287n. *See also* Willow, Pacific

Salix lutea, **7**: 14n, **8**: 81n. *See also* Willow, yellow

Salix nigra, **2**: 368n, **4**: 325n, **8**: 359n. *See also* Willow, black

Salix rigida, **4**: 75n, 325n, **7**: 14n. *See also* Willow, diamond

Salix scouleriana, **6**: 29n, **8**: 81n. *See also* Willow, Scouler

Salix sessilifolia, **7**: 14n. *See also* Willow, northwest

Salix sitchensis, **6**: 29n. *See also* Willow, Sitka

Salix sp., **9**: 17n, **11**: 230n. *See also* Willows

Salmo clarkii. See Oncorhynchus clarki

Salmo gairdneri, **5**: 147n, **7**: 241n, **8**: 37n. *See also* Trout, steelhead

Salmon: abundance, **3**: 369, **5**: 4, 286–88, **7**: 291, **9**: 240–42, **10**: 149, 153, 155, 157, 159, **11**: 357–59, 361–62; as food, **5**: 83, 128–29, 131, 135, 138–39, 146, 152, 155, 167–69, 174–75, 177, 219, 222–23, 226, 229, 232, 233n, 277, 286, 303, **7**: 327, 329, **9**: 228, 253, 258, 292, 316, **10**: 130, 132–34, 136, 157–58, 169, 179, **11**: 289, 291, 326–28, 331–32, 338, 348, 350–52, 360, 393, 400, 439; and Indians, **5**: 85n, 122–23, 130, 137–39, 175, 204–5, 228n, 233–34, 238, 251, 259, 286–88, 290, 323, 325, 338, **6**: 36, 76, 118, 180, 184, 192, 196, 203, 211, 214, 480, 487, **7**: 97–100, 106, 109, 113, 121, 134, 142, 144, 145n, 160–61, 174, 176, 205, 217–18, 245, 269, 286–87, 320–21, **9**: 205, 212, 215, 223, 235, 238, 240–41, 248, 295, 297, **10**: 129–30, 132–34, 136, 158, 165, 169, 175, 183–85, 207, 215, **11**: 272, 274, 315–16, 330, 332–35, 341–42, 349, 358–59, 362–64, 366, 371, 380, 385, 439; scarcity, **5**: 89, 153, 192, **6**: 308, 310, **7**: 131, **8**: 37, 45–46, **9**: 316; fished for, **5**: 138, 141n, 145, 174, 177, 183, **6**: 42–43, **9**: 212, 229–30, 314, **10**: 129, 215, **11**: 286, 291, 295, 332, 335; as trade item, **5**: 175, 227, 234–35, **6**: 76, 187, 203–5, **7**: 279, 293, 326, 329, **9**: 263, 326, **10**: 165, 184–85, **11**: 380; purchased, **5**: 175, 234, **6**: 192, 196, **9**: 214, 216, 228, 231, 233, 235, 237, 239, 242, 317, **10**: 169, 175, 184–85, 235, **11**: 293, 295, 327, 329–30, 335–38, 341–42, 344–46, 348–49, 355–56, 366, 370–71, 376, 395, 408; behavior, **5**: 286–87, 290n,

331, 349, 351, **10**: 161, 207, 231; as gift, **6**: 74; migration, **6**: 336, 338, 414n, **7**: 38, 49–50, 52, 53n, 107, 205, 207, 256, 258, 269, 271, 276, 278, 319, 331–32; observed, **6**: 407, **7**: 269, 271, 289–90, **10**: 241; mentioned, **5**: 86n, 141n, 331, **6**: 296n, 423, 425, **7**: 323, 325, 330n, **9**: 206n, 216n, 245, **10**: 130n, 155n, 206n, 233n, 235n, **11**: 273, 275, 294

Salmon, chinook, **7**: 125n

Salmon, coho, **5**: 290n, **6**: 407, 409n, 421, 423, 425, 425n, **7**: 44, 47n, 102–3, 131, **10**: 157n, **11**: 358n

Salmon, king, **6**: 410, 412, 414n

Salmon, silver, **7**: 47n

Salmon, sockeye, **5**: 290n, **6**: 40–41, 41n, 407, 410–13, 414–15, 414n, **10**: 157n, **11**: 358n

Salmonberry, **6**: 102, 104n, 298, 299n, **7**: 13–14, 15n, 22n, 47n, 55, 77, 94, 96n

Salmon Creek, **6**: 21n, **9**: 250n, **10**: 167n, **11**: 387n

Salmonidae sp., **4**: 415. *See also* Whitefish

Salmon (Columbia, Lewis's) River, **11**: 286n, 290–91, 293–94, 294n, 296n, 347n

Salmon (Lewis's, Main Fork Lewis's, Southeast Fork of Columbia, West Fork Lewis's) River, **1**: 10–11, **3**: 298n, 382, **5**: 75n, 81, 86n, 88, 94n, 115, 131n, 140, 141n, 145–46, 147n, 152–56, 157n, 164n, 169, 175, 179, 179n, 183–84, 255, 260n, **6**: 308–10, 311n, 314, 316, 451, 465, 482, **7**: 233n, 249, 251, 326–27, 329, 330n, 341, **8**: 26, 27n, 167, 172, **9**: 211n, 231, 316–17, 316n, 317n, 318n, **10**: 129, 129n, 130n, 131n, 132–33, 133n, 135n, 152n, 160n, 173, 174n

Salmon River Mountains, **5**: 94n, 140, 141n

Salt: sources, **2**: 118, 119n, 219–20, 282, 283n, **3**: 92, 345, 349–50, 473–75, **4**: 22, **9**: 11; and traders, **2**: 134, 144; listed, **2**: 200, 202, 217, **6**: 113; sent for, **2**: 211, 212n, **6**: 230, 237, 322; making, **2**: 282, **3**: 473, **6**: 116, 138, 140, 140n, 166–67, 171, 195, 275–76, **9**: 256, 259, 263–64, 266, 268–73, **10**: 186–88, 191, 193–94, **11**: 403, 407–10, 414–17, 419, 421–22, 431; and Indians, **3**: 161, 163, **9**: 65, 213, **11**: 288–89; use, **4**: 131, 303, **6**: 211–12, 245–46; cache, **4**: 269, 275, 279, **8**: 138; need for, **6**: 84–85, 441–42; scarcity, **6**: 228–29, **8**: 37, 61, 63, **10**: 150, 184, **11**: 398, 407, 409; quantity, **6**: 235–36, 321, 324, 333, 335; brought in, **6**: 242–43; mentioned, **3**: 100, **5**: 131, **6**: 38, 177, **8**: 38n, 118–19, **9**: 155, 376, **11**: 412. *See also* Saltmaking Camp

Salt Creek, **2**: 403, 404n

Saltgrass, seashore, **6**: 305, 307, 307n

Salt licks, **3**: 61–63, 64n, 340–41, 474

Saltmaking, **2**: 147, 205, 220, 221, 221n, 283, 285

Saltmaking Camp (Oreg.): established, **6**: 2, 140, 166–67, **9**: 263, 263n, **11**: 408; maps, **6**: 127n; site, **6**: 140n, 192n, 471; arrive at, **6**: 175, 177, 188; party at, **6**: 194–95, 200, 223n, 230–31, 235–36, 237–40, 275–76, 297, 307, 309, 312, 314, 325–26, 328–29, **9**: 266, 268–72, **10**: 185, 186n, 187–91, **11**: 409–10, 410n, 412, 414, 419–22, 419n; conditions at, **6**: 242–43, 253, 255, 276, 321, 324, **9**: 271–72, **10**: 192–93; abandoned, **6**: 333, 335, **9**: 273n, **10**: 193, 194n; dis-

tances, **6**: 460; evacuated, **11**: 422n; mentioned, **6**: 162–64, 172n, 293, 295, **10**: 186, 187n, **11**: 413, 416–17, 431

Saltpeter, **3**: 350, 474. *See also* Medicine

Salt River, **3**: 345, 347, 349, 352, 384n, 394

Salts. *See* Medicine

Salts, Epsom, **3**: 475. *See also* Medicine, salts

Salts, Glauber's, **3**: 50, 184–85, 186n, 363, 418, 475, 481, **4**: 22, 27, 36, 41, 109, 111n, **5**: 25–26. *See also* Medicine, salts; Salts, mineral

Salts, mineral, **4**: 22, 23–24n, 34, 36, 39, 41–42, 41n, 46, 47n, 52, 60, 81, 84n, 117, 120, 120n, 121, 123, 130, 140, 143, 144n, 161, 163n, 164, 171, 179, 181–83, 195, 198, 202, 205, 207n, 208–9, 210n, 216, 227, 232, 234n, 255, 257n, 318, **5**: 37, 39n. *See also* Medicine, salts; Salts, Epsom; Salts, Glauber's

Salts, tartar. *See* Salts, mineral

Salt Water River, **2**: 219

Salve. *See* Medicine

Salvelinus fontinalis, **2**: 484n, **4**: 289n, **5**: 125n, **9**: 207n. *See also* Trout, brook

Salvia lyrata, **7**: 338n. *See also* Cancerroot

Salvia officinalis, **4**: 40n. *See also* Sage, garden

Sambucus canadensis, **6**: 286n, **8**: 81n. *See also* Elderberry, common

Sambucus cerulea, **6**: 104n, **7**: 198n, **10**: 142n, **11**: 310n. *See also* Elderberry, blue

Sambucus glauca, **10**: 142n. *See also* Elderberry, blue

Sambucus racemosa, **6**: 104n, **7**: 47n, **10**: 142n. *See also* Elderberry, black; Elderberry, red

Sand, **3**: 348, 473, **4**: 24n, 26–27, 40n, 45, 47n, 65–66, 117, 130, 135n, 140, 145n, 146, 159, 163n, 238, 240, 241n, 296n, **5**: 52n, 85n, 88,

140, 141n, 275, 348, 373, **6**: 230n, **8**: 88, 113, 203n, 231, 238, 248

Sand (Big Dry) Creek (McCone County, Mont.), **4**: 117, 119, 120n, **6**: 447, 462, **8**: 381, 400

Sand Coulee Creek (Flattery Run), **4**: 307, 308n, 309n, 310, 312, 316, **8**: 106n, **9**: 171n, 338n, **10**: 104n, 252n, **11**: 208n

Sand Creek (Little Dry River) (Custer County, Mont.), **8**: 251, 254, 255n, 256n, 407

Sand Creek (Pine Brook) (Dawson County, Mont.), **8**: 267–68, 270n, 389, 406

Sand Creek (Rosebud County, Mont.), **8**: 242, 244, 246n

Sand Creek (Yellowstone County, Mont.), **8**: 231, 234n

Sand (Little Dog) Creek (Fergus County, Mont.), **4**: 189, 192n, **9**: 154, 154n, **10**: 91, 91n, **11**: 166–67, 167n

Sanders, Albert E., **12**: 6

Sand Hill River, **2**: 219

Sand Island, **6**: 49–50, 51n, **11**: 394n

Sand or Sandy Lake, **3**: 439, 442, 480

Sandpiper, pectoral, **3**: 132n, **9**: 63n

Sandpiper, spotted, **6**: 382–83, 383n

Sandpiper, stilt, **3**: 132n, **9**: 63n

Sandpiper, upland, **4**: 419n, **8**: 75, 78n

Sandpipers, **9**: 63

Sandrush, **5**: 8, 10n, 45, **9**: 191, 191n

Sandstone (freestone), **2**: 103, 104n, 293n, 369–70, 373n, 383–85, 386n, 391–92, 393n, 394, 465–67, 467n, 469, 471, 474, 501, **3**: 181n, 476, **4**: 18n, 27, 40n, 47n, 144n, 145n, 198, 200, 200n, 205, 207n, 209, 210n, 225–26, 230, 233n, 288n, 299n, **5**: 27, 29, 29n, 30n, 52n, 102n, 140, 141n, 148n, **6**:

67n, 179n, 185n, **8:** 65n,
98n, 118n, 122n, 123n,
124n, 171n, 190, 193n, 217,
221, 228n, 231, 234n, 255n,
256n, 261n, 271, 274, 275n,
9: 37, **11:** 169–70
Sandstone, Dakota, **2:** 467,
467n, 469, 471n
Sandstone, Eagle, **8:** 193n,
208n, 223n
Sandstone, Horsethief, **8:** 126n
Sandstone, Virgelle, **8:** 122n
Sandstone Bluffs, **4:** 232
Sandwich Islands, **6:** 307n
Sandy Creek, **2:** 147, 150n, **5:**
86n
Sandy (Quicksand) River, **6:**
11–13, 18, 14n, 24, 55, 59,
83–84, 101n, 112, 229, 233,
298, 298n, 324, 325n 457,
461, 469, 484, 493, **7:** 39, 41,
41n, 46, 48–52, 54, 56, 62,
66, 71, 74, 77, 113, 118, 120,
8: 386, 405, 415, **9:** 232, 249,
249n, 284–86, 284n, 288,
311n, 368n, **10:** 165, 166n,
173, 174n, 204–5, 204n,
206n, **11:** 382–83, 384n,
437–38, 437n
Sangre de Cristo Range, **2:** 442n
Sanpoil (Hi-high-e-nim-mo) Indians, **6:** 480, 488, 491
Sans Arc Indians. *See* Sioux Indians, Sans Arc
Santa Fe, N. Mex., **2:** 438–39,
442n, **3:** 228n, 349, **8:** 363,
364n
Santee Sioux Indians. *See* Sioux
Indians, Santee
Saone Sioux Indians. *See* Sioux
Indians, Saone
Sapphire Mountains, **5:** 191,
191n, **8:** 162, 162n, **9:** 220,
221n, **11:** 305–6, 306n
Sapsucker, red-breasted, **6:**
379–80, 381n, **7:** 9, 11n
Sapsucker, yellow-bellied, **3:**
307n, **4:** 95n
Sarcobatus vermiculatus, **4:** 145n,
5: 52n, **6:** 373n. *See also*
Greasewood
Sardinia, **10:** 93n
Sarpy (Artk-tar-ha) Creek (La-

biche's River), **3:** 365, 374,
383, **8:** 236, 239, 241n, 390,
407
Saskatchewan River, **3:** 214n,
363, 431, 433–34, 444, **4:**
60, 62, 103, 106, 124, 188,
204, 214n, 222, 224, 248,
270, **7:** 219n, 258, **8:** 120n,
123, 131, 294, **9:** 159, 159n,
10: 67n
Sassafras, **2:** 69, 69n, **6:** 174, 197
Sassafras albidum, **2:** 69n. *See also*
Sassafras
Saucier, François, **2:** 180, 180n,
232n
Sauger, **2:** 433n, **4:** 278, 279n,
280, 286, 309, 347, 371
Saugrain, Antoine François, **2:**
147n, 243, 243–44n
Sauke Prairie, **2:** 310–11
Sauk (Saukee) Indians, **2:** 181,
181n, 212, 235, 279, 295–
96, 299n, 302–3, 306, 327,
524, **3:** 340, 394–95, 406–7,
411–17, 439, 448, 483, **9:**
380–81, 380n
Sauvie (Wapato) Island, **6:** 20n,
21n, 24n, 25n, 186n, 457,
461, 470, 475, 477–78, 484,
490, 494, **7:** 26–27, 31n, 32–
34, 36n, 37n, 41, 55, 59–60,
62, 81–83, **8:** 405, 415, **9:**
283, 283n, **10:** 166, 167n,
203, 204n, **11:** 387n, 437,
437n
Sawa-haini village, **3:** 153n, **10:**
270, 270n, **8:** 315, 317n
Saws, **2:** 137, 141, 157n, **3:** 240,
9: 166, **11:** 193–94
Sawtooth Creek, **8:** 163, 164n
Sawyers, **8:** 147, 148n, 350, 355
Sayornis saya, **7:** 195n. *See also*
Phoebe, Say's
Scad-dal Indians. *See* Klickitat
Indians
Scaffolds, **4:** 289, **5:** 146, 274–
76, 281–82, 286–88, 298,
304, 306, 309, 335, **7:** 54, 56,
66, 79, 86–88, 224, **8:** 17,
20, 32, 34, 108, 211, **9:** 91,
238, 288, 324, **10:** 36, 60,
162, **11:** 217, 224–25, 350–
51, 354, 358–59, 362, 413

Scalopus sp., **6:** 355n. *See also*
Mole, eastern
Scalp Creek, **10:** 37, 37n
Scalps, **3:** 116, 119, 121–22,
5: 127, 159, 351, **7:** 253,
255, **10:** 47, 228, **11:** 88–
89, 289–90
Scannon. *See* Seaman
Scapanus sp., **6:** 355n. *See also*
Mole, western
Scaphirhynchus platorynchus,
2: 72n. *See also* Sturgeon,
shovelnose
Scappoose Bay, **7:** 31n
Scarabaeidae, **7:** 312n. *See also*
Beetles
Scarlet, **4:** 105. *See also* Clothing
Sceloporus occidentalis, **6:** 405n, **7:**
165n. *See also* Lizard, western
fence
Schist (shistus), **3:** 474, 476–77
Schuyler, A. E., **12:** 6
Schuylkill River, **4:** 291, 296n
Scimitar, **7:** 31n. *See also* Swords
Scirpus acutus, **4:** 422n, **5:** 21n,
10: 16on. *See also* Bulrush,
western; Tule
Scirpus sp., **6:** 29n, 307n, **7:**
159n. *See also* Bulrushes;
Rushes
Scirpus validus, **5:** 21n, **10:** 16on.
See also Tule
Sciurus carolinensis, **2:** 79n, **3:**
54n, **8:** 13n, **9:** 55n. *See also*
Squirrel, gray
Sciurus griseus, **5:** 344n, **6:** 317n,
7: 129n, **9:** 246n, **10:** 159n,
11: 374n. *See also* Squirrel,
western gray
Sciurus niger, **3:** 57n, **6:** 347n, **8:**
333n, **9:** 56n, **11:** 71n. *See also*
Squirrel, fox
Scott, Hugh, **6:** 33on
Scott's pills. *See* Medicine
Scrapers, **9:** 113, 134
Screws, **4:** 306, **6:** 146–47, **11:**
207
Scrofula. *See* Medical problems
Scumar-qua-up, **6:** 155, 159n
Scurf pea, lemon, **3:** 464, 469
Scurf pea, silver-leaf, **3:** 460,
464, 471
Scurvy. *See* Medical problems

Seader (and similar spellings). *See* Cedar

Seal, harbor, **5**: 4, 327, 328n, 329, 337, 339, 366, 369, 366, 369, 379, 380n, **6**: 10n, 13, 14n, 55, 313, 315, 317n, 340–42, 342n, 457, **7**: 12–13, 39, 40, 41n, **9**: 242n, 243, 243n, 266, 369n, **10**: 161, 162n, 164, **11**: 365–66, 367n, 383–87, 391, 397–98

Seal Islands. *See* Karlson Island; Marsh Island

Seal River. *See* Washougal River

Seaman, **2**: 79, 80n, 82, 89, 347, 350, 509, **3**: 7, 9,**4**: 60, 66, 68, 85, 113, 115, 166, 168, 215, 218, 309, 336, 338, 383, 411, 430, **5**: 112, 115, **7**: 1, 105, 109, 226, 230, 280–81, **8**: 92n, 95, 110, 139n, **9**: 25, 25n, 133, 137, 150, 157, 307, 374n. *See also* Monture (Seaman's) Creek

Sea sickness. *See* Medical problems

Seaweed, **6**: 431

Second Bear (Matocoquepan), **3**: 113, **10**: 45, 45n, **11**: 85, 86n

Sedge, needle leaf, **5**: 21n

Sedge, thread-leaved, **4**: 140–41, 145n, **5**: 21n, 67n

Sedges, **4**: 430, **5**: 10n, 18, 21n, 45, 60n, **6**: 77n, 144n, 216–17, 217n, 304, 307

Sedum stenopetalum, **8**: 81n. *See also* Stonecrop, wormleaf

Seeing Snake (Mar-book She-a-O-ke-ah), **3**: 276n, 284, 284n

Sego Island, **3**: 37, 39n

Sego lily, **5**: 224n

Sehrt Creek, **2**: 249–50, 251n

Seines, **5**: 119, **7**: 182, 184, 343–44, 346n, **10**: 159

Selasphorus platycercus, **8**: 27n. *See also* Hummingbird, broad-tailed

Selasphorus rufus, **7**: 47n. *See also* Hummingbird, rufous

Selenite, **4**: 131, 134, 135n, 140, 144n, 202, 207n, 208, 210n, 234n

Sentinel Butte Formation, **4**: 18n, 21n, 24n, 40n, 47n, 50n, 53n, 63n, 76n

Sepulchre Rock. *See* Lower Memaloose Island

Serpent Creek, **5**: 211n, **8**: 56–57, 58n

Serviceberry: abundance, **2**: 216, 217n, **3**: 481,**4**: 406, 414, 417, **5**: 107, **9**: 309, **10**: 121, 126, 135, 147, 249, **11**: 293–95, 308–9; habitat, **4**: 70; observed, **4**: 94, 388, 391, **5**: 31–32, 36, 81, 83, 116, 241, **7**: 110, 111n, 113, 192–93, **8**: 10–11, 13n, 71, 79, 334, **9**: 187, 187n, 190, 203, 215–16, **10**: 118, 141–42, 238, **11**: 241, 242n, 270–71; described, **4**: 392; as food, **5**: 32, 81, 162, **11**: 289–91, 299–300; gathered, **5**: 106; and Indians, **5**: 142, **9**: 208, 213, 218, **10**: 130, **11**: 286–87, 299–300, 308–9; mentioned, **3**: 492n, **4**: 57n, 396–97n, **5**: 35n, **6**: 45–46n, **7**: 114n, **10**: 119n

Serviceberry, eastern. *See* Juneberry

Serviceberry Valley, **8**: 175, 176n

Setaria italica, **7**: 337n. *See also* Foxtail

Sevenbark, **8**: 12–13n, 71, 79. *See also* Ninebark

Seven Blackfoot (Burnt Lodge, Rattlesnake) Creek, **4**: 159, 161, 163n, **6**: 448, 463, **8**: 382, 400, **9**: 149, 149n, **10**: 89, 89n, **11**: 159–60, 160n

Seven Devils Mountains, **8**: 27n

Sevenmile Creek, **4**: 187n, **7**: 252, 255n, **9**: 153, 153n, **10**: 91n

Seventh Point Coulee (Pine Creek), **4**: 147–48, 149n, **6**: 448, 463, **8**: 381, 400, **9**: 147, 147n, **11**: 154, 154n

Sewelel. *See* Beaver, mountain

Sextants, **1**: 4, **2**: 91, 92n, 97, 110, 122n, 135–38, 145, 158, 410–12, 414n, **3**: 273,

4: 25, 222, **6**: 277, 317, **7**: 349. *See also* Instruments, scientific

Sexton (East Lacrush) Creek, **2**: 105, 109n

Seybert, Adam, **3**: 472

Shad, gizzard, **4**: 278, 279n, 332, 347, 414

Shadwell Creek, **8**: 272, 274n

Sha-ha-la Indians. *See* Watlala Indians

Shahaptian language, **5**: 222, 225n, 263n, 284n, 292–94, 307n, 319n, 326n, 329, 336n, 344–45, **7**: 145n, 151n, 158, 159n, 162n, 168n, 169n, 177n, 181n, 219n, 343n, 348n, **9**: 240n, **10**: 158n, 163n, 200n, 213n, 215n, 216n, **11**: 356n, 374n

Shâh-hâr-wâr-cap, **6**: 192, 196, 198n, **9**: 265, 266n, **11**: 411, 412n

The Shake Hand, **3**: 19, 21n, 23–24, 28–29, 33, 36n, **9**: 48n, 51n

Shale, **2**: 373n, 471–72, 474, 475n, **4**: 18n, 24n, 47n, 144n, 288n, 296n, 299n, 336, 337n, 419, 421n, 422, **5**: 30n, 102n, **8**: 98n, 119n, 124n, 217, 223, 227, 234n, 261n, 351n, **9**: 189, 189n, **10**: 117, 117n

Shale, Bearpaw, **4**: 107n, 120n, 129n, 135n, 144n, 148n, 163n, 179n, 207n, 210n, **8**: 227, 229n, 240n, 279n

Shale, Carlile, **2**: 506n, **3**: 13n, 15n, **8**: 216, 220, 221n

Shale, Claggett, **4**: 200n, 207n, 233n, 234n, 257n, 264n, **8**: 217, 221, 223n, 279n

Shale, Graneros, **3**: 13n

Shale, Greyson, **4**: 406n, 425n

Shale, Marias River, **4**: 233n, 257n, 282n, 296n, **8**: 114n, 118n

Shale, Niobrara, **8**: 216, 220, 221n

Shale, Otoe, **2**: 393n

Shale, Pierre, **3**: 48n, 51n, 52n, 57, 60n, 67–68, 68n, 69n,

96n, 99n, 146n, **8**: 262n, 321n

Shale, Spokane, **4**: 425n

Shaler, William, **6**: 29n

Shal-lât-to (and similar spellings) Indians. *See* Klickitat Indians

Shallon (and similar spellings). *See* Salal

Shallow Bay. *See* Grays Bay

Shannetahque (and similar spellings). *See* Thistle, edible

Shannon, George: assists Biddle, **2**: 37; listed, **2**: 148, 187–88, 194, 197, 199, 255, **4**: 9, 11, **8**: 162n, 179, **11**: 4n, 7n, 187n, 203n, 393n, 395n, 400n, 408n, 414n, 419n, 420n, 424n, 428n; fishing, **2**: 181; duties, **2**: 190, **7**: 139, 141, **8**: 284; sent out, **2**: 205, 476–77, **3**: 1, 13–14, 272n, **4**: 329, **5**: 53–55, 57, 59–62, 116n, 167, 169, **6**: 44–47, 60, **7**: 86–87, 131, 133–34, 143–44, **8**: 34–36, 170, 209, 211–12, 329, **9**: 38, 109, 172, 254, 286, 332, **10**: 28, 170, 181, 241, 255, 265; in permanent party, **2**: 229n; hunting, **2**: 260, 422, 423n, 497, **3**: 8–9, 11, 271, 271n, **4**: 96, 98–99, 309, 327, 332–33, **6**: 16, 117–18, 124, 138, 140, 177, 190, 194–95, 221, 226–27, 229, 239–40, 242, 244n, 275–76, 279–80, 287–88, 317–18, 324, 328–29, 342, 344, 351, 353, 358, 360, 365, 368n, 414–16, 418, 420n, **7**: 71, 74, 86, 92, 95, 257–60, 262, 264, 266, 268, 271n, 273–74, 277, 279, 281, 289, 297, 299, 326, 328, **8**: 17, 165, 182, 190, 195, 209, 284–85, 290, 322, 327, 337, 361, **9**: 8, 30, 42, 45, 59, 170, 173, 263, 267–68, 272, 273n, 274, 310, 312, 315, 322, 355, 357, **10**: 31, 39, 105, 123, 181, 184, 188–89, 192, 205, 227–29, 235, 238, 271, 273–74, **11**: 45, 62, 74,

74n, 120, 203, 209–11, 261–62, 408, 414–15, 420, 423–24, 423n, 428; returns, **2**: 499, **3**: 65–66, 273, 274n, **6**: 48, 50, **7**: 88, 335–36, **8**: 46–47, 218, 283, 295, 323, 328, 351, **9**: 58–59, 109, 199, 253, 266–67, 270, 273, 277, 313, 319, 326, 331, **10**: 70, 105, 133, 171, 190, 195, 207, 229n, 230, 232–33, 236, 239, 243n, **11**: 59, 60n, 72–74, 120, 188, 261–62, 393–94, 396, 413, 415, 418; separated, **2**: 502, **8**: 39, 41, 44–45, 47, 290, 323, 331, **11**: 209–11; biographical sketch, **2**: 521–22; one of "nine young men from Kentucky," **2**: 529n; lost, **3**: 1, 16, 19–22, 21n, 40, 44–45, 48, 50, 51n, 71, 73n, 74, **9**: 46–47, 50, 54–55, 197–98, **10**: 36, 38, **11**: 64, 69–70, 257–62; court-martial member, **3**: 170; medical problems, **3**: 309, 309n, **8**: 365; scouting, **4**: 250, 256, **6**: 62, 65, 92, 116, 117n, **9**: 253–54, 257, **10**: 98, 175, 178, **11**: 186–89, 393, 395, 400, 403; information from, **4**: 333, **8**: 166n, 209, 218, 222n, **9**: 268; and Indians, **6**: 48, 50; votes, **6**: 83; and saltmaking camp, **6**: 162–64, 172n, 179, 194–95, **9**: 259, **10**: 185, 187; and species, **6**: 319, 321–23, **8**: 285, **11**: 421, 421n; accidents, **7**: 308, 310, **10**: 234; loses tomahawk, **8**: 165, 289, **9**: 331; creek named for, **8**: 228n, 328, **9**: 367n, **11**: 75; loses ammunition, **8**: 359; trade, **9**: 294, 324, **10**: 213; mentioned, **2**: 66n, 153n, 510, 544–45, **3**: 36n, **8**: 37, 164, **9**: 39n, 170n, 253n, 254n, 255n, 257n, 259n, 263n, 266n, 271n, 272n, 274n, 277n, 279, 286n, 294n, 310n, 312n, 315n, 320n, 332n, 356n, 357n,

396n, **10**: 28n, 31n, 36n, 38n, 39n, 70n, 98n, 105n, 106n, 123n, 133n, 170n, 171n, 175n, 179n, 181n, 182n, 184n, 186n, 187n, 188n, 190n, 192n, 195n, 206n, 208n, 213n, 228n, 229n, 230n, 232n, 233n, 234n, 235n, 236n, 238n, 239n, 241n, 243, 256n, 265n, 271n, 273n, 274n, **11**: 76n, 120n, 394n, 403n, 413n, 415n

Sha-no-ma, **6**: 154, 159n

Shan-wap-pom (and similar spellings) Indians. *See* Klickitat Indians

Shappellel (and similar spellings). *See* Cous

Sharbono (and similar spellings). *See* Charbonneau

Shaved Prairie, **2**: 219

Shaw-natahque (and similar spellings). *See* Thistle, edible

Shawnee Indians, Absentee, **2**: 89, 90n, 111–12, 113n

Shawnee (Shawonie) Indians, **2**: 69n, 90n, 93, 107, 109, 174n, 516, 524, **3**: 391, 446, 449, **5**: 121

Sheep. *See* Goat, mountain

Sheep, Audubon's mountain, **4**: 75n

Sheep, bighorn (argali, ibex): horns, **3**: 117, 119, 260, 330–31, **4**: 71, 74, 275, **5**: 150, **9**: 126, 166, 337, **10**: 75; informed of, **3**: 133, 135, 482, **7**: 112–13, 114n; skins, **3**: 261, 396–444 passim, 482, 484, 488, **5**: 126–27, 134, 139, 259, **6**: 146–47, **7**: 112–13, 114n, **8**: 145, **9**: 205, 208, 218, 224, 337, 344, **10**: 131, 215, **11**: 276–77, 280–81, 299, 329–30; observed, **4**: 71, 74, 75n, 85, 87, 136, 139, 201, 208–9, 394, 396, 399, 401, 403, 414, 434, **5**: 19, 160, 187, **7**: 327, 329, **8**: 66, 68, 255, 272, **9**: 140, 160, 185–86, 192, 217, 316, 343, 349, **10**: 84, 113, 235,

Sheep, bighorn (argali, ibex)
(*continued*)
 11: 141, 175, 230–31, 248,
  299–30; behavior, **4**: 85–86,
  194–95, 198, 212, 397, **8**:
  175, **11**: 141, 170, 229–31;
  hunted, **4**: 86, 193, 196–98,
  202, 205, 207, 211, 213, 227,
  229, 232, 236, 238, 240, **5**:
  27, 29, **6**: 448–49; described,
  4: 193–98, **8**: 140, **9**: 155l,
  10: 92, **11**: 169–70; habitat,
  4: 194–95, 397, **8**: 140, 175;
  specimens, **4**: 199n, **8**: 418,
  419, **10**: 260; abundance, **4**:
  213, 215, 227, 229, 232, **8**:
  140, 225, 232, 276, **9**: 156,
  190, 331, 336, **11**: 242–43;
  and Indians, **5**: 94n, 150, **7**:
  145, 147–48, 202–3, **8**: 232,
  9: 205, 218, 229, **10**: 131,
  215, **11**: 276–77, 280–81,
  299, 329–30; hunted, **8**: 141,
  163, 165, 225, 276, 281–82,
  334, **9**: 154–56, 193, 312n,
  336, **10**: 92, 96, 260–61, **11**:
  168–71, 175–76, 180–82,
  230, 249–50, 281; scarcity,
  8: 238; food, **11**: 171; mentioned, **3**: 120n, 137n, 261n,
  4: 51, 200n, 207n, **5**: 21n, **8**:
  69n, 226, 274n, 417, 418n,
  9: 127n, 140n, **10**: 84n, 92n,
  93n, 148, **11**: 6n, 141n
Sheep, common, **4**: 193, 197
Sheep, mountain. *See* Goat,
 mountain
Sheep Coulee, **4**: 255, 257n
Sheep Creek, **4**: 150, 150n, **9**:
 147, 147n, **10**: 88, 88n
Sheepeater Indians. *See* Tukudika Indians
Sheep Island, **5**: 304, 307n
Sheep Mountain, **8**: 188n
Sheep Nose Point, **2**: 309n,
 311n
Sheep Shed Coulee (Crevis
 Creek), **4**: 221n, 224n, **9**:
 159n, **10**: 96n, **11**: 179n
Sheheke. *See* Big White
Shelathwell, **6**: 72, 73n, 154,
 159n, 333n

Shelewele (and similar spellings). *See* Salal
Shell Creek (Goose Egg Lake
 Run) (Mont.), **4**: 30, 33n,
 6: 447, 462, **8**: 381, 399
Shell Creek (Nebr.), **3**: 351–52,
 384n
Shellfish, **9**: 163
Shells, **5**: 89, 114, 122, 128,
 134–35, 222, 259, 261, 289,
 318, 359, 361, 369, 373–74,
 7: 10, 108, 253, 255, **8**: 314,
 318–19, **9**: 205, 289, 309,
 10: 176. *See also* Clothing
Shelton (Beef) Island, **2**: 259n
She-ne-tock-we (and similar
 spellings). *See* Thistle, edible
Shepherd Butte, **4**: 260n
Shepherdia argentea, **2**: 499n,
 3: 107n, **4**: 28n, 469, **5**: 40n,
 8: 115n, **9**: 44n, **10**: 30n,
 11: 61n. *See also* Buffaloberry
Sheppards Dell, **10**: 207n
Sherman Peak, **5**: 214n, 217n,
 9: 226, 226n
Sherman Saddle, **8**: 34n, **9**:
 324n, **10**: 241n
Sheyenne (Chien, Shayen,
 Shaha) River, **2**: 219, **3**: 169,
 171n
Shields, **3**: 289, **5**: 80, 122, 150–
 51, **8**: 135, **9**: 342. *See also*
 Arms and ammunition
Shields, John: hunting, **2**: 139,
 158, 167, 254, 260, 261n,
 502, **3**: 28, 70–72, 92–93,
 95n, 98, 99n, 146–47, 286,
 288, **4**: 258, 331, 334, **5**: 87,
 102, 104, 109, 202, 211,
 214n, 229–30, 356, **6**: 351,
 353, 358, 360, 365, 368n,
 391, 393, 403, 443, **7**: 116–
 17, 132, 226, 230, 260, 262,
 265, 268, 271n, 272–73,
 275–76, 278–79, 284, 286,
 288, 326, 328, 333–34, **8**:
 21–23, 65–66, 68, 165–66,
 172, 174, 181–82, 202, 209,
 212, 219, 224, 232, 238, 245,
 273, 283, 285–87, 290, 320,
 322, 326, 328, **9**: 33, 55, 59,
 62, 112–13, 225, 265, 274,

291, 312, 315, 322, 326,
 328–29, 331, **10**: 24, 39,
 39n, 143, 147, 164, 199, 210,
 212, 223, 229, 231, 235, 244,
 246n, 271, 273, **11**: 27, 49,
 80, 320–21, 327–28, 424,
 426; sent out, **2**: 140, 152,
 173, 202, 308, 494, **3**: 7, 9,
 16, 48–49, **4**: 327, **5**: 64, 68,
 70, 73, **8**: 34–35, 51–52,
 205, 208, **9**: 199, 276, 325,
 375, **10**: 9, 41, 106, 244,
 244n, 255, **11**: 61, 78–79,
 410; returns, **2**: 141, 269–70,
 500, **3**: 19–20, **7**: 291, 294,
 8: 37–38, **9**: 64, 319, 322, **10**:
 42, 195–96, 200, 228, 230–
 33, 236, 238–39, 242, **11**:
 28, 190–91; listed, **2**: 147,
 187–88, 194, 197, 199, 255,
 4: 9, 11, **6**: 172n, **8**: 162n,
 179, 277, **11**: 4n, 7n, 62n,
 187n, 210n, 411n, 424n;
 shooting match, **2**: 157;
 blacksmithing, **2**: 175, 176n,
 524, **3**: 262n, **4**: 275, 306, **6**:
 158, 441–42, **7**: 93n, 95, **8**:
 74–75, 79–80, **9**: 107, 107n,
 165, **10**: 71, 268, **11**: 125,
 129, 192–94; discipline, **2**:
 178, 183, 194, 200n; court-
 martialed, **2**: 182; in permanent party, **2**: 229n; scouting,
 2: 310, 315–16, **4**: 250, 256,
 5: 61–62, **9**: 44, **10**: 98, 123,
 11: 186–90, 261; biographical sketch, **2**: 522; one of
 "nine young men from Kentucky," **2**: 529; information
 from, **3**: 50, **4**: 171, **7**: 3, 283–
 84, **8**: 165, 166n; court-martial member, **3**: 170; medical
 problems, **3**: 240, **4**: 96, 98;
 and mineralogical speci-
 mens, **3**: 478; creek named
 for, **4**: 299n, **11**: 199n; and
 iron-frame boat, **4**: 323, 330,
 336–37, 343, 349, 351; duties, **4**: 331, 333–34, **6**: 395–
 96, **8**: 170, **10**: 105, 107, 241,
 11: 209, 214; votes, **6**: 83;
 and species, **6**: 390, 398, 400,

401n; fishing, **6**: 451; and Indians, **7**: 105, 109; loses horse, **8**: 34–35; river named for, **8**: 188n, **9**: 168, 168n, **10**: 102n; and saltmaking camp, **10**: 187; mentioned, **3**: 141, 142n, **5**: 69, **6**: 401, **9**: xiv, 44n, 165n, 226n, 265n, 274n, 276n, 279, 291n, 312n, 315n, 373–74n, 375n, 386n, **10**: 9n, 25n, 42n, 43n, 71n, 98n, 105n, 107n, 123n, 144n, 147n, 164n, 188n, 195n, 196n, 200n, 210n, 212n, 224n, 229n, 230n, 231n, 232n, 233n, 235n, 236n, 239n, 241n, 242n, 244n, 256n, 271n, 273n, **11**: 27n, 125n, 193n, 214n, 321n, 329n, 426n

Shields, William Bayard, **2**: 74, 75n

Shields Creek, **5**: 186–87n

Shields River, **8**: 180n, 184, 186, 187n, 188n, 191, 197n, 392, 409

Shil-lar-la-wit. *See* Shelathwell

Shirts, **2**: 318, **3**: 79, **4**: 294, **5**: 104, 231–32, **6**: 137, 187, 205, 390, 407, **7**: 147–48, 158, 162, 249–50, 349, **8**: 83, 88, 219, 351, **9**: 47, 123, 205–6, 208, 301, 359, 362, **10**: 67, 193, **11**: 113, 276, 280–81, 301–2. *See also* Clothing

Shives. *See* Chive, wild

Shoalwater Bay. *See* Willapa Bay

Shocatilicum, **6**: 184, 185n

Shoe Indians. *See* Hidatsa Indians, Awaxawi

Shoemate. *See* Sumac, smooth

Shoes, **2**: 154, **3**: 486, **5**: 114, **6**: 104, 130, **7**: 344–45, 346n. *See also* Clothing

Shonkin Creek (Snow River), **4**: 256, 257n, 287, 289n, **6**: 449, 464, **8**: 382, 401, **9**: 167, 167n, **10**: 101, 102n, **11**: 195–96, 196n

Shonkinite, **4**: 233n

Shortgrass Prairie, **8**: 188n

Short (Little) Narrows, **5**: 336n, 337, 340n, **6**: 455, 469, **8**: 385, 404, **9**: 232, 294, **10**: 173, 174n, 213, **11**: 370n. *See also* Columbia River, The Dalles of the

Short Rapids, **6**: 455, 468, **8**: 385, 403

Shoshone Cove, **5**: 2, 65–66, 67n, 71, 72n, 73, 97, 104, 117–18, 124, 133, 141, 149, 158, 163n, 166–68, 181, **8**: 172, 173n, **9**: 210, 210n, **10**: 127, 127n, **11**: 284n

Shoshone Indians, Lemhi, **5**: 85n

Shoshone Indians, Northern, **5**: 85n, 94n

Shoshone Indians, Western, **5**: 85n

Shoshone (Snake) Indians: encountered, **1**: 10, **4**: 407, **5**: 2, 68–69, 77–79, 114, 131, 181, 260n, **8**: 96n, **9**: 110, 204, **10**: 126, 127n, 129, **11**: 272–74, 275n, 289–90; and maps, **1**: 11; and horses, **2**: 7, **3**: 369, **5**: 160–61; trade, **2**: 7, **3**: 428, 484, **5**: 3, 81, 92, 95n, 106, 111, 117–18, 135, 158, **7**: 136, 148, **8**: 201, 278, 388–89, **11**: 276–77, 280–81, 293; relations with the party, **2**: 7, **5**: 3, 70, 83, 96–97, 102, 104–106, 109, 111, 114–15, 117, 121, 123, 125–6, 128, 131, 135, 137–39, 142, 144–46, 148–49, 158–59, 164–68, 171, 173–75, 177, 179, **7**: 221, 223, 227–28, 231, 248, 313, 315, **8**: 169–70, **9**: 206–8, 210, 212–14, **10**: 130, 133–34, 222, 230, 234, **11**: 272–76, 278–93, 295, 313, 340; search for, **2**: 22, **4**: 4, 398, 401, 407–10, 418, 420, 430, 432, 435–38, **5**: 18, 20, 23–25, 24n, 59, 62, **9**: 188, 190, 195, 200, **10**: 120, 120n, **11**: 236–37, 243–44, 261–63; war, **3**: 207n, 208, 210, 234,

276, 313, 395, 400, 402–44, 430–31, **5**: 8–9, 83, 91–92, 122–24, 125n, 127, 159, 164n, 168, 197, 242, **6**: 155, **7**: 211, 213, 229, 247, 250–51, 251n, 278, 280, **8**: 40, 42, 48, 132n, 195, 278, 302–4, **9**: 110n, 192, 213, 222, 300, 317n, **10**: 128, 140, 235, **11**: 246–47, 280–81, 289–91, 308–9; located, **3**: 213n, 368–69, 386, **5**: 89, **6**: 311, 313–15, 451, 495, **7**: 227, 231, 334n, **8**: 40, 42, 413, **9**: 190, 332, **10**: 160, 160n, **11**: 195, 237–38, 289; language, **3**: 228, **5**: 69, 72n, 85n, 86n, 94n, 116–17n, 188n, 224n, 256, 260n, **6**: 13, 14n, 317n, **7**: 21n, 242, 244, 269–70, 271n, **8**: 53, 55n, 90n, 161, 175, 176n, 235n, **9**: 219n, 306n, **10**: 223, **11**: 4n, 8n, 138, 138n, 195, 302n; Sacagawea and, **3**: 229n, 312, 327; peace, **3**: 234, **7**: 334, 341, **8**: 47, 301, **9**: 320; name, **3**: 328n, **4**: 401n, **5**: 115, 116n, 159, **10**: 78n, 160n, 214n, **11**: 286; historical sketch, **3**: 435–36, **5**: 85–86n, 119–23; listed, **3**: 449; appearance, **3**: 488, **5**: 121; signs, **4**: 4, **5**: 71, 73, 168, **8**: 163, 165, **11**: 237, 257; hunting, **4**: 237, **5**: 87–88, 123, 130, 148–49, 164–65, **8**: 182, **9**: 209–10, **11**: 283, 292; camps, **4**: 386–87, **5**: 70, 78, 87, 113, 130–31, 132n, 135, 138–39, 142–3, 146, 159, 162–63, 167–69, 174, 174n, 177, 179, 181, **9**: 203; information from, **4**: 410n, **5**: 89–91, 94n, 100, 109, 113, 115, 148n, 153, 156, 164n, 175, **6**: 3, 310, 316, **7**: 182, 184, **8**: 2, 40, 42, 115n, 177, **9**: 214, **10**: 128–29, **11**: 273–74, 291, 374n; gifts, **5**: 70, 77, 78–79, 81, 90, 105, 112, 123–24, 129–

Shoshone (Snake) Indians
(*continued*)
30, 144–45, **8**: 314; lodges,
5: 73, 80, 83, 92, 121, 128,
130–31, 139, 167, 172, **10**:
128–29; clothes, **5**: 78, 79,
94n, 112, 114, 117–18, 121–
24, 126–28, 131n, 133–35,
139, 145, 149, 158, 189, **7**:
62, 124–25, 145, 148, 253,
255, **9**: 205, **11**: 276–77;
ceremonies, **5**: 79–81, 86n,
96–97, 112, 114–15, 128,
130, 150–51, 165; arms and
ammunition, **5**: 80, 122,
150–51, 160, **11**: 276; councils, **5**: 81, 111–12, 130, 143–
44, 165, 178; customs, **5**: 83,
92, 96, 112, 119–22, 140,
150–51, 171, **6**: 273–74, **7**:
341, 343n, 249, **9**: 212, **11**:
286–88; food, **5**: 95, 103,
112, 115, 117, 143, 148–49,
172, 175, **8**: 50–51, 167, **10**:
128, 134, **11**: 283–84, 287,
289; chiefs, **5**: 112, 117–20,
143–44, 166, **9**: 205, 208,
11: 277n, 280, 285–87;
villages, **5**: 116n, 128, 154,
172, 178, 178n, 182, 182n,
10: 133, 134n, **11**: 285, 295;
numbers, **5**: 120, 178, **6**:
479–80, 482, 487; medical
problems, **5**: 122; fishing, **5**:
137, 139, 175, 230, **11**: 281,
295; artifacts, **5**: 149–50, **10**:
134; tobacco, **6**: 123, 147;
and animals, **6**: 313, 315–16;
as interpreters, **7**: 178, 180,
211, 213, 243–44; men-
tioned, **4**: 1, 9, 11, 14, 216,
299, 319, 344, 359, 412, 416,
5: 1, 116, 155, 183, 255, **6**:
433, 437, 473, 483, 489, 491,
7: 215n, **8**: 43n, 165, 393, **9**:
152n, 236, 279, 304–5, 307,
316, **10**: 77–78, 129, 222n,
11: 114n, 275n, 345–46. *See
also* Sacagawea; Old Toby
Shoshone River, **3**: 385n, **8**:
193n, 235n
Shot. *See* Balls, bullets, and shot

Sho-ta-harro-ra, **9**: 95n
Shotguns, **2**: 214n. *See also* Arms
and ammunition
Sho-to Indians. *See* Kanasisi
Indians
Shoulders. *See* Medical
problems
Shoveler, northern, **7**: 166, 168,
169n, 226, 233n
Shrew, short-tailed, **3**: 331n
Shrike, loggerhead, **4**: 276,
277n
Shrike, white-rumped, **4**: 277n
Shrub-steppe region, **7**: 172n,
190n, 204n
Sialia currucoides, **6**: 131n. *See
also* Bluebird, mountain
Sialia sialis, **4**: 277n. *See also*
Bluebird, eastern
Sibley's Island, **3**: 186–88, 188n
Sidehill Calf, **8**: 134, 136n
Sign language, **5**: 2, 79, 85n, 88,
94n, 114, 142, 188n, 196–
97, 224n, 226, 230–31, 278,
287, 289, 296, 303, 305,
307n, 346n
Siletz River, **6**: 202n
Silica, **6**: 179n, 193
Silk, **3**: 309, **9**: 369n
Silkgrass, **7**: 146–47, 149
Silt, **4**: 135n, 241n, 296n, **5**:
85n, **6**: 230n, **8**: 114n
Siltstone, **4**: 145n, 299n, **5**:
102n, **6**: 67n, **8**: 261n
Silver, **4**: 375, **7**: 341, 343n,
8: 363, **9**: 364, **10**: 280
Silverberry, **8**: 93, 94n
Silverfish, **2**: 483, 484n, 485–
86, 486n
Silver King Mountain, **10**: 250n
Silversage. *See* Sagebrush, silver
Silver-weed, **7**: 55, 61n, 335,
337
Simlins, **3**: 154n, **11**: 91–92,
92n, 106. *See also* Squashes
Simms Creek, **8**: 99n, **10**: 251n
Simulium sp., **4**: 377n, **5**: 10n. *See
also* Gnat, buffalo
Simulium vittatum, **10**: 244n. *See
also* Fly, black
Sinquefield (and similar spell-
ings). *See* Silver-weed

Siouan language, **3**: 27, 32, 34n,
50n, 206n, 234n, 384n, 489–
90, 492n, **4**: 214n, **8**: 235n
Siouan language, Chiwere
group, **2**: 192n, 299n, 425n,
437n, 442n
Siouan language, Dhegiha
group, **2**: 267n, 281n, 425n,
442n, 482n
Sioux City, Iowa, **9**: xvii
Sioux Indians: trade, **1**: 6, 8, **2**:
442, **3**: 88n, 101–2, 103n,
133, 135, 140, 163, 166n,
238, 356–57, 385n, 401,
487, **4**: 272, **5**: 121, 150, **8**:
317, 346, **10**: 13, **11**: 81n;
speech for, **2**: 191–92, **3**: 21–
24, 156–57; listed, **2**: 195; located, **2**: 252, 440, **3**: 89–90,
238; encountered, **2**: 264n,
3: 16–17, 20, 104, 106–8,
165, 167, 169, 191, 222,
223n; war, **2**: 306, 362, 440,
456, 507, **3**: 3, 26n, 27, 56n,
154n, 160–63, 175, 187,
191, 196–97, 201n, 207n,
213–14n, 222, 233–34, 241,
243–46, 250n, 251–52, 272,
284, 292, 295–97, 299, 304–
5, 307, 312, 317, 331, 398–
99, 401–8, 426–28, 430,
433, 437–43, 482-, **4**: 10–11,
8: 228n, 298–99, 301–2,
304, 306, 308, 311–15, 319,
323, 380, 486, **10**: 74; language, **2**: 438, 458, 463n,
484n, **3**: 27, 32, 34n, 35n,
114n, 123n, 137n, 230n,
235, 384n, 490, **8**: 329–30;
search for, **2**: 483–84, 487–
88, **3**: 8, 11, **10**: 28; customs,
2: 504–5, **3**: 22, 23n, 26n,
115–22, 161, 163–64, **6**:
169, 191, **8**: 349–50n; relations with the party, **2**: 519,
3: 140, 299; villages, **3**: 19,
122, **8**: 322, 323n; chiefs, **3**:
21n, 111, 258, **8**: 74, 77, 156,
212; tipis and lodges, **3**: 22,
103n; warrior societies, **3**:
23–26, 25–26n, 113, 114n;
councils, **3**: 24, 26, 29–31,

111–20, 123n; divisions, **3**: 27, 32–33, 35–36n, 109n; peace, **3**: 32; historical sketch, **3**: 35–36n, 415–18; camps, **3**: 89–90, 99, 167, **8**: 310; clothes, **3**: 117, 488; police, **3**: 119, 489; distances, **3**: 180; stealing horses, **3**: 196–97, 292, 295, 305–7; character, **3**: 276; hunting, **3**: 484–85, **8**: 321; appearance, **3**: 487; mentioned, **2**: 7, 294, 295n, 444n, **3**: 156n, 167n, 236n, 330, 408–20, 481, **4**: 35, 38, 88n, **10**: 60, 61n, **11**: 110n

Sioux Indians, Blackfeet, **3**: 23n, 109n

Sioux Indians, Brulé (Bois Brule), **3**: 19, 21n, 27, 32, 109n, 118–19, 140n, 399, 415, 418, 420, 448, **8**: 157, 159n, **9**: 48, 51n, 357–58, **10**: 50, 50n, **11**: 67, 67n

Sioux Indians, Hunkpapa, **3**: 109n

Sioux Indians, Mdewakanton (Min-da-war-car-ton), **3**: 35–36n, 410–11, 419, 448

Sioux Indians, Miniconjou (Min-na-Kine-az-zo), **3**: 109n, 416–17, 420, 448

Sioux Indians, Oglala (O-kan-dan-das), **3**: 109n, 415–16, 420, 448

Sioux Indians, Sans Arc, **3**: 109n

Sioux Indians, Santee, **3**: 35–36n, 46n, **11**: 69n

Sioux Indians, Saone (Sah-o-ne), **3**: 35n, 417–18, 420, 448

Sioux Indians, Sisseton (Sis-sa-tone), **3**: 35n, 304, 356–401, 412–13, 419, 448

Sioux Indians, Teton: encountered, **3**: 2, 104, 106–8, 126, 128–29, 138–39, 144–45, 148, 191, 222, **8**: 4, 329–30, 332, 335, **9**: 64–65, 67, 355, **10**: 43, 58, 274, **11**: 82, 96–97, 103; relations with the party, **3**: 2, 117, 121, 123–25,

161, 191, 245–46, 284, 295, 329, 356, 418, 486, **8**: 330–31, **9**: 65–71, 73, 76–77, 356, 356n, **10**: 45–49, 47n, 51–52, 73, 272n, 274n, **11**: 83–93, 108–9, 125–26; bands, **3**: 35–36n, 171n; language, **3**: 35n, **10**: 44, **11**: 93n; camps, **3**: 99, **8**: 322; trade, **3**: 101–2, 258n, 356, 413, 483–84, **8**: 158n, 288, 351, 360n; villages, **3**: 109, 132n, **11**: 87; chiefs, **3**: 111, 128, 130, 258n, 419–20, **9**: 65, 66n, 67, 126, **10**: 45–46, 47n, **11**: 85; confrontation, **3**: 111–14, 123–24, 131, 486; councils, **3**: 108–9, 111–12, 115–16, 118, 121–22, **9**: 69, **10**: 45-, **11**: 85–86; prisoners, **3**: 115, 118–19, 121–23; customs, **3**: 115–17, 119, 121, **8**: 331, 332n; appearance, **3**: 117, **9**: 69; war, **3**: 117, 119, 191, 222, 297, 299, 304, 329, 398–99, 401, 483, **9**: 69, 99, 102, 114–15, 119, **10**: 48n, 63, 73, **11**: 88–89, 108–9, 110n, 125–27; speech for, **3**: 129; historical sketch, **3**: 415–18; character, **3**: 418, 483; located, **3**: 419; listed, **3**: 448; signs, **8**: 323; **11**: 127; danger from, **8**: 324; relations with U. S., **8**: 357–58; trade, **9**: 64, 64n, 359; arms and ammunition, **9**: 71, **11**: 89–90; name, **10**: 44, **11**: 83–84; food, **10**: 46; information from, **10**: 48, **11**: 90–91; clothes, **10**: 58; artifacts, **11**: 80–81, 88–89; mentioned, **3**: 56n, 89–90, 109n, **8**: 337–38, **10**: 44n, 272, **11**: 84n

Sioux Indians, Two Kettles, **3**: 109n

Sioux Indians, Wahpeton (Wah-pa-tone), **3**: 35n, 408–9, 419, 448

Sioux Indians, Wapekute (Wâh-pa-coo-tar), **3**: 35–36n, 411–12, 419, 448

Sioux Indians, Yankton: councils, **3**: 1, 16–17, 21, 23–24, 26, 28–29, 33–34, **8**: 4, 342, 344n, **9**: 48–50; relations with the party, **3**: 16–17, 22, **8**: 329, 338, **10**: 31–33, 50, 50n, 274–75, 275n, **11**: 63–67, 63n; encountered, **3**: 19, 21n, **8**: 338, **9**: 45–46, 89, 357; language, **3**: 35n, **9**: 51n, 75; bands, **3**: 140n, 419; war, **3**: 304; trade, **3**: 356, 401, 411–13, 23n, **9**: 13, 13n, 358–59, 361; chiefs, **3**: 419–20, **9**: 48–51, 51n; listed, **3**: 448, **11**: 174; information about, **8**: 288; villages, **9**: 45–46; lodges, **9**: 46–47; customs, **9**: 47; peace, **9**: 48–50; gifts, **9**: 48–50, 357; mentioned, **3**: 23n, 398–99, 413–14, **8**: 344, 351, 360, **9**: 357, **11**: 67n

Sioux Indians, Yanktonai (Yanktons-Ah-nah), **3**: 35n, 36n, 353, 356, 384n, 407, 412–15, 420, 448, 484

Sioux Pass of the Three Rivers. *See* Three Rivers of the Sioux Pass

Sioux River, **3**: 7–8, 11, 23, 27, 32, 94, 180, 476

Siparyann Spring Creek, **4**: 191, 192n, **9**: 154, 154n

Siskin, pine, **4**: 269n

Sisseton Sioux Indians. *See* Sioux Indians, Sisseton

Sitanion hystrix, **4**: 333n. *See also* Squirrel tail

Sitka. *See* New Archangel

Siuslawan language, **6**: 237n

Siuslaw (She-a-stuck-kle) Indians, **6**: 237n, 432n, 476, 485, 491

Sixbit Creek, **5**: 223n, **9**: 227n, **10**: 145n, **11**: 325n

Sixmile Coulee, **10**: 97, 97n, **11**: 183, 183n

Sixteenmile (Howard's) Creek, **4**: 430–31, 433n, **6**: 450, 465, **8**: 186, 188n, **10**: 118, 118n

Skâddât (and similar spellings) Indians. *See* Klickitat Indians

Skalkaho (Horse Valley) Creek, **5**: 191n, **6**: 452, 466

Skamanyak (*sk!Emaniak*) village, **5**: 358, 363n

Skamokawa site, **6**: 33, 34n

Skate, big, **6**: 175, 177, 178n, 407, 410, 412, 414n

Skeets-so-mish Indians. *See* Skit-swish Indians

Skelley (or Shellie), **6**: 155–56, 427

Sketches, Historical and Descriptive, of Louisiana (Stoddard), **2**: 145n

Skewers, **6**: 215–16

Skillute (and similar spellings) Indians. *See* Cowlitz Indians; Watlala Indians; Wishram-Wasco Indians

Skin. *See* Medical problems

Skipanon River, **6**: 95, 98n, 117–18, 117n, 276n, 312, 316n, 325–26, 327n, **10**: 193n

Skiri Pawnee Indians. *See* Pawnee Indians, Loup or Skiri

Skitswish (Skeet-so-mish) Indians, **6**: 480, 488, 492, **7**: 216–17, 219n

Skull Creek, **2**: 400n, **3**: 352, 384n

Skunk, eastern spotted, **6**: 355n

Skunk, striped, **5**: 140n, **6**: 313, 315, 317n, 355, 356n, 360

Skunks, **3**: 80, 85n, 115, 117, **4**: 195, 198, 200n, **5**: 329, 335, **7**: 47n, 62, 70n, **9**: 155, 155n

Sk!in village, **7**: 145–46, 151n

Slate, **2**: 391–92, **3**: 17, 88n, 476–77, **4**: 296n, 421n, 424

Slaughterhouse Creek, **8**: 246n

Slave River, **10**: 6n

Slavery. *See* Indians, customs; *specific Indian tribes*

Sleds, **9**: 103, 105, 111–12, 114–17, **10**: 43, 65–67, 73, **11**: 111, 123, 125, 127

Sleepy Branch (Coal, Charbonea) Creek, **2**: 321–22, 322n, **9**: 17, 17n, 383, **11**: 30, 30n

Sleet. *See* Weather conditions

Sleighs, **3**: 265, 271–72, 285–86, 288, 291–93, 295–96, 299, **4**: 54, 56

Slipper, lady's, **8**: 66, 69n, 80

Slipper, mountain lady's, **8**: 66, 69n, 80

Sloe, **7**: 344, 346n

Slug, Pacific woods, **6**: 145, 146n, 147

Smackshop (and similar spellings) Indians. *See* Wishram-Wasco Indians

Small Lake, **3**: 168

Smallpox. *See* Medical problems

Smartweed, **8**: 416, 418n

Smilacina racemosa, **6**: 242n. *See also* Solomon's seal, false

Smilacina stellata, **6**: 242n. *See also* Solomon's seal, false

Smilax hispida, **8**: 418n. *See also* Greenbriar, bristly

Smith, Robert, **4**: 382, 385, 386n, **9**: 184n, **10**: 112n, **11**: 228n

Smith, Silas B., **6**: 123n, 185n

Smith Creek (Rosebud County, Mont.), **8**: 246n

Smith Creek (Oreg.), **11**: 438n

Smith (Ibex) Creek (Richland County, Mont.), **8**: 270, 272–73, 274–75n, 389, 406

Smith Point, **7**: 8, 9n

Smith River, **4**: 381n, 382, 385, 386n, 417, **6**: 449, 464, **9**: 184, 184n, 337, 337n, **10**: 112, 112n, **11**: 227, 228n

Smockshop (and similar spellings) Indians. *See* Wishram-Wasco Indians

Smoke house, **3**: 238

Snag Island, **3**: 64n

Snags, **8**: 350, 354–56, 359, 363

Snails, **6**: 96, 402, 405n, 408, **7**: 43, 46n

Snake, garter, **2**: 185, 186n, **7**: 24–25, 28, 31n

Snake, Great Basin gopher, **7**: 265, 266n

Snake, Pacific red-sided garter, **6**: 22, 24, 101n, 405n, **7**: 24–

25, 26n, **9**: 282, 282n, **10**: 203, 203n, **11**: 435n

Snake, smooth green, **8**: 374, 375n

Snake, wandering garter, **4**: 423, 425n

Snake, western hog-nosed, **4**: 421, 422n, **8**: 264, 266n

Snakebites. *See* Medical problems

Snake (E-pe,-Âh-zhah, Miry) Creek (McLean County, N. Dak.), **3**: 362–63, 373, 381, 491, **4**: 16–17, 18n, 19n, **6**: 447, 462, **8**: 297, 298n, 381, 399, **9**: 128, 128n, 349n, **10**: 267n, **11**: 134, 134n

Snake Indians. *See* Northern Paiute Indians; Paiute Indians; Shoshone Indians

Snake (Ki-moo-e-nim, Lewis's, Southeast Branch of Columbia) River: and maps, **1**: 10–11, **2**: 7, **4**: 13n, 75n, **6**: 309, 430–31, **7**: 190n, 227, 231, 233n, 315n; arrive at, **5**: 4, 255–56, 258, **7**: 205–6, **9**: 236, 236n, 304, **10**: 152, 221, **11**: 346; described, **5**: 89, 227, 260n, 292, **6**: 311, 311n, **8**: 26, 166, 297, **10**: 152, 155, **11**: 346–47, 355–56; characteristics, **5**: 255–56, 277, **7**: 186n, 202–3, 204n, 205, 207, 208n, **11**: 358–59; conditions, **5**: 256, 264–66, 268–69, 274–75, 282–83, **10**: 156; navigational problems on, **5**: 265–66, 271, 275–76, 282–83, **8**: 40, 42, **9**: 237–39, **10**: 153–55, **11**: 348–55; distances, **5**: 278–83, 373–74, **6**: 446, 453, 461, **7**: 197, **8**: 388, **10**: 173, **11**: 431; and Indians, **5**: 289, **6**: 204, 474, 479, 482, 487, 491, **7**: 35, 37n, 38, 65, 129, 169n, 173–74, 176, 206, 208, 214n, 220n, 229, 242, 247, 278, 280–81, 286–87, 326–27, 338–39, 341, 346–49, 348n, **8**: 40, 42, 88, 278, **9**:

238–39, **11**: 349–51, 349n, 350n, 355–56, 373; animals, **6**: 368, 370, 413–15, **7**: 278, 280, 290–91, 293, 319–20, 323, 325, 327, 331–32; explored, **7**: 2, 209n, **9**: 316, 317n, 319; listed, **8**: 381, 384–85, 402–3, 415; directions to, **9**: 214, 298, **11**: 292; name, **9**: 240, 240n, **10**: 152, **11**: 356–57, 356n; trading on, **9**: 315; mentioned, **5**: 76n, 95n, 228n, 230, 231n, 243, 243n, 245, 263n, 272n, 278, 284n, 287, 294, 300n, 318, 353n, 365, 376, **6**: 467–68, **7**: 54, 56, 60n, 127, 130n, 149, 177n, 182, 184, 224, 329, 330n, **8**: 27n, 43n, 277, 279n, 412, **9**: 211n, 215n, 232, 239n, 300n, 305, 305n, 315n, 317n, 318n, **10**: 132n, 135n, 152n, 153n, 154n, 157n, 158n, 160n, 200n, 217n, 218, 219n, 221, 221n, 222n, 226n, 233n, 235, 235n, **11**: 286n, 292n, 347n, 352n

Snake River Plain, **5**: 89–90, 94n, **8**: 43n, **10**: 226n

Snakeroot, seneca, **7**: 283, 285n

Snakes, **2**: 300–301, 301n, 319, 320n, 345, 347, 349n, 453, 459, **3**: 53, 54n, 180, 304, **4**: 423, **5**: 67n, **6**: 94, 96, 137–38, 145, 147, 259, 402, 408, 458, **7**: 24–25, 308–9, 311, **9**: 20, 136, 189, 381, 385, **10**: 18, **11**: 239, 435. *See also specific species*

Snakeweed, broom, **3**: 464–65, 469

Snell Creek, **8**: 249n

Sniabar (and similar spellings) River. *See* Sni River

Sni (Euebaux's, Eue-bert's, Eubert's) River, **2**: 311–13, 312n, 314n, **3**: 343, 370, 377, **8**: 378, 395, **9**: 15, 15n, 368n, 382, **10**: 16n

Snipe, common, **6**: 382–83, 383n

Snow. *See* Weather conditions

Snowberries, **8**: 117

Snowberry, common, **5**: 77, 85n, 218, 224n, **7**: 47n, 112, 114n, 188, 190, **8**: 10–11, 13n, 79, 118n, 128

Snowberry, western, **2**: 433–34, 435n, **3**: 468, **4**: 57n, **5**: 36, 39n, 77, 85n, **8**: 118n

Snowblindness. *See* Medical problems, eyes

Snow (Brown Bear Defeated) Creek, **4**: 151, 154–55, 155n, 156n, **6**: 448, 463, **8**: 381, 400, **9**: 148n, **10**: 88, 89n, **11**: 155, 157, 158n

Snowcrest Range, **5**: 87n

Snow Mountains. *See* Bitterroot Mountains

Snow-on-the-mountain, **3**: 458, 463, 468

Snowshoes, **7**: 106. *See also* Clothing

Snowy Mountains. *See* Lewis Range

Soap, **2**: 156, 201n, 203, 217, **6**: 230–31. *See also* Medicine

Soap, Castile, **7**: 212, 215n

Soapweed, **3**: 43n

Socket, **10**: 213, 214n

Socks, **6**: 103, 130, 137, **11**: 318. *See also* Clothing

Soda, **3**: 473–74

Sodium bicarbonate, **4**: 23n, 120n, **5**: 39n

Sodium carbonate, **4**: 135n

Sodium chloride, **4**: 23n

Sodium hydroxide, **7**: 215n

Sodium sulphate, **4**: 23n, 120n, **5**: 39n

Soft Rock Creek, **5**: 191n

Sokulk Indians. *See* Wanapam Indians

Soldier River, **2**: 448–49, 452–53, 452n, 454n, **3**: 354, 371, 379, **8**: 352n, 353, 353n, 374, 379, 397, **9**: 35, 35n, 359n, 367n, 392, **10**: 26, 26n

Solidago missouriensis, **9**: 199n. *See also* Goldenrod, Missouri

Sol-me, **6**: 45, 45n, 235–36, 237n, 240–42, 242n, 495.

See also Bunchberry; Solomon's seal, false

Solomon's Creek, **3**: 345

Solomon's (de Selamen, de Salamin) Island, **2**: 364–65, 365n, **9**: 23, 23n

Solomon's seal, **6**: 240–42, 242n

Solomon's seal, false, **6**: 235–36, 240–42, 242n

Somerset House (Elbow Fort), **2**: 226n

Son of the Little Calf (Fils de Petit Veau), **3**: 278, 278n

Sonora Island. *See* Sun (Fair Sun, Good Sun) Island

Sorbus scopulina, **8**: 12n. *See also* Ash, Greene mountain

Sorbus stichensis, **5**: 223n. *See also* Ash, Pacific mountain

Sorghum halepense, **7**: 337n. *See also* Grass, Johnson-

Sorrel, garden, **10**: 198n

Sosone. *See* Shoshone Indians

Sotheby's, **12**: 5

Soto, **6**: 148n, **7**: 61n

Soulard, Antoine, **1**: 5, 7

Soulier Noir (Black Shoe). *See* Hidatsa Indians, Awaxawi

Sounds. *See* Rocky Mountains, sounds from

Soup, **4**: 303, **5**: 222. *See also* Medicine

Soup, portable, **4**: 334–35, **5**: 211, 214n, 215, **9**: 174–75, 177, 223–26, **10**: 142–44, 142n, **11**: 212–13, 315–24, 316n

Soup Creek, **4**: 410n, **10**: 115n, **11**: 235n

Sourdough Creek, **8**: 392, 409

Souris (Mouse) River, **2**: 220, 225, 226n, **3**: 262, 262n, 364, 429–32, 491, 492n, **4**: 16, 42–43, **6**: 447, **8**: 289, 289n, 381

South Blackbird Creek, **3**: 379, 384n

South Boulder (Frazer's) Creek, **5**: 28–29, 30n, 48n, **6**: 450, 465, **8**: 175, 176n, **9**: 193, 194n, **11**: 250–51, 251n

South Dakota, camps in: Union County, **2**: 499n, 502n, **8**: 347n; Clay County, **2**: 503n, 507n, **3**: 15n; Yankton County, **3**: 18n, **8**: 344n, 345n; Bon Homme County, **3**: 39n, 43n; Charles Mix County, **3**: 51n, 52n, 57n, 64n, **8**: 332n, 333n; Gregory County, **3**: 57n, 60n, 64n, 66n, **8**: 332n; Brule County, **3**: 67n, 69n, 76n, **8**: 327n; Lyman County, **3**: 74n, 79n, 88n, 91n, **8**: 324n, 326n; Hughes County, **3**: 95n, 99n, 103n, 107n, 109n, 114n, 125n, **8**: 323n; Stanley County, **3**: 120n, 125n, 127n; Sully County, **3**: 127n, 130n, 140n; Dewey County, **3**: 136n, 140n, 142n, 144n, 150n, **8**: 322n; Potter County, **3**: 142n, 144n, 146n, **8**: 321n; Walworth County, **3**: 148n, 150n, **8**: 320n; Corson County, **3**: 154n, 160n; Campbell County, **3**: 166n, 171n, **8**: 307n, 311n; Carson County, **8**: 307n; Buffalo County, **8**: 326n, 329n

Southerland (Gibson's) Creek, **10**: 88, 89n

Southernwood, **4**: 35, 40n, 419n. *See also* Sagebrush, big; Sagebrush, silver

South Fork Clearwater River, **1**: 11, **7**: 289, 290n, 325n

South Gabourie Creek, **2**: 123, 124n

South Mountain Creek, **6**: 448, 463, **8**: 382, 400

South Omaha Creek, **9**: 39n

South Pass, **8**: 358n, 368n

South Platte (Ringing Water) River, **3**: 349–52, 384n

South Saskatchewan River, **3**: 236n, **8**: 119, 120n

South Table Creek, **2**: 394–96, 397n, **9**: 27n, 388n, **11**: 42n

Spain, **1**: 4–5, 8, 13, **2**: 2, 4–5, 59, 106–7, 180n, 234n, 343n, 442n, 478n, **3**: 116,

118, 483, **6**: 86n. *See also* Spanish

Spancel, **9**: 294, 295n

Spaniels, **6**: 120, 122n

Spanish, **2**: 8, 93, 94n, 101, 241, 439, **3**: 29–31, 56n, 133, 135, 137n, 151, 154n, 228n, 315n, 363–64, 428, 435–38, 484, **5**: 91–92, 94n, 95n, 124, 149, 161, **6**: 36n, 148n, 160n, 311, 314, 316, **7**: 61n, 130n, **8**: 277, 279n, 302, 303n, 346, 347n, 348n, 356n, 363, 364n, 367, 368n, **9**: 23, 49–50, 140, 205, 213, 309, 316, 352, 361–62, 364, **10**: 231, 231n, 235, 235n, 279–80, **11**: 13n, 273, 275–77, 275n, 288–89. *See also* New Mexico; Spain

Spanish language, **2**: 281n

Sparrow, fox, **6**: 164n

Sparrow, golden-crowned, **6**: 164n

Sparrow, song, **6**: 382–83, 383n

Sparrows, **4**: 254, 349n, **6**: 365, **7**: 196, 198, 339, 345, **8**: 38, 93, 117, 210

Spartina pectinata, **2**: 373n, **3**: 167n. *See also* Cordgrass, prairie

Spearfish Lake, **7**: 141n, **9**: 294n, **10**: 212n

Spear Island, **3**: 60n

Spears, **2**: 71, **3**: 28, 122, 296, **5**: 141n, 149, **6**: 17, 206, 208, 210, **8**: 38, **9**: 71, **10**: 131, **11**: 178. *See also* Arms and ammunition; Lances

Specie. *See* Coins

Spermophilus beecheyi, **7**: 129n, **9**: 293n, **10**: 212n. *See also* Squirrel, California ground

Spermophilus columbianus, **7**: 282n, **8**: 13n, **10**: 239n. *See also* Squirrel, Columbian ground

Spermophilus richardsonii, **4**: 18n, **7**: 296n. *See also* Squirrel, Richardson's ground

Spermophilus tridecemlineatus, **4**: 368n, **6**: 347n, **10**: 110n. *See*

also Squirrel, thirteen-lined ground

Sphyrapicus ruber, **6**: 381n, **7**: 11n. *See also* Sapsucker, red-breasted

Sphyrapicus varius, **3**: 307n, **4**: 95n. *See also* Sapsucker, yellow-bellied

Spice bush (spicewood), **2**: 185, 186n, 208

Spiders, **6**: 94, 96, **7**: 43, 46n, 76

Spilogale putorius, **6**: 355n. *See also* Skunk, eastern spotted

Spirit (d'Esprit) Lake, **2**: 458, 463n

Spirit Mound, **2**: 504–5, 507n, **3**: 1, 7, 9–11, 12n, **9**: 43, 44n, **10**: 31, 31n, **11**: 61, 61n

Spirits. *See* Liquor

Split Rock Creek. *See* Perchee Creek

Split Rock Island, **2**: 281–82

Spokane (Hi-high-e-nim-mo, Lar-ti-e-to) Indians, **6**: 480, 488, 492

Spokane Hills, **10**: 115, 115n, 116n, **11**: 235, 236n

Spokane (Pott's Valley, Pryor's Valley) Creek, **4**: 406n, 410n, 412–13, 415n, **6**: 450, 464, 495, **9**: 187, 187n, **10**: 115, 115n, **11**: 235, 235n

Spokane River, **7**: 219n

Spoon Creek, **5**: 191n

Spoons, **5**: 150, 252, **6**: 134, 215–17, **7**: 96, 99, 146, **9**: 295, **10**: 268, **11**: 129n, 352–53

Spring beauty, western, **8**: 50–51, 52n

Spring Coulee, **10**: 97, **11**: 183, 183n

Spring Creek (Cass County, Nebr.), **2**: 400n, **9**: 28n, **11**: 42n

Spring Creek (Charles Mix County, S. Dak.), **3**: 60n, **10**: 37n, **11**: 71, 72n

Spring Creek (Lewis and Clark County, Mont.), **8**: 95, 96n, 102

Spring (Little Dry) Creek (Mc-

Cone County, Mont.), **4**: 117, 119–20, 120n, **6**: 447, 462, **8**: 381, 400

Spring (Stone Idol) Creek (Campbell County, S. Dak.), **3**: 168–69, 171n, 361, 373, 381, **8**: 311n, 380, 399, **9**: 84, 84n, 352n, 367n, **10**: 54, 55n, 269n, **11**: 99, 100n

Spring (White Bluff) Creek (Nebr.), **3**: 351–52, 384n

Spring Hill, **5**: 210n, **8**: 58n, **9**: 225n, 327, 327n, **10**: 245, 245n

Spruce, **4**: 186, 189, 191, 201, 346, **5**: 238, **9**: 186, **10**: 117, 135, 166–67, 176, **11**: 171, 175, 232, 235, 377–78, 381–82, 385–86, 402

Spruce, Engelmann, **4**: 396, 397n, **5**: 191, 195n, 201, 202n, 204–5, 205n, 209, 210n, 215, 238, **6**: 19n, **8**: 7, 11, 12n, **9**: 153–54, 154n, 224–25, 224n, **10**: 114, 114n, 117, 136, 137n, 142, 144, 147, 181, **11**: 316–20, 318n, 322, 396

Spruce, Sitka (spruce pine), **5**: 355–56, 358n, **6**: 3, 7, 9, 15, 19n, 26, 42–44, 45n, 77n, 124n, 176, 276–78, 278n, 291–93, 293n, 325–26, 327n, 398, 400, 401n, **7**: 76, 78n, **9**: 259, 259n, **10**: 189, 189n, **11**: 403n

Spruce, Sitka, vegetation zone, **6**: 45n, 104n, 284n, 307n

Spuck. *See* Otter, sea

Squân-nar-oo (and similar spellings) Indians. *See* Klickitat Indians

Square Butte (Barn Mountain), **4**: 253–54, 257n, 268

Square Butte (Fort Mountain), **4**: 383, 385, 386n, **8**: 95, 96n, 107, 291, 383, 401, **9**: 184, 185n, **11**: 228, 228n

Square Butte (Hunting) Creek, **3**: 191, 192n, 293, 295n, 373, 381, **10**: 72n, **11**: 124n

Squash, crookneck, **3**: 154n

Squash, hubbard, **3**: 148n

Squash, summer, **8**: 298, 300n

Squashberry, **5**: 354n

Squashes, **3**: 146–47, 148n, 151, 159–60, 162–63, 252–53, 261, 403, 483, **5**: 144, 147n, **8**: 315, **9**: 76–79, 82, 82n, 92–93, 106, 350, 350n, **10**: 51, 53, 267–68, **11**: 98, 115, 132

Squaw (Blowing Fly) Creek (Mont.), **4**: 170, 172–73, 175n, **6**: 448, 463, **9**: 151, 151n, **10**: 90, 90n, **11**: 162, 163n

Squaw Creek (Idaho), **5**: 154–56, 157n

Squawfish, northern, **7**: 131, 135n

Squawmash. *See* Camas

Squirrel, barking. *See* Prairie dog

Squirrel, California ground, **7**: 129n, **9**: 293, 293n, **10**: 212, 212n

Squirrel, Columbian ground, **7**: 3, 282, 282n, 291–92, 294–96, 296n, **8**: 10–11, 13n, 76, 93, 94n, 102, 125, 125n, 162, 162n, 166, 168n, 332n, **10**: 238, 239n

Squirrel, Douglas's, **6**: 313, 315, 317n, 345, 347n, 348

Squirrel, fox, **3**: 55, 57n, **6**: 345, 347n, **8**: 333, 333n, 417, 418n, **9**: 56, 56n, **11**: 71, 71n

Squirrel, gray, **2**: 79, 79n, 80, 80n, 82–83, 183, **3**: 53, 54n, **8**: 10–11, 13n, 80, 416, 418n, **9**: 55, 55n

Squirrel, large gray. *See* Squirrel, western gray

Squirrel, red, **6**: 345, 347n, 348

Squirrel, Richardson's ground, **4**: 18n, 259n, **7**: 291–92, 294–96, 296n

Squirrel, Richardson's red, **5**: 214n, **6**: 101–2, 104n, 313, 315, 317n, 345, 347n, 348, **7**: 257, 259, 260n, **8**: 66, 69n, 87, 89, 90n

Squirrel, thirteen-lined ground,

4: 2, 367, 368n, **6**: 346, 347n, 348, **10**: 110, 110n

Squirrel, western gray, **5**: 341, 343, 344n, 354, 357n, **6**: 313, 315, 317n, 345, 347, 347n, **7**: 126, 129n, 145, 147–48, **9**: 245, 246n, 293, 293n, **10**: 159, 159n, **11**: 372–73, 374n

Squirrels, **3**: 66, 330, 482, **5**: 153, 344–45, **6**: 206, 329, 334, 347n, 351, 354, **8**: 75, **9**: 310, 355, **10**: 135, 175, 162–63, 187, **11**: 363–64, 395

Squirrel tail, **4**: 333n

Starvation Creek, **5**: 357n

Starved to Death (White) Creek, **8**: 236, 239, 241n, 390, 407

Station Camp (Wash.), **6**: 112, 458, 470. *See also* Chinook Point

"A Statistical View of the Indian Nations" (Jefferson), **3**: 387

Staubach Creek, **4**: 416, 418n

Steam. *See* Medicine

Steel, **7**: 220, 222, 225n. *See also* Flints

Steiger Creek. *See* Reservation Creek

Stelgidopteryx serripennis, **3**: 13n. *See also* Swallow, northern rough-winged

Stellula calliope, **7**: 47n. *See also* Hummingbird, calliope

Stember Creek, **7**: 208n

Steppe region, **7**: 204n

Sterna antillarum, **2**: 452n. *See also* Tern, least

Sterna forsteri, **6**: 387n, **8**: 151n. *See also* Tern, Forster's

Steubenville, Ohio, **2**: 73, 73n

Stickney Creek (Gun Brook), **4**: 399, 402n, **6**: 450, 464, **10**: 114, 114n

Stil-la-sha, **6**: 73, 76–77n

Stillwater (Rosebud) River, **8**: 203n, 204–6, 207–8n, 391, 408

Stinking Bird River, **2**: 219

Stipa comata, **4**: 433n, **5**: 21n. *See also* Grass, needle and thread

Stirrups, **5**: 97, 103, 149, 161, **7**: 165, 167

Stizostedion canadense, **2**: 433n, **4**: 279n. *See also* Sauger

Stizostedion vitreum, **2**: 433n. *See also* Walleye

Stock-home. *See* Tah-cum

Stoddard, Amos, **2**: 141n, 145, 145n, 168n, 190n, 193, 212, 240, 243, 243n, 295n, 417n, 510, 516, 520–22, 524, **3**: 464, **8**: 368n, **9**: 6, 6n, 361, **11**: 10n, 22–23, 23n

Stonecat, **2**: 484n, **10**: 29n

Stonecrop, wormleaf, **8**: 81n

Stone Indians. *See* Assiniboine Indians

Stone River. *See* Little Sioux River

Stone Walls of the Missouri River. *See* Missouri River, White Cliffs of the

Stony Point, **9**: 57n, **10**: 37n, **11**: 72n

Stores. *See* Provisions

Stork, wood, **6**: 13, 14n

Storms. *See* Weather conditions

Stove (Teel) Creek, **3**: 142, 144n, **9**: 76, 76n, **10**: 50, 50n, **11**: 95, 95n

Stoves, **3**: 288, 289n

Strains. *See* Medical problems

Strait of Juan de Fuca, **6**: 416n

Stratford Hill, **8**: 205, 208n

Straw, **5**: 250, 327, 331, **6**: 55, **7**: 38, 40, 57, 79, 144–47, 149, 153, 164, 210, 216, 218, 233, 235, 263, 335, 337

Strawberries, **7**: 55, 77, 193, 335, 337, **8**: 71–72, 73n, **9**: 326, **10**: 141, **11**: 198

Strawberry, wild, **2**: 216, 217n, **4**: 237–38n, **7**: 61n, 338n, **8**: 73n, **10**: 102, 102n, 238, 238n, **11**: 38, 38n, 199n

Strawberry, woodland, **4**: 237–38n, **5**: 359–60, 362, 364n, **6**: 9n, 54, **7**: 61n, 338n, **8**: 73n, **10**: 102n, 238n, **11**: 199n

Strawberry Island, **5**: 283n. *See also* Hamilton Island

Strehlow Island, **9**: 56n, **11**: 71n

Strix nebulosa, **7**: 282n. *See also* Owl, great gray

Strophostyles helvola, **8**: 360n. *See also* Bean, wild

Struck by the Ree (Parnarne Arparbe, Pan-dan-apappy), **3**: 29, 34, 37n, **9**: 49–50, 51n

Stuart, Robert, **7**: 17n, **8**: 358n, 368n

Sturgeon, green, **6**: 68, 70, 70n, **9**: 275n, **10**: 195n, **11**: 396, 396n, 425n

Sturgeon, shovelnose, **2**: 71, 72n

Sturgeon, white, **6**: 342, 346, 346n, **7**: 12–13, 14n, 15–16, 18, 27, 32, 34–36, 38, 49, 52, 130, 135n, **9**: 275n, **10**: 195n, **11**: 425n

Sturgeon River, **10**: 67n

Sturgeons, **6**: 72, 74, 121, 180, 184, 206, 209, 344, 346, 351, 353, 358, 360, 364, 368, 370, 378–80, 402–3, **9**: 250, 275–76, 281–82, 369n, **10**: 195, 197, 201–2, **11**: 385–86, 423, 423n, 425, 427, 434–35

Sturnella magna, **4**: 326n, **6**: 381n. *See also* Meadowlark, eastern

Sturnella neglecta, **3**: 12n, **4**: 29n, **6**: 381n, **7**: 195n. *See also* Meadowlark, western

Sucker, mountain, **5**: 13n, **6**: 407, 409n, 414–15, **7**: 245, 246n, **8**: 189–90, 193n

Sucker, northern (bottlenose, mullet), **5**: 37, 39, 39n, 119, 124n, **6**: 407, 409n, 414–15, **9**: 208, 209n

Suckers (mullets), **2**: 486n, **4**: 333n, **7**: 174, 176, 177n, 182, 184, **9**: 174n, 298, 298n, 300, **11**: 211–12, 212n

Suet, **4**: 334. *See also* Dumplings, suet

Sugar, **2**: 144, 175, 203, 217, **3**: 161, 163, **4**: 140, 143, **5**: 144, **6**: 113, **8**: 363

Sugar (Labeenie, Bennet's, Benoit) Creek, **2**: 321–22, 322n, **9**: 17, 17n, 383, **10**: 17, 17n, **11**: 30, 30n

Sugar Loaf, **2**: 114–15, 114n

Sugarloaf Butte, **3**: 184–85, 186n

Sugar Loaf Rock (Mine Hill), **2**: 277n, **10**: 12n, **11**: 18n

Sugar of lead. *See* Medicine, lead acetate

Sugar (Shugar) Rapid, **2**: 219

Sula Peak, **5**: 190n

Sulfate, **8**: 120n

Sulfide, ferrous, **2**: 502n

Sulphur, **4**: 19, 21n, 34, 39, 40n, 45, 47n, 300, **10**: 78, 78n, **11**: 199–200, 313. *See* Medicine

Sulphur dioxide, **4**: 21n

Sulphuric acid. *See* Medicine

Sulphur (Sacagawea) Springs, **4**: 300, 302n, 306, **9**: 169, 169n, **10**: 103, 103n, **11**: 199–200, 201n

Sumac, **4**: 388, 392, 417

Sumac, aromatic, **3**: 465, 470, **8**: 238, 240n

Sumac, dwarf, **6**: 240–41, 242n

Sumac, skunkbush, **4**: 391n, **5**: 85n

Sumac, smooth (shoemate), **3**: 43n, **4**: 391n, **7**: 188, 190, 191n, **8**: 10–11, 12n, 417, 418n

Summit Creek, **5**: 357n

Sunburn. *See* Medical problems

Sun Dance, **3**: 190n, **4**: 379n, **10**: 111, 111n

Sunday Creek (Dry River), **8**: 251, 254, 256n, 390, 407

Sunday Island, **4**: 37, 40, 41n

Sun dog, **3**: 255n

Sun (Fair Sun, Good Sun) Island, **2**: 383–85, 386n, 479, **9**: 26, 26n, 80, **11**: 174

Sunfish, **2**: 350

Sunfish, American, **2**: 432, 433n

Sunfish Creek, **2**: 78–79, 78–79n

Sunflower, annual, **7**: 122n

Sunflower, common, **4**: 383, 385, 386n, 391, 399, **9**: 38, 39n, **10**: 131n

Sunflower, Cusick's, **7**: 122n

Sunflower, Nuttall, **5**: 58, 60n, 143, 147n, 172, 174n, **8**: 52n, 119, 120n, **9**: 212, 212n, **10**: 131n, **11**: 260, 261n, 286–87, 288n

Sunflower, plains, **8**: 120n

Sunflower, stiff, **8**: 120n

Sunflowers, **7**: 122–23n, 154, 227, **8**: 72, 120n, 143, 190, 193n, 264, **9**: 90, 198, 201, **10**: 130, 134, **11**: 266–67. *See also* Balsamroot

Sunken Village, **6**: 20–21n

Sun (Mah-pah-pah,-ah-zhah, Medicine) River: and maps, **1**: 9, 11; described, **3**: 367–68, **4**: 293, 319, **8**: 98, 103, 109, 382, **9**: 171, **11**: 204, 206; distances, **3**: 374, **6**: 449, **8**: 104, 382–83; listed, **3**: 382, **6**: 464, **8**: 401, 412; arrive at, **4**: 291, 293, 307, **9**: 338, 339n; conditions, **4**: 333; route to, **5**: 163, 164n; and Indians, **7**: 342, 343n, **9**: 175, 228; hunting on, **8**: 97, 99, **9**: 170, 170n, 172–73, **10**: 104–6, 104n, 251, 251n, **11**: 203–4, 203n, 209–11; animals, **8**: 99, 112; camped on, **10**: 251–52, 251n, 252n; mentioned, **4**: 270, 296n, 304, 309, 312–13, 316, 320, 324, 324n, 326–27, 329, 366–68, 388, **5**: 196, **8**: 85, 87n, 98n, 99n, 100n, 103, 104n, 107, 111, 291, **10**: 105n, 106n

Sunstroke. *See* Medical problems

Supplies. *See* Provisions

Susquehanna River, **4**: 324, **6**: 395, 397

Sutherland (Gibson's) Creek, **4**: 151, 153–155, 155n, **6**: 448, 463, **8**: 381, 400, **9**: 147, 148n, **10**: 88, 89n, **11**: 155–56, 157n

Suzie Creek, **7**: 241n

Swallow, bank, **2**: 386n, **3**: 13n, **7**: 45, 47n, **8**: 210, 210n, **9**: 34, 35n, 190, 191n, 194, **11**: 242–43, 244n, 251–52

Swallow, barn, **3**: 131, 132n, **8**: 266, 267n

Swallow, cliff, **4**: 226, 231, 233n, 436, **11**: 181–82, 182n

Swallow, northern rough-winged, **3**: 13n

Swallows, **4**: 281

Swan, large. *See* Swan, trumpeter

Swan, small. *See* Swan, tundra

Swan, trumpeter, **2**: 142n, **4**: 21n, 411, 415n, **6**: 11, 13, 14n, 161–62, 383, 385, 395–96, 397n, **7**: 11n, 23, 25, 28, **9**: 138, 138n, **11**: 140n, 235, 235n

Swan, tundra (whistling), **2**: 142n, **4**: 21n, **5**: 350, 352, 354n, **6**: 11, 13, 14n, 161–62, 383, 385, 395–96, 397n, **7**: 11n, 28, 30, **9**: 247, 247n, 249, 250, 251, 264, **10**: 164, 164n, **11**: 140n, 377, 378n

Swan, William, **2**: 85, 85n

Swan (Goodrich's, Otter) Creek, **3**: 146–47, 147–48n, 360, 373, 380, **9**: 77, 77n, **10**: 51, 52n, **11**: 96, 96n, 97n

Swan Range, **10**: 249, 249n

Swan River House, **2**: 225, 226n

Swans: observed, **2**: 142, 355–56, **3**: 147, 184–85, 233, 237, 249, 319, 326, **4**: 23, 58, 103, 105, **6**: 9, 11, **7**: 46, **8**: 92, 101, **11**: 381–87, 399, 436; abundance, **2**: 173, 177, 429, 432, **4**: 30, 49, 79, **6**: 11, 13, 35, 88, 92, **9**: 187, **10**: 166, 168, **11**: 140, 384–86; scarcity, **2**: 208, **6**: 73, **7**: 9; food, **2**: 222; hunted, **2**: 298, **6**: 11–12, 22–23, 91–92, **9**: 187, **11**: 383, 387, 390, 410; and Indians, **3**: 116, 118, **11**: 395; mentioned, **6**: 21, 74, 171, 207, 209, 261, 391, 393, **9**: 51n

Sweat baths. *See* Medical problems; Medicine

Sweathouse Creek, **8**: 161, 162n

Sweating. *See* Medical problems; Medicine

Sweeney Creek (Ravalli County, Mont.), **8**: 162n

Sweeney Creek (Wood Brook) (Rosebud County, Mont.), **8**: 242–43, 245, 246n, 390, 407

Sweetgrass, **4**: 54, 57n, **5**: 122, 135, 140, 141n, 259, 260n, **8**: 218, 222n

Sweet Grass Creek (Otter River), **8**: 194–96, 197n, 391, 408

Sweetgrass Hills, **4**: 258, 259n 260n, **8**: 115, 116n, 117, 118n, 119, 131, 136, 235n, **10**: 100, 100n

Sweetwater River, **8**: 235n

Swelling. *See* Medical problems

Swepeton (and similar spellings), **6**: 155–56, 416, 416n, 427, 436, 439, **7**: 106, 109, 110n

Swift Bird (White Brant, White Goat) Creek, **3**: 144–45, 146n, **9**: 76, 76n, **10**: 51, 51n, **11**: 95, 96n

Swivels. *See* Cannons; Cannons, swivel

Swords, **2**: 205, **3**: 112–13, **5**: 346, 351, **6**: 15, **7**: 28, 31n, 36, 38n, 147–48, 165, 177, 179, **9**: 299, 369n, **11**: 89–90, 375. *See also* Arms and ammunition

Sycamore, **2**: 313, 314n, 392, 428, 430, **8**: 355n, 359, 416–17, 418n, **9**: 8, 9n, 361, **10**: 10, 11n

Sylvilagus floridanus, **2**: 156n, **4**: 75n, **6**: 317n, **9**: 17n. *See also* Cottontail, eastern

Sylvilagus nuttallii, **4**: 75n, **6**: 317n, **8**: 168n, **9**: 332n. *See also* Cottontail, Nuttall

Symphoricarpos albus, **5**: 85n, **7**: 47n, **8**: 13n, **12**: 6, 10n. *See also* Snowberry, common

Symphoricarpos occidentalis, **2**: 435n, **3**: 468, **4**: 57n, **5**: 39n, **8**: 118n. *See also* Snowberry, western

Symphoricarpos orbiculatus, **2**: 435n, **3**: 468. *See also* Coralberry

A Synonymized Checklist of the Vascular Flora of the United States, Canada, and Greenland (Kartesz), **12**: 7

Syphilis. *See* Medical problems, venereal disease

Syringa, Lewis's, **5**: 71–72, 73n, **8**: 10–11, 12–13n, 79

Syringa vulgaris, **2**: 210n. *See also* Lilac

T

Ta-ba-bone, **5**: 2, 69, 72n, 77–78. *See also* Shoshone Indians

Tabanidae, **7**: 312n. *See also* Flies

Tabanus sp., **5**: 58n, **7**: 312n, **8**: 144n, **11**: 259n. *See also* Fly, horse; Greenhead

Tabeau, Pierre-Antoine, **1**: 8, **2**: 221, 221n, 253n, 309n, **3**: 114n, 154n, 155, 155–56n, 156–57, 157n, 161, 163, 181n, 252, 304–5, 305n, 309–10, 461–62, **4**: 7, 11, **8**: 369n, **9**: 79, 82n, 119, 126, **10**: 52, 52n, 74n, **11**: 97–98, 98n

Table Mountain, **8**: 96n, **10**: 251n

Tables Requisite to be Used with the Nautical Ephermeris for Finding the Latitude and Longitude at Sea (Maskelyn), **2**: 87n

Tabo Creek, **2**: 308–9, 309n, **9**: 15, 15n, 382, **10**: 15, **11**: 26, 26n

Taboe, **8**: 369, 369n

Tacoutche-Tesse River. *See* Fraser River

Tafia, **3**: 247, 247n, 261, **9**: 100–102, 100n, 106. *See also* Rum

Tah-cum, **6**: 154, 159n, 330, 332, 333n, **10**: 194, 194n

Tail of Calumet Bird (Man-nes-surree, Man-se-rus-se), **3**: 212, 213n, 241, **9**: 98n

Talc, **4**: 135n, 233n, **5**: 86n

Tallamon. *See* Callamon

Tallow, **3**: 297, 466, **6**: 107, 201–2, **8**: 153, **9**: 181, 380, **10**: 110, **11**: 220–22. *See also* Grease

Tamarack, **8**: 12n. *See* Larch, western

Tambourines, **3**: 116, 119, **9**: 48n, 107

Tamiasciurus douglasii, **6**: 317n. *See also* Squirrel, Douglas's

Tamiasciurus hudsonicus, **6**: 347n. *See also* Squirrel, red

Tamiasciurus hudsonicus richardsoni, **5**: 214n, **6**: 104n, **7**: 260n, **8**: 69n. *See also* Squirrel, Richardson's red

Tamias striatus, **6**: 347n. *See also* Chipmunk, eastern

Tanacetum, **5**: 21n. *See also* Tansy

Tanacetum vulgare, **4**: 262n, **7**: 338n. *See also* Tansy, common

Tanager, western, **7**: 3, 339–40, 342n, 345–46

Tanner Creek, **9**: 248, 248n, **11**: 380–81, 382n

Tanner's ooze, **6**: 102, 104n, 175, 197, 346

Tanning, **6**: 230–31, 232n

Tansey Creek, **6**: 276n

Tansy, **5**: 21n, **7**: 335, 337, **9**: 163, 192. *See also* Yarrow, western

Tansy, common, **4**: 252n, 262n, **7**: 338n

Tansy River. *See* Teton River

Tapanash Indians. *See* Tenino Indians

Tappage Pawnee Indians. *See* Pawnee Indians, Tappage or Pitahawirata

Taptate (and similar spellings) River. *See* Yakima River

Tar, **4**: 349–51, 354, 356, 359, 359n, 362, 371, **9**: 181, 181n, **11**: 217, 221–22, 221n

Taricha granulosa, **6**: 405n. *See also* Newt, rough-skinned

Tarkio River, **2**: 368n, 374–75, 376n, **8**: 378, 396, **9**: 24, 24n, 387, **11**: 39, 39n. *See also* Big Tarkio Creek

Tarpaulin, **9**: 95

Tarromonee, **3**: 29–30, 37n

Tartar, cream of. *See* Medicine, potassium bitartrate

Tartar emetic. *See* Medicine, emetic

Tartary, **10**: 93n

Tavern Creek, **2**: 246, 248, 249n, 264n, **9**: 7, 7n, 375, **10**: 9

Tavern Island, **2**: 245, 246n, 248

Tavern Rock, **2**: 246, 248, 249n, **3**: 370, 376, **9**: 7, 368n, 375, **11**: 12

Tawnish-e-o, **3**: 212, 214n

Taxidea taxus, **2**: 173n, **3**: 12n, **5**: 189n, **6**: 21n, **8**: 203n, **9**: 32n, **10**: 24n, **11**: 48n. *See also* Badger

Tayon, Charles, **2**: 232, 234n, 241, 243

Tea. *See* Medicine

Tea Island, **4**: 195, 199

Teakettles, **7**: 108. *See also* Kettles

Teal, blue-winged, **3**: 69, 69n, 221, 223n, **4**: 46, 47n, **5**: 271, 272n, 274–75, **6**: 383, 384n, 385, 398–99, 400–401

Teals, **6**: 383, 384n, 398–400

Techumtas Island, **5**: 304, 307n

Teeth. *See* Medical problems, teeth

Telegraph Creek Formation, **4**: 386n, **8**: 118n, 122n

Telescopes (spy glass), **2**: 410–11, **3**: 273, **5**: 68, 70, **7**: 242, 244, **8**: 113, 128, 329, **9**: 121, **11**: 248–49

Tenasillahe Island, **6**: 32, 34n, 58, **7**: 11n, **10**: 201n, **11**: 433n

Tendoy Mountains, **5**: 52n, **8**: 167, 168n

Tenino (E-nee-shur, Wah-how-pum) Indians: appearance, **5**: 315, 318, 319n, **7**: 162; relations with the party, **5**: 315, 318, 323, 328, 342–43, **7**: 142, 144–46, 148–49, 159, 161, 163, **9**: 296–97, 296n, 297n, **11**: 364–66; customs, **5**: 318, 319n, 323, 331, **6**: 201–2, 313, 315, 455, 483,

7: 160–62, 10: 160–61, 11: 364–66, 367n; villages, 5: 326n, 340n, 7: 127, 131, 139, 142, 145, 149, 152, 154–55, 157, 159, 161, 10: 214n, 215n; lodges, 5: 329; language, 5: 333, 342, 344–45, 7: 145n, 160–61, 162n, 216, 218; gifts, 5: 341–43; chiefs, 5: 341–42, 7: 139; hunting, 5: 342; name, 5: 344–45; listed, 6: 455, 468–69, 474, 483, 490, 8: 385, 403; trade, 7: 134, 163; clothes, 7: 145, 148, 160, 162; lodges, 7: 145, 149; mentioned, 5: 344, 369, 7: 130n, 151n, 10: 213n

Tennessee, 2: 139, 139n

Tennessee River, 2: 147

Tents, 2: 83, 213, 332, 4: 215, 275, 365, 6: 91, 7: 104, 171, 247, 256, 262–63, 275–76, 285, 8: 346, 367. See also Medicine; Tipis

Tepahcus, 3: 217n

Tern, Forster's, 6: 387n, 8: 151n

Tern, least, 2: 450–51, 452n

Terrapin Island, 2: 282–83, 283n

Terrapin. See specific species of turtles

Tetoharsky, 5: 249, 250n, 252, 278, 294, 296, 298, 304–5, 328–29, 335, 336n, 338, 7: 206–7, 209n, 9: 234, 234n, 304, 305n, 10: 151, 151n, 221–22, 222n, 11: 339–41, 341n, 349–50, 358–59, 371

Teton River. See Bad River

Teton (Rose, Tansy) River, 4: 247, 249–52, 252n, 257n, 259, 260n, 261, 277, 8: 113–16, 115n, 128, 132n, 136, 137n, 139n, 292, 9: 161, 162n, 163, 164n, 165, 10: 98–99, 98n, 99n, 258, 258n

Teton Sioux Indians. See Sioux Indians, Teton

Thalaspi arvense, 3: 466. See also Pennycress, field

Thaleichthys pacificus, 6: 346n,

7: 14n, 9: 275n, 10: 194n, 11: 423n. See also Eulachon

Thamnophis elegans, 7: 31n. See also Snake, garter

Thamnophis elegans vagrans, 4: 425n. See also Snake, wandering garter

Thamnophis ordinoides, 7: 31n. See also Snake, garter

Thamnophis sirtalis, 2: 186n, 7: 31n. See also Snake, garter

Thamnophis sirtalis concinnus, 6: 101n, 7: 26n, 9: 282n, 10: 203n, 11: 435n. See also Snake, Pacific red-sided garter

Theade Creek (Dry Brook), 8: 247–48, 250n

The Dalles of the Columbia River. See Columbia River, The Dalles of the

The Needles, 6: 185n

Thermometers, 2: 6, 69–70, 69n, 145, 146–47n, 169, 186n, 244n, 316n, 3: 13n, 132n, 4: 348, 416, 5: 186, 241, 243n, 6: 259, 9: 104, 153–54, 188, 203, 11: 236–37, 237n, 270–71. See also Weather observations

Thermopsis, mountain, 5: 60n, 106–7, 108n, 8: 28, 30, 30n

Thermopsis montana, 5: 60n, 8: 30n. See also Thermopsis, mountain

Thermopsis rhombifolia, 4: 53n. See also Pea, golden

Thibault, 8: 369n

Thighs. See Medical problems

Thimbleberry, 7: 96n

Thimbles, 5: 294, 296, 6: 113, 7: 137

Thirteenmile (Buffalo) Creek, 8: 267, 269, 270n, 389, 406

Thistle, edible (shaw-natahque), 6: 74, 76, 77n, 78n, 123, 123n, 139, 146–47, 183, 224, 226–27, 227n, 233, 495, 7: 55, 60–61n, 77, 9: 291, 292n

Thistle, elk, 4: 420, 422n, 5: 21n, 9: 188, 189n, 11: 237–38, 238n

Thistle, wavyleaf, 5: 21n

Thistles, 5: 18, 58, 9: 38, 39n, 192, 198, 11: 248, 260

Thomas (Riffle) Island, 11: 25, 25n

Thomomys talpoides, 4: 18n, 7: 225n. See also Gopher, northern pocket

Thompson, David, 1: 5, 3: 92, 201n, 205n, 273n, 275n, 297n, 4: 28n, 7: 61n, 8: 364n, 10: 63n, 157n, 272–73n

Thompson, John B.: listed, 2: 148, 187, 189, 195, 197, 199, 255, 4: 9, 11, 8: 74, 77, 86n, 139n, 11: 4n, 7n, 419n; hunting, 2: 158, 6: 296–97, 409–11, 414–15, 10: 192–93, 198, 11: 419–20; returns, 2: 173, 9: 272; in permanent party, 2: 229n; court-martial member, 2: 329; duties, 2: 357, 359–60, 475n, 8: 107, 291, 10: 254; biographical sketch, 2: 522; creek named for, 4: 211–14, 214n, 9: 157n, 11: 176n; accidents, 5: 251, 11: 341, 343; votes, 6: 83; sent out, 6: 365, 367, 7: 271–72, 9: 271, 274, 285, 330, 10: 205, 247; scouting, 7: 54, 57, 60n, 11: 438–39; and Indians, 7: 105, 109; and species, 8: 99, 10: 252n; death, 8: 364n; trading, 9: 312, 10: 230; medical problems, 11: 343n; mentioned, 8: 43–44, 9: 271n, 272n, 274n, 279, 285n, 313n, 330n, 338, 338n, 395n, 10: 193n, 198n, 206n, 230n, 248n, 254n, 11: 421n, 440n

Thompson Creek, 10: 186–87, 186n

Thompson Falls, 10: 246, 246n

Thompson River, 2: 299n

Thomson, James, 4: 285, 288n

Thongs. See Ropes

Thorn, fleshy. See Greasewood

Thorn, large leaf. See Salmonberry

Thorn, pulpy leaf. *See* Grease-
wood
Thorn, white. *See* Hawthorn,
black
Thornton, Edward, **1**: 5, **3**: 225n
Thrasher (thrush), brown, **4**:
236, 237n, 265, **8**: 107, 107n
Thread, **6**: 173n, 192, 214, 216,
7: 275–76
Three Eagles, **5**: 188n
Three Forks of the Missouri
River. *See* Missouri River,
Three Forks of the
Threemile Creek, **2**: 336, 340n
Threemile Rapids, **7**: 141n, **9**:
294n
Three Rivers of the Sioux Pass,
3: 91n, 358, 372, 380, **9**:
367n, **10**: 41, 41n
Three Sisters, **10**: 43, 43n
3000 Mile Island, **5**: 71–72,
73n, **8**: 175, 176n, **10**: 124,
124n, **11**: 264–65, 265n
Throats. *See* Medical problems,
colds and sore throats
Throngs. *See* Rope
Thrush, hermit, **2**: 277n
Thrush, varied, **5**: 217, 223n,
6: 254–56, 257n, 261, 262n,
363, 365n, 379–80, 381n
Thuja plicata, **5**: 210n, **6**: 28n,
7: 37n, **8**: 26n, **9**: 224n, **10**:
145n, **11**: 316n. *See also* Redcedar, western
Thunder. *See* Weather
conditions
Thwaites, Reuben Gold, **1**: 3–6,
10–11, **2**: 9–10, 19, 28, 39–
42, 52, 536, 538–39, 542,
544, **3**: 387, 472, **4**: 175n,
9: xvii, **11**: xvi, 20n
Tibeau, **8**: 369n
Tick, American dog, **2**: 305n
Tick, lone star, **2**: 305n
Ticks, **2**: 272, 304, 306, 318, **10**:
185, 185n
Tides. *See* Weather conditions,
wind, waves, and tides
Tilia americana, **2**: 314n, **8**:
345n, **9**: 31n. *See also* Linden
Till, glacial, **4**: 24n, 29n, 53n,
107n, 120n, 123n, 129n,

257n, 282n, **8**: 114n, 118n,
119–20n
Tillamook Head (Clark's Point
of View), **6**: 67, 68n, 76n,
120, 122n, 176, 178, 178n,
182–83, 184n, 188, 193–94,
460, 471, 493, **9**: 266, 266n,
10: 186, 186n, **11**: 411–12,
412n
Tillamook (Kilamox) Bay, **6**:
98n, 184, 184n, 185n, 461,
471
Tillamook (Kilamox) Indians:
food, **6**: 2, 180, 193, 230–31;
customs, **6**: 99n, 168–69,
180, 182, 185n, 190–91,
194, 365–67, 435, 439; located, **6**: 112, 144n, 154,
184n, 201–2, 284, 460–
61, 471, **10**: 187, **11**: 412n;
chiefs, **6**: 154, 159n, 495;
language, **6**: 154, 180, 184,
186n, 194, 202n, 236, 237n,
430–32, 432n, 476, 485;
trade, **6**: 162–63, 180, 183,
188–89, 195, 199, 224, **7**:
83; relations with the party,
6: 166–67, 177, 190, 194, **7**:
187–88; lodges, **6**: 166–67,
180, 184; appearance, **6**:
168, 180, 184, 190, 432–34,
437–38; clothes, **6**: 180, 184,
194, 432–36, 438–40; ca-
noes, **6**: 180, 265, 271–72,
436; villages, **6**: 180–84,
185n, 461, **11**: 412; historical
sketch, **6**: 184n; bands, **6**:
202n, 236; artifacts, **6**: 208,
210; arms and ammunition,
6: 208–10; head deformation, **6**: 433, 437; visits, **6**:
444; numbers, **6**: 475, 485;
prisoners, **6**: 476; mentioned, **6**: 115n, 143, 164n,
176, 192n, 262n, 286, 427,
490, **7**: 89n, **10**: 188n, 199,
200n
Tillamook (Kilamox) River, **6**:
461, 471, **7**: 26, 31n, 34, 83,
89n
Timber (Bratton's, Rattlesnake)
Creek, **4**: 159–62, 163n, **6**:

448, 463, **8**: 381, 400, **10**: 89,
89n
Timm Mountain. *See* Mount
Hood
Timothy, **2**: 305n, 374–75,
377–78, 487, **3**: 457, 465,
5: 58, 60n, **7**: 208n, **10**: 133,
133n, 138n. *See also* Canarygrass, reed
Timothy, alpine, **10**: 138, 138n
Tin, **2**: 153, **3**: 237, **7**: 102–3,
158, 160–61, **9**: 333, **11**:
341–42
Tin Cup Creek, **5**: 190n, 194, **8**:
163, 164n, **11**: 304–5, 305n
Tintinger Slough, **4**: 391n, **10**:
113n, **11**: 229n
Tipis, **3**: 22, 101, 103n, 109n,
428, **4**: 10, 12n, 38–39, 139,
160–62, 378, 388, 394, **5**: 8,
80, 139, 272, **6**: 127, **7**: 238,
240, 241n, 262, 264n, **8**:
305, 307n, 310, **9**: 47, 69,
70n, 73, 218, 229, 308,
308n, **10**: 270, **11**: 299–301,
329, 331. *See also* Indians,
lodges; Tents
Tippets, **5**: 104, 122, 127–28,
131n, **7**: 253, 255, **9**: 206,
206n, **11**: 277n. *See also*
Clothing
Tipulidae, **2**: 186n, **6**: 139n, **10**:
185n. *See also* Fly, crane
Titian, **4**: 285
Tlashgenemaki Village, **6**: 34n
Toad, American, **7**: 309, 311,
312n
Toad, Fowler's, **7**: 309, 311,
312n
Toad, horned. *See* Lizard, pigmy
horned
Toad, western, **7**: 3, 309, 311,
312n
Toads, **7**: 302, 305
Tobacco: gifts, **2**: 212, 300, 416,
435, 455–56, 477, 492, **3**:
21–22, 26, 31, 34, 104, 106,
123–24, 126, 128–30, 132,
142–45, 155, 160, 162, 164,
203–4, 222, 227, 235, 242,
251–52, 290, 310, **4**: 11, **5**:
112, 188, 188n, 227, 231,

244–45, 277, **6**: 137, **7**: 208, **8**: 314–15, 317, **9**: 46–47, 50, 65, 67, 73–74, 100, 113, 262, 358, **10**: 32, 47–48, 184, **11**: 64–65, 407; purchased, **2**: 237, **8**: 348, **10**: 275; wet, **2**: 261; smoked or chewed, **3**: 24, 116, 120n, 130, 460, 464, **4**: 324, **5**: 80, **8**: 172, **9**: 69, 78; cultivated, **3**: 151–52, 161, 163, 331n, 401, 403, 460–61, **9**: 79; and Indians, **3**: 160, 166n, 460–61, 464, 470–71, 471–72n, **4**: 54, 57n, **5**: 80–81, 86n, 97, **6**: 123, 179, 192, 196, **8**: 312, **10**: 53, **11**: 90–92; seeds, **3**: 330, 331n, 460–61, 464, 471–72n; as trade item, **3**: 401, 484, **6**: 134, 146–47, 187, 192, 205, 426, 428, **7**: 15–16, **8**: 132, **9**: 71–72, 100, 104, 111, 121, 271, 277, **11**: 90–92, 429n; scarcity, **7**: 15–16, **10**: 196; cached, **8**: 172–73; mentioned, **2**: 494n, **6**: 113, 244, **7**: 17n, **9**: 82n, 134n, 271n, 369n, 373–74n, **10**: 53n, 76, 255

Tobacco (Hall's Strand) Creek, **4**: 50, **6**: 447, 462, **8**: 283n, 287n, 381, 400, **9**: 348n, **10**: 80, 81n, 265n, **11**: 136, 136n

Tobacco Garden (Pumice Stone) Creek, **8**: 287n

Tobacco Root Mountains, **4**: 428, 429n, **5**: 20, 20n, 29n, **9**: 192, 193n, 194n, **10**: 119–20, 119n, 121n, **11**: 241–42, 242n, 250–51, 251n

Toby. *See* Old Toby

To-che-wah-Coo Indians, **3**: 136, 137n

Todd, **2**: 156

Todd, Andrew, **1**: 5

Toehead Island, **9**: 57n, **11**: 72n

Tomahawk (Image Canoe) Island, **6**: 20n, **7**: 33–35, 36n, 54, 56, 58–60, 81, 83, **10**: 166, 167n, **11**: 384–85, 387n, 440n

Tomahawks: cached, **2**: 83; dis-

tributed, **2**: 192; lost, **2**: 194, 428n, **3**: 188, 222, **4**: 341, 343, **5**: 32, 249, 271–72, **7**: 102–3, 322, 324, 326, 328, **8**: 165, 289, **9**: 31, 122, 177, 235, 238, 319, 331, **11**: 47, 250; as trade item, **3**: 3, 262n, 280n, **7**: 106, 109, 158, 164, 253, 346–47, **9**: 369n, **10**: 71; stolen, **3**: 296, **7**: 33, 35, 96, 99, 146, 151–52, 154, 322, 325–26, 328, **9**: 122, 288, 295, **10**: 213, **11**: 385–86; use, **5**: 71–72, **7**: 163, **8**: 39, 41; found, **5**: 138–39, **8**: 165, 290; as weapon, **7**: 210, 212; as gift, **9**: 303; mentioned, **2**: 497, **5**: 112, **6**: 15, 17–18, 117, 293, 295, 457, **9**: 34n, 49, 205, 306, **10**: 50n, 209n, **11**: 128n, 276. *See also* Arms and ammunition

To-mar-lar, **6**: 148n

Tomlinson, Joseph, Jr., **2**: 78n

Tongs, **4**: 275

Tongue (Le-ze-ka) River, **3**: 234n, 365, 374, 382, **8**: 247–49, 250n, 277–79, 390, 407

Tongue Point (Point William), **4**: 71, 73, **6**: 37n, 41n, 76n, 90–91, 91n, 101, 104, 151n, 441, 443, 459, 471, 472n, **7**: 7–8, 8n, **8**: 387, 405, **9**: 257, 257n, 280, 280n, **10**: 178, 178n, 201, 201n, **11**: 399, 399n, 400n, 432, 432n

Tongue River Member, **8**: 255n, 261n, 262n, 275n

Tongues. *See* Wagons

Tonquin, **6**: 94n

Tonsillitis. *See* Medical problems

Tonti, Henri de, **2**: 150n

Tonwontonga village, **2**: 476–80, 478n, 482n, 483, 499n, **9**: 39n, **10**: 28, 28n, **11**: 55, 55n. *See also* Omaha Indians

Too-et-te-con'l. *See* Cameahwait

Too-ite-coon, **5**: 86n

Tools, **2**: 218, **3**: 303, **4**: 269, 271, 274–75, 279, 279n 323, 334–35, **5**: 113, 115, **6**: 158,

203–4, **7**: 93n, **9**: 118, 182, **11**: 212–13, 222–24, 420. *See also* Equipment; Instruments, scientific; *specific tools;* Utensils, cooking

Toone, **10**: 59, 59n. *See also* Eagles Feather

Toothaches. *See* Medical problems, teeth

Toowar Sar Indians, **3**: 136, 138n

Touchet River, **7**: 187–89, 190n, 198n, 199, 201, 201n, 203, 204n, **9**: 301, 301n, 302n, 303, 303n, **10**: 218, 218n, 219n, 220, 220n

Towanahiook (and similar spellings) Indians. *See* Paiute Indians

Towanahiook (and similar spellings) River. *See* Deschutes River

Tower. *See* Eagle Rock; Old Baldy

Tower Creek, **5**: 141n, 144, 147n, 169, 179, 179n, 183, **6**: 451, 466, 493, **9**: 215, 215n, 231, **10**: 130n, 134, 135n, 173, 174n, **11**: 293–94, 294n

Tower Mountain, **4**: 258, 268

Tow-er-quottons Creek, **6**: 461, 471

Tower Rock, **2**: 112–15, 114n

Towhead Gulch (Potts' Creek), **4**: 402n, 407–8, 410n, 412–13, **6**: 450, 464

Towline. *See* Rope, tow

Tow-wall, **6**: 73, 77n, 112

Toxostoma rufum, **4**: 237n, **8**: 107n. *See also* Thrasher, brown

Trachoma. *See* Medical problems; Medical problems, eyes

Traders: French, **1**: 3, **3**: 114n, 270n, 305n, **10**: 9; information from, **1**: 5, 8–9, **2**: 8, **3**: 3, 34n, 37n, 268n, 269, 311, 385n, 386, **6**: 73n, 329, 333n, **8**: 235n, **11**: xiv; and maps, **1**: 8, **3**: 3; from St. Louis, **2**: 2, **3**: 270n, 483; Ca-

Traders (*continued*)
nadian, **2**: 3, **3**: 3, 214n, 363, 433, **5**: 95n; and Indians, **2**: 7, 93–94, 470n, 482n, **3**: 2, 27, 30–32, 34, 114n, 139, 153–54n, 163, 208n, 214n, 247, 311n, 393–94, 396–97, 402–7, 409–14, 418, 425–27, 432–33, 441–42, 444, 483–84, 487, **6**: 2, 19, 40–41, 48n, 50, 148n, 168, 179, 202–4, 206, 208, **7**: 106, 109, 129, 289, **8**: 132n, 294, **9**: 305, **11**: 276–77, 299–300, 330, 355–57, 362, 369–70, 392, 433; suppliers, **2**: 70n; encountered, **2**: 102, 259–60, 266, 277, 279, 286–87, 294, 300, **3**: 181–82, **4**: 20, **8**: 4, 362, 362n, **10**: 49; American, **3**: 54n, **7**: 215n; boats, **3**: 106n; food, **3**: 120n; robbed, **3**: 181–82, 192–93, 209–10; visits, **3**: 236; British, **3**: 311n; information about, **4**: 272, **6**: 47, 50, 62, 66, 84–85, 186–87, 190, 201, **11**: 395, 433; Spanish, **5**: 94n, 95n; signs, **5**: 312–13n; and messages, **6**: 4, 430–31; explorations, **6**: 36n, 37n; listed, **6**: 155–56, 159–60n, 427, **7**: 110n, **8**: 288; mentioned, **3**: 183n, 267, 291n, 305n, **5**: 131n, 307n, **6**: 36, 314, 316, 428n, 441–42, **7**: 3, 130n. *See also* Hudson's Bay Company; *individual traders;* Missouri Fur Company; North West Company
Trading establishments, **3**: 25n, 137n, 171n, 196–97, 221, 223n, 235, 353, 363, 368, 403, 422, 441–43, 483, 487, **4**: 30, 33–35, 39, 77, 80n, **5**: 8, **6**: 94n, 187, 191n, 205, 307n, **7**: 242, 244, 248, 301, **8**: 74, 77, 213–14, 278, 353, 362n, 388–89, 412. *See also* Hudson's Bay Company; North West Company
Trail (Glade) Creek, **5**: 2, 74, 76n, 170n, **6**: 451, 465, **8**:

166–67, 168n, 169n, 393–94, 410, **9**: 211, 211n, 331, 332n, **10**: 127, 128n, 172, 174n, **11**: 284, 284n, 286n
Traps, **3**: 217–19, 227, **4**: 275, 279, **5**: 119, 126, **6**: 161–62, 196, 296n, 430–31, **7**: 196, 198, 227, 230, 284, **8**: 138, 295, 302, **9**: 32, 59, 108, 110, 128–29, 131–34, 136, 163, 166, 206–7, 265, 300–301, 342, 348, 352, **10**: 220, **11**: 71, 75–76, 102, 104, 143, 186–87, 194, 278–79, 397, 411
Trask River, **6**: 185n
Travelers' Rest Creek. *See* Lolo (Travelers' Rest) Creek
Travelers' Rest (Idaho): and maps, **1**: 10–11, **7**: 74n; arrive at, **1**: 10, **2**: 29, **5**: 192–94, 196n, **8**: 1, 66, **9**: 221, 329, **10**: 140, 246, **11**: 307; and journal-keeping methods, **2**: 23; depart, **2**: 23, **8**: 3, 263, 290; and Indians, **5**: 196, **7**: 331–32, **8**: 34–35, 53, 56–57, 88, **9**: 221, 338n, **10**: 247, **11**: 308; latitude, **5**: 196, **9**: 222, **10**: 140, **11**: 310; location, **5**: 196n, **9**: 221n, 329n, **10**: 140n, 246n, **11**: 308n; distances, **6**: 472–73n, **8**: 66, 82; route to, **7**: 249, 323, 325, 334n, **8**: 24, 46–47, 56–57, 69n, 88; and species, **8**: 66, 68, 79, 80n; mentioned, **6**: 432n, **8**: 24n, 69n, 104n, 162n, 296n, 372n, **10**: 255n
Travois, **3**: 489, 492n, **9**: 64, 64n, **10**: 42, 43n, 48, **11**: 81, 82n, 176–78
Tree Frog Creek, **2**: 336, 338, 340n
Tree River, **2**: 219
Trenchers, **5**: 311, **6**: 118–19, **7**: 59, 82
Triceratops, **8**: 229n
Trifolium longipes, **5**: 60n, **8**: 80n, **9**: 330n. *See also* Clover, longstalk

Trifolium macrocephalum, **10**: 216n. *See also* Clover, large-head
Trifolium microcephalum, **8**: 80n. *See also* Clover, small-head
Trifolium pratense, **10**: 216n. *See also* Clover, red
Trifolium sp., **5**: 108n. *See also* Clover
Tringa melanoleuca, **4**: 136n. *See also* Yellowlegs, greater
Trionyx spiniferus hartwegi, **4**: 207n, **8**: 250n, **9**: 156n. *See also* Turtle, Western spiny softshell
Tripod, **2**: 94n. *See also* Instruments, scientific
Triteleia grandiflora, **7**: 135n. *See also* Hyacinth, wild
Triticum sp., **6**: 368n. *See also* Wheat
Troglodytes troglodytes, **4**: 269n, **6**: 94n. *See also* Wren, winter
Trousers, **6**: 187, 205. *See also* Clothing
Trout, **5**: 13n, 37, 39, 84, 98, 106, 118, 126, 144, 159, 331, **6**: 211, 214, **7**: 227, 231, **9**: 174, 201, 203, 210, 253, **10**: 125, **11**: 266–67, 269–70
Trout, brook, **2**: 484n, **4**: 286, 288–89n, **5**: 119, 125n, **9**: 207, 207n
Trout, cutthroat, **4**: 2, 286–87, 288n, 296, 299, 309, 332, 414, **5**: 13n, 119, 125n, **6**: 407, 409n, 413, 415, **8**: 125, 126n, **9**: 168, 169n, 207–8, 207n, 209n, **10**: 125, 125n, **11**: 199–200, 201n, 211–12, 277–78, 278n, 286–87, 392
Trout, salmon. *See* Trout, steelhead
Trout, steelhead, **5**: 4, 144, 147n, 331, 341, 343, 344n, **6**: 3, 27, 30, 42–43, 45, 407, 409n, 413–15, 414n, **7**: 237, 241n, 245, 278–80, 280n, **8**: 35, 37–39, 37n, 41, **9**: 208, 209n, 245, 246n, 252, 289, 290n, 298, 300, 324–25, 325n, **10**: 241, 242n, 243, **11**: 372–73, 374n

Trout, white salmon. *See* Salmon, coho

Trout Creek, **4**: 410n, **7**: 151n, **9**: 187, 187n, **10**: 115, 115n, 116n, **11**: 235n

Troutdale Formation, **6**: 94n

Trucks. *See* Wagons

Trudeau, Zenon, **2**: 138n, **3**: 56n

Truffles, **4**: 126

Trumbull, John, **3**: 214n

Trumpets. *See* Horns, tin

Trunks, **5**: 207, **8**: 107–8, 164

Truteau, Jean Baptiste, **1**: 5, **3**: 54–56, 56n, 198n, 270n, **9**: 56n, **10**: 37n, **11**: 71n

Tsuga heterophylla, **6**: 45n, **7**: 37n, **10**: 206n. *See also* Hemlock, western

Tsuga mertensiana, **5**: 210n. *See also* Hemlock, mountain

Tucannon River (Ki-moo-e-nim Creek), **5**: 266, 268, 268n, 281, **6**: 453, 467, 493, **7**: 202–3, 204n, **8**: 384, 403, **9**: 238, 238n, 240n, 304, 304n, 315n, **10**: 154, 154n, 173, 174n, 221, 221n

Tuckerman, Edward, **12**: 5, 7–8

Tuffs, **5**: 102n, 148n, 157n

Tuffs, ashfall, **4**: 397n

Tukudika (Broken Moccasin?) Indians, **5**: 89–90, 94n, **9**: 214, 214n, **11**: 290–91, 291n

Tule, **5**: 21n, **10**: 160n

Tulip tree, **2**: 78, 78n, 102

Tullock (Muddy) Creek, **8**: 231–32, 234n

Tullock Member, **8**: 246n, 250n, 255n, 256n, 261n, 262n

Tumbling Bluff. *See* Hell Creek Formation

Tumors. *See* Medical problems, abscesses and boils

Tunica Indians, **3**: 447, 450

Tunnachemootoolt (and similar spellings). *See* Broken Arm

Tuque (La Freeau) Creek, **2**: 251–52, 252n

Turdus migratorius, **4**: 96n, **5**: 29n, **6**: 257n, **7**: 47n, **8**: 78n. *See also* Robin, American

Turf bogs. *See* Peat bogs

Turkey, white, **3**: 85, 86n, 133, 135, 137n

Turkey, wild, **2**: 131, 132n, 139–42, 158, 166, 300–301, 301n, 313, 333, 336, 339, 419, 429–30, 447–48, 464, **3**: 48–49, 55, 77, 86n, 96, 137n, 141, **4**: 411, **5**: 129, 131, 163, 287, **8**: 318, 325–26, 325n, 345, 355, 359, 365, 417, 418n, **9**: 15–16, 15n, 30, 35, 37, 54–56, 358, 360, 364, 383, **10**: 27, 27n, 278, 280, **11**: 27–28, 28n, 44–45, 69–71

Turkey-beard, **8**: 55n

Turkey Creek, **2**: 277n

Turkey Island, **2**: 123, 124n

Turner, George, **1**: 5, **2**: 233, 234n

Turnip, prairie. *See* Breadroot

Turnips, **2**: 140

Turtle, painted, **4**: 331, 333n

Turtle, western spiny softshell, **4**: 201, 205, 207n, **8**: 248, 250n, **9**: 155, 156n

Turtle Mountain, **2**: 220. *See also* Killdeer Mountains

Turtle River, **2**: 219

Turtles, **3**: 180, **6**: 63

Tushepaw (and similar spellings) Indians. *See* Flathead Indians

Tuttle, Ebenezer, **2**: 229n, 256, 415, 417n, 511, 522, **4**: 12n

Tututni (Han-na-kal-lal, Luck-kar-So) Indians, **6**: 477, 477n, 486, 491

Tweedy Mountain, **8**: 169n

Tweezers, **9**: 369n

Twin Creek, **5**: 187n

Twisted Hair (Walamotinin): and maps, **1**: 11; meets Clark, **5**: 226–27; information from, **5**: 228n, 230, 296, 298, 327, **7**: 229, 239–40, **11**: 371; name, **5**: 228n; relations with the party, **5**: 229–30, 232–33, 328–29, **7**: 2, 228, 233, 243–44, 248–51, 323, 325, 337, 342, **9**: 234, 307, **10**: 151, 223, **11**: 329–30, 338–40, 358–59; gifts, **5**: 231; camp, **5**: 233n; guide, **5**: 249, 250n, 252, 294, **10**: 222n, **11**: 349–50; duties, **5**: 278, 304–5, 338; interpreter, **5**: 296, 336n; peace, **5**: 335; village, **7**: 206, 235–36, 338, **9**: 315n; brother, **7**: 216–18, 220, 222, 227, 234–35; and Cut Nose, **7**: 228–32; and Broken Arm, **7**: 229–30, 232; sons, **8**: 48n, **11**: 338; mentioned, **9**: 234n, **10**: 151n, 224n, **11**: 339n, 341n

Two Calf Creek, **4**: 195, 199n, **9**: 154, 155n, **10**: 92, 92n, **11**: 167–68, 169n, **11**: 331n

Two Kettles Sioux Indians. *See* Sioux Indians, Two Kettles

Two Medicine Formation, **8**: 98n, 122n

Two Medicine River (Main or South Branch Marias River), **8**: 2, 121, 121n, 122n, 124n, 125n, 126–28, 127n, 130–31, 132n, 133n, 135, 137n, 292–93, 295

Two Muddy River. *See* Auxvasse (Big Miry) River; Muddy (Little Miry) Creek

Two Tailed Calumet Bird (Eapanopa), **3**: 212, 213n

Tympanuchus cupido, **2**: 90n, **6**: 368n. *See also* Prairie-chicken, greater

Tympanuchus cupido cupido, **2**: 90n. *See also* Hen, heath

Tympanuchus cupido pinnatus, **2**: 90n, **8**: 149n. *See also* Prairie-chicken, greater

Tympanuchus phasianellus, **3**: 50n, **4**: 44n, **5**: 76n, **6**: 368n, **8**: 78n, **9**: 123n. *See also* Grouse, sharp-tailed

Tympanuchus phasianellus columbianus, **6**: 368n. *See also* Grouse, Columbian sharp-tailed

Typha latifolia, **4**: 422n, **5**: 21n, **6**: 29n, **7**: 159n, **9**: 229n, **10**: 160n, **11**: 331n. *See also* Cattail, common

Tyrannosaurus, **8**: 229n

Tyrannus tyrannus, **4**: 238n, **6**: 131n, **8**: 78n. *See also* Kingbird; Kingbird, eastern
Tyrannus verticalis, **4**: 277n, **8**: 27n. *See also* Kingbird, western
Tywappity Bottom, **2**: 101–2, 104n, 109n

U

Ulcers. *See* Medical problems, abscesses and boils
Ulmus americana, **3**: 184n, **4**: 19n, **8**: 151n, **9**: 27n, **10**: 32n. *See also* Elm, American
Ulmus rubra, **2**: 349n, **8**: 345n. *See also* Elm, slippery
Ulmus thomasi, **8**: 359n. *See also* Elm, rock
Umatilla (Youmalolam) Indians: villages, **5**: 284n, 301, 303, 305–6, 319n, **7**: 164n, 168n, 172n, **9**: 297, 297n, **11**: 356n; gifts, **5**: 301, 303, 305–6; relations with the party, **5**: 301, 303–6, 309; appearance, **5**: 303, 306; language, **5**: 303, 306, 307n, 317, 319n; numbers, **5**: 303, 306, 309; clothes, **5**: 303, 306, 309–11; fishing, **5**: 303, 309; lodges, **5**: 304–5, 309, 311–12, 313n, 317, 375; located, **5**: 307n; food, **5**: 309; information from, **5**: 309; customs, **10**: 158, 158n; mentioned, **11**: 360–62, 361n
Umatilla (Youmalolam) River, **1**: 10, **7**: 172–73n, 173, 177n, 182, 184, **6**: 480, 487, **5**: 307n, 312n, **8**: 415, **10**: 216n
Umbelliferae, **7**: 266n. *See also* Parsley
Umbrellas, **4**: 341, 343, **9**: 177, **10**: 108
Umpqua Indians, **6**: 237n, 432n
Umpqua River Basin, **7**: 70n

Union Creek, **8**: 90, 92n, 101
Unionidae, **2**: 484n, **4**: 333n, **6**: 409n, **9**: 174n, **11**: 175n. *See also* Mussels
University of Pennsylvania, **12**: 2
Unknown Creek, **8**: 235, 238, 241n
Uppah. *See* Cous
Upper Chinookan language, **6**: 2on, 21n, 25n, 34n, 41n, 76n, **7**: 31n, 36n, 6on, 61n, 62n, 7on, 10on, 111n, 122n, 125n, **9**: 245, 25on, **10**: 167n, 185n, 203n, 204n, 211n. *See also* Chinookan language; Lower Chinookan language
Upper Chinookan (Multnomah) Indians, **7**: 31n, 36n, 41n, 6on, 61n, 62n, 10on, 122n, **8**: 386–87, 405
Upper Deer (Thigh Snagged) Creek, **8**: 194, 196, 198n, 391, 409
Upper Holter Lake, **11**: 233n
Upper Memaloose Island, **7**: 121n
Upper Oven Island, **2**: 393n. *See also* Oven Islands
Upper portage camp (Mont.), **4**: 3, 308, 309n, 326, 326n, 330, 334, 335n, 350, **8**: 2, **9**: 171–72, 172n, 173–74, 177–82, 338, 338n, **10**: 104n, 105n, 111n, 112, 253, **11**: 207–10, 208n, 213n, 218n, 223–25, 223n, 225n. *See also* White Bear Islands
Upper Sevenmile Creek, **8**: 267, 269, 27on
Urn-tree, **2**: 309n
Ursus americanus, **2**: 142n, **3**: 492n, **4**: 45n, **6**: 293n, **7**: 53n, 315n, **8**: 21n, **9**: 11n, **10**: 15n, **11**: 20n. *See also* Bear, black
Ursus cinnamomeus, **7**: 315n. *See also* Bear, cinnamon
Ursus horribilis, **3**: 39n, **4**: 34n, **6**: 317n, **7**: 259–6on, **8**: 26n, **9**: 51n, **10**: 33n, **11**: 103n. *See also* Bear, grizzly

Urtica dioica, **2**: 277n, **4**: 381n, **6**: 29n, **7**: 47n, **10**: 202n. *See also* Nettle, stinging; Nettle, tall
Ute (Alitan of the West) Indians, **3**: 328n, 395, 436–37, 449
Utensils, cooking, **2**: 6, 189, 256, 360, **4**: 157, **5**: 150, **6**: 333, 335. *See also* Indians; *specific Indian tribes; specific utensils*
Utz site, **2**: 299n, 304n

V

Vaccinium membranaceum, **5**: 224n, **6**: 286n, **8**: 3on. *See also* Huckleberry, mountain
Vaccinium ovatum, **6**: 239n, **7**: 47n. *See also* Huckleberry, evergreen
Vaccinium oxycoccos, **6**: 77n. *See also* Cranberry, wild
Vaccinium scoparium, **8**: 61n. *See also* Grouseberry
Vaccinium sp., **7**: 115n. *See also* Huckleberries
Valeriana, edible, **5**: 143, 147n
Valeriana edulis, **5**: 147n. *See also* Valeriana, edible
Vallé, Jean, **1**: 8, **3**: 133, 135, 136–37n, 138–39, **8**: 321n, **9**: 74–75, 75n, **10**: 49, 49n, 5on, **11**: 93, 93n
Vancouver, George, **1**: 4–5, 16n, 21, **2**: 2, **5**: 301n, **6**: 1, 14n, 2on, 29n, 46–47, 47n, 50, 51n, 87n, 115n, 16on, **7**: 61n, **9**: 249n, **10**: 166, 166n, **11**: 384n
Vancouver Island, **1**: 4, **6**: 191n, 272n, 307n
Vancouver Lake, **6**: 21n
Vanilla, common, **6**: 175, 178n, 197, **8**: 218
Vanilla fragrans, **6**: 178n. *See also* Vanilla, common
Van Meter Ditch (Indian Creek), **9**: 14, 14n

Varnish, **6**: 206, 210n

Vaughan, John, **3**: 450–51, 462, 472, **12**: 3, 6, 9n

Vaughn, Joseph (Joshua or Josiah?), **2**: 144n

Velella sp., **6**: 425n. *See also* Jellyfish

Venereal disease. *See* Medical problems

Veneridae, **6**: 409n. *See also* Clams

Venison. *See* Deer, as food

Vérendrye, Sieur de la (Pierre Gaultier de Varennes), **2**: 226n, **3**: 201n

Vermillion, **5**: 78–79, **7**: 249, 275. *See also* Paint

Vermillion (Black Paint) River (Kans.), **3**: 344, 383–84n

Vermillion (White Stone) River (S. Dak.), **2**: 61, 503n, 504–5, 507, 507n, 508n, **3**: 1, 7–11, 12n, 355, 372, 379, 431, 447, **8**: 346, 347n, 379, 397, 416, **9**: 44, 44n, 358–59, 358n, 367n, **10**: 30, 30n, **11**: 61, 61n

Vespula maculifrons, **7**: 312n. *See also* Yellow jacket

Vespula pensylvanica, **7**: 312n, **9**: 227n, **11**: 325n. *See also* Yellow jacket, western

Vests, **3**: 310, **6**: 137, 346. *See also* Clothing

Vetch, sweet, **7**: 338n

Vial, Pedro, **8**: 364n

Viburnum, **8**: 359n. *See also* Arrowwood

Viburnum edule, **5**: 354n. *See also* Squashberry

Viburnum lentago, **3**: 223n. *See also* Nannyberry

Viburnum opulus, **3**: 492n, **5**: 354n. *See also* Cranberry, high bush

Viburnum prunifolium, **2**: 309n, **3**: 223n, **8**: 359n. *See also* Haw, black

Viburnum rufidulum, **2**: 309n, **3**: 223n. *See also* Haw, southern black

Viburnum trilobum, **5**: 354n,

6: 45n, **10**: 161n, **11**: 370n. *See also* Cranberrybush, American

Viento Creek, **5**: 357n

Ville Monteau Island, **2**: 278–79, 281n

Vimy Ridge, **4**: 256, 257n, 279n

Vine, pea. *See* Peanut, hog

Vine Creek, **5**: 187n

Vinegar, **2**: 156

Vingt-un Island, **2**: 233, 234n

Viola sp., **7**: 195n

Violet. *See* Dog's-tooth-violet

Violin. *See* Fiddle

Vitis aestivalis, **2**: 379n, 452n. *See also* Grape, summer

Vitis cinerea, **2**: 379n. *See also* Grape, grayback

Vitis labrusca, **2**: 452n. *See also* Grape, concord

Vitis riparia, **2**: 373n, 452n, **8**: 240n, 418n, **9**: 9n, **10**: 11n, **11**: 68n. *See also* Grape, riverbank

Vitis sp., **2**: 293n, 379n, **8**: 266n, 359n, 418n. *See also* Grapes

Vitis vulpina, **2**: 452n. *See also* Grape, winter

Vitriol, white. *See* Medicine, zinc sulphate

Vivaldi, Canon de, **2**: 543, **11**: xvi

Volcanics, Goble, **6**: 28n

Volcano, **3**: 70–71, 73n. *See also* Ionia Volcano

Von Steuben, Friedrich Wilhelm, **2**: 73n

Voorhis, Eleanor Glasgow, **1**: 3, **2**: 40, 538

Voorhis, Julia Clark, **1**: 3, **2**: 40, 538

Voorhis Collection, Missouri Historical Society, **1**: 4, 11, 19n. 135, **2**: 34, 40–41, 220n, 538, **3**: 160n, 167n, 213n, 217n, 220n, 225n, 479, 492n, **8**: 215n, 415n

Voorhis journals: and maps, **1**: 10, **5**: 300n, 326n, 336n; Voorhis No. 2, **2**: 28–29, 32, 35, 538–39, 555, 560, **4**: 139n, **6**: 248n, 253n, 290n,

7: 38n, 46n, 48n, 61n, 70n; Voorhis No. 3, **2**: 28–29, 32, 538–39, 560, **6**: 248n, 253n, **7**: 74n, 145n, 151n, 155n, 173n, 187n, 194n, 233n, 245n, 322n, 342n, 343n; discussed, **2**: 40, 538; Voorhis No. 4, **2**: 171n, 538–39, 562, **4**: 12–13n, **5**: 366n, **6**: 446, 473, 488n, **8**: 376–77, 410–11n, 418n; Voorhis No. 1, **2**: 359n, 538, 555, **4**: 11, 12–13n, 129n, 139n, 234n, 269n, 302n, 305n, 309n, 317n, 321n, 350n, 359, 359n; First Draft, **8**: 180n, 279n. *See also* Codex journals; Elkskin-bound Journal; Field Notes; First Draft

Voyages from Montreal through the Continent of North America, to the Frozen and Pacific Oceans (Mackenzie), **2**: 3

Vulpes fulva, **3**: 66n. *See also* Fox, red

Vulpes velox, **4**: 40n, **6**: 317n, **8**: 132n, **9**: 181n, **10**: 110n, **11**: 221n. *See also* Fox, swift

Vulpes vulpes, **4**: 234n, **5**: 141n, **6**: 192n, 330n. *See also* Fox, red

Vulter River, **3**: 355

Vulture. *See* Condor, California

Vulture, turkey, **4**: 347, 349n, **7**: 97–98, 100n, 113, **8**: 23, 23n, 359, 419, **9**: 322, 322n

W

Wabash River, **2**: 112, 147

Wabaunsee Group, **2**: 373n, 393n, 399n

Wabonsie (Pigeon) Creek, **2**: 398, 400n, **9**: 389, 389n

Wackkicum Indians. *See* Wahkiakum Indians

Wagonhammer Creek, **5**: 144, 146, 147n

Wagons, **2**: 137–39, 142, 156, **4**: 3, 300–303, 305–6, 323, 325–26, 326n, 328, 330, 332–33, 338–40, 344–45, 371, **8**: 394, **9**: 169–70, 173–78, 339–40, **10**: 103–4, 254, 256–57, **11**: 201–3, 208–13, 216

Wah-clel-lah Indians, **7**: 96–97, 99–100, 100n, 104–8, 111, 113. *See also* Watlala Indians

Wahclellar Village. *See* Watlala Indians

Wah-how-pum Indians. *See* Tenino Indians

Wahkiakum (Wackkicum, Warci-a-cum) Indians: language, **6**: 31–32, 41n, 50, 89; food, **6**: 32; clothes, **6**: 32, 34n, 75, 89, 142, 144, 251, 432–36, 438–40; appearance, **6**: 32, 89, 432–34, 437–38, **7**: 10; lodges, **6**: 32–33, 34n, 221n; head deformation, **6**: 32, 433, 437; villages, **6**: 33, 33n, 34n, 37n, 42n, 58, 155, **7**: 10, 11n, 13, **8**: 387, 405, **9**: 251, 251n, **10**: 168, 168n, **11**: 389–90, 390n; name, **6**: 33n; camps, **6**: 34n; historical sketch, **6**: 34n; canoes, **6**: 34n, 142, 147, 263, 270, 436; located, **6**: 34n, 155, 458–59, 470; relations with the party, **6**: 46–47, 146–47; trade, **6**: 50, 142, 144–45, 147. **7**: 13, 15–16, **9**: 263, **11**: 408; visits, **6**: 142, 144–47, **7**: 13, 15–16; chiefs, **6**: 155, 159n; tattooing, **6**: 435, 439; numbers, **6**: 475, 485; and other Indians, **7**: 18, 20; mentioned, **6**: 281, 401–3, 474, 490, **9**: 263n, **11**: 408n, 409n

Wahlala village, **5**: 355, 357n

Wah-na-a-chee River. *See* Wenatchee River

Waho-erha village, **3**: 156n, 160, 162, 166n, **10**: 54, 54n

Wahpeton Sioux Indians. *See* Sioux Indians, Wahpeton

Waistcoats, **8**: 45–46. *See also* Clothing

Wakarusa (Wor-rah-ruza) River, **3**: 344, 383n

Wakashan language, **6**: 416n

Wakenda (Snag) Island, **2**: 304–5, 305n

Wakenda (Snake) Creek, **2**: 300–301, 301n, **3**: 343, 370, 377, **8**: 378, 395, **9**: 13, 13n, 368n, 380, **10**: 14, 14n

Walker Island, **6**: 27, 28n, **7**: 17n, **9**: 281n, **10**: 202n, **11**: 434n

Wallace Island, **6**: 29n, 30n. *See also* Puget Island

Wallacut (Chinook) River, **6**: 62, 66, 67n, 68–70, 71n, 113, 475, 485, **9**: 254, 255n, **10**: 173, 175, 175n

Wal-lal__-le, **7**: 15–16, 17n

Walla Walla (and similar spellings) Indians. *See* Walula Indians

Walla Walla (Waller Waller) River, **1**: 10, **5**: 294, 298, 300n, 301n, 307n, 374, **6**: 454, 468, 480, 487, **7**: 2, 169n, 177n, 181–84, 186n, 187, 187n, 189, 190n, **8**: 385, 403, 415, **9**: 241n, 298n, 300–301, 300n, 301n, **10**: 158n, 217n, 218, 218n, 220, **11**: 360n

Waller's Ripple, **2**: 69, 69n

Wallets, **8**: 419

Walleye, **2**: 433n

Wallowa Mountains, **8**: 27n

Walnut, black, **2**: 80n, 315n, **8**: 349, 350n, 354, 355n, 416, 418n, **9**: 10, 10n, 20, 20n, 31–32, 377, 377n, **10**: 11, 11n

Walnut, white. *See* Butternut

Walnut Creek, **2**: 344, 345n

Walnuts, **2**: 79, 275, 286, 313–14, 388, 407, 429–30, **8**: 354, 359, **9**: 12, **11**: 138n

Walton, Mary Lee, **2**: 542, **9**: xvii

Walula (Walla Walla) Indians: villages, **5**: 284n, **7**: 166–67, 170–71, 172n, 173, 175, 185, **9**: 298, 298n, **10**: 216, 217n; encountered, **5**: 291, 296, **9**: 240–41, 298, **10**:

157–58, 216–17, **11**: 355, 358–60; lodges, **5**: 294–96, 298, 300, 300n, **7**: 176; fishing, **5**: 294–96, **7**: 181–82, 184; gifts, **5**: 296, 301, 303; councils, **5**: 296, 303; relations with the party, **5**: 296, **7**: 2, 170–71, 173–74, 176, 178–80, 187, 189, 196–98, 200–201, 203–4, **9**: 241–42, 299–301, 303, **10**: 220; chiefs, **5**: 301, 307n, 298, 300, **6**: 148n, **7**: 173–74, 176, **9**: 241, 241n, 299, 300n; listed, **6**: 474, 483, 490; historical sketch, **7**: 169n; food, **7**: 174, 176, 200–201, 201n; medical problems, **7**: 178, 180, 181n, 186; customs, **7**: 178–81; artifacts, **7**: 181–82; appearance, **7**: 183; clothes, **7**: 183, 185; peace, **8**: 47; distances, **8**: 385; language, **9**: 240, **10**: 157; visits, **10**: 158; trading, **9**: 242, 302; mentioned, **7**: 303, **9**: 296, 296n, **10**: 158n, 218n, 220n, **11**: 356n, 361n

Wampum, **2**: 455–56, **3**: 23–24, 210–11, 318, **4**: 11, **5**: 291, 296, 301, 303, 306, 373, **6**: 135–36, 172n, 215–16, 436, 439, **7**: 50, 53, 53n, 147–48, 151n, 224, 249–50, 253, 341

Wanapam (Sokulk) Indians, **5**: 278, 284n, 287, 292, 294, 326n, **6**: 313, 315, 454, 468, 474, 482, 487, 489, **9**: 239, 239n, 240, 240n, **10**: 156–58, 157n, 158n, 160, 160n, **11**: 355–58, 356n, 364, 367n

Wanatarwer Indians, **3**: 217n

Wannershia, **6**: 235n

Wanutarie (and similar spellings) Indians. *See* Hidatsa Indians

Wapato: as food, **6**: 15, 17, 44, 84, 106, 152–53, 368, 370, 378–79, 402–3, **7**: 19–20, **9**: 276, **10**: 166, 167n; habitat, **6**: 24, 229, 233, **7**: 28, 30, 32, 34; as trade item, **6**: 25, 27, 30–31, 33, 49–50, 74, 79,

89, 106, 123, 142, 144, 146–47, 184, 185n, 336–37, 7: 9–10, 15–16, 28, 30, 32, 34–36, 76–77, 80–81, 97, 99, 10: 185, 11: 408, 411; and Indians, 6: 32, 53, 76, 87, 89, 154, 193, 195–96, 199, 234, 461, 7: 12–13, 27–28, 30, 36, 38, 40, 57, 59, 79, 82, 92–93, 98–99, 9: 281–82, 287, 10: 206, 11: 433; as gift, 6: 60, 72, 74, 192, 7: 15–16, 18–19, 28, 58, 80; scarcity, 6: 165–66; purchased, 9: 249, 250n, 257, 263, 265, 274–75, 283, 285, 10: 178, 184, 202–3, 11: 385–86, 387n, 481, 425–27, 436; mentioned, 5: 326n, 6: 19n, 20n, 7: 11n, 36n, 9: 287n

Wapato Indians, 7: 89n

Wapekute Sioux Indians. *See* Sioux Indians, Wapekute

Wappetoe (and similar spellings). *See* Wapato

Wappetoe (and similar spellings) Island. *See* Sauvie Island

Wapshilla Ridge, 9: 317n

Waq!Emap village, 5: 336n

War-ci-a-cum (and similar spellings) Indians. *See* Wahkiakum Indians

Wareington, Warrington, Warvington (and similar spellings). *See* Warfington

Warfington, Richard, 2: 14–15, 139n, 141n, 148, 151n, 164, 188–89, 190n, 191n, 195, 198–99, 212, 215n, 229n, 256, 258, 347, 415, 417n, 475n, 511, 520–23, 3: 7, 9, 21n, 79n, 106n, 333–34, 4: 1, 7, 11, 12n, 8: 289n, 9: 44, 45n, 57, 11: 62n, 132

War-ho-ba Creek, 3: 344

War-ho-lote, 6: 154, 159n

War-ka-res-so-ra, 3: 212

Warkiacum Indians. *See* Wahkiakum Indians

Warm Spring Creek (Beaverhead County, Mont.), 8: 170, 171n, 9: 333, 333n

Warm Springs (Flour Camp)

Creek (Ravalli County, Mont.), 5: 190n, 8: 164, 165n, 393, 410, 9: 220n, 10: 138n, 11: 304n, 6: 452, 466

Warm Springs River, 7: 151n

Warner. *See* Werner

War-re-con-ne River. *See* Beaver Creek

Warren Creek, 5: 357n

Wartoocheworkkoo Indians, 3: 217n

Warzinggo, 3: 113, 10: 45, 45n, 11: 85, 86n

Wasco Indians, 5: 346n, 369. *See also* Wishram-Wasco Indians

Washington, camps in: Whitman County, 5: 260n, 264n, 266n, 7: 209n; Franklin County, 5: 269n, 272n, 276n, 284n, Walla Walla County, 5: 300n, 7: 186n, 190n, 198n; Klickitat County, 5: 313n, 320n, 326n, 336n, 7: 122n, 141n, 145n, 155n, 159n, 162n, 164n, 169n; Skamania County, 5: 353n, 358n, 380n, 7: 104n, 114n, 117n; Clark County, 6: 21n, 7: 31n, 36n, 41n, 70n; Wahkiakum County, 6: 34n, 87n; Wahkiakum-Pacific counties, 6: 37n; Pacific County, 6: 40n, 51n, 59n, 67–68n, 71n, 73n; Benton County, 7: 169n, 172n, 177n; Columbia County, 7: 201n; Garfield County, 7: 204n

Washington, D.C., 3: 153n, 213n, 214n, 225n, 230, 231n, 258n, 8: 4, 22, 74, 77, 212, 303n, 316n, 344n, 357, 358n, 419, 9: xvi, 59, 10: xv, 38, 76n, 260, 270n, 12: 3

Washington, George, 5: 112, 7: 238

Washougal (Seal) River, 6: 11–12, 14n, 457, 469, 7: 39–41, 41n, 70n, 8: 386, 405, 415, 9: 284, 284n, 10: 204n, 205n, 11: 382–83, 384n, 437, 437n

Wasps, 7: 309, 311, 312n

Watap, 6: 262, 267, 272n, 325, 327, 436, 440

Watches, pocket, 4: 65–66, 341, 343, 6: 81, 165, 7: 242, 244, 9: 177. *See also* Chronometers

Water, eye. *See* Medicine

Water, mineral. *See* Medicine

Watercress, 7: 55, 61n, 77

Waterfowl, 6: 30, 32, 65, 147, 259, 261, 363–64, 387–88, 7: 45, 46. *See also specific species*

Waterhold Creek, 3: 74n

Water lily, white, 2: 224, 225n

Watermelons, 2: 75, 435–36, 437–38n, 439, 9: 78, 82n

Watersoon Indians. *See* Hidatsa Indians, Awaxawi

Watkins Creek, 2: 130–31, 132n

Watlala (Clahcellah, Shahhala, Skillute, Wahclellar) Indians: and maps, 1: 11; villages, 6: 8, 17, 20n, 21, 55–56, 7: 19, 57, 64, 79, 81, 83, 90–92, 96, 98–99, 101–2, 103n, 111, 113, 131, 134, 136, 142–43, 154, 8: 385–87, 404–5, 9: 249, 250n, 283, 284n, 10: 204–5, 204n, 206n, 208, 208n, 11: 384–85, 387n, 434–35, 435n, 437, 437n, 439, 440n; historical sketch, 6: 10n; located, 6: 10n, 201, 456–58, 469–70, 7: 18, 20, 9: 250n, 284n; clothes, 6: 19, 186, 249, 251, 253n, 7: 18, 20, 38, 40, 67, 101–3, 113, 145; food, 6: 19; language, 6: 19, 7: 18, 20, 38–40, 111, 113, 114n, 218; head deformation, 6: 19; canoes, 6: 55, 147; lodges, 6: 56, 7: 38–40, 97–99, 107, 110–11, 145, 149; relations with the party, 6: 146–47, 7: 18–20, 57–58, 64, 80–81, 83–84, 90, 92, 96, 98–100, 104–6, 109, 113, 152, 9: 288–89, 289n, 290n, 11: 385, 408, 408n, 409n; visits, 6: 146–47; trade, 6: 147, 203–4, 224, 7: 20, 149, 9: 263, 10: 185; numbers, 6: 475, 478, 483–85, 7: 18, 20, 114n; name, 7:

Watlala (Clahcellah, Shahhala, Skillute, Wahclellar) Indians (*continued*)
14n, 21n, 22n, 41n, 100n, 130n; war, **7**: 18, 20; customs, **7**: 38–39, 108, 110n, 137–41, 144, 154; information from, **7**: 54, 56, **10**: 166, 167n; movements, **7**: 80; appearance, **7**: 97, 107, 110, 147; chiefs, **7**: 113; and horses, **7**: 143; mentioned, **6**: 474, 490, **7**: 12, 61n, 151n, **9**: 263n, **10**: 185n

Wattasoon (and similar spellings) Indians. *See* Hidatsa Indians, Awaxawi

Waubash River, **3**: 406

Wau-pe-ur, **2**: 439, 441

Waves. *See* Weather conditions, wind, waves, and tides

Wax, **7**: 215n, **11**: 426

Waxwing, cedar, **3**: 249, 250n, **4**: 92–93, 95n

Wayne, Anthony, **2**: 85n, 90n, 107, 140n, 513, **8**: 347n, 358n, 371n

Waystrips, **4**: 344, 346n, 349, 351

Waytom Lake. *See* Lake Pend Oreille

Weapons. *See* Arms and ammunition

We-ark-koomt (and similar spellings). *See* Apash Wyakaikt

Wears (Nightingale Creek) Creek, **2**: 275–76, 276n, **9**: 10, 10n

Weasel, long-tailed, **3**: 232, 232n, 330, **5**: 92, 95n, 127–28, 139, **6**: 137, 138n, **7**: 134, 135n, **9**: 206, 206n, **11**: 276–77, 277n

Weasels, **6**: 330n, 355n

Weather conditions: fog, **2**: 67, 70, 72–73, 83, 300, 321, 380, 464, **3**: 99–102, **4**: 166, 168, **6**: 10–12, 30–31, 33, **8**: 337, 373, **9**: 17, 47, 249, 383, 393, **10**: 27, 37, 165, 206, **11**: 40, 65–66, 382–83; wind, **2**: 73, 93, 145, 293, 317–18, 502–3, **3**: 128–30, 134–35,

139–41, 154–55, 179–80, 207, 221–23, 225, 248, 290, 481, **4**: 2, 13, 29–30, 51–59, 62–66, 68, 77–78, 96, 98, 121, 123, 136, 139–40, 144, 146–47, 149–50, 152, 154, 176, 179, 181, 207, 209, 221, 223, 237, 335, 351, 354n, 375–76, 378, **5**: 346–47, **8**: 106–7, 126, 143–44, 149, 154, 160, 167, 177, 210, 224, 226, 248, 263–66, 268, 282–83, 287, 295, 307–11, 320–21, 332, 335, 344–46, 358–59, 361, 373; rain, **2**: 76, 127, 139, **3**: 76, 140, **4**: 3, 262–63, 333, 338–39, 341–43, **5**: 56, 355–56, **6**: 2, 22, 24, 38, 40–44, 47–48, 69, 79, 90, 107–8, 126–27, 429–30, 432, 436, 440–42, 444, **7**: 8, 98, 100, 104, 108, 183, 186, 235–36, 266, 268, 270, 273–76, **8**: 1, 25, 71–72, 98, 126–27, 139–41, 143–44, 149, 154, 167, 224, 253, 263–66, 268, 283–84, 292, 310, 317, 320, 332, 334–35, 346, 348, 369, 374, **9**: 24, 37, 124, 164, 175–76, 183, 238, 252–53, 256, 261–62, 272–73, 279, 322, 324, 340, 346, 356, 387, 392, **10**: 10, 20, 25, 27, 74, 101, 108, 124, 136, 164, 167, 169–70, 178, 180, 183, 187, 189, 193, 199, 251, 257, **11**: 21, 26, 28, 39, 99, 104, 154–55, 158, 189, 210–11, 215, 298, 350–51, 391–93, 402, 405, 414, 418, 430, 434; storms, **2**: 131, 240–41, 307, 315, 373–78, 447–48, 452–53, **4**: 176, 345, **6**: 37, 39, 92, 100–101, 101n, 108, 118, 126–27, 135, 138, 163, 259, 344, 347, 349; sleet, **2**: 139, **10**: 58; heat, **2**: 334, **3**: 9, **8**: 361–62, **11**: 28; ice, **3**: 219, 235–37, 242, 294, **5**: 187, **9**: 96, **10**: 71–72, 74, 91, **11**: 123, 128; cold, **3**: 240, 256, 271, **4**: 102, **8**: 143, 166, 264, **9**: 101, 105, 108, 203, 207,

211, 217, 261, **10**: 64–65, 136, 165, **11**: 109, 111, 118, 121, 123, 142–44, 299–300; snow, **3**: 242, 246, 255, **5**: 3, 207, 209–10, 213, 242, **6**: 130, 239, 241–42, 244, 260, 262, 267, **7**: 3, 202–4, 235–37, 239, 248–49, 262–63, 267–68, 273–74, 301, 319, 337, **8**: 1, 10, 24, 28–29, 31–33, 39–42, 52–54, 55n, 56–61, 61n, 69, 71, 79, 88, 124n, 143–44, 162, 166–67, 171–72, 177, 181–82, 184–85, 187, 193, 205, 224, 264, 383–84, 388–89, 392, 413, **9**: 99, 101, 141, 164, 211, 224, 323, 325–26, **10**: 58, 62, 66, 85, 137, 143, 183, 190, 223–24, 227, 240, 244–45, **11**: 109, 142–43, 318–20, 415; floods, **4**: 3, 341–43; hail, **4**: 3, 342–43, 345, 349n, **5**: 23, 66–67, **6**: 43–44, 100, 126–27, 130, 133–35, 163, 432, 436, **7**: 202–4, 235, 319, **8**: 144, **9**: 124, 175–76, 178, 180, 324, 332, 342–43, **10**: 58, 107, 124, **11**: 214–16, 219, 263–64; dry air, **4**: 221–22, 224n; wind, waves, and tides, **6**: 1, 32–33, 35–43, 46, 48–50, 53, 60, 73, 75, 79, 86–87, 90–92, 100, 103–4, 107–9, 126–27, 130, 138, 142–43, 150, 171, 181, 199, 201–2, 275–76, 312, 314, 344, 347, 349, 364, 387, 390, 395–96, 401–2, 421–23, 441–42, **7**: 9, 12–13, 15–16, 39, 43, 94–96, 98, 100, 115–17, 157–58, 163, 167, 183, 186, 235–36, **9**: 24, 43, 75, 78, 101, 133–34, 136, 138, 141, 147–48, 152, 156, 158, 175–76, 182–83, 202, 235–36, 238, 251–53, 256–57, 259, 262, 273, 276, 279, 281, 288, 332, 336–37, 346, 353, 356, 359, 390, 392, **10**: 11, 13, 16, 20, 25, 27, 50, 56, 60, 80–82, 86–88, 90, 101, 152, 156n,

162–63, 166–71, 176, 180, 187, 193, 193n, 201, 207, 214, 263, 269, 271, **11**: 16n, 21–22, 28–29, 39, 60, 94, 101, 105, 107, 117, 121, 136–38, 140, 142–44, 148, 151–52, 154–57, 163–65, 177–79, 204, 222–24, 373–75, 384–85, 388, 390–91, 393, 397, 402–3, 405, 413–14, 417, 421–22, 431, 433–34; general, **6**: 84, 86, 243, 426–27; frost, **9**: 96, 135, 142, 147, 153, 206–7, 217, 334, **10**: 81, 85, 127, 221, **11**: 144, 403; thunder, **9**: 157. *See also* Great Plains

Weather Diary, **2**: 20, 171–72n, 177–78n, 186n, 209–10n, 216–17n, 224–25n, 336n, 433n, 537, 555, **4**: 95n, **8**: 353n, **9**: 374n, **12**: 1

Weather observations: explanation, **2**: 168–69; January 1804, **2**: 169–71; February 1804, **2**: 176–77; March 1804, **2**: 184–85; April 1804, **2**: 207–9; May 1804, **2**: 216; June 1804, **2**: 335–36; July 1804, **2**: 432; September 1804, **3**: 130–32; October 1804, **3**: 220–23; November 1804, **3**: 247–50; December 1804, **3**: 264–65; January 1805, **3**: 281–83; February 1805, **3**: 305–7; March 1805, **3**: 324–26; April 1805, **4**: 91–95; May 1805, **4**: 234–37; June 1805, **4**: 346–48; July 1805, **5**: 22–24; August 1805, **5**: 180–82; September 1805, **5**: 240–42; October 1805, **5**: 364–65; November 1805, **6**: 99–101; December 1805, **6**: 148–51; January 1806, **6**: 258–62; February 1806, **6**: 362–65; March 1806, **7**: 42–46; April 1806, **7**: 191–94; May 1806, **7**: 318–21; June 1806, **8**: 70; July 1806 (Lewis), **8**: 142–43; August 1806 (Lewis), **8**: 159–60; July 1806 (Clark),

8: 262–63; August 1806 (Clark), **8**: 269, 333–34; September 1806, **8**: 373; mentioned, **2**: 68n, 150, 157–58, 164–68, 171n, 417–18, **3**: 13n, 91n, 327, **4**: 100–102, 118, 211–12, 219, 221–22, 224n, 319–20, 350–51, 358–59, 361–62, 364, 416

Weeping Water (*l'Eau qui pleure*) Creek, **2**: 397–99, 399n, **3**: 347, 371, 378, **8**: 378, 396, **9**: 28, 28n, 367n, 389, **10**: 22, 22n, **11**: 41–42, 42n

Wehee Shaw Indians, **3**: 136, 138n

Weimar, **10**: xvii

Weippe Prairie (Camas Flats, Quawmash Flats): arrive at, **1**: 10, **2**: 24, **5**: 3, 224n, 231n, **9**: 228, 228n, 321, 321n, **10**: 146, 147n, 237, 237n, **11**: 326, 328, 328n; and Indians, **7**: 269–70, **8**: 7, 10–11, **10**: 237, 237n, **11**: 326, 328; sent to, **7**: 282, 284, 286–87, 297, 299, 323, 325–26, 328; hunting on, **7**: 331–34, 344, **8**: 44–45, **9**: 325–26, 326n, **10**: 243; distances, **8**: 66, **9**: 231; described, **8**: 69; conditions, **8**: 69; listed, **8**: 384, **9**: 311n, **10**: 173, 174n; camped on, **9**: 325–26, 326n, **10**: 146; return to, **10**: 242, 243n; mentioned, **6**: 467, **7**: 271n, 302n, 332n, **8**: 1, 12n, 25, 35–37, 39, 41, 43, 45n, 69n, 72, 73n, 77, 162, 162n, 402, **10**: 239

Weirs, fish, **5**: 122, 137–38, 141n, 174, 174n, 179n, 204–5, 227, 238, **7**: 181, 183–85, 187n, **8**: 31, 33, **11**: 289n, 293, 315, 316n

Weiser, Peter: drunk, **2**: 144; listed, **2**: 148–49, 188–89, 195, 198–99, 255, **4**: 9, 11, **8**: 139n, 162n, **11**: 4n, 7n, 395n, 408n; shooting match, **2**: 157; discipline, **2**: 179, **3**: 170; in permanent party, **2**: 229n; duties, **2**: 472, 474, **7**:

133–34; biographical sketch, **2**: 523; creek named for, **4**: 163–66, **9**: 150n; medical problems, **5**: 158, **6**: 35, **7**: 261–63, 265, **8**: 138, **9**: 209, **11**: 283; sent out, **6**: 60, 281, 284n, **7**: 125, 129n, 258, 271–72, 291, 296n, 327, 329, **8**: 46–47, 179, 180n, **9**: 270, 285, 315, 335, **10**: 192, 205, 227, 255, **11**: 407–8, 418–19, 423, 423n; scouting, **6**: 62, 65, **7**: 54, 57, 60n, **9**: 254, **10**: 175, **11**: 395, 438–39; votes, **6**: 83; and saltmaking camp, **6**: 139–40, 166–67, 297, **9**: 263, 263n, 271, **10**: 184, 187, 193n; separated, **6**: 152, 161–64; returns, **6**: 284–85, 370, **7**: 326, 329, **8**: 48, 50, **9**: 264, 265n, **10**: 192n, 195, 235, 243, **11**: 396, 410, 410n, 424; hunting, **6**: 290–91, 293, 295, **7**: 71, 74, **9**: 271, 286, **10**: 205; fishing, **6**: 353, 355n, **10**: 194; and Indians, **7**: 327, 329; accidents, **8**: 332, **9**: 340, **10**: 257; trading, **9**: 293, 312, **10**: 212, 230, 233n; mentioned, **2**: 190n, 211n, **6**: 172n, **9**: 255n, 265n, 270n, 271n, 279, 285n, 286n, 293n, 313n, 336n, **10**: 175n, 184n, 188n, 192n, 195n, 206n, 212n, 228n, 230n, 235n, 243n, 255n, 257n, **11**: 284n, 411n, 418n, 419n, 425n, 440n

Wellsburg (Charlestown), W. Va., **2**: 73, 74n, 513, **10**: xv, xvi

Wells Island, **2**: 79, 79n

Welsh Indians, **1**: 6, **3**: 201n, **9**: xv, 218–19, **10**: 60n, **11**: 303, 304n, 439, 440n

Wenatchee (Wah-na-a-chee) River, **6**: 487

Wendover Ridge (Snowy Mountain), **5**: 207n, **8**: 383, 402, **9**: 224n, **11**: 316, 318n

Wenser (and similar spellings). *See* Windsor

We-ock-sock Indians. *See* White Salmon Indians

Werner, William: listed, **2**: 148, 187, 189, 195, 197, 199, 255, **3**: 170, **4**: 9, 11, **8**: 74, 77, 86n, 110, 139n, **11**: 4n, 7n; discipline, **2**: 150, 194; hunting, **2**: 158; in permanent party, **2**: 229n; court-martialed, **2**: 235–37, **11**: xv; duties, **2**: 357, 360, **6**: 177, **8**: 291, **10**: 254; sent out, **2**: 476–77, **6**: 169, 172n, **9**: 265, 338, **10**: 28, 188, 247, **11**: 410, 411n; biographical sketch, **2**: 523–24; creek named for, **4**: 133, 135, **10**: 87n, 249n, **11**: 151n; votes, **6**: 84; medical problems, **6**: 122; and saltmaking camp, **6**: 177, 230–31, 242–43, **9**: 268, **10**: 187, 189, **11**: 414, 414n; separated, **6**: 237, **7**: 129n, 139, 141; returns, **6**: 448, **8**: 107, **9**: 269, **10**: 190, **11**: 416, 416n; loses tomahawk, **9**: 122; river named for, **9**: 145, 145n; volunteers, **9**: 330, 330n; trading, **10**: 212; mentioned, **9**: 122n, 265n, 268n, 269n, 279, 293n, 338n, **10**: 28n, 188n, 189n, 190n, 212n, 248n, 254n

Werner Creek, **10**: 114, 114n

West Butte, **8**: 117, 118n

West Florida, **10**: 6n

West Fork Bitterroot River (West Fork Clark's River), **5**: 186n, 188n, 190n, **9**: 331n, **8**: 48, 163–64, 164n, 165n, 393, 410, 415, **10**: 139n, **11**: 305n

West Pintlar Peak, **8**: 165, 166n

West Twin Creek, **8**: 90, 92n, 101

West Virginia, camps in: Hancock County, **2**: 72n; Ohio County, **2**: 74n; Marshall County, **2**: 76n, 78n; Tyler County, **2**: 80n; Wood County, **2**: 83n; Jackson County, **2**: 83n

Wetepahato Indians. *See* Kiowa Indians

Weterhoo River. *See* Grand River

Weucha (and similar spellings) (La Librator), **9**: 47–48, 50, 51n

Whale, blue, **6**: 185n, **9**: 265–66, 266n, **10**: 187, 188n, **11**: 407, 410–12, 412n

Whales: seeking, **2**: 32–33, **6**: 167–68, 171, 172n, 176–77, 182–84, 192, 262; as trade item, **6**: 2, 167–68, 180, 183, 193, 221–22, 235–36; remains, **6**: 66, 320, 322; bones, **6**: 68, 70, 183, 407–8; and Indians, **6**: 141, 143, 162–63, 166, 176, 178, 180, 183, 185n, 188–89, 193, 199, 229, 233, 407–8, 409n, 416, 416n, 495, **9**: 265–66, 270, 270n, 273, **11**: 422; information about, **6**: 141, 143, **9**: 262, **10**: 184; oil, **6**: 141–42, 175, 178n, 197, **7**: 82, 83, 89n; as food, **6**: 166–68, 188–89, 193, 235–36, **11**: 417; scarcity, **6**: 245–46; figures, **6**: 246, 249; mentioned, **6**: 68n, 144n, 198n, **9**: 273n, **11**: 413n, 417n

Wharton, **2**: 138

Wheat, **2**: 102, 219, **5**: 8, **6**: 228, 368n

Wheat, Carl I., **1**: 13

Wheatgrass, bluebunch, **5**: 228n, **6**: 366–68, 368n, **7**: 204n, **8**: 38n

Wheatgrasses, **7**: 338n

Wheeler, Olin D., **6**: 123n, **7**: 259n

Wheeler Draw, **7**: 237n, **10**: 224n

Wheeling, W. Va., **2**: 71, 73–76, 74n, 81

Wheels, **8**: 108, 292, 414. *See also* Wagons

Whetstones, **2**: 291, 293n

Whins. *See* Sagebrush, big

Whip, **5**: 70, 103, 142

Whip-poor-will, **2**: 276–77n, 335, 336n, 353, **3**: 178, 179n, **4**: 346n, **8**: 374, 375n, **9**: 21, 21n. *See also* Poorwill, common

Whip-poor-will (Toone), **3**: 156n, 190

Whips, **7**: 217–18

Whiskey, **2**: 66, 101, 140–41, 156, 157n, 165, 175, 179, 200–201, 212, 238, 245–46, 300, 329–30, 332, 348, 439, 441, 489, 491–95, 515, 518, **3**: 30–31, 33, 111, 113, 128, 130, 144–45, 157n, 227, 247, **8**: 351, 355, 363, 367, **9**: 27, 28n, 50, 55, 96, 359, 361–62, 364–65, **10**: 68, 277–78, 280, **11**: 24–25, 41, 109–10. *See also* Alcoholic beverages

Whiskey (Fourth of July) Creek, **2**: 346–47, 349n

White, George W., **2**: 543

White, Isaac, **2**: 229n, 256, 415, 417n, 511, 524, **4**: 12n

White Bear. *See* White Crane

White Bear Cliff, **3**: 38, 39n

White Bear Island Rapid. *See* Yellow Bear Rapids

White Bear Islands, **1**: 9, 11, **4**: 28n, 308, 309n, 310, 316–18, 325, 329, 334, 345, 350, 356, 372, 377n, 378–79, 383, 388, 394, **6**: 354, 356, 449, 464, **8**: 104, 106–8, 106n, 107n, 108n, 111, 119, 139, 291, **9**: 171, 171n, 174, 179, 181, 183n, 338, 338n, **10**: 108, 252, 252n, 253n, **11**: 204–5, 210–11, 217, 218n. *See also* Upper portage camp

White Beaver (Muddy) Creek, **8**: 198, 200, 202, 203n, 391, 408

White Brant Island. *See* Lady Island

White Buffalo Robe Unfolded (Ta-tuck-copinrehas), **3**: 209, 211–12, 213n, 311, **8**: 298, 300n

White Catfish Camp (Iowa), **8**: 353

White Cliffs of the Missouri

River. *See* Missouri River, White Cliffs of the

White Crane (Martoree, Mot, thouge), **3**: 19, 29, 33, 37n, **9**: 49–50, 51n

White Earth (Ok-hah-Âh-zhâh) River, **3**: 363, 374, 382, 431, **4**: 46, 47n, 59n, 63n, 69, **8**: 157n, **9**: 135n, 348n, **10**: 82n, 265n, **11**: 137n. *See also* Little Muddy River

Whitefish, **4**: 415n, **6**: 344, 346n, 349

White Hair, **3**: 138n

White Horse (Shon Guss Còn), **2**: 441, 443n

Whitehouse, Joseph: journal, **2**: 40–42, 190n, 240n, 243n, 285n, 288n, 295n, 309n, 356n, 423n, 435n, 503n, 510, 521, 543–45, 566–67, **3**: 57, 60n, 66n, 273n, 276n, **4**: 100n, 252n, 288n, 299n, 359n, 374n, 379n, 410n, **6**: 59n, **9**: 9n, 29n, 32n, 48n, 58n, 149n, 150n, 162n, 164n, 168n, 179n, 212n, 217n, 266n, 269n, 272n, 286n, 336n, **10**: xii–xiii, 11n, 12n, 17n, 23n, 24n, 25n, 61n, 62n, 70n, 71n, 92n, 102n, 109n, 157n, 172n, 194n, 199n, **11**: xii–xvi, 4–8n, 11n, 12n, 14n, 15n, 16n, 17n, 18n, 20n, 24n, 25n, 26n, 29n, 30n, 32n, 33n, 34n, 35n, 36n, 37n, 39n, 41n, 42n, 43n, 44n, 47n, 48n, 49n, 51n, 53n, 54n, 56n, 57n, 61n, 62n, 68n, 71n, 73n, 74n, 77n, 87n, 93n, 94n, 95–96n, 97n, 98n, 101n, 105n, 107n, 110n, 112n, 113n, 114n, 115n, 117n, 118n, 122n, 123n, 124n, 125n, 126n, 128n, 129n, 135n, 137n, 138n, 142n, 144n, 149n, 150n, 166n, 170n, 175n, 189n, 193n, 196n, 207n, 208–9n, 219n, 222n, 223n, 224n, 232n, 234n, 238n, 251n, 261n, 264n, 275n, 294n, 295n, 302n, 304n, 308n, 311n, 316n, 319n, 336n, 349n, 350n, 352n, 358n, 372n, 388, 389n, 390n, 393n, 394n, 397n, 402n, 421n, 425n, 428–29n, 432n, 436n, 437n, 440n; listed, **2**: 148, 188, 194–96, 198–99, 255, **4**: 9, 11, **8**: 139n, 162n, **11**: 4n, 7n; duties, **2**: 152, **10**: 107, **11**: 213–15, 220–21, 280–81; discipline, **2**: 194; in permanent party, **2**: 229n; court-martial member, **2**: 236; separated, **2**: 261, 264, 264n, **4**: 96, 100n, **6**: 125, **11**: 14–15, 142, 142n; accidents, **2**: 422, 423n, **5**: 53–54, **9**: 109, 197, **10**: 70, **11**: 354–55; biographical sketch, **2**: 524; hunting, **3**: 271, 272n, **6**: 312, 314, 323–24, **10**: 229, **11**: 14–15, 185–86, 420–21; medical problems, **3**: 273, 275, 276n, **4**: 287, 289n, 334, 336, **9**: 174–75, **10**: 107, **11**: 47, 120–21, 196–97, 212–13, 240–41, 257–58, 416; information from, **3**: 273n, **4**: 158n; and Indians, **3**: 315, **7**: 343–45, **11**: 129n; scouting, **4**: 247, **7**: 54, 57, 60n, **10**: 97, **11**: 184–86, 186n, 438–39; and iron-frame boat, **4**: 336–37, 343, 349; sent out, **4**: 371, 378, **7**: 268–70, **8**: 45–46, 179, 180n, **9**: 161, 269, 272, 285, 320, 335, **10**: 110, 183, 190, 206, 236, 255, **11**: 88, 195–96, 213, 236–37, 421–22, 421n; creek named for, **4**: 420, **9**: 188n, **11**: 238n; and species, **5**: 202n, **6**: 327, **11**: 138n, 195, 213, 223–24, 224n, 233, 326, 328, 329n; votes, **6**: 84; returns, **6**: 126, **8**: 21–22, 46–47, **9**: 272, 326, **10**: 237, **11**: 89, 120, 184, 186, 209, 210n, 213n, 236–37, 422; gifts, **6**: 137; loses horse, **8**: 7, 10, 14, 17, **10**: 238, 238n; lost, **9**: 8–9, 261; stays behind, **10**: 10; and saltmaking camp, **10**: 194; mentioned, **2**: 59, 141, 141n, 239, **5**: 211n, **9**: xii–xiii, 279, 285n, 320n, 336n, 396n, **10**: 10n, 70n, 98n, 107n, 110n, 183n, 190n, 206n, 230n, 237n, 255n, **11**: xiv–xv, 76n, 107n, 173, 214n, 420n, 421n

Whitehouse Pond, **9**: 224, 224n, **11**: 316–17, 318n

White River, **1**: 6–7, 12, **2**: 18, 485, **3**: 1, 31, 74–75, 76n, 77–78, 79n, 82–83, 95–96, 358–59, 372, 375, 380, 415, 419, **7**: 127, 130n, 149, 151n, 182, 184, 186n, **8**: 327n, 328, 328n, 380, 398, 411, 417, **9**: 60, 60n, 355n, 367n, **10**: 39–40, 273, **11**: 75–76, 76n, 172

White Salmon River (Canoe Creek), **5**: 352, 354n, 378, **6**: 456, 469, **7**: 118, 120, 122n, **9**: 292n

White Salmon (We-ock-sock, Wil-la-cum) Indians, **5**: 353–54n, **7**: 118–21, 122n, **9**: 292n, **10**: 164n, 210, 211n, **11**: 376–77, 377n

White Sand Creek. *See* Colt Killed Creek

Whiteside, William, **2**: 144, 145n, 150, 168

White Stone River. *See* Vermillion River

Whitetail Creek, **8**: 248, 249n

Whitetail Deer (Birth) Creek, **5**: 33–35, 35n, 49

White Water River, **2**: 113n

White Wolf, **3**: 318, 319n

Whiting. *See* Limestone, Grand Tower

Whitlow. *See* Medical problems, fingers

Whitney, Thomas, **2**: 92n

Whoopup Creek, **8**: 258, 261, 262n

Whortleberry, **8**: 61n

Wichita (Pawnee Pick) Indians, **3**: 138n, 395, 445, 449, 490

Wigle Creek, **9**: 39n

Wildcat (Me-war-ton-nen-gar)
Creek, **3**: 344, 384n
Wild Goose Rapids, **9**: 317n,
317n
Wild Oats River, **2**: 219
Wild rye, **3**: 148–49, 463, **8**:
143, 218
Wild rye, basin, **5**: 58, 60n,
6: 366, 368, 368n, **7**: 188,
191n, 335–36, 337n, **8**: 187,
188n, 222n
Wild rye, Canada, **2**: 364–65,
365n, 374–75, 487, 488n,
3: 144–45, 146n, 457, 463,
468, **5**: 60n, **7**: 335, 337,
338n, **8**: 222n, **9**: 23–24,
23n, **11**: 38n
Wild rye, slender, **3**: 468
Wild rye, Virginia, **3**: 468
Wilkinson, **2**: 81
Wilkinson, Ann Biddle, **8**: 370,
370n
Wilkinson, James, **8**: 346, 347n,
347–48n, 348n, 351, 355,
355–56n, 362–63, 362n,
364n, 370, 370n, **9**: 366n
Wilkinson, James B., **8**: 355,
355n
Wil-la-cum Indians. *See* White
Salmon Indians
Willamette Falls, **7**: 60n, 66,
70n, 82, 86, 93, 96–97, 99,
9: 286n, **11**: 439, 440n
Willamette (Multnomah) River:
and maps, **1**: 10–11; explored, **2**: 28, **7**: 1, 57, 59, 79,
9: 285, **10**: 205, **11**: 438–39;
information about, **6**: 311,
311n, **9**: 285, **10**: 205, **11**:
438–39; and Indians, **6**: 314,
317n, 478–80, 483–84,
486–87, 491, **7**: 54–56, 59,
60n, 70n, 81, 86, 89n, 96–
97, 119, 121, 122n, **8**: 277,
279n, 387, 405, 412, 415;
distances, **6**: 457, **7**: 60, 82–
83, **10**: 206n; located, **6**: 470;
valley, **7**: 22n, 48, 51, 53n;
characteristics, **7**: 41, 41n,
48, 51, 59–60, 64, 66, 77,
81–83, 86, 127, 130n, 149,
182, 184, 186n; plants, **7**: 60,
104n; maps, **7**: 92–93, 315n;

mentioned, **6**: 1, 13, 14n, **9**:
285n, **10**: 205n, **11**: 440n
Willapa Bay, **6**: 51n, 68–69,
70n, 77n, **10**: 200n
Willard, Alexander: returns, **2**:
141, 181–82, 251, 304, **7**:
131, 235, **8**: 138, 328, **9**: 59,
264, 265n, 271, 307, **10**: 228,
236, 262, **11**: 204–6, 410,
410n, 419, 419n; drunk, **2**:
143, 143n; listed, **2**: 148–49,
188–89, 195–96, 198–99,
255, **4**: 9, 11, **8**: 139n, 162n,
11: 4n, 7n, 393n, 408n,
414n; blacksmithing, **2**: 175,
176n, **3**: 262n, **9**: 107, 107n;
sent out, **2**: 191, **4**: 302, 304,
305n, **6**: 42–45, 47, **7**: 125,
129n, 133–39, 236, **8**: 179,
180n, **9**: 6, 169, 335, 341–
42, **10**: 103, 143, 170–71,
255, 258, **11**: 11, 320–21,
407–8; in permanent party,
2: 229n; court-martialed, **2**:
369–71, 373n, **9**: 24, 24n;
loses gun, **2**: 426–27, 428n;
biographical sketch, **2**: 524;
journal, **2**: 545, **10**: xiii; accidents, **4**: 308, **8**: 147–48,
332, **9**: 345, **10**: 192, 192n;
hunting, **4**: 324, **6**: 221, 228,
229n, 235–36, 253, 255,
293, 295, **7**: 260, 262, 323,
325, 331, **8**: 22–23, 25–26,
147, 178–79, 326–27, **9**:
33, 171, 267, 319, 322–23,
336, 343, 345, **10**: 189, 191n,
235, 239, 273, **11**: 414, 416n;
creek named for, **5**: 98,
102n, **9**: 203n, **11**: 270n; and
horses, **5**: 211, **7**: 143; scouting, **6**: 48, **9**: 253, **11**: 201,
393; and Indians, **6**: 48, 50,
7: 275–76, 312, 314; votes,
6: 83; and saltmaking camp,
6: 138, 140, 166–67, **9**: 263,
263n, **10**: 184, 192; separated, **6**: 152, 161–64, **8**:
147; medical problems, **6**:
293, 295, 332–33, 335–37,
347, 349, 356–57, 393, 441–
43, **7**: 10, 30, **9**: 274, **10**: 203,
11: 419n, 424; discovers

creek, **6**: 451; loses tomahawk and rifle, **9**: 31, **11**: 47;
trading, **9**: 293, **10**: 212, 234;
192n; stays behind, **10**: 262;
and species, **11**: 204–5; mentioned, **9**: xiii, 6n, 169n,
253n, 267n, 271n, 279,
293n, 319n, 336n, 396n,
10: 103n, 144n, 170n, 171n,
184n, 189n, 203n, 212n,
229n, 234n, 235n, 236n,
239n, 240n, 255n, 258n,
262n, 263n, 273n, **11**: xiii,
11n, 202n, 321n, 394n, 424n
Willet, **4**: 132, 134–35, 135–
36n
Williams Creek, **8**: 251, 254,
257n
Williamson Island, **2**: 79, 79n
Willoughby Creek, **5**: 191n
Willow, Bebb, **8**: 79, 81n
Willow, black, **2**: 368n, **4**: 325n,
8: 359, 359n
Willow, broad-, large-, or wide-
leaved, **4**: 70, 75n, 94, 96,
176, 351, 417, 419. *See also*
Willow, diamond; Willow,
peached-leaved
Willow, Columbia River, **7**: 192,
194n
Willow, cotton. *See* Cottonwood,
narrowleaf
Willow, coyote. *See* Willow,
sandbar
Willow, diamond, **4**: 75n, **7**: 14n
Willow, narrow leaf. *See* Willow,
sandbar
Willow, northwest, **7**: 14n, 193,
194n, 195n
Willow, Pacific, **6**: 29n, **7**: 14n,
19, 21, 22n, 32, 55, 77, 112–
13, 188–89, 192, 194, 194n,
335, 337, **8**: 161, 162n, **9**:
287, 287n
Willow, peach-leaved (broad
leaf, large, sweet, wide leaf),
2: 367, 368n, **3**: 455–56,
463, 467, **4**: 75n, 325–26,
325n, 334, 372, 417, 419,
435, **7**: 14n, **8**: 162n
Willow, red. *See* Dogwood, red
osier
Willow, sandbar (narrow leaf,

small leaf), **2**: 367, 368n, **3**: 454–56, 463, 467, **4**: 26, 28n, 54, 57n, 70, 75n, 96n, 142, 324, 325n, 417, 419, 435, **5**: 36, 39n, 57, 58n, 261, 263n, **7**: 194n, **8**: 79, 81n, 117

Willow, Scouler, **6**: 29n, **8**: 79, 81n

Willow, Sitka, **6**: 29n

Willow, sweet. *See* Willow, Pacific

Willow, weeping, **2**: 208–9, 210n

Willow, wide leaf. *See* Willow, peach-leaved

Willow, yellow (broad-leaved), **4**: 75n, 324, 325n, 417, **7**: 14n, 194n, **8**: 79, 81n

Willow Creek (Gilliam County, Oreg.), **5**: 312, 313n, **6**: 468

Willow Creek (Glacier County, Mont.), **8**: 127, 132n, 293

Willow Creek (Gun Brook River) (Lewis and Clark County, Mont.), **4**: 404, 406n, **9**: 186, 186n, **11**: 232–33, 233n

Willow Creek (Liberty County, Mont.), **8**: 116–17, 117n, 118n

Willow Creek (Philosophy River) (Gallatin County, Mont.), **4**: 428, 429n, 433n, **5**: 17n, 18–20, 20n, **6**: 450, 465, **9**: 192, 192n, 193n, 200, **10**: 119, 119n, 120n, **11**: 247–48, 247n, 249n, 263–64

Willow Creek (Ravalli County, Mont.), **5**: 191n

Willow Ridge, **8**: 34n, 55n, **9**: 323, 324n, 327, 327n, **10**: 241n, 244, 245n

Willows: observed, **2**: 89, 92, 105, 250, 253, 321–23, 343–44, 353, 355, 366, 375, 383–84, 397–98, 405, 407, 424, 428, 430, 444, 446–47, 449, 453–55, 457, 464–67, 469–70, 472, 474–76, 494, 496–98, 502–6, **3**: 9, 11, 13, 19–20, 38, 49, 54–55, 57–58, 68, 87, 96, 104–5, 114, 126–

27, 133–34, 139, 144–47, 149–50, 152, 169, 176–77, 184–86, 190, **4**: 17, 48, 52–53, 55, 57–59, 61, 63, 78–79, 90, 93, 108–10, 114–15, 119–20, 133–34, 147–48, 167, 169, 172, 175, 180, 184, 186, 217, 219, 242, 244, 250, 358, 383, 388, 421, 424–25, **5**: 19, 39, 46–47, 60, 71, 81, 97, 106, 108, 118, 265, 274–75, 282, 287, 298, 303, 306, 312, 374–75, **6**: 26–27, **7**: 13–14, 22, 25, 60, 83, 192, 197, 202–3, **8**: 83, **9**: 38, 59, 78, 145, 153, 185, 192, 195, 198, 210, 242, 246, 251, 257, **10**: 26, 59, 94, 105, 114, 153, 216, 218, **11**: 154, 156, 158–59, 161–62, 227, 229–30, 239, 248, 255–56, 259–60, 262, 284, 348–49, 355–56, 361; discussed, **2**: 313, 367; as food, **2**: 320–22, **3**: 294, **4**: 46, 124, 104, 235, **8**: 276; as drag, **2**: 483; use, **3**: 161, 163, 461, 489, **4**: 263, 278, 330, 337, 349, 378, 386, 403, **5**: 15, 32, 59, 64–66, 70, 75, 84, 105, 107, 111, 113, 119, 278, 296, 300, 315, **6**: 74, 77n, **7**: 262, 275, 283, **9**: 204–5, 208, 297–98, **10**: 104, 159, 256, **11**: 271, 273, 275, 280–81, 359–60, 362; abundance, **3**: 188, **4**: 125, 414, **8**: 189, 192, 310, **10**: 55, 94, 113, 116, 227, **11**: 239, 308–9; described, **3**: 452; habitat, **4**: 26, 39, 70, 73, 96, 216, 401, **8**: 79, 95, 102, 186–87, 200, 203, 238, 272, 322; scarcity, **4**: 159, 163, 165, 222–24, **8**: 128, **9**: 159, 201, 236–37, 239; and Indians, **5**: 73, 80, 83, 114, 137, 151, 340, **7**: 146–47, 149, 181–84, 230–31, 253–54, **9**: 215, 223, 300, **10**: 53, 128, 134, 154, **11**: 98, 315; and animals, **5**: 98, **6**: 360–61, 366, 368, **9**: 17; as fuel, **7**: 163–64, 166–68, 170–71;

camped by, **9**: 23, 241, 287; mentioned, **2**: 315n, **4**: 2, 20, 151, 255, 305, **8**: 110, 154–56, **9**: 17n, 185n, **10**: 22, 113n, **11**: 230n

Wilson, Alexander, **6**: 37n, **7**: 302n

Wilson Creek, **7**: 201n, **8**: 247–48, 249–50n

Wilson (Kilamox) River, **6**: 185n, 461, 471

Wilson's riffle, **2**: 80

Winans, Lineaus, **4**: 277n

Wind. *See* Weather conditions

Wind (Cruzatte's) River (Wash.), **1**: 10, **5**: 354, 356, 357n, 379, **6**: 112, 115n, 456, 469, **7**: 106, 110n, 115–17, 117n, **8**: 386, 404, **9**: 247, 247n, 291, 291n, **10**: 164, 164n, 210, 210n, **11**: 377–78, 379n

Wind River (Wyo.), **8**: 235n

Windlass, **3**: 285, 302, **9**: 118

Windsor, Richard: drunk, **2**: 144; listed, **2**: 148, 187, 189, 195, 197, 199, 255, **4**: 9, 11, **6**: 83, **8**: 162n, 179, **9**: 279, 395–96n, **11**: 4n, 7n; shooting match, **2**: 157; separated, **2**: 165; returns, **2**: 166, **6**: 325–26, **7**: 152, **8**: 218, 284; hunting, **2**: 166, 173, **6**: 321, 324, **7**: 54, 56, 60n, 71, 74, 76–77, **8**: 179, **9**: 284, 285n, **10**: 205, **11**: 421, 421n, 438, 440n; in permanent party, **2**: 229n; court-martial member, **2**: 236; biographical sketch, **2**: 524–25; creek named for, **4**: 202, 206, 207n, **9**: 156n, **10**: 93n, **11**: 170n; scouting, **4**: 250, **10**: 98; duties, **4**: 256; sent out, **4**: 260, **5**: 116n, **6**: 172n, **8**: 211–12, **10**: 205, 255, **11**: 186–87, 187n, 410, 411n; accidents, **4**: 262–63; medical problems, **5**: 167, 169, 175, 175n; and Indians, **7**: 277, 279; damages rifle, **8**: 27–29, 75; and species, **8**: 285, 286n; and saltmaking camp, **9**: 264, 265n, **10**: 187;

Windsor, Richard (*continued*)
horses stolen, **10**: 265; mentioned, **6**: 86n, **10**: 98n, 205n, 206n, 256n, 265n
Windust Caves, **5**: 272n
Windy Island, **4**: 176, 179, 179n
Windy Saddle, **9**: 323n
Wine, **2**: 167, 312, **9**: 361–62. *See also* Alcoholic beverages
Winn, Thomas M., **9**: 395n
Winnebago Indians, **3**: 490, 492n
Winnipeg River, **4**: 40n, **10**: 67n
Winship, Charles, **6**: 160n
Winship, Jonathan, **6**: 160n
Wipers. *See* Cloth, wiping
Wires, **5**: 261, **9**: 369n, **6**: 74, 144, 173n, 187, 196, 205, 385, **7**: 158, 160
Wisconsin, State Historical Society of, **2**: 39–40, 542, 550, **9**: xvii
Wisconsin River, **3**: 357, 407, 409
Wisdom River. *See* Big Hole River
Wiser (and similar spellings). *See* Weiser
Wishram-Wasco (Chil-luck-kit-te-quaw, Echelute, Elute, E-skel-lute, Skillute, Smackshop) Indians: villages, **5**: 329, 333, 336n, 340n, 346–48, 348n, 350–51, 353n, 378, **6**: 455–56, **7**: 79, 123–24, 126–28, 130n, **8**: 386, 404, **9**: 243, 247n, **10**: 161–63, 161n, 163n, 164n, 211, 211n, **11**: 369, 370n, 371, 375, 375n, 377n; encountered, **5**: 329, 333, **7**: 98–99, 107, 110; lodges, **5**: 333, 335, 348–50, **7**: 65, 70n, 84, 127; relations with the party, **5**: 333, 336–39, 345, 348, **7**: 128, 136, 141, **9**: 243–46, 244n, 294–95, **10**: 161–63, 213–14, **11**: 365–77; peace, **5**: 335; gifts, **5**: 335, 337, 348, 351; food, **5**: 335, 347–48; language, **5**: 336n, 344–45, 347, 351, **6**: 19, **7**: 85, 100n, 119, 121, 122n, 130n,

11: 372–73, 374n; chiefs, **5**: 338–39, 348, 350–51; clothes, **5**: 339, 351, **7**: 118–20, 127–29; name, **5**: 344–45, 369, **7**: 70n, 100n, 130n; trade, **5**: 346–47, 351, **6**: 201–2, **7**: 98–100, 129, 133; located, **5**: 346n, **6**: 313, 315, 469; customs, **5**: 347, 353n, **7**: 145n, **9**: 294–95, **11**: 369, 372, 373; artifacts, **5**: 347–48, 351; numbers, **5**: 348, 351, **6**: 475, 481, 483; fishing, **5**: 349; arms and ammunition, **5**: 351; war, **5**: 351, **7**: 119; canoes, **6**: 263, 270; and horses, **6**: 313, 315; appearance, **7**: 118–20; listed, **8**: 415; information from, **11**: 366–67, 371–72; mentioned, **6**: 10n, 395–96, 477n, 490, **9**: 246n, **11**: 368
Wistar, Caspar, **2**: 6
Withington Creek, **5**: 132n, **10**: 129, 129n
Wiyot Indians, **6**: 432n
Wolf, gray (large, yellow, white): observed, **2**: 333–34, 402–3, 497, **3**: 55, 75, **4**: 48–49, 112, **8**: 108, 115; hunted, **2**: 355–56, 397–98, **3**: 96, **6**: 449, **8**: 97, **9**: 18, **10**: 17, 42, **11**: 32; skins, **3**: 98; habitat, **3**: 482; and Indians, **3**: 485, **6**: 308, 210, **7**: 145, 147–48; as trade item, **4**: 34, 38; abundance, **4**: 112; behavior, **4**: 112–13, **5**: 55; listed, **6**: 312–13, 315, **8**: 416, 419; described, **6**: 331, 335; mentioned, **2**: 335n, 356n, 399n, **3**: 57n, 76n, 88n, **4**: 40n, 116n, **5**: 55n, **6**: 210n, 317n, 333n, **7**: 151n, **8**: 98n, 108n, 116n, 418n, **9**: 18n, **10**: 17n, **11**: 32n
Wolf, prairie. *See* Coyote
Wolf, small. *See* Coyote
Wolfberry. *See* Snowberry, western
Wolf Calf, **8**: 133n
Wolf Creek (N. Dak.), **4**: 19n

Wolf Creek (S. Dak.), **3**: 380, **8**: 398
Wolf (Lackwater) Creek (Mont.), **4**: 118–19, 121n, **6**: 447, 462
Wolf (Loup) Creek (Wolf River) (Kans.), **2**: 362–64, 363n, **8**: 356, 357n, 378, 396, **9**: 22–23, 23n, 367n, 386, **10**: 19, 19n, **11**: 37–38, 37n
Wolf Island (Strong Water Point), **2**: 310–11, 312n, **9**: 15n, **10**: 15, 15n, **11**: 27, 27n
Wolf Man (Ar-rat-tana-mock-She), **3**: 212, 213n, 214n
Wolf Point, **10**: 86n, 263n
Wolf Rapid, **8**: 257–59, 261n, 262n, 277, 390, 406
Wolf River. *See* Loup River
Wolomped River, **6**: 115n
Wolpard. *See* Woolford
Wolverine, **3**: 415–44 passim, **4**: 296n, **5**: 76n
Wolves: as trade item, **3**: 27, 32, 393–444 passim, **4**: 34, 38, **8**: 294, **9**: 106, 110; abundance, **3**: 55, 80, 253, **4**: 126, 128, 217, 219, **8**: 97–99, 113, 146, 148, 219, 225, 272, 310, 326, **9**: 158, 163, **10**: 72, **11**: 124, 212–13; observed, **3**: 57n, 75, 76n, 78–79, 82, 88n, 147, 185, **4**: 48–49, 87, 90, 114, 256, 258–59, 280, **7**: 171, **8**: 117–18, 128, 180, 210, 258, 272, **9**: 42, 174, 384, **10**: 109, 251, **11**: 33, 188–89; food, **3**: 77, 187–88, 292, **4**: 75, 78, 111, 113, 303, **6**: 200–201, **7**: 267, **8**: 150, 208, **11**: 177–78; hunted, **3**: 96, 98, 144–45, 267, 269, **4**: 126, 128, 151, 155, 217, 219, 363–66, **8**: 126, **9**: 22, 55, 88, 106, 108–10, 116, 180, 227, **10**: 19, 41, 57, 69–70, 146, **11**: 30, 32, 36, 70, 77, 80–81, 103, 117, 120–21, 162–63, 177–78, 220, 325–26; skins, **3**: 98, **4**: 364–66, **5**: 350, 352, **8**: 131, 294, **9**: 106, 110, **11**: 81; be-

havior, **3**: 181n, 187–88, 253–55, 293–94, 300, **4**: 60, 63, 85, 87, 195, 198, 217, 219, 247, 289, 306, 326, 397, **8**: 211, 356, **10**: 37, 72, 253, 258, **11**: 124, 177–78, 320; and Indians, **5**: 122, 124, 139, 340, 350, 352, **7**: 219; as food, **6**: 166, **9**: 108, **10**: 146, **11**: 117; danger from, **8**: 285, 286n; mentioned, **3**: 87, **4**: 34n, 67, **5**: 95, 155, **6**: 319, **8**: 98n, 108n, 145, 175, **9**: 110, 114, 136, 139, 155, 225, 307, **10**: 93n, **11**: 32n

Wood, Maria, **4**: 2, 220n, 266, **9**: 161n, **10**: 97n, **11**: 184n

Wood, opalized, **5**: 147n

Wood, petrified, **4**: 27, 45, 47n, 60, 83

Wood, red. *See* Dogwood, red osier

Woodchuck, **5**: 131n, **7**: 165n, **9**: 32, 32n, 377

Wood Island. *See* Cabaret Island

Wood (Pelican) Island, **2**: 457–59, 463n, **11**: 53

Woodman Creek, **5**: 199n, 201, 201n, 237, **9**: 222, 222n, **10**: 140n, **11**: 311n

Woodpecker, black. *See* Woodpecker, Lewis's

Woodpecker, Cabanis's, **8**: 27n

Woodpecker, downy, **4**: 95n, **7**: 78n

Woodpecker, hairy, **4**: 95n, **7**: 78n, **8**: 25, 27n

Woodpecker, lark. *See* Flicker, northern

Woodpecker, Lewis's, **4**: 407, 410n, **5**: 4, 33, 35, 35n, 217, 223n, **7**: 3, 265, 266n, 293, 296, 297n, **8**: 75, 78n, **10**: 238, 239n

Woodpecker, pileated, **5**: 195n, **6**: 379–80, 381n, **7**: 75–76, 78n, **8**: 25, 27n, **9**: 221, 221n, **11**: 308n

Woodpecker, red-headed, **4**: 237, 238n, **5**: 195n, **7**: 293, 296, 297n, **8**: 143, 144n, 146, **9**: 221, 221n, **10**: 238, 239n, **11**: 308n

Woodpecker, Rocky Mountain hairy, **8**: 27n

Woodpeckers, **3**: 306, **7**: 76, **8**: 93, **11**: 307

Woodrat, bushy-tailed, **4**: 352, 354, 354n, **6**: 354, 355n, 356, **9**: 179, 179n

Woodrat, eastern, **2**: 266, 267n, 355–56, 356n, **6**: 354, 355n, 356, **10**: 19, 19n

Wood River (Ill.). *See* Dubois River; Camp Dubois

Woodrush, smooth, **8**: 60–61, 61n

Woodtick, Rocky Mountain, **7**: 75, 77, 78n, **10**: 185n

Woodward (Beacon Rock) Creek, **6**: 469, **8**: 386, 404, **9**: 288, 289n

Woolens, **2**: 327, **6**: 137, 138n. *See also* Clothing

Woolery's Ripple, **2**: 67, 68n

Woolford (Wolpard), Adam, **2**: 202, 202n, 207, 211, **8**: 418, 419n

Worbington (and similar spellings). *See* Warfington

Work Creek, **8**: 194, 196, 197n, 198n

Worms, **6**: 94, 96, **7**: 293, 296

Wormwood, **4**: 35, 40n

Wormwood, silky, **3**: 469

Worner (and similar spellings). *See* Werner

Worrell (Werness), Stephen, **2**: 240, 243, 243n, **9**: 6, 6n, **11**: 10n

Worrington, Worthington, Worthyton, Woverington (and similar spellings). *See* Warfington

Wounds. *See* Medical problems

Wovington (and similar spellings). *See* Warfington

Wren, winter, **4**: 269n, **6**: 94, 94n, 162–63, 164n, 262n, 363–65, 365n, 379, 381, 381n

Wrens, **3**: 11, 13n, **4**: 265

Wurttemburg, Paul, Prince of, **3**: 228n, 291n

Wy-ach-hich village, **7**: 109, 110–11n, 114n. *See also* Yehuh Indians

X

Xanthium strumarium, **2**: 379n. *See also* Cocklebur

Xerophyllum asphodeloides, **8**: 55n. *See also* Turkey-beard

Xerophyllum tenax, **5**: 326n, **6**: 9n, **7**: 100n, **8**: 55n, **9**: 241n, **10**: 160n, **11**: 396n. *See also* Beargrass

X Y Company, **3**: 241n, 308, 308n, 402–4, 429–32, 441–43

Y

Yâck-kâh. *See* Bear, black

Yahache (You-ilt) Indians, **6**: 476, 485, 491

Yakima (Chimnapam, Cuts-sah-nim, Pish-quit-pah) Indians: and maps, **2**: 25; councils, **5**: 278, **10**: 158; ceremonies, **5**: 278, **9**: 239; encountered, **5**: 278, **7**: 178–80, **9**: 239, **10**: 156–58, 217, **11**: 355–56; clothes, **5**: 278, 286, 289; gifts, **5**: 278, 288, 291; relations with the party, **5**: 278, 285–88, 290, **7**: 165–67, 178–80, 185, **9**: 239, **11**: 356–58; historical sketch, **5**: 284n; information from, **5**: 285, 288, 296; lodges, **5**: 285–88, 290, 294, **9**: 239; clothes, **5**: 286, 289, **7**: 35, 37n, 165–67, 183; language, **5**: 287, 290n, 292, 294, **7**: 168n, **9**: 240, 240n; customs, **5**: 289, **7**: 178–81; head deformation, **5**: 289, **7**: 166–67; appearance, **5**: 289, 291; medical problems, **5**: 289, 291n; artifacts, **5**: 290; chiefs, **5**: 291; name, **5**: 292, 369, **7**: 181n; location, **6**: 313, 315, **10**: 158n, **11**: 356n; distances, **6**: 454;

Yakima Indians (*continued*)
listed, **6**: 454, 468, 490–91;
villages, **6**: 468, 474, 483,
487, **7**: 130n, 165–66; bands,
7: 168n; mentioned, **9**: 239n,
10: 157n, 217n

Yakima (Tapteete) River, **1**: 10–
11, **5**: 284n, 286–88, 290n,
292, 296, **6**: 474, 483, 487, **7**:
129, 130n, 132, 151n, 181n,
10: 217n

Yale University, **1**: 4, 11–12,
19n. 135, **2**: 41, 538, 542,
12: 6

Yampah, Gairdner's, **5**: 172,
174n, **7**: 264–65, 266n,
269–70, 271n

Yankton Sioux Indians. *See*
Sioux Indians, Yankton

Yanktonai Sioux Indians. *See*
Sioux Indians, Yanktonai

Yaquina (Lick-a-wi, Yorick-cone)
Indians, **6**: 201, 202n, 237n,
432n, 476, 485, 490

Yarrow, western, **7**: 338n, **9**:
164n, **11**: 188–89, 189n, 248

Ye-e-al-po (and similar spellings) Indians. *See* Cayuse
Indians

Y-eh-huh village, **5**: 355, 357n,
7: 106, 110n, 115, 117, 117n

Yehuh Indians, **5**: 355, 357n, **7**:
108–10, 112–13, 114n, 117,
8: 386, **9**: 247, 247n, **10**:
164n, **11**: 377–80, 378n.
See also Watlala Indians

Yelleppit, **2**: 542, **5**: 296, 300–
301, 303, 307n, **6**: 148n,
454, 468, **7**: 2, 173–74, 176–
79, 177n, 181, 183, 187, 189,
9: 241, 241n, 299, 300n, **10**:
158, 158n, **11**: 360, 361n

Yellow Bear Rapids, **8**: 252–53,
255, 255n, 390, 407

Yellow jacket, western, **7**: 309,
311, 312n, **9**: 227, 227n, **11**:
324–25, 325n

Yellowlegs, greater, **4**: 136n,
419n

Yellow Medicine River, **3**: 411

Yellow Ochre Creek. *See* Brush
Creek

Yellowstone (Meé,-ah_-zah, Rochejhone) River: and maps,
1: 8, 11–13, **8**: 299n; explored, **2**: 8, 29, **4**: 69, **6**: 3,
7: 334n, **8**: 1–3, **9**: 137,
137n, 138n, 334–35, 334n,
346, 346n, 349, **11**: 138–39,
138n, 139n; described, **2**:
30, **3**: 364, **4**: 69, 69n, 71–73,
76n, 78–79, **8**: 187, 189,
200, 217, 232, 248, 271, 361,
9: 138, **11**: 139; and members of the party, **2**: 516, 523,
10: 254–55, 256n, 264n,
265–66, 265n, 267n; traders
on, **3**: 198n, 242n, 311n; and
Indians, **3**: 234n, 400, 402–
3, 405, 421–33, 436, 484, **5**:
80, 91, 149, **7**: 242, 245n,
342, 343n, **8**: 2, 74, 77, 159n,
215n, 279n, 388–89, 415,
10: 138; sketches, **3**: 269,
270n, **8**: 287; affluents, **3**:
349, 351, 363, 365, 374, 381–
82, 385n, **7**: 74n, 185, **8**: 225,
240n, 241n, 245n, 246n,
255n, 256n, 257n, 261n,
262n, 270n; listed, **3**: 479, **6**:
462, **8**: 381, 392, 400, 406–
9; arrive at, **4**: 1, 67, **8**: 150,
10: 83, 263; conditions, **4**:
69–70, 71–74, 76–77, **8**:
175, 190, 210n, 219, 248,
264–65, 278, 283, 334;
plants, **4**: 91n, **8**: 416–17;
latitude, **6**: 447, 496, **8**: 191,
414, **11**: 139; distances, **6**:
447, **8**: 149, 183, 185–86,
207n, 275–77, 389, 394,
412; animals, **8**: 90, 150, 186,
195, 248, 278, 310, 417;
hunting on, **8**: 146, 276, 281,
284, 287–88, 295, **9**: 349;
characteristics, **8**: 151n, 183,
186, 231, 243, 273–74,
280n; set out for, **10**: 82–83;
and botanical specimens, **12**:
1; mentioned, **2**: 31, **3**: 291n,
298n, 334–36, 367–68,
491n, **4**: 20, 26, 32, 66–68,
69n, 75n, 134, 170–71, 173,
175n, 188, 204, 222, 270,

480, **6**: 86n, 311n, **7**: 182,
8: 43n, 78n, 86n, 146, 156,
158n, 174, 174n, 183n, 184,
188n, 192n, 193n, 204,
208n, 211n, 221n, 222n,
228n, 229n, 234n, 235n,
249n, 250n, 275n, 279n,
280, 281n, 282, 285, 316n,
366, 376, 415n, **9**: 151, 352,
10: 83n, 84, 247, 264n, **11**:
140

Yellowstone Plateau, **5**: 60n, **8**:
43n, 203n, 303n

Yellowstone River, Falls of, **8**:
277, 279n

Yoom-park-kar-tim, **7**: 242–44,
245n

York: duties, **2**: 141; accompa-
nies Clark, **2**: 193, 505, **3**:
277; listed, **2**: 194–95, 347,
4: 9, 11, **8**: 74, 162n, 179,
277, **11**: 4n, 8n, 187n, 395n;
collects food, **2**: 278–79;
medical problems, **2**: 310,
3: 8, 255, **4**: 365–66, **6**: 125,
135, 140–41, 143, **7**: 261,
263, 265, **10**: 65, 65n, 135;
cares for Floyd, **2**: 492; hunting, **2**: 504, 506n, **3**: 58, 89–
90, **8**: 209, 219, **9**: 172, **10**:
37, 114, 179, **11**: 207–8; biographical sketch, **2**: 525, **6**:
53–54; in permanent party,
3: 4, 327; sent out, **3**: 7, 9, **4**:
340, 342, **6**: 60, **7**: 289–90,
325, 328, **9**: 176–77, 259,
285, **10**: 114, 205, **11**: 402;
and Indians, **3**: 155–57,
157n, 174, 199, 208, 267,
5: 3, 106, 112, 115, 188n, **7**:
294, **9**: 85, **10**: 68; accidents,
4: 3, 215, **11**: 215–16; scouting, **4**: 250, 256, 398, 401, **6**:
62, 65, **7**: 54, 57, 60n, **9**: 186,
254, **10**: 98, 175, **11**: 186–
89, 230–31, 395, 438–39;
and lower portage camp, **4**:
325; dancing, **5**: 341, 343;
separated, **4**: 341, **6**: 109,
114; votes, **6**: 2, 84, 86n; fishing, **6**: 105, **11**: 401, 401n;
and species, **7**: 43, **8**: 264;

returns, **7**: 297, 299, **9**: 177, **10**: 233, **11**: 188, 396; creek named for, **8**: 253, 256n; stays behind, **10**: 181n; trading, **10**: 233; mentioned, **2**: 59, 141n, 229n, 218, 509–10, 518, **3**: 316n, **4**: 343, 409, **6**: 450, **9**: 45n, 172, 172n, 186n, 255n, 279, 285n, **10**: 37n, 68n, 77n, 98n, 108n, 114n, 175n, 206n, 233n, **11**: 62n, 208n, 216n, 440n

York's 8 Islands, **6**: 450, 464

Youens (and similar spellings). *See* Ewen

Youmalolam (and similar spellings) River. *See* Umatilla River

Young, Sir George, **6**: 115n

Youngs (Kilhow-a-nah-kle) River, **6**: 95, 98n, 114, 115n, 164, 164n, 317–18, 321n, 381–83, 384n, 391, 393, 398, 400, **9**: 274, 274n, 276n, **10**: 195, 195n, 197n, **11**: 424, 424n, 427n

Youngs (Meriwether's) Bay, **6**: 92–93, 94n, 95–96, 108–9, 114–15, 115n, 133, 133n, 147, 164, 171, 199, 275–76, 276n, 318, 384n, 398–99, 402–3, 409, 411, 459, 471, **7**: 7–8, 9n, **8**: 387–88, 406, **9**: 259, 259n, 280, **10**: 180, 181n, 195n, 197, 197n, **11**: 402, 402n, 427n

Youngs Point, **8**: 408

Youngs River Falls, **6**: 383, 384n, **10**: 195, 195n, **11**: 424n

Yucca, **5**: 131n

Yucca glauca, **3**: 43n. *See also* Soapweed

Yurok Indians, **6**: 432n

Yutan site, **2**: 400n

Z

Zanthoxylum americanum, **8**: 359n. *See also* Ash, prickly

Zea maise, **5**: 147n. *See also* Corn

Zenaida macroura, **4**: 237n, **5**: 214n, **6**: 381n, **7**: 297n, **8**: 78n, **10**: 111n. *See also* Dove, mourning

Zinc, **2**: 277n

Zinc sulphate, **4**: 139n, **10**: 230n. *See also* Medicine

Zizania aquatic, **3**: 469. *See also* Rice, wild

Zonotrichia atricapilla, **6**: 164n. *See also* Sparrow, golden-crowned

Appendix: Corrections

ATLAS VOLUME

p. 5: "Secretary of State Albert Gallatin" should be "Secretary of Treasury Albert Gallatin"

p. 11: "Shaddot" should be "Skaddot"

p. 18n. 84: "December 18 and 19, 1805, and January 5 and 7, 1806" should be "December 18 and 19, 1804" and "January 5 and 7, 1805"

p. 19n. 137: "The George Drouillard Maps of 1801" should be "The George Drouillard Maps of 1808"

Maps 1a and 1b: designation "Michigan" should be "Wisconsin"

Map 1e: caption should include maps 91–93

Map 96: caption "Shaddot" should be "Skaddot"

Maps 99 and 100: caption "May 9" should be "May 29"

VOLUME 2

pp. 54 & 65: Blaze Cenas was related by marriage to Felix Brunot, which would explain his presence on Brunot's Island. By 1808 Cenas was living in New Orleans.

p. 78n. 4: "*saccaharinum*" should be "*saccharinum*"

p. 82n. 3: "Hocking Port" should be "Hockingport"

p. 90n. 2: "Houck, 1 : 208–20" should be "Houck, 1 : 208–10"

p. 111n. 1: "Clark's identification" should be "Lewis's identification"

p. 134n. 1: "octant mentioned by Clark on December 3, 1803" should be "octant mentioned by Lewis on December 3, 1803"

p. 181n. 2: Goodrich's "[Toe?]" may be "roe" for fish eggs.

p. 186n. 15: "*Chironmidae*" should be "Chironomidae"

p. 210n. 19: "(see above n. 12)" should be "(see above n. 16)"

p. 214n. 2: the letter "F" may be more than a doodle; it may stand for "fusil," the French term for muskets.

p. 217n. 6: "(Michx.)" should be "(Michx. f.)"

p. 276n. 3: Coon Creek is no more; Wears Creek and Coon Creek are now one and the same, called Wears Creek, at Jefferson City. Clark's "Nightingale Creek" may be an unnamed stream one mile west of Moreau River, between that stream and Boggs Creek. For a discussion of the creeks in question and the possible identification of Clark's "nightingale," see James Wallace, "The Mystery of Clark's Nightingale," *We Proceeded On* 26 (May 2000): 18–25.

p. 277n. 4: Cedar Creek does not flow into Turkey Creek; they are separate streams.

p. 277n. 6: "Meadow[s] Creek" should be "Workman Creek"

p. 277n. 11: The note should read: In northwestern Cole County, in the vicinity of Sugar Loaf Rock, which is Clark's "Mine Hill" of the second entry's course and distance table and between modern Workman Creek and Meadows Creek.

p. 293n. 8: "April 5, 1804" should be "April 4, 1804"

p. 295n. 3: "Irving (Astor), 97–100" should be "Irving (Astor), 117–20"

p. 299n. 5: "notes for June 13" should be "notes for June 15"

p. 307n. 1: Whitehouse confirms that Colter killed a bear.

p. 314n. 4: "March." should be "Marsh."

p. 357n. 7: "Cutright (LCPN), 94" should be "Cutright (LCPN), 64"

pp. 416–17: there are two textual notes "3"; the one on p. 416 is unnecessary and in error

pp. 429–30, 431n. 5: the "little Dogs of the Prarie" and "Prarie Dogs" from the text should be identified in the note as prairie dog, *Cynomys ludovicianus.*

p. 431n. 3: "Koch." should be "Koch"

p. 484n. 2: "Pigeon Creek, in Thurston County" should be "Omaha Creek, Dakota County"

p. 488n. 2: Canada wildrye is incorrect; it should be reed canarygrass (see June 16, 1804). The other grasses Clark mentions may be specimens of *Elymus* sp. and *Agropyron* sp.

p. 507n. 10: "MRC map 9" should be "MRC map 29"

p. 512: "Jean-Baptiste Charbonneau" should be "Jean Baptiste Charbonneau"; he apparently did not use the hyphen in his name.

p. 517 (in entry for Joseph and Reubin Field): "July 17" should be "July 27"

p. 518 (in entry for François Labiche): "Charles Mackenzie" should be "Charles McKenzie"

VOLUME 3

p. vii: "Woodcook" should be "Woodcock"

p. 1: According to the party's estimate, Shannon had been missing since August 27

p. 19n. 7: "August 17" should be "August 27"

p. 23n. 1: "Irving (Astor), 97–100" should be "Irving (Astor), 117–20"

p. 36: "Ronda (LCAI), 23–16" should be "Ronda (LCAI), 23–26"

p. 51n. 10: *"Pituophis melanolecus"* should be *"Pituophis melanoleucus"*

pp. 54nn. 2, 6, and 372: "Tower" is now called "Old Baldy"

p. 63n. 2: "pleisosaur" should be "plesiosaur"

p. 67n. 3: should read "The camp was apparently a short distance north of the Lyman-Gregory county line."

p. 79n. 7: reference to paper birch (*Betula papyrifera*) as not being on the White River may be in error. The "Sticks" may have washed down from areas of the White River drainage where the birch existed two hundred years ago.

p. 103n. 4: "Mattison (BB), 241–63" should be "Mattison (BB), 261–63"

p. 109n. 4: "Hodge, 1:736" should be "Hodge, 2:736"

p. 142n. 2: "Potter and Dewey counties" should be "Potter and Sully counties"

p. 144n. 4: "Stove" Creek may be "Stone" Creek

p. 146n. 2: The darker birds may not be brant, since they are uncommon in South Dakota. It is not clear what bird Clark saw, but it may have been a "blue" phase snow goose.

p. 155n. 1: "Pierre-Antoione" should be "Pierre-Antoine"

p. 160n. 2: "Cathead Creek" became "Fisher Creek"

p. 175n. 4: "Long Soldier Creek" became "Onemile Creek"

p. 184n. 8: "Cutright (LCPN), 85–86" should be "Cutright (LCPN), 83–84"

p. 190n. 1: "Killdeer range" should be "Killdeer Mountains"

p. 201n. 5: "Ronda (LCAI), 67–132" should be "Ronda (LCAI), 67–112"

p. 206n. 5: Clark's "Michillinicknac" (p. 203) is likely Fort Michilimackinac located at modern St. Ignace, Mackinac County, Michigan, and controlled by the British from 1761 to 1781. "Michilimackinac Island" in the note is actually Mackinac Island but is not an appropriate reference.

p. 227n. 3: "Clark's interlineation" should be "Biddle's interlineation"

p. 229n. 2: "(See above, October 14, 1804)" should be "(See above, October 13, 1804)"

p. 297n. 2: "Thompson, 36" should be "Glover, 36"

p. 354: "Liard" should be identified as *liard amere,* narrowleaf cottonwood, *Populus angustifolia.*

p. 376: Camp Dubois (Camp Wood) is not "Probably beneath Missouri River" but "Probably beneath Mississippi River."

pp. 383–84n. 10: no identification for "Solomon's Creek" (p. 345); it is present Solomon River

p. 467, item 15, and p. 468, item 16: *"Petatostemum"* should be *"Petalostemon"*

p. 469, item 32: *"Gutierrezia sarothrae"* should be *"Chrysothamnus nauseosus"*

p. 471, item 47: *Juniperas* should be *Juniperus*

VOLUME 4

p. 19n. 15: "arrow wood is *Cornus sericea* L. red osier dogwood" should be "arrow wood is probably nannyberry, *Viburnum lentago* L."

p. 28n. 11: add, "The 'black flint' is probably Knife River flint carried by the Missouri River to this area from secondary deposits in North Dakota."

p. 50: add a note to identify "Halls Strand Lake" as named for Hugh Hall, a member of the party; it is today's Tobacco Creek, Williams County, North Dakota.

p. 53n. 6: "*zebethicus*" should be "*zibethicus*"

p. 91n. 3: "golden current" should be "golden currant"

p. 91n. 4: "Richland County" should be "Roosevelt County"

p. 102n. 4: "Richland County" should be "Roosevelt County"

p. 107n. 8: "Red Water Creek, in Richland County" should be "Red Water River, McCone County"

p. 111n. 5: "AOU, 61" should be "AOU, 611"

p. 129n. 7: "Cutright (LCPN), 265" is not relevant to this material.

p. 200n. 8: add that Goodrich's Island is later Dry Island.

p. 221n. 3: "Clark's wording" should be "Lewis's wording"

p. 250n. 10: add "It is probably an abbreviation for haversack."

p. 257n. 5: add that the common snipe used for comparison is *Gallinago gallinago* [AOU, 230]

p. 262n. 2: Clark's tansy may also be western yarrow, *Achillea millefolium* L.

p. 269n. 1: "Criswell, 53" should be "Criswell, xcv, 53"

p. 279n. 1: The *Cracon du Nez* is more properly a part of Rowe Bench, while Vimy Ridge is to the southwest of that feature and to the north of Fort Benton; both are north of the Teton River.

p. 317n. 1: "July 17–19" should be "June 17–19"

p. 321n. 4: "Biddle later suggested to Clark" should be "Clark later suggested to Biddle"

p. 322, figure 3: "Malstrom" should be "Malmstrom"

p. 368n. 4: The term "BB" may not refer to Bristol Blue but to a range of sizes as in A, AA, B, BB.

p. 386n. 5: "Wienm." should be "Weinm."

p. 418n. 1: another possibility is *Allium canadense* L.

p. 420n. 2: "Later Duck, or Gurnett, Creek" should be "Ray Creek"

p. 429n. 7: for a discussion of the campsite for this day see "Re-interpreting July 25, 1805 . . . Where is the Campsite?" *We Proceeded On* 16 (February 1990): 22–24

VOLUME 5

p. 8, first line: the line "do much walking . . . would command" is out of place and does not belong here; it is a repeat of last line of p. 1

p. 30n. 12: "South Boulder Creek" should be "South Boulder River"

p. 39n. 8: add "mountain whitefish, *Prosopium williamsoni*,"

as a possibility in addition to northern sucker

p. 72n. 2: "Printer" should be "Painter"

p. 124n. 1: add "mountain whitefish, *Prosopium williamsoni*," as a possibility in addition to northern sucker

p. 147n. 6: "Nuttall sunflower" should be "western spring beauty, *Claytonia lanceolata* Pursh"

p. 147n. 12: Clark's route on Salmon reconnaissance is discussed in J. Wilmer Rigby, "Where the Mountains Come Close to the Rivers," *We Proceeded On* 16 (February 1990): 25–26.

p. 147n. 13: it is actually Lewis that is giving the description here, but he got it from Clark, whom he quotes.

p. 186, l. 8 from top: Clark says the thermometer broke this day (September 3, 1805), but in the remarks section of the captains' weather diary (p. 241) the date is given as September 6. Moreover, the men record temperatures in the weather table for September 4 and 5.

p. 187n. 1: it is probably not correct to say that the party "ascended" Saddle Mountain, but rather that they made their way adjacent to it.

p. 195n. 4: the honeysuckle is perhaps more likely, Utah honeysuckle, *Lonicera utahensis* Wats., or bearberry honeysuckle, *L. involucrata* (Rich.) Banks *ex* Spreng.

p. 210n. 3: "Englemann" should be "Engelmann"

p. 210n. 3: add western larch as one of the possible eight species.

p. 223n. 2: *"Sorbus sitchensis"* (incorrectly spelled) may not be correct; Greene mountain ash, *S. scopulina* Greene is more likely.

p. 224n. 11: alder may be thin-leaved alder, *Alnus incana* (L.) Moench

p. 243n. 12: possibilities for the rose include, nootka rose, *Rosa nutkana* Presl, and wood rose, *R. gymnocarpa* Nutt. in T. & G.; *"Rhus"* should be *"Rubus"* and the possibilities include, thimbleberry *Rubus parviflorus* Nutt., red raspberry, *R. idaeus* L., or black raspberry, *R. leucodermis* Dougl. ex T. & G.

p. 252n. 1: It appears that the peace medal, supposedly at the American Museum of Natural History, has been lost for some time.

p. 260n. 5: "Spaulding" should be "Spalding"

p. 269n. 5: The peace medal is no longer at Washington State University; it is on loan for display to the Nez Perce National Historical Park, Spalding, Idaho.

p. 266n. 6: "and were several hundred feet thick" should be "and were up to several hundred feet thick"

p. 272n. 5: Pine Tree Rapids was probably an earlier rapids that the party passed. It may have been Clark's "bad rapid on which 3 Canoes Struck" (p. 269). The "island and bad rapid" is probably in the area of Rescue Island Rapids.

p. 313n. 9: "February 6, 1806" should be "March 6, 1806"

p. 319n. 9: "Olive Creek" probably should be "Rock Creek"

p. 326n. 5: For Eneeshurs "Tapanash" should be "Teninos"

p. 340n. 6: "cut through a downfaulted block of basalt" should be "cut through an easily eroded zone of basalt"

p. 353n. 5: "Memaloose Island" should be "Lower Memaloose Island"

p. 363n. 1: "composed of middle to lower Miocene olivine basalt" should be "composed of Pliocene or Pleistocene olivine basalt"

VOLUME 6

p. vii, item 30: *"Pseudotsuga taxifolia"* should be *"Pseudotsuga menziesii"*

p. 10, l. 2 from bottom: "Collins killed a Duck" should be "Collins killed a Buck"

p. 14n. 7: The wood stork may not be a valid identification since its range is well south of Lewis and Clark's path.

p. 14n. 7: *"auritas"* should be *"auritus"*

p. 20n. 11: Mount St. Helens was not named after the island of St. Helena but after Baron St. Helens (Alleyne Fitzherbert, 1753–1839), Britain's ambassador to Spain.

p. 28n. 9: "Lewis's laurel" should be "Clark's laurel"

p. 28n. 9, and 98n. 14: Clark's laurel may be salal, *Gaultheria shallon* Pursh. On February 4, 1806 (p. 276), Lewis wrote that the salal "resembles the lorel in some measure," and on February 8, 1806 (pp. 287–88), he described the salal in detail and notes that he had "heretofore taken [it] to be a species of loral."

p. 29n. 12: Hooker willow, *Salix hookeriana* Barratt *ex* Hook., is another common willow species in the area.

p. 40n. 1: "except for a short move on November 12" should be added after "November 15"

p. 104n. 10: *"Physocarpa"* should be *"Physocarpus"*

p. 115n. 7: "southeast of Astoria" should be "southwest of Astoria"

p. 120n. 1: Revision for this note: Cuscalah's village correlates with the Clatsop settlement of *Ne-ah-ko-win* or *niakiwanqi* on the coast north of the Necanicum estuary near present Camp Rilea. The term *"niakiwanqi"* has been interpreted as "where there is killing," a possible reference to the Kathlamet myth "War Against the Klatsop" in which this village was attacked. The village is shown on *Atlas* map 84 and on fig. 9.

p. 129, fig. 9: Revision for this note: Neawanna (Ne-er ca wen a ca) Creek in the area Clark visited on December 9–10, 1805.

p. 133n. 1: "the abandoned house could have been near Point Adams" should be "the abandoned house may have been in the vicinity of Point Adams near present Astoria, Oregon."

p. 159n. 6: Revision for this note: The "small river" mentioned by Clark probably refers to the Tillamook (Kilamox) River, one of several streams that drain into Tillamook Bay, Tillamook County, Oregon; shown on *Atlas* map 85.

p. 173n. 6: Revision for this note: Clark camped at the forks of Neawanna (Ne-er ca wen a ca) Creek, whose configuration has changed since Clark's time. *Atlas* map 84; figs. 9, 13.

p. 177 ll. 12–13 from the top: New note for the text: "a Short distance up this river on the N E Side is the remains of an old village of Clatsops." This village probably correlates with the Clatsop village of *Nehaynehum* or *nikanikm*.

p. 229n. 2: Gass may have been with one of the parties of hunters; see Gass's entry of this day.

p. 237n. 5: "*Arcostaphylos*" should be "*Arctostaphylos*"

p. 286n. 4: Oval-leaf blueberry, *Vaccinium ovalifolium* Sm., may be a better candidate for Lewis's huckleberry than the mountain huckleberry, a montane species which Lewis may have seen upriver near the Cascades.

p. 291 fig. 30: "*Pseudotsuga taxifolia*" should be "*Pseudotsuga menziesii*"

p. 296n. 1: "Oregon white ash" should be "Oregon ash"

p. 298n. 2: "Pacific blackberry" may be "salmonberry"

p. 327n. 2: "February 4, 1805" should be "February 4, 1806"

p. 397n. 3: "March Island" should be "Marsh Island"

p. 398n. 4: "*Astagus*" should be "*Astacus*"

p. 444n. 2: Red huckleberry, *Vaccinium parvifolium* Sm., or oval-leaf blueberry, *Vaccinium ovalifolium* Sm., are probably better candidates for Lewis's

huckleberry than mountain huckleberry, a montane species.

p. 490, item 21: "Hull-loo-et-tell" is incorrectly identified as "Watlala Chinookans"; they are Salishan Cowlitz

p. 491, item 38: the four tribes designated "Pisquows or Kittitas" should be identified as Klickitats

VOLUME 7

p. 9nn. 5–7: notes do not match text (p. 7); the information in n. 6 should be in n. 5, the information in n. 7 should be in n. 6, and the information in n. 5 should be in n. 7.

p. 9n. 11: "October 25, 1806" should be "October 25, 1805"

p. 31n. 8: "November 5, 1806" should be "November 5, 1805"

p. 36n. 1: "*sagitilifolia*" should be "*sagittifolia*"

p. 70n. 8: "October 24, 1806" should be "October 24, 1805"

p. 115n. 16: "California rhododendron, *Rhododendron macrophyllum* G. Don" may be "salal, *Gaultheria shallon* Pursh" (see correction for volume 6, p. 28n. 9).

p. 122n. 10: "October 29, 1806" should be "October 29, 1805"

p. 141n. 2: the letters "EM" should not be here (probably from reading the proofreader's note to put in an "em" space at this point).

p. 151n. 9: "Metotius River" should be "Metolius River"

p. 169n. 1: "October 19, 1806" should be "October 19, 1805"

p. 191n. 11: "Little (MWH), 2-NW" should be "Little (MWH), 22-NW"

p. 191n. 12: change to "Probably the Columbia hawthorn, *Crataegus columbiana* How."

p. 195n. 11: "Hitchcock et al., 7:488–90" should be "Hitchcock et al., 1:788–90"

p. 266n. 1: The "fennel" gathered by Sacagawea is more likely western sweet-cicely. *osmorhiza occidentalis* (Nutt. *ex* Torr & Gray) Torr.

p. 215n. 7: "American Numismatic Society" should have been "American Museum of Natural History," but it appears that the peace medal supposedly at the American Museum of Natural History has been lost for some time.

p. 330n. 6: Ordway party went westerly not "easterly" (2 times)

VOLUME 8

pp. 8–9, Map of Expedition's Route: Canoe Camp, July 19–24, 1806 (Clark), should be on Yellowstone River, not on Clearwater

p. 78n. 8: "*Eremophola*" should be "*Eremophila*"

p. 80n. 2: larger clover is largehead clover, *T. macrocephalum* (Pursh) Poiret. Hitchcock et al., 3:366; Cutright (LCPN), 421. Longstalk clover is incorrect. Red clover used for comparison is *T. pratense* L.

p. 197n. 1: Figure 5 (p. 199) is an inverted sketch map of Clark's route on the Yellowstone River for July 17–18, 1806, and can be reconciled to *Atlas* map 107. Clark's camp of July 17 is marked on the *Atlas* map as "Encamped

7th July 1806," while on figure 5 that night's camp is indicated by one of Clark's campsite symbols near the left-middle of the sheet. Above that on the *Atlas* map are three islands across from White Beaver Creek ("Muddy Creek"), Stillwater County, Montana. The same three islands are shown on figure 5 near the lower left hand corner, where "Muddy Creek" is not named.

p. 350n. 6: "*Junglans*" should be "*Juglans*"

p. 354n. 3: "Pottawatomie" should be "Pottawattamie"

p. 361n. 3: Ordway says on north side, so it would be in Clay County.

VOLUME 9

p. 75n. 3: Ordway may have thought Vallé was from St. Charles, *Petite Côte*

p. 130n. 2: Little Missouri River is in Dunn County.

p. 131n. 2: "*zebethicus*" should be "*zibethicus*"

p. 142n. 2: "Richland County" should be "Roosevelt County"

p. 154n. 3: "Armalls" should be "Armells"

p. 164n. 1: "July 12" should be "June 12"

p. 164n. 4: "*mellefolium*" should be "*millefolium*"

p. 241n. 2: "beargrass, *Xerophyllum tenax* (Pursh) Nutt." may be incorrect; the following should be substituted or added, "western bulrush, *Scirpus acutus* Muhl. *ex* Bigelow"

p. 247n. 2: "*califorianus*" should be "*californianus*"

VOLUME 10

p. 75n. 1: "April 13, 1805" should be "April 3, 1805"

p. 79n. 1: Little Missouri River is in Dunn County.

p. 84n. 1: "Brockton, Richland County" should be "Brockton, Roosevelt County"

p. 85n. 2: "McCone County" should be "Roosevelt County"

p. 136n. 1: "*Dendragapagus*" should be "*Dendragapus*"

VOLUME 11

p. 8n. 8: Whitehouse's "pettiaugers" (p. 1) is from the French, *petit auge,* "small trough"

p. 72n. 1: "pleisosaur" should be "plesiosaur"

p. 135n. 1: Little Missouri River is in Dunn County.

p. 141n. 1: "Brockton, Richland County" should be "Brockton, Roosevelt County"

p. 143n. 2: "Richland County" should be "Roosevelt County"

p. 145n. 2: "McCone County" should be "Roosevelt County"

p. 175n. 3: "*arvenis*" should be "*arvensis*"

VOLUME 12

p. 6, col. 1, l. 15 from top: "Three forks of the Missouri River" should be "Great Falls of the Missouri River"